The Mammoth Book of HOW IT HAPPENED Battles

Edited by

RICHARD RUSSELL LAWRENCE

ROBINSON

London

Constable & Robinson Ltd
3 The Lanchesters
162 Fulham Palace Road
London W6 9ER
www.constablerobinson.com

First published in the UK by Robinson,
an imprint of Constable & Robinson Ltd 2002

A copy of the British Library Cataloguing in Publication Data is available from the British Library.

ISBN 1–84119–479–4

Printed and bound in the EU

CONTENTS

Introduction

"The field was so enveloped in smoke that nothing was discernible"
Harry Smith's description of the Battle of Waterloo.

This collection of accounts of famous battles is intended to explain what happened and what it was like to be involved in them. Often an account either gives an overview of what happened or an impression of what it was like. For example, if the eyewitness was a commanding officer, the account is more likely to be an overview of the battle than an account of the same battle by a soldier who served in the ranks. The overview can tell us what happened but seldom tells us what it was like. An account by a soldier from the ranks or a junior officer is more likely to tell us what it was like, but often does not give us a picture of what happened. Surely the ideal account of a battle combines both.

The main substance of this book is eyewitness accounts. The introductions and linking text are intended to put the accounts into context and to provide explanation where it would be useful. The maps are intended to help the reader understand the location of the battlefields and the strategic development of the campaigns and battles. In historical terms eyewitness accounts are primary sources. A few of the accounts are secondary sources written by someone who was not there but based on the accounts of those who were. The accounts of Thucydides fall into this category. Some are a combination of first-hand experience and the experience of others who were there. The accounts of the battles of the Coral Sea and Midway are of this nature.

As an editor it is possible to add to the description of what happened. Occasionally the eyewitness does so himself with the benefit of hindsight. Thomas's accounts of the Peninsular war regiment did this when he described, for example, the Lines of Torres Vedras. Thomas was a private in the British 43rd regiment. Another account from the same period was by a different "Thomas". This one was a private in the Highland Light Infantry, the 71st regiment. By contrast, his account of the Battle of Waterloo is remarkable because the writer had so little idea of what was happening beyond his own personal experience. He actually fell asleep during a direct artillery bombardment. Both accounts by "Thomas" are also remarkable simply because the writer only identified himself by his first name.

The Recollections of Rifleman Harris were written after his military service was over. He wrote them while working as a cobbler in Richmond Street, Soho, London. He limited his account to "the things which happened immediately around me, and that I think, is as much as a private soldier can be expected to do."

This viewpoint is very different from that of an American Civil War general such as Abner Doubleday. His accounts mainly took the form of an overview of events. His overviews become enlivened when he was present at the place and moment of crisis. This happened at the battles of Chancellorsville and Gettysburg. The problem Doubleday's accounts present is that of remembering on which side each commander fought. Contemporary accounts of that war often identified the unit by the commander's name. Identification is made more difficult by changes of command during the battle. These were frequently brought about by death or injury to the previous commander.

Where possible, this collection has used several eyewitnesses to describe what happened and what it was like.

An eyewitness account is by its nature contemporary to the event. It may present cross-cultural difficulties when we read the account. For example, technical terms change and may no longer mean the same thing or have a modern equivalent. What interested readers then may not interest us as much now. For example, the Ancient Greek accounts are more concerned with the overview than what it was like. Perhaps contemporaries didn't need to be told because they knew from experience. Consequently we are left with very little material which tells us what it was like. The chapter on the Hoplite experience attempts to combine what little we have.

Other cross-cultural difficulties are more easily remedied. For example the words cavalry and infantry are of Italian (*cavalleria*) and French (*infanterie*) origin. They came into common English use after the English Civil War. It is therefore inappropriate to use them to describe events which happened before their introduction. It is appropriate, and more interesting, to use the contemporary expressions, Horse and Foot. These were still in common use during the Napoleonic wars. Earlier Froissart used the words "knights" and "foot soldiery" to distinguish between Horse and Foot at the battle of Crécy. Some of our distinctions such as that between regulars and part-time soldiers do not translate into the Ancient Greek culture in which military experience was normal for citizens from boyhood.

Among the many surprises in the eyewitness accounts was this piece of ironic humour from the Spanish-American war of 1898:

> Not all of the Indians were from the Indian Territory. One of the gamest fighters and best soldiers in the regiment was Pollock, a full-blooded Pawnee. I never suspected him of having a sense of humor until one day, at the end of our stay in Cuba, as he was sitting in the Adjutant's tent working over the returns, there turned up a trooper of the First who had been acting as barber. Eying him with immovable face Pollock asked, in a guttural voice, "Do you cut hair?" The man answered "Yes"; and Pollock continued, "Then you'd better cut mine," muttering, in an explanatory soliloquy, "Don't want to wear my hair long like a wild Indian when I'm in civilized warfare."

Richard Russell Lawrence

Sword and Shield
Ancient and Medieval Periods

Ancient

The Greek Hoplite Battle Experience

The ancient Greek way of waging war involved fighting on foot in heavy armour. The heavily armoured Greek foot soldier was called a Hoplite. The name Hoplite came from the Greek word *hoplon. Hoplon* meant shield, armour or weapons. Each soldier provided his own armour and weapons. To do so he had to be wealthy enough to afford them. He also had to be able to take the time off to go on campaign. This was possible for men of modest means in a society in which slavery was normal. Those rich enough to also afford a horse could fight as cavalry. Originally the property qualification of the hoplite class was ownership of a pair of oxen. The ability to fight as a hoplite gave a man the social standing of a gentleman. The army of each Greek city state was a levy which was called out when required. So the armies of the Greek city states were composed of part-time soldiers, with one exception.

Of all Greek hoplites only the Spartans were full-time soldiers. The Spartans' superiority came from this. Slavery was common to all the Greek city states but the Spartans had an entire subject population, the helots, to allow them more time for soldiering.

The weapons of the hoplite were the sword and the spear. His armour consisted of helmet, shield, body armour and greaves. The helmet covered the head down to the back of the neck and the whole face. The actual word the Greeks used for the hoplite shield was *aspis*. The shield was round, bowl-shaped and one metre wide. It protected the man from shoulder to knee. It was made of oak and faced with bronze. The support arm band and the grip cords were positioned so that the shield protected the left hand side of the holder and the right hand side of the next man. In close order the formation made a solid wall. The body armour was a corset around the body and broad

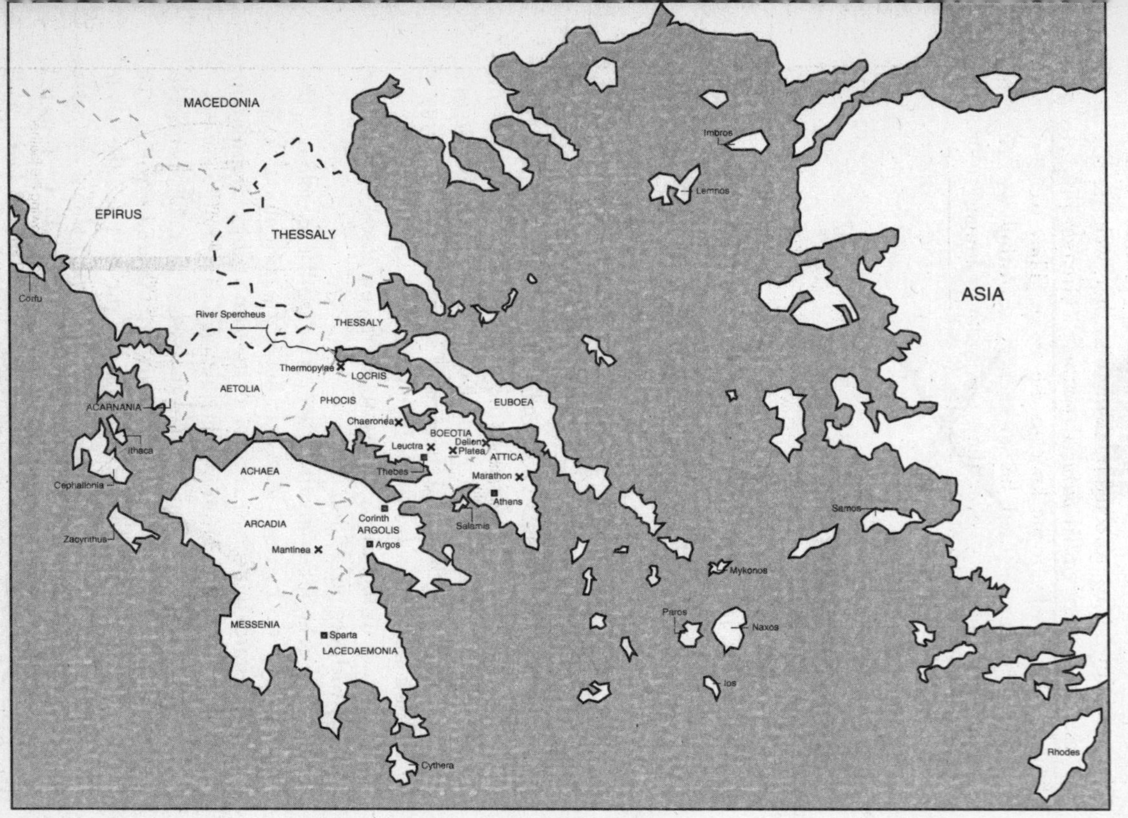

Map of Ancient Greece

shoulder straps. The body armour was made of leather, covered with metal plates. The body armour was worn over a tunic (*chiton*). From the waist down was protected by strips of leather, weighted by metal plates. These were called *pteruges* (feathers). Greaves protected the front of the legs from the knee to the ankle. They were made of bronze. The hoplite used his spear first, thrusting with it. The advantage of the spear over the sword was its longer reach. The

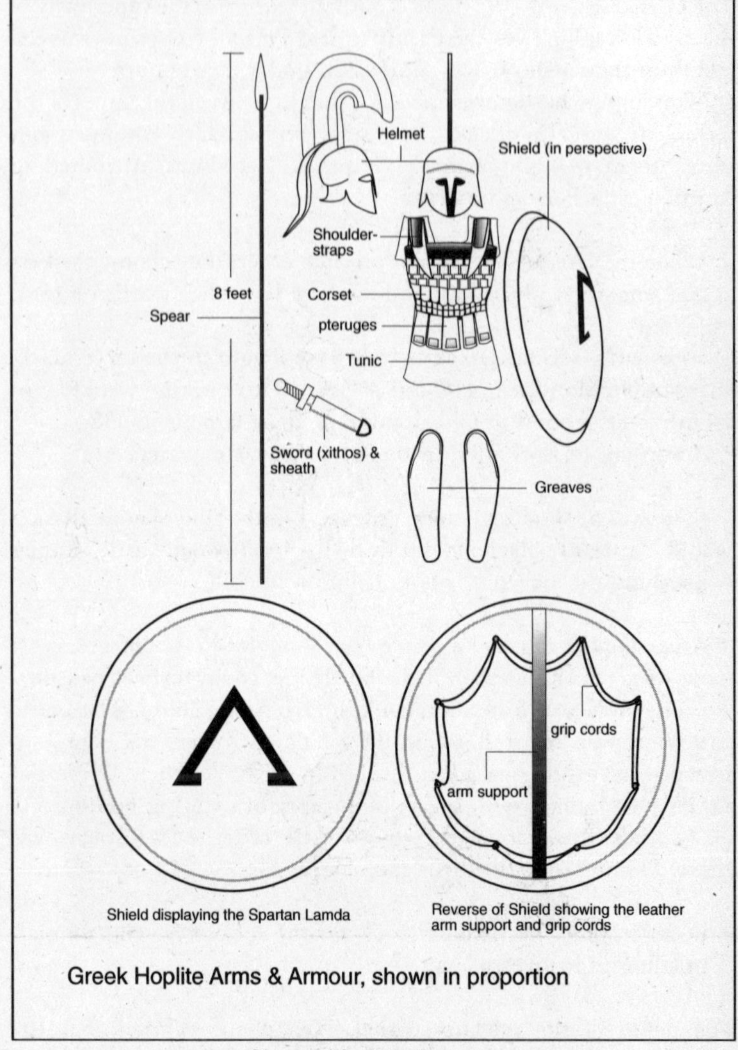

Diagram of Greek Hoplite armour

spear was eight feet long. When the spear had been dropped or broken, he drew his sword. The sword (*xithos*) was relatively short for thrusting.

The superiority of the hoplite over soldiers from outside Greece was demonstrated by the Greek victory over the huge hordes of Persian soldiers at Marathon (490 BC). At Marathon the Persians lost 6,400 men and an unrecorded number of wounded and prisoners. The Greeks lost only 192 dead. Another measure of the superiority of the Greek hoplite over the lightly armed Persian conscripts was the length of the battle. It was all over in under three hours.

Most hoplite battles were actually fought between the forces of the Greek city states themselves. Both sides were similarly equipped so it suited them to fight on an even plain. Herodotus attributed to Mardonios, a Persian observer:

> When the Greeks declare war on each other, they choose the best and smoothest place and go down and have their battle on that.

Consequently several Greek battles were fought in the same place, for example Mantinea (418 and 362 BC). Three battles were fought on the same ground at Chaeronea, the most famous in 338 BC.

According to Euripides, in the Greek battle experience:

> there was no shouting, nor yet silence, but the kind of noise passion and battle are likely to produce . . . each man hardly knows anything except what is happening to himself.

Greek hoplites formed a battle line, shoulder to shoulder, several ranks deep. Each member of the battle line could turn. When they did this, the whole formation could march as a column. The battle formation was referred to as the phalanx. When the signal to advance was given, one side advanced towards the other. The initial advance took place with spears in an upright carrying position. As the two sides drew closer to each other, the order to level spears was given. Plutarch described the moment at Platea (478 BC) when:

> in an instant the phalanx took on the look of a wild animal, bristling as it turns at bay.

The depth of the phalanx varied. Xenophon reported that the Spartans' opponents had some discussion before deciding to form up sixteen deep at the battle of Nemea. The Boeotians made their formation "really deep", perhaps twenty-five, as at Delion. By comparison, the Theban tactics at Leuctra were unconventional. Polynaeus reported Epaminondas made his formation "fifty shields deep".

The speed of the advance probably broke into a run when they got within missile range.

When the attacking formation got within missile range, they were pelted with whatever was available, the hoplites' camp followers usually doubled as slingers or light archers. (after throwing whatever they had, they sheltered behind the phalanx). These light infantry were called *gymnets* which means "naked." They were armed with javelins (throwing spears), slings or bows and arrows. They carried only a small round shield, the *pelte*.

Peltasts were a late form of Greek light infantry armed with the *pelte* and javelins. Their tactic was to approach within range, throw their javelins and retreat before the enemy reached them. They were victorious against Spartan hoplites at Lekhaion in 390 BC.

The hoplites themselves did not throw their spears, which were for stabbing and thrusting. Many such battles were actually decided almost before they began by one side or the other running away. One of the characters in a play by Euripedes remarked:

> It is common for fear to strike with panic an army under arms and in its ranks, before the spears touch . . . the test of a man's courage was not the bow.

– "the bow" meant the missile stage of the conflict.

Once battle was joined the fray became impersonal: Euripides has Theseus say in one of his plays that one question he will not ask, in case he is laughed at, is who met whom in battle.

Demosthenes said no one who flees from a battle line ever blamed himself but the general, his neighbours and everyone else, but he continued:

> They are none the less, of course, defeated by all who flee, for it was open to the man who blames the others to stand and if each man did this they would win.

The integrity of the battle line was to be maintained, especially when the lines closed with each other. Thucydides reported that leaving the line was to be discouraged because:

independent action is always likely to give a man a good excuse for saving his own skin

The fighting continued until both sides had virtually wiped each other out. According to Xenophon, an Athenian soldier and historian (born about 430 BC):

each fought and fell in their places . . . With foot set beside, pressing shield to shield, crest against crest, helmet against helmet, chest against chest:

Xenophon described Spartans against Thebans at the second battle of Chaeronea:

crashing their shields together they shoved, fought, slew and died.

It is not known exactly what form this shoving took. It is possible the rear rank men put their shields against the backs of the men in front and pushed. Xenophon recommended that the best men were put in the front and rear ranks so that the worst men in the middle could be:

led by the former and shoved by the latter.

Shoving was vital because taking one step back could be fatal. Once it had begun, the backward movement seems to have been extraordinarily difficult to stop. According to Thucydides the Thebans at Delion secured their victory as "they followed up, little by little as they shoved".

According to Polynaeus, Epaminondas at Leuctra called for "One pace more".

Commanders were of the same class as the rank and file and fought in the battle line themselves. Generals got killed in the front line in Greek battles. Epaminondas, the Theban general who beat the Spartans at Leuctra, was killed at the second battle of Mantineia; Pelopidas at Cynoscephelae; both Athenian generals were killed at the first battle of Mantineia.

Men in battle were not shy of shouting advice to their officers, kings included.

The physical exertion was considerable; in one of Euripedes' plays, Hecuba described Hector after battle: the stain on the rim of his shield was caused by the sweat of his face "as he endured the toils of battle."

Morale was a vital factor. At the crucial moment before the battle formations actually clashed, panic was easily spread. Pindar related, at such a time, "even the sons of God are not immune."

Once men started to run away it affected their comrades in arms. Xenophon reported that Epaminondas maintained the principle:

> It is very hard to find men willing to stand when they see some of their own side in flight.

Tyrtaios explained that, for the victors:

> it is easy to pierce the back of a fleeing man.

Xenophon described a fleeing mob of Argives as:

> frightened, panic-stricken, presenting their unprotected sides, no one turning to fight but all doing everything to assist in their own slaughter.

Due to the nature of his arms and armour the hoplite's right-hand side was unprotected. His shield protected his own left-hand side and the right-hand side of the man on his left. Turning your back to the enemy was a disgrace as well as being potentially lethal. It was a point of honour in Greek society to receive "all your wounds in front".

Hoplite versus hoplite battles seem to have had a relatively low casualty rate. Perhaps this was because hoplites were unsuited to pursuit due to the sheer weight of their equipment. They were also vulnerable to counter-attack by cavalry or light infantry. Even the Spartans were accustomed to only pursue their enemies for a short distance.

The small area where the actual encounter took place was grim. Aischylos described:

> Clotted gore lying on the soil of Plataia . . . heaps of corpses bearing witness to the eyes of mortals to the third generation.

Herodotus saw skeletons from an earlier battle at Pelousion during Kambyses' invasion of Egypt.

Xenophon described the battlefield after the second battle of Chaeronea:

> When the battle was over, one could see where they had crashed into each other, the earth stained with blood, bodies of friend and foe lying with each other, shattered shields, broken spears, swords bare of sheaths, some on the ground, some in the body, some still in the hand.

Herodotus makes it clear that, individually, the Spartans were superior to the soldiers of any other Greek city state. The Spartans were:

> second to none, though together they were the best of all men.

Xenophon testified that Spartan battle tactics were too complicated for others to attempt in the presence of the enemy. Complicated maneouvres included counter-marching (reversing direction) and back-wheeling.

The other Greeks feared the Spartans. They regarded them as invincible. Plutarch explained that the Spartans were so confident that they were:

> irresistible in spirit and, because of this, when they came to grips, terrifying to opponents who themselves did not think with equal forces they stood a chance with Spartiates.

The mere sight of the Spartans' shields was enough to dismay their opponents. Thucydides explains that, although they heavily outnumbered them, the Athenians at Sphakteria (425 BC) went ashore 'obsessed by the idea they were going against Spartans.'

The Spartans' shields were identified by the Greek letter Lamda. This resembled an inverted V. The Spartan state was actually called Lacedaemonia. They called themselves Lacedaemonians. Sparta was the capital city.

An epitaph for Megistias, an Arkanian seer, who chose to stand with the Spartans at Thermopylae, reveals the respect in which the Spartans were held for their fighting qualities:

> This is the memorial of the famed Megistias, whom on a day the Medes slew, having crossed the Spercheus river. He was a seer, who all the time knowing well the fate approaching, had not the heart to desert the captains of Sparta.

At Thermopylae, in 480 BC, a small force of Spartans had all died defending a pass into Greece from an invading Persian army so large it was reported to have drunk the rivers dry. Xenophon reported that Procles, addressing the Athenian assembly in favour of an alliance with Sparta against the Thebans (370 BC), said:

> Are there any others you would be more glad to have as your comrade-in-arms than these men whose countrymen, standing at Thermopylae, chose to a man to die fighting rather than to live and let the barbarian into Greece?

The Battle of Delion 424 BC

In 431 BC the rivalry between Athens and Sparta became a full-scale war, subsequently known as the Peloponnesian War. The Boeotian cities and states had formed themselves into a federation known as the Boeotian League. The League included Thebes, Thespia, Chaeronea and Orchomenos. The Boeotian League was allied with the Spartans. In 424 BC the Athenians were making a two-pronged attack on the Boeotians. The Athenian general, Hippokrates, had led out the full Athenian army into Boeotia to join with another general, Demosthenes. The campaign went wrong. As Hippokrates set out to return home from Delion, the Boeotian army, under Pagondas, prepared to attack him.

In 424 BC Thucydides was an Athenian general. He was subsequently exiled for losing an important city to the Spartans. He spent the rest of the War collecting evidence and talking with participants in the various actions. Thucydides:

When the approach of the Boeotians was reported to Hippokrates at Delion, he sent orders to his army to take up battle formation, and shortly afterwards joined them himself, leaving three hundred cavalry at Delion to guard the place from attack and to watch for a chance of attacking the Boeotians during the battle. The Boeotians posted a detachment to deal with these, and when they were ready appeared over the crest of the hill, grounded their arms and halted in their predetermined order. They numbered seven thousand hoplites, ten thousand and more light-armed troops, a thousand horse and five hundred peltasts. On the right wing were those from Thebes and district; in the centre the Haliartioi, Koronaioi, Kopaies and other lake-side dwellers; on the left the Thespies, Tanagraioi, and Orchomenioi. The cavalry and light troops were on the wings. The Thebans were drawn up twenty-five shields deep, the rest as they pleased. So much for the Thebans.

> The Athenian hoplites were drawn up eight shields deep, their numbers were about equal to the Boeotians, and their cavalry was on the wings. The Athenians had no regular light-armed troops present on this occasion, nor did the city possess any. Those who had joined the invasion far outnumbered the enemy, but were for the most part unarmed; they were a general expedition of foreign residents and citizens, and as they had been the first to start home very few were present . . .

Hippokrates began to encourage his army.

> These were Hippokrates' words of encouragement, but he only got halfway down the line when he had to break off as the Boeotians, after a few more hurried words from Pagondas, struck up the paean and advanced down the hill. The Athenians advanced to meet them and closed at a run. The wings of neither army came to blows, being held up by water-courses. The rest fought stubbornly, shield thrusting against shield. The Boeotian left, as far as the centre, was worsted by the Athenians, the Thespies being particularly hard-pressed. The troops next to them in the line gave way, they were encircled in a narrow space and cut down in hand-to-hand fighting. Some of the Athenians were confused by the encircling movement and mistakenly killed each other. The Boeotians were thus worsted in this part of the field and retreated towards the fighting, but on the right wing where the Thebans were, they got the better of the Athenians, pushed them back slowly at first and followed them up. It so happened also that Pagondas, seeing his left was in trouble, sent two squadrons of cavalry round under the hill where they could not be seen, and their sudden appearance caused the victorious Athenian wing to panic, thinking that another army was advancing against them. What with this and the Theban pressure and breakthrough on the right the whole Athenian army took flight.

The Peloponnesian War continued for another 20 years. Athens lost her fleet, the main source of her power, and finally surrendered to Sparta in 404 BC.

The First Battle of Mantineia 418 BC

The two leading Greek city states were Athens and Sparta. Their rivalry resulted in a long drawn-out war, known as the Peloponnesian War. The First battle of Mantineia happened in 418 BC between Sparta and Athens and her allies, Argos and Mantineia. The Skiritai were long-standing allies of the Spartans. They came from the mountains immediately north of the Spartan capital city.

Agis was the Spartan king and commander in chief. A polemarch was a senior Spartan officer, in command of 600 men. Under the polemarch were four *lochagoi* who each commanded a *lochos* of 150 men. Under each of the *lochagoi* were two *pentekonteres*, who each commanded 75 men. Under each of the *pentekonteres* were two *enomotarchs*, who each commanded 36 men. Thucydides:

> The next day the Argives and their allies formed up in battle order, ready for the enemy. The Spartans, returning from the water to their old camp by the temple of Herakles, found themselves at close quarters with the enemy already drawn up for battle and advancing from the hill. This caused them greater alarm than any other occasion on record. There was little time for preparation, and they formed ranks in haste, under the orders of Agis. For it is their rule that when a king is in command all orders are given by him. He instructs the *polemarkhoi*, they give the word to the *Iokhagoi*, they to the *pentekonteres*, they in turn to the *enomotia*. All necessary orders are passed on through the same channels and quickly reach the ranks. For almost the whole Spartan army with a few exceptions consists of officers serving under officers and responsibility for seeing that orders are carried out is widely delegated . . .
>
> Before they actually engaged, the generals on either side spoke a few words of encouragement . . . The Spartans meanwhile sang war-songs and exchanged words of individual encouragement reminding each other of their proven courage and well aware that long training in action is more effective than a few words of encouragement, however well delivered.
>
> After this they joined battle, the Argives and their allies advan-

cing with vigour and fury, the Spartans slowly to the sound of pipes, a standing institution in their army, not for religious reasons but to make them advance evenly, keeping time, without breaking ranks as large armies are apt to do at the moment of impact.

As they were approaching each other, Agis decided on the following manoeuvre. All armies have a common tendency as they go into action; they get pushed out towards the right, and overlap the enemy left with their own right wing, because each man seeks protection for his own uncovered right-hand side from the shield of his right-hand neighbour, thinking that the more closely the shields are locked the safer he will be. The man primarily responsible is the man on the extreme right of the front line, who keeps trying to keep his own unarmed side away from the enemy; the rest follow him with the same motive. On the present occasion the Mantineians far outflanked the Skiritai, and the Spartans and Tegeans outflanked the Athenians still further, their force being correspondingly larger. Agis was afraid that his left would be surrounded, and that the Mantineians were outflanking it too far; he therefore ordered the Skiritai and the Brasideioi to move out of their position in the line and level up the front with the Mantineians, while he passed word to the two generals Hipponoidas and Aristokles to move two companies from the right wing to fill the gap, thinking he had men to spare on his right and that he would strengthen the line facing the Mantineians . . .

The flight and retreat however was pressed neither hard nor long. The Spartans fight long and stubbornly until they have routed the enemy, but that once done their pursuit is short and brief.

That, or something very much like it, was the course of the battle, which was the greatest that had occurred for a long time among the Greeks and involved the most famous of their cities. The Spartans took up a position in front of the enemy dead, and proceeded at once to set up a trophy and strip the bodies of the fallen. Their own dead they took up and carried to Tegea, where they buried them; the enemy dead they gave back under truce. The Argives, Orneatai and Kleonaioi lost seven hundred killed, the Mantineians two hundred, the Athenians and men of Aigine two hundred with both generals. On the Spartan side the allies suffered no losses worth mentioning; of the Spartans themselves it was reported that three hundred were killed, but the true figure was difficult to find out.

The Battle of Lekhaion 390 BC

One of the first times the Spartans were beaten was at Lekhaion in 390 BC. A force of special light-armed troops, called *peltasts*, under the command of the Athenian general Iphikrates, cut to pieces a division of the Spartan army near Corinth. Peltasts were armed with javelins, throwing spears. Xenophon:

> The generals in Corinth, Kallias the son of Hipponikos who commanded the Athenian hoplites, and Iphikrates who commanded the *peltasts*, when they saw that the Spartans were few in number and unescorted by *peltasts* or cavalry, decided that it was safe enough to attack them with their own *peltasts*. If they marched along the road, they could be attacked on their unprotected side with javelins and destroyed; and if they turned in pursuit it would be easy enough for the *peltasts* with their light equipment to get away from hoplites.
>
> Kallias drew up his hoplites close to the city and Iphikrates with his *peltasts* attacked the Spartan regiment. Under this assault by javelin some of the Spartans were wounded and some killed, and the shield-bearers were ordered to pick them up and carry them to Lekhaion; and they were the only men in the regiment to get away safely. The general then ordered the first ten year-groups to drive off their assailants.
>
> They went after them, but failed to catch any of them. They were hoplites chasing *peltasts* who had a javelin throw's start, and Iphikrates had given orders that they were to retire before the hoplites got to grips with them. Besides, the hoplites became scattered in their efforts at pursuit, and when they turned to retire Iphikrates' men wheeled round and attacked them again, some from the front and some from the flank, running along to expose their unprotected side. In the first pursuit nine or ten of the *peltasts*' javelins struck home, which encouraged them to attack still more boldly.
>
> As the Spartans continued to suffer casualties, their general ordered the first fifteen year-groups to the attack and pursuit. But when they turned to retire they suffered more casualties than before. They had already lost all their best men, when the cavalry appeared and they attempted a joint pursuit. The *peltasts* turned to run, but the cavalry mismanaged their attack. Instead of pressing their pursuit till they had inflicted casualties they kept a continuous front with the hoplites both in advance and retreat.

The Spartans continued to pursue the same tactics with the same result, becoming fewer and less resolute while their assailants became bolder and more numerous.

At last in desperation they formed up on a small hill, about half a mile from the sea and two miles from Lekhaion. The men of Lekhaion, when they saw them, embarked in small boats and sailed along till they were opposite the hill. The Spartans were already desperate; they were suffering acutely and being killed without being able to retaliate, and when they finally saw the hoplites coming up they broke and ran. Some plunged into the sea and a few managed to escape to Lekhaion with the cavalry; but in the whole engagement and in the subsequent flight about two hundred and fifty of them were killed.

The Battle of Leuktra 371 BC

There were other developments in Ancient Greek warfare. The Theban general, Epaminondas, was an innovator. He defeated the Spartans at Leuktra by concentrating his forces on one side of his line of battle. The Spartans, on that side, were forced back. Xenophon:

As there was level ground between the two armies, the Spartans stationed their cavalry in front of their phalanx and the Thebans stationed theirs opposite them.

The Theban cavalry was in good training as a result of their wars against the Orkhomenioi and Thespies, but the Spartan cavalry at that particular time was in poor shape.

As far as the infantry is concerned, the Spartans are said to have drawn up each half-company three files abreast, so that their phalanx was not more than twelve deep. The Thebans on the other hand were drawn up not less than fifty shields deep, reckoning that if they defeated those around the king the rest would be easy.

When Kleombrotos the Spartan began the advance, and before his troops were aware that he had done so, the cavalry had already joined battle and the Spartans had been quickly worsted. In their flight they ran into their own hoplites, who were at the same time attacked by the Thebans. None the less the troops round Kleombrotos at first had the best of the fighting . . .

> But Demon the *polemarkhos* was killed and Sphodrias one of the king's council and his son Kleonymos fell also; the king's hoplites and the troops known as the "Polemarkhos Own" were pushed back by the massed weight of the Thebans, and when they saw their right wing thus forced back the Spartan left turned and fled.

Another translation of Xenophon's account used the term "gave way" in place of "turned and fled". However Leuktra marked the end of Sparta's domination of the Greek city states and the beginning of Thebes' period of ascendancy. All the Greek city states were eventually dominated by Macedon. In 338 BC the Macedonians led by King Phillip defeated the Thebans and the Athenians at Chaeronea.

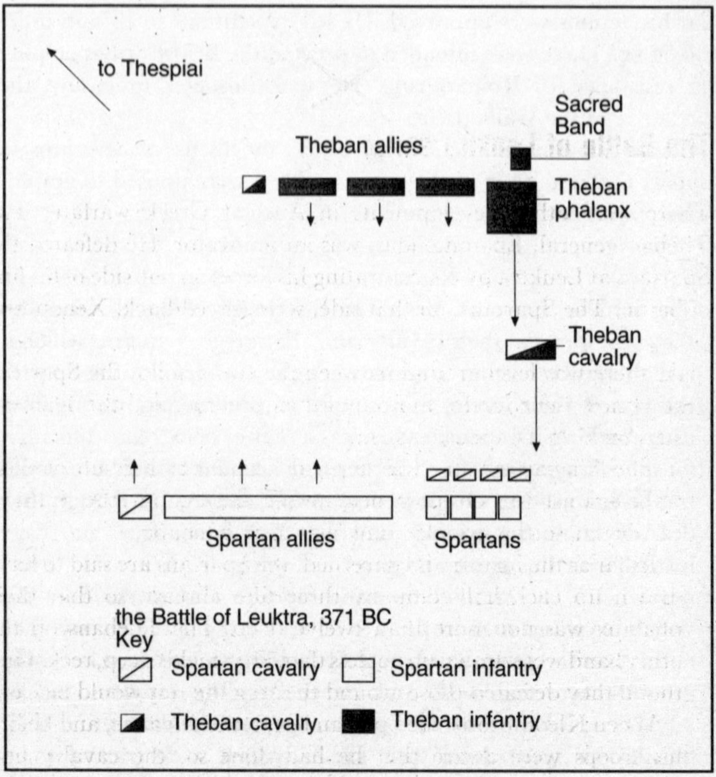

to Thespiai
Sacred Band
Theban allies
Theban phalanx
Theban cavalry
Spartan allies
Spartans
the Battle of Leuktra, 371 BC
Key
Spartan cavalry
Spartan infantry
Theban cavalry
Theban infantry

Map of the Battle of Leuktra

The First Invasion of Britain 54 BC

G. Julius Caesar (102–44BC) was a Roman politician and soldier. He used his military achievements to support his political aims. A contemporary described him as 'a realist to his fingertips'. He was a member of Rome's principal political body, the Senate. In 60 BC he formed a political alliance with Crassus, Rome's richest senator and Pompey, Rome's most successful general. In 59 BC Caesar was appointed governor of Rome's provinces in Gaul (France). As a Roman governor he was the commander of Rome's military forces in the area. He used them to extend Roman control to the whole of Gaul. This was actually exceeding his authority. He sent back reports on his campaigns to Rome. These so impressed the Romans that his actions were approved. He led expeditions to Britain in 55 and 54 BC. These were intended to prevent the British tribes helping the resistance to Roman rule. He took hostages to ensure the obedience of the Gallic tribes.

Caesar showed his tactical awareness by his use of warships to support the landing of his legionaries. They were unused to amphibious operations:

> The natives, however, perceived the design of the Romans. So they sent forward their cavalry and charioteers – an arm which it is their regular custom to employ in fights – and, following up with the rest of their forces, they sought to prevent our troops from disembarking. Disembarkation was a matter of extreme difficulty, for the following reasons. The ships, on account of their size, could not be run ashore, except in deep water; the troops, though they did not know the ground, had not their hands free, and were loaded with the great and grievous weight of their arms – had nevertheless at one and the same time to leap down from the vessels, to stand firm in the waves, and to fight the enemy. The enemy, on the other hand, had all their limbs free, and knew the ground exceeding well; and either standing on dry land or advancing a little way into the water, they boldly hurled their missiles, or spurred on their horses, which were trained to it. Frightened by all this, and wholly inexperienced in this sort of fighting, our troops did not press on with the same fire and force as they were accustomed to show in land engagements.
>
> When Caesar remarked this, he commanded the ships of war

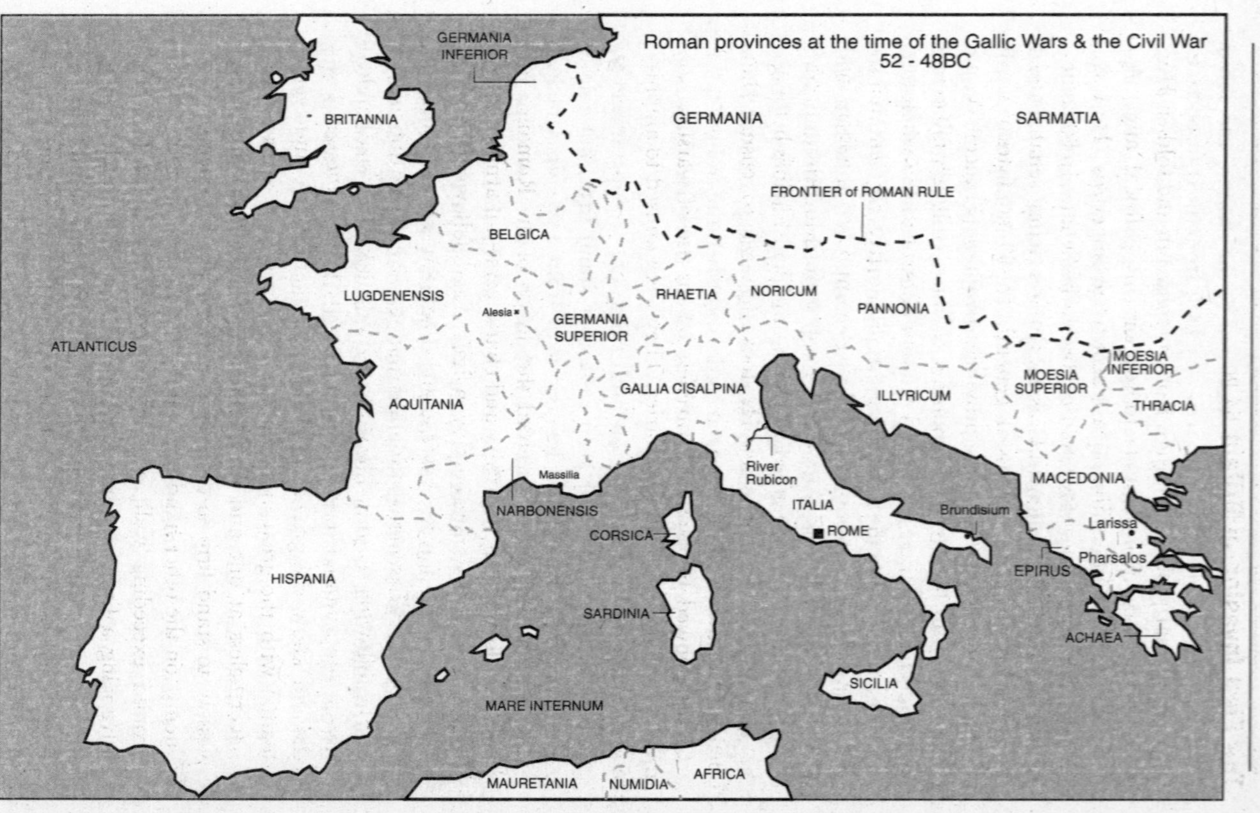

Map of Roman Provinces 52–48 BC

(which were less familiar in appearance to the natives, and could move more freely at need) to remove a little from the transports, to row at speed, and to bring up on the exposed flank of the enemy; and thence to drive and clear them off with slings, arrows, and artillery. This movement proved of great service to our troops; for the natives, frightened by the shape of the ships, the motion of the oars, and the unfamiliar type of the artillery, came to a halt, and retired, but only for a little pace. And then, while our troops still hung back, chiefly on account of the depth of the sea, the eagle bearer of the Tenth Legion, after a prayer to heaven to bless the legion by his act, cried: "Leap down, soldiers, unless you wish to betray your eagle to the enemy; it shall be told that I at any rate did my duty to my country and my general." When he had said this with a loud voice, he cast himself forth from the ship, and began to bear the eagle against the enemy. Then our troops exhorted one another not to allow so dire a disgrace, and leapt down from the ship with one accord. And when the troops on the nearest ships saw them, they likewise followed on, and drew near to the enemy.

The fighting was fierce on both sides. Our troops, however, because they could not keep rank, nor stand firm, nor follow their proper standards – for any man from any ship attached himself to whatever standard he chanced upon – were in considerable disorder. But the enemy knew all the shallows, and as soon as they had observed from the shore a party of soldiers disembarking one by one from a ship, they spurred on their horses and attacked them while they were in difficulties, many surrounding few, while others hurled missiles into a whole party from the exposed flank. Caesar noticed this; and, causing the boats of the warships, and likewise the scout-vessels, to be manned with soldiers, he sent them to support any parties whom he had observed to be in distress. The moment our men stood firm on dry land, they charged with all their comrades close behind, and put the enemy to rout; but they could not pursue very far, because the cavalry had not been able to hold on their course and make the island.

The Battle of Alesia 52 BC

In 52 BC a Gallic leader, Vercingetorix, formed an alliance against the Roman invaders of Gaul. Caesar:

> . . . in the fields he held a levy of beggars and outcasts. Then, having got together a body of this sort, he brought over to his own way of thinking all the members of his state whom he approached, urging them to take up arms for the sake of the general liberty; and having collected large forces, he cast out of the state his opponents by whom he had been expelled a short time before. He was greeted as "King" by his followers. He sent out deputations in every direction, adjuring the tribesmen to remain loyal to him. He speedily added to his side the Senones, Parisii, Pictones, Cadurci, Turoni, Aulerci, Lemovices, Andi, and all the other maritime tribes; by consent of all, the command was bestowed upon him.

Caesar received reports of Vercingetorix' rebellion and began to gather his forces. Moving fast Caesar won several victories. Vercingetorix tried to deprive the Romans of supplies:

> Having experienced three continuous reverses – at Vellaunodunum, Cenabum, and Noviodunum – Vercingetorix summoned his followers to a convention. He pointed out that the campaign must be conducted in far different fashion from hitherto. By every possible means they must endeavour to prevent the Romans from obtaining forage and supplies. The task was easy, because the Gauls had an abundance of horsemen and were assisted by the season of the year. The forage could not be cut; the enemy must of necessity scatter to seek it from the homesteads; and all these detachments could be picked off daily by the horsemen.

Eventually Caesar pursued Vercingetorix' army to a hill camp at Alesia. This was a natural fortress. The sides of the hill were too steep for a direct attack. Caesar's army of 70,000 men besieged Alesia. The Roman army was excellent at siege warfare. Caesar:

> The actual stronghold of Alesia was set atop of a hill, in a very lofty situation, apparently impregnable save by blockade. The bases of the hill were washed on two separate sides by rivers. Before the town a plain extended for a length of about three miles;

on all the other sides there were hills surrounding the town at a short distance, and equal to it in height. Under the wall, on the side which looked eastward, the forces of the Gauls had entirely occupied all this intervening space; and had made in front a ditch and a rough wall six feet high. The perimeter of the siege-works which the Romans were beginning had a length of eleven miles. Camps had been pitched at convenient spots, and three-and-twenty forts had been constructed on the line. In these piquets would be posted by day to prevent any sudden sortie; by night the same stations were held by sentries and strong garrisons.

Vercingetorix had requested help from the other Gauls:

Caesar had report of this from deserters and prisoners, and determined on the following types of entrenchments. He dug a trench 20 feet wide with perpendicular sides, in such fashion that the bottom thereof was just as broad as the distance from edge to edge at the surface. He set back the rest of the siege-works 400 paces from the trench; for as he had of necessity included so large an area, and the whole of the works could not easily be manned by a ring-fence of troops, his intention was to provide against any sudden rush of the enemy's host by night upon the entrenchments, or any chance of directing their missiles by day upon our troops engaged on the works. Behind this interval he dug all round two trenches, 15 feet broad and of equal-depth; and the inner one, where the ground was level with the plain or sank below it, he filled with water diverted from the river. Behind the trenches he constructed a ramp and palisade 12 feet high; to this he added a breastwork and battlements, with large fraises projecting at the junctions of screens and ramp, to check the upward advance of the enemy; and all round the works he set turrets at intervals of 80 feet.

As it was necessary that at one and the same time timber and corn should be procured, and lines of such extent constructed, our forces, having to proceed to a considerable distance from camp, were reduced in number; and sometimes the Gauls would try to make an attempt upon our works by a sortie in force from several gates of the town. Caesar, therefore, thought proper to make a further addition to these works, in order that the lines might be defensible by a smaller number of troops. Accordingly, trunks or very stout branches of trees were cut, and the tops thereof barked and sharpened, and continuous trenches five feet deep were dug.

Into these the stumps were sunk and fastened at the bottom so that they could not be torn up, while the bough-ends were left projecting. They were in rows of five fastened and entangled together, and anyone who pushed into them must impale himself on the sharpest

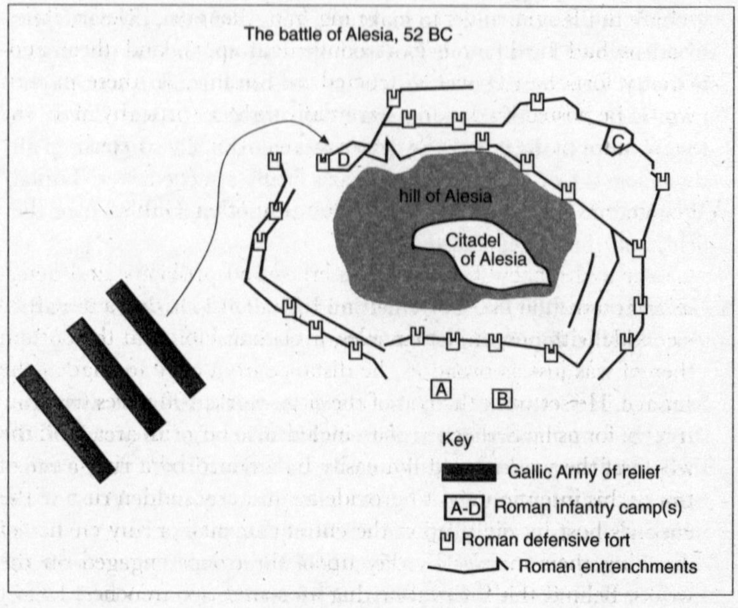

Map of the Battle of Alesia

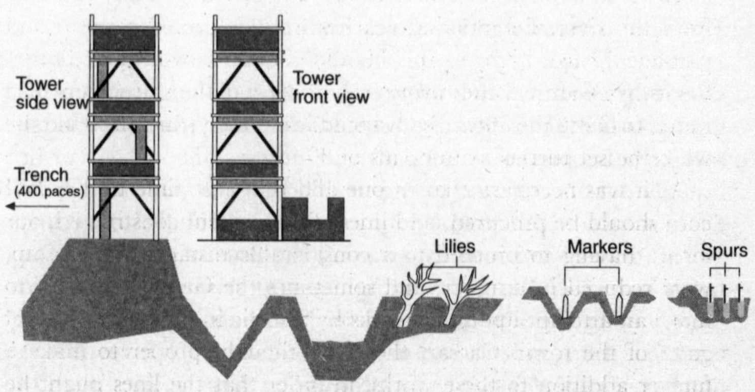

Roman entrenchments at Alesia

of stakes. These they called 'markers'. In front of these, in diagonal rows arranged like a figure of five, four pits three feet deep were dug, sloping inwards slightly to the bottom. In these, tapering stakes as thick as a man's thigh, sharpened at the top and fire-hardened, were sunk so as to project no more than four fingers' breadth from the ground; at the same time, to make all strong and firm, the earth was trodden down hard for one foot from the bottom, and the remainder of the pit was covered over with twigs and brushwood to conceal the trap. Eight rows of this kind were dug, three feet apart. From its resemblance to the flower the device was called a 'lily'. In front of all these, logs a foot long, with iron hooks firmly attached, were buried altogether in the ground and scattered at brief intervals all over the field, and these they called 'spurs'.

A Gallic army of 80,000 horsemen and 250,000 footmen was gathered under the command of Commius. Caesar:

Meanwhile Commius and the other leaders entrusted with the supreme command reached the neighbourhood of Alesia with all their force and, seizing a hill outside, halted not more than a mile from our entrenchments. The day after they brought their horsemen out of camp and filled the whole of that plain which we have described as extending for a length of three miles; their force of footmen they posted a little way back from the spot, on the higher ground.

Caesar had to guard against attack from both sides. Caesar:

Caesar disposed the whole army on both faces of the entrenchments in such fashion that, if occasion should arise, each man could know and keep his proper station; then he ordered the cavalry to be brought out of camp and to engage. There was a view down from all the camps, which occupied the top of the surrounding ridge, and all the troops were intently awaiting the issue of the fight. The Gauls had placed archers and light-armed skirmishers here and there among the horsemen to give immediate support to their comrades if driven back and to resist the charge of our cavalry. A number of men, wounded unexpectedly by these troops, began to withdraw from the fight. When the Gauls were confident that their own men were getting the better of the battle, and saw ours hard pressed by numbers, with shouts and yells on every side – those who were confined by the entrenchments as well as the others who had come up to their assistance – they sought to inspirit their countrymen. As the action was proceeding in sight of all, and no deed, of honour or dishonour, could escape notice, both sides were stirred to courage by desire of praise and fear of disgrace. The fight lasted, and the victory was doubtful, from noon almost to sunset; then the Germans in one part of the field massed their troops of horse, charged the enemy and routed them, and when they had been put to flight the archers were surrounded and slain. Likewise, from the other parts of the field, our troops pursued the retreating enemy right up to their camp, giving them no chance of rallying. But the Gauls who had come forth from Alesia, almost despairing of victory, sadly withdrew again into the town.

The Gauls tried a night attack. This was unsuccessful due to the Roman entrenchments and artillery. Caesar:

While the Gauls were some distance from the entrenchment they had more advantage from the quantity of their missiles; then, when they came up closer, they were soon caught unawares on the 'spurs', or they sank into the pits and were impaled, or they were shot by artillery pikes from the rampart and the turrets, and so perished on every side. Many a man was wounded, but the entrenchment was nowhere penetrated; and when daybreak drew nigh, fearing that they might be surrounded on their exposed flank by a sortie from the camps above them, they retired to their comrades. Meanwhile the inner force brought out the appliances which had been prepared by Vercingetorix for a sortie, and filled in the nearer trenches; but they lingered too long in the execution of the business, and, or ever they could get near the entrenchments, they learnt that their countrymen had withdrawn. So without success they returned to the town.

The Gauls then attacked one of the Roman camps which was outside the Roman entrenchments. Caesar:

When from the citadel of Alesia Vercingetorix observed his countrymen, he moved out of the town, taking with him the hurdles, poles, mantlets, grappling-hooks, and all the other appliances prepared for the sally. The fight went on simultaneously in all places, and all expedients were attempted, with a rapid

> concentration on that section which was seen to be least strong. With lines so extensive the Roman army was strung out, and at several points defence proved difficult. The shouting which arose in rear of the fighting line did much to scare our troops, as they saw that the risk to themselves depended on the success of others; for, as a rule, what is out of sight disturbs men's minds more seriously than what they see.
>
> Caesar found a suitable spot from which he could see what was proceeding in each quarter. To parties distressed he sent up supports.

Caesar's tactical control was vital. He sent his cavalry to attack Commius' army from the rear. Finally he fought himself. His men were inspired both by his leadership and participation. Caesar:

> Caesar first sent young Brutus with some cohorts, and then Gaius Fabius, lieutenant-general, with others; last of all, as the fight raged more fiercely, he himself brought up fresh troops to reinforce. The battle restored, and the enemy repulsed, he hastened to the quarter whither he had sent Labienus. He withdrew four cohorts from the nearest fort, and ordered part of the cavalry to follow him, part to go round the outer entrenchments and attack the enemy in rear. Labienus, finding that neither ramps nor trenches could resist the rush of the enemy, collected together forty cohorts, which had been withdrawn from the nearest posts and by chance presented themselves, and sent messengers to inform Caesar what he thought it proper to do. Caesar hurried on to take part in the action.
>
> His coming was known by the colour of his cloak, which it was his habit to wear in action as a distinguishing mark; and the troops of cavalry and the cohorts which he had ordered to follow him were noticed, because from the upper levels these downward slopes and depressions were visible. Thereupon the enemy joined battle: a shout was raised on both sides, and taken up by an answering shout from the rampart and the whole of the entrenchments. Our troops discarded their pikes and got to work with their swords. Suddenly the cavalry was noticed in the rear; other cohorts drew near. The enemy turned to flee; the cavalry met them in flight, and a great slaughter ensued. Sedulius, commander and chief of the Lemovices, was killed; Vercassivellaunus the Arvernian was captured alive in the rout; 74 war-standards were brought in to Caesar; of the vast host few returned safe to camp. The others beheld from the town

the slaughter and rout of their countrymen, and, in despair of safety, recalled their force from the entrenchments. Directly they heard what had happened the Gauls fled from their camp. And if the troops had not been worn out by frequent reinforcing and the whole day's effort, the entire force of the enemy could have been destroyed. The cavalry were sent off just after midnight and caught up the rearguard: a great number were taken and slain, the rest fled away into the different states.

The next day Vercingetorix surrendered. When the news reached Rome, a public thanksgiving of twenty days was granted. Caesar eventually became the dictator (sole ruler) of Rome. He was assassinated in 44 BC.

The Battle of Pharsalos 48 BC

After his conquest of Gaul, Julius Caesar had only one political rival, Pompey. In 49 BC, Caesar started a civil war when he marched into Italy. He left six of his best legions behind in case legions loyal to Pompey attacked him from Spain. Pompey's forces, in Italy, were spread out and could only retreat in front of Caesar's army. Finally Pompey shipped his forces to Greece from Brindisi, abandoning Italy to Caesar.

Caesar defeated Pompey's lieutenants' forces in Spain. Pompey's lieutenant, Varus, defeated Caesar's lieutenant, Curio, in Africa.

In 48 BC Caesar crossed over to Greece with seven legions but few cavalry. After an indecisive campaign in Epirus, Caesar moved to Thessaly, in Northern Greece. Pompey followed. Both armies pitched their camps near to each other, on a plain near Pharsalos.

On the left of Caesar's position was the river, Enipeus. His right was open. Caesar arranged his army in three lines. He placed a 'fourth line' of six cohorts on his right. The first two lines were to attack. The third and fourth lines were to remain stationary; the third line was a reserve. The fourth line was a guard against a possible attack on his flank and rear.

When Caesar's first and second lines attacked, Pompey sent his cavalry and light troops to attack Caesar's right flank and rear. Caesar continued his *Commentarii* to cover the Civil War. Caesar:

But when our men, on the giving of the signal, had run forward with javelins levelled and had observed that the Pompeians were not advancing against them, profiting by the experience they had gained in former battles, they spontaneously checked their speed and halted in about the middle of the space, so that they might not approach the foe with their vigour exhausted; and after a brief interval, again renewing their rapid advance, they discharged their javelins and quickly drew their swords, according to Caesar's directions. Nor indeed did the Pompelans fail to meet the emergency. For they parried the shower of missiles and withstood the attack of the legions without breaking their ranks, and after discharging their javelins had recourse to their swords. At the same time the horse on Pompeius' left wing, according to orders, charged in a body, and the whole multitude of archers poured forth. Our cavalry, failing to withstand their attack, gradually quitted their position and retired. Pompeius' cavalry pressed forward all the more eagerly, and deploying by squadrons began to surround our lines on their exposed flank. Caesar, observing it, gave the signal to his fourth line, which he had composed of six cohorts. These advanced rapidly and with colours flying attacked Pompeius' horse with such fury that not one of them stood his ground, and all, wheeling round, not only quitted the position but forthwith in hurried flight made for the highest hills. When these were dislodged all the archers and slingers, left defenceless, without support, were slain. With the same onslaught the cohorts surrounded the left wing, the Pompeians still fighting and continuing their resistance in their lines, and attacked them in the rear.

At the same time Caesar ordered the third line, which had been undisturbed and up to that time had retained its position, to advance. So, as they had come up fresh and vigorous in place of the exhausted troops, while others were attacking in the rear, the Pompeians could not hold their ground and turned to flight in mass. Nor was Caesar wrong in thinking that the victory would originate with those cohorts which had been posted opposite the cavalry in the fourth line, as he had himself stated in exhorting his troops; for it was by them that the cavalry was first repulsed, by them that the archers and slingers were slaughtered, by them that the Pompeian force was surrounded on the left and the rout first started. But Pompeius, when he saw his cavalry beaten back and that part of his force in which he had most confidence panic-stricken, mistrusting the rest also, left the field and straightway rode off to the camp. To the centurions whom he had placed on duty at the praetorian gate he exclaimed in a loud voice that the troops might hear: "Protect the camp and defend it carefully if anything goes amiss. I am going round the other gates and encouraging the guards of the camp." Having said this, he betook himself to the general's headquarters, mistrusting his fortunes and yet waiting to see the issue.

When the Pompeians were driven in flight within the rampart, Caesar, thinking that no respite should be given them in their terror, urged his men to take advantage of the kindness of fortune and attack the camp. And though fatigued by the great heat, for the action had been prolonged till noon, they nevertheless obeyed his command, with a spirit ready for every toil. The camp was being

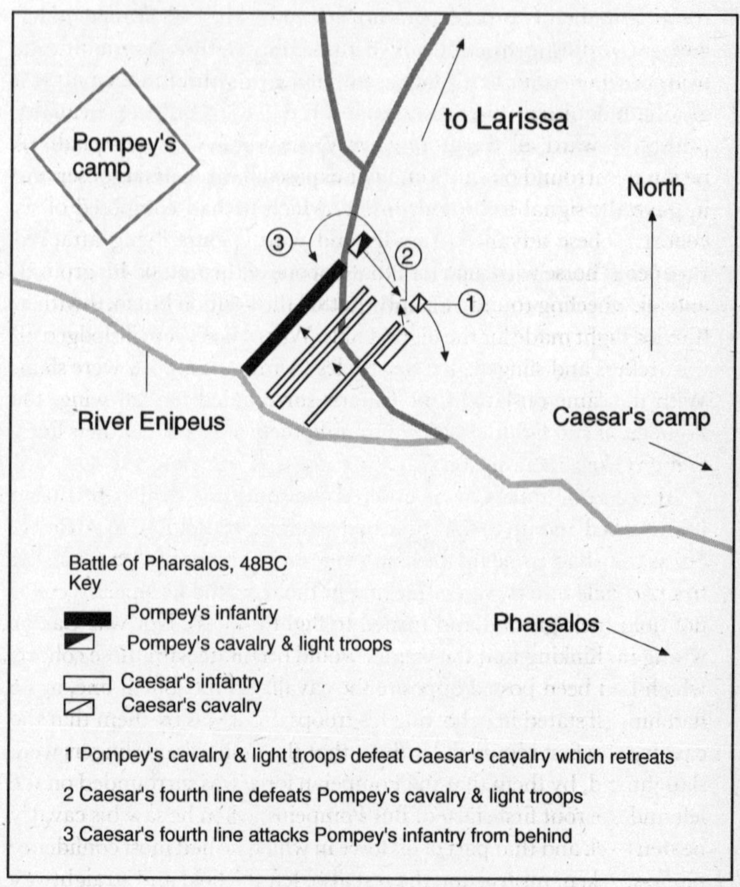

Map of the Battle of Pharsalos

zealously defended by the cohorts which had been left there on guard, and much more keenly still by the Thracians and barbaric auxiliaries. For the soldiers who had fled from the battlefield, panic-stricken in spirit and exhausted by fatigue, many of them having thrown away their arms and their military standards, were thinking more of further flight than of the defence of the camp. Nor could those who had planted themselves on the rampart stand up any longer against the multitude of javelins, but, worn out by wounds, quitted their position, and forthwith all, following the guidance of centurions and military tribunes, fled for refuge to some very lofty hills that stretched up to the camp.

. . . Pompeius, procuring a horse and tearing off his insignia as Imperator, flung himself out of the camp by the decuman gate and, putting spurs to his horse, hurried straight off to Larisa. Nor did be halt there, but, coming across a few of his men in flight, with undiminished speed, not stopping his course at night, arrives at the sea with a retinue of thirty horsemen and embarks on board a cornship . . .

Pompey was murdered shortly after he arrived in Egypt. Caesar was master of the Roman world until his own death, four years later.

Medieval – The Crusades

The Battle of Dorylaeum 1 July 1097

The Roman Empire had been divided into two parts in 395. Rome remained the capital of the Western part. Rome declined but the Eastern Roman Empire had continued uninterrupted. Its capital was Constantinople. The city was also known as Byzantium. It drew much of its strength, in revenues and manpower, from Asia Minor, fertile provinces which were known as Anatolia. Its territories were threatened by the incursions of a nomadic people known as the Seljuk Turks. Later, they were also known as Saracens. In 1071 the Turks destroyed the main army of the Eastern Roman Empire at the battle of Manzikert. The result of the battle was the permanent loss of the provinces of Anatolia.

The Seljuk Turks were Sunnite Muslims. They acknowledged the authority of the Abbassid Caliphs in Baghdad. Further south, Jerusalem was held by Egyptian Muslims who were Shi'ites. They acknowledged the authority of the Fatimid Caliphs in Cairo.

In 1093 the Emperor, Alexius I Comnenus, wrote a letter to Count Robert of Flanders in which he appealed for help against the encroaching Turks:

> O illustrious count and great consoler of the faith, I am writing to inform Your Prudence that the very saintly empire of the Greek Christians is daily being persecuted by the Pechenegs and the Turks . . . The blood of Christians flows in unheard-of scenes of carnage . . .
>
> Therefore in the name of God and because of the true piety of the generality of Greek Christians, we implore you to bring to this

> city all the faithful soldiers of Christ . . . Bring me aid and bring aid to the Greek Christians.
>
> By coming, you will find your reward in heaven and, if you do not come, God will condemn you.

At the Council of Clermont, in 1095, Pope Urban II, called for an army to travel to the East. The response was the military expedition known as the First Crusade. Armies, led by Godfrey of Bouillon, Raymond of Toulouse, Robert, Duke of Normandy and the Norman Lords, Bohemond and Tancred, journeyed east.

The armies of the First Crusade were marching through Asia Minor. They had forced Nicaea to surrender. The country was desolate. To make foraging easier the armies split into two columns. One column was encamped near the ruined town of Dorylaeum when swarms of Turks appeared from all directions. They were all horse-archers. The crusader knights began to withdraw towards their camp. Fulcher of Chartres was an eyewitness:

> But, what they thought was a deliberate move on our part – was really involuntary, and the result of despair. For, crushed one against another like sheep penned up in a fold, helpless and panic-stricken, we were shut in by the Turks on every side, and had not the courage to break out at any point. The air was filled with shouts and screams, partly from the combatants, partly from the multitude in the camp. Already we had lost all hope of saving ourselves, and were owning our sins and commending ourselves to God's mercy. Believing themselves at the point to die, many men left the ranks and asked for absolution from the nearest priest. It was to little purpose that our chiefs, Robert of Normandy, Stephen of Blois, and Bohemund kept striving to beat back the infidels, and sometimes charged out against them. The Turks had closed in, and were attacking us with the greatest audacity.

Messages had been sent to the other column which was not far away. They now came charging into the Turks at full speed, taking them in the flank and the rear. The Turks panicked and were routed.

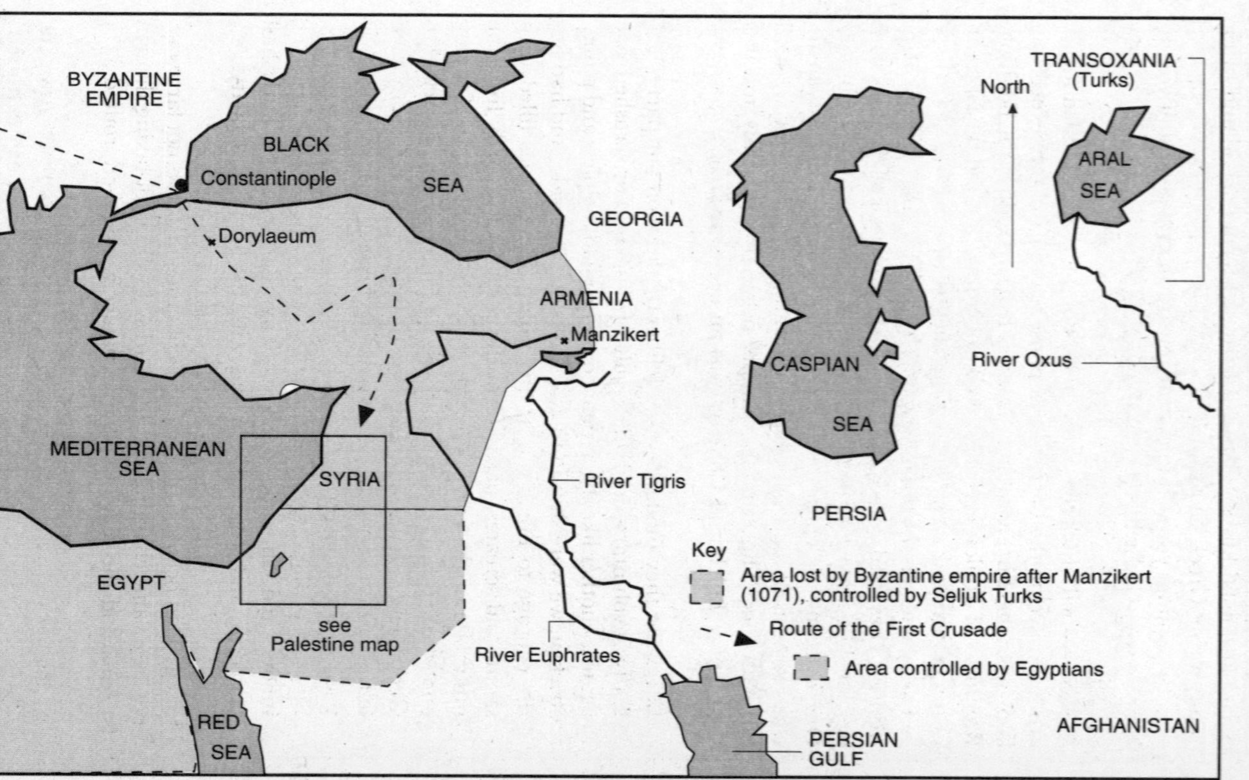

Map of Asia Minor at the time of the Crusades

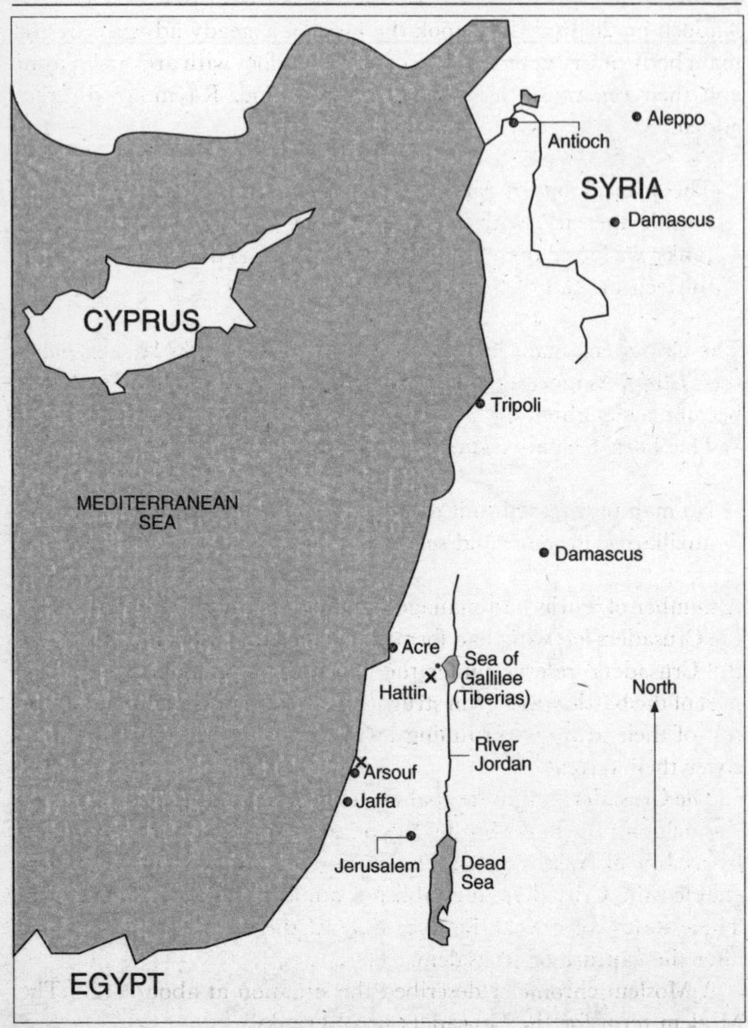

Map of Palestine at the time of the Crusades

The Battle of Antioch 28 June 1098

Their victory at Dorylaeum allowed the Crusaders to reach Antioch which they besieged during the winter of 1097–8. They captured Antioch by treachery on 4 June 1098. They then defeated an army of Turks which arrived after the city had fallen to them. The battle of

Antioch on 28 June 1098 took the form of a steady advance by the main body of Crusaders, in line of battle, on foot with archers in front and their remaining mounted knights behind. Raymond d'Agiles added:

> The princes had arranged eight corps, but when we had got outside the city, with every man able to bear arms put in the ranks; we found there were five more corps, so that we fought with thirteen instead of the original eight.

The Crusaders' main line of battle pushed the Turks back towards their camp. As more and more Turks broke away and fled, the battle became a slaughter.

The Turk Kemal-ed-din was quoted as saying:

> No man of rank fell, but there was a horrid slaughter of our foot auxiliaries, grooms, and servants.

A number of Turks had managed to cross in front of the hills before the Crusaders left wing had formed. These Turks were able to attack the Crusaders' reserve under the Norman leader Bohemund. This part of the battle was a grim struggle until the Turks realised that the rest of their army was running away. They set fire to the grass to cover their retreat.

The Crusaders' ultimate goal was to recapture Jerusalem. The city was held not by Turks but by Egyptians. The Crusaders captured it by assault in August 1099. The capture of Antioch and Jerusalem enabled the Crusaders to establish a number of states of their own. These states were weak because most of the Crusaders went home after the capture of Jerusalem.

A Moslem chronicler described the situation at about 1127. The Moslem term for the Crusaders was "Franks":

> The power of the Franks extended from Mardin and Scheikstan in Mesopotamia as far as El-Arish on the frontier of Egypt, and all the provinces of Syria only Aleppo, Emesa, Hamah, and Damascus were still unconquered. Their bands raided as far as Amida in the province of Diarbekir and in that of El Jezireh [Upper Mesopotamia] as far as Nisibis and Ras-Ain. The Mussulmans of Rakkah and Haran were exposed to their oppression; and the victims of their barbarous violence. All the roads to Damascus

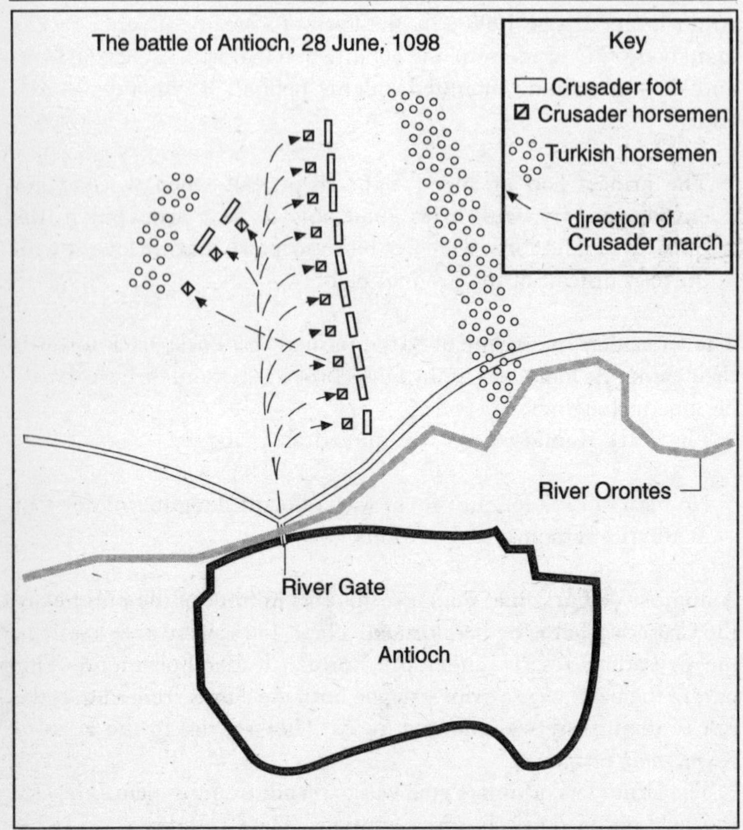

Map of the Battle of Antioch

except that which passes by Rahaba (Rehoboth) and the desert were infested by their plundering parties. Merchants and travellers had to hide among the rocks and the wilderness, or to trust themselves and their goods to the mercy of the Bedouins. Things were growing worse and worse – and the Christians had begun to impose a fixed blackmail on the surviving Moslem towns which the latter paid to be quit of their devastations . . . They took a regular tribute from all the territory of Aleppo as far as the mill outside the garden-gate – only 20 paces from the city itself. Then Almighty God casting his eyes on the Mussulman emirs and noting the contempt in which the true faith had fallen saw that these princes were too weak to undertake the defence of the true religion and resolved

> to raise up against the Christians a man capable of punishing them and exacting a due vengeance for their crimes.

The "man capable of punishing them" was the governor of Mosul, Zengi. He retook the northernmost crusader state of Edessa in 1144. In 1146–7 a Second Crusade failed to capture Damascus. The Moslem leaders were involved in a power struggle. Eventually the Moslem states were united under Yussuf Salah-ed-din (Saladin).

The Battle of Tiberias (Hattin) 3–4 July 1187

In 1187 Saladin invaded the kingdom of Jerusalem. He besieged the castle of Tiberias, by the Sea of Gallilee (also known as Lake Tiberias). On 3 July the entire Crusader army left camp at Saffuriyah and advanced to the relief of the garrison. They were surrounded by thousands of Turkish horse-bowmen. The main force of the Turks was between the crusaders and the Sea of Gallilee. Men and horses were desperately thirsty. King Guy of Jerusalem's nerve failed and he ordered his army to pitch camp. Ralph of Coggleshall recorded that Raymond Count of Tripoli, exclaimed:

> Alas, Lord God! The war is ended we are all delivered over to death, and the realm is ruined.

The Turks shot arrows into the camp that night and set fire to the dry grass upwind. Boha-ed-din described the Crusaders' situation from the Moslem point-of-view:

> God fed the Christians with the bread of tears, and gave them to drink without stint the cup of repentance, till the dawn of tribulation came again.

The next day, the Crusaders tried to get to the nearest source of water, the village of Hattin. It was vital that the infantry remained with the horsemen to support them with their cross-bows. The infantry deserted the horsemen, climbing a hill and refusing to come down. The king tried to move on with his horsemen towards the Sea of Gallilee. Ralph of Coggleshall:

> Then the king, seeing that the infantry would not return, and that without them he could not prevail against the arrows of the Turks, ordered his men to halt and pitch their tents. So the battles broke up, and all huddled together in a confused mass around the True Cross.

Raymond, Count of Tripoli, and the leading horsemen, one third of the army, tried to charge through the Turks. According to Ralph of Coggleshall, Raymond cried:

> The battle is hopelessly lost; let every man save himself if he can.

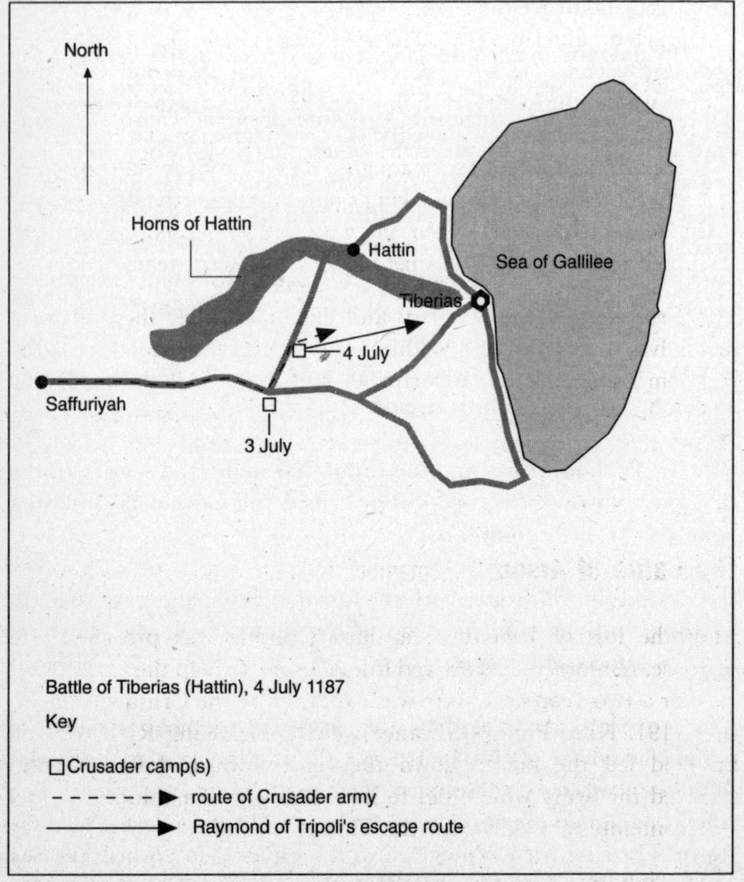

Map of the Battle of Tiberias

They managed to burst through the horse-bowmen and escaped. Saladin's son, Malek-el-Afdal described the fate of the remaining Crusaders:

> When the king of the Franks and his Knights, found themselves pressed together on a hillock on the side of the hill of Kurn-Hattin, I was with my father. I saw the Franks make a gallant charge at those of the Moslems who were nearest them, and drive them back close to the spot where we stood. I looked at my father and saw that he was deeply moved; he changed colour, grasped his beard in hand, and moved forward crying, "Let us prove the devil a liar." At these words our men precipitated themselves upon the Franks, and drove them back up the hillside. I began myself to be overjoyed, and to cry, "They fly! they fly!" But the enemy presently came back to the charge, and for a second time cut their way to the foot of the hill; when they were again driven back, I began to cry afresh, "They fly! they fly!" Then my father looked at me and said, "Hold your tongue, and do not say that they are really routed till you see the king's tent fall." Shortly after we saw the tent come down; then my father dismounted, prostrated himself to the earth in thanks to God, and wept tears of joy.

The Crusaders were so thirsty and exhausted that they allowed themselves to be captured. Within a few months the whole Crusader kingdom except for a few fortresses had fallen. All the available soldiers had been lost in the battle. King Guy was released in 1188. He set about gathering forces to recover some of his lost realm.

The Battle of Arsouf 7 September 1191

After the loss of Jerusalem, a third Crusade was preached. In response, reinforcements arrived from Europe to help the Crusaders.

After a two-year siege Acre was captured by the Crusaders on 12 July 1191. King Philip of France went home. King Richard I of England led the march down the coast towards Jaffa. Saladin attacked the army which had to march slowly in a column.

A contemporary described the Turkish tactics:

> The infidels, not weighed down with heavy armour like our knights, but always able to outstrip them in pace, were a constant

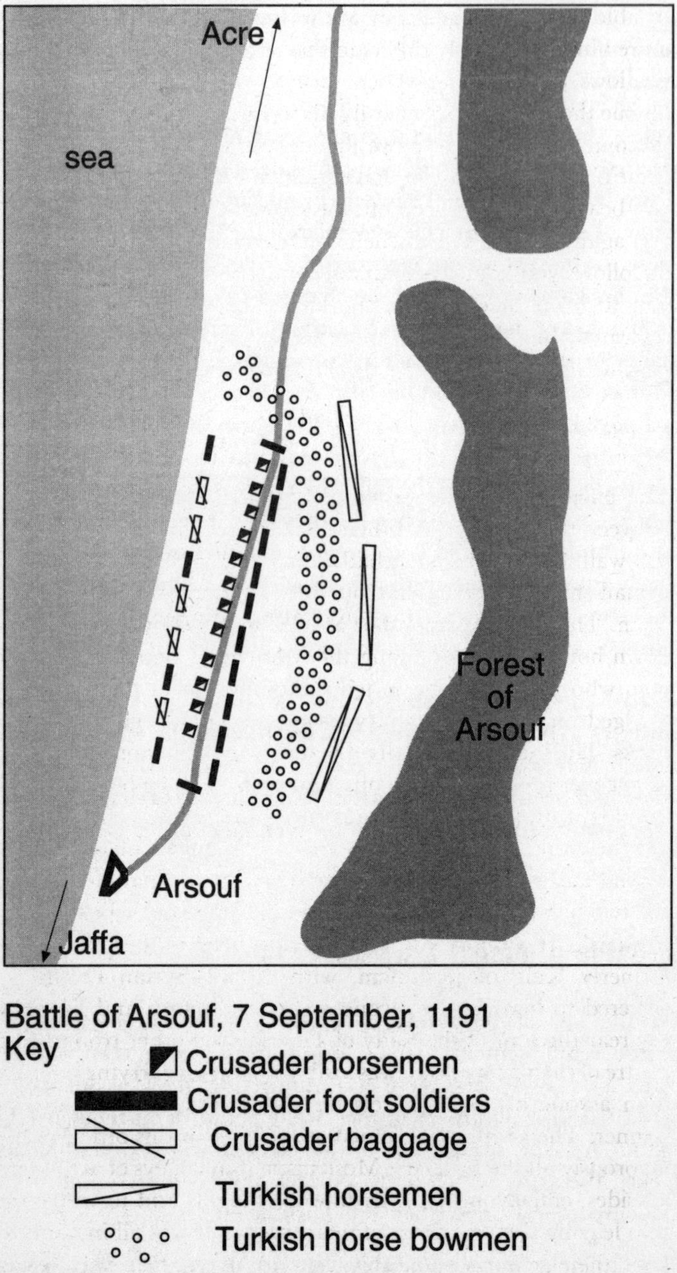

Acre
sea
Forest of Arsouf
Arsouf
Jaffa

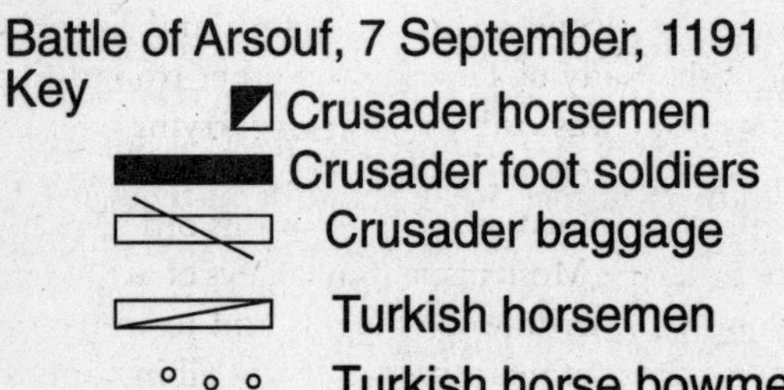

Map of the Battle of Arsouf

trouble. When charged they are wont to fly, and their horses are more nimble than any others in the world; one may liken them to swallows for swiftness. When they see that you have ceased to pursue them, they no longer fly but return upon you; they are like tiresome flies which you can flap away for a moment, but which come back the instant you have stopped hitting at them: as long as you beat about they keep off: the moment you cease, they are on you again. So the Turk, when you wheel about after driving him off follows you home without a second's delay, but will fly again if you turn on them. When the king rode at them, they always retreated, but they hung about our rear, and sometimes did us mischief, not unfrequently disabling some of our men.

Boha-ed-din witnessed the crusaders' march:

The enemy moved in order of battle: their infantry marched between them and us and their cavalry, keeping as level and firm as a wall. Each foot-soldier had a thick cassock of felt, and under it a mail-shirt so strong that our arrows made no impression on them. They, meanwhile, shot at us with crossbows, which struck down horse and man among the Moslems. I noted among them men who had from one to ten shafts sticking in their backs, yet trudged on at their ordinary pace and did not fall out of their ranks. The infantry were divided into two halves: one marched so as to cover the cavalry, the other moved along the beach and took no part in the fighting, but rested itself.

When the first half was wearied, it changed places with the second and got its turn of repose. The cavalry marched between the two halves of the infantry, and only came out when it wished to charge. It was formed in three main corps: in the van was Guy, formerly King of Jerusalem, with all the Syrian Franks who adhered to him; in the second were the English and French; in the rear the sons of the Lady of Tiberias and other troops. In the centre of their army there was visible a waggon carrying a tower as high as one of our minarets on which was planted the king's banner. The Franks' continued to advance in this order, fighting vigorously all the time: the Moslems sent in volleys of arrows from all sides, endeavouring to irritate the knights and to worry them into leaving their rampart of infantry. But it was all in vain: they kept their temper admirably and went on their way without hurrying themselves in the least, while their fleet sailed along

> the coast parallel with them, till they arrived at their camping-place for the night. They never marched a long stage, because they had to spare the foot-soldiers, of whom the half not actively engaged was carrying the baggage and tents, so great was their want of beasts of burden. It was impossible not to admire the patience which these people showed: they bore crushing fatigue, though they had no proper military administration, and were getting no personal advantage. And so they finally pitched their camp on the farther side of the river of Caesarea.

Saladin was waiting for an opportunity to make a serious attack. He hid his main force in one of the few forests in the area, the "wood of Arsouf".

On 7 September, King Richard divided the army into twelve divisions; each had its foot soldiers in the outer ranks, the cross-bowmen in the front rank. A squadron of horsemen were behind the foot soldiers and the baggage was carried by those nearest the sea. They were well on their way when Saladin's main army came out of the woods.

A contemporary described their appearance:

> All over the face of the land you could see the well-ordered bands of the Turks, myriads of parti-coloured banners, marshalled in troops and squadrons; of mailed men alone there appeared to be more than 20,000. With unswerving course, swifter than eagles, they swept down upon our line of march. The air was turned black by the dust that their hoofs cast up. Before the face of each emir went his musicians, making a horrid din with horns, trumpets, drums, cymbals; and all manner of brazen instruments while the troops behind pressed on with howls and cries of war. For the Infidels think that the louder the noise, the bolder grows the spirit of the warrior. So did the cursed Turks beset us before, behind and on the flank, and they pressed in so close that for two miles around there was not a spot of the bare earth visible; all was covered by the thick array of the enemy.

They closed in to within range of their bows and shot continually. The last Crusader division suffered most. Although the infantry shot back, so many horses and men were wounded that the last division began to charge. The movement spread up the column. The Turks, taken by surprise, panicked. Boha-ed-din:

> On a sudden, we saw the cavalry of the enemy, who were now drawn together in three main masses, brandish their lances; raise their war-cry, and dash out at us. The infantry suddenly opened up gaps in their line to let them pass through.
>
> On our side the rout was complete. I was myself in the centre: that corps having fled in confusion, I thought to take refuge with the left wing, which was the nearest to me; but when I reached it, I found it also in full retreat, and making off no less quickly than the centre. Then I rode to the right wing, but this had been routed even more thoroughly than the left. I turned accordingly to the spot where the Sultan's bodyguard should have served as a rallying-point for the rest. The banners were still upright and the drum beating, but only 17 horsemen were round them.

After the battle, the Crusaders were able to regain the whole coastland of Southern Palestine. The war ended in a treaty.

Medieval – 100 Years War

The Battle of Crecy 1346

The English kings had claims to lands in France, since 1066. King John lost Normandy in 1204. In 1152, the English king Henry II acquired Aquitaine through his marriage to the heiress, Eleanor. This brought them into direct conflict with the French king who was technically the overlord of all owners of French land. The conflict between the national sovereigns resulted in a period of intermittent warfare known as the Hundred Years War.

In July 1346 the English king Edward III crossed over to France to protect his interests there. He brought with him an army of 4,000 men at arms, 12,000 archers and 6,000 Welsh light infantry.

The French relied on mounted men at arms. The English had 30 years' experience of fighting the Welsh and the Scots. As a result they had changed their style of fighting. They had learnt to use the southern Welsh long bow. A skilled archer could load and shoot its three-foot-long arrow in ten seconds. The longbow's three-foot-long arrow was easily capable of piercing the chain mail armour of the time. It could pierce four inches of oak and was effective at 250 yards' range. They had also learnt that even men at arms defended best on foot.

Edward III marched through Normandy and then retreated towards Flanders, aware that King Philip of France was nearby with a large French army.

At Crecy-en-Ponthieu he found a good defensive position on a hill between the villages of Crecy and Wadicourt. The French army was following from Abbeville. On 26 August 1346 they arrived, led by Genoese crossbowmen from the French fleet, followed next by the

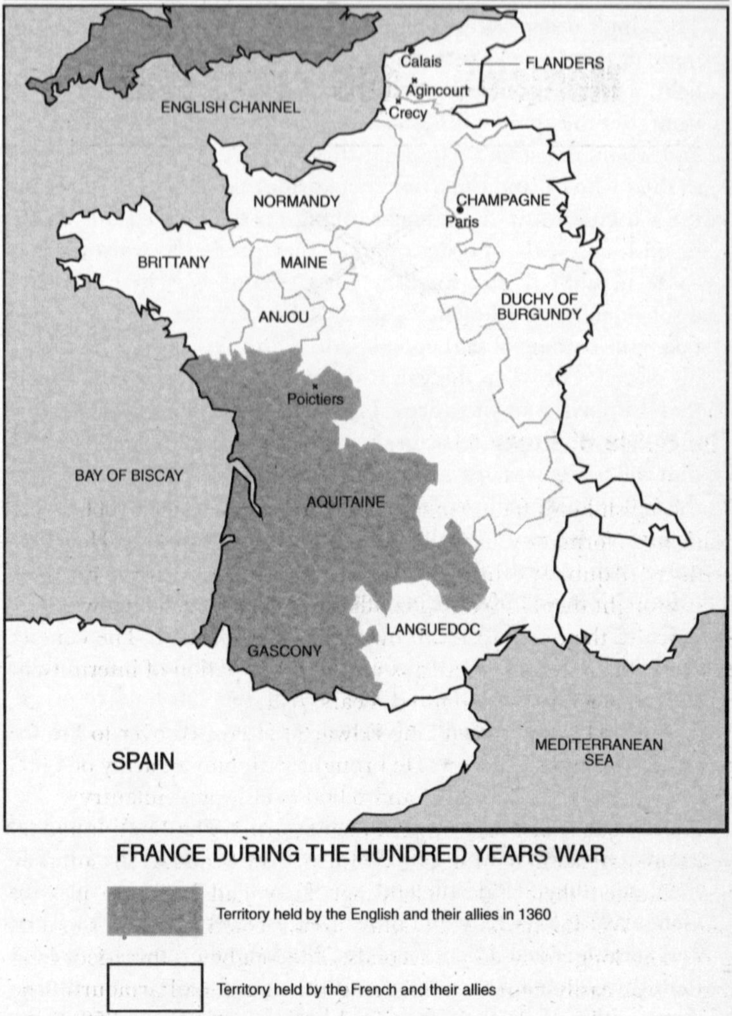

FRANCE DURING THE HUNDRED YEARS WAR

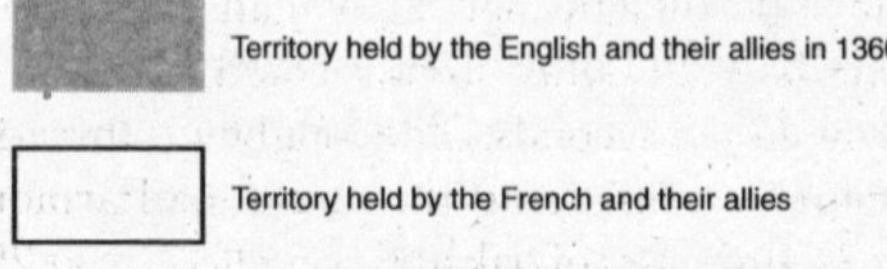

Map of France during the 100 Years War

mounted men at arms. Volunteers on foot followed last. They outnumbered the English by at least three to one. The mounted men at arms were grouped in formations called "battles".

The contemporary chronicler Jean de Froissart was a secretary to the English Royal Court. He provided a detailed account of the battle:

> The king's orders were soon passed around among his lords, but none of them would turn back, for each wished to be first in the field. The van would not retire because they had got so far to the front, but they halted. But those behind them kept riding forward; and would not stop, saying that they would get as far to the front as their fellows, and that from mere pride and jealousy. And when the vanguard saw the others pushing on they would not be left behind, and without order or array they pressed forward till they came in sight of the English. Great shame was it to see such disobedience, and better would it have been for all if they had taken the counsel of that good knight who advised the king to stay his march. For when the van came suddenly in face of the enemy they stopped, and then drew back a space in such disarray that they rushed in upon those in their rear so that all behind thought that the battle was begun, and the vanguard already routed. And the foot soldiery of the cities and communes who covered the roads behind as far as Abbeville, and were more than 20,000 strong, drew their swords and began to cry, "Death to those English traitors! Not one of them shall ever get back to England."

The French arrived on the battlefield in confusion. A sudden thunderstorm drenched both sides. When the sunshine returned, the Genoese crossbowmen advanced up the valley towards the English. Froissart:

> When the Genoways were assembled together and began to approach, they made a great leap and cry to abash the Englishmen, but they stood still and stirred not for all that: then the Genoways again the second time made another leap and a fell cry, and stept forward a little, and the Englishmen removed not one foot: thirdly, again they leapt and cried, and went forth till they came within shot; then they shot fiercely with their cross-bows. Then the English archers stept forth one pace and let fly their arrows so wholly [together] and so thick, that it seemed snow. When the Genoways felt the arrows piercing through heads, arms and breasts, many of them cast down their cross-bows and did cut their strings and returned discomfited. When the French king saw them fly away, he said: "Slay these rascals, for they shall let and trouble us without reason." Then ye should have seen the men of arms dash in among them and killed a great number of them: and ever still the Englishmen shot whereas they saw thickest press; the

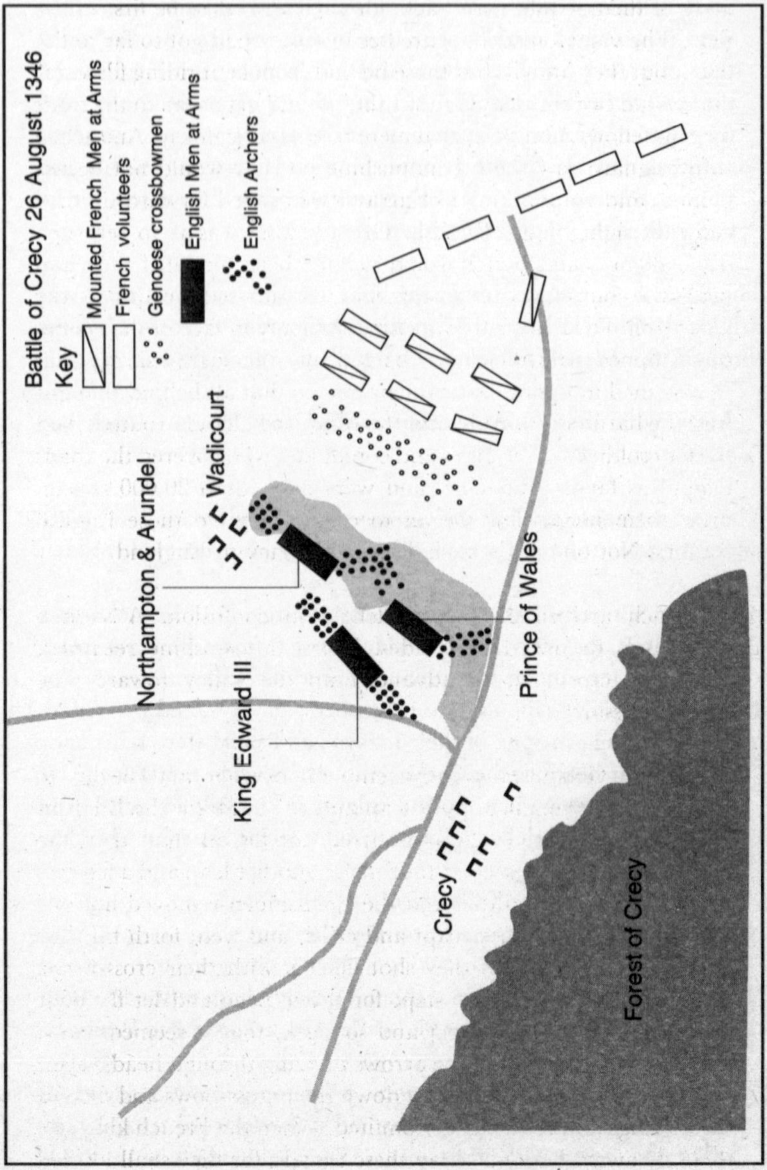

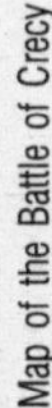

Map of the Battle of Crecy

> sharp arrows ran into the men of arms and into their horses, and many fell, horse and men, among the Genoways, and when they were down, they could not relieve again, the press was so thick that one overthrew another. And also among the Englishmen there were certain rascals that went afoot with great knives, and they went in among the men of arms, and slew and murdered many as they lay on the ground, both earls, barons, knights and squires, whereof the king of England was after displeased, for he had rather they had been taken prisoners.

The French horsemen imagined that treason or cowardice was driving them back. Instead of opening their ranks to let the Genoese through, the French horsemen charged into them, crying:

> Away with these faint-hearted rabble! they do but block our advance.

They were unable to clear the Genoese out of their way. They were under a constant hail of arrows from the English archery. Froissart:

> For the bowmen let fly among them at large, and did not lose a single shaft, for every arrow told on horse or man, piercing head, or arm, or leg among the riders and sending the horses mad. For some stood stock-still, and others rushed sideways, and most of all began backing in spite of their masters and some were rearing or tossing their heads at the arrows; and others when they felt the bit threw themselves down. So the knights in the first French battle fell, slain or sore stricken, almost without seeing the men who slew them.

None of the French horsemen reached the English.

The rest of the battle was a series of chaotic charges. In the second charge. King John of Bohemia, though nearly blind, refused to hold back. He said to the knights at his bridle-rein, according to Froissart:

> Then he said: "Sirs, ye are my men, my companions and friends in this journey: I require you bring me so far forward, that I may strike one stroke with my sword." They said they would do his commandment, and to the intent that they should not lose him in the press, they tied all their reins of their bridles each to other and set the king before to accomplish his desire, and so they went on

> their enemies. The lord Charles of Bohemia his son, who wrote himself king of Almaine and bare the arms, he came in good order to the battle; but when he saw that the matter went awry on their party, he departed, I cannot tell you which way. The king his father was so far forward that he strake a stroke with his sword, yea and more than four, and fought valiantly and so did his company; and they adventured themselves so forward, that they were there all slain, and the next day they were found in the place about the king, and all their horses tied each to other.

Each group of French knights worked its way to the front and charged at the English but soon fell back. The English archers inflicted most of the casualties, shooting at the flanks of each "battle". The French tried to reach the English men at arms as they advanced. The arrows killed or dismounted the outer riders, but the central section of each squadron, protected by their fellows' bodies, often reached the front of either the Prince of Wales's or Arundel's dismounted knights and pressed hard upon them. The main stress seems to have fallen on the southern formation commanded by the Prince of Wales because they were nearest. One attack was conducted with such vigour that requests were sent for help to the king. Froissart:

> The day of the battle certain Frenchmen and Almains perforce opened the archers of the prince's battle and came and fought with the men of arms hand to hand. Then the second battle of the Englishmen came to succour the prince's battle, the which was time, for they had as then much ado; and they with the prince sent a messenger to the king, who was on a little windmill hill. Then the knight said to the king: "Sir, the Earl of Warwick and the earl of Oxford, Sir Raynold Cobham and other, such as be about the prince, your son, are fiercely fought withal and are sore handled; wherefore they desire you that you and your battle will come and aid them; for if the Frenchmen increase, as they doubt they will, your son and they shall have much ado." Then the king said: "Is my son dead or hurt or on the earth felled?" "No, sir," quoth the knight, "but he is hardly matched; wherefore he hath need of your aid." "Well," said the king, "return to him and to them that sent you hither, and say to them that they send no more to me for any adventure that falleth, as long as my son is alive: and also say to them that they suffer him this day to win his spurs."

According to Baker of Swinbrook, another contemporary chronicler, the prince himself was beaten to his knees. The Earl of Arundel pushed forward to align his troops alongside those of the prince. Baker of Swinbrook reported fifteen or sixteen separate attacks before the sun set and the French gradually withdrew.

The Battle of Poictiers 19 September 1356

In the summer of 1356 Prince Edward, the Prince of Wales, was leading a raid through the Loire valley. King John of France had assembled an army to intercept him. On 17 September they came into contact. The English army was composed of archers, men at arms and some Gascon light troops. It had an immense baggage train to carry the plunder from its raid. 18 September was spent in negotiations through the mediation of the Cardinal of Perigord "to spare the effusion of Christian blood by a treaty of peace." Nothing was achieved. Chandos Herald described the Prince's intentions:

> The prince put his men in order, and willingly would he have avoided an action, if he could have managed it. But he saw well what he had to do: accordingly he summoned the Earl of Warwick, gave him charge of the van, and said to him, "You shall first go over the passage and take our baggage in charge: I will ride after you with all my knights, that if you meet with any mischance we may reinforce you: and the Earl of Salisbury shall follow behind and lead our rear-battle. Let us each be upon our guard, and, in case the French fall upon us, let every man dismount as quickly as he can, to fight on foot." So they settled the matter over night, and in the morning the prince left his quarters and set out to ride away, for on this day he did not think to fight, but thought that rather he could avoid an action.

On 19 September the French king sent forward some knights to report on the strength and position of the English. According to Froissart, a contemporary chronicler, the knights reported that the English were:

> strongly posted along a road with a hedge and a ditch beside it, with the hedge lined with archers and the men at-arms drawn up

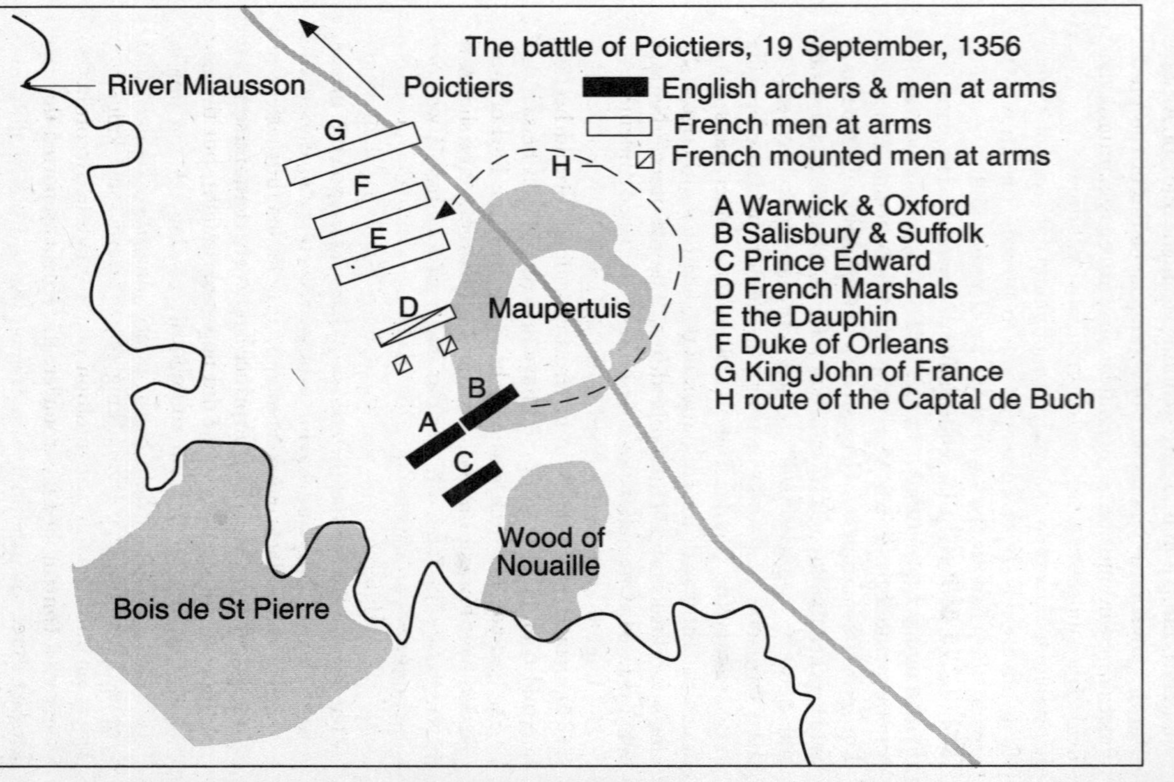

Map of the Battle of Poictiers

> behind among the vines and thorn bushes, all on foot; the hedge had but one gap in it, where four knights might ride abreast save at this point there was no way of getting at the English except by breaking through the archers, who were never easy to dislodge.

King John told his men at arms to dismount and fight on foot. Only a small advance body of horsemen was to precede the army. The ground they had to cross was thick with bushes and trees which might have disordered a large formation of horsemen. His army was divided into five formations ("battles"). The first formation was 300 horsemen, under the two Marshals, D'Audrehem and Clermont. The second formation was German men at arms under the Counts of Saarbrucken, Nidau and Nassau. They also had 2,000 crossbowmen and 2,000 "sergeants à pied" armed with darts and javelins. The third formation was 4,000 men at arms under the Dauphin (the king's eldest son, Charles Duke of Normandy) and the Duke of Bourbon. The fourth formation was 3,000 men at arms under the king's brother, Philip, Duke of Orleans. The fifth formation was 6,000 men at arms under the king himself.

The English army was formed in three "battles". Each "battle" was composed of 1,000 men at arms, 1,000 archers and a few hundred Gascon light troops. The leading battle was commanded by the earls of Warwick and Oxford. The main battle was commanded by the prince himself. The rearward battle was commanded by the earls of Salisbury & Suffolk. Baker of Swinbrook, another contemporary chronicler:

> The Prince's battle and the convoy of baggage passed the stream at a narrow ford, and having crossed the valley made its way through the hedges and ditches and occupied the hill, where he was hidden from view by the thicket, and yet himself commanded a view of the enemy. The French, seeing the Prince's banner clearly in sight at first, then gradually moving off and finally concealed from their sight by the intervening ridge, thought that he was retreating.

Seeing the English begin to withdraw, King John ordered the advance. The advance body of horsemen reached the English line, charged at full speed and were shot down by the English archers. The survivors joined the second formation in their attack on the English line along the hedge in front of their position. The English rearguard under the Earl of Salisbury held them until Prince Edward and the Earl of Warwick's battles returned. A flanking movement by archers led by the Earl of Oxford completed the rout of the first main "battle" who retired in disorder. The third formation then attacked the entire length of the English line along the hedge. Prince Edward had to commit his own "battle" except for a reserve of 400 men at arms. The struggle was long and hard but eventually the French retreated, pursued by a few rash English knights.

The fourth formation under the Duke of Orleans was completely dismayed by this setback and fled too. The king's battle was equal in size to the entire English army who were in disarray.

Baker of Swinbrook described the English line at this moment:

> Some were carrying the wounded to the rear and laying them under the shelter of the trees and thickets, others were replacing their broken swords and lances from the spoils of the slain; archers were trying to replenish their store of arrows even pulling them out of the bodies of the dead and wounded. There was in the whole host no one who was not either hurt or utterly worn out with the battle, save only the reserve of 400 men whom Edward still kept about his standard.

Seeing that the French were sending their last reserves into the battle, Prince Edward decided to attack. He put the 400 men of his reserve in front and charged down the slope with his entire army. He sent a Gascon nobleman, the Capital de Buch, with about 150 men around the French flank to attack them from behind. The two sides clashed at the foot of the slope. The English archers joined in the hand to hand combat as soon as they had shot all their arrows. The Captal de Buch and his small force attacking the French from behind made the difference. The French began to retreat. The French King and his nobles resisted until virtually all who fought for him were either captured or killed. Finally the king and his youngest son were taken prisoner. According to Baker of Swinbrook, the battle lasted seven hours:

> The first attack had commenced at prime, and the last of the English had not returned from pursuit till vespers.

At the Treaty of Bretigny, in 1360, King John conceded Poitou,

Angoumois, Limousin, Rouergue and other districts – in fact most of the duchy of Aquitaine, lost 200 years before. The English retained Calais.

The Battle of Agincourt 25 October 1415

In the summer of 1415, King Henry V of England invaded France. England still held Calais, Bordeaux and other territory in the south.

The English army sailed on 11 August. 8,000 archers and 2,000 men at arms landed in Normandy near Harfleur. They besieged the town which surrendered on 22 September. It was too late in the year to march on Paris and Bordeaux. The King decided to march north to Calais, 120 miles away, across the river Somme. The French defended the river crossings until the English managed to cross the river on 19 October. In the evening of 24 October they found the French army in a position ahead of them across the road to Calais. The English army camped around the village of Maisoncelles. At first light the archers and men at arms took up battle positions between two woods.

The two armies were about 1,000 yards apart. The French army was entirely formed of mounted and dismounted men at arms. For four hours both armies held their positions. King Henry led the English forward to within bowshot of the French (perhaps 250 yards). The English archers planted their defensive stakes and began to shoot at the French. In retaliation the mounted French men at arms on the wings began to charge the English line. They failed to break the English line, suffered losses from the archery and turned back. Many of them crashed into the first line of dismounted French men at arms. Despite this they crowded forward in three groups to attack the English men at arms. The English men at arms were now in front of the archers who joined in the hand-to-hand combat. Their mobility was an advantage against the heavily armoured French men at arms. The French second line came up to join in. The French superiority in numbers actually hampered them, men behind pressing the men in front so that they could not move freely and faced several opponents at once. The French had shortened their lances to fight on foot. They had to step over fallen bodies to reach the English who had full length lances. The English archers moved forward to

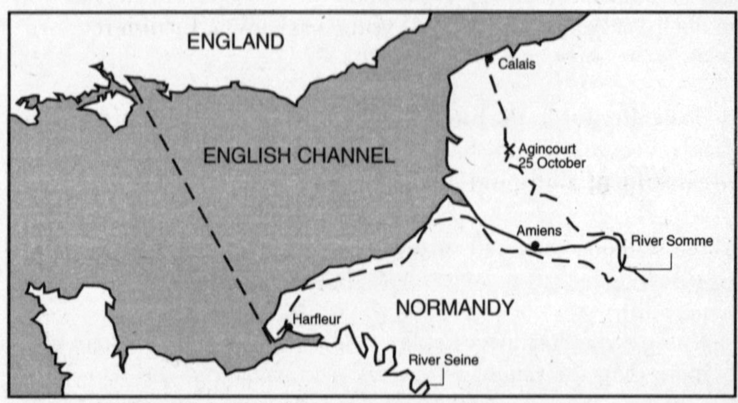

Above: AGINCOURT CAMPAIGN MAP 9 August–29 October 1415

– – – – English route

Right: Battle of Agincourt
25 October, 1415
Key

woods
Dismounted Men-at-Arms
Cavalry
Archers

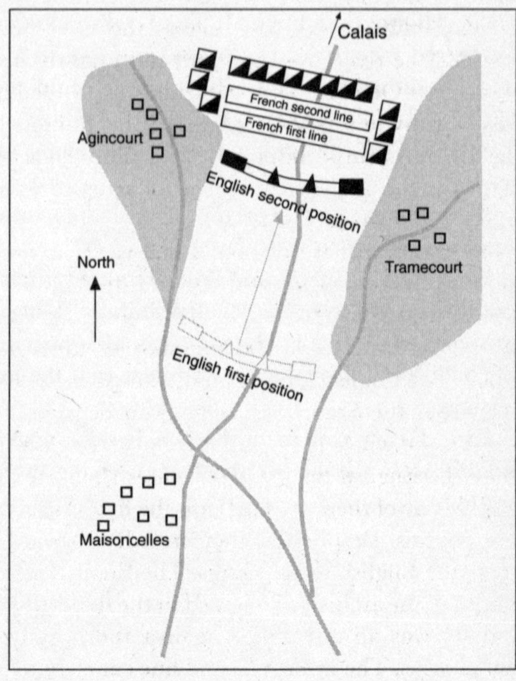

Map of the Battle of Agincourt

attack the flanks of the French columns. These were so tightly packed by men pushing they had difficulty in defending themselves.

St Remy, a French man at arms:

> Soon afterwards, the English archers perceiving the disorder of the advance guard and, hastening to the place where the fugitives came from, killed and disabled the French.

Many of the French had surrendered. A contemporary manuscript reported:

> Some, even of the more noble . . . that day surrendered themselves more than ten times.

According to contemporary accounts the bodies of the French lay piled "Higher than a man". The English climbed these heaps "and butchered the adversaries below with swords axes and other weapons". Soon after midday the English could move freely over the battlefield, pulling "Down the heaps of bodies to separate the living from the dead, proposing to keep the living as slaves, to be ransomed".

King Henry had kept the English line intact as a precaution against the French third line.

Faced by this threat and an unexpected attack on the unguarded English baggage by the local peasantry, King Henry ordered the prisoners to be killed. The most valuable prisoners were spared and the killing called off once it was clear that the French third line was leaving.

King Henry called the French heralds who confirmed that the English were the victors and told the King the name of the nearest castle, Agincourt.

Horse and Musket
English Civil War to American Civil War

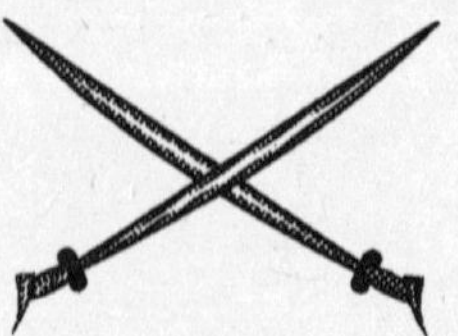

English Civil War

English Civil War – Introduction and Chronology

The long struggle between the King, Charles I, and Parliament became a war about issues such as politics and religion. Individuals, from all classes and regions, had to choose between the king's party and that of Parliament.

The contemporary term for mounted soldiers was "horse". Those who fought on foot were referred to as "foot"; hence "horse, foot and guns".

22 August 1642

King Charles I raised his standard at Nottingham. This was a symbolical declaration that he intended to impose his authority on Parliament by force of arms.

23 September

Powick Bridge
The first clash of arms of the war was a skirmish between the horse of Prince Rupert and the horse of Lord Essex's Parliamentary army under Nathaniel Fiennes.

23 October

The battle of Edgehill
The first major battle of the war between the Parliamentary army under Lord Essex and the Royalist army. Both armies were about 14,500 strong. Essex had to withdraw, leaving the road to London open to the king.

12–13 November

Brentford and Turnham Green

The Royalists took possession of Brentford but the next day the king's progress into London was held up by a large Parliamentarian army at Turnham Green. The Parliamentarian army included the London trained bands, 18,000 well-drilled militia. King Charles' army was too weak because of cold and hunger to attack such a large force. The king withdrew to Reading.

19 January 1643

Bradock Down

The Royalists, Sir Ralph Hopton and Sir Basil Grenville, defeated Parliamentarian forces under the Earl of Stamford in Cornwall.

5 July

Lansdown

The Royalists, Sir Ralph Hopton and Sir Basil Grenville, defeated Parliamentarian forces under Sir William Waller near Bath. Sir Basil Grenvile was killed.

13 July

Roundway Down

Sir Ralph Hopton received reinforcements and defeated the Parliamentarians threatening Devizes at Roundway Down.

20 September

First battle of Newbury

The Royalists got between the Parliamentarian army under Lord Essex and London. The battle was a draw. The Royalists were short of ammunition and withdrew during the night.

29 March 1644

Cheriton

Cheriton was the first decisive victory for parliament, in the west, near Winchester. Sir William Waller's army defeated the forces of Sir Ralph Hopton and Lord Forth.

2 July

The battle of Marston Moor

The Royalist army under Prince Rupert relieved York which was besieged by a combined Parliamentarian and Scottish army. He then faced the combined Parliamentarian and Scottish army, whose commanders delayed, then attacked in the evening. Cromwell's horse won on the left then returned to break the Duke of Newcastle's foot in the centre. The Royalists had lost the north.

27 October

Second battle of Newbury

King Charles was marching back to Oxford from the west. His way was blocked by a large Parliamentarian army under Lord Manchester. A flanking attack by Sir William Waller failed and the battle ended indecisively. King Charles withdrew to Oxford.

14 June 1645

The battle of Naseby

Parliament's New Model Army under Sir Thomas Fairfax decisively defeated the king and Prince Rupert. The Parliamentarian army outnumbered the Royalists by 13,000 to 6,500. Cromwell's horse won on the Parliamentarian right and the Royalists' foot in the centre were eventually overpowered and captured. The king's main field army had ceased to exist.

10 July

Langport

After Naseby, Leicester surrendered to Parliament. Parliament's army, under Fairfax, was sent to relieve Taunton. The Royalist besieging army, under Lord Goring, withdrew. Fairfax attacked Goring near Langport and broke the Royalists. Cromwell's horse joined in the pursuit. Goring's army had been the king's last hope.

The king gave himself up to the Scots early in May 1646. Even in captivity he continued to intrigue with resistance to Parliament. He was tried and executed for treason in January 1649.

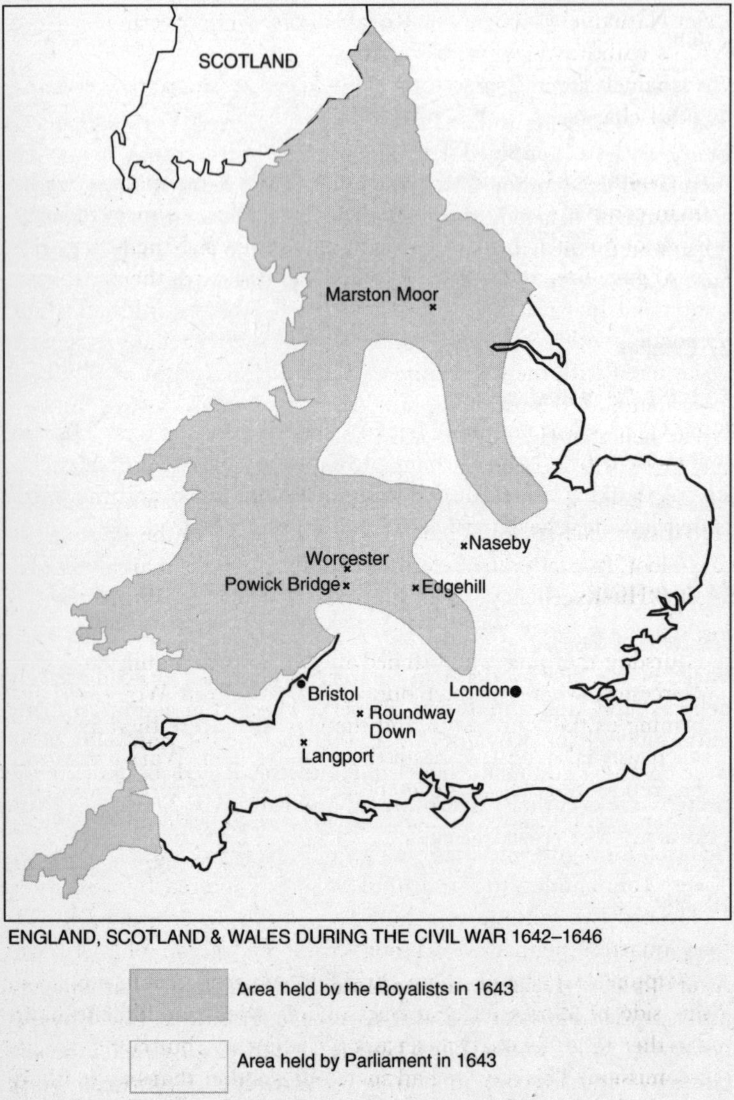

SCOTLAND
Marston Moor
Naseby
Worcester
Powick Bridge
Edgehill
Bristol
London
Roundway Down
Langport

ENGLAND, SCOTLAND & WALES DURING THE CIVIL WAR 1642–1646

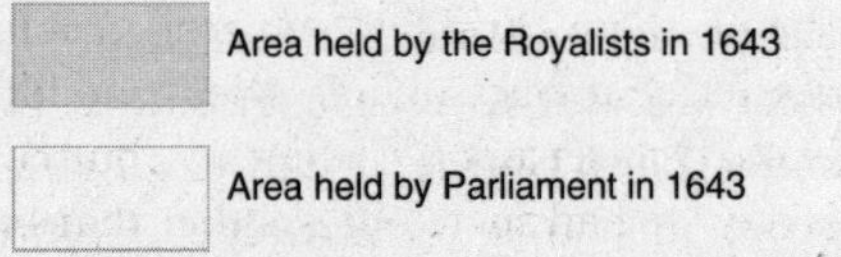

Map of England, Scotland and Wales during the English Civil War

The Battle of Powick Bridge 23 September 1642

The first battle of the English Civil War was a skirmish between the Royalist horse under Prince Rupert and the Parliamentarian horse under Nathaniel Fiennes. The Royalist horse were covering Sir John Byron's withdrawal from Worcester.

Nathaniel Fiennes described how his own troop received the Royalist charge:

> As soon as Sir Lewis Dive's troop had discharged upon us, we let them come up very near that their horses noses almost touched those of our first rank before ours gave fire, and then they (our men) gave fire, and very well to my thinking, with their carbines, after fell in with their swords pell mell into the midst of their enemies, with good hope to have broken them (being pretty well shattered with the first charge of their carbines). But of a sudden we found all the troops on both sides of us melted away, and our rear being carried away with them.

Fiennes' horse were ahead of the main Parliamentarian army under Lord Essex. Nehemiah Wharton was a sergeant in the Parliamentarian foot. In a letter, he described conditions on the march, as Lord Essex ("His Excellency") and his army approached Worcester:

> Thursday morning we marched in the front four miles towards Worcester, where we met one riding post from Worcester, informing us that our troops and the Cavaliers were there in fight; but it was false, only to haste the captains from Warwick. Upon this report our whole regiment ran shouting for two miles together, and crying, 'To Worcester, to Worcester!' and desired to march all night: but after we had marched two miles further we were commanded to stand until our forces passed by, and then marched two miles further into Assincantlo, where we could get no quarter, neither bread nor drink, by reason of the Lord Compton's late being there. Friday we marched four miles on this side of Worcester, but our soldiers cried out for one hour together to go forward to set upon the enemy, but could get no commission. This day we had such foul weather that before I had marched one mile I was wet to the skin. This day our horse forces, namely, Sir William Belford, Col. Sands, Col. Vines, Col. Clarke, Major Duglas, kept all the passages over the Severn, and by that means kept in the Cavaliers, who often assayed to fly, but were repelled. Those commanders sent to His Excellency for three field pieces, and offered with them to keep them in on that side until we had surrounded them: but they were denied this day. Towards

even Prince Rupert entered the city at a bye passage with eighteen troops of horse, most of the city crying, "Welcome, welcome!" but principally the mayor, who desired to entertain him; but he answered, "God damn him, he would not stay, but would go wash his hands in the blood of the Roundheads", and immediately set some to lie in ambush, and with the rest sallied out upon our forces; and immediately Col. Sands came on bravely, even unto the breast of their chief commander, and discharged. The rest undauntedly followed, but their forces immediately fled, and our followed them, and by the ambushment were beset before and behind, so that the battle was very hot, and many fell on both sides. Some of our chief commanders, as Col. Sands and Duglas, was wounded, and are since both dead. The chief amongst the Cavaliers were Prince Rupert, who, I hear, was wounded, the Lord Craven, and the Lord of Northampton. Our wounded men they brought into the city, and stripped, stabbed, and slashed their dead bodies in a most barbarous manner and imbrued their hands in their blood. They also at their return met a young gentleman, a Parliament man, as I am informed – his name I cannot learn – and stabbed him on horseback with many wounds, and trampled upon him, and also most maliciously shot his horse. This even, our general's troop of gentlemen, going to quarter themselves about the country, were betrayed and beset by the enemy, and, overmuch timorous, immediately fled so confusedly that some broke their horses' necks, others their own; some were taken, others slain; and scarce half of them escaped; which is such a blot upon them as nothing but some desperate exploit will wipe off. Hearing this news, we immediately cried out to march unto them, and forthwith drew out a forlorn hope – some out of every company – and sent them before, intending to march after them; but about eleven of the clock, the enemies fled, and our hope returned. Here we abode all night, where we had small comfort, for it rained hard. Our food was fruit, for those who could get it; our drink, water; our beds, the earth; our canopy, the clouds; but we pulled up the hedges, pales and gates, and made some good fires; his Excellency promising us that, if the country relieved us not the day following, he would fire their towns. Thus we continued singing of psalms until the morning. Saturday morning we marched into Worcester – our regiment in the rear of the waggons – the rain continuing the whole day, and the way so base that we went up to the ankles in thick clay; and, about four of the

> clock after noon, entered the city, where we found 28 dead men, which we buried – some of them Cavaliers – and these were all that we can find slain on our side. This evening, by lot, our company watched one of the gates, and also the day following, until even. This evening, his Excellency's guard entered the mayor's house, and took him prisoner, who is now more guarded than regarded. Sabbath day morning our soldiers entered a vault of the College, where his Excellency was to hear a sermon, and found eleven barrels of gunpowder and a pot of bullets. This day Mr Marshall Sedgewick & Co., preached about the city, but I, being upon the court of guard, could not hear them. This evening his Excellency proclaimed that no soldier should plunder either church or private house, upon pain of death. We shortly expect a pitched battle which if the Cavaliers will but stand, will be very hot; for we are all much enraged against them for their barbarisms, and shall shew them little mercy.

The Royalists retreated. Nehemiah Wharton took part in the first "pitched battle" of the war, the battle of Edgehill, on 23 October, 1642. It is thought that Nehemiah Wharton was killed at Edgehill, because no more letters survive.

The Battle of Edgehill 23 October 1642

The Royalist horse won on the left and the right. In the centre the foot of neither side was able to win. After three hours both sides had had enough. Presumably, Nehemiah Wharton, in the Parliamentarian foot, was killed; he did not write any more letters.

The commander of the Royalist horse at Edgehill, Prince Rupert, had served abroad where he had learnt that it was more effective to charge first and to hold your fire. Sir Richard Bulstrode described Prince Rupert's orders at Edgehill:

> Prince Rupert passed from one wing to the other, giving positive orders to the horse to march as close as possible, keeping their ranks with sword in hand to receive the enemy's shot without firing either carbine or pistol till we broke in amongst the enemy, and then to make use of our firearms as need should require; which order was punctually observed.

Another Royalist, Lord Bernard Stuart, described what happened. The Parliamentary horse:

> stood still all the while upon the hill, expecting the charge, so that we were fain to charge them up hill and leap over some five or six hedges and ditches; upon our approach they gave fire with their cannon lined amongst their horse, (their) dragooners, carbines and pistols, but finding that did nothing to dismay the king's horse and that they came more roundly to them with all their fire reserved, just when our men charged they all began to turn head.

The Battle of Roundway Down 13 July 1643

The Western Parliamentarian army under Sir William Waller was besieging Devizes in Wiltshire. The Royalists received reinforcements of horse under Lord Wilmot. At Roundway Down, two miles north of Devizes, the Royalist forces fought the Western Parliamentarian army under Sir William Waller. The Royalist horse defeated the Parliamentarian horse. The abandoned Parliamentarian foot soldiers surrendered, losing their cannon, much of their ammunition and their baggage. Richard Atkyns was a Royalist who was serving as an officer in Prince Maurice's regiment of horse. After the war Atkyns wrote:

> We advanced a full trot, three deep, and kept in order: the enemy kept their station and their right wing of horse, being cuirassiers, were I am sure in such close order that Punchinello himself had he been there could not have got in to them.

The result was that the cuirassiers were outflanked and routed. (Punchinello is a character in a traditional childrens' game – in which the children sing a rhyme, 'Punchinello, funny fellow'.):

> They being six deep in close order but three deep and open (by reason of our sudden charge), we were without them at both ends.

Atkyns himself fought a running battle against the Parliamentarian cavalry commander, Sir Arthur Hesilrige. The cuirassiers were horsemen who wore full armour. They were Hesilrige's own regiment. Atkyns was unable to hurt Hesilrige because of his armour:

> He cut my horse's nose that you might put your finger in the wound, and gave me such a blow on the inside of my arm amongst the veins that I could hardly hold my sword

The Battle of Marston Moor 2 July 1644

It was usual for battles to begin with artillery fire. The army's report to Parliament narrated:

> Our ordnance, about two o'clock, began to play upon the brigade of horse that were nearest, and did some execution upon them, which forced the enemy to leave that ground, and remove to a greater distance.

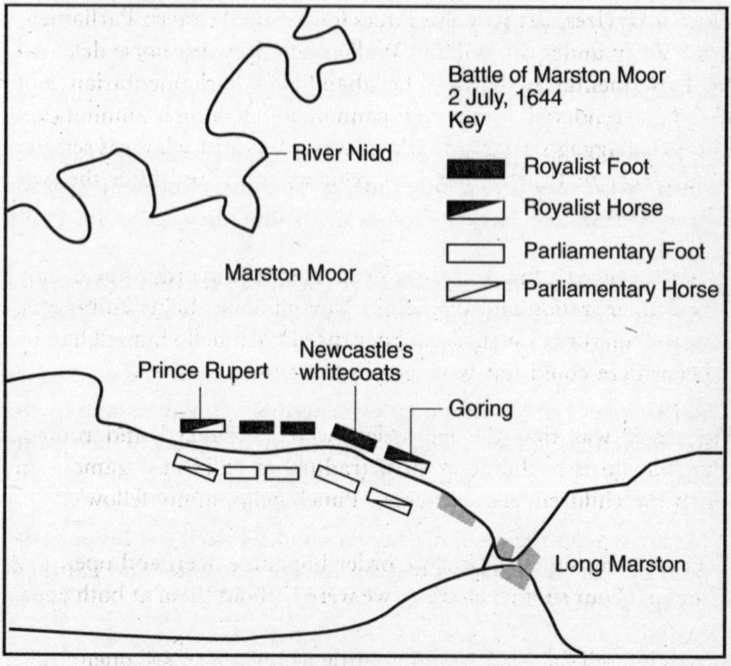

Map of the Battle of Marston Moor

After the Parliamentarian horse on their left had driven their opponents off, they were kept under control and were able to attack the Royalists in the centre and on the right. Among the numerous new developments of the period were dragoons. Dragoons were horsemen who fought on foot, armed with both muskets and swords. At Marston Moor, a Scottish regiment of dragoons under a Colonel Frazer (Frizell) were highly effective. They prepared the way for the advance of Cromwell's horse by driving some musketeers out of a ditch across Cromwell's path. The army's report to Parliament narrated:

> By the good management of Col. Frizell, they acted their part so well that at the first assault they beat the enemy from the ditch, and shortly after killed a great many, and put the rest to rout.

After Cromwell charged Prince Rupert's division of horse, on the Royalist left, Scout-master Watson described:

> they stood, at sword's point a pretty while, hacking at one another, but at last it pleased God he brake through them, scattering them like a little dust.

Other narrators described:

> The enemy, being many of them, if not the greatest part gentlemen, stood very firm a long time, coming to a close fight with the sword, standing like an iron wall so that they were not easily broken.
>
> The horse on both sides behaved with the greatest bravery, for having discharged their pistols and flung them at each others' heads they fell to it with the sword.

Later Colonel Frizell's dragoons were needed to break a stand by the Duke of Newcastle's foot, who were distinctive because of their white coats:

> At last a Scots regiment of dragoons under Frizell was brought up, and by their shot made a way for the horse to enter and put them to the sword.

The Battle of Naseby 14 June 1645

After Marston Moor the king still had an army at Oxford and another in the south-west of England under Lord Goring and Hopton. Parliamentarian forces outnumbered the Royalists. The main Parliamentarian force, the New Model army, was still being formed. The foot were mainly conscripts without battle experience but the Parliamentarian horse was, perhaps, better than the Royalist. This was because the Parliamentarian army was better supplied.

Prince Rupert captured Leicester, but the Royalist army was weakened by having to leave a garrison behind and also by desertion. The Royalists were unable to evade the main Parliamentarian army. They were outnumbered by 13,000 to 6,500. The Royalist army took position on the Naseby ridge. Cromwell suggested to Fairfax that the Parliamentarian army take position on some high ground to the west:

> Let us, I beseech you, draw back to yonder hill, which will encourage the enemy to charge us, which they cannot do in that place without absolute ruin.

Fairfax agreed and the army moved position. Before the battle, Joshua Sprigge, Fairfax's chaplain, recalled:

> that seeing the horse were near 6,000, and were to be fought in two wings, his excellency would be pleased to make Colonel Ireton Commissary-general of horse, and to appoint him command of the left wing that day, the command of the right wing being as much as the lieutenant-general could apply himself unto.

Colonel Okey was in command of a regiment of dragoons. He described the time before the battle, when he was "watching every night with my regiment upon their quarters, having the forlorn guard every night".

Sir Edward Walker narrated that Prince Rupert wished to know whether it was true Fairfax was advancing to fight: whereupon Ruce, the scout-master, was sent to discover, "who in a short time returned with a lie in his mouth, that he had been two or three miles forward, and could neither discover nor hear of the rebels."

Prince Rupert went to see for himself, just as the Parliamentarian army was changing position. He decided to attack them before they were well positioned.

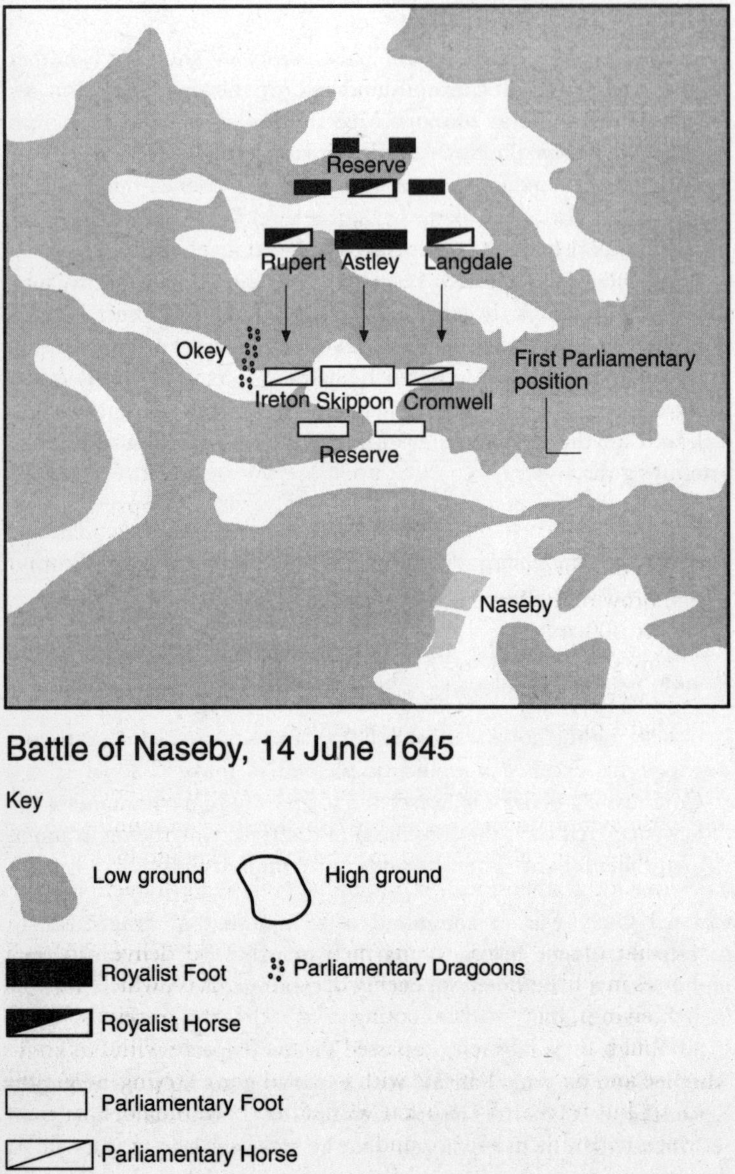

Reserve
Rupert
Astley
Langdale
Okey
First Parliamentary position
Ireton
Skippon
Cromwell
Reserve
Naseby
Battle of Naseby, 14 June 1645
Key
Low ground
High ground
Royalist Foot
Parliamentary Dragoons
Royalist Horse
Parliamentary Foot
Parliamentary Horse

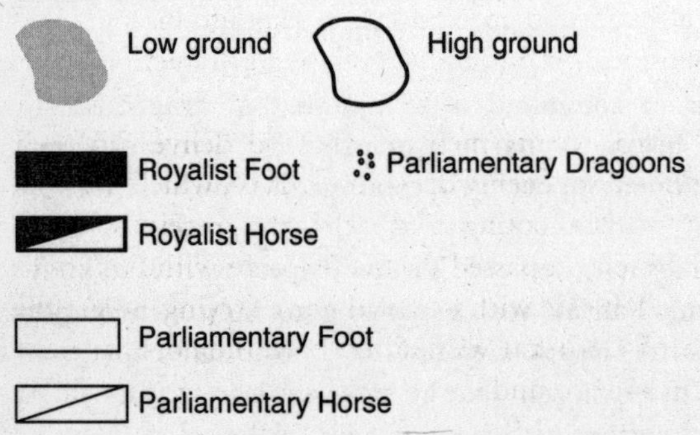

Map of the Battle of Naseby

There was very little artillery fire at the beginning. The army's report to Parliament narrated:

> Being come within cannon-shot the ordnance began to play but that being found at Marston Moor and other places but a loss of time, we resolved not to want daylight as usual, but to charge with the first.

A battle was also usually preceded by a movement called "getting the wind of the enemy". The Parliamentarians clearly saw the Royalists advancing to attack them – Joshua Sprigge narrated, "and the wind blowing somewhat westwardly, by the enemy's advance so much on their right hand it was evident he designed to get the wind of us."

This was met by a counter movement. The purpose of this was to get into a position where the wind would blow the smoke of the enemy's guns and muskets back upon his own troops. It was safer to attack the enemy under cover of the smoke. Joshua Sprigge:

> Upon the enemy's approach, the parliament army marched up to the brow of the hill, having placed: a forlorn of foot, consisting of about 300 musketeers, down the steep of the hill towards the enemy somewhat more than a carbine shot from the main battle, who were ordered to retreat to the battle whensoever they should be hard pressed upon by the enemy.

Colonel Okey and his regiment of dragoons was half a mile behind the Parliamentary army in a meadow distributing ammunition to his men when Cromwell came and ordered him to remount his men, and take up a forward position on the left flank of the Parliamentary line:

> By that time I could get my men to light and deliver up their horses in a little close, the enemy drew towards us, which my men perceiving, they with shooting and rejoycing received them, although they were encompassed on the one side with the king's horse and on the other side with foot and horse (trying) to get the close; but it pleased God that we beat off both the horse and the foot . . . and kept our ground.

Okey's dragoons were in a position to make flanking fire on Prince Rupert's horse. Despite this advantage Ireton's horse were forced back. When the pikemen charged, the musketeers, instead of halting to reload, fell upon the enemy side by side with them, using their muskets as clubs. Sir Edward Walker, a Royalist, recalled:

> The foot on either side, hardly saw each other till they were within carbine shot, and so only made one volley; ours falling in with sword and butt end of the musket did notable execution, insomuch as I saw their colours fall and their foot in great disorder.

The Parliamentarian centre was in disarray when Fairfax, himself and Colonel Skippon brought up the reserve. Colonel Skippon had been wounded, Fairfax told him to retire. Skippon replied that [He] "would not stir so long as a man could stand".

The Royalist infantry were winning in the centre.

Cromwell had been so successful on the right that he was able to send some of his horse in pursuit and also to bring back some of his well-disciplined horse to attack the flank of the Royalist infantry in the centre.

Sir Edward Walker described the pursuit:

> Four of the Rebel Bodies in close and good order followed this defeated wing.

The king took personal command of his reserves but he was restrained by the Earl of Carnwath, who said, "Will you go upon your death?" The command "march to the right hand" was heard. This was taken to mean "Everyone to shift for himself". Sir Edward Walker narrated that the reserves:

> turned about and ran on the spur almost a quarter of a mile and there the word being given to make a stand we did so, though the body could never be rallied.

Okey and his dragoons were able to join the defeat of the Royalists:

> I lost not one man but three wounded in all my regiment.

The king had lost his army and his papers which Parliament published as evidence of his guilt.

The Battle of Langport 10 July 1645

The second battle in which the New Model Army fought was Langport. It was one in which artillery played a really important part, and all three arms worked together effectively. Goring, the Royalist leader, was endeavouring to cover the retreat of his baggage and his train to the fortified town of Bridgwater. Goring's army was posted on one ridge, that of Fairfax on another, and between the two armies lay a valley and a stream through which a narrow lane led up to the Royalist position. Goring had filled the enclosures on each side of the lane with his musketeers, and stationed his horse on the brow of the hill where the lane reached the plateau. He had only two guns on the hill; the rest were on the way to Bridgwater. Fairfax's artillery began the action, silenced the two guns and forced Goring to draw his main body farther back. Joshua Sprigge described:

> A good while before the foot engaged our ordnance began to play, doing great execution upon the body of the enemy's army, both horse and foot, who stood in good order on the hill about musket shot from the pass, forcing them to draw off their ordnance and their horse to remove their ground.

The musketeers Goring had placed in the valley were left unsupported. The army report to Parliament described:

> Our cannon, did very good service, and made the other side of the hill so hot that they could not come down to relieve their men.

Fairfax's infantry then drove the Royalist musketeers out of the enclosures, and made it possible for his horse to gallop up the lane and fight the Royalist horse on the high ground beyond it. Six troops of Cromwell's Ironsides under Major Bethel led the charge. The army's report to Parliament narrated:

> Bethel upon command given, led on his own troop through the water, which was deep, and, dirty, and very narrow, the enemy having a very large body at the top of the lane many times over his numbers, charged them with as much gallantry as ever I saw in my life, forcing them with the sword to give ground; which made way for Capt. Evanson's troop to draw out of the lane and front with him, driving the enemy's great body and their reserve up the

hill; but a very great fresh body of the enemy's horse coming upon them forced them to retreat to Captain Grove who was their reserve, who drawing his men close received the enemy with much bravery and resolution, and gave liberty to his friends to rally and front with him, who all three charged the enemy's numerous bodies very furiously, and routed them quite; made way for our musketeers to run up the hedges and gall the enemy, and for Major Desborough to draw his three troops out of the lane and front with Bethel. Upon which six troops divers mighty bodies of the enemy's came, and having disputed it soundly with their swords, the foot marching up furiously, and the other troops careered, God took away the enemy's courage and away they run. Of which charge of Major Bethell's, I heard the General, Lieutenant-General, and all the chief officers that saw it, say it was one of the bravest that ever their eyes beheld.

American War of Independence

The American War of Independence – Introduction and Chronology

Tension between American settlers and their British rulers had been increasing since the 17th century. A major revolt, Bacon's rebellion, had taken place in Virginia in 1676. The British government tried to increase revenue from the colonies by measures such as the Stamp Act of 1765. This Act was eventually repealed. In 1773 a tax on tea was imposed. This led to an act of resistance known as The Boston Tea Party. A group of Americans, dressed as Indians, boarded a merchant ship in Boston harbour. They threw its cargo of tea into the harbour. The British government deprived Boston of its port revenues until the damage was paid for and quartered troops in the town itself.

In 1774 the settlers convened a congress at Philadelphia to secure redress for their grievances. This was known as the Continental Congress. The first armed clash took place at Concord and Lexington, near Boston, in April 1775.

In May 1775 the Continental Congress decided to put the 13 colonies in a state of defence. George Washington was appointed commander-in chief of their forces. At first, these forces consisted of armed citizens (militia) ready to serve at one minute's notice. They were called minutemen. Later, their army was referred to as the Continental Army or, when it became permanent, the Continental Line.

Americans who remained loyal to the British were referred to as Loyalists or Tories. Americans who sought Independence were sometimes called Whigs; in Britain, Whigs were the political

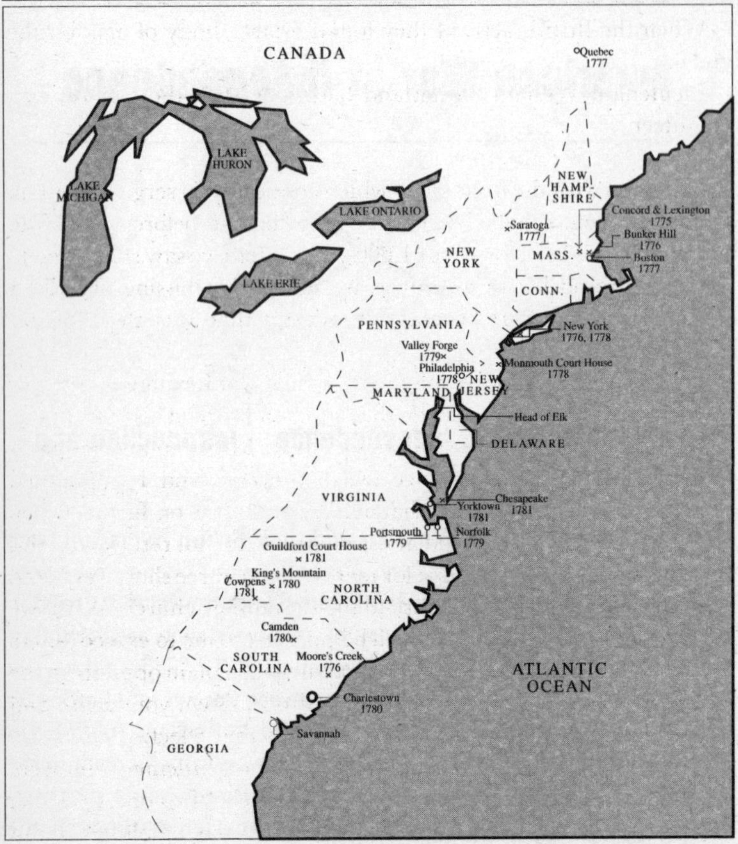

Map of North America during the American War of Independence

opponents of Tories. More often the Americans called themselves Patriots. Sometimes they were called Rebels. The British forces were also referred to as King's Troops or Redcoats.

The Battle of Lexington 19 March 1775

On 19 March 1775 the British commander-in-chief and military governor, General Gage, sent a column of troops to capture two leading dissidents, Samuel Adams and John Hancock, who were known to be in the village of Lexington.

When the British arrived they found a large body of men on the green.

Lieutenant William Sutherland had gone with the column as a volunteer:

> I went on with the front party which consisted of a sergeant and six or eight men. I shall observe here that the road before you go into Lexington is level for about 1,000 yards. Here we saw shots fired to the right and left of us, but as we heard no whissing of balls, I conclude they were to alarm the body that was there of our approach.
>
> On coming within gunshot of the village of Lexington, a fellow from the corner of the road on the right hand cocked his piece at me, but burnt priming. I immediately called to Mr Adair and the party to observe this circumstance which they did and I acquainted Major Pitcairn of it immediately. We still went on further when three shots more were fired at us, which we did not return, and this is the sacred truth as I hope for mercy. These three shots were fired from a corner of a large house to the right of the church. When we came up to the main body, which appeared to me to exceed 400 in and about the village, who were drawn up in a plain opposite to the Church, several officers called out, "Throw down your arms, and you shall come to no harm", or words to that effect.
>
> They refusing to act instantaneously, the gentlemen who were on horseback rode in amongst them of which I was one, at which instant I heard Major Pitcairn's voice call out, "Soldiers, don't fire, keep your ranks, form and surround them." Instantly some of the villains who got over the hedge fired at us which our men for the first time returned, which set my horse a-going who galloped with me down a road above 600 yards, among the middle of them before I turned him . . . In consequence of their discovering themselves, our Grenadiers gave them a smart fire.

The British knew the Americans were keeping military stores at the nearby village of Concord. They marched to Concord to seize them.

At Concord the American were waiting for them. Amos Barrett was a 20-year-old corporal in David Brown's Concord minutemen company:

> We at Concord heard they was a-coming. The Bell rung at 3 o'clock for an alarm. As I was then a Minuteman, I was soon in town and found my captain and the rest of my company at the

> post. It wasn't long before there was other minute companies. One company, I believe, of minute-men was raised in almost every town to stand at a minute's warning. Before sunrise there was, I believe, 150 of us and more of all that was there. When we was on the hill by the bridge, there was about 80 or 90 British came to the bridge and there made a halt. After a while they begun to tear up the plank of the bridge. Major Buttrick said if we were all of his mind, he would drive them away from the bridge; they should not tear that up. We all said we would go. We then wasn't loaded; we were all ordered to load – and had strict orders not to fire till they fired first, then to fire as fast as we could. They stayed about ten minutes and then marched back, and we after them. After a while we found them a-marching back towards Boston. We was soon after them. When they got about a mile and a half to a road that comes from Bedford and Billerica, they was waylaid and a great many killed. When I got there, a great many lay dead and the road was bloody.

A relief column came from Boston under Lord Percy to escort the first column back to Boston. The return march was described by Lieutenant John Barker of the King's Own Regiment:

> We were fired on from all sides, but mostly from the rear, where people had hid themselves in houses till we had passed and then fired. The country was an amazing strong one, full of hills, woods, stone walls, &c, which the rebels did not fail to take advantage of; for they were all lined with people who kept up an incessant fire upon us, as we did too upon them but not with the same advantage, for they were so concealed there was hardly any seeing them. In this way we marched between nine and ten miles, their numbers increasing from all parts, while ours was reducing by deaths, wounds and fatigue, and we were totally surrounded with such an incessant fire as it's impossible to conceive; our ammunition was likewise near expended.
>
> In this critical situation we perceived the 1st Brigade coming to our assistance: it consisted of the 4th, 23rd, and 47th regiments and the battalion of marines, with two field pieces, 6-pounders. We were now obliged to force almost every house in the road, for the Rebels had taken possession of them and galled us exceedingly, but they suffered for their temerity, for all that was found in the houses were put to death.

At that time, Frederick Mackenzie was a Lieutenant of the Royal Welch Fusiliers, (the 23rd regiment):

> During the whole of the march from Lexington, the Rebels kept an incessant irregular fire from all points on the column, which was more galling as our flanking parties, which at first were placed at sufficient distances to cover the march of it, were at last, from the different obstructions they occassionally met with, obliged to keep almost close to it. Our men had very few opportunities of getting good shots at the Rebels, as they hardly ever fired but under cover of some stone wall, from behind a tree, or out of a house; and the moment they had fired they lay down out of sight until they had loaded again, or the column had passed. In the road indeed in our rear, they were most numerous, and came on pretty close, frequently calling out, "King Hancock forever".
>
> Many of them were killed in the houses on the road side from whence they fired; in some, seven or eight men were destroyed. Some houses were forced open in which no person could be discovered, but when the column had passed, numbers sallied forth from some place in which they had lain concealed, fired at the rear guard, and augmented the numbers which followed us. If we had had time to set fire to those houses, many rebels must have perished in them, but as night drew on, Lord Percy thought it best to continue the march. Many houses were plundered by the soldiers, notwithstanding the efforts of the officers to prevent it. I have no doubt that this inflamed the Rebels, and made many of them follow us farther than they otherwise would have done. By all accounts some soldiers who stayed too long in the houses, were killed in the very act of plundering by those who lay concealed in them.

An anonymous observer, writing from the British ships in Boston harbour, wrote:

> even women had firelocks. One was seen to fire a blunderbuss between her father and her husband from their windows.

Both British and Americans were appalled. Deacon Joseph Adams escaped during the hubbub, his wife Hannah wrote:

> divers of them entered our house by bursting open the doors, and three of the soldiers broke into the room in which I was laid on

> my bed, being scarcely able to walk from my bed to the fire and not having been to my chamber door from my time being delivered in childbirth to that time. One of the said soldiers immediately opened my bed curtains with his bayonet fixed and pointing . . . to my breast. I immediately cried out, 'For the Lord's sake, don't kill me!' He replied, 'Damn you.' One that stood near said, 'We will not hurt the woman if she will go out of the house, but we will surely burn it.' I immediately arose, threw a blanket over me, went out, and crawled into a corn-house near the door with my infant in my arms, where I remained until they were gone. They immediately set the house on fire, in which I had left five children and no other person; but the fire was happily extinguished when the house was in the utmost danger of being utterly consumed.

The redcoats raided Cooper's Tavern, and made no distinction between minutemen and customers. An unsigned account described:

> The King's Regular troops . . . fired more than one hundred bullets into the house where we dwell, through doors, windows, etc. Then a number of them entered the house where we and two aged gentlemen were, all unarmed. We escaped with our lives into the cellar. The two aged gentlemen were immediately most barbarously and inhumanely murdered by them, being stabbed through in many places, their heads mauled, skulls broke, and their brains beat out on the floor and walls of the house.

General Gage described the event to Lord Barrington, the Secretary of War.

> I have now nothing to trouble your lordship with, but of an affair that happened here on the 19th instant. I having intelligence of a large quantity of military stores, being collected at Concord, for the avowed purpose, of supplying a body of troops, to act in opposition to his Majesty's government; I got the grenadiers, and light infantry out of town, under the command of Lieutenant Colonel Smith of the 10th Regiment, and Major Pitcairne of the Marines, with as much secrecy a possible, on the 18th at night; and the next morning, by eight companys of the 4th, the same number of the 23rd 47th, and Marines under the command of

Lord Percy. It appears from the firing of alarm guns and ringing of bells, that the march of Lieutenant Colonel Smith was discovered, and he was opposed, by a body of men, within six miles of Concord: some few of whom first began to fire upon his advanced companys, which brought on a fire from the troops, that dispersed the body opposed to them, and they proceeded to Concord, where they destroyed all the military stores they could find. On the return of the troops, they were attacked from all quarters, where any cover was to be found, from whence it was practicable to annoy them; and they were so fatigued with their march, that it was with difficulty they could keep out their flanking partys, to remove the enemy at a distance, so that they were at length, a good deal pressed. Lord Percy then arrived opportunely to their assistance, with his brigade, and two pieces of cannon. And not withstanding a continual skirmish for the space of fifteen miles, receiving fire from every hill, fence, house, barn &c his lordship kept the enemy off and brought the troops to Charles Town from whence they were ferryed over to Boston. Too much praise cannot be given to Lord Percy, for his remarkable activity and conduct during the whole day. Lieutenant Colonel Smith, and Major Pitcairne, did everything men could do, as did all the officers in general, and the men behaved with their usual intrepidity.

The whole country was assembled in arms with surprizing expedition, and several thousand are now assembled about this town, threatening an attack, and getting up artillery: and we are very busy in making preparations to oppose them . . .

At Lexington and Concord the British lost 73 men with 200 wounded, the Americans 49, with 46 wounded.

By the Spring of 1775 armed citizens from the New England countryside were surrounding Boston.

A siege of Boston began. By June, 1775, 7,000 men, had dug themselves in, were sniping at British sentries and firing on British guard ships, occasionally a cannon shot thudded into their lines. They did not always react wisely, as the nineteen-year-old John Trumbull, son of the Governor of Connecticut, recounts:

The entire army, if it deserved the name, was but an assemblage of brave, enthusiastic, undisciplined country lads; the officers in general; quite as ignorant of military life as the troops, excepting

> a few elderly men, who had seen some irregular service among the provincials, under Lord Amherst. Our first occupation was to secure our positions, by constructing fieldworks for defense. Nothing of military importance occurred for some time; the enemy occasionally fired upon our working parties, whenever they approached too nigh to their works; and in order to familiarize our raw soldiers to this exposure, a small reward was offered in general orders, for every ball fired by the enemy, which should be picked up and brought to head-quarters. This soon produced the intended effect – a fearless emulation among the men; but it produced also a very unfortunate result; for when the soldiers saw a ball, after having struck and rebounded from the ground several times (en ricochet) roll sluggishly along, they would run and place a foot before it, to stop it, not aware that a heavy ball retains a sufficient impetus to overcome such an obstacle. The consequence was, that several brave lads lost their feet, which were crushed by the weight of the rolling shot. The order was of course withdrawn, and they were cautioned against touching a ball, until it was entirely at rest.

Sir William Howe replaced Gage as British commander-in-chief in September 1775. Two other Generals arrived with him. They were Sir William Clinton and John Burgoyne. Washington had been appointed commander-in-chief of the American forces. The Americans fortified Bunker's Hill overlooking Boston harbor.

The Battle of Bunker Hill 17 June 1775

> It was a dear bought victory. Another such would have ruined us.
> – General Sir William Clinton

The Boston Committee of Safety decided on 15 June to occupy Bunker Hill and Breed's Hill. From Breed's Hill, small cannon could threaten Boston and its shipping.

Howe attempted to drive the Americans off the heights.

Amos Farnsworth was in the Massachusetts militia:

> As the enemy approached, our men was not only exposed to the attack of the very numerous musketry, but to the heavy fire of the

battery on Corps-Hill, 4 or 5 men of war, several armed boats or floating batteries in Mistick-River, and a number of field pieces. Not withstanding, we within the intrenchment, and at a breast work without, sustained the enemy's attacks with great bravery and resolution, killed and wounded great numbers, and repulsed them several times; and after bearing, for about 2 hours as severe and heavy a fire as perhaps was ever known, and many having fired away all their ammunition, and having no reinforsement, althoe thare was a great boddy of men nie by, we ware over-powered by numbers and obliged to leave the intrenchment, retreating about sunset to a small distance over Charlestown Neck.

NB. I did not leave the intrenchment until the enemy got in. I then retreated ten or fifteen rods; then I receved a wound in my rite arm, the bawl gowing through a little below my elbow breaking the little shel bone. Another bawl struck my back, taking a piece of skin about as big as a penny. But I got to Cambridge that night. The town of Charlestown supposed to contain about 300 dwelling-houses, a great number of which ware large and elegant, besides 150 or 200 other buildings, are almost all laid in ashes by the barbarity and wanton cruelty of that infernal villain Thomas Gage.

Oh, the goodness of God in preserving my life althoe thay fell on my right hand and my left! O, may this act of deliverance of thine, oh God, lead me never to distrust thee; but may I ever trust in thee and put confidence in no arm of flesh! I was in great pane the first night with my wound.

Colonel William Prescott commanded at Bunker Hill. He reported:

About an hour after the enemy landed, they began to march to the attack in three columns. I commanded my Lieutenant-Col Robinson and Major Woods, each with a detachment, to flank the enemy, who I have reason to think, behaved with prudence and courage. I was now left with perhaps 150 men in the fort. The enemy advanced and fired very hotly on the fort and, meeting with a warm reception, there was a very smart firing on both sides. After a considerable time, finding our ammunition was almost spent, I commanded a cessation till the enemy advanced within 30 yards, when we gave them such a hot fire that they were obliged to retire nearly 150 yards before they could rally and come up again to the attack.

> Our ammunition being nearly exhausted, could keep up only a scattering fire. The enemy, being numerous, surrounded our little fort with their bayonets. We was obliged to retreat through them, while they kept up as hot a fire as it was possible for them to make. We, having very few bayonets, could make no resistance. We kept the fort about one hour and twenty minutes after the attack with small arms . . .

Robert Steele was a drummer boy in an American regiment from Cambridge:

> I beat to "Yankee Doodle" when we mustered for Bunker Hill that morning . . . the British . . . marched with rather a slow step nearly up to our entrenchment, and the battle began. The conflict was sharp, but the British soon retreated with a quicker step than they came up, leaving some of their killed and wounded in sight of us. They retreated towards where they landed and formed again . . . came up again and a second battle ensued which was harder and longer than the first, but being but a lad and this the first engagement I was ever in, I cannot remember much more . . . than great noise and confusion. One or two circumstances I can, however, distinctly remember.
>
> About the time the British retreated the second time, I was standing side of Benjamin Ballard, a Boston boy about my age, who had a gun in his hands, when one of our sergeants came up to us and said, 'You are young and spry, run in a moment to some of the stores and bring some rum. Major Moore is badly wounded. Go as quick as possible.'
>
> We threw down our implements of war and run as fast as we could and passed over the hill.

Bunker Hill was a British victory. But the British had lost far more men than they could afford. General Clinton admitted, "It was a dear-bought victory, another such would have ruined us."

The British lost 1150 men, out of 2500 engaged, and 92 officers. All of Howe's staff officers were killed or wounded on Bunker Hill.

The Continental Congress called for volunteers. The strength of the rebellion further south made the Governor of Virginia take refuge aboard a ship. The British fleet bombarded Norfolk.

Conditions became so bad in Boston that the British abandoned it in March 1776.

The Battle of Brandywine 11 September 1776

Sir William Howe realized he needed to take the initiative. On 1 July he left New York with 15,000 men. He intended to capture Philadelphia. Travelling by sea he disembarked at Head of Elk in Maryland, 55 miles away from Philadelphia. Washington marched his army across country and positioned it between the city and the enemy.

Washington positioned his men on the Brandywine Creek, outside Philadelphia. Howe turned the American right flank as he had at Long Island. It all went according to plan as Major John André, a British staff officer, recorded.

The plan was that General Knyphausen, at Chad's Ford, should distract the enemy on the opposite side of the Creek, by a cannonade which would make him presume the whole British army was attacking, whilst the other column should be performing the detour. Lord Cornwallis's wing being engaged was to be the signal for the troops under General Knyphausen to cross the ford when they were to push their advantage.

Washington was deceived by this manoeuvre. Colonel Timothy Pickering recorded in his journal:

> September 11th This morning a cannonade took place, the enemy having advanced to the heights opposite to those occupied by us, on the other side of the ford . . . The enemy made no attempt to cross at this place.
>
> The enemy remaining paraded on the distant heights, and continuing the cannonade, induced me to think they did not intend to cross at Chad's Ford, but only to amuse us while their main army crossed at some other place. The event proved the conjecture right. The enemy's main body crossed the Brandywine six or eight miles above, on our right. The General had intelligence of this by some messenger; but it was contradicted by others; and, the information remaining a long time surprisingly uncertain, it was late before a disposition was made to receive the enemy on that quarter.
>
> The whole army this night retired to Chester. It was fortunate for us that the night came on, for under its cover the fatigued stragglers and some wounded made their escape.

The Americans lost over 1,000 men, the British 500. Joseph Clark of Princeton recorded in his diary:

> The sun was set when I left the hill from whence I saw the fate of the day. His Excellency I saw within 200 yards of the enemy, with but a small party about him, and they drawing off from their station, our army broke at the right, and night coming on, adding a gloom to our misfortunes, amidst the noise of cannon, the hurry of people, and wagons driving in confusion from the field, I came off with a heart full of distress. In painful anxiety I took with hasty step the gloomy path from the field, and travelled 15 miles to Chester, where I slept two hours upon a couple of chairs . . .

The Battle of Paoli, 1777

Further up-river and 23 miles west of Philadelphia, near Paoli, 1,500 men under Anthony Wayne were attacked by Major-General Grey's forces with unloaded muskets. British and Hessian bayonets inflicted 300 casualties and not a shot was fired.

Captain John André described the British success:

> On approaching the right of the camp we perceived the line of fires, and the Light Infantry being ordered to form the front, rushed along the line putting to the bayonet all they came up with, and overtaking the main herd of the fugitives, stabbed great numbers and pressed on their rear till it was thought prudent to order them to desist.
>
> Near 200 must have been killed, and a great number wounded. 71 prisoners were brought off; 40 of them badly wounded were left at different houses on the road. A major, a captain and two lieutenants were amongst the prisoners. We lost Captain Wolfe killed and one or two private men; four or five were wounded, one an officer, Lieut. Hunter of the 52d Light Company.

Major Samuel Hay of the Continental Army wrote about the attack:

> We lay the 18th and 19th undisturbed, but, on the 20th, at 12 o'clock at night, the enemy marched out, and so unguarded was

our camp that they were amongst us before we either formed in any manner for our safety, or attempted to retreat, notwithstanding the General had full intelligence of their designs two hours before they came out. The enemy rushed on with fixed bayonets and made the use of them they intended. So you may figure to yourself what followed. The party lost 300 privates in killed, wounded and missing, besides commissioned and non-commissioned officers. Our loss is Col. Grier, Captain Wilson and Lieutenant Irvine wounded (but none of them dangerously) and 61 non-commissioned and privates killed and wounded, which was just half the men we had on the ground fit for duty.

The 22nd, I went to the ground to see the wounded. The scene was shocking – the poor men groaning under their wounds, which were all by stabs of bayonets and cuts of Light-Horsemen's swords. Col Grier is wounded in the side by a bayonet, superficially slanting to the breast bone. Captain Wilson's stabbed in the side, but not dangerous, and it did not take the guts or belly. He got also a bad stroke on the head with the cock nail of the locks of a musket. Andrew Irvine was run through the fleshy part of the thigh with a bayonet. They are all lying near David Jones' tavern. I left Captain McDowell with them to dress and take care of them, and they all are in a fair way of recovery. Major LaMar, of the 4th Regiment, was killed, and some other inferior officers.

Congress left Philadelphia before Howe arrived, after conferring dictatorial powers on Washington. On 27 September, Cornwallis led his men into Philadelphia with bands playing. They would stay nine months. Benjamin Franklin, in Paris, was not disheartened. When told that Howe had taken Philadelphia, he replied: "No! Philadelphia captured Howe!"

Howe's main force was at Germantown, five miles outside the city, so that they could protect supply routes.

Washington, who had withdrawn steadily before him, tried a surprise attack, on the same lines as at Trenton. His attacks were held up by a strong point on his flank, "the Chew House".

Colonel Timothy Pickering described the event in his journal:

This house of Chew's was a strong stone building and exceedingly commodious, having windows on every side, so that you could not approach it without being exposed to a severe fire; which, in fact, was well directed and killed and wounded a great many of our

> officers and men. Several of our pieces, six-pounders, were brought up within musket-shot of it, and fired round balls at it, but in vain: the enemy, I imagine, were very little hurt; they still kept possession.

American casualties exceeded British – 700 to 530. Adam Stephen, a gallant Virginian, was convicted of "unofficerlike behaviour" and drunkenness and dismissed the service – his troops had panicked and their firing was confused. A French officer noted:

> The principal advantage of General Howe's army over General Washington's in the two battles fought by them, must be ascribed to their being more trained to the use of the bayonet. The American army know their superior dexterity in firing well, and rely entirely upon it. The British army know it likewise, and dread it. Hence in all engagements the British soldiers rush on with the bayonet after one fire, and seldom fail of throwing the Americans into confusion. Habit, which forms men to do anything, I am persuaded would soon render these brave people as firm at the approaches of a bayonet, as the whistling of a musket ball. General [Charles] Lee, I am told, took great pains to eradicate the universal prejudice he found among the Americans, in favor of terminating the war with fire arms alone. "We must learn to face our enemies," said he, "man to man in the open field, or we shall never beat them." The late General Montgomery, who served his apprenticeship in the British Army, knew so well that nothing but the bayonet would ever rout troops that had been trained to it, that he once proposed in the Convention of New York, of which he was a member, that directions should be given, both in Europe and in this country, to make all muskets intended for the American soldiers two inches longer than the muskets now in use in the British Army, in order that they may have an advantage of their enemy, in a charge with bayonets, for, he said, "Britain will never yield but to the push of the bayonet."

Saratoga 19 September–7 October, 1777

General Burgoyne, had 7,000 men in Canada. He moved south

slowly from fort to fort. In July, 1777 he took 24 days to cover 23 miles, harassed by Americans and their Indian allies.

General Horatio Gates was in command of the American forces in the area. He was an ex-British regular, competent, popular, cautious – Burgoyne called him "the old midwife."

Gates had moved forward to occupy a strong point, named Bemis Heights. As Gates' numbers grew steadily, Burgoyne's fell from disease and desertion. His horses were dying of starvation; uniforms and boots were wearing out, the men's rations of salt pork and flour were running out.

Burgoyne attacked Freeman's Farm on 19 September. Although remaining in occupation of the field, British losses were heavier than American, due to Daniel Morgan's sharpshooters and the initiative of Benedict Arnold. Captain Wakefield had vivid memories of the attack.

> I shall never never forget the opening scene of the first day's conflict. The riflemen and light infantry were ordered to clear the woods of the Indians. Arnold rode up, and with his sword pointing to the enemy emerging from the woods into an opening partially cleared, covered with stumps and fallen timber, addressing Morgan, he said, "Colonel Morgan, you and I have seen too many redskins to be deceived by that garb of paint and feathers; they are asses in lions' skins, Canadians and Tories; let your riflemen cure them of their borrowed plumes."
>
> And so they did; for in less than fifteen minutes the "Wagon Boy", with his Virginia riflemen, sent the painted devils with a howl back to the British lines. Morgan was in his glory, catching the inspiration of Arnold, as he thrilled his men; when he hurled them against the enemy, he astonished the English and Germans with the deadly fire of his rifles.

Nothing could exceed the bravery of Arnold on this day; he seemed the very genius of war. Infuriated by the conflict and maddened by Gates' refusal to send reinforcements, which he repeatedly called for, and knowing he was meeting the brunt of the battle, he seemed inspired with the fury of a demon.

Saratoga consisted of three battles, Freeman's Farm, Bemis Heights and Saratoga.

Lieutenant Anburey was aware that Burgoyne's forces lost some of their manpower:

The Indians were running from wood to wood, and just as soon as our regiment had formed in the skirts of one, several of them came up, and by their signs were conversing about the severe fire on our right. Soon after the enemy attacked us, and at the very first fire the Indians run off through the woods.

From the situation of the ground, and their being perfectly acquainted with it, the whole of our troops could not be brought to engage together, which was a very material disadvantage, though everything possible was tried to remedy that inconvenience, but to no effect. Such an explosion of fire I never had any idea of before, and the heavy artillery joining in concert like great peals of thunder, assisted by the echoes of the woods, almost deafened us with the noise. To an unconcerned spectator, it must have had the most awful and glorious appearance, the different battalions moving to relieve each other, some being pressed and almost broke by their superior numbers. The crash of cannon and musketry never ceased till darkness parted us, when they retired to their camp, leaving us masters of the field; but it was a dear-bought victory if I can give it that name as we lost many brave men. The 62nd had scarce 10 men a company left, and other regiments suffered much, and no very great advantage, honor excepted, was gained by the day.

Anburey had to bury the dead. He saw:

fifteen, sixteen and twenty buried in one hole . . . heads, legs and arms above ground. No other distinction is paid to officer or private, than the officers are put in a hole by themselves. Our army abounded with young officers, in the subaltern line, and in the course of this unpleasant duty, three of the 20th Regiment were interred together, the age of the eldest not exceeding seventeen. This friendly office to the dead, though it greatly affects the feeling, was nothing to the scenes in bringing in the wounded; the one were past all pain, the other in the most excruciating torments, sending forth dreadful groans. They had remained out all night, and from the loss of blood and want of nourishment, were upon the point of expiring. Some of them begged they might lay and die, others again were insensible, some upon the least movement were put in the most horrid tortures, and all had near a mile to be conveyed to the hospitals; others at their last gasp, who for want of our timely assistance must have inevitably expired. These poor creatures, perishing with cold and weltering in their blood, displayed such a scene, it must be a heart of adamant that could not be affected by it, even to a degree of weakness.

In the course of the late action, Lieutenant Harvey of the 62nd, a youth of sixteen and a nephew of the Adjutant General of the same name, received several wounds and was repeatedly ordered off the field by Colonel Anstruther. But his heroic ardor would not allow him to quit the battle, while he could stand and see his brave lads fighting beside him. A ball striking one of his legs, his removal became absolutely necessary, and while they were conveying him away, another wounded him mortally. In this situation the Surgeon recommended him to take a powerful dose of opium, to avoid a seven or eight hours of most exquisite torture. This he immediately consented to, and when the Colonel entered the tent with Major Harnage, who were both wounded, they asked whether he had any affairs they could settle for him? His reply was, "That being a minor, everything was already adjusted." But he had one request, which he had just life enough to utter, "Tell my uncle I died like a soldier!"

Burgoyne hesitated about his next move. He was relying on support from General Clinton in New York.

General Clinton never came. He did not move to support Burgoyne until 5 October. He got within forty miles of Albany by mid-October; Saratoga was thirty miles to its north.

On 7 October, Burgoyne tried a flanking movement, which failed. The Americans attacked frontally in the second battle of Saratoga. The British line held but their losses were heavy (600 out of 1500 engaged). Burgoyne withdrew to open ground around Saratoga; Gates did not give battle but kept up a constant bombardment.

It rained incessantly; guns and wagons had to be abandoned, cattle were nearly starved for want of forage and the bridges had been destroyed by the enemy. The men were exhausted and dispirited, hungry and soaked. And they were retreating. Burgoyne surrendered, calling it "a convention not a capitulation".

Sergeant Roger Lamb of the 9th regiment of the British army:

Taking all the results of this battle, if we had reason to boast of it, our advantages from it were very few indeed. In fact, difficulty and danger appeared to grow out of it. The intricacy of the ground before us increased at every step. Our scouting, reconnoitring and foraging parties encountered perils uncalculated and unseen before. Our enemy, being at home, was well used to the places, and thus possessed of every local advantage that favours an army.

To procure provisions, and forage, without sending out large parties or bodies of soldiers, became impossible, and, therefore, the Indians themselves, who were attached to march with and reinforce us, began to desert. Plunder and freebooting was greatly their object, and to be debarred from that, as they found themselves, they turned away from privations and regular warfare, which they were disused to maintain. Of this we had evidence, for as a party of our troops posted near a wood were severely galled on the right of our line by the fire of the enemy, the Indians who accompanied us seemed to hold a consultation among themselves, precipitately retreated, and abandoned the army altogether.

In this circumstance of our military affairs, the Canadians and Colonists reinforcing us afforded no effectual assistance; they evidently betrayed their wishes of withdrawing from our forces, not being previously made up in mind for the severity and hardships of war, in the inveterate and wasting progress of its continuance, which, instead of favouring them with comfortable prospects of a returning tranquility, assumed day by day a more ferocious and unpromising aspect. Such then being the gloomy face of affairs in the great cause at issue, and the Colonial armies becoming daily stronger and more formidable opponents to us, it was not surprising that the tribes of Indians and the corps of loyal Colonists along with us should feel disheartened and relax their efforts in his Majesty's service.

The Battle of Valley Forge December 1776

Burgoyne's surrender at Saratoga influenced the French government to openly support the American cause. Sir William Howe remained in Philadelphia. Washington took his men into winter camp twenty miles away from Philadelphia, at Valley Forge. Albigence Waldo of Connecticut, a surgeon, provided a vivid description of the experience in his diary:

Dec 12th We are ordered to march over the river – it snows – I'm sick – eat nothing – no whiskey – no baggage – Lord – Lord – Lord. The army were till sunrise crossing the river – some at the wagon bridge and some at the raft bridge below. Cold and uncomfortable.

Dec 14th Poor food – hard lodging – cold weather – fatigue – nasty clothes – nasty cookery – vomit half my time – smoked out of my senses – the Devil's in it – I can't endure it – why are we sent here to starve and freeze – what sweet felicities have I left at home – a charming wife – pretty children – good food – good cookery – all agreeable – all harmonious. Here, all confusion – smoke and cold – hunger and filthiness – a pox on my bad luck. Here comes a bowl of beef soup – full of burnt leaves and dirt, sickish enough to make a Hector spew – away with it Boys – I'll live like the chameleon upon air.

Dec 15th Quiet. Eat persimmons, found myself better for their lenient operation What have you for dinner, boys? "Nothing but fire cake & water, Sir." – "Gentlemen, the supper is ready." What is your supper, lads? "Fire cake & water, Sir." What have you got for breakfast, lads? "Fire cake and water, Sir." The Lord send that our Commissary of Purchases may live on fire cake and water, till their glutted guts are turned to pasteboard.

Dec 25th Christmas We are still in tents – when we ought to be in huts – the poor sick, suffer much in tents this cold weather –

Dec 28th Yesterday, upwards of 50 officers in General Greene's Division resigned their commission, six or seven of our regiment are doing the like today. All this is occasion'd by officers' families being so much neglected at home on account of provisions. Their wages will not by considerable purchase a few trifling comfortables here in camp, and maintain their families at home, while such extravagant prices are demanded for the common necessaries of life . . . When the officer has been fatiguing through the wet and cold and returns to his tent where he finds a letter directed to him from his wife, fill'd with the most heartaching, tender complaints a woman is capable of writing, acquainting him with the incredible difficulty with which she procures a little bread for herself and children, and finally concluding with expressions bordering on despair of procuring a sufficiency of food to keep soul & body together through the winter – that the money is of little consequence to her – that she begs him to consider that charity begins at home, and not suffer his family to perish with want, in the midst of plenty.

Dr Benjamin Rush, another doctor, described what he saw:

> The encampment dirty and stinking, no forage for 7 days – 1,500 horses died from ye want of it. 3 Ounces of meal and 3 pounds of flour in 7 days. The Commander-in-Chief and all ye Major Generals live in houses out of ye camp.

The Battle of Monmouth Courthouse June 1778

France allied itself with the Americans in February 1778. Washington and his army received the news in May. Howe was replaced by Sir Henry Clinton. Clinton withdrew from Philadelphia and began to retreat towards New York. Washington and his army followed them, catching them up at Monmouth Courthouse. General Charles Lee was under orders to attack the British rearguard but instead he retreated. Private Joseph Martin was among those ordered to retreat:

> We had not retreated far before we came to a defile, a muddy sloughy brook; while the artillery were passing this place, we sat down by the road side; – in a few minutes the Commander-in-chief and Suit crossed the road just where we were sitting. I heard him ask our officers, "by whose order the troops were retreating," and being answered, "by Gen. Lee's," he said something, but as he was moving forward all the time this was passing, he was too far off for me to hear it distinctly; those that were nearer to him said that his words were "D-n him"; whether he did thus express himself or not I do not know; it was certainly very unlike him, but he seemed at the instant to be in a great passion his looks if not his words seemed to indicate as much.

A Maryland captain observed Washington confront General Lee:

> General Washington rode up and upbraided General Lee for his dastardly conduct. General Washington demanded of General Lee the reason for the retreat, to which General Lee replied: "Sir, these troops are not able to meet British grenadiers."
>
> "Sir," said General Washington, much excited, "they are able,

and by God they shall do it," and immediately gave orders to countermarch the column.

Monmouth Courthouse was the longest battle of the war fought in extremely hot weather. Each side lost about 350 officers and men. The British lost 60 men from sunstroke. It was the last major battle in the north. Washington and his army returned to Philadelphia in triumph.

The British colonies in the West Indies were in danger from the French fleet and a French invasion of England was a possibility which had to be guarded against. The French had 21 battleships in American and West Indian waters. The British only had 11. There was an additional naval threat from American privateers, armed vessels licensed to capture British merchant ships.

Bonhomme Richard v Serapis 23 September 1779

In 1779 Great Britain faced an invasion threat from France, supported by the Spanish fleet. The American ambassador in Paris, Benjamin Franklin encouraged the American captain, John Paul Jones, to raid the English coast. Franklin helped Jones to get a ship with which to attack British shipping. He was finally given an ex-Indiaman, a strongly built vessel, capable of mounting heavy guns. She was fitted out at L'Orient in France and renamed the *Bonhomme Richard.*

A captured British officer wrote a letter dated 15 June:

> Capt. Paul Jones, who some time since landed in Scotland and other places, has fitted out an Old East Indiaman, to mount 50 guns, and has had her full manned except about 40. She is to carry 300; most of them are English prisoners, who are allowed to enter on board the American vessel. Numbers of them, I am sure, would never have gone on board, but for the bad treatment they experienced in prison. The above ship is to sail in consort with an American frigate called the *Alliance*.

Jones put to sea in August with a squadron, comprising the *Pallas*, a French 32-gun frigate, the *Vengeance*, a French 14-gun brig, the *Alliance*, an American 36–gun frigate – and the flagship, the *Bonhomme Richard.*

On 23 September, off Flamborough Head, he found a merchant

fleet of 40 ships returning from the Baltic, escorted by the *Serapis* of 44 guns, and the *Countess of Scarborough*, of 22. The merchant fleet scurried to safety but Jones engaged the *Serapis*. The *Serapis* was a two-decked 44-gun ship, a very poor class of ship whose guns and equipment were in bad condition.

Lieutenant Richard Dale was commanding a battery of twelve-pounders on the *Bonhomme Richard*. He described the action:

> At about eight, being within hail, the *Serapis* demanded, "What ship is that?"
>
> He was answered, "I can't hear what you say."
>
> Immediately after, the *Serapis* hailed again, "What ship is that? Answer immediately, or I shall be under the necessity of firing into you."
>
> At this moment I received orders from Commodore Jones to commence the action with a broadside, which indeed appeared to be simultaneous on board both ships. Our position being to windward of the *Serapis*, we passed ahead of her, and the *Serapis* coming up on our larboard quarter, the action commenced abreast of each other. The *Serapis* soon passed ahead of the *Bonhomme Richard*, and when he thought he had gained a distance sufficient to go down athwart the fore foot to rake us, found he had not enough distance, and that the *Bonhomme Richard* would be aboard him, put his helm a-lee, which brought the two ships on a line, and the *Bonhomme Richard*, having head way, ran her bows into the stern of the *Serapis*.
>
> We had remained in this situation but a few minutes when we were again hailed by the *Serapis*, "Has your ship struck?"
>
> To which Captain Jones answered, "I have not yet begun to fight!"
>
> As we were unable to bring a single gun to bear upon the *Serapis* our top-sails were backed while, those of the *Serapis* being filled, the ships separated. The *Serapis* bore short round upon her heel, and her jibboom ran into the mizen rigging of the *Bonhomme Richard*. In this situation the ships were made fast together with a hawser, the bowsprit of the *Serapis* to the mizen-mast of the *Bonhomme Richard*, and the action recommenced from the starboard sides of the two ships. With a view of separating the ships, the *Serapis* let go her anchor, which manoeuver brought her head and the stern of the *Bonhomme Richard* to the wind, while the ships lay closely pressed against each other.
>
> A novelty in naval combats was now presented to many wit-

nesses, but to few admirers. The rammers were run into the respective ships to enable the men to load after the lower ports of the *Serapis* had been blown away, to make room for running out their guns, and in this situation the ships remained until between 10 and 11 o'clock pm, when the engagement terminated by the surrender of the *Serapis*.

From the commencement to the termination of the action there was not a man on board the *Bonhomme Richard* ignorant of the superiority of the *Serapis*, both in weight of metal and in the qualities of the crews. The crew of that ship was picked seamen, and the ship itself had been only a few months off the stocks, whereas the crew of the *Bonhomme Richard* consisted of part Americans, English and French, and a part of Maltese, Portuguese and Malays, these latter contributing by their want of naval skill and knowledge of the English language to depress rather than to elevate a just hope of success in a combat under such circumstances.

Neither the consideration of the relative force of the ships, the fact of the blowing up of the gundeck above them by the bursting of two of the 18-pounders, nor the alarm that the ship was sinking, could depress the ardor or change the determination of the brave Captain Jones, his officers and men. Neither the repeated broadsides of the *Alliance*, given with the view of sinking or disabling the *Bonhomme Richard*, the frequent necessity of suspending the combat to extinguish the flames, which several times were within a few inches of the magazine, nor the liberation by the master-at-arms of nearly 500 prisoners, could change or weaken the purpose of the American commander. At the moment of the liberation of the prisoners, one of them, a commander of a 20-gun ship taken a few days before, passed through the ports on board the *Serapis* and informed Captain Pearson that if he would hold out only a little while longer, the ship alongside would either strike or sink, and that all the prisoners had been released to save their lives. The combat was accordingly continued with renewed ardor by the *Serapis*.

The *Alliance* was now under the stern of the *Serapis* and able to fire into her unnopposed:

The fire from the tops of the *Bonhomme Richard* was conducted with so much skill and effect as to destroy ultimately every man who appeared upon the quarter deck of the *Serapis*, and induced her commander to order the survivors to go below. Not even under

> the shelter of the decks were they more secure. The powder-monkies of the *Serapis*, finding no officer to receive the 18-pound cartridges brought from the magazines, threw them on the main deck and went for more. These cartridges being scattered along the deck and numbers of them broken, it so happened that some of the hand-grenades thrown from the main-yard of the *Bonhomme Richard*, which was directly over the main-hatch of the *Serapis*, fell upon this powder and produced a most awful explosion. The effect was tremendous; more than 20 of the enemy were blown to pieces, and many stood with only the collars of their shirts upon their bodies. In less than an hour afterwards, the flag of England, which had been nailed to the mast of the *Serapis*, was struck by Captain Pearson's own hand, as none of his people would venture aloft on this duty; and this too when more than 1,500 persons were witnessing the conflict, and the humiliating termination of it, from Scarborough and Flamborough Head.

Midshipman Nathaniel Fanning, perched in the maintop of the *Bonhomme Richard*, had a different view:

> It was, however, some time before the enemy's colours were struck. The captain of the *Serapis* gave repeated orders for one of his crew to ascend the quarter-deck and haul down the English flag, but no one would stir to do it. They told the captain they were afraid of our riflemen, believing that all our men who were seen with muskets were of that description. The captain of the *Serapis* therefore ascended the quarter-deck and hauled down the very flag which he had nailed to the flag-staff a little before the commencement of the battle, and which flag he had at that time, in the presence of his principal officers, swore he never would strike to that infamous pirate J. P. Jones.
>
> The enemy's flag being struck, Captain Jones ordered Richard Dale, his first lieutenant, to select out of our crew a number of men and take possession of the prize, which was immediately put into execution. Several of our men (I believe three) were killed by the English on board of the *Serapis* after she had struck her colours.

The *Bonhomme Richard* was so badly damaged that she sank immediately.

The Battle of Stony Point July 1779

In May, 1779 Sir Henry Clinton sent a force to devastate Virginia whose beef fed the Continental army and whose tobacco financed Congress' credit abroad. Portsmouth, New Haven and Norfolk were raided.

The New York Journal reported that the redcoats:

> plundered the houses of everything they could carry away or convert to their own use, and broke or destroyed every whole article of household goods and furniture, together with the window glass and sashes.

Washington was at Middlebrook in New Jersey, in case Clinton came south from New York. Clinton had 12,000 men and was launching raids in the Hudson valley. In July, the Americans attacked a British post at Stony Point.

Nathanael Greene described the attack:

> I wrote you a hasty account yesterday of a surprise General Wayne has effected on the garrison at this place. He marched about two o'clock in the afternoon from Fort Montgomery with part of the light infantry of the army, amounting to about 1,400 men. The garrison consisted of between 5 and 600 men, including officers. The attack was made about midnight and conducted with great spirit and enterprise, the troops marching up in the face of an exceeding heavy fire with cannon and musketry, without discharging a gun. This is thought to be the perfection of discipline and will for ever immortalize Gen. Wayne, as it would do honor to the first general in Europe. The place is as difficult of access as any you ever saw, strongly fortified with lines and secured with a double row of abatis. The post actually looks more formidable on the ground than it can be made by description, and, contrary to almost all other events of this nature, increases our surprize by viewing the place and the circumstances.
>
> The darkness of the night favoured the attack and made our loss much less than might have been expected. The whole business was done with fixed bayonets. Our loss in killed and wounded amounted to 90 men, including officers – eight only of which were killed. Gen. Wayne got a slight wound (upon the side of the head) and three or four other officers – among the number is

Lieut. Col. Hay, of Pennsylvania – but they are all in a fair way of recovery.

The Battle of Savannah September 1779

In the south the British had regained Savannah and were in control of Georgia. The Comte d'Estaing had arrived with a French fleet, fresh from capturing St Vincent and Grenada in the West Indies. Benjamin Lincoln was the American general in command in the south. He had two thousand men. He marched on Savannah in September 1779.

Comte d'Estaing insisted upon an all-out assault, despite the objections of Lincoln. Major Thomas Pinckney of the South Carolina militia blamed d'Estaing for the fiasco that followed:

> By the time the French column had arrived at the open space, day had fairly broke, when Count d'Estaing, without waiting until the other columns had arrived at their positions, placed himself at the head of his first column and rushed forward to the attack. But this body was so severely galled by the grape shot from the batteries as they advanced, and by both grape shot and musketry when they reached the abatis that, in spite of the efforts of the officers, the column got into confusion and broke away to their left toward the wood in that direction. The second and third French column shared successively the same fate, having the additional discouragement of seeing, as they marched to the attack, the repulse and loss of their comrades who had preceded them.
>
> Count Pulaski who, with the cavalry, preceded the right column of the Americans, proceeded gallantly until stopped by the abatis, and before he could force through it, received his mortal wound. In the meantime, Colonel Laurens at the head of the light infantry, followed by the 2nd South Carolina Regiment and 1st Battalion Charlestown militia, attacked the Spring Hill redoubt, got into the ditch and planted the colors of the 2nd Regiment on the berm, but the parapet was too steep for them to scale it under so heavy a fire, and after much slaughter they were driven out of the ditch.
>
> By this time the 2nd American column, headed by General McIntosh, to which I was attached, arrived at the foot of the

> Spring Hill redoubt, and such a scene of confusion as there appeared is not often equalled. Count d'Estaing was wounded in the arm, and endeavoring to rally his men, a few of whom with a drummer he had collected. General McIntosh did not speak French, but desired me to inform the Commander-in-Chief that his column was fresh, and that he wished his directions, where, under the present circumstances, he should make the attack. The Count ordered that we should move more to the left, and by no means to interfere with the troops he was endeavoring to rally. In pursuing this direction we were thrown too much to the left, and before we could reach Spring Hill redoubt, we had to pass through Yamacraw Swamp, then wet and boggy, with the galley at the mouth annoying our left flank with grape shot.
>
> While struggling through this morass, the firing slacked, and it was reported that the whole army had retired. I was sent by General McIntosh to look out from the Spring Hill, where I found not an assailant standing. On reporting this to the General, he ordered a retreat, which was effected without too much loss, notwithstanding the heavy fire of grape shot with which we were followed.

The loss of both armies in killed and wounded amounted to 637 French and 457 Americans . . . The loss of the British amounted only to 55.

Franco-American co-operation had failed. A Loyalist officer, John Harris Cruger, put it:

> They came in so full of confidence of succeeding, that they were at some loss where to lay the blame, each abusing the other for deceiving them.
>
> We are all hands sufferers by this unfortunate invasion. The difference is we have acquired glory and our Enemies, Disgrace.

The Battle of Camden 15 August 1780

In 1780, Washington's army had wintered at Morristown. The British had received reinforcements under Cornwallis. Clinton now embarked on a southern campaign. He besieged Charlestown which surrendered in May 1780. Congress appointed Horatio Gates

Commander in the South. Gates had been the victor at Saratoga. Washington preferred Nathanael Greene to Gates. Gates marched on the town of Camden on the night of 15 August, by way of Gum Swamp. Cornwallis had arrived to take command and was determined to attack Gates. He also marched by way of Gum Swamp. At two in the morning, to each part's surprise, the two armies collided. Gates ordered the deputy adjutant general, Colonel Otho Williams, to call a council of war. Colonel Otho Williams:

> The General's astonishment could not be concealed. He ordered the deputy adjutant general to call another council of war. All the general officers immediately assembled in the rear of the line; the unwelcome news was communicated to them. General Gates said, "Gentlemen, what is best to be done?" All were mute for a few moments, when the gallant Stevens exclaimed, "Gentlemen, is it not too late now to do anything but fight?" No other advice was offered, and the General desired the gentlemen would repair to their respective commands.
>
> Frequent skirmishes happened during the night between the two advanced parties, which served to discover the relative situation of the two armies, and as a prelude to what was to take place in the morning. General Stevens, observing the enemy to rush on, put his men in mind of their bayonets; but, the impetuosity with which they advanced, firing and huzzaing, threw the whole body of the militia into such a panic, that they generally threw down their loaded arms and fled in the utmost consternation. The unworthy example of the Virginians was almost instantly followed by the North Carolinians; only a small part of the brigade, commanded by Brigadier General Gregory, made a short pause. A part of Dixon's regiment, of that brigade, next in line to the second Maryland brigade, fired two or three rounds of cartridge. But a great majority of the militia (at least two-thirds of the army) fled without firing a shot.
>
> The second Maryland brigade, including the battalion of Delawares, on the right, were engaged with the enemy's left, which they opposed with a very great firmness. They even advanced upon them and had taken a number of prisoners, when their companions of the first brigade (which formed the second line) being greatly outflanked, and charged by superior numbers, were obliged to give ground.
>
> The enemy, having collected their corps, and directing their

whole force against these two devoted brigades, a tremendous fire of musketry was, for some time, kept up on both sides with equal perseverance and obstinacy, until Lord Cornwallis, perceiving there was no cavalry opposed to him, pushed forward his dragoons and his infantry charging at the same moment with fixed bayonets, put an end to the contest.

His victory was complete. All the artillery and a great number of prisoners fell into his hands. Many fine fellows lay on the field, and the rout of the remainder was entire (not even a company retired in any order), every one escaped as he could. If, in this affair, the militia fled too soon, the regulars may be thought almost blamable for remaining too long on the field, especially after all hope of victory must have been despaired of . . .

The torrent of unarmed militia bore away with it Generals Gates, Caswell, and a number of the others, who soon saw that all was lost.

General Gates, at first, conceived a hope that he might rally at Clermont a sufficient number to cover the retreat of the regulars, but the farther they fled the more they were dispersed, and the generals soon found themselves abandoned by all but their aides . . .

The Battle of King's Mountain 14 October 1780

After the battle of Camden, Cornwallis moved north. On his left flank were 1,000 loyalists led by Major Patrick Ferguson. Hearing that a much larger Patriot force of Mountain men was looking for them, he took up a defensive position on King's Mountain, an outlying spur of the Blue Ridge near the borders of North Carolina and South Carolina.

Ferguson was caught unprepared by the American advance through the woods to King's Mountain. Captain Alexander Chesney, a South Carolina Loyalist officer, had been on reconnaissance:

So rapid was their attack that I was in the act of dismounting to report that all was quiet and the pickets on the alert when we heard their firing [on the pickets] about half a mile off I immediately paraded the men and posted the officers.

King's Mountain, from its height, would have enabled us to

> oppose a superior force with advantage, had it nor been covered with wood, which sheltered the Americans and enabled them to fight in their favorite manner. In fact, after driving in our pickets, they were able to advance . . . to the crest . . . in perfect safety, until they took post and opened an irregular but destructive fire from behind trees and other cover.

Thomas Young was an American 16-year-old private, who had lost his shoes but fought his way up the north slope:

> The orders were at the firing of the first gun, for every man to raise a whoop, rush forward, and fight his way as best he could. When our division came up to the northern base of the mountain, Colonel Roebuck drew us a little to the left and commenced the attack. I well remember how I behaved. Ben Hollingworth and myself took right up the side of the mountain, and fought from tree to tree, our way to the summit. I recollect I stood behind one tree and fired until the bark was nearly all knocked off, and my eyes pretty well filled with it. One fellow shaved me pretty close, for his bullet took a piece out of my gun stock.
>
> Before I was aware of it, I found myself apparently between my own regiment and the enemy, as I judged, from seeing the paper the Whigs wore in their hats, and the pine knots the Tories wore in theirs, these being the badges of distinction.
>
> On top of the mountain, in the thickest of the fight, I saw Colonel Williams fall, and a braver or better man never died upon the field of battle. I had seen him fall but once before that day; it was in the beginning of the action, as he charged by me at full speed around the mountain. Towards the summit a ball struck his horse just under the jaw, when he commenced stamping as if he were in a nest of yellow jackets. Colonel Williams threw his reins over the animal's neck, sprang to the ground, and dashed onward.
>
> The moment I heard the cry that Colonel Williams was shot, I ran to his assistance, for I loved him as a father; he had been ever so kind to me and almost always carried a cake in his pocket for me and his little son, Joseph. They carried him into a tent, and sprinkled some water in his face. He revived, and his first words were, "For God's sake, boys, don't give up the hill!" . . . I left him in the arms of his son, Daniel, and returned to the field to revenge his fate.

Robert Henry was in another American regiment:

> We then advanced up the hill close to the Tory lines. There was a log across a hollow that I took my stand by and, stepping one step back, I was safe from British fire. I there maintained firing until the British charged bayonets . . . The Fork boys fired and did considerable execution. I was preparing to fire when one of the British advancing, I stepped [back] and was in the act of cocking my gun when his bayonet was running along the barrel of my gun, and gave me a thrust through my hand and into my thigh. My antagonist and I both fell. The Fork boys retreated and loaded their guns. I was then lying under the smoke and it appeared that some of them were not more than a gun's length in front of the bayonets, and the farthest could not have been more than twenty feet in front when they discharged their rifles. It was said that every one dropped his man. The British then retreated in great haste, and were pursued by the Fork boys.
>
> William Caldwell saw my condition, and pulled the bayonet out of my thigh, but it hung to my hand; he gave my hand a kick and it went out. The thrust gave me much pain, but the pulling of it was much more severe. With my well hand I picked up my gun and found her discharged. I suppose that when the soldier made the thrust, I gripped the trigger and discharged her; the load must have passed through his bladder and cut a main artery of his back, as he bled profusely . . .

In Colonel Shelby's column was the boy James Collins:

> Their leader, Ferguson, came in full view, within a rifle shot as if to encourage his men, who by this time were falling very fast; he soon disappeared. We took to the hill a third time; the enemy gave way.
>
> When he had gotten near the top, some of our leaders roared out: "Hurrah, my brave fellows! Advance! They are crying for quarter!"

The American Colonel Shelby described Ferguson's death:

> Still Ferguson's proud heart could not think of surrender. He swore "he never would yield to such a d—banditti," and rushed from his men, sword in hand, and cut away until his sword was broken and he was shot down. His men, seeing their leader fall,

immediately surrendered. The British loss, in killed and prisoners, was 1,105.

Collins continued:

> By this time the right and left had gained the top of the cliff – the enemy was completely hemmed in on all sides, and no chance of escaping. Besides, their leader had fallen. They soon threw down their arms and surrendered. After the fight was over, the situation of the poor Tories appeared to be really pitiable; the dead lay in heaps on all sides, while the groans of the wounded were heard in every direction. I could not help turning away from the scene before me, with horror, and though exulting in victory, could not refrain from shedding tears.
>
> On examining the body of their great chief, it appeared that almost 50 rifles must have been leveled at him at the same time. Seven rifle balls had passed through his body, both his arms were broken, and his hat and clothing were literally shot to pieces. Their great elevation above us had proved their ruin; they overshot us altogether, scarce touching a man except those on horseback, while every rifle from below seemed to have the desired effect. In this conflict I had fired my rifle six times, while others perhaps fired nine or ten.

He confirmed the scale of the casualties:

> The wives and children of the poor Tories came in, in great numbers. Their husbands, fathers, and brothers lay dead in heaps, while others lay wounded or dying . . . We proceeded to bury the dead, but it was badly done. They were thrown into convenient piles and covered with old logs, the bark of old trees and rocks, yet not so as to secure them from becoming a prey to the beasts of the forest, or the vultures of the air; and the wolves [later] became so plenty, that it was dangerous for anyone to be out at night for several miles around. Also the hogs in the neighborhood gathered into the place to devour the flesh of men, in-as-much as numbers chose to live on little meat rather than eat their hogs, though they were fat. Half of the dogs in the country were said to be mad and were put to death. I saw myself in passing the place, a few weeks after, all parts of the human frame . . . scattered in every direction . . .

> In the evening, there was a distribution . . . of the plunder, and we were dismissed. My father and myself drew two fine horses, two guns, and some articles of clothing with a share of powder and lead. Every man repaired to his tent or home. It seemed like a calm after a heavy storm . . . and for a short time, every man could visit his home, or his neighbor without being afraid . . .

On the same day as the battle of King's Mountain, Gates was replaced as commander of the Southern army by Nathanael Green.

The Battle of Cowpens 17 January 1781

In 1780, a French fleet had arrived at Newport, Rhode Island and landed 6,000 French troops under the Comte de Rochambeau. Rochambeau was ordered to obey Washington's orders and campaign plans. At home, the British were resisting the French invasion threat by a close blockade of French ports, which also cut off further reinforcements to North America. The war was becoming a world war for the British. Her enemies then included the Spanish, French, Dutch and Russians.

Washington put his army into winter quarters along the Hudson river. Nathanael Green was now in command of the American forces in the south. The war was becoming increasingly ruthless. The British cavalry commander, Banastre Tarleton, used terror tactics.

Nathanael Green sent a Patriot force under Daniel Morgan to attack troops from Cornwallis' army under the notorious Lieutenant Colonel Banastre Tarleton. One of Morgan's columns had attacked 250 Loyalists at Hammond's Store and killed or wounded 150 of them without a single loss. Cornwallis, at Winnsboro, sent Tarleton in pursuit. On 16 January 1781, Morgan made a stand at Cowpens. Tarleton ordered a frontal attack with the bayonet which was intended to make the new militia run. They did not run, as James Collins told:

> About sunrise on the 17th of January, 1781, the enemy came in full view. The sight, to me at least, seemed somewhat imposing. They halted for a short time, and then advanced rapidly as if certain of victory. The militia under Pickins and Moffitt was posted on the right of the regulars some distance in advance, while

Washington's cavalry was stationed in the rear. We gave the enemy one fire; when they charged us with their bayonets, we gave way and retreated for our horses. Tarleton's cavalry pursued us. "Now," thought I, "my hide is in the loft."

Just as we got to our horses, they overtook us and began to make a few hacks at some, however without doing much injury. They, in their haste, had pretty much scattered, perhaps thinking they would have another Fishing Creek frolic, but in a few moments Col Washington's cavalry was among them like a whirlwind, and the poor fellows began to keel from their horses without being able to remount. The shock was so sudden and violent they could not stand it and immediately betook themselves to fight. There was no time to rally, and they appeared to be as hard to stop as a drove of wild Choctaw steers going to a Pennsylvania market. In a few moments the clashing of swords was out of hearing and quickly out of sight.

By this time both lines of the infantry were warmly engaged and we, being relieved from the pursuit of the enemy, began to rally and prepare to redeem our credit, when Morgan rode up in front and, waving his sword, cried out, "Form, form, my brave fellows! Give them more fire and the day is ours. Old Morgan was never beaten."

We then advanced briskly and gained the right flank of the enemy, and they, being hard pressed in front by Howard and falling very fast, could not stand it long. They began to throw down their arms and surrender themselves prisoners of war. The whole army, except Tarleton and his horsemen, fell into the hands of Morgan, together with all the baggage . . .

General Daniel Morgan wrote to Nathanael Greene from Cain Creek:

The troops I have the honour to command have been so fortunate as to obtain a complete victory over a detachment from the British army, commanded by Lieut. Col. Tarleton. The action happened on the 17th inst., about sunrise, at the Cowpens. It, perhaps, would be well to remark, for the honour of the American arms, that although the progress of this corps was marked with burning and devastation, and although they waged the most cruel warfare, not a man was killed, wounded or even insulted after he surrendered. Had not Britons during this contest received so many lessons of humanity, I should flatter myself that this might teach them a little. But I fear they are incorrigible.

The British lost in one hour 1,000 men killed, wounded or captured, two three-pounder cannon, 800 muskets, 35 wagons of stores, 100 horses and 60 slaves. The Americans lost only 12 lives.

Morgan moved to rejoin Greene and the main body of the Continental army. He and his men had to cross swollen streams and march on muddy, icy roads. The rendezvous was to be at Guilford Courthouse. Morgan covered 100 miles in five days, leaving behind him fords made impassable by felled trees. Cornwallis with 2,500 men gave chase. His men travelled light, having been told to burn all unnecessary stores, including rum.

The Battle of Guilford Courthouse 15 March 1781

"Another such victory would destroy the British army".
Charles James Fox

The two opposing armies of Greene and Cornwallis were now in Virginia. Spring brought Greene some reinforcements and a mood of optimism, caught by the young Virginian, St George Tucker, who had risen from private to major of militia, in a letter to his wife:

The lark is up, the morning gray, and I am seated by a smoky fire to let my dearest Fanny know that her soldier is as blithe as the mockingbird which is at this moment tuning his pipe within a dozen yards of me. If the fatigues of the remainder of the campaign sit as well upon my limbs as those which I have hitherto experienced, you may be assured that I shall return to Cumberland the most portly, genteel fellow that the country will be able to boast of

The battle of Guilford Courthouse in March was similar to Cowpens, although Cornwallis claimed the victory since he kept the field. Greene reported:

The battle was fought at or near Guilford Court-House, the very place from whence we began our retreat after the Light Infantry joined the army from the Pedee. The battle was long, obstinate and bloody. We were obliged to give up the ground and lost our artillery, but the enemy have been so soundly beaten that they dare not move towards us since the action, notwithstanding we lay within ten miles of him for two days. Except the ground and the artillery, they have gained no advantage. On the contrary, they are little short of being ruined. The enemy's loss in killed and wounded cannot be less than between 6 and 700, perhaps more.

Victory was long doubtful, and had the North Carolina militia done their duty, it was certain. They had the most advantageous position I ever saw, and left it without making scarcely the shadow of opposition. Their general and field officers exerted themselves, but the men would not stand. Many threw away their arms and fled with the utmost precipitation, even before a gun was fired at them. The Virginia militia behaved nobly and annoyed the enemy greatly. The horse, at different times in the course of the day, performed wonders. Indeed, the horse is our great safeguard, and without them the militia could not keep the field in this country . . . Never did an army labour under so many disadvantages as this; but the fortitude and patience of the officers and soldiery rise superior to all difficulties. We have little to eat, less to drink, and lodge in the woods in the midst of smoke. Indeed, our fatigue is excessive. I was so much overcome night before last that I fainted.

Our army is in good spirits, but the militia are leaving us in great numbers to return home to kiss their wives and sweethearts.

I have never felt an easy moment since the enemy crossed the Catawba until since the defeat of the 15th, but now I am perfectly easy, being persuaded it is out of the enemy's power to do us any great injury. Indeed, I think they will retire as soon as they can get off their wounded. My love to your family and all friends . . .

Cornwallis had about 2,200 men and was actually outnumbered. Sergeant Roger Lamb had escaped after Burgoyne's surrender at Saratoga and was back with the British army. He had been sent south to join a newly formed Brigade, commanded by Colonel Webster. He wrote:

Colonel [Webster] rode on to the front and gave the word, "Charge!" Instantly, the movement was made in excellent order, in a smart run, with arms charged. When arrived within 40 yards of the enemy's lines, it was perceived that their whole force had their arms presented and resting on a rail fence . . . They were taking aim with the nicest precision.

At this awful period, a general pause took place. Both parties surveyed each other for the moment with the most anxious suspense. Nothing speaks the general more than seizing on decisive moments:

Colonel Webster rode forward in the front of the Twenty-third Regiment and said . . . "Come on, my brave fusiliers" . . . They rushed forward amidst the enemy's fire. Dreadful was the havoc on both sides . . .

At last the Americans gave way and the brigade advanced to the attack of their second line.

The second line, 300 yards behind the first, gave way, but the Greene's men behind it remained firm. They even counter-attacked, but Greene would not risk following up the counter-attack – to lose would be to lose an army. With one horse already shot under him, and now, Cornwallis, mounted on his second horse, was in the middle of the action. Finally he ordered his artillery to fire grapeshot at the Continental Line, halting them and driving them back. His artillery was indiscriminate and killed many men – on both sides. At the end, however, Cornwallis remained in possession of the battlefield. As such he was able to claim a victory.

Major Henry Lee (the father of Robert E. Lee) for the Americans left an account of the battlefield afterwards:

The night . . . was rainy, dark, and cold. The dead unburied, the wounded unsheltered, the groans of the dying and the shrieks of the living, cast a deeper shade over the gloom of nature. The victorious troops, without tents and without food, participated in sufferings which they could not relieve. The ensuing morning was spent in performing the last offices to the dead and in providing comfort for the wounded . . . The British general regarded with equal attention friends and foes. As soon as this service was over, he put his army in motion for New Garden, where his rear guard with his baggage met him. All his wounded, incapable of moving (about 70 . . .) he left to the humanity of General Greene.

Cornwallis had lost a quarter of his army (killed, wounded or missing) and was 250 miles from his base, at Yorktown. Charles James Fox echoed Clinton's comment after Bunker Hill, "Another such victory would destroy the British army".

Cornwallis, withdrew to the coast at Wilmington, and Greene moved south to reconquer South Carolina and Georgia.

Frederick Mackenzie, observing the campaign from New York, wrote:

> Greene is however entitled to great praise for his wonderful exertions; the more he is beaten, the further he advances in the end. He has been indefatigable in collecting troops and leading them to be defeated. Greene is this, to be the Fabius of the age, and the people of this country almost adore him.

Or as Greene put it himself, "We fight, get beat, rise and fight again."

Greene wrote to George Washington in March from his headquarters on Deep River:

> In this critical and distressing situation, I am determined to carry the war immediately into South Carolina. The enemy will be obliged to follow us or give up their posts in that State. If the former takes place it will draw the war out of this State and give it an opportunity to raise its proportion of men. If they leave their posts to fall, they must lose more than they can gain here. If we continue in this State, the enemy will hold their possessions in both. All things considered, I think the movement is warranted by the soundest reasons, both political and military. The manoeuvre will be critical and dangerous, and the troops exposed to every hardship. But as I share it with them, I hope they will bear up under it with that magnanimity which has already supported them, and for which they deserve everything of their country.

Cornwallis still had a number of fortified positions in North Carolina and South Carolina at Camden, Augusta, Ninety Six, Orangeburg and Fort La Motte. But his troops were scattered across what was now plainly hostile territory. He began a retreat to the coast which would eventually bring him to Yorktown. Clinton, the British commander-in-chief, in New York, feared a joint French and American attack against New York or Virginia. He wanted to establish an anchorage for battleships in Chesapeake Bay. It was because of this that Cornwallis chose to fortify Yorktown.

The Battle of Yorktown September-October 1781

"We cannot hope to make a very long resistance."

Lord Cornwallis

Yorktown was the British base of operations for their attempts to reconquer the southern United States. Yorktown lay at the mouth of the James River in Chesapeake Bay, Virginia.

George Washington was sufficiently confident of the support of the French fleet to risk attacking Cornwallis' army at Yorktown. In fact, he planned the Yorktown campaign aboard the *Ville de Paris*, flagship of the French fleet.

The British Admiral Thomas Graves was searching for the French fleet off New England, in fog.

The British forces, under Lord Cornwallis, were in retreat after taking heavy casualties at the recent battles of Cowpens and Guildford Courthouse; Cornwallis' troops hoped to find their own fleet offshore at Yorktown.

To Lord Cornwallis' dismay, the French fleet, not the British, had arrived in Chesapeake Bay on 2 September. This was the fleet commanded by the Comte de Grasse, from the West Indies. It consisted of 29 battleships. When the British fleet arrived, they were outnumbered. On 5 September they failed to drive the French away. They remained offshore but the battle of the Chesapeake was not renewed. On 14 September eight more French battleships arrived under the Comte de Baras. The British fleet sailed back to New York to refit.

The French fleet bombarded Cornwallis' defences at Yorktown. They also landed siege equipment and 4,000 French troops to reinforce the Americans. Washington moved quickly and decisively to attack the British from the landward side. Cornwallis' 7,000 British soldiers were now outnumbered by 15,000 French and Americans. The British were cut off and under siege.

Dr James Thatcher described Washington's plan:

> The great secret respecting our late preparation and movements can now be explained. It was a judiciously concerted strategem calculated to menace and alarm Sir Henry Clinton for the safety of the garrison of New York, and induce him to recall a part of his troops from Virginia, for his own defence; or perhaps, keeping an eye on the city, to attempt its capture, provided that by the arrival of a French fleet, favorable circumstances should present. The deception has proved completely successful; a part of Cornwallis' troops are reported to have returned to New York. His Excellency General Washington, having succeeded in a masterly piece of generalship, has now the satisfaction of leaving his adversary to ruminate on his own mortifying situation, and to anticipate the perilous fate which awaits his friend, Lord Cornwallis, in a different quarter.

Colonel St George Tucker, still serving with the Virginia militia, wrote to his wife on 5 September:

> Hear then, my Fanny, from me what perhaps you have not heard yet from good authority. About the middle of last week 29 ships of the line and four frigates arrived in our bay, with 4,000 land forces sent to our assistance by Louis the Great. Besides these there are 3,000 marines to be landed in case of an emergency. Of the fleet there are 10 sixty-fours; 18 seventy-fours, and one ship of an hundred and ten guns! A fleet of 12 sail of the line has arrived in the West Indies to keep the enemy still employed in that quarter. Of the troops, 3,500 landed at James Town three days ago and are now on their march to this city. 500 are left on board to land at York River. The fleet lies from Lynnhaven bay to the mouth of York River, and some, we are informed, have proceeded within two or three miles of the town. The British fleet still lies at York, and their land forces are now in the town.
>
> Nor is this all, for, to my great suprise and pleasure, I was this morning informed from undoubted authority that General Washington is at the Head of Elk with 5,000 troops, which are to be embarked from thence in transports sent there for that purpose, of which the Marquis last night received official accounts from General Washington in a letter dated at Chatham.

The siege began on 28 September. Cornwallis immediately withdrew

to his outer defences. On 9 October, his earthworks were bombarded by French guns. Washington touched off the first shot. Cornwallis wrote: "We cannot hope to make a very long resistance."
Inside Yorktown was Captain Samuel Graham of the 76th Regiment of Foot, who had come to Virginia with his Highland regiment early in the spring. So far he had thoroughly enjoyed the Virginia campaign: now that he faced besiegement, his ardour only increased, as did that of his comrades:

> On 28 September, information was given by a picket . . . that the enemy were advancing in force by the Williamsburg road. The army immediately took post in the outward were fired from our fieldpieces. The French also felt the redoubt on our right flank, defended by the Twenty-third and a party of marines, but did not persist. The two armies remained some time in this position observing each other. In ours there was but one wish, that they would advance. While standing with a brother captain . . . we overheard a soliloquy of an old Highland gentleman, a lieutenant, who drawing his sword, said to himself, "Come on, Maister Washington, I'm unco' glad to see you. I've been offered money for my commission, but I could na think of gangin' hame without a sight of you! Come on!"

Captain James Duncan's diary reported:

> A militia man this day, possessed of more bravery than prudence, stood constantly on the parapet and d—his soul if he would dodge for the buggers. He had escaped longer than could have been expected, and growing foolhardy, brandished his spade at every ball that was fired till, unfortunately, a ball came and put an end to his capers.

Dr James Thatcher recounted in his journal:

> From the 10th to the 15th (of October), a tremendous and incessant firing from the American and French batteries is kept up, and the enemy return the fire, but with little effect. A red-hot shell from the French battery set fire to the Charon, a British 44-gun ship, and two or three smaller vessels at anchor in the river, which were consumed in the night. From the bank of the river I had a fine view of this splendid conflagration.

During the assault, the British kept up an incessant firing of cannon and musketry from their whole line. His Excellency General Washington, Generals Lincoln and Knox, with their aids having dismounted, were standing in an exposed situation waiting the result.

Colonel Cobb, one of General Washington's aids, solicitous for his safety, said to His Excellency, "Sir, you are too much exposed here. Had you not better step a little back?"

"Colonel Cobb," replied his Excellency, "if you are afraid, you have liberty to step back."

Colonel Philip van Cortlandt, of the 2nd New York Regiment, remembered:

> . . . the first gun which was fired I could distinctly hear pass through the town . . . I could hear the ball strike from house to house, and I was afterwards informed that it went through the one where many of the officers were at dinner, and over the tables, discomposing the dishes, and either killed or wounded the one at the head of the table. And I also heard that the gun was fired by the Commander-in-Chief, who was designedly present in the battery for the express purpose of putting the first match.

That night, Lieutenant Ebenezer Denny thought:

> The scene viewed from the camp now was grand . . . A number of shells from the works of both parties passing high in the air and descending in a curve, each with a long train of fire, exhibited a brilliant spectacle.

Meanwhile, Stephen Popp in the British lines remembered:

> We could find no refuge in or out of the town. The people fled to the waterside and hid in hastily contrived shelters on the banks, but many of them were killed by bursting bombs. More than 80 were thus lost, besides many wounded, and their houses utterly destroyed. Our ships suffered, too, under the heavy fire, for the enemy fired in one day 3,600 shot from their heavy guns and batteries. Soldiers and sailors deserted in great numbers. The Hessian Regiment von Bose lost heavily, although it was in our

> rear in the second line, but in full range of the enemy's fire. Our two regiments lost very heavily too. The Light Infantry posted at an angle had the worst position and the heaviest loss. Sailors and marines all served in defending our lines on shore.

Two British redoubts, were taken, one by the French, and one by the Americans. The American assault was led by a detachment of sappers and miners. This detachment included Sergeant Martin:

> We arrived at the trenches a little before sunset. I saw several officers fixing bayonets on long staves. I then concluded we were about to make a general assault upon the enemy's works, but before dark I was informed of the whole plan.
>
> The sappers and miners were furnished with axes and were to proceed infront and cut a passage for the troops through the abatis . . . At dark the detachment . . . advanced beyond the trenches and lay down on the ground to await the signal for . . . the attack, which was to be three shells from a certain battery . . . All the batteries in our line were silent, and we lay anxiously waiting for the signal . . . Our watchword was, "Rochambeau". Being pronounced, 'Ro-sham-bow', it sounded when pronounced quick like, "Rush on boys."
>
> We had not lain here long before the signal was given for us and the French . . . the three shells with their fiery trains mounting the air in quick succession. The word, "up up" was then reiterated through the detachment. We . . . moved toward the redoubt we were to attack with unloaded muskets.

In October Cornwallis complained to Clinton that:

> My situation now becomes very critical. We dare not show a gun to their old batteries, and I expect that their new ones will open tomorrow morning. Experience has shown that our fresh earthen works do not resist their powerful artillery, so that we shall soon be exposed to an assault in ruined works, in a bad position, and with weakened numbers. The safety of the place is, therefore, so precarious that I cannot recommend that the fleet and army should run great risk in endeavouring to save us.

Ebenezer Denny wrote on 17 October:

> Before relief came I had the pleasure of seeing a drummer mount the enemy's parapet and beat a parley, and immediately an officer, holding up a white handkerchief, made his appearance outside their works. The drummer accompanied him, beating. Our batteries ceased. An officer from our lines ran and met the other and tied the handkerchief over his eyes. The drummer (was) sent back, and the British officer conducted to a house in rear of our lines. Firing ceased totally.

Letters were passed between Cornwallis and Washington on 17 October:

> SIR,
> I propose a cessation of hostilities for twenty-four hours, and that two officers may be appointed by each side, to meet at Mr Moore's house, to settle terms for the surrender of the posts of York and Gloucester –
>
> I have the honor to be, &c.
>
> CORNWALLIS
>
> MY LORD,
> I have had the honor of receiving your Lordship's letter of this date. An ardent desire to spare the further effusion of blood will readily incline me to listen to such terms for the surrender of your posts of York and Gloucester, as are admissible.
>
> I wish, previously to the meeting of commissioners, that your Lordship's proposals in writing may be sent to the American lines, for which purpose a suspension of hostilities, during two hours from the delivery of this letter, will be granted.
>
> I have the honor to be, &c.
> GEORGE WASHINGTON

St George Tucker recorded the memorable day:

> At dawn of day [the eighteenth] the British gave us a serenade with the bagpipes, I believe, and were answered by the French with the band of the Regiment of Deux-Ponts. As soon as the sun rose, one of the most striking pictures of war was displayed . . .

> From the point of Rock battery on one side our lines completely manned and our works crowded with soldiers were exhibited to view. Opposite these at the distance of 200 yards, you were presented with a sight of the British works, their parapets crowded with officers looking at those who were assembled at the top of our works. The Secretary's [Thomas Nelson's] house with one of the corners broke off and many large holes through the roof and walls, part of which seemed tottering . . . afforded a striking instance of the destruction occasioned by war. Many other houses in the vicinity contributed to accomplish the scene.

On 19 October 1781 the surrender took place. Lord Cornwallis was not well enough to appear at the moment of surrender. Clinton arrived with a rescue fleet five days too late.

"Yorktown" was the second time an entire British army surrendered to the Americans. A year later, a peace treaty had been drawn up and the Americans had won the war.

French Revolutionary and Napoleonic Wars

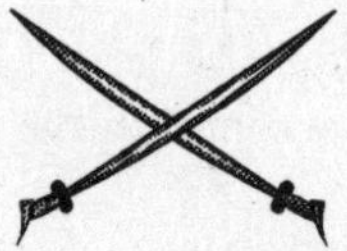

French Revolutionary and Napoleonic Wars – Introduction and Chronology

The French Revolutionary and Napoleonic Wars were a series of conflicts which lasted from 1792–1815. From 1793–1815 there were only two periods when France and Great Britain were at peace with each other. These were the Peace of Amiens (1802–3) and between Napoleon's surrender in 1814 and his return from exile in 1815. From 1792–1802, the wars are known as the French Revolutionary Wars. After the Peace of Amiens (1802–4) the wars are known as the Napoleonic Wars. Apart from this brief period of peace, Great Britain was at the heart of a series of alliances against France. Even without allies, Great Britain opposed France and her allies alone. The alliances against France were known as Coalitions.

A pattern emerged early in the wars: on land the French were victorious but at sea the British were in control. The British quickly enforced a naval blockade of French ports to deprive France of imports of food and raw materials. The British were able to do this because of the superiority of their fleet, the Royal Navy, to that of the French. The French fleet had lost many of its experienced officers in the upheaval of the French Revolution. The British policy of continuous blockade meant that their ships and crews were always at sea. The result was the British gained greater skill and experience at sea at the cost of worn-out ships and men. The demand for seamen strained British relations with other seafaring nations. The United States of America fought a separate war with Great Britain just when the struggle with France was at a critical stage. This separate conflict is known as the War of 1812.

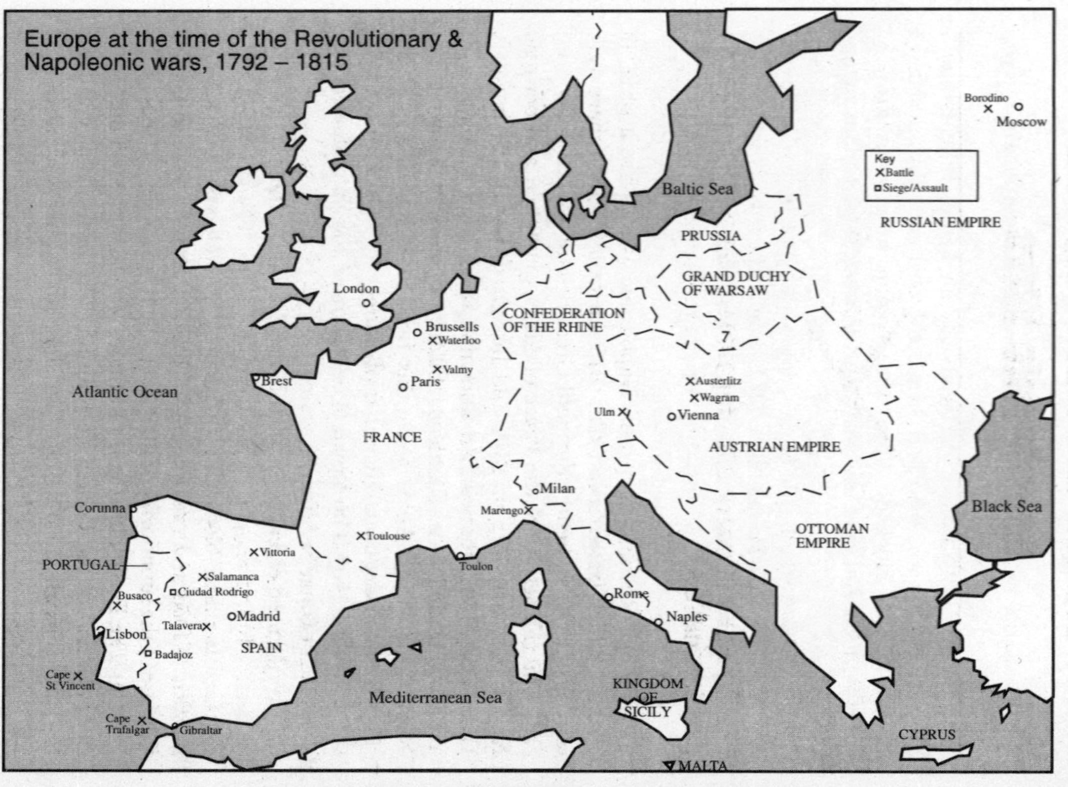

Map of Europe during the French Revolutionary and Napoleonic Wars

The War of the First Coalition

20 April 1792 France declared war on Austria, which allied with Prussia.

At the battle of Valmy, 1792, the French Revolutionary forces repelled the Prussians.

1 February 1793 France declared war on Britain, the United Provinces and Spain, who had joined the coalition. Britain's first concern was to blockade Brest and Toulon to prevent France importing food and raw materials, and to seize West Indian sugar islands.

1 June 1794 At the Battle of the Glorious First of June, the Royal Navy intercepted a French fleet, off Ushant, which was escorting a grain convoy from America; the Royal Navy captured four French battleships and sank another but the grain reached France.

27 July Antwerp fell and the Dutch in the Austrian Netherlands surrendered.

January 1795 France invaded and defeated the United Provinces; they became the Batavian Republic.

16 May Treaty of Basel; Prussia and Spain made peace with France.

19 August 1796 Treaty of San Ildefonso: Spain allied with France; the British Mediterranean fleet abandoned Corsica and withdrew to Gibraltar.

8 October Spain declared war on Britain.

14 February 1797 The Royal Navy defeated the Spanish fleet at the Battle of Cape St Vincent.

18 April Peace of Leoben: Austria and France agreed to a cease-fire.

11 October The Royal Navy defeated the (Dutch) fleet of the Batavian Republic, at the Battle of Camperdown. It was sailing in support of French invasion plans.

17 October Treaty of Campo Formio: the Austrian Netherlands became part of France.

1 July 1798 Forty thousand French troops under Bonaparte landed in Egypt.

1–2 August The Royal Navy, under Nelson, destroyed the French fleet at the Battle of the Nile.

In October Napoleon left his army and returned to France.

The War of the Second Coalition

29 December Russia allied with Britain; joined by Naples, Portugal, the Ottoman Empire, and the Vatican.

22 June 1799 Austria joined the Second Coalition.

27 August to 7 October 1799 Forty-five thousand British and Russian troops failed to take the Netherlands, but the Batavian fleet was captured. Russia left the coalition.

5 September 1800 Britain recaptured Malta which the French had seized in 1798.

16 December 1800 Russia, Prussia, Denmark, and Sweden formed the anti-British League of Armed Neutrality, denying her Baltic naval supplies and grain.

25 December Austria made peace with France again.

9 February 1801 At the Peace of Luneville France's borders were agreed to be the Rhine, Alps, and Pyrenees.

8 March 1801 General Sir Ralph Abercromby landed an army at Aboukir.

31 August The French, left in Egypt, finally surrendered.

2 April, The Royal Navy, under Nelson, destroyed the Danish fleet at the Battle of Copenhagen; Alexander I dissolved the League of Armed Neutrality and made peace.

2 October Cessation of hostilities between Britain and France.

27 March 1802 Peace of Amiens: Britain agreed to return all colonial gains except Ceylon and Trinidad. Britain was to evacuate Malta but kept it.

French Revolutionary War – Introduction

The French had been involved in a series of wars throughout the eighteenth century. By the mid 1780s the French monarchy was in a financial crisis. In an attempt to raise funds it allowed the States General to be revived. This was supposed to be a body of elected representatives who would consent to additional taxes. Their consent would help to raise revenue for the virtually bankrupt Royal administration. The States General proved unco-operative. In 1789 it refused to be dismissed. The Paris crowd rioted and took the Bastille, a royal fortress in the city. Throughout France, popular dissent swept away the existing order of rights and privileges. The

French king, Louis XVI, was forced to accept a constitution. Austria and Prussia which were ruled by monarchs, threatened developments in France. France was governed by the Revolutionary Convention. On 20 April 1792, the Convention declared war on Austria. Allied Austrian and Prussian forces quickly crossed the frontier and began to march on Paris. Their aim was to restore the power of the French monarchy. Against the Austrian and Prussian forces the French relied on their National Guard, a force of armed citizens.

The Battle of Valmy 1792

At the battle of Valmy, in North East France, the Prussian general, the Duke of Brunswick, lost his nerve and withdrew after a long artillery duel.

Goethe, the German poet, witnessed the battle and wrote:

> From today and from this place there begins a new epoch in the history of the world.

Charles François was a volunteer in one of the Paris battalions of the National Guard. He had joined up 16 days before the battle:

> We of the volunteer battalion, although in line with veterans, lost few men. We manoeuvred like our comrades, and did some shooting, which much amused us, and made us wish the enemy would take his revenge. He did not fail to try. About 4 o'clock in the afternoon, having received reinforcements, he came on in the same order as in the morning, but was received with such a hot fusillade that he was obliged to retreat with heavy loss. A battery of 24 guns – eight- and twelve-pounders – at the Valmy mill crushed them and completed the victory. Firing ceased about nine in the evening, when the Prussians were in full retreat, which was difficult for them, for they were shut in to such a degree that some of them had to lay down their arms, and we nearly captured the King. I do not know why we did not profit by our success, pursue them, and capture their train. The enemy was beaten, and surrounded on every side; it was said that we might have made the King of Prussia sign a peace. Instead of pursuing them, we remained on the field of battle, which was covered with dead and

wounded. The battalion to which I belonged had 27 killed and 67 wounded. We of the 5th Paris battalion afterwards returned to the camp at Sainte Menehould; but there were absolutely no provisions for us. I even had to pay five francs in cash for a loaf of bad army bread.

I received a ball just above the right ear, which, however, only just grazed the skin and went clean through my hat. I was very proud of that hat, and kept it for a long time. Thus, after serving only 16 days, we were amongst the victors of Valmy.

French forces advanced on the Austrian Netherlands (Belgium), and seized it after the battle of Jemappes (6 November 1792), while other French forces captured Mainz and advanced on Frankfurt.

Late in 1792 the Convention issued a decree offering assistance to all peoples wishing to recover their liberty. After the Revolutionary Convention executed King Louis XVI, the King of Great Britain, George III, ordered the French Ambassador to leave. On 1 February 1793, France declared war on Britain and Holland, and on 7 March on Spain. The British fleet, the Royal Navy, soon established a blockade of the French Channel ports. The French were defeated at Neerwinden (18 March) by the Austrians, and a revolt broke out in the Vendée; the French forces lost Mainz to the Prussians (23 July). Toulon, the main French naval base in the south of France, surrendered to combined British and Spanish forces.

In response to these threats, the first Committee of Public Safety was created on 6 April, and a levée en masse (a draft of able-bodied men between 18 and 25) was decreed in August. The Committee, inspired by the leadership of Lazare Carnot, raised armies of approximately 750,000 men; revolutionary commissioners were attached to the commands; defeated generals were executed "to encourage" the others.

French forces were sent to recapture Toulon. They included a young artillery officer named Napoleon Bonaparte.

The final conflict took place on the night of 16–17 December; Bonaparte's horse was shot dead under him but the British and Spanish were overwhelmed. The ships weighed anchor under the fire of Bonaparte's guns.

By the end of 1793 foreign forces had been driven from France. A pattern began to emerge with the French victorious by land and the British in control at sea. In 1794 the French, under new commanders, Jourdan and Pichegru, attacked. On 26 June 1794 General

Jourdan defeated the Austrians at Fleurus and moved along the Rhine as far as Mannheim; Pichegru seized the Low Countries. Under French control Holland was transformed into the Batavian Republic and made peace. Prussia made a separate peace (the first Treaty of Basel), ceding the left bank of the Rhine to France. At the second Treaty of Basel, Spain made peace on 22 July 1794.

The Battle of the Glorious First of June 1 June 1794

At sea the British blockade was proving effective. France badly needed imports of food and raw materials. A vital grain convoy was expected from America. The French fleet had to risk battle to ensure its arrival. They were intercepted by the Royal Navy west of Ushant at the end of May, 1794. On 1 June 1794 the British fleet, under Admiral Lord Howe, attacked the French fleet of 26 ships protecting the convoy. The convoy escaped safely to Brest but the British captured six French battleships and sunk a seventh. Lord Howe's flagship was the *Queen Charlotte*. In the *Queen Charlotte* he deliberately broke through the French line to prevent them escaping by turning down wind.

William Parker was 12 years old. He was serving as a midshipman aboard the British battleship *Orion*, 74 (guns). He wrote an account of the battle in a letter to his father:

> Lord Howe always likes to begin in the morning and let us have a whole day at it. The next morning early the signal was made to form the line of battle; we beat to quarters and got up sufficiently of powder and shot to engage the enemy. The enemy also formed their line to leeward. Upon our making observations on the enemy's fleet we found that one of their three-deck ships was missing, but counted 28 sail-of-the-line, which was two more than they had on May 29. We supposed the Isle d'Aix squadron had joined them, and the ship that we had disabled on the 29th had bore up for Brest or sunk, and some thought the *Audacious* must have taken one of them, and took her away from the fleet, as she was missing May 30; but the best joke was that the French Commander-in-Chief had the impudence to say to those ships who joined him that he had thrashed us on the 29th completely, and that he only wanted to have another little dust with us before

he should carry us all into Brest. Our fleet was formed, and we only waited to get near enough to the enemy to begin.

At eight the action began, and the firing from the enemy was very smart before we could engage the ship that came to our turn to engage, as every ship is to have one because our line is formed ahead, and theirs is formed also. Suppose their first or leading ship is a 100 guns and ours a 74, our ship must engage her. I believe we were the ninth or tenth ship; our lot fell to an 80-gun ship, so we would not waste our powder and shot by firing at other ships, though I am sorry to say they fired very smartly at us and unluckily killed two men before we fired a gun, which so exasperated our men that they kept singing out, "For God's sake, brave captain, let us fire! Consider, sir, two poor souls are slaughtered already." But Captain Duckworth would not let them fire till we came abreast of the ship we were to engage, when Captain Duckworth cried out, "Fire, my boys, fire!" upon which our enraged boys gave them such an extraordinary warm reception that I really believe it struck the rascals with the panic. The French ever since the 29th (because we so much damaged one of their ships) called us the little devil and the little black ribband, as we have a black streak painted on our side. They made the signal for three or four of their ships to come down and sink us, and if we struck to them to give us no quarter; but all this did not in the least dishearten our ship's company, and we kept up a very smart fire when some of the enemy's masts and yards went over their side, which we gave credit for some of our doing.

The smoke was so thick that we could not at all times see the ships engaging ahead and astern. Our main-topmast and main-yard being carried away by the enemy's shot, the Frenchmen gave three cheers, upon which our ship's company, to show they did not mind it, returned them the three cheers, and after that gave them a furious broadside. About this time a musket ball came and struck Captain Duckworth between the bottom part of his thumb and finger, but very slightly, so that he only wrapped a handkerchief about it, and it is now almost quite well. But to proceed with my account: at about ten the *Queen* (*Charlotte*) broke their line again, and we gave three cheers at our quarters; and now we engaged whichever ship we could best. A ship of 80 guns, which we had poured three or four broadsides into on May 29, we saw drawing ahead on our lee quarter to fire into us, which ship our ship's company had a great desire to have made strike to us on the

29th, and now quite rejoiced at having an opportunity of engaging her again, gave three cheers at their quarters, and began a very smart firing at their former antagonist.

Their firing was not very smart, though she contrived to send a red-hot shot into the captain's cabin where I am quartered, which kept rolling about and burning everybody, when gallant Mears, our first lieutenant, took it up in his speaking trumpet and threw it overboard. At last being so very close to her we supposed her men had left their quarters as Frenchmen do not like close quarters. She bore down to leeward of the fleet, being very much disabled. The French fleet then ran away like cowardly rascals and we made all the sail we could.

Lord Howe ordered our ships that were not very much disabled to take the prizes in tow, and our own dismasted ships, who were erecting jury masts as fast as possible. But I forgot to tell you that the ship which struck to us was so much disabled that she could not live much longer upon the water, but gave a dreadful reel and lay down on her broadside. We were afraid to send any boats to help them, because they would have sunk her by too many poor souls getting into her at once. You could plainly perceive the poor wretches climbing over to windward and crying most dreadfully. She then righted a little, and then her head went down gradually, and she sunk. She after that rosen a little and then sunk, so that no more was seen of her. Oh, my dear father! when you consider five or six hundred souls destroyed in that shocking manner, it will make your very heart relent. Our own men were a great many of them in tears and groaning, they said God bless them. Oh, that we had come into a thousand engagements sooner than so many poor souls should be at once destroyed in that shocking manner. I really think it would have rent the hardest of hearts.

Most of our brave boys have undone all the good they ever did. They contrived to smuggle a great deal of liquor into the ship and, with the joy of the victory, most of the ship's company got so drunk that they mutinied. They said that they would have liberty to go ashore. They released the English prisoners out of irons. Every officer belonging to the ship was sent for. The Captain almost broke his heart about it. Seven of the ringleaders were seized by the officers and twenty others, when they were put in irons; and the next morning, when they were told of their night's proceedings they all cried like children. They punished the twenty with two dozen lashes each, and the seven were kept in irons to be

> hung, if tried by a Court Martial; but Captain Duckworth came on board today and said that, as he was of a forgiving temper, he gave them into the hands of the ship's company, that he looked up to them with love for the services they had done him . . .

Under the newly established Directory, France attacked in three directions: southeastward from Belgium and Holland under Jourdan; into Southern Germany under Moreau; and into Italy. During 1795 the French defeated the allies on all fronts, but in 1796 the new Austrian commander, Archduke Charles, defeated first Jourdan, then Moreau, both of whom had retreated to the Rhine by September, 1796.

Political developments in France had been affected both by the wars and popular developments in Paris. The period of the Terror coincided with the threat of foreign invasion (1793–4). The political situation stabilised as Revolutionary France's armies pushed back her enemies. As the threat lessened a more moderate form of government, the Directory, took power. There were still opportunities to be taken. One officer who took his opportunities was Napoleon Bonaparte. On 10 May 1795 he was in Paris just as a mob was about to overthrow the government. He surrounded the building in which the government was meeting with cannon. A few shots were enough to prevent a political coup d'etat. Napoleon later referred to this incident as a "whiff of grapeshot". His immediate reward was the command of a French army division. On 3 February 1796 Napoleon was given command of the Army of Italy.

On 3 March 1796 Napoleon joined his army at Nice, but found them undernourished, ill-clothed, and undisciplined. To give them confidence, Napoleon told them:

> You have neither shoes, coats or shirts, almost no bread and your magazines are empty. Those of the enemy are bursting with everything; they are yours if you want them, you can do it, let's go!

On 5 October 1796 Napoleon defeated the Austrian army at Lodi. He personally led French troops across a well-defended bridge spanning the River Adda. Victorious at Rivoli, he captured Mantua. On 17 October 1797, without the authorization of the Directory, Napoleon signed the Treaty of Campo-Formio with Austria.

France created Republics in Switzerland and Italy. A Second

Coalition against France was formed by Russia, Austria, Britain, Turkey, Portugal, and Naples.

In 1797 France was in control of the Dutch and Spanish fleets. The French hoped that a combination of their own fleet and those of the Dutch and Spanish would be able to overwhelm the British fleet in the English Channél. This would allow the French to invade England.

In February 1797 the Spanish fleet was ordered to prepare to join the Dutch and French fleets for the invasion of England. On 14 February a British fleet under Admiral Sir John Jervis intercepted the Spanish fleet off Cape St Vincent.

The Battle of Cape St Vincent 14 February 1797

George Samuel Parsons had entered the Royal Navy as a 12-year-old in July 1795. Parsons was a midshipman aboard *HMS Barfleur*, 98 (guns).

> During the long night of the 13th of February, we heard many heavy guns to wind-ward, and felt perfectly certain that they proceeded from the Spanish fleet, which could not be very remote. The day dawned in the east, and "Up all hammocks, ahoy!" resounded through the decks of His Majesty's Ship *Barfleur*. Some were sent aloft to barricade the tops, while the remainder were stowed with unusual care as a bulwark round the upper decks. Great haze had prevailed during the night, and it still continued. General signal flying on board the *Victory* for the fleet to make all sail on the starboard tack, preserving a close order of sailing in two lines, a vice-admiral leading each line, with Sir John in the *Victory* two points on the weather-bow, our two frigates and *La Bonne Citoyenne* sloop, under a press of sail, to windward. At nine, the latter made the signal for a strange fleet to windward; then, that they were 27 ships of the line and ten frigates, with a cloud of small craft, and that they were the Spanish fleet, under Don Cordova. These intimations of approaching battle were received by the British squadron with reiterated cheers; and so beautifully close was our order of sailing, that the flying jib-boom of the ship astern projected over the taffrail of her leader. Signal was made for the *Culloden* to chase to windward, and after a short

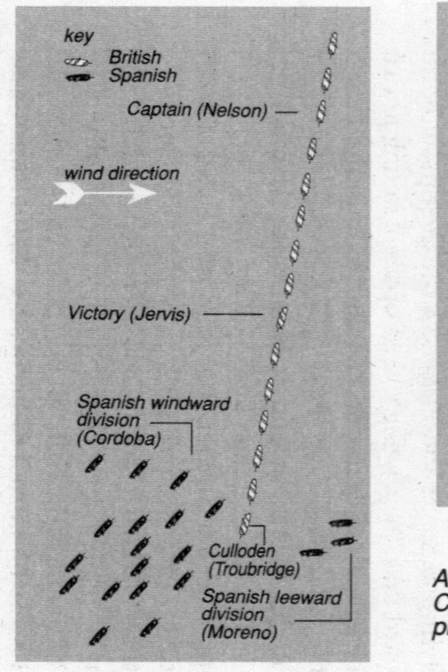

At 11.35 am, The British line attacks the Spanish

At 1.05 pm, Commodore Nelson, in HMS Captain, 74, leaves the British line to prevent the Spanish from escaping

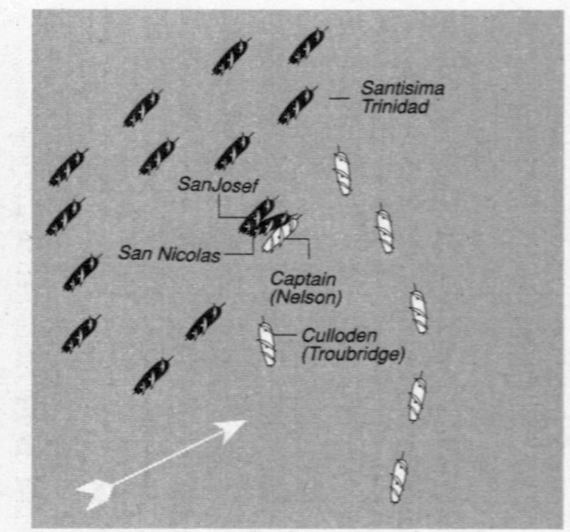

At 1.15 pm, the fastest British ships support Commodore Nelson, in HMS Captain, 74

Battle of Cape St Vincent, 14 February, 1797

Map of the Battle of Cape St Vincent

period, to form the line of battle, without regard to the established order, by which manoeuvre Captain Troubridge led the British line; and one more competent could not have been selected. Here we must admire that wonderful tact, and knowledge of human nature, possessed by Sir John Jervis. Naval etiquette has established the senior captain as better fitted to lead, from his experience, and he is so placed in the established order of battle; but practice has sometimes proved the fallacy of such a theory; and Sir John, without offending, placed at the head of his line, one of the most perfect seamen, though, as his subsequent end proved, too daring, even to rashness. This ill-fated officer took the *Culloden* home from Malta, when she had been declared not seaworthy, and tried the same in the *Blenheim* from India, and has never since been heard of – no doubt he fell a victim to his rash daring. But on the 14th of February, no man could have led the British line better, or better have proved the unrivalled judgment of Sir John Jervis.

"I have a glimpse through the fog of their leeward line," called Signal-Lieutenant Edghill, from the mainyard, "and they loom like Beachy Head in a fog. By my soul, they are thumpers, for I distinctly make out four tier of ports in one of them, bearing an admiral's flag."

"Don Cordova, in the *Santissima Trinidad*," said the vice-admiral; "and I trust in Providence that we shall reduce this mountain into a mole hill before sunset."

The British had formed one of the most beautiful and close lines ever beheld. The fog drew up like a curtain, and disclosed the grandest sight I ever witnessed. The Spanish fleet, close on our weather bow, were making the most awkward attempts to form their line of battle, and they looked a complete forest huddled together; their commander-in-chief, covered with signals, and running free on his leeward line, using his utmost endeavours to get them into order; but they seemed confusion worse confounded. I was certainly very young, but felt so elated as to walk on my toes, by way of appearing taller, as I bore oranges to the admiral and captain, selecting some for myself, which I stored in a snug corner in the stern-galley, as a corps de reserve. The breeze was just sufficient to cause all the sails to sleep, and we were close hauled on the starboard tack, with royals set, heading up for the Spanish fleet. Our supporting ship, in the well-formed line, happened to be the *Captain*, and Captain Dacres hailed to say that he was desired by the vice-admiral to express his pleasure at being supported by Sir Horatio Nelson.

It wanted some time of noon when the *Culloden* opened her fire on the Spanish van, and our gallant fifteen, so close together, soon imitated her example. The roar was like heavy thunder, and the ship reeled and shook as if she was inclined to fall in pieces. I felt a choking sensation from the smell and smoke of gunpowder, and did serious execution on the oranges. This uproar and blinding appeared to me to have lasted a considerable time; but I judged more from my feelings than my watch, when I heard our active signal-lieutenant report the *Culloden*'s signal to tack and break through the enemy's line, and the fleet to follow in succession. Down went the *Culloden*'s helm, and she dashed through, as reported, for my vision was dazzled, between the nineteenth and twentieth ship of the enemy, closely followed by the *Colossus*, whose foreyard was shot away in the slings, as she was in stays.

"The *Captain* has put her helm down," called the signal-luff.

"Only in the wind," said the vice-admiral; "she will box off directly."

The admiral was wrong, and Commodore Sir Horatio Nelson went clean about, and dashed in among the Spanish van, totally unsupported, leaving a break in the British line – conduct totally unprecedented, and only to be justified by the most complete success with which it was crowned. After losing sight for some time of the little *Captain* among the leviathans of Spain, one of them, by some chance, appeared close under our stern; just as I had applied one of my select store of oranges to my mouth, she opened an ill-directed fire, apparently into the admiral's stern-galley, that I was viewing her from. The first bang caused a cessation of my labours, the second made me drop a remarkably fine Maltese orange, which rolled away and was no more seen, and the third made me close my commanders on the quarter-deck, bearing to each an orange. An opening in the Spanish forest now showed the *Captain* on board of two Spanish ships, large enough to hoist her in, and to our astonishment and joy, a tattered Union Jack fluttered above their sweeping ensigns. The commodore had made a bridge of one, to capture the other, and both were prizes to the *Captain*, Sir Horatio Nelson.

At this time, the fleets being much intermingled, Sir John bore up in the *Victory* to rake the *Salvador del Mundo*, who carried a rear-admiral's flag, and had been roughly used by the *Excellent*, which had passed on to assist the *Orion*, engaged by the *Santissima Trinidad*. What a smashing broadside was sent into the unfortunate Spaniard's stern by the *Victory*! and before she could digest such a dose, we delivered another, which caused the Spanish flag to be quickly lowered, leaving our following friend to take possession of her.

When the British squadron passed through the Spanish fleet, they cut out eight ships of the line, who then tacked, and kept hovering to windward of their distressed friends. The rear division now perceived the imminent peril of their commander-in-chief who was dismasted and very hard pressed; indeed, it was roundly asserted that he struck his colours, and re-hoisted them on the rear division bearing down to his succour. The *Conde Reigle*, who led this division, ranging up alongside of His Majesty's Ship *Britannia*, received one of the most destructive broadsides, and hauled her wind in a great hurry, taking no further part in the action.

The time now nearly five p.m., and two first-rates and two second-rates showed the gay Union of England fluttering over the ensign of Spain. Our prizes and disabled ships had fallen to leeward, and as the day was closing, Sir John, who must have been amazed at his own success, made the signal for the fleet to reform the line of battle to leeward, and bore up in the *Victory* to close them, and formed his line just to windward of his prizes, between them and the Spanish fleet, which still remained in the greatest disorder, their commander-in-chief, in the *Santissima*, with only her mainmast and mainyard standing. I believe the slaughter on board her so unprecedented, that Don Cordova, on shifting his flag, stated he had left 400 of his men dead on her decks. The captured ships had suffered much, and certainly took a glutton's share of beating with apathetic composure, their return being very feeble. Had the daring and heroic soul of Nelson been infused into the breast of every British commander on that glorious day, every one of their gorgeous ensigns would have bowed to the Jack of England, and Sir John Jervis would have been created a duke, instead of Earl St Vincent.

The Battle of the Nile 1 August 1798

In December 1797 Napoleon Bonaparte took command of the French army intended for the invasion of England. He found the invasion preparations to be inadequate. The British were experiencing their own problems. There were mutinies by the seamen of two of the Royal Navy's main fleets. The seamen wanted improved pay and better conditions. Despite this, on 11 October, the Royal Navy defeated the Dutch fleet at the Battle of Camperdown. Formally the Dutch fleet was that of the Batavian Republic. It was sailing in support of French invasion plans.

In 1798 France had no enemy on mainland Europe. Her armies were positioned along the English Channel with little hope of crossing it successfully. Napoleon Bonaparte suggested a plan to attack the British by way capturing Egypt and then India. The Directory were convinced and authorised him to proceed.

By 1 July 1798 40,000 French troops under Bonaparte had landed in Egypt. Nelson had been promoted to the rank of Rear-Admiral after the battle of Cape St Vincent. He was given a squadron of 14 battleships to pursue the French and foil their plans. His flagship was *HMS Vanguard*, 74 (guns), commanded by Captain Edward Berry. Nelson guessed the intentions of the French correctly but was unable to find them. On 26 June 1798 Nelson wrote to George Baldwin, the British Consul at Alexandria. He asked him if he had any more information about the French:

> Sir,
> The French having possessed themselves of Malta, on Friday, the 15th of this month, the next day, the whole Fleet, consisting of sixteen Sail of the Line, Frigates, Bomb-vessels, &c. and near 300 Transports, left the Island. I only heard this unpleasant news on the 2nd, off Cape Passaro. As Sicily was not their object, and the wind blew fresh from the westward, from the time they sailed, it was clear that their destination was to the eastward; and I think their object is, to possess themselves of some port in Egypt and to fix themselves at the head of the Red Sea, in order to get a formidable Army into India; and, in concert with Tippoo Saib, to drive us, if possible, from India. But I have reason to believe, from not seeing a Vessel, that they have heard of my coming up the Mediterranean, and are got safe into Corfu. But still I am most exceedingly anxious to know from you if any reports or prepara-

tions have been made in Egypt for them; or any Vessels prepared in the Red Sea, to carry them to India, where, from the prevailing winds at this season, they would soon arrive; or any other information you would be good enough to give me, I shall hold myself much obliged.

I am, Sir, &c.
HORATIO NELSON

On 1 August 1798 Nelson found the French fleet. The French fleet of 13 battleships was at anchor in Aboukir Bay at the mouth of the river Nile. The French had anchored in a defensive line down one side of the bay. The captain of the leading British battleship, *HMS Zealous*, 74, noticed that it would be possible to sail down the landward side of the French line. This side was unprotected. This would allow the British battleships to attack each French battleship from both sides simultaneously. The British arrived at dusk and attacked at 6.20 p.m. The battle continued until the French flagship, *L'Orient*, 120, blew up at 10 p.m. There was a terrible pause in the battle. Samuel Grant, a purser in the British battleship *Goliath*, described the explosion:

It was the most melancholy but at the same time most beautiful sight I ever beheld.

By dawn all the French battleships but two had been captured or destroyed. The British battleships were too battered to prevent their escape. Nelson wrote to Earl St Vincent, the Royal Navy's Commander-in-Chief in the Mediterranean:

My Lord,
Almighty God has blessed his Majesty's Arms in the late Battle, by a great Victory over the Fleet of the Enemy, who I attacked at sunset on the 1st of August, off the Mouth of the Nile. The Enemy were moored in a strong Line of Battle for defending the entrance of the Bay, (of Shoals,) flanked by numerous Gun-boats, four Frigates, and a Battery of Guns and Mortars on an Island in their Van; but nothing could withstand the Squadron your Lordship did me the honour to place under my command. Their high state of discipline is well known to you, and with the judgment of the

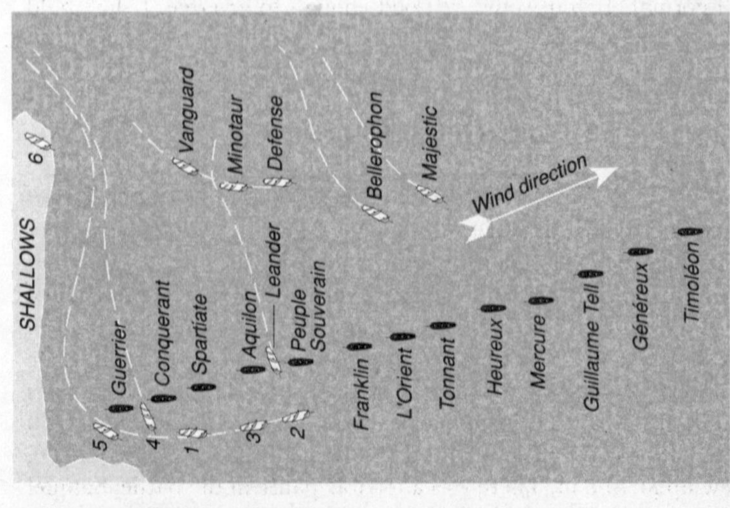

The battle of the Nile 1 August, 1798

Above at 6.20pm:

(1) On her Captain's initiative HMS Goliath sails inside the French line followed by
(2) HMS Zealous
(3) HMS Orion
(4) HMS Audacious
(5) HMS Theseus
(6) is HMS Culloden which ran aground on the shallows at the entrance to the bay

Right: the rest of the British fleet attacks from the seaward side as planned

Map of the Battle of the Nile

Captains, together with their valour, and that of the Officers and Men of every description, it was absolutely irresistible. Could anything from my pen add to the character of the Captains, I would write it with pleasure, but that is impossible.

I have to regret the loss of Captain Westcott of the *Majestic*, who was killed early in the Action; but the Ship was continued to be so well fought by her First Lieutenant, Mr Cuthbert, that I have given him an order to command her till your Lordship's pleasure is known.

The Ships of the Enemy, all but their two rear Ships, are nearly dismasted: and those two, with two Frigates, I am sorry to say, made their escape; nor was it, I assure you, in my power to prevent them. Captain Hood most handsomely endeavoured to do it, but I had no Ship in a condition to support the *Zealous*, and I was obliged to call her in.

The support and assistance I have received from Captain Berry cannot be sufficiently expressed. I was wounded in the head, and obliged to be carried off the deck; but the service suffered no loss by that event; Captain Berry was fully equal to the important service then going on, and to him I must beg leave to refer you for every information relative to this Victory. He will present you with the Flag of the Second in Command, that of the Commander-in-Chief being burnt in *L'Orient*.

L'Orient was the flagship of the French Commander-in-Chief, Admiral Brueys.

The British battleships destroyed or captured 11 of the 13 French battleships; French casualties and prisoners numbered some 6,200. Without a fleet the French army in Egypt was cut off. Their successes on land had no strategic effect.

The Battle of Marengo 14 June 1800

Napoleon Bonaparte left his army and returned to France in October.

France defeated Naples and transformed it into the Parthenopean Republic (January 1799), but in Northern Italy the Austrians and the Russians drove out the French, and in August 1799 General Suvorov crossed the Alps into Switzerland, where Archduke Charles had already won (4–7 June) a victory at Zürich over Masséna. However, disunity between the Austrians and the Russians resulted in disastrous defeats in Switzerland, and Suvorov returned to Russia.

On his return to France Bonaparte was involved in the political coup d'etat of 18 Brumaire (9–10 November 1799). Under the new regime France was to be governed by three Consuls. Bonaparte became First Consul. The coalition against France was weakened by Russia's withdrawal, and Napoleon feverishly prepared a campaign to recoup French losses. Napoleon's second Italian campaign began on 15 May 1800 by crossing the St Bernard Pass. The cannon were enveloped in hollow tree trunks, and dragged across the ice and snow by French soldiers because there were not enough mules for the task and the peasants refused to undertake the arduous work. Napoleon rode a mule at the head of the rearguard, wrapped in a grey great-coat.

Jean-Roch Coignet was conscripted on 23 August 1799. He was put in the Grenadier company of the first battalion of the 96th Demi-Brigade. In his memoirs Coignet described dragging the guns across the Alps:

> The next morning at daybreak, our master placed us twenties at our pieces, ten on each side of a gun. I was put in the first place, to the right, in front; it was the most dangerous side, because it was next to the precipices. Then we started with our three pieces. Two men carried each axle-tree, two carried a wheel, four carried the upper part of the caisson, eight carried the chest, eight others the muskets. Every one had his special duty and position. It was a most terrible journey. From time to time there were commands of "Halt," or "Advance," and not a word was spoken. All this was mere pastime, but when we reached the snow, matters became more serious. The road was covered with ice which cut our shoes, and our gunner could not manage his piece; it slipped constantly. He was obliged to mount it anew. This man needed all his courage to be able to hold out: "Halt!" "Advance!" he cried every moment, and all moved on in silence.
>
> We had gone over a league of this terrible road, and it was necessary to give us a moment to rest and to put on some new shoes, for those we had on were in tatters, and also to take a bite of our biscuits. As I was taking my string from around my neck so as to take one off, the string broke, and all my biscuits went rolling down the precipice. How grieved I was to find myself without

bread, and how my 40 comrades laughed at my misfortune! "Come," said our gunner, "we must make up a feed for our leading horse, he understands the word of command." This made my comrades laugh again. "All right," they answered, "let each of us give a biscuit to our lead horse!" Then I recovered my spirits. I thanked them with all my heart and found myself richer than my comrades. We started off again well shod. "Come, my horses," said our gunner, "fall in, advance! When we reach the snow fields, we shall move more easily and not have so much trouble."

We did reach those terrible fields of perpetual snow, and found less difficulty; our gun-trough slid along more rapidly. General Chambarlhac came up with us and wanted to hasten us; he stood by the gunner and assumed the tone of command, but was ill received. "You don't command my piece," said the gunner. "I alone am responsible for it. Go your own way! These grenadiers do not belong to you for the present; I alone command them." The general went up to the gunner, but the latter commanded him to halt. "If you do not move out of my way I will knock you down with one blow of my crowbar. Move on, or I will throw you over the precipice!"

He was compelled to go away, and after the greatest exertion we reached the foot of the monastery. For 400 feet the ascent is very rapid, and we could see that some troops had gone on ahead of us. The road had been opened and paths cut out leading to the monastery. We left our guns there, and 400 of us grenadiers with a party of our officers entered the house of God, where men devoted to the cause of humanity are stationed to give aid and comfort to travellers. Their dogs are always on hand to guide unfortunate creatures who may have fallen in the avalanches of snow, and conduct them to this house, where every necessary comfort is provided.

While our colonel and other officers were in the halls beside bright fires, we received from these venerable men a bucket of wine for every twelve men, and a quarter of a pound of Gruyère cheese and a loaf of bread for each. We were lodged in the large corridors. The good monks did everything that they possibly could; and I believe they were well treated.

For our part, we pressed the good fathers' hands when we parted from them, and embraced their dogs, which caressed us as if they knew us. I cannot find words to express the veneration I feel for those men.

By 20 May 1800 Bonaparte's army had crossed the Alps and were reassembling. French forces under Lannes faced the army of the Austrian General Ott at Montebello, and after a hard-fought engagement the Austrian force was defeated.

Montebello was Jean-Roch Coignet's first battle:

We again marched down to the Po. The Austrians seized upon the heights before reaching Montebello. Their artillery cut down our troops as they came up. We were obliged send the 24th and 43rd half-brigades forward to take possession of the position. General Lannes finally succeeded driving them back toward Montebello, and pursued them all night. The next morning he gave them another greeting, and our half-brigade occupied the heights which had cost so much to take, for they were twice as strong as we were. Next morning we started out to follow in the wake of that immense advance-guard, and we were stationed about half a league in rear of Montebello, in a broad walk in a beautiful plantation of mulberry-trees. There we were made to stack arms.

We were regaling ourselves upon the ripe fruit with which the trees were loaded, when suddenly at eleven o'clock we heard cannonading. We thought it was very far off. But were mistaken, it was coming nearer to us. An aide-de-camp came up with orders for us to advance as rapidly as possible The general was hard pressed on all sides. "To arms," said our colonel, "fall in, my brave regiment! Our turn has come to distinguish ourselves." And we shouted, "Hurrah for our colonel and all our brave officers!" Our captain, with his 174 grenadiers, said, "I will answer for company. I will march at their head."

We were made to march by platoons, and load our muskets as we were marching, and here I put the first cartridge in my musket. I made the sign of the cross with my cartridge, and it brought me good luck. We reached the entrance of the village of Montebello, where we saw a great many wounded soldiers, and then we heard the drums beating the charge.

I was in the first platoon in the third rank, according to my height. As we were going out of the village, a cannon gave us a volley of grape-shot, which did no one any harm. I ducked my head at the sound of the gun, but my sergeant-major slapped me on the knapsack with his sabre, and said, "No ducking!" – "No, there shan't be!" I answered.

After the first discharge, Captain Merle cried, "To right and left into the trenches," so as to prevent our receiving another volley. As I did not hear the captain's command, I was left entirely exposed. I rushed past our drummers, towards the gun, and fell upon the gunners. They were loading again, and did not see me. I bayoneted all five of them, then leaped upon the piece, and my captain embraced me as he went by. He told me to guard my cannon, which I did, and our battalions dashed upon the enemy. It was a bloody affair of bayonets, with firing by platoons. The men of our brigade fought like lions.

I did not remain long in that position. General Berthier came galloping up, and said to me, "What are you doing there?" – "General, you see what I've done. This gun is mine, I took it all by myself." – "Do you want something to eat? "Yes, General." (He talked through his nose.) Then he turned to his groom, and said, "Give him some bread." And taking out a little green memorandum-book, he asked me my name. "Jean-Roch Coignet." – "Your half-brigade?" "Ninety-sixth." – "Your battalion?" – "The first." "Your company?" – "First." – "Your captain?" – "Merle." "Tell your captain to bring you to see the Consul at ten o'clock. Leave your gun and go and find him."

Then he galloped off, and I, delighted, went as fast as my legs would take me to rejoin my company, which had turned into a road to the right. This road was a sunk road, bordered on each side with hedges and occupied by some Austrian grenadiers. Our grenadiers were fighting them with bayonets. They were in complete disorder. I went up to my captain, and told him that my name had been taken down.

"That is good," said he. "Now, come through this opening, So that we can get ahead of the company; they are marching too fast, they will be cut off. Follow me." We went together through the opening. About a hundred steps off, on the other side of the road, there was a large wild pear-tree, and behind it a Hungarian grenadier, who was waiting till my captain came in front of him to fire upon him. But as he saw him, he cried to me. "Fire, grenadier." As I was behind the Hungarian, I took aim at a distance of only ten paces, and he fell, stone dead. Then my captain embraced me. "Don't leave me today," said he; "you have saved my life." And we hastened on to get ahead of the company which had advanced too rapidly.

A sergeant came out from the road as we had. Three grenadiers surrounded him. I ran to help him. They had hold of him, and called on me to surrender. I pointed my musket at them with my left hand and, using my right as a lever, plunged my bayonet into the belly of first one and then a second of the grenadiers. The third was thrown down by sergeant, who took him by the head, and laid him flat. The captain finished the work. The sergeant recovered his belt and his watch, and in his turn plundered the three Austrians. We left him to look after himself; and put on his clothes, and hastened forward to get in front of the company, which was filing into an open field, where the captain once more took command, and rejoined the battalion, which was advancing at a quick step.

We were encumbered with 300 Prisoners, who had surrendered on the sunk road. We turned them over to some of the hussars de la mort who had escaped, for they had been cut to pieces that morning, and only 200 out of 1,000 were left. We took more prisoners; we did not know what to do with them; no one wanted to take charge of them, and they went along unguarded. They were routed completely. They ceased firing upon us, and ran like rabbits especially the cavalry, which caused a panic throughout the infantry. The Consul came up in time to see the battle won, and General Lannes covered with blood (he looked dreadful) for he had been constantly in the thick of the fight, and it was he who made the last charge. If we had had two regiments of cavalry, all their infantry might have been taken.

That evening, the captain took me by the arm, presented me to the colonel, and told him what I had done during the day. He answered, "Why, captain, I knew nothing about this!" then he shook me by the hand, and said, "I must make a note of it." – "General Berthier wishes to present him to the Consul at ten o'clock this evening," said my captain; "I am to take him." – "Ah! I am glad of it, grenadier."

We went to see General Berthier, and my captain said to him, "Here is my grenadier who captured the gun, and since then he has saved my life and that of my first sergeant. He killed three Hungarian grenadiers." – "I will present him to the Consul." Then General Berthier and my captain went to see the Consul, and after talking a while with him they called me in. The Consul came up to me, and took me by the ear. I thought he was going to scold me, but, on the contrary, he was very kind; and still holding me by the ear, he said, "How long have you been in the service?" – "This is my first battle." – "Ah, indeed! it is a good beginning. Berthier, put him down for a musket of honour. You are too young to be in my Guard; for that, one must have made four campaigns. Berthier, make a note of him at once, and put it on the file. You may go now," said he to me, "but you shall one day be one of my guards."

Then my captain took me away, and we went off arm in arm as if I had been his equal. "Can you write?" said he. – "No, captain." – "Oh, that is a pity; if you did, your fortune would be made. But, never mind, you will be specially remembered." – "Thank you, captain."

The French army continued to advance. They arrived at a village called Marengo:

On the 12th our two half-brigades came up on our right and our division was reunited. We were told that the the village was Marengo. In the morning the breakfast drum beat. What joy! 27 wagons filled with bread had arrived. What happiness for the starving men! Everyone was willing to do extra duty. But what was our disappointment! The bread was all damp and mouldy. We put up with it though.

On the 13th, at break of day, we were made to march forward into an open plain, and at two o'clock we were placed in line of battle and piled arms. Aides-de-camp arrived from our right, who flew around in every direction. A general engagement was beginning; the 24th half-brigade was detached and sent forward unsupported. It marched a long distance, came up with the Austrians, and had a serious encounter, in which it lost heavily. It was obliged to form square in order to resist the attack of the enemy. Bonaparte abandoned it in this terrible position. It was said that he desired to leave it to be destroyed. The reason was this. At time of the battle of Montebello, this half-brigade, having been ordered to advance by General Lannes, began by firing upon its officers. The soldiers spared only one lieutenant. I do not know what could have been the motive for this terrible vengeance. The Consul, informed of what had taken place, concealed his indignation. He could not give way to it when in face of the enemy. The lieutenant who had survived the destruction of his comrades was appointed captain; the staff immediately reformed. But, nevertheless, it was understood that Bonaparte had not forgotten.

About five or six o'clock in the evening we were sent to extricate the 24th. When we arrived, soldiers and officers heaped insults upon us, declaring that we had wantonly left them to destruction, as if it depended upon us to march to their assistance. They had been overwhelmed. I suppose they had lost half their men; but this did not prevent their fighting still better the next day.

The Austrians had occupied the city of Alessandria. All night long we were under arms; the outposts were placed as far forward as possible, and small covering – parties advanced. On the 14th, at three o'clock in the morning, they surprised two of our small posts of four men and killed them. This was the signal for the morning reveille. At four o'clock there was firing on our right. Our drums beat to arm: all along the line, and the aides-de-camp came and ordered us to form our lines of battle. We were made to fall back a little behind a fine field of wheat, which was on a slightly rising ground and concealed us, and there we waited a little while. Suddenly their sharpshooters came out from behind the willows and from the marshes, and then the artillery opened fire. A shell burst in the first company and killed seven men; a bullet killed the orderly near General Chambarlhac, who galloped off at full speed. We saw him no more all day.

A little general came up, who had fine moustaches: he found our colonel, and asked where was our general. We answered, "He is gone." – "Very well, I will take command of the division." And he immediately took charge of the company of grenadiers of whom I was one, and led us to the attack in one rank. We opened fire. "Do not halt while loading," said he. "I will recall you by beat of drum." And he hastened to rejoin his division. He had scarcely returned to his post when the column of Austrians started from behind the willows, deployed in front of us, fired by battalions, and riddled us with small shot. Our little general answered, and there we were between two fires, sacrificed . . . I ran behind a big willow-tree, and fired into that column, but I could not stand it. The balls came from every direction and I was obliged to lie down with my head on the ground in order to shield myself from the small shot, which were making the twigs fall all over me; I was covered with them; I believed myself lost.

Fortunately our whole division now advanced by battalions. I got up and found myself in a musket-company; I continued in it all the rest of the day, for not more than fourteen of our 170 grenadiers remained; the rest were killed or wounded. We were obliged to resume our first position, riddled by small shot. Everything fell upon those who held the left wing of the army, opposite the high road to Alessandria, and we had the most difficult position to maintain. They constantly endeavoured to outflank us, and we were obliged to close up continually, in order to prevent them from surprising us in the rear.

Our colonel ran up and down the line, inspiring us with his presence; our captain, who had lost his company and who was wounded in the arm, performed the duties of orderly officer to our intrepid general. We could not see one another in the smoke. The guns set the wheatfield on fire, and this caused a general commotion in the ranks. Some cartridge-boxes exploded; we were obliged to fall back and form again as quickly as possible. This weakened our position, but the situation was restored by the intrepidity of our chiefs, who looked out for everything.

In the centre of the division was a barn surrounded by high walls, where a regiment of Austrian dragoons had concealed themselves; they burst upon a battalion of the 43rd brigade and surrounded it; every man of it was captured and taken to Alessandria. Fortunately General Kellermann came up with his dragoons and restored order. His charges silenced the Austrian cavalry.

Nevertheless, their numerous artillery overwhelmed us and we could hold out no longer. Our ranks were thinned visibly; all about us there were only wounded men to be seen and the soldiers who bore them away did not return to their ranks; this weakened us very much. We had to yield ground. Their columns were constantly reinforced; no one came to our support. Our musket-barrels were so hot that it was impossible to load for fear of igniting the cartridges. There was nothing for it but to piss into the barrels to cool and then to dry them by pouring in loose powder and set it alight unrammed. Then, as soon as we could fire again, we retired in good order. Our cartridges were giving out and we had already lost an ambulance when the consular guard arrived with 800 men having their linen overalls filled with cartridges; they passed along our rear and gave us the cartridges. This saved our lives.

Then our fire redoubled and the Consul appeared; we felt ourselves strong again. He placed his guard in line in the centre of the army and sent it forward. They immediately held the enemy, forming square and marching in battle order. The splendid horse-grenadiers came up at a gallop, charged the enemy at once and cut their cavalry to pieces. Ah! that gave us a moment to breathe, it gave us confidence for an hour. But not being able to hold out against consular horse-grenadiers, they turned upon our half-brigade and drove in the first platoons; sabring them. I received such a blow from a sabre on my neck that my queue was almost cut off; fortunately I had the thickest one in the regiment. My epaulet was cut off with a piece of my coat and shirt, and the flesh a little scratched. I fell head over heels into a ditch.

The cavalry charges were terrible. Kellermann made three in succession with his dragoons; he led them forward and led them back. The whole of that body of cavalry leaped over me as I lay stunned in the ditch. I got rid of my knapsack, my cartridge-pouch, and my sabre. I took hold of the tail of a retreating dragoon's horse; leaving all my belongings in the ditch I made a few strides behind that horse which carried away and then fell senseless, not being able to breathe any longer. But, thank God, I was saved! But for my head of hair which I still have at 72 years of age, I should been killed.

I had time to find a musket, a cartridge-pouch, and a knapsack (the ground was covered with them). I resumed my place in the second company of grenadiers, who received me with cordiality. The captain came and shook hands with me. "I thought you were lost, my brave fellow," said he; "you got a famous sabre stroke, for you have no queue and your shoulder is badly hurt. You must go to the rear." – "I thank you, I have plenty of cartridges, and I am going to revenge myself upon such troopers as I meet; they have done me too much harm; they shall pay for it."

We retreated in good order, but the battalions were visibly reduced, and quite ready to give up but for the encouragement of their officers. We held out till noon without being disordered. Looking behind, we saw the Consul seated on the bank of the ditch by the highway to Alessandria, holding his horse by the bridle, and flirting up little stones with his riding-whip. The cannon-balls which rolled along the road he did not seem to see. When we came near him he mounted his horse and set off at a gallop behind our ranks. "Courage, soldiers," said he, "the reserves are coming. Stand firm!" Then he was off to the right of the army. The soldiers were shouting, "Vive Bonapartet". But the plain was filled with the dead and wounded, for we had no time to gather them up; we had to face in all directions battalion fire from echelons formed in the rear, arrested the enemy, but those cursed cartridges would no longer go into our fouled and heated musket barrels. We had to piss into them again. This caused us to lose time.

My brave captain, Merle, passed behind the second battalion, and the captain said to him, "I have one of your grenadiers; he has received a famous sabre-cut." – "Where is he? Bring him out, so that I may see him. Ah! it is you, is it, Coignet?" – "Yes, captain." – "I thought you were among the dead, I saw you fall into the ditch." – "They gave me a famous sabre-cut; see, they have cut off my queue." – "Look here, feel in my knapsack, take my 'life-preserver', and drink a cup of rum to restore you. This evening, if we live, I shall come and seek you out." – "Now I am saved for the day, captain; I shall fight finely." The other captain said, "I wanted him to go to the rear, but he would not." – "I can readily believe it; he saved my life at Montebello." They took me by the hand. There's nothing like appreciation! I shall feel the value of it all my life.

Meanwhile, do all we could, we were beginning to fail. It was two o'clock. "The battle is lost," said our officers, when suddenly an aide-de-camp arrived at a sweeping gallop. He cried, "Where is the First Consul? The reserves are up. Courage! you will be reinforced at once, within half an hour." Then up came the Consul. "Steady," said he, as he passed along, "reserves are at hand." Our poor little platoons gazed down the road to Montebello every time we turned around.

Finally came the joyful cry, "Here they are, here they are!" That splendid division came up carrying arms. It was like a forest swayed by the wind. The troops marched at a steady pace, with batteries of guns in the spaces between the half-brigades, and a regiment of heavy cavalry bringing up the rear. Having reached their position, they took possession of it as though they had chosen it expressly for their line of battle. On our left, to the left of the highway, a very tall hedge concealed them; not even the cavalry could be seen.

Meanwhile we continued our withdrawal. The Consul gave his orders, and the Austrians came along as though on their way home, with sloped arms; they paid no attention to us; they believed us to be utterly routed. We had gone hundred paces past the division of General Desaix the Austrians were also about to pass the line, when the thunderbolt descended upon the head of their column grape shot, shells, and musket-fire rained upon them. Our drums beat a general charge; the whole line wheeled about about and ran forward. We did not shout, we yelled.

The men of the brave 96th demi-brigade dashed like rabbits through the hedge; they rushed with their bayonets upon the Hungarian grenadiers, and gave them no time to recover. The 30th and 59th fell in their turn upon the enemy and took 4,000 prisoners. The regiment of heavy cavalry charged in turn. Their whole army was routed. Every man did his duty, but the 9th excelled them all. Our other cavalry came up, and rushed in solid column upon the Austrian cavalry, whom they so completely routed that they rode off at full gallop to Alessandria. An Austrian division coming from the right wing charged us with bayonets. We ran up also and crossed bayonets with them. We overcame them, and I received a small cut in the right eyelid, as I was parrying a thrust from a grenadier. I did not miss him, but the blood blinded my eyes (they had a grudge against my head that day). It was a small matter. I continued to march and did not suffer from it. We followed them until nine o'clock in the evening: we threw them into the ditches full of water. Their bodies served as a bridge upon which others could cross over. It was frightful to see these unfortunate wretches drowning, and the bridge all blocked with them. We could hear nothing but their cries; they were cut off from the city, and we took their wagon-trains and guns. At ten o'clock, my captain sent his servant to ask me to take supper with him, and my eye was dressed and my hair put in good condition.

We slept on the battlefield, and the next day at four o'clock in the morning, a party with flags of truce came out of the city. They demanded an armistice, and went to the headquarters of the Consul. They were well escorted. The camp became gay once more. I said to my captain, "If you please, I would like to go to headquarters." – "What for?" "I have some acquaintances among the guard. Let me have a man to go with me." – "But it's a long way." – "No matter, we will return early, I promise you." – "Very well, go."

We set out, our sabres at our sides.

At Marengo, the Austrians lost approximately 7,000 troops taken prisoner; in addition they lost another 7,000 killed and wounded. French losses were upwards of 7,000 – about a quarter of the troops deployed.

The French had success elsewhere; in Germany, Moreau crossed the Rhine and defeated the allies at Hohenlinden (3 December 1800).

9 February 1801, at the Peace of Lunéville, Austria was forced to make peace with France.

Hostilities between Britain and France ceased on 2 October 1801.

On 27 March 1802 a peace treaty was agreed at Amiens.

Napoleonic Wars 1804–15

The bullet that is to kill me has not yet been moulded.
Napoleon Bonaparte (1769–1821)

Napoleon Bonaparte said this in reply to his brother Joseph, King of Spain, who had asked whether he had ever been hit by a cannonball, in 1814.

Napoleon Bonaparte took advantage of the Peace of Amiens to strengthen his political position by first being made Consul for life in 1802 and finally being crowned Emperor in 1804.

During the Peace of Amiens it became clear to Britain that France under Napoleon was building up her forces to invade England. In April 1803 Britain declared war on France. Spain was forced into an alliance with France. On 12 December 1804 Spain declared war on Britain. Once again France tried to use the combined fleets of France and Spain to gain control of the English Channel while an invasion crossing took place.

The responsibility for preventing the fleets of France and Spain from combining belonged to Admiral Lord Nelson. As a reward for his achievements, Nelson had been made a Viscount. In 1803 he was given command of Royal Naval forces in the Mediterranean. Vice-Admiral Pierre Villeneuve was appointed commander-in-chief of the French and Spanish fleets, once they had combined. Nelson blockaded Villeneuve's French fleet in Toulon for two years. The French fleet escaped in March 1805. Nelson chased them for six months, crossing the Atlantic to the West Indies and back again.

By October Napoleon had cancelled the invasion of England and ordered Villeneuve with the combined French and Spanish fleets to Naples, to support an attack on Austria. He left Cadiz on 19

October. At 6 a.m. on the 21 October Nelson's fleet caught up with the combined French and Spanish fleets off Cape Trafalgar.

The Battle of Trafalgar 21 October 1805

Nelson's tactics were intended to bring his entire fleet into action against the centre and rear of the combined French and Spanish fleets. This would give the advantage to his smaller fleet.

Nelson ordered his fleet to attack in two columns (files) of ships. This was a bold tactic which would expose his ships to the broadsides of the enemy while they were unable to return fire. To avoid wasting time they were to form the columns in the order in which they were sailing when the order was given. In his own words:

> the order of sailing is to be the order of battle.
>
> If the enemy's fleet should be seen to windward in line of battle . . . they will probably be so extended that their van could not succour their rear. I should therefore probably make the second in command's signal to lead through, about their twelfth ship from the rear . . . My line would cut through about their centre . . . The whole impression of the British fleet must be to overpower [from] two or three ships ahead of their commander-in-chief, supposed to be in the centre, to the rear of the fleet. I will suppose twenty sail of the enemy's line to be untouched; it must be some time before they could perform a manoeuvre to bring their force compact to attack any part of the British fleet engaged, or to succour their own ships . . . In case signals can neither be seen nor perfectly understood, no captain can do very wrong if he places his ship alongside that of an enemy.

Nelson described his captains' reaction to his plan:

> When I came to explain to them the Nelson touch, it was like an electric shock. Some shed tears. All approved. It was new. It was magic. It was simple.

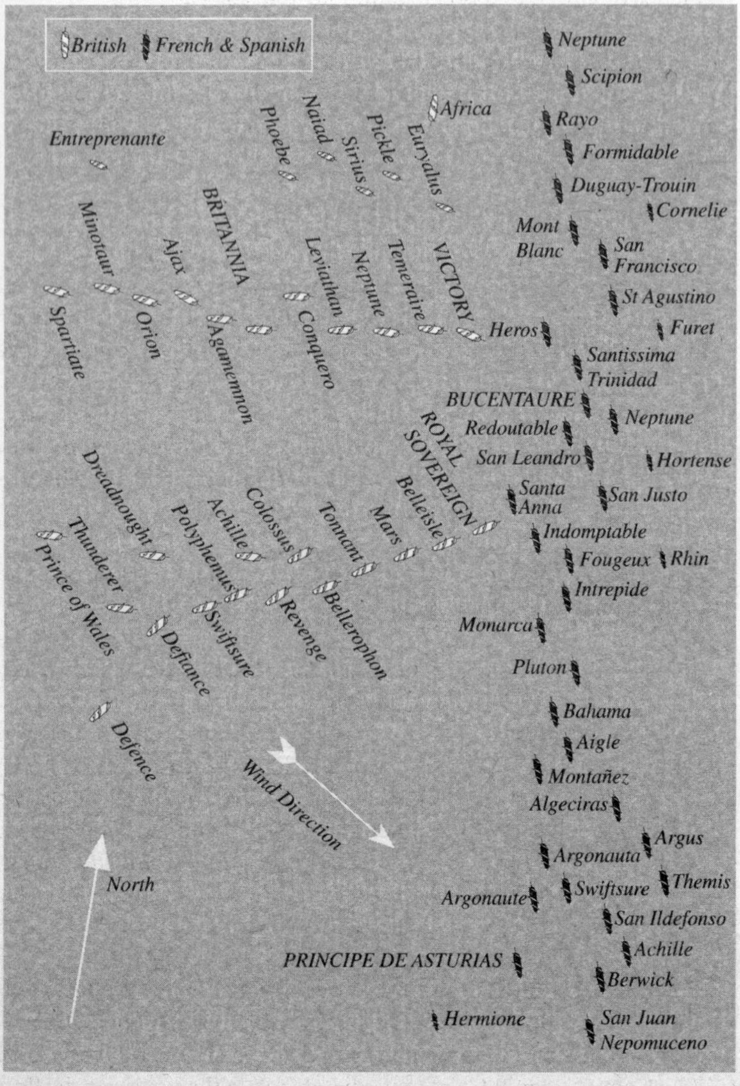

Battle of Trafalgar 21 October, 1805, about 11.30am. The British fleet attacks in two columns. The names of FLAGSHIPS are in CAPITALS

Map of the Battle of Trafalgar

Villeneuve guessed Nelson's plan, and told his captains:

> The British fleet will not be formed in line of battle according to the usage of former days. Nelson . . . will seek to break our line, envelop our rear, and overpower with groups of his ships as many of ours as he can isolate or cut off.

Nelson prayed in his cabin, before the battle:

> May the Great God, whom I worship, grant to my Country, and to the benefit of Europe a great and glorious victory; and may no misconduct in any one tarnish it; and may humanity after Victory be the predominant feature in the British Fleet. For myself, individually, I commit my life to Him who made me, and may his blessing light upon my endeavours for serving my country faithfully. To Him I resign myself and the just cause which is entrusted to me to defend. Amen. Amen. Amen.

Nelson himself went round the *Victory* encouraging the crew. Seaman Brown remembered that he said:

> It will be a glorious day for England whoever lives to see it.

The winds were very light so the approach was very slow. Nelson in his flagship, *HMS Victory*, 100 was leading the weather (upwind) column. His second in command was leading the leeward (downwind) column. His second in command was Admiral Collingwood. Collingwood's flagship, *HMS Royal Sovereign*, 100 was the first British battleship to break through the enemy's line of battle. In his despatch after Trafalgar, Collingwood wrote:

> On Monday the 21st instant, at day-light, when Cape Trafalgar bore E. by S. about seven leagues, the enemy was discovered six or seven miles to the Eastwards, the wind about West, and very light; the Commander in Chief immediately made the signal for the fleet to bear up in two columns, as they are formed in order of sailing; a mode of attack his Lordship had previously directed, to avoid the inconvenience and delay in forming a line of battle in the usual manner. The enemy's line consisted of 33 ships (of which 18 were French and 15 Spanish), Commanded in Chief by Admiral Villeneuve. The Spaniards, under the direction of Gravina, wore

with their heads to the northwards, and formed their line of battle with great coolness and correctness; but as the mode of attack was unusual, so the structure of their line was new. As the mode of our attack had been previously determined on, and communicated to the Flag Officers, and Captains, few signals were necessary, and none were made, except to direct close order as the lines bore down. The Commander in Chief in the *Victory*, led the weather column, and the *Royal Sovereign*, which bore my flag, the lee.

The action began at twelve o'clock, by the leading ships of the column breaking through the enemy's line, the Commander in Chief about the tenth ship from the van, the Second in Command about the twelfth from the rear, leaving the van of the enemy unoccupied; the succeeding ships breaking through, in all parts, astern of their leaders, and engaging the enemy at the muzzles of their guns; the conflict was severe; the enemy's ships were fought with a gallantry highly honourable to their Officers; but the attack on them was irresistible, and it pleased the Almighty Disposer of all events to grant his Majesty's arms a complete and glorious victory.

About three p.m. many of the enemy's ships, having struck their colours, their line gave way; Admiral Gravina, with ten ships joining their frigates to leeward, stood towards Cadiz. The five headmost ships in the van tacked, and standing to the Southward, to windward of the British line, were engaged, and the sternmost of them taken; the others went off, leaving to his Majesty's squadron 19 ships of the line.

After such a Victory, it may appear unnecessary to enter into encomiums on the particular parts taken by the several Commanders; the conclusion says more on the subject than I have the language to express; the spirit which animated all was the same: when all exert themselves zealously in their country's service, all deserve that their high merits should stand recorded; and never was high merit more conspicuous than in the battle I have described.

I am, & c.

(signed) C. Collingwood; HMS *Euryalus*, October 22, 1805

Collingwood's flagship, HMS *Royal Sovereign*, had lost all its masts in the battle so he had moved to a another ship, HMS *Euryalus*.

HMS *Victory* was a three decker. Its cannon were mounted on three decks; these were the upper deck, the middle deck and the lower deck. Royal Marine Roteley was stationed on HMS *Victory's* middle deck. Usually, the guncrews manned the guns on one side only but occasionally the guncrews had to "fight both sides".

> We were engaging on both sides. Every gun was going off. A man should witness a battle from the middle deck of of a three-decker for it beggars all description. It bewilders the sight and hearing. There was the fire from above besides the deck I was upon. The guns recoiling with violence, the reports louder than thunder, the decks heaving and the sides straining. I fancied myself in the infernal regions where every man appeared a devil. The cries of the wounded rang through all parts of the ship. Two of the boys stationed on the quarter-deck were killed. A man who saw one of them killed told me afterwards, his powder caught fire and burnt the flesh almost off his face. The brave Bosun was fastening a stopper to a backstay when a ball took his head off. Our men kept cheering with all their might. I confess, I cheered too, though I scarcely knew for what.

William Beatty, the surgeon of Nelson's flagship, described the battle and Nelson's death:

> The enemy began to fire on the *Royal Sovereign* at thirty minutes past eleven o'clock; in ten minutes after which, she got under the stern of the *St Anna*, and commenced a fire on her. Lieutenant Pasco, signal officer of the *Victory*, was heard to say while looking through his glass, "There is a topgallant yard gone." Lordship eagerly asked, "Whose topgallant yard is gone? Is it the *Royal Sovereign's*?" and on being answered by Lieutenant Pasco in the negative, and that it was the enemy's, he smiled, and said: "Collingwood is doing well."
>
> At fifty minutes past eleven, the enemy opened their fire on the commander in chief. They shewed great coolness in the commencement of the battle; for as the *Victory* approached their line, their ships lying immediately ahead of her and across her bows fired only one gun at a time, to ascertain whether she was yet within their range. This was frequently repeated by eight or nine of their ships, till at length a shot passed through the *Victory*'s main topgallant sail; the hole in which being discovered by the enemy, they immediately opened their broadsides, supporting an awful and tremendous fire.

In a very short time afterwards, Mr Scott, public secretary to the commander in chief, was killed by a cannon shot while in conversation with Captain Hardy. Lord Nelson being then near them; Captain Adair of the marines, with the assistance of a seaman, endeavoured to remove the body from his Lordship's sight: but he had already observed the fall of his secretary; and now said with anxiety, "Is that poor Scott that is gone?" and on being answered in the affirmative by Captain Adair, he replied, "Poor fellow!"

Lord Nelson and Captain Hardy walked the quarterdeck in conversation for some time after this, while the enemy kept up an incessant raking fire.

A double-headed shot struck one of the parties of marines drawn up on the poop, and killed eight of them; when his Lordship, perceiving this, ordered Captain Adair to disperse his men round the ship that they might not suffer so much from being together.

In a few minutes afterwards a shot struck the forebrace bits on the quarter deck, and passed between Lord Nelson and Captain Hardy; a splinter from the bits bruising Captain Hardy's foot, and tearing the buckle from his shoe. They both instantly stopped; and were observed by the officers on deck to survey each other with inquiring looks, each supposing the other to be wounded. His Lordship then smiled, and said: "This is too warm work, Hardy, to last long"; and declared that "through all the battles he had been in, he had never witnessed more cool courage than was displayed by the *Victory*'s crew on this occasion."

The *Victory* by this time, having approached close to the enemy's van, had suffered very severely without firing a single gun: she had lost about 20 men killed, and had about 30 wounded. Her mizzen topmast, and all her studding sails and their booms on both sides were shot away; the enemy's fire being chiefly directed at her rigging, with a view to disable her before she could close with them.

At four minutes past twelve o'clock, she opened her fire, from both sides of her decks, upon the enemy; when Captain Hardy represented to his Lordship, that "it appeared impracticable to pass through the enemy's line without going on board some one of their ships."

Lord Nelson answered, "I cannot help it: it does not signify which we run on board of; go on board which you please; take your choice."

At twenty minutes past twelve, the tiller ropes being shot away: Mr Atkinson, the master, was ordered below to get the helm put to port; which being done, the *Victory* was soon run on board the *Redoubtable* of 74 guns.

On coming alongside and nearly on board of her, that ship fired her broadside into the *Victory*, and immediately let down her lower deck ports; which, as has been since learnt, was done to prevent her from being boarded through them by the *Victory*'s crew.

She never fired a great gun after this single broadside.

A few minutes after this, the *Temeraire* fell likewise on board of the *Redoubtable*, on the side opposite to the *Victory*; having also an enemy's ship, said to be *La Fougueux*, on board of her on her other side: so that the extraordinary and unprecedented circumstance occurred here, of four ships of the line being on board of each other in the heat of battle; forming as compact a tier as if they had been moored together, their heads lying all the same way. The *Temeraire*, as was just before mentioned, was between the *Redoubtable* and *La Fougueux*.

The *Redoubtable* commenced a heavy fire of musketry from the tops, which was continued for a considerable time with destructive effect to the *Victory's* crew. Her great guns however being silent, it was supposed at different times that she had surrendered; and in consequence of this opinion, the *Victory* twice ceased firing upon her by orders transmitted from the quarter deck.

At this period, scarcely a person in the *Victory* escaped unhurt who was exposed to the enemy's musketry; but there were frequent huzzas and cheers from between the decks, in token of the surrender of different of the enemy's ships. An incessant fire was kept up from both sides of the *Victory*: her larboard guns played upon the *Santissima Trinidad* and the *Bucentaure*; and the starboard guns of the middle and lower decks were depressed, and fired with a diminished charge of powder, and three shot each, into the *Redoubtable*. This mode of firing was adopted by Lieutenants Williams, King, Yule, and Brown, to obviate the danger of the *Temeraire's* suffering from the *Victory's* shot passing through the *Redoubtable*; which must have been the case if the usual quantity of powder, and the common elevation, had been given to the guns.

A circumstance occurred in this situation which showed in a most striking manner the cool intrepidity of the officers and men stationed on the lower deck of the *Victory*. When the guns on this deck were run out, their muzzles came into contact with the *Redoubtable's* side; and consequently at every discharge there was reason to fear that the enemy would take fire, and both the *Victory* and the *Temeraire* be involved in her flames. Here then was seen the astonishing spectacle of the fireman of each gun standing ready with a bucket full of water, which as soon as his gun was discharged he dashed into the enemy through the holes made in her side by the shot.

It was from this ship (the *Redoubtable*) that Lord Nelson received his mortal wound. About fifteen minutes past one o'clock, which was in the heat of the engagement, he was walking the middle of the quarter deck with Captain Hardy, and in the act of turning near the hatchway with his face towards the stern of the *Victory*, when the fatal ball was fired from the enemy's mizzen top; which, from the situation of the two ships (lying on board of each other), was brought just abaft, and rather below, the *Victory*'s main yard, and of course not more than fifteen yards distant from that part of the deck where his Lordship stood. The ball struck the epaulette on his left shoulder, and penetrated his chest. He fell with his face on the deck. Captain Hardy, who was on his right (the side furthest from the enemy) and (had) advanced some steps before his Lordship, on turning round, saw the serjeant.major (Secker) of Marines with two seamen raising him from the deck; where he had fallen on the same spot on which, a little before, his secretary had breathed his last, with whose blood his Lordship's clothes were much soiled.

Captain Hardy expressed a hope that he was not severely wounded; to which the gallant chief replied:

"They have done for me at last, Hardy."

"I hope not," answered Captain Hardy.

"Yes," replied his Lordship; "my backbone is shot through."

Captain Hardy ordered the seamen to carry the admiral to the cockpit; and now two incidents occurred strikingly characteristic of this great man, and strongly marking that energy and reflection which in his heroic mind rose superior even to the immediate consideration of his present awful condition. While the men were carrying him down the ladder from the middle deck, his Lordship observed that the tiller ropes were not yet replaced; and desired one of the midshipmen stationed there to go upon the quarterdeck and remind Captain Hardy of that circumstance and request that new ones should be immediately rove. Having delivered this order, he took his handkerchief from his pocket and covered his face with it, that he might be conveyed to the cockpit at this crisis unnoticed by the crew.

Several wounded officers, and about 40 men, were likewise carried to the surgeon for assistance just at this time; and some others had breathed their last during their conveyance below. Among the latter were Lieutenant William Andrew Ram, and Mr Whipple, captain's clerk. The surgeon had just examined these two officers, and found that they were dead; when his attention was arrested by several of the wounded calling to him, "Mr Beatty, Lord Nelson is here: Mr Beatty, the admiral is wounded."

The surgeon now, on looking round, saw the handkerchief fall from his Lordship's face; when the stars on his coat, which also had been covered by it, appeared. Mr Burke the purser, and the surgeon, ran immediately to the assistance of his Lordship; and took him from the arms of the seamen who had carried him below. In conveying him to one of the midshipmen's berths, they stumbled; but recovered themselves without falling. Lord Nelson then inquired who were supporting him; and when the surgeon informed him, his Lordship replied, "Ah, Mr Beatty! You can do nothing for me. I have but a short time to live: my back is shot through."

The surgeon said, "he hoped the wound was not so dangerous as his Lordship imagined, and that he might still survive long to enjoy his glorious victory."

The Rev. Dr Scott, who had been absent in another part of the cockpit administering lemonade to the wounded, now came instantly to his Lordship; and in the anguish of grief wrung his hands, and said: "Alas, Beatty, how prophetic you were!" alluding to the apprehensions expressed by the surgeon for his Lordship's safety previous to the battle.

23 French and Spanish battleships were destroyed or captured. 4,500 French and Spanish sailors were killed or wounded and 20,000 taken prisoner. Only 449 British sailors were killed or wounded. But despite the success few in the British fleet were celebrating because, at 4.30 p.m., Nelson had died.

Russia and Austria had joined the British in a new coalition after Napoleon abandoned his plans to invade England and turned his armies against the Austro-Russian forces. Napoleon's military genius lay in maneouvre and rapid marches. Since becoming First Consul he had been Commander-in-Chief of France's military forces. He was at the head of a nation in arms. He called his new military force the Grand Armée. He knew that the Austrians and Russians were advancing against him. He was anxious to defeat the Austrians before the Russians could arrive to reinforce them. There was also the threat that a Prussian army of 200,000 men would join forces against the French. He marched his Grand Armée from its camps on the French coast into Germany before the Austrians realised he was on the move. Napoleon's Grand Armée was the best trained and equipped force he ever had. It had spent the years from 1803–5 in camp, training and building up its resources. As a result it blended enthusiasm, youth and experience in its ranks.

Jean Baptiste Barres was a soldier in the French Imperial Guard. In his memoirs he wrote:

> We left Paris quite content to go campaigning rather than march to Boulogne. I was especially so, for war was the one thing I wanted. I was young, full of health and courage, and I thought one could wish for nothing better than to fight against all possible odds; moreover, I was broken to marching; everything conspired to make me regard a campaign as a pleasant excursion, on which, even if one lost one's head, arms, or legs, one should at least find some diversion. I wanted, too, to see the country, the siege of a fortress, a battlefield. I reasoned, in those days, like a child. And at the moment of writing this, the boredom which is consuming me in cantonments (at Schonbrunn) and four months of marching about, months of fatigue and wretchedness, have proved to me that nothing is more hideous, more miserable, than war. And yet our sufferings in the Guard are not to be compared with those of the line.

Barres fell ill on the march. He lost his appetite and became feverish. He refused to go into hospital, or even ride in the carts accompanying the column. Despite this, he reached Strasbourg "still intoxicated with glory". He noted:

> Several of my colleagues, not more unwell than I was, stayed behind in the hospitals and there found their deaths . . . Woe to those who go into hospital on campaign! They are isolated and forgotten, and tedium slays them rather than their sickness.

At Strasbourg the troops were issued with fifty cartridges each, four days' supplies and their campaigning equipment. As they crossed the Rhine Barres had:

> a secret feeling of contentment when I recalled to memory all the noble feats of arms which its banks had seen. Then warlike reminiscences made me long for a few glorious encounters in which I might satisfy my eager impatience.

But he remembered that, one night, after a long march:

> I was so weary that I could neither eat nor sleep. I began to regret Paris.

A few days later he briefly fell out on the march and could not find his unit for several days; when he finally rejoined his regiment he received a warm welcome:

> Ah, it is a nasty thing to be lost in the midst of an army on the march!

Barres saw a farm thoroughly plundered and half demolished for firewood to keep the troops warm. He was shocked at his first sight of the destructiveness of war:

> I shed tears over the fate of these poor villagers, who had in a moment lost all their possessions. But what I saw later caused me to regard them as still happy in their misfortune. As I was a novice in the military art, all that was contrary to the principles in which I had been trained surprised me; but I had time, afterwards, to become accustomed to such things.

The Grand Armée was 210,000 strong. It surprised an Austrian army of 60,000 men at Ulm. The Austrians, under General Mack, surrendered. On 15 November it marched into the Austrian capital Vienna. Barres had not taken part in the fighting before the Austrian surrender at Ulm although:

> I should have been glad if we had fought, in order to prove that even if one were new to such work one had as much love of glory as the veterans.

Instead there were more marches as the French army marched on up the valley of the Danube, Barres had to camp in the open in bad weather:

> I did not find it very fascinating; it is a dismal way of going to bed . . . no straw on which to lie, little wood for burning, and a north wind that was like a wind of Lapland. I passed a wretched night; roasted on one side, frozen on the other. That was all the rest I got.

One Austrian army had been defeated but the Russian army was still coming up to support the remaining Austrian forces. The Russian army retreated and:

> drew us perforce into the most frightful country, and this, above all, at a time of the year unsuitable for marching. I confess frankly that this departure displeased me sorely.

The Battle of Austerlitz 2 December 1805

Napoleon was a master of exploiting terrain. He pursued the retreating Austrian army north of Vienna into an area of hills, rivers and shallow lakes near the town of Austerlitz. The Austrian army was joined by a Russian army under Kutusov. Napoleon had only 50,000 soldiers with him. He had himself examined the ground on which he intended to lure the Austrian and Russian forces into a trap. On 1 December he held the high ground of the Pratzen Heights. He then pulled his forces back into the valley below. He deliberately let his enemy see that his numbers were half theirs. The misty conditions helped him to allow the Austrian and Russian commanders to see what he wanted them to see but not what he wanted to conceal. French reinforcements of 25,000 men had just arrived from Vienna under the cover of the mist. Napoleon wanted to lure the Austrian and Russian commanders into attacking his right wing. His right wing lay on broken ground by the Golden Creek at the foot of the Pratzen Heights. Once they were involved with his right he expected them to weaken their centre to reinforce their attack on his right.

Battle of Austerlitz, 2 December 1805

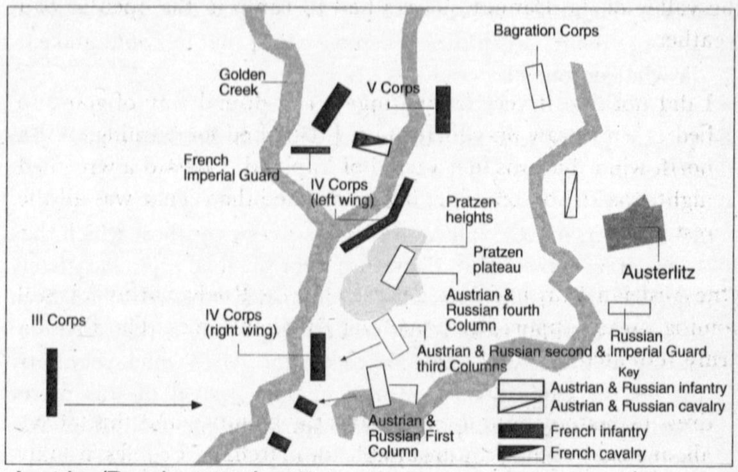

Austrian/Russian attack at 7am

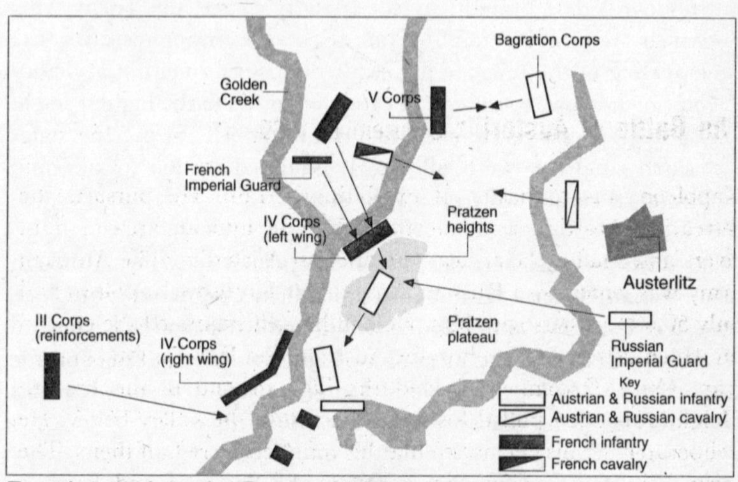

French attack on the Pratzen Heights at 7.45am
Final attack by Russian Imperial Guard also shown

Map of the Battle of Austerlitz 1805

The night before the battle Napoleon himself went round his camp to encourage his men. They were tired by their exertions but the Emperor's presence inspired them. In the words of Charles François, a French soldier since 1792:

The emperor knew of our wants and our fatigues, which he shared. He said that "it is to spare their blood that I make them undergo these hardships." When we heard that he could make us do what no one else could.

Baron Le Jeune was an officer on Marshal Berthier's staff. He described his bivouac that night:

The soldiers merrily talked over past successes or those which they counted on achieving in the future. Our bivouac was a very lively one, for one of our comrades, M. Longchamps, who had been detained in France, had only been able to join us that day, and during his journey he had composed some verses which very aptly hit off the rapidity of our march. The arrival of this merry companion, who brought letters from home for each of us, was the most charming episode of the day.

The letters from our families, the portraits, and in some cases the love letters brought by the friendly singer, the Tokay wine which we drank straight from the casks through straws, the crackling of the bivouac fire, with the presentiment of a victory on the morrow, combined to raise our spirits to the highest pitch. By degrees, however, one after the other fell asleep, the songs ceased, and we were all closely-wrapped in our cloaks and stretched comfortably on a little straw.

The allied generals were deceived by Napoleon's scheme. Although the Russian General Kutusov was the allied Commander-in-Chief, the Austrian staff planned the Austrians and Russian attack. General Langeron described the meeting at Kutusov's headquarters on the night before the battle. General Langeron was a French Royalist exile serving as an officer in the Russian army:

General Weyrother came in. He had an immense map, showing the neighbourhood of Brijnn and Austerlitz in the greatest precision and detail. He spread it on the large table, and read his dispositions to us in a loud voice, and with a boastful manner which betrayed smug self-satisfaction. He might have been a form-master reading a lesson to his pupils, though he was far from being a good teacher. We had found Kutusov half asleep in a chair when we arrived at his house, and by the time we came to leave he had dozed off completely. Buxhowden was standing. He listened to what was being said, though it must have gone in one ear and out the other. Miloradovich spoke not a word. Prebyshevsky kept in the background, and only Dokhturov examined the map with any attention.

The Austrian and Russian commanders did exactly what Napoleon wanted them to do. On 2 December 1805, the Austrian and Russians attacked in four columns. At dawn the leading troops of the first allied column attacked the right of the French IV Corps which was in at the foot of the Pratzen Heights. It was followed by the second and third allied columns. The fourth Austrian and Russian column advanced towards the Pratzen Heights.

The right of the French IV Corps began to fall back without breaking. By 10 a.m., the allies had nearly broken through the French lines. The French reinforcements (their III Corps) arrived just in time to salvage the situation. As Napoleon had expected, the fourth Austrian and Russians column had to send troops down to reinforce the attack on the French right.

At about 7.45 a.m., just after the allied reinforcements started in motion down the slopes of the plateau, the left of the French IV Corps surged through the morning's thick fog and attacked the right flank of the fourth Austrian and Russian column on the Pratzen Heights.

Major-General Stutterheim described two Russian attacks in the struggle for the Pratzen Heights:

> The action then became very warm, and it was attempted to regain the ground that had been lost by the advanced guard. The Russians made an attack; opened their fire at too great a distance, and without much effect, while the French columns continued to advance without firing a shot; but when at a distance of about a hundred paces, they opened a fire of musketry which became general, and very destructive.
>
> There was no other chance of turning the fate of the day but a general and desperate attack at the point of the bayonet. The Austrian Brigades, with that of General Kamensky, charged the enemy; the Russians shouting, according to their usual custom; but the French received them with steadiness, and a well-supported fire, which made a dreadful carnage in the compact ranks of the Russians. General Miloradovich, on his side, advanced upon the right; but the Generals Berg and Repninsky being

> wounded, their troops had lost that confidence in themselves, without which nothing is to be done in war. The ardour of this attack soon evaporated. The superior numbers of the enemy, and his steadiness, soon changed it to a slow uncertain pace, accompanied by an ill-directed fire of musketry.

Napoleon's troops succeeded in advancing to the top of the Pratzen Heights.

The Austrians and Russians still had troops on the Pratzen Heights; unfortunately they were already marching down into the valley. Some of their troops attacking in the valley had to be sent back to defend the the Pratzen Heights.

In the fighting in the valley a French artillery battery was overrun by allied cavalry. Its officer described the struggle:

> The soldiers threw themselves beneath the ammunition carts and the pieces, while the gunners defended themselves with their rammers. For a time the infantry was unable to shoot, because the mass of Kellermann's cavalry stood in the way, but once the field was clear they opened a rolling fire at 30 paces. At that moment I was at bay among my draught-horses, fighting hand to hand with a Russian officer. He had severed the little finger of my right hand with a blow of his sword, but all at once his horse collapsed, struck by a musket ball. The officer cast himself at my stirrups and cried out, "We are heroes after all, aren't we?" He repeated these words several times and kept by my side, regarding himself as my prisoner.

Both sides brought up reinforcements. The Austrian and Russian troops assaulting the French right were being attacked on both flanks. In one last bold but fruitless attempt at relief, the Russian Imperial Guard charged up the plateau but was turned back. Avoiding total ruin, the Austrian and Russian troops retreated in all directions.

The allied reinforcements were defeated after a bitter fight. Now, the French assault on the flank received fresh reserves of its own, as the I Corps joined the divisions of the IV Corps. Napoleon now established his command post on the peak of Pratzen Plateau to observe the destruction of the Austrian and Russian armies.

Napoleon himself said to a captured Russian artillery officer:

There is no disgrace in being beaten by the French.

A French soldier, Thiebault, described the rout:

> Until the last hour we did not take prisoners. Our orders were to stick at nothing, not to take any risks. Not a single enemy remained to our rear.

The French lost 9,000 casualties. The Austrian and Russian armies lost 13,000 casualties and 12,000 prisoners. On 4 December Austria surrendered; the Russian army retreated back to Russia.

In 1806 Napoleon seized the kingdom of Naples and made his elder brother Joseph king; converted the Dutch Republic into the kingdom of Holland for his brother Louis, and established the Confederation of the Rhine (most of the German states) of which he was protector. Prussia then allied itself with Russia and attacked the confederation. Napoleon destroyed the Prussian army at Jena and Auerstädt (1806) and the Russian army at Friedland. At the Treaty of Tilsit (July 1807), Napoleon made an ally of Tsar Alexander I and greatly reduced the size of Prussia. He also added new states to the empire: the kingdom of Westphalia, under his brother Jerome, the duchy of Warsaw, and others.

On 27 October 1807, in the Treaty of Fontainebleu, France and Spanish made an alliance against Portugal. Under the terms of the Treaty, the Spanish allowed a French army to march through Spain to conquer Portugal.

By December 1807 a French army had conquered Portugal. On 19 March 1808 it forced the Spanish king, Charles IV, to abdicate in favour of his son, Ferdinand VII. On 6 May, Ferdinand VII was imprisoned by the French and abdicated; he was replaced by Napoleon's brother Joseph. On 2 May there was a riot in Madrid. This was brutally suppressed by the French. Popular uprisings against the French began. This was the beginning of the Peninsular War.

Napoleon's Russian Campaign 1812

Great Britain's naval blockade extended to the ports of every country involved in the war with France. It was effective economic warfare. In retaliation, Napoleon imposed a "Continental System". This was

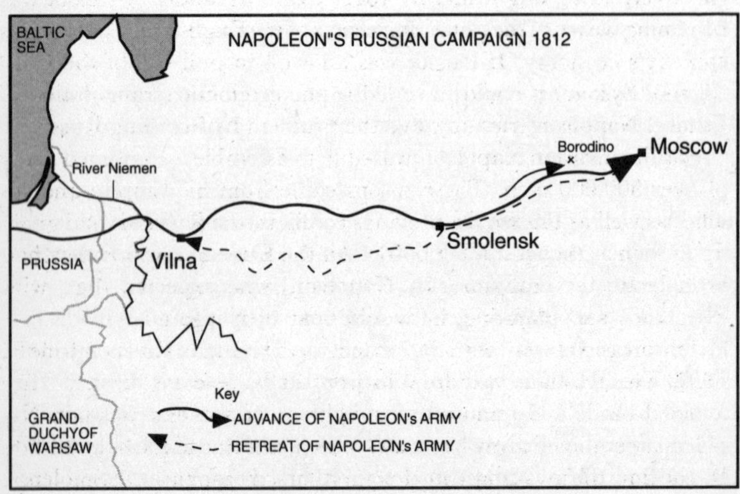

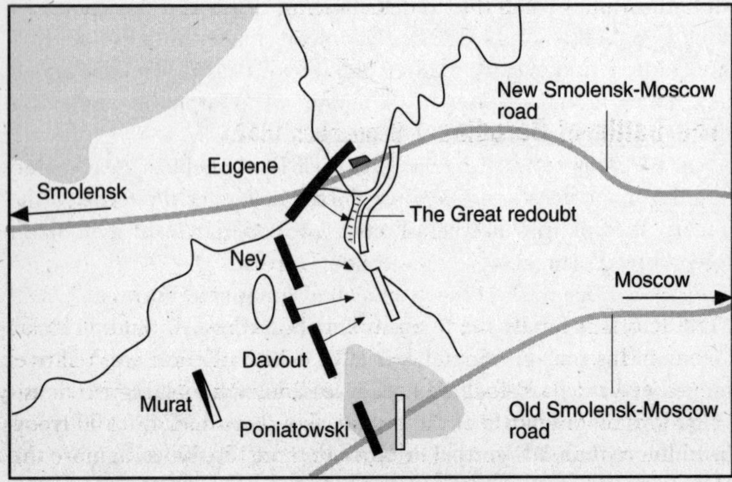

Battle of Borodino, 7 September 1812 key

Maps of Napoleon's Russian Campaign 1812 and the Battle of Borodino

a ban on all trade with Great Britain and her allies. The war was effectively strangling trade. By 1812, Czar Alexander of Russia was becoming weary of the punishing effects of the English blockade on his country's economy. If Russia was allowed to pull out of the Continental System, it could have led to the economic strangulation of France. Napoleon tried to solve the problem by invading Russia.

For the invasion Napoleon was able to assemble a combined army of over 500,000 men. These troops came from his Empire and his allies as well as France. In previous conflicts, the Russians had given up as soon as they lost a big battle. All the Russian commanders had been beaten several times by Napoleon, who expected that, with extra men and planning, he would beat them again.

The invasion began with the crossing of the Niemen River on June 24 1812. The Russians withdrew in front of Napoleon's armies. They avoided battle and removed all supplies. The weather was hot. Napoleon's combined army lost many of its horses due to the hot weather. By the time the invading army fought its first major battle at Smolensk, it had shrunk by half due to detachments, death and desertion.

The Battle of Borodino 7 September 1812

A hellish day
Nadezhda Durova

The Russians finally made a stand at Borodino, 70 miles (110 km) west of Moscow, on 7 September 1812. The battlefield was relatively small. It was a hard-fought battle of attrition with the highest density of troops of any battle of the period. Napoleon had 130,000 troops, with more than 500 guns, The Russians had 120,000 with more than 600 guns. There was almost no attempt to manoeuvre for position. The French made frontal attacks against the Russian defences. The Russians stood their ground. There was a very high proportion of artillery on both sides. The Russians concentrated some of theirs in a central redoubt which the French attacked.

Baron Lejeune described one of the unsuccessful French attacks:

> All this time the formidable artillery of the redoubts in the centre of the enemy's line was working such fearful havoc in our ranks,

that it became of the utmost importance to take the largest of these redoubts and spike its guns. The sappers of the engineers, therefore, beneath a hail of grapeshot, flung several little trestle bridges across the Kaluga stream protecting the base of the ridge, and the Morand division crossed the ravine with their aid and managed to get at the enemy. The first brigade of this division, led by General Bonamy, scaled the height and the entrenchments, deployed successfully in the redoubt, and killed the artillerymen at their guns. But the Russians came to the rescue in great force, and General Bonamy, after receiving seventeen bayonet wounds, fell disabled, and as he was taken prisoner he had the grief of seeing all his men either killed or driven back. The remainder of the Morand division was only able to protect the retreat of the few who escaped in disorder.

The smoke and the noise of the battle of Borodino was remarkable. Nadezhda Durova, a woman disguised as a man, described the the battle of Borodino as:

A hellish day! I have gone almost deaf from the savage, unceasing roar of both artilleries. Nobody paid any attention to the bullets which were whistling, whining, hissing and showering down on us like hail. Even those wounded by them did not hear them; we had other worries!

Lieutenant Roth von Schreckenstein was in the Saxon Zastrow Cuirassiers in Napoleon's army. His horse was killed in the battle:

I looked about for another horse, but those nearest to me had been wounded. One Russian horse which I did mount refused to move, even when I clapped spurs to it, so I was on the point of moving off on foot, pistol in hand, without really knowing which way to flee, because, owing either to an illusion stemming from fear or else because they were really there, I could see enemies on all sides. The thought of being captured and ill-treated overwhelmed me, and I gripped my pistol in much the same way as a person who is drowning clutches at the nearest straw. At very best this weapon would enable me to sell my liberty or my life more dearly. By some fortunate chance a riderless horse came past with a troop of Life Guards, so close that I was able to grab hold of it and escape with a swarm of horsemen who were withdrawing. Skill at vaulting

> stood me in very good stead, because I had no time left in which to mount in the normal way, and I was thankful when I eventually managed to reach the middle of the saddle.

The Russians retired in good order but evacuated Moscow. Napoleon and his main army entered the city. The Russians did not make a peace offer. Napoleon was faced with a dilemma. He couldn't get back to his supplies in western Russia, East Prussia and Poland before winter. If he stayed in Moscow his army might starve. In his absence the political situation in France could get worse.

On 19 October the French began to retreat west. They were forced to return by the same route they had come, through lands they had already drained of resources. After five weeks they met up with fresh troops east of Borisov. By the time they reached the Berezina River, the main army had dwindled to 60,000 troops. Constant attacks, severe cold and deprivation had turned much of the main army into a mass of fugitives.

Charles François:

> Some days before we reached Smolensk, our cavalry had almost entirely disappeared. A good part of our artillery and baggage had been abandoned on the road. All our cavalry men left, who had looked so fine six months previously, were on foot with the stragglers. There was no discipline; all military rank was destroyed. Generals, superior officers and subalterns no longer cared for the soldiers who had contributed to their glory. The men themselves asked nothing but death. Such a request was often made to me, and I had not the strength to recommend them to take courage, or even to weep for them.
>
> Those who, like myself, had still a little strength, were tortured by hunger, and we ran after the horses, watching for them to fall; when we threw ourselves upon them like wolves, fighting for bits of flesh. To cook this miserable food, we had to seek everywhere for wood. Often it refused to light, or else the wind blew it out. This search for food took all the time we had for rest. Worn out for want of sleep and long marches, we had nothing but the snow to lie on. Generals, officers, and privates were mixed pell-mell, huddled against one another. There were some, who nearly dead with fatigue, stood all night like spectres, round the faggots, when they had been able to light them.

The crossing of the Berezina River was a catastrophe in which half the remaining 60,000 troops died. Half the 30,000 survivors died in the following weeks as temperatures dropped. By the time the few thousand remaining men abandoned their wagons and artillery west of Vilna, the army had ceased to exist. Survivors of the various contingents simply deserted and walked home or wandered to the closest friendly depots.

Peninsula War 1808–1814

The Peninsular War

On 4 June 1808 Spain declared war on France, and on 4 July made peace with Britain. Britain sent troops to support her new ally. On 1 August 1808 a British expeditionary force of 8,740 troops landed at the mouth of the Mondego river in Portugal. They were under the command of Lieutenant General Sir Arthur Wellesley. Four days later, Wellesley's army was reinforced by a further 4,750 troops.

By 10 August, the combined army of 13,500 men was marching on Lisbon. They were joined by 2,000 Portuguese troops under the command of Colonel Trant, a British officer in the Portuguese service. Wellesley reached Alcobaça on the 14th. He was fully aware that a French army under General Delaborde stood in his path one day's march away at Obidos. On 16 December Delaborde positioned his force of some 4,350 men along a low ridge east of Roliça, 6 km south of Obidos.

The Battle of Roliça 17 December 1808

Wellesley advanced from Obidos in a formation with two wings thrust forward. The wings were commanded by Trant and Ferguson. Before his forces were outflanked by Trant and Ferguson, the French general, Delaborde, fell back to a much stronger position on the heights above the village of Columbeira.

Both the French and the British used light infantry as skirmishers. These troops advanced in open order to shoot at the enemy's

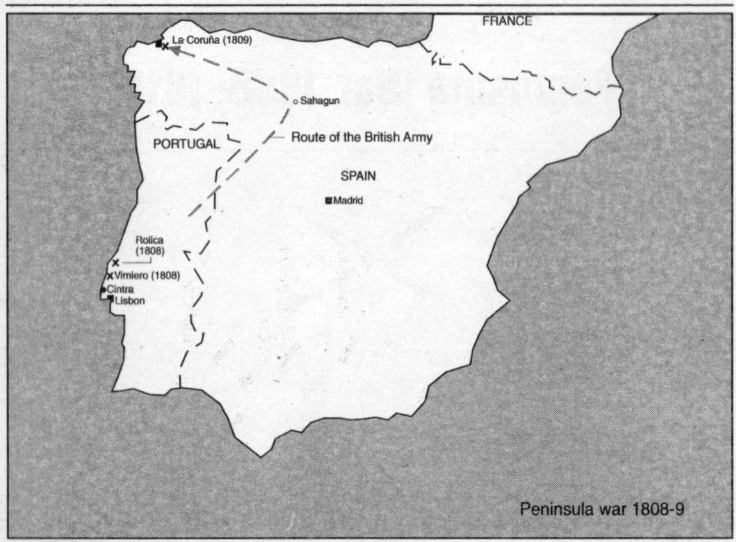

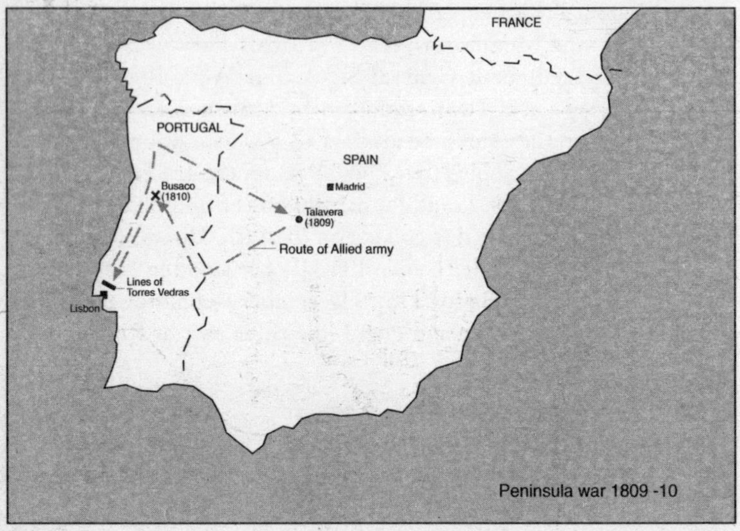

Map of the Peninsular Campaign 1808–10

formations before the main formations clashed. The result was a duel between the skirmishers of each side. The winners pushed back their opponents and were then able to aim their muskets at the main formations of their enemy. The targets of this aimed musket fire were usually the officers and sergeants. The British and their allies armed

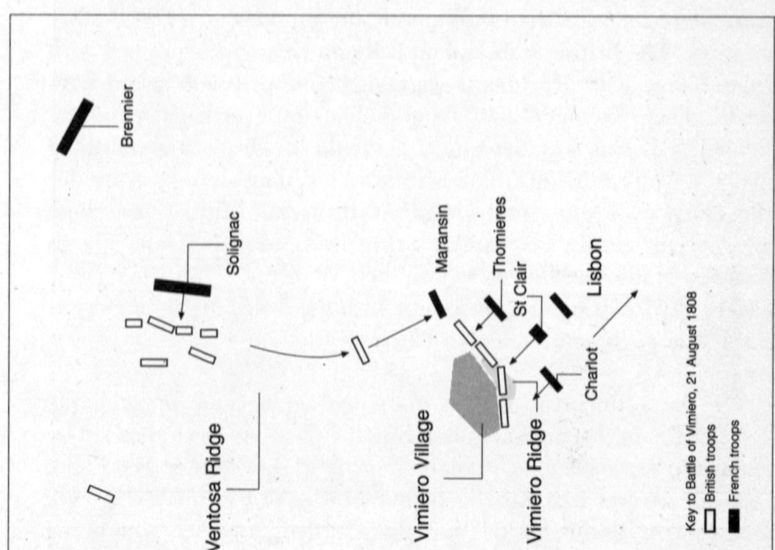

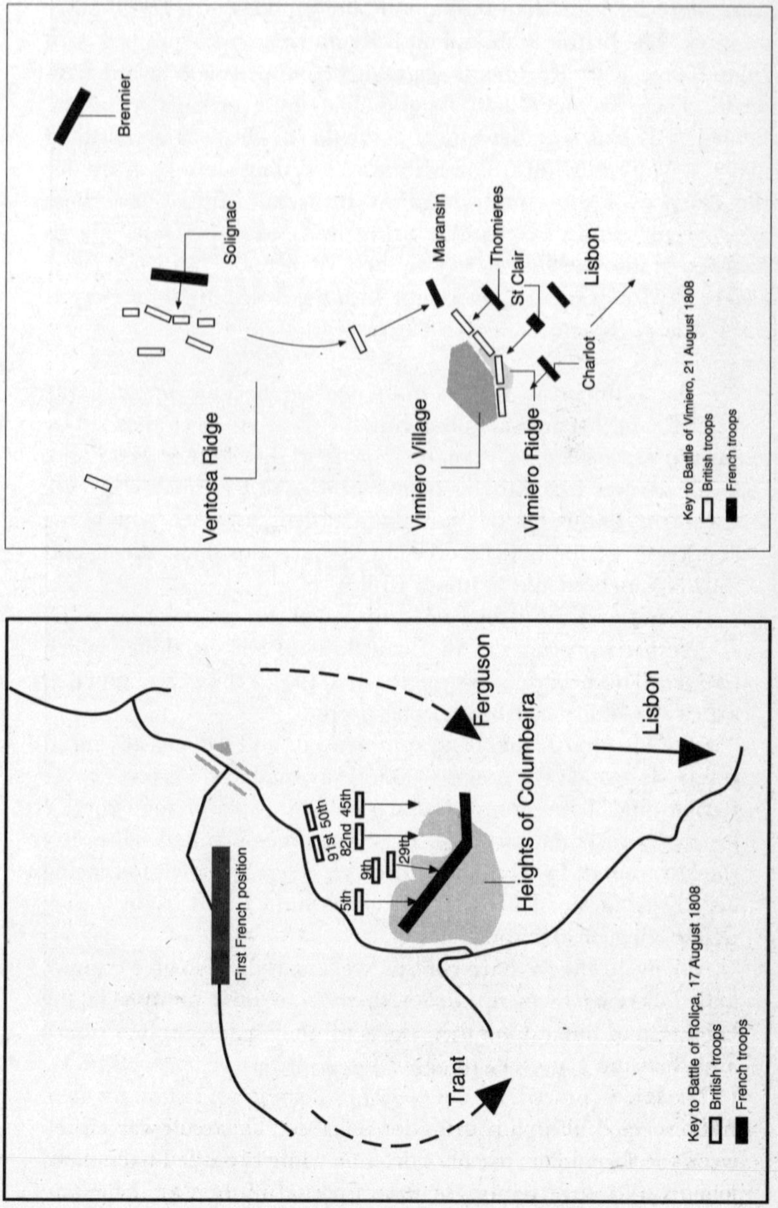

Map of the Battles of Roliça and Vimeiro

some of their light troops with rifles. Rifles had longer range and were more accurate than the smoothbore muskets used by all other infantry. The British 95th and 60th Regiments were equipped with rifles. These Rifle Regiments were also equipped with sword bayonets. These bayonets had handles like those of cavalry sabres. Benjamin Harris was the son of a shepherd who was conscripted into the Militia in 1802. The Militia was Britain's reseve army, for the defence of the country against invasion. Militia men were allowed to transfer to regular army units as volunteers. Harris transferred into the 95th Rifle Regiment. Rifleman Harris had come ashore at Mondego bay. He fought with the British light infantry at the battle of Roliça. Rifleman Harris:

> On the 17th, being still in front, we again came up with the French, and I remember observing the pleasing effect afforded by the sun's rays glancing upon their arms, as they formed in order of battle to receive us. Moving on in extended order, under whatever cover the nature of the ground afforded, together with some companies of the 60th, we began a sharp fire upon them; and thus commenced the battle of Roliça.
>
> I do not pretend to give a description of this or any other battle I have been present at. All I can do is to tell the things which happened immediately around me, and that, I think, is as much as a Private soldier can be expected to do.
>
> Soon afterwards the firing commenced, and we had advanced pretty close upon the enemy. Taking advantage of whatever cover I could find, I threw myself down behind a small bank, where I lay so secure, that, although the Frenchmen's bullets fell pretty thickly around, I was enabled to knock several over without being dislodged; in fact I fired away every round I had in my pouch whilst lying on this spot.
>
> At length, after a sharp contest, we forced them to give ground, and, following them up, drove them from their position in the heights, and hung upon their skirts till they made another stand, and then the game began again.
>
> The Rifles, indeed, fought well this day and we lost many men. They seemed in high spirits, and delighted at having driven the enemy before them. Joseph Cochan was by my side loading and firing very industriously about this period of the day. Thirsting with heat and action, he lifted his canteen to his mouth. "Here's to you, old boy," he said, as he took a pull at its contents. As he did so

> a bullet went through the canteen and, perforating his brain, killed him in a moment. Another man fell close to him almost immediately, struck by a ball in the thigh.

Wellesley intended his centre to assault the French position on the heights only after Trant and Ferguson were in position on both flanks.

The 29th Regiment led by Lt-Col. George Lake forged on ahead of any supporting troops. They came under fire from three sides but reached the brow of the hill before being broken by a French charge. The impetuous Colonel Lake was killed while 6 officers and 30 other ranks were captured. An anonymous account in the Regimental history remembered:

> The French suddenly rose up and opened their fire, which their officers seemed endeavouring to restrain, and apparently urging them on to the charge, as we observed them knocking down the men's firelocks with their swords. But they did not advance.
>
> Colonel Lake called out, "Don't fire, men; don't fire; wait a little, we shall soon charge," (meaning when more companies should come up), adding, "The bayonet is the true weapon for a British soldier" . . . but he was killed, and the companies on the right opened their fire and a desperate engagement ensued.

The survivors of the 29th fell back down the hillside into the ranks of the supporting 9th Regiment. By now, Wellesley had ordered the 5th, 9th, 82nd and 45th Regiments into a frontal attack against the heights. Two hours of bitter fighting followed. The French threw back three assaults before the British finally gained firm footholds along the crest. By this time Ferguson was finally in a position to threaten Delaborde's right flank, Delaborde skillfully disengaged from the battle. French losses amounted to 600 men killed or wounded and three guns; of the 474 British and Portugese killed, wounded or taken prisoner, nearly half were from the 29th Regiment.

Battle of Vimeiro 21 August 1808

Wellesley's army was advancing towards Lisbon. About 9 a.m. on the morning of 21 August, Marshall Junot's army was revealed in dense clouds of dust. It was manoeuvering east of Vimeiro so as to threaten the British left flank. Wellesley had ample time to counter the threat by moving the bulk of his forces from the western ridge to the ridge running north-east from Vimeiro through Ventosa. Junot started a divided attack in which his main force would be thrust against Vimeiro Hill while Brennier's brigade was sent northwards to turn Wellesley's left. Prompted by the sight of British troops occupying the Ventosa ridge in force, Junot then dispatched Solignac northwards in support of Brennier.

The first French attack was launched against Vimeiro Hill. The brigades of Thomières and Charlot, advancing in columns and screened by tirailleurs, gradually pushed the thick British skirmishing line back from the foot of the hill, only to be overwhelmed by the fire of the enveloping lines of British infantry.

Among the British skirmishers was Rifleman Harris. When the battle started, Harris was mending shoes. In his regiment he had a secondary skill which was extremely valuable. He was able to repair boots and shoes. Rifleman Harris:

> I myself was very soon so hotly engaged, loading and firing away, enveloped in the smoke I created, and the cloud which hung about me from the continued fire of my comrades, that I could see nothing for a few minutes but the red flash of my own piece amongst the white vapour clinging to my very clothes. This has often seemed to me the greatest drawback upon our present system of fighting; for whilst in such state, on a calm day, until some friendly breeze of wind clears the space around, a soldier knows no more of his position and what is about to happen in his front, or what has happened (even amongst his own companions) than the very dead lying around. The Rifles, as usual, were pretty busy in this battle.
>
> The French, in great numbers, came steadily down upon us, and we pelted away upon them like a shower of leaden hail. Under any cover we could find we lay; firing one moment, jumping up and running for it the next; and, when we could see before us, we observed the cannon-balls making a lane through the enemy's columns as they advanced, huzzaing and shouting like madmen.
>
> Such is my remembrance of the commencement of the battle of Vimeiro. The battle began on a fine bright day, and the sun played on the arms of the enemy's battalions, as they came on, as if they had been tipped with gold. The battle became general; the

smoke thickened around, and often I was obliged to stop firing, and dash it aside from my face, and try in vain to get a sight of what was going on, whilst groans and shouts and a noise of cannon and musketry appeared almost to shake the very ground. It seemed hell upon earth, I thought . . .

A man named John Low stood before me at this moment, and he turned round during a pause in our exertions, and addressed me: "Harris, you humbug," he said, "you have got plenty of money about you, I know; for you are always staying about and picking up what you can find on the field. But I think this will be your last field-day, old boy. A good many of us will catch it, I suspect, to-day." "You are right, Low," I said. "I have got nine guineas in my pack, and if I am shot to-day, and you yourself escape, it's quite at your service. In the meantime, however, if you see any symptoms of my wishing to flinch in this business I hope you will shoot me with your own hand." Low, as well as myself, survived this battle, and after it was over, whilst we sat down with our comrades and rested, amongst other matters talked over, Low told them of our conversation during the heat of the day, and the money I had collected, and the Rifles from that time had a great respect for me. It is, indeed, singular, how a man loses or gains caste with his comrades from his behaviour, and how closely he is observed in the field. The officers, too, are commented upon and closely observed.

The men are very proud of those who are brave in the field, and kind and considerate to the soldiers under them. An act of kindness done by an officer has often during the battle been the cause of his life being saved. Nay, whatever folks may say upon the matter, I know from experience, that in our army the men like best to be officered by gentlemen, whose education has rendered them more kind in manners than your coarse officer, sprung from obscure origin, and whose style is brutal and overbearing.

During this day I myself narrowly escaped being killed by our own dragoons, for somehow or other, in the confusion, I fell whilst they were charging, and the whole squadron thundering past just missed me, as I lay amongst the dead and wounded. Tired and overweighted with knapsack and all my shoe-making implements, I lay where had fallen for a short time, and watched the cavalry as they gained the enemy. I observed a fine, gallant-looking officer leading them on in that charge. He was a brave fellow, and bore himself like a hero; with his sword waving in the air, cheered the men on, as he went dashing upon the enemy, and hewing and slashing at them in tremendous style. I watched for him as the dragoons came off after that charge, but saw him no more; he had fallen. Fine fellow! his conduct indeed made an impression upon me that I shall never forget, and I was told afterwards that he was a brother of Sir John Eustace.

A French soldier was lying beside me at this time; he was badly wounded and, hearing him moan as he lay, after I had done looking at the cavalry, I turned my attention to him and, getting up, lifted his head, and poured some water into his mouth. He was dying fast; but he thanked me in a foreign language, which, although I did not exactly understand, I could easily make out by the look he gave me. Mullins, of the Rifles, who stepped up whilst I supported his head, d–d me for a fool for my pains. "Better knock out his brains, Harris," said he; "he has done us mischief enough, I'll be bound, for it, today."

After the battle I strolled about the field in order to see if there was anything to be found worth picking up amongst the dead. The first thing I saw was a three-pronged silver fork, which, as it lay by itself, had most likely been dropped by some person who had been on the look-out before me. A little further on I saw a French soldier sitting against a small rise in the ground or bank. He was wounded in the throat, and appeared very faint, the bosom of his coat being saturated, with the blood which had flowed down. By his side lay his cap, and close to that was a bundle containing a quantity of gold and silver crosses, which I concluded he had plundered from some convent or church. He looked the picture of a sacrilegious thief, dying hopelessly, and overtaken by divine wrath. I kicked over his cap, which was also full of plunder, but I declined taking anything from him. I felt fearful of incurring the wrath of Heaven for the like offence, so I left him, and passed on. A little further off lay an officer of the 50th regiment. I knew him by sight, and recognised him as he lay. He was quite dead, and lying on his back. He had been plundered, and his clothes were torn open. Three bullet-holes were close together in the pit of his stomach: beside him lay an empty pocket-book, and his epaulette had been pulled from his shoulder.

I had moved on but a few paces when I recollected that perhaps the officer's shoes might serve me, my own being considerably the worse for wear, so I returned again, went back, pulled one of his shoes off, and knelt down on one knee to try it on. It was not much better than my own; however, I determined on the exchange, and proceeded to take off its fellow. As I did so I was startled by the sharp report of a firelock, and, at the same moment, a bullet whistled close by my head. Instantly starting up, I turned, and looked in the direction whence the shot had come. There was no person near me in this part of the field. The dead and the dying lay thickly all around; but nothing else could I see. I looked to the priming of my rifle, and again turned to the dead officer of the 50th. It was evident that some plundering scoundrel had taken a shot at me, and the fact of his doing so proclaimed him one of the enemy. To distinguish him amongst the bodies strewn about was impossible; perhaps he might himself be one of the wounded. Hardly had I effected the exchange, put on the dead officer's shoes, and resumed my rifle, when another shot took place, and a second ball whistled past me. This time I was ready, and turning quickly I saw my man: he was just about to squat down behind a small mound, about twenty paces from me. I took a haphazard shot at him, and instantly knocked him over. I immediately ran up to him; he had fallen on his face, and I heaved him over on his back, bestrode his body, and drew my sword bayonet, There was, however, no occasion for the precaution as he was even then in the agonies of death.

It was a relief to me to find I had not been mistaken. He was a French light-infantryman, and I therefore took it in the way of business – he had attempted my life, and lost his own. It was the fortune of war; so, stooping down, with my sword I cut the green string that sustained his calibash, and took a hearty pull to quench my thirst.

Undaunted, Junot renewed the attack by sending St Clair's two battalions of grenadiers against the midpoint of the British line on the hill. Again the British infantry threw back the attack by converging so as to fire into the French column from three sides.

In a final act of desperation, Junot sent Maransin's two battalions of grenadiers directly against Vimeiro village, only to see them caught in fire from both flanks as Wellesley ordered troops to move down from the Ventosa ridge. After vicious, close-range fighting in the streets of the village, the grenadiers were compelled to retire.

The actions at Vimeiro Hill were virtually at an end before Junot's flanking force arrived at a position where it could threaten the flank of the British forces. When they finally arrived one brigade was met by shattering musketry fire; the other brigade was thrown back in turn.

By midday, the battle for Vimeiro was at an end. Out of a force of some 18,800, British and Portugese casualties numbered only 720. In contrast, French losses were estimated at 2,000 from a force of 13,050; at least 13 of their 23 guns had been captured.

Unfortunately the British High Command had sent not one, but two generals senior to Wellesley to take over from him. The opportunity for the British-Portuguese army to follow up the victory with an advance on Lisbon was lost as Wellesley ceded command to the cautious Sir Henry Burrard. Burrard was himself replaced by General Hew Dalrymple. Burrard and Dalrymple negotiated a truce with the French. Under the terms of the truce, Marshal Junot agreed that the entire French army in Portugal (25,747 troops) would be evacuated back to France by the Royal Navy. Wellesley protested at this. The arrangement was known as the Convention of Cintra. Wellesley, Burrard and Dalrymple had to return to England to face a court of inquiry.

Sir John Moore was left in command of the British expeditionary force of 30,000 in Portugal.

In November 1808, Napoleon himself arrived in Spain at the head of 200,000 veteran troops. Moore struck towards Burgos and the northern flank of Napoleon's army. He succeeded in drawing French forces away from southern Spain before being forced to retreat towards the coast where he hoped the Royal Navy would be able to evacuate his army. Napoleon was marching towards him with 80,000 men.

The Retreat to Coruña

I hope the (British) people will be satisfied.

Sir John Moore

Moore had reached Sahagun in northern Spain before he discovered that Napoleon was advancing against him with 80,000 men led by Marshall Ney's VI Corps. Moore ordered a retreat to Coruña on the coast. Rifleman Harris' battalion left Sahagun on Christmas Day 1808. The officer in command of Harris' Brigade was General Robert Craufurd. Craufurd believed in stern discipline and disliked retreating. Harris and his fellow soldiers realised there was something wrong from Craufurd's "severe look and scowling eye". Rifleman Harris:

> "Keep your ranks there, men!" he said, spurring his horse towards some Riflemen who were avoiding a small rivulet. "Keep your ranks and move on – no straggling from the main body."
>
> We pushed on all that day without halting; and I recollect the first thing that struck us as somewhat odd was our passing one of the commissariat wagons, overturned and stuck fast in the mud, and which was abandoned without an effort to save any of its contents. A sergeant of the 92nd Highlanders, just about this time, fell dead with fatigue, and no one stopped, as we passed, to offer him any assistance. Night came down upon us, without our having tasted food, or halted – I speak for myself, and those around me – and all night long we continued this dreadful march. Men began to look into each other's faces, and ask the question, "Are we ever to be halted again?" and many of the weaker sort were now seen to stagger, make a few desperate efforts, and then fall, perhaps to rise no more. Most of us had devoured all we carried in our haversacks, and endeavoured to catch up anything we could snatch from hut or cottage in our route. Many, even at this period, would have struggled from the ranks, and perished, had not Craufurd held them together with a firm rein. One such bold and stern commander in the East during a memorable disaster, and that devoted army had reached its refuge unbroken! Thus we staggered on, night and day, for about four days, before we discovered the reason of this continued forced march. The discovery was made to our company by a good-tempered, jolly fellow, named Patrick M'Lauchlan. He inquired of an officer, marching directly in his front, the destination intended.
>
> "By J—s! Musther Hills," I heard him say, "where the d–l is this you're taking us to?"
>
> "To England, M'Lauchlan," replied the officer "if we can get there."
>
> The information M'Lauchlan obtained from Lieutenant Hill quickly spread amongst us, and we now began to see more clearly the horrors of our situation, and the men to murmur at not being permitted to turn and stand at bay, cursing the French and swearing they would rather die ten thousand deaths, with their rifles in their hands in opposition, than endure the present toil. We

were in the rear at this time, and following that part of the army which made for Vigo, whilst the other portion of the British, being on the main road to Coruña, were at this moment closely pursued and harassed by the enemy, as I should judge from the continued thunder of their cannon and rattle of their musketry. Craufurd seemed to sniff the sound of battle from afar with peculiar feelings. He halted us for a few minutes occasionally when the distant clamour became more distinct and his face turned towards the sound and seemed to light up and become less stern. It was then indeed that every poor fellow clutched his weapon more firmly, and wished for a sight of the enemy.

Before long they had their wish: the enemy's cavalry were on our skirts that night; and as we rushed out of a small village, the name of which I cannot now recollect, we turned to bay. Behind broken-down carts and tumbrils, huge trunks of trees, and everything we could scrape together, the Rifles lay and blazed away at the advancing cavalry, whilst the inhabitants, suddenly aroused from their beds to behold their village almost on fire with our continued discharges, and nearly distracted with the sound, ran from their houses, crying, "Viva l'Englisa!" and "Viva la Franca!" in a breath; men, women, and children flying to the open country in their alarm.

We passed the night thus engaged, holding our own as well as we could, together with the 43rd Light Infantry, the 52nd, a portion of the German Legion – part of the 10th Hussars, and the 15th Dragoons. Towards morning we moved down towards a small bridge, still followed by the enemy, whom, however, we had sharply galled, and obliged to be more wary in their efforts. The rain was pouring down in torrents on this morning I recollect, and we remained many hours with our arms ported, standing in this manner, and staring the French cavalry in the face, the water actually running out of the muzzles of our rifles.

General Craufurd's light infantry brigade and General Alten's King's German Legion had been detached from the main column at Astorga and ordered to march to the port of Vigo, just south of Coruña. The King's German Legion were troops from German states ruled by King George. They were allowed to serve with the British Army abroad. They proved to be excellent troops.

Rifleman Harris described some of the horrors of the march:

> Being constantly in rear of the main body, the scenes of distress and misery I witnessed were dreadful to contemplate, particularly amongst the women and children, who were lagging and falling behind, their husbands and fathers being in the main body in our front.

Like many others, Rifleman Harris suffered from hunger and fatigue on the march. Eventually he fell out but was able to hobble to a peasant's hut where he was given some food:

> All they gave me was some coarse black bread, and a pitcher of sour wine. It was, however, acceptable to a half-famished man; and I felt greatly revived by it.

The next day Harris was able to follow the retreating army.

On 16 January 1809 the transports arrived at Coruña. The British army was in defensive positions outside the city. A French force of 20,000 men attacked the 14,000 men of the British army. The 43rd Regiment were also part of Craufurd's light brigade. A private called Thomas was serving in the 43rd:

> Sir John Moore, while earnestly watching the result of the battle about the village of Elvina, was struck on the left breast by a cannon shot. The shock threw him from his horse with violence. He rose again in a sitting posture. His eye was still fixed on the regiments engaged in his front; and in a few moments, when he was satisfied that the troops were gaining ground, his countenance brightened, and he suffered himself to be taken to the rear. The dreadful nature of the injury he had received was then noticed; the shoulder was shattered in pieces, and the muscles of the breast torn into long strips, which were interlaced by their recoil from the strain and dragging of the shot. As the soldiers placed him in a blanket his sword got entangled, and the hilt entered the wound. Captain Hardinge, a staff officer, who was near, attempted to take it off; but the dying man stopped him, saying, "It is as well as it is. I had rather it should go out of the field with me." In that manner Sir John was borne from the fight.

Rifleman William Green wrote that:

> The roar of the cannon and the roll of musketry was so loud, that without great attention the word of command could scarcely be given, and the sound of the bugle hardly heard.

The British gained ground and could claim a victory. That night they retreated into the citadel and began boarding the waiting ships. That night Sir John Moore died and was buried. Thomas remembered another problem they endured on the retreat, apart from lack of food and fatigue:

> Another serious difficulty arose from the circumstance that our retreat was conducted in winter: the roads for an immense distance had been torn into deep ruts by the wheels of the baggage waggons and cannon, and rendered rough by the trampling of cavalry horses; severe frost then set in, when the rough and rugged surface was suddenly hardened into ice. Meantime my shoes were worn out, and as they would no longer hold together, I was compelled to march bare-footed: this was severe, and the sensation produced was singularly painful. In the frozen condition of the ground every step seemed to place my feet on flint: scarcely able to move, and yet forbidden to stay, the Sergeant of my company, a worthy fellow, proposed to lend me a pair of shoes, but his kindness was unavailing; on attempting to put them on, they would not fit my feet. How it was that I was sustained under these difficulties, I knew not then; but now I know: the Almighty was my support, though I was heedless of his help. "His arm unseen conveyed me safe", and I feel at this moment some satisfaction, which I hope may be pardoned, that though heavily pressed with the sufferings of those days, I never fell out of the line of march, or impeded the public service by imbecility of purpose, or disposition to flinch from duty. Previous to embarkation I was provided with the article needed; and, praised be the Lord, I have never wanted a pair of shoes from that day to this. On getting into the boat which conveyed me on board the ship, determined to forget my former vexations, I threw my old shoes into the sea, and there, like my past troubles, they were soon out of sight and forgotten.

Rifleman Harris finally caught up with the army when the evacuation was almost over:

> As it was, when I did manage to gain the sea-shore, it was by the aid of my rifle that I could stand, and my eyes were now so dim and heavy that with difficulty I made out a boat which seemed the last that had put off.
>
> Fearful of being left half blind in the lurch, I took off my cap,

and placed it on the muzzle of my rifle as a signal, for I was totally unable to call out. Luckily, Lieutenant Cox, who was aboard the boat; saw me, and ordered the men to return, and, making one more effort, I walked into the water, and a sailor stretching his body over the gunwale, seized me as if I had been an infant, and hauled me on board. His words were characteristic of the English sailor, I thought.

"Hollo there, you lazy lubber!" he said, as he grasped hold of me, "who the h–ll do you think is to stay humbugging all day for such a fellow as you?"

The boat, I found, was crowded with our exhausted men, who lay helplessly at the bottom, the heavy sea every moment drenching them to the skin. As soon as we reached the vessel's side, the sailors immediately aided us to get on board, which in our exhausted state was not a very easy matter, as they were obliged to place ropes in our hands, and heave us up by setting their shoulders under us, and hoisting away as if they had been pushing bales of goods on board.

"Heave away!" cried one of the boat's crew, as I clung to a rope, quite unable to pull myself up, "heave away, you lubber!"

The tar placed his shoulder beneath me as he spoke, and hoisted me up against the ship's side; I lost my grasp of the rope and should have fallen into the sea had it not been for two of the crew. These men grasped me as I was falling, and drew me into the porthole like a bundle of foul clothes, tearing away my belt and bayonet in the effort, which fell into the sea.

Harris fell asleep a few minutes later and returned to England. Later in 1809 he was sent on the expedition to Walcheren. He was one of many soldiers whose health was ruined on this ineffectual expedition. He left the army as an invalid. He wrote his "recollections" while working as a cobbler in Richmond Street, Soho, London.

On 22 April 1809 Sir Arthur Wellesley rejoined the British Army in Portugal. The Portuguese army was being reconstructed by the British General William Beresford. On 16 May 1809 Wellesley was able to lead 30,000 British and 16,000 Portuguese troops against the French in northern Portugal; the French under Marshal Soult retreated into Spain.

The Battle of Talavera 21–22 July 1809

The British–Portuguese Army marched into Spain for action against the French in combination with a Spanish army led by General Cuesta. They were faced by two French armies. The nearest was commanded by Marshal Soult. He had 30,000 men. Marshal Victor and King Joseph were not far away with another 25,000 men. The British–Portuguese Army and the Spanish Army faced Victor's army on 23 July but the Spanish refused to move because it was a Sunday. A few days later Victor's army was back but now it been reinforced by King Joseph. The combined French armies outnumbered Wellesley's British–Portuguese Army by 46,000 to 20,600.

Cuesta's Spanish army held prepared positions at the southern end of the allied line. The French tried a night attack against the Medellin Hill on the northern end of the allied line.

A second attack against the Medellin shortly after dawn the following day was also repulsed.

There was now a lull in the fighting for several hours as the French command reassessed the situation. News had reached Joseph of a move by the Spanish General Venegas towards Madrid. A decisive victory was now essential in order to release forces to counter this new threat. Accordingly, Joseph ordered a full-scale assault against the British–Portugese line.

General Chambray described the attack from the French point of view:

> The French charged with shouldered arms as was their custom. When they arrived at short range, and the English line remained motionless, some hesitation was seen in the march. The officers and NCOs shouted at the soldiers, "Forward; march; don't fire." Some even cried, "They're surrendering." The forward movement was therefore resumed; but it was not until extremely close range of the English line that the latter started a two-rank fire which carried destruction into the heart of the French line, stopped its movement, and produced some disorder.
>
> While the officers shouted to the soldiers, "Forward: don't fire," (although firing set in nevertheless), the English suddenly stopped their own fire and charged with the bayonet. Everything was favourable to them; orderliness, impetus, and the resolution to fight with the bayonet. Among the French, on the other hand, there was no longer any impetus, but disorder and surprise caused by the enemy's unexpected resolve: flight was inevitable.

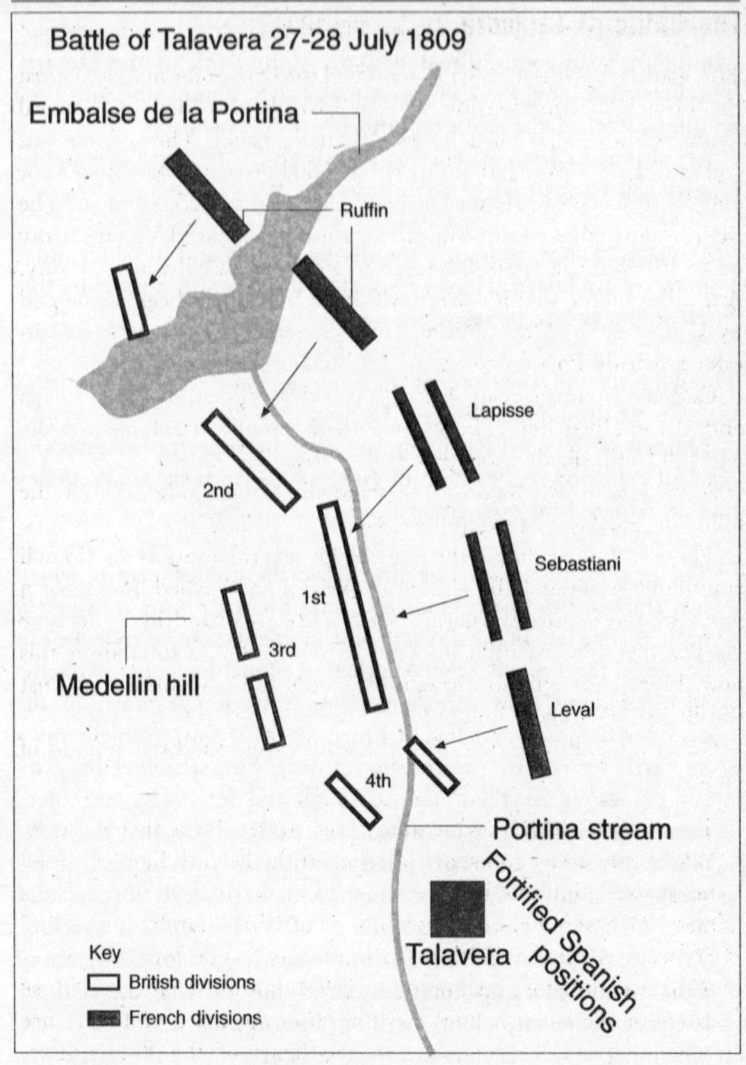

Map of the Battle of Talavera

The French had attacked in two waves. The men of the British First Division pursued the defeated French first wave with wild enthusiasm. Only Cameron's brigade halted just beyond the Portina brook: the other three brigades continued the chase in complete disorder, and became vulnerable. The French artillery on the Cascajal heights opened a heavy enfilading fire on Low and Langwerth's brigades, inflicting very heavy casualties, while Latour-Maubourg's dragoons threatened the right flank of the Guards. The French second wave of Lapisse and Sebastiani's divisions then counter-attacked the scattered and breathless men.

According to John Aitchison, an ensign in the 3rd Guards, the Guards fell back in fairly good order:

> We faced about, retired to the ravine, slower and in better order than we advanced. Here we made a stand and did considerable execution before being again forced to retreat.

The Guards did not lose as heavily on Low and Langwerth's brigades of the King's German Legion.

Thomas of the 43rd Regiment, recently been promoted corporal. He had returned to Portugal in June 1809. He believed Wellesley had anticipated his own troops' impetuous pursuit:

> The next grand attack was directed to the English centre, which was thrown into great confusion, and for some time completely broken. The fate of the day for some moments seemed to incline in favour of the French, when suddenly Colonel Donellan, with the 48th regiment, was seen advancing thrugh the midst of the disordered masses. At first it appeared as if this regiment must be carried away by the retiring crowds; but, wheeling back by companies, it let them pass through the intervals, and then, resuming its firm and beautiful line, marched against the right of the pursuing columns, plied them with such a destructive musketry, and closed upon them with a pace so regular and steady, that the forward movement of the French was checked. The Guards and the Germans immediately rallied; a brigade of light cavalry came up from the second line at a trot; the artillery battered the enemy's flanks without intermission and the French, beginning to waver, soon lost their advantage, and the battle was restored.
>
> The annals of warfare often tell us that in all actions there is one critical and decisive moment which will give the victory to the General who knows how to discover and secure it. When the Guards first made their rash charge, Sir Arthur Wellesley, foreseeing the issue of it, had ordered the 48th down from the hill, although a rough battle was going on there, and at the same time he ordered Cotton's light cavalry to advance. These dispositions

> gained the day. The French relaxed their efforts by degrees; the fire of the English grew hotter; and their loud and confident shouts, sure augury of success, were heard along the whole line. The French army soon after retired to the position from whence it had descended to the attack. This retrograde movement was covered by skirmishers, and increasing fire of artillery; and the British, reduced to less than 14,000 men, and exhausted by toil and want of food, were unable to pursue.
>
> The battle was scarcely over when the dry grass and shrubs taking fire, a volume of flame passed with inconceivable rapidity across a part of the field, scorching in its course both the dead and wounded. The loss of the British in the course of this severe action and previous skirmishing was upwards of 6,000 men killed and wounded. That of the French, as afterwards appeared in a manuscript of Marshal Jourdan, was rather more than 7,300.

The next morning, the French had gone. Although Victor was left to hold the line of the Alberche, the bulk of Joseph's army retired to defend Madrid against the threat of a Spanish army under Venegas.

The French casualties were 7,300 at Talavera. Wellesley's were 5,400. Another French army under Soult threatened him. He was compelled to retreat towards Portugal and safety.

In February 1810 Marshall Victor was replaced by Massena who arrived with reinforcements from France. It was during the winter of 1809–10 that Wellesley, now Lord Wellington, began to prepare a secure defensive position in southern Portugal.

In his Memoirs, Thomas observed:

> When his Lordship required 30,000 men for the defence of Portugal, he considered the number that could be fed rather than what was necessary to fight the enemy. On this principle he asserted that success must depend on the exertions and devotedness of the native forces. Two points were to be secured at the very onset. One was, to concert measures by which sustenance might be secured for the united British and Portuguese army; and the other, to devise plans by which the enemy should be deprived of supplies, whenever and wherever he entered the country. In effecting this latter purpose it was demanded (for the exactions of war are necessarily rigorous) that the people should destroy their mills, remove their boats, break down their bridges, lay waste their fields, abandon their dwellings, and carry off their

property, on whatever line the invader should penetrate; while the entire population, converted into soldiers and closing on the rear and flanks, should cut off all resources, excepting those carried in the midst of the troops. These were hard sayings; but they were dictated by stern necessity, and were positively required for the safety of the kingdom. The call was obeyed. Part of the public property was sacrificed, in order that the whole might, in some form or other, eventually be restored and rendered safe. In pursuance of the comprehensive plans adopted by the British leader, it was necessary to find a position, covering Lisbon, where the allied forces could neither be turned by the flanks, nor forced in front by numbers, nor reduced by famine. The mountains filling the tongue of land upon which Lisbon is situated furnished this key-stone to the arch of defence. Lord Wellington then conceived the design of turning these vast mountains into one stupendous and impregnable citadel on which to deposit the independence of the whole Peninsula. The works were forthwith commenced. Intrenchments, inundations, and redoubts, covered more than 500 square miles of mountainous country lying between the Tagus and the ocean. The actual force under Lord Wellington cannot be estimated higher than 80,000 men, while the frontier he had to defend, reckoning from Braganza to Ayamonte, was 400 miles long. The British forces included in the above were under 30,000. Every probable movement of the enemy was previously considered: at the same time the English Commander was aware how many counter-combinations were to be expected in a contest with 80,000 French veterans, having a competent General at their head. Hence, to secure embarkation in the event of disaster, a third line of entrenchments was prepared, and 24,000 tons of shipping were constantly kept in the river to receive the British forces.

Thomas was involved in a fight defending a bridge over the river Coa on 24 July 1810:

The most dangerous crisis had now arrived: this was on the evening of 24 July, which was stormy, and proved to be a memorable period. Our whole force under arms consisted of 4,000 infantry, 11,000 cavalry, and six guns; and the position occupied was about one mile and a half in length, extending in an oblique line towards the Coa. The cavalry piquets were upon the plain in front, the right on some broken ground, and the left resting on an nufim shed tower 800 yards from Almeida: the rear was on the edge of the ravine forming the channel of the Coa, and the bridge was more than a mile distant in the bottom of the chasm. The lightning towards midnight became unusually vivid. Having been under arms for several hours, we were drenched with rain: as the day dawned a few pistol-shots in front, followed by an order for the cavalry reserve and the guns to advance, gave notice of the enemy's approach; and as the morning cleared, 24,000 French infantry, 5,000 cavalry, and 30 pieces of artillery were observed marching from Turones. Our line was immediately contracted, and brought under the edge of the ravine: in an instant 4,000 hostile cavalry swept the plain, and our regiment was unaccountably placed within an enclosure of solid masonry at least ten feet high, situated on the left of the road, with but one narrow outlet about half musket-shot down the ravine. While thus shut up the firing in front redoubled, the cavalry, the artillery, and the Cacadores successively passed by in retreat, and the sharp clang of the 95th Rifle was heard along the edge of the plain above. A few moments later and we should have been surrounded; but here, as in every other part of the field, the quickness and knowledge of the battalion officer remedied the faults of the General. In little more than a minute, by united effort, we contrived to loosen some large stones, when, by a powerful exertion, we burst the enclosure, and the regiment, reformed in column of companies, was the next instant up with the Riflemen. There was no room to array the line, no time for anything but battle; every Captain carried off his company as an independent body, the whole presenting a mass of skirmishers, acting in small parties and under no regular command, yet each confident in the courage and discipline of those on his right and left, and all regulating their movements by a common discretion. Having the advantage of ground and number, the enemy broke over the edge of the ravine; their guns, ranged along the summit, played hotly with grape; and their Hussars, galloping over the glacis of Almeida, poured down the road, sabring every thing in their way. The British regiments, however, extricated themselves from their perilous situation. Falling back slowly, and yet stopping and fighting whenever opportunity offered, they made their way through a rugged country, tangled with vineyards, in despite of the enemy, who was so fierce and eager, that even the horsemen rode in among the enclosures, striking at us, as we mounted the walls, or scrambled over the rocks. Just then, I found myself within pistol-shot of the enemy, while my passage was checked by a deep chasm or ravine: as not a moment was to be lost, I contrived to mount to the edge, and, having gained the opposite side, put myself in a crouching position, and managed to slide down the steep and slippery descent without injury. On approaching the river, a more open space presented itself; but the left wing being harder pressed, and having the shortest distance, the bridge was so crowded as to be impassable: here therefore we made a stand. The post was maintained until the enemy, gathering in great numbers, made a second burst, when the companies fell back. At this moment the right wing of the 52d was seen marching towards the bridge, which was still crowded with the passing troops, when M'Leod, a very young man, immediately turned his horse round, called to the troops to follow, and, taking off his cap, rode with a shout towards the enemy. The suddenness of the thing, and the distinguished action of the man, produced the effect he designed: we all rushed after him, cheering and charging as if a whole army were behind to sustain us; the enemy's skirmishers, amazed at this unexpected movement, were directly checked. The conflict was tremendous: thrice we repulsed the enemy at the point of the bayonet. M'Leod was in the hottest of the battle, and a ball passed through the collar of his coat; still he was to be seen with a pistol in his right hand, among the last to retire. At length the bugle sounded for retreat: just then, my left-hand man, one of the stoutest in the regiment, was hit by a musket shot – he threw his head back, and was instantly dead. I fired at the fellow who shot my comrade; and before I could reload, my pay-sergeant, Thomas, received a ball in the thigh, and earnestly implored me to carry him away. As the enemy was not far off, such a load was by no means desirable: but he was my friend; I therefore took him up; and though several shots were directed to us, they all missed, and I was able, though encumbered with such weight, to carry him safely over the bridge. At length the assistance of another soldier was procured: we then carried the wounded man between us, when he was placed on a car. He returned me sincere thanks, and, what was just then much better, gave me his canteen, out of which I was permitted to take a draught of rum: how refreshing it was, can be fully known only to myself. As the regiments passed the bridge, they planted themselves in loose order on the side of the mountain; the artillery drew up on the summit, and the cavalry were disposed in parties on the roads to the right, because two miles higher up the stream there were fords, and beyond them the bridge of Castello Bom. The French skirmishers, swarming on the right bank, opened a biting fire, which was returned as bitterly; the artillery on both sides played across the ravine, the sounds were repeated by numberless echoes; and the smoke, rising slowly, resolved itself into an immense arch, sparkling with the whifling phases of the flying shells. The enemy despatched a Dragoon to try the depth of the stream above; but two shots from the 52d killed man and horse, and the carcases floating down the river discovered that it was impassable. The monotonous tones of a French drum were then heard; and in another second the head of a column was at the long narrow bridge. A drummer, and an officer in splendid uniform, leaped forward together, and the whole rushed on with loud cries. The depth of the ravine at first deceived the soldiers' aim on our side, and two-thirds of the passage were won before an English shot had brought down an enemy. A few paces onward the line of death was traced, and the whole of the leading French section fell as one man. Still the gallant column pressed forward, but no foot could pass that terrible line: the killed and wounded rolled together, until the heap rose nearly to a level with the parapet. Our shouts now rose loudly, but they were confidently answered; and in half an hour a second column, more numerous than the first, again crowded the bridge. This time the range was better judged, and ere half the distance was passed, the multitude was again torn, shattered, dispersed, and slain: ten or twelve men only succeeded in crossing, and took shelter under the rocks at the brink of the river. The skirmishing was renewed, and a French surgeon, coming down to the very foot of the bridge, waved his handkerchief, and commenced dressing the wounded under the hottest fire: the appeal was heard; every musket turned from him, although his still undaunted countrymen were preparing for a third attempt. This last effort was comparatively feeble, and soon failed. The combat was nevertheless continued by the French, as a point of honour to cover the escape of those who had passed the bridge, and by the English from ignorance of their object. One of the enemy's guns was dismantled; a powder magazine blew up; and many continued to fall on both sides till four o'clock, when a heavy rain caused a momentary cessation of fire the men among the rocks returned unmolested to their own party, the fight ceased, and we retired behind the Pinkel river. On our side upwards of 300 were killed or wounded. The French lost more than 1,000 men.

Wellington hoped that the Fortress town of Almeida would hold up the French advance. Thomas:

A sad disaster happened at time. Almeida was besieged by Massena in person, at the head of a powerful army. The place, though regularly constructed with six bastions, ravines, an excellent ditch and covered way, was extremely defective: with the exception of some damp casemates in one of the bastions, there was no magazine for the powder. The garrison consisted of about four thousand men. On 18 July the trenches were begun; and on the morning of the 26th, the second parallel being commenced, 65 pieces of artillery mounted on ten batteries threw in their fire. Many houses were soon in flames, and the garrison was unable to extinguish them; the counter fire was, however, briskly maintained, little military damage was sustained, and towards evening the cannonade slackened on both sides; but just after dark; the ground suddenly trembled, the castle burst into a thousand pieces, and gave vent to a column of smoke and fire: presently the whole town sunk into a shapeless mass of ruin. Treason or accident had caused the magazine to explode; and the devastation was incredible. Five hundred persons were struck dead on the instant; only six houses remained standing; and the surviving garrison, aghast at the terrible commotion, disregarded all exhortations to rally. An immediate surrender was the necessary result.

The invasion of Portugal by the French now assumed a most serious aspect. Massena's command extended from the banks of the Tagus to the Bay of Biscay, and the number of his troops exceeded 110,000 men. The view was discouraging, and was so felt by the British Ministry at home. Massena could bring 60,000 veterans into the field, while the British force was scarcely 50,000, more than half of which consisted of untried men. The Sierra Busaco was the place on which Lord Wellington fixed for his position. A succession of ascending ridges lead to this mountain, which is separated from the last by a chasm so profound, that the unassisted eye could hardly distinguish the movement of troops in the bottom. When this formidable position was chosen, some officers expressed their fears that Massena would not assail it.

"But if he do, I shall beat him," was the reply of the English leader; who was well assured that the Prince would attack. Massena was in fact anxious of a battle, and indulged in a vision, in which he beheld the allies fly before his face.

The Battle of Busaco 27 September 1810

Wellington formed his infantry and artillery on the Sierra Busaco. He left his cavalry on the plain, below, guarding his rear. Massena attacked confidently. He formed his troops into columns preceded by skirmishers.

In his official dispatch Wellington wrote:

At 6 in the morning of the 27th, the enemy made two desperate attacks upon our position, the one on the right, the other on the left of the highest part of the Sierra. The attack upon the right was made by two divisions of the 2nd Corps, on that part of the Sierra occupied by the 3rd division of infantry. One division of French infantry arrived at the top of the ridge, where it was attacked in the most gallant manner by the 88th regiment, under the command of Lieut. Colonel Wallace, the 45th, under the command of Lieut. Colonel the Hon. R. Meade, and by the 8th Portuguese regiment, under the command of Lieut. Colonel Douglas, directed by Major General Picton. These three corps advanced with the bayonet and drove the enemy's division from the advantageous ground which they had obtained. The other division of the 2nd Corps attacked further on the right, by the road leading by St Antonio de Cantaro, also in front of Major General Picton's division. These were repulsed, before they could reach the top of the ridge, by the 74th, under the command of Lieut. Colonel the Hon. R. Trench, and the brigade of Portuguese infantry of the 9th and 21st regiments, under the command of Colonel Champelmond, directed by Colonel Mackinnon. Major General Leith also moved to his left to the support of Major General Picton, and aided in the defeat of the enemy by the 3rd battalion of Royals, the 1st battalion of the 9th, and the 2nd battalion of the 38th regiments. In these attacks Major Generals Leith and Picton, Colonels Mackinnon and Champelmond, of the Portuguese

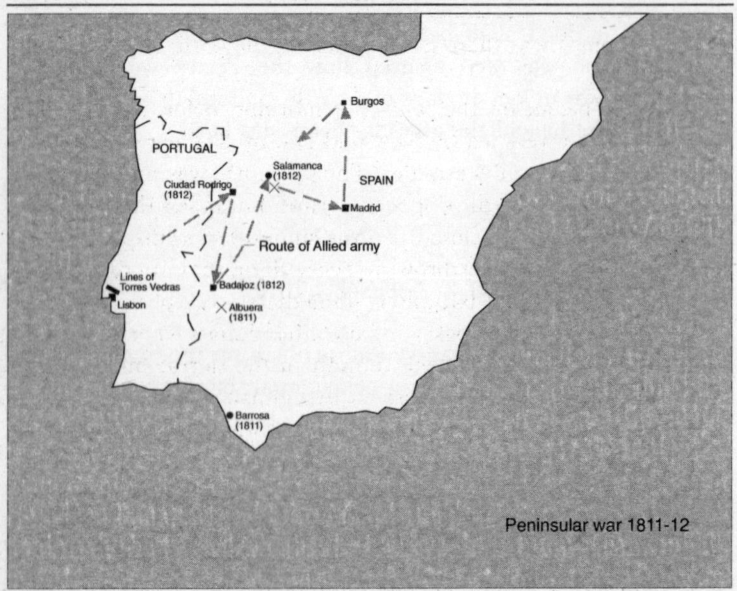

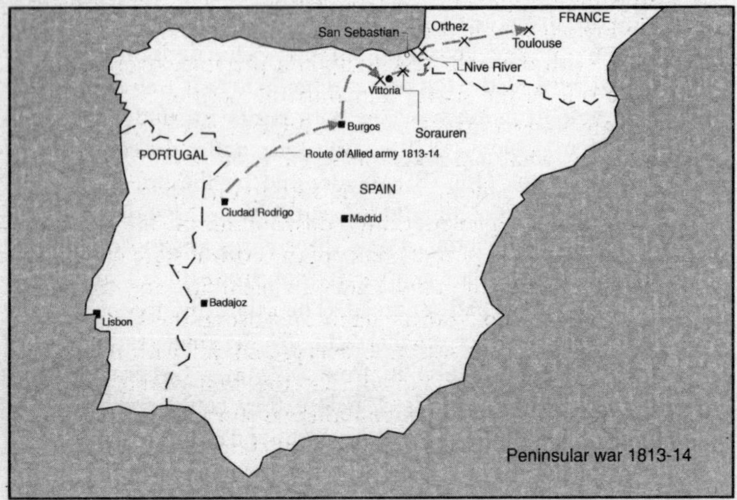

Maps of the Peninsular War 1811–12, 1813–14

service, who was wounded, Lieut. Colonel Wallace, Lieut. Colonel the Hon. R. Meade, Lieut. Colonel Sutton, of the 9th Portuguese, Major Smyth of the 45th, who was afterwards killed, Lieut. Colonel Douglas, and Major Birmingham, of the 8th Portuguese regiment, distinguished themselves.

Corporal Thomas was there in the ranks of the 43rd:

> The attack began on the following morning before day-break. Three columns were led by Ney, and two by Reynier, the points being about three miles asunder. The resistance was spirited, and six guns played along the slope with grape; but in less than half an hour the French were close upon the summit, so swiftly did they scale the mountain, overthrowing every thing that opposed their progress. The leading battalions immediately established themselves upon the higher rocks, and a confused mass wheeled to the right, intending to sweep the summit of the sierra; but at that moment Lord Wellington directed two guns to open with grape upon their flank, while a heavy musketry was poured into their front; and in a little time the 45th and 88th regiments charged so furiously that even fresh men could not have with stood them. The French, quite spent with their previous exertion, opened a straggling fire, and both parties, mingling together, went down the mountain side with mighty clamour and confusion; the dead and dying strewing the way, even to the bottom of the valley. Meanwhile the French who had first gained the summit had reformed their ranks, with the right resting upon a precipice overhanging the reverse side of the sierra; and thus the position was in fact gained, if any reserve had been at hand; but just then General Leith, who saw what had taken place, came on rapidly. Keeping the Royals in reserve, he directed the 38th to turn the right of the French; but the precipice prevented this; and meanwhile Colonel Cameron, informed by a staff officer of the critical state of affairs, formed the 9th regiment in line under a violent fire, and, without returning a single shot, ran in upon and drove the Grenadiers from the rocks with irresistible bravery, and yet with excellent discipline; refraining from pursuit, lest the crest of the position should be again lost, for the mountain was so rugged that it was impossible to judge clearly of the general state of the action.
>
> On that side, however, the victory was secure. Ney's attack was equally unsuccessful. From the abutment of the mountain on which the light division was placed, the lower parts of the valley could be discerned. The table-land was sufficiently hollow to conceal the 43d and 52d regiments, drawn up in a line; and a quarter of a mile behind them, but on higher ground, and close to the convent, a brigade of German infantry appeared to be the only solid line of resistance on this part of the position. In front of the

two British regiments, some rocks over-hanging the descent furnished natural embrasures, in which the guns of the division were placed, and the whole face of the hill was planted with the skirmishers of the Rifle Corps, and of the two Portuguese Cacadore battalions. While it was yet dark, on listening attentively, we heard a straggling musketry in the deep hollows separating the armies; and when the light broke, the three divisions of the 6th corps were observed entering the woods below, and throwing forward a profusion of skirmishers soon afterwards. The French ascended with wonderful cheerfulness, and though the light troops plied them unceasingly with musketry, and the artillery bullets swept through their ranks, the order of advance was never disturbed. Ross's guns were worked with incredible swiftness, yet their range was contracted every round, and the enemy's shot came singing up in a sharper key, until the skirmishers, breathless, and begrimed with powder, rushed over the edge of the ascent, when the artillery suddenly drew back, and the victorious cries of the French were heard within a few yards of the summit. Crauford, who, standing alone on one of the rocks, had been intently watching the progress of the attack, then turned, and in a quick shrill tone desired the two regiments in reserve to charge. The next moment 1,800 British bayonets went over the hill. Our shouts startled the French column; and yet so truly brave were the hostile leaders, that each man of the first section raised his musket, and two officers and ten men fell before them, so unerring was their aim. They could do no more: we were on them with resistless impetuosity. The head of their column was violently overturned, and driven upon the rear; both flanks were lapped over by our wings; and three terrible discharges at five yards distance completed the rout. In a few minutes a long line of carcases and broken arms indicated the line of retreat. The main body of the British stood fast, but several companies followed in pursuit down the mountain. Before two o'clock, Crauford having assented to a momentary truce, parties of both armies were mixed amicably together, searching for the wounded men. Towards evening, however, a French company having impudently seized a village within half musket-shot of our division, and refusing to retire, it so incensed Crauford, that, turning twelve guns on the village, he overwhelmed it with bullets for half an hour. A company of the 43d was then sent down, who cleared the place in a few minutes.

The Allied lines had overwhelmed the French columns. The French columns had experienced the firepower of the British and Portuguese infantry, including three volleys fired at five yards' range and charging with bayonets.

Lieutenant Charles Booth of the 43rd wrote a description a few weeks after the battle. In his description of the three volleys fired at five yards' range, he says the bayonet charge actually came before:

> the most destructive flanking fire . . . ever witnessed.
>
> In the part of the line occupied by the Light Division and about 200 yards immediately to its front two columns of the enemy – supposed about 5,000 each – were met by the two left-hand companies of the 43rd, and the right two of the 52nd. The front of their columns alone – chiefly composed of officers – stood the charge; the rest took to their heels, throwing away their arms, pouches, &c. Our men did not stand to take prisoners; what were taken were those left in our rear in the hurry of pressing forward in the charge. The flanks of the 43rd and 52nd in their charge met only the enemy's skirmishers who had by superior numbers driven in the 95th Rifles but a few seconds before the charge of the division.
>
> These poor fellows were all glad enough to give themselves up as prisoners, our men not being allowed to fire a shot at them. The advanced part of the charging line – the four companies first mentioned – after throwing themselves into the midst of the enemy's retreating columns, killing, wounding, and in short felling to the ground lots of them, were with great difficulty halted, and then commenced from the flanks of the whole division the most destructive flanking fire that I believe was ever witnessed. Not a tenth part of their whole force would have escaped had not the four companies, by precipitating themselves too far in front of the general line, exposed themselves to the fire of their comrades, and thus prevented more than 300 firelocks on each flank of the division from being brought into action. The flanks, and in fact every other part of the division (except the four centre companies), had to pass over in the charge some very steep rugged ground, where, not meeting anything but the enemy's skirmishers, they pushed on head-over-heels, until the descent became almost perpendicular. At this time they were halted, and had a fine view of what was going on in the centre.

Despite the result of the battle Wellington continued to retreat south and Massena continued to advance. Until a few days before he arrived at the Lines of Torres Vedras, Massena still had no idea of what lay ahead.

Pelet, Massena's senior aide-de-camp, is reported to have said:

> On arriving at Sobral, instead of the "undulating accessible plateaux" that we had been told to expect, we saw steeply scarped mountains and deep ravines, a road-passage only a few paces broad, and on each side walls of rock crowned with everything that could be accomplished in the way of field fortifications garnished with artillery; then at last it was plainly demonstrated to us that we could not attack the Lines of Montechique with the 35,000 or 36,000 men that still remained of the army. For, even if we had forced some point of the Lines, we should not have had enough men left to seize and occupy Lisbon.

Corporal Thomas:

> Massena was astonished at the extent and strength of works, the existence of which had only become known to him five days before he came upon them. He employed several days in examining their nature, and was as much at a loss at the end of his inspection as at the beginning. The heights of Alhandra he judged unattackable; but the valleys of Calandrix and Aruda attracted his attention. There were here frequent skirmishes with the light division to oblige Crauford to show his force; but by making Aruda an advanced post, he rendered it impossible to discover his true position without a serious affair; and in a short time the division, with prodigious labour, secured the position, in a manner which was spoken of with admiration. Across the ravine on the left, a loose stone wall, 16 feet thick, and 40 feet high, was raised: and across the great valley of Aruda, a double line of abattis was drawn; not composed, as is usual, of the limbs of trees, but of full-grown oaks and chestnuts, dug up with all their roots and branches, dragged by main force for several hundred yards, and then reset and crossed, so that no human strength could break through. Breast-works at convenient distances, to defend this line of trees, were then cast up; and along the summit of the mountain, for the space of nearly three miles, including the salient points, other stone walls, six feet high, and four in thickness, with

> banquettes, were built, so that a good defence might have been made against the attacks of 20,000 men. The increased strength of the works in general soon convinced Massena that it was impracticable to force the lines without great reinforcements; and towards the end of October the hospitals, stores, and other incumbrances of the French army, were removed to Santarem.

Wellington had insisted that the country outside the Lines of Torres Vedras be stripped of all food and supplies. Consequently, the French army would have nothing to eat or feed for its horses and animals. In November 1810, the French retreated to Santarem. By the Spring of 1811, lack of supplies and the imminent arrival of British reinforcements forced the French to retreat further. This time it was Wellington's army which pushed the French out of Portugal. Harry Smith was a lieutenant in the 95th Rifle regiment. He was acting as an Aide de Camp (ADC) to Colonel Beckwith. Colonel Sydney Beckwith was the commanding officer of Smith's battalion of the 95th Rifle regiment.

> I found the army in hourly expectation to move, and the Captain of my Company – Leach – was gone sick to the rear, so I said to my Colonel, "I must be no longer A.D.C., sir. However grateful I am, my Company wants me." "Ah, now you can walk a little, you leave me! Go and be d–d to you but I love you for the desire." Off I started, and the very next day we marched [6 March 1811], Massena retreating out of Portugal, and many is the skirmish we had. My leg was so painful, the wound open, and I was so lame. When others could lie down I was on horseback, on a dear little Spanish horse given me by James Stewart, afterwards an animal of still greater renown.

At Sabugal, the Light Division was involved in a flanking movement against the French rearguard. Corporal Thomas:

> At daylight on 8 April our nearness to the enemy indicated the approach of another collision. The English General, having 10,000 men pivoted on the 5th Division at Sabugal, designed to turn Reynier's left, and surround him before he could be succoured. This well-concerted plan was marred by one of those accidents to which war is always liable, and brought on the combat of Sabugal, one of the hottest in which I was ever engaged.

The morning was so foggy that the troops could not gain their respective posts of attack with that simultaneous regularity which is so essential to success. Colonel Beckwith, who commanded the first brigade, halted at a ford to await orders, and at that moment a staff-officer rode up, and somewhat hastily asked why he did not attack. The thing appeared rash; but with an enemy in front he could make no reply; and instantly passing the river, which was deep and rapid, mounted a steep wooded hill on the other side. Many of the men were up to their middle in water; and a dark heavy rain coming on, it was impossible for some time to distinguish friends from foes. The attack was thus made too soon; for owing to the obscurity, none of the divisions of the army had reached their respective posts; and Beckwith having only one bayonet regiment, and four companies of Riflemen, was advancing against more than 12,000 infantry supported by cavalry and artillery. Scarcely had the Riflemen reached the top of the hill, when a compact and strong body of French drove them back upon the 43d. The weather cleared at that instant, and Beckwith at once saw and felt all his danger; but, well-supported as he was, it was met with a heart that nothing could shake. Leading a fierce charge, he beat back the enemy, and the summit of the hill was attained; but at the same moment two French guns opened with grape, at the distance of a hundred yards: a fresh body appeared in front, and considerable forces upon either flank of the regiment. Fortunately, Reynier, little expecting to be attacked, had, for the convenience of water, placed his principal masses in the low ground, behind the height on which the action commenced; his renewed attack was therefore uphill; yet the musketry, heavy from the beginning, now increased to a storm. The French mounted the acclivity with great clamour; and it was evident that nothing but the most desperate fighting could save the regiment from destruction. Captain Hopkins, commanding a flank company of the 43d, immediately ran out to the right, and with admirable presence of mind seized a small eminence close to the French guns and commanding the ascent by which the French troops were approaching. His first fire was so sharp that the assailants were thrown into confusion: they rallied, and were again confounded by the volleys of this company: a third time they endeavoured to form an attack, when Hopkins, with a sudden charge, increased the disorder; and at the same moment the two battalions of the 52d regiment, which had been attracted by the fire, entered the line. Meantime the centre and left of the 43rd were furiously engaged, and excited beyond all former precedent. Beckwith, wounded in the head, and with the blood streaming down his face, rode amongst the foremost of the skirmishers, directing all with ability, and praising the men in a loud, cheerful tone. I was close to him at the time. One of our company called out, "Old Sydney is wounded." Beckwith heard the remark, and instantly replied, "But he won't leave you: fight on, my brave fellows; we shall beat them." The musket bullets flew thicker and closer every instant; but the French fell fast: a second charge cleared the hill, a howitzer was taken, and the British skirmishers were even advanced a short way down the hill, when small bodies of French cavalry came galloping in from all parts, and obliged them to take refuge in the main body of the regiment. Having brought down a Frenchman by a random shot, I advanced close to the poor fellow as he lay on his side. Never shall I forget the alarm that was pictured on his countenance: he thought I was going to bayonet him, to avert which he held out his knapsack, containing most likely all his worldly substance, by way of appeasing my wrath. Unwilling to injure a fallen foe, I did not take his life, and in a few seconds he was protected by a charge of cavalry.

Harry Smith was acting as a company commander before Sabugal:

In a few days, as we had got well up to the French rear-guard and were about to attack, a General Order was received, to my astonishment, appointing me Brigade Major to the 2nd Light Brigade, not dear old Sydney's. He expected it, since he and Colonel Pakenham (dear Sir Edward!) were trying to do something for me on account of my lame leg. Beckwith says, "Now give your Company over to Layton, and set off immediately to Colonel Drummond," who commanded the Brigade. Hardly had I reached it, when such a cannonade commenced, knocking the 52nd about in a way I never saw before and hardly since. We were soon all engaged, and drove the French, with very hard fighting, into and over the river, with a severe loss in killed, prisoners, and drowned.

A very heavy fight it was, ending just before dark. I said to my Brigadier, "Have you any orders for the picquets, sir?" He was an old Guardsman, the kindest though oddest fellow possible. "Pray, Mr Smith, are you my Brigade Major?" "I believe so, sir." "Then let me tell you, it is your duty to post the picquets, and mine to have a d–d good dinner for you every day." We soon understood each other. He cooked the dinner often himself, and I commanded the Brigade.

Our next great fight was a bitter one, Sabugal [3 April]. I shall never forget the German 1st Hussars, my old friends, moving on that day; their singing was melodious. Sir W. Erskine commanded the cavalry and Light Division, a near-sighted old ass, and we got meléed with Reynier's corps d'armee strongly posted on heights above Sabugal, and attacked when the Duke intended we should have moved round their left to Quadraseyes, as the 5th, 4th, and 3rd Divisions were to attack their front in the centre of their position. However, we began, and never was more gallantry mutually displayed by friend and foe than on this occasion, particularly by dear old Beckwith and his 1st Brigade. Some guns were taken and retaken several times. A French officer on a grey horse was most gallant. Old Beckwith, in a voice like thunder, roared out to the Riflemen, "Shoot that fellow, will you?" In a moment he and his horse were knocked over, and Sydney exclaimed, "Alas! you were a noble fellow."

My Brigadier, as I soon discovered, left the command to me, so I led away, and we came in for a pretty good share in preventing Reynier's turning the left of Beckwith's Brigade. Fortunately, the 5th Division got into action just in time, for the French at the moment were squeezing us awfully. The Light Division, under the shout of old Beckwith, rushed on with an impetuosity nothing could resist, for, so checked had we been, our bloods were really up, and we paid off the enemy most awfully. Such a scene of slaughter as there was on one hill would appal a modern soldier. The night came on most awfully wet, and the 5th and Light Division were sent back to Sabugal for shelter. Most dilapidated the place was, but the roofs were on, and Sir W. Gomm, A.Q.M.G. of the 5th, and I divided the town between us, our poor wounded lying out in the rain and cold all night. The next morning was fine, and as the sun rose we marched over the field of battle. Our soldiers' blood was then cool, and it was beautiful to hear the remarks of sympathy for the distress of the numerous dying and wounded all around us. Oh, you kings and usurpers should view these scenes and moderate ambition!

On 3 and 5 May 1811 Massena counter attacked at Fuentes de Onoro.

John Kincaid was a lieutenant in the 2nd battalion of the 95th Rifles. He had arrived in the peninsula in the spring of 1810. The Light Division was sent to support the 7th Division which had become separated from the rest of the allied army:

The day began to dawn, this fine May morning, with a rattling fire of musketry on the extreme right of our position, which the enemy had attacked, and to which point our division was rapidly moved.

Our battalion was thrown into a wood, a little to the left and front of the division engaged, and was instantly warmly opposed to the French skirmishers; in the course of which I was struck with a musket-ball on the left breast, which made me stagger a yard or two backward, and, as I felt no pain, I concluded that I was dangerously wounded; but it turned out to be owing to my not being hurt. While our operations here were confined to a tame skirmish, and our view to the oaks with which we were mingled, we found, by the evidence of our ears, that the division which we had come to support was involved in a more serious onset, for there was the successive rattle of artillery, the wild hurrah of charging squadrons, and the repulsing volley of musketry; until Lord Wellington, finding his right too much extended, directed the 7th division to fall back behind the small river Turones, and ours to join the main body of the army. The execution of our movement presented a magnificent military spectacle, as the plain, between us and the right of the army, was by this time in the possession of the French cavalry, and, while we were retiring through it with the order and precision of a common field-day, they kept dancing around us, and every instant threatening a charge, without daring to execute it.

We took up our new position at a right angle of the then right of the British line, on which our left rested, and with our right on the Turones. The enemy followed our movement with a heavy column of infantry; but when they came near enough to exchange shots they did not seem to like our looks, as we occupied a low ridge of broken rocks, against which even a rat could scarcely have hoped to advance alive; and they again fell back, and opened a tremendous fire of artillery, which was returned by a battery of our guns. In the course of a short time, seeing no further demonstration against this part of the position, our division was withdrawn, and placed in reserve in rear of the centre.

The battle continued to rage with fury in and about Fuentes, whilst we were lying by our arms under a burning sun, some stray cannon-shot passing over and about us, whose progress we watched for want of other employment.

The allied cavalry were also involved in supporting the Light and 7th Divisions. Francis Hall was an officer in the 14th Light Dragoons at Fuentes de Onoro:

I had been carrying a message when the first charge took place, and returned in the midst of the melée. It was literally "auferre, trudidare, rapere." Horses whose riders had been killed or overthrown ran wildly across the field or lay panting in their blood. The general recontre was sub-divided into partial combats. Two heavy Dragoons were in the act of felling a Chasseur with their broad swords; his chaco [shako] resisted several blows, but he at length dropped. Another was hanging in the stirrup, while his horse was hurried off by a German Hussar, eager to plunder his valise. Some were driving two or three slashed prisoners to the rear: one wretch was dragged on foot between two Dragoons, but as he was unable to keep pace with their horses, and the enemy were now forming for a second charge, he was cut down.

We again formed in line, and a second charge was led on by Captain Brotherton . . . He rode at the French officer, who was in front of his men, but the latter made a few steps on one side and politely let him pass. We were soon completely intermixed. Our men had evidently the advantage as individuals. Their broad swords, ably wielded, flashed over the Frenchmen's heads, and obliged them to cower to their saddle bows. The alarm was, indeed, greater than the hurt, for their cloaks were so well rolled across their left shoulders, that it was no easy matter to give a mortal stroke with the broad edge of a sabre, whereas their swords, which were straight and pointed, though their effect on the eyes was less formidable, were capable of inflicting a much severer wound. Many, however, turned their horses, and our men shouted in the pursuit; but it was quite clear that, go which way they might, we were but scattered drops amid their host, and could not possibly arrest their progress. We again, therefore, went about, and retired towards the Guards, who were formed in squares on the right of our line of infantry.

Massena had failed to re-conquer Portugal. He was replaced by Marshal Marmont. In southern Spain Marshal Soult advanced northwards to join forces with Marmont. He was intercepted at Albuera by a British–Portuguese force under Beresford. Soult retreated after Albuera. Although Soult remained a threat he was unable to achieve anything during the rest of 1811.

On 8 January 1812, Wellington began to advance into Spain. He needed to capture two fortress towns on the Portuguese border. The first of these towns was Ciudad Rodrigo. Corporal Thomas:

> The new year opened with uncommon effort on the side of the British forces in Spain. Lord Wellington, whose means of collecting information were extensive and correct, had discovered that a considerable reduction had taken place in the French army. The Imperial Guards, 17,000 strong, were required for the Russian war, and had returned to France; so that the force in the Peninsula was diminished by 60,000 men. Marmont was also deceived by what appeared to him the careless winter attitude of the allies, and Ciudad Rodrigo was left unprotected.

Harry Smith:

> The siege was carried on by four Divisions: the 1st, 3rd, 4th, and Light, cantoned as near Ciudad Rodrigo as possible. One Division was on duty at a time, and each had to ford the Agueda the day it was for duty. The Light was at El Bodon. We had a distance of nine miles to march every fourth day, and back on the fifth, so that we had only three days' halt. The frost was excessive, and there was some little snow, but fortunately the weather was fine above head.
>
> The Light Division stormed the little breach on the evening of 19 January (nine o'clock). I was supping with my dear friend Captain Uniacke, and brother Tom, his only subaltern not wounded. When I parted from Uniacke he was a noble, light-hearted fellow – he says, "Harry, you will be a Captain before morning." Little, poor fellow, did he think he was to make the vacancy. I was senior subaltern of the 95th, and I went to General Craufurd and volunteered the forlorn hope that was given to Gurwood. Craufurd said, "Why, you cannot go; you, a Major of Brigade, a senior Lieutenant, you are sure to get a Company. No, I must give it to a younger officer." This was to me a laborious

night. Just as my Brigade had to march, I discovered the Engineer officer had not brought up the ladders, fascines, and bundles of hay, and old George Simmons was sent for them.

In ascending the breach, I got on a ravelin at the head of the 43rd and 52nd, moving in column together. Colborne pulled me down again, and up the right breach we ascended. I saw the great breach, stormed by the 3rd Division, was ably defended, and a line behind a work which, as soon as we rushed along the ramparts, we could enfilade. I seized a Company of the 43rd and rushed on the flank, and opened a fire which destroyed every man behind the works. My conduct caused great annoyance to the Captain, Duffy, with whom I had some very high words; but the Company obeyed me, and then ran on with poor Uniacke's Company to meet the 3rd Division, or rather clear the ramparts to aid them, when the horrid explosion took place which killed General Mackinnon of the 3rd Division on the spot and many soldiers, awfully scorching others. I and Uniacke were much scorched, but some splinters of an ammunition chest lacerated him and caused his death three days after the storm. Tom, my brother, was not hurt.

I shall never forget the concussion when it struck me, throwing me back many feet into a lot of charged fuses of shells, which in the confusion I took for shells. But a gallant fellow, a Sergeant MacCurrie, 52nd Regiment, soon put me right, and prevented me leaping into the ditch. My cocked hat was blown away, my clothes all singed; however the sergeant, a noble fellow, lent me a catskin forage-cap, and on we rushed to meet the 3rd Division, which we soon did. It was headed by a great, big thundering Grenadier of the 88th, a Lieutenant Stewart, and one of his men seized me by the throat as if I were a kitten, crying out, "You French—." Luckily, he left me room in the windpipe to d—his eyes, or the bayonet would have been through me in a moment. Gurwood got great credit here unfairly. Willie Johnstone and poor Uniacke were the two first on the ramparts, Gurwood having been knocked down in the breach and momentarily stunned, which enabled them to get before him. However, Gurwood's a sharp fellow, and he cut off in search of the Governor, and brought his sword to the Duke, and Lord Fitzroy Somerset buckled it on him in the breach. Gurwood made the most of it.

Corporal Thomas was also in the assault on 19 January 1812:

All the troops reached their different posts without seeming to attract the attention of the enemy; but before the signal was given, and while Lord Wellington was still at the convent of Francisco, the attack on the right commenced, and was instantly taken up along the whole line. The space between the army and the ditch was then ravaged by a tempest of grape from the ramparts. The storming parties of the third division jumped out of the parallel when the first shout arose; but so rapid had been the movements on their right, that before they could reach the ditch, three regiments had already scoured the fausse-braye, and were pushing up the great breach, amid the bursting of shells, the whistling of grape and muskets, and the shrill cries of the French, who were driven fighting behind the retrenchments. There, however, they rallied, and, aided by the musketry from the houses, made hard battle for their post; none would go back on either side, and yet the British could not get forward; and men and officers, falling in heaps, choked up the passage, which was incessantly raked with grape from two guns flanking the top of the breach at the distance of a few yards. It was now our turn. We had 300 yards to clear; but, impatient of delay, we did not wait for the hay-bags, but swiftly ran to the crest of the glacis, jumped down the scarp, a depth of eleven feet, and rushed up the faussebraye, under a smashing discharge of grape and musketry. The bottom of the ditch was dark and intricate, and the forlorn hope took too much to their left; but the storming party went straight to the breach, which was so contracted, that a gun placed lengthwise across the top nearly blocked up the opening. Here the forlorn hope rejoined the stormers; but when two-thirds of the ascent were gained, the leading men, crushed together by the narrowness of the place, staggered under the weight of the enemy's fire. Our Commander, Major Napier, was at this moment struck to the earth by a grapeshot, which shattered his arm, but he called on his men to trust to their bayonets; and all the officers simultaneously sprang to the front, when the charge was renewed with a furious shout, and the entrance was gained. The supporting regiments then came up in sections abreast, and the place was won. During the contest, which lasted only for a few minutes after the fausse-braye was passed, the fighting had continued at the great breach with unabated violence; but when the 43d, and the stormers of the light division, came pouring down on the right flank of the French, the latter yielded to the storm; at the same moment

> the explosion of three wall-magazines destroyed many persons, and the third division with a mighty effort broke through the retrenchments. The garrison fought for a short time in the streets, but finally fled to the castle, where an officer, who, though wounded, had been amongst the foremost at the lesser breach, received the Governor's sword. The allies now plunged into the streets from all quarters; after which, throwing off the restraints of discipline, frightful excesses were committed. The town was fired in three or four places; the soldiers menaced their officers, and shot each other; many were killed in the market-place; intoxication soon increased the disorder; and at last, the fury rising to an absolute madness, a fire was wilfully lighted in the middle of the great magazine, when the town, and all in it, would have been blown to atoms, but for the energetic courage of some officers and a few soldiers, who still preserved their senses. 300 French had fallen; 1,500 were made prisoners; and beside the immense store of ammunition, above 150 pieces of artillery were captured in the place. The whole loss of the allies was about 1,200 soldiers, and 90 officers; and of these above 650 men, and 60 officers, had been slain or hurt in the breaches. General Crauford and General Mackinnon were killed.

General Crauford had been the outstanding commander of the Light Brigade which had been expanded into the Light Division. He was replaced as commander of the Light Division by General Count Alten of the King's German Legion.

The Siege of Badajoz 17 March–6 April 1812

Wellington marched south to Badajoz. Badajoz was much larger than Ciudad Rodrigo and preparations for an assault took longer. The garrison was nearly 5,000 strong. Badajoz had already successfully withstood two sieges. Its walls were 50 feet high. Each angle was protected by a strong fortification. These fortifications were called bastions. In front of the fortifications was a glacis. This was a slope which could make solid shot bounce harmlessly. On the glacis were Ravellins. These were triangular structures designed to split up and confuse the attacking troops. In front of the glacis was a wide ditch. When the bombardment began, the garrison replied with artillery

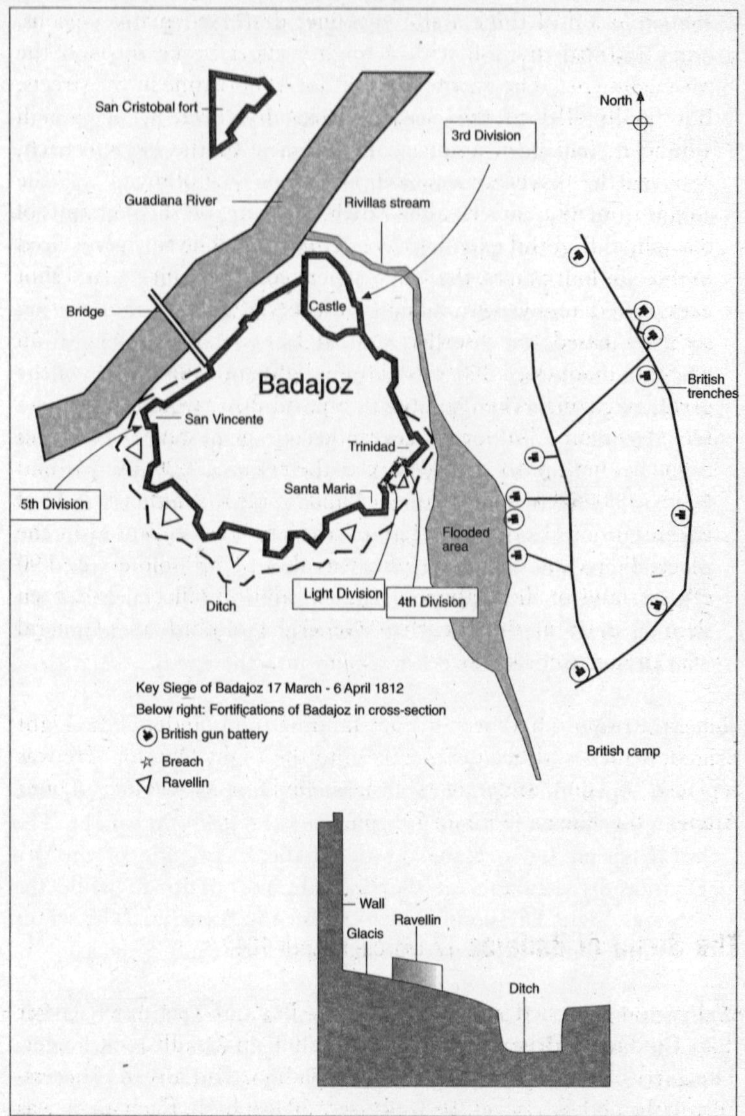

Map of the siege of Badajoz

fire to interfere with the heavy artillery which was trying to knock down enough wall to make breaches. Before the infantry could attack through the breaches, they had to dig trenches and build gun emplacements.

Rifleman Edward Costello described working in the trenches around Badajoz:

> The greatest annoyance we experienced during the siege arose from the shells thrown at us from the town. Our works effectually screened us from the round-shot; but these dangerous missiles, falling into the trenches where we worked, and exploding, frequently did great mischief. Immediately a shell fell, every man threw himself flat upon the ground until it had burst. Tom Crawley, I remember, though tolerably fearless with reference to other shot, had a most inveterate dislike to those deadly visitors. His fears made him believe that more of them were thrown where he chanced to be than in any other part of the trenches. At night, in particular, Tom was always on the *qui vive*: as soon as he beheld a shell coming he would call out, "Here's another brute – lookout!" and instantly fall on his face. This, however, did not always protect us, for the head was no sooner on the ground, than its presence was again required, to watch the falling splinters. These, from their composing large portions of the metal of the missile, descended with great violence, and were sometimes of themselves sufficient to crush a man into the earth.

Kincaid wrote:

> On 6 April three practicable breaches had been effected, and arrangements were made for assaulting the town that night. The 3rd Division by escalade, at the castle; a brigade of the 5th Division by escalade, at the opposite side of town; while the 4th and Light Divisions were to storm the breaches. The whole were ordered to be formed for the attack at eight o'clock.

The breaches were between the Santa Maria and Trinidad bastions.

In the assault, Rifleman Costello had to help carry a ladder and a "grass-bag". The "grass-bag" was to help the attackers to get across the ditch.

> A Sergeant Fleming coming up, informed Major O'Hare that a ladder party was wanted. "Take the right files of the leading sections," was the prompt order of the Major. No sooner said than done, I and my front-rank men were immediately tapped on the shoulder for the ladder party. I now gave up all hope of ever

returning. At Rodrigo, as before stated, we had fatigue parties for the ladders, but now the case was altered; besides which the ladders, now in preparation, were much longer than those employed at that fortress.

The word was now given to the ladder party to move forward. We were accompanied at each side by two men with hatchets to cut down any obstacle that might oppose them, such as chevaux-de-frise.

There were six of us supporting the ladder allotted to me, and I contrived to carry my grass-bag before me. We had proceeded but a short distance when we heard the sound of voices on our right, upon which we halted and, supposing they might be enemies, I disengaged myself from the ladder and, cocking my rifle, prepared for action. Luckily we soon discovered our mistake, as one of our party cried, – "Take care! "Tis the stormers of the 4th division coming to join us." This proved to be the case. This brief alarm over, we continued advancing towards the walls, the Rifles, as before, keeping in front. We had to pass Fort San Roche on our left, near to the tower, and as we approached it the French sentry challenged. This was instantly followed by a shot from the fort and another from the walls of the town. A moment afterwards, a fire-ball was thrown out, which threw a bright red glare of light around us, and instantly a volley of grapeshot, canister, and small arms poured in among us as we stood on the glacis, at a distance of about 30 yards from the walls.

Corporal Thomas was also in the main assault on the breaches:

On 3 April it was evident that crisis of the siege drew nigh. The British guns being all turned against the curtain, the masonry crumbled rapidly away; in two hours a yawning breach appeared; and Lord Wellington, having examined the points of attack in person, gave the order for assault. The soldiers then made themselves ready for the approaching combat, one of the most fierce and terrible ever exhibited in the annals of war.

We were now selected and classified for the actual assault. The difficulty was not to procure men enough, but how to refuse applications, for all were ready. Nor were these offers founded in ignorance of the nature of the expected service; the candidates were not such novices. The watch-word of Nelson was not forgotten – "England expects every man to do his duty" – and the resolution which everywhere prevailed was entered into with a thorough consciousness that life was then scarcely worth an hour's purchase. And yet every countenance was bright, for every heart was firm; and it was clear that the elevation and strength of mind so universally prevalent, was the effect of principle, well considered, and approved. Indeed, there was no stimulus at hand to produce superficial excitement; no drops of Scheidam to generate Dutch courage the men were kept in the utmost silence and order. It is true, here and there a soldier might be perceived stealing from the trenches, with a little refreshment in his canteen for the friend with whom he was to part; and in return, more than one message, the last to be delivered on earth, was sent from many a brave man to mother, wife, or some other valued relative, with directions that if killed, the knapsack of a certain number, with its contents, should be duly forwarded. The night was dry, but clouded; the air thick with watery exhalations from the river; the ramparts and the trenches were unusually still, yet a low murmur pervaded the latter, and in the former, lights were seen to flit here and there; while the deep voices of the sentinels at times proclaimed that all was well in Badajos. The French, confiding in Phillipon's direful skill, watched from their lofty station the approach of enemies, whom they had twice before baffled, and now hoped to drive a third time, blasted and ruined, from the walls. At ten o'clock the whole of the works were to have been simultaneously assailed, and it was hoped that the strength of the enemy would shrivel before this fiery girdle; but the disappointments of war are many. An unforeseen accident delayed the attack of the 5th Division; and a lighted carcass thrown from the castle falling close to where the men of the 3rd Division were drawn up, discovered their array, and obliged them to anticipate the signal by half an hour. Then, every thing being suddenly disturbed, the double columns of the 4th and Light Divisions also moved silently and swiftly against the breaches; and the guard of the trenches, rushing forward with a shout, encompassed the San Roque with fire, and broke in so violently that scarcely any resistance was made. General Kempt passed the Rivellas in single files by a narrow bridge, under a terrible musketry; and then reforming and running up the rugged hill, had reached the foot of the castle, when he fell severely wounded, and being carried back to the trenches, met Picton, who hastened forward to take the command. Meanwhile his troops spreading along the front reared their ladders, some against the lofty castle, some against the adjoining front on the left, and with incredible courage ascended amidst showers of heavy stones, logs of wood, and bursting shells rolled off the parapet; while from the flanks the enemy plied his musketry with fearful rapidity, and in front with pikes and bayonets stabbing the leading assailants, or pushed the ladders from the walls; and all this attended with deafening shouts, and the crash of breaking ladders, and the shriek of soldiers crushed by violent falls. Still, swarming round the remaining ladders, these undaunted veterans strove who should first climb; until all being overturned, the French shouted victory, and the British, baffled but untamed, fell back a few paces, and took shelter under the rugged edge of the hill. Here, when the broken ranks were somewhat reformed, the heroic Colonel Ridge, springing forward, called with stentorian voice on his men to follow; and, seizing a ladder, once more raised it against the castle, yet to the right of the former attack, where the wall was lower, and an embrasure offered some facility. A second ladder was soon placed alongside the first by the Grenadier officer Canch; and the next instant he and Ridge were on the rampart: the shouting troops pressed after them; the garrison, amazed, and in a manner surprised, were driven fighting through the double gate into the town, and the castle was won. A reinforcement sent from the French reserve then came up, a sharp action followed, both sides fired through the gate, and the enemy retired; but Ridge fell, and no man died that night with greater honour.

During these events, the tumult at the breaches was such, as if the very earth had been rent asunder, and its central fires were bursting up uncontrolled. The two divisions had reached the glacis in silence; as yet no stir was heard, and darkness covered the breaches. Some hay-packs were then thrown, several ladders placed, and the forlorn hopes and storming parties of the light division, about 500 in all, had descended into the ditch without opposition, when a bright flame shooting upwards displayed all the terror of the scene. The ramparts, crowded with dark figures, and glittering arms, were on the one side; and on the other the red columns of the British, deep and broad, were coming on like streams of burning lava. A crash immediately followed, and the storming parties were dashed to pieces with incredible violence by the explosion of hundreds of shells and powder barrels. The place which fell to my lot was just in the centre of this hurly-burly. With what similitude to illustrate our condition at that moment, I know not. The regular discharge of musketry at given distances, and the usual clash of arms, in field-warfare, is rather rough, to say the least of it; but the collision of hostile forces in open space, where the combatants may evade approaching ruin, is civil pastime compared with this deadly ditch-conflict. Each of the men fought as if the issue of the assault depended on his single arm. As to timidity, the thing was unknown: every drum-boy acted well. Shielded by Eternal Mercy, all undeserving as I was, my life was preserved. Not that it then appeared even to myself worth consideration. All thought of self-protection was banished from the corps in general. Every nerve and muscle was strained to the utmost tension in the struggle; among the whole body there appeared to be only one heart; and in the attempt to reach the ramparts all other considerations merged. But what an assemblage of furies; the excitement was indescribable. Fancying that the man immediately behind myself did not press forward with sufficient energy, I turned round, and with imprecations of which the bare remembrance causes regret, I declared that if he did not push on I would shoot him. Most likely I was wrong, not only in language but in opinion: I have since thought the man did his best but in the raging of such a tempest, mistakes were easily made, and the mere notion of defective effort ignited the passions.

For one instant we stood on the brink of the ditch, amazed at the terrific sight; then with a shout that matched even the sound of the explosion, the men flew down the ladders, or, disdaining their aid, leaped, unmindful of the depth, into the gulf below. The fourth division came running after, and followed with like fury: there were, however, only five ladders for both columns, which were close together; and a deep cut made in the bottom of the ditch as far as the counter-guard of the Trinidad was filled with water from the inundation; into this watery snare the head of the fourth division fell, and it is said that above 100 of the Fusileers, the men of Albuera, were there smothered. Great was the confusion at this juncture; for now the ravelin was crowded with men of both divisions, and while some continued to fire, others ran down and jumped towards the breach; many also passed between the ravelin and the counter-guard of the Trinidad; the two divisions got mingled; and the reserves, who should have remained at the quarries, also came pouring in, until the ditch was quite filled – the rear still crowding forward, and all cheering vehemently. The enemy's shouts were also loud and terrible; and

> the bursting of shells and of grenades, the roaring of the guns from the flanks, answered by the iron howitzers from the battery of the parallel, the heavy rolls and explosion of the powder-barrels, the flight of the blazing splinters, the loud exhortations of the officers, and the continued clatter of the muskets, made a maddening din.

At midnight Lord Wellington ordered the main assaulting force to retreat from the ditch for a second assault. He knew, by then, that the Castle had been captured and wished to ensure that the garrison would be unable to hold out in the town itself. The 5th Division was assaulting another bastion, that of San Vincente. They had managed to get onto the ramparts and were able to advance into the town. French troops were sent to oppose them, weakening the defence at the breaches. The men of the 4th and Light Divisions continued to attack there. Corporal Thomas was wounded:

> At length the French were beaten back, other parties entered the place and finally, General Viellande, and Phillipon, who was wounded, seeing all ruined, passed the bridge with a few hundred soldiers, and entered San Cristoval, where they all surrendered early the next morning, upon summons, to Lord Somerset, who had with great readiness pushed through the town to the drawbridge before they had time to organize further resistance.
>
> In these protracted conflicts many of the finest soldiers in the British army met their fate, and fell in the firm and vigorous discharge of their duty. Of these, numbers might have been preserved had they chosen to have fallen back; but it was with them a point of honour to gain the breach or die on the spot. So wonderful is the resolution of a noble heart; and so much the more is it to be regretted, that power, so morally invincible, should be employed in the sad purpose of human destruction. For my own part, my mind had been unhesitatingly made up from the first shot that was fired, that so long as life and consciousness continued, I would fulfil my commission to the best of my ability. As the battle grew hot I caught the contagion that burned all around, and in this desperate and murderous mood advanced to the breach of Trinidad. My pride perhaps wanted to be repressed; and while in the act of marching, I was wounded in the left thigh by a musket-shot, which remains unextracted to this day, and will probably go with me to the grave. At first, not disposed to heed the

casualty, I affected to despise such a trifle, and continued to fight on. Nature, however, refused her support; and after firing a few times, I felt myself getting weak and feverish. What rendered my situation worse, was, that at that precise moment the report of an unexpected sally of the French was circulated. Had that been realized, my doom would have been sealed, as I could neither resist nor retreat. In this condition, faint with loss of blood, I contrived to descend into the ditch with the help of my musket. Meanwhile the depth of water by some added inundation had been increased, and no ladder was to be discovered for my ascent on the opposite side. Unwilling to die there, I made another effort, and at length observed a ladder standing in front of the ditch. Unable to get up with my musket, I reluctantly left that behind, and scrambled up with extreme difficulty. Numerous shots were fired at me while ascending, and I perceived bullets whistling through the rounds of the ladder, but not one of them struck me. But I was sadly grieved at the loss of my musket: it had been a faithful friend to me: I seldom knew it to fail in the hour of need: the number on it was 77. Having succeeded in gaining the summit, I found, to my surprise, a young man belonging to the gallant Napier's company, who kindly offered his arm, and supported me to the field-hospital. May the Almighty think upon and reward this timely benefactor! He was amongst the bravest where all were brave, and, though unhurt, had stood in the forefront and pinnacle at the severest point of strife. With so large an influx of patients, it will be supposed that the hospital attentions were not very prompt: I was placed on the ground, with many others in a worse condition than myself; to await my turn for surgical assistance. After some hours I found that unless my wound ceased bleeding I should not long survive: this, with a little contrivance, I managed to effect. But the most intolerable sensation was that of raging thirst: all my worldly substance, ten times valued, would have been no price at all for a draught of water. Meantime the frost was so severe that my limbs appeared to be deprived of flexibility and motion. In the course of the night, hearing a deep moan at a little distance, I called out, "Who is there?" and was answered, "It's me, Tom." The voice was familiar, and I found it was that of Patrick Murphy, an old comrade and countryman, in Dalzell's company, who had fought most nobly through several campaigns. He had been miserably burnt while endeavouring to force the breach, and suffered extremely. In the course of a day or two we were placed in military spring-waggons, and conveyed to Elvas. We were afterwards transferred to bullock-carts: a mode of conveyance not remarkable either for comfort or speed; the carriages were clumsily constructed, and ensured very little in the way of easy riding; added to which, we moved only at the rate of about one mile an hour.

Thomas recovered. He was sent home and promoted to sergeant in the second (home) battalion of his regiment, the 43rd. Like most British regiments, the 43rd had only two battalions. The first was the active service battalion. The second battalion stayed at home to raise and train recruits. These were then sent to the first battalion as reinforcements. He finally retired from the army in 1823.

The French forces in Spain still far outnumbered Wellington's army but he was able to advance because most of them were spread out trying to contain Spanish regular and guerilla forces all over the country. On 17 June Wellington's army entered the university town of Salamanca. Only Marmont's army was in the vicinity. The two armies maneouvred for several weeks trying to get some kind of tactical advantage.

The Battle of Salamanca 22 July, 1812

On 22 July Marmont tried to outflank Wellington. Wellington noticed that Marmont's leading corps had got far enough ahead of the others to leave a gap which he could exploit. He immediately ordered the Third Division to attack, supported by a brigade of heavy cavalry. In his official despatch he wrote:

The extension of his line to his left, however, and its advance upon our right, notwithstanding that his troops still occupied very strong ground, and his position was well defended by cannon, gave me an opportunity of attacking him, for which I had long been anxious. I reinforced our right with the 5th Division, under Lieut. General Leith, which I placed behind the village of Arapiles, on the right of the 4th Division, and with the 6th and 7th Divisions in reserve; and as soon as these troops had taken their station, I ordered Major General the Hon. E. Pakenham to move forward with the 3rd Division and General D'Urban's cavalry,

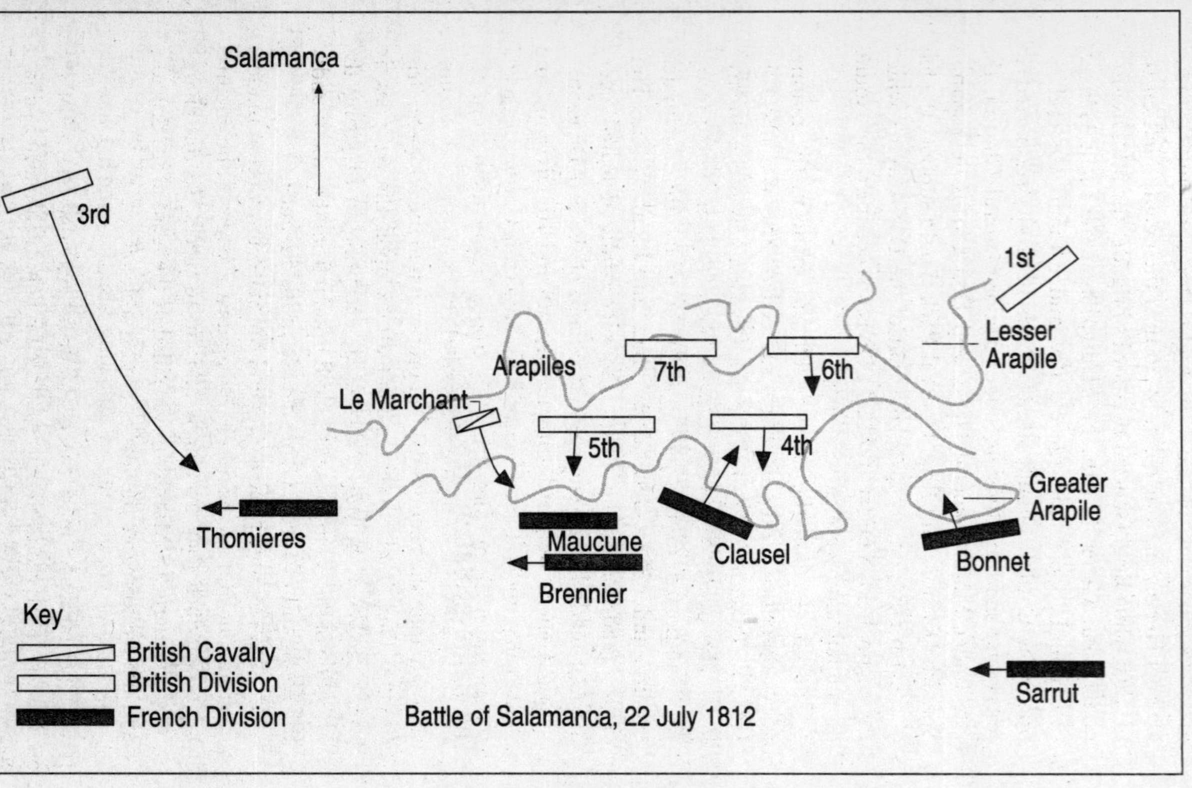

Map of the Battle of Salamanca

and two squadrons of the 14th Light Dragoons, under Lieut. Colonel Hervey, in four columns, to turn the enemy's left on the heights; while Brig. General Bradford's brigade, the 5th Division, under Lieut. General Leith, the 4th division, under Lieut. General the Hon. L. Cole, and the cavalry under Lieut. General Sir Stapleton Cotton, should attack them in front, supported in reserve by the 6th Division, under Major General Clinton, the 7th, under Major General Hope, and Don Carlos de España's Spanish Division; and Brig. General Pack should support the left of the 4th Division, by attacking that of the Dos Arapiles which the enemy held. The 1st and Light Divisions occupied the ground on the left, and were in reserve.

The attack upon the enemy's left was made in the manner above described, and completely succeeded. Major General the Hon. E. Pakenham formed the 3rd Division across the enemy's flank, and overthrew every thing opposed to him. These troops were supported in the most gallant style by the Portuguese cavalry, under Brig. General D'Urban, and Lieut. Colonel Hervey's squadrons of the 14th, who successfully defeated every attempt made by the enemy on the flank of the 3rd Division.

Brig. General Bradford's brigade, the 5th and 4th Divisions, and the cavalry under Lieut. General Sir Stapleton Cotton, attacked the enemy in front, and drove his troops before them from one height to another, bringing forward their right, so as to acquire strength upon the enemy's flank in proportion to the advance. Brig. General Pack made a very gallant attack upon the Arapiles, in which, however, he did not succeed, excepting in diverting the attention of the enemy's corps placed upon it from the troops under the command of Lieut. General Cole in his advance.

The cavalry under Lieut. General Sir Stapleton Cotton made a most gallant and successful charge against a body of the enemy's infantry, which they overthrew and cut to pieces. In this charge Major General Le Marchant was killed at the head of his brigade; and I have to regret the loss of a most able officer.

It was, perhaps, the most successful British cavalry charge of the entire war. It arrived in time to rout the French. Lieutenant William Bragg of the 3rd King's Own Dragoons was in the charge:

I escaped perfectly sound, Wind and Limb, together with the Little Bay Mare who carried me through the Day delightfully and

I believe to her Speed and Activity I may in a great measure attribute my marvellous escape, as I at one Time had to gallop along the whole Front of a French Brigade retreating in double quick step.

. . . Lord Wellington gave the Signal for a general Attack . . . Immediately upon this, our Right and Left turned theirs, the Enemy were driven from the Hills and the Cavalry advanced upon the Backs of the Infantry. Our Brigade literally rode over the Regiments in their Front and dashed through the Wood at a Gallop, the Infantry cheering us in all Directions. We quickly came up with the French Columns and charged their Rear. Hundreds threw down their Arms, their Cavalry ran away, and most of the Artillery jumped upon the Horses and followed the Cavalry. One or two charges mixed up the whole Brigade, it being impossible to see for Dust and Smoak, but this kind of Attack – so novel and unexpected – threw the French into confusion and gave our Infantry Time to get another Battle at them, when they served it out nicely, making them fly in all directions. We lost our General in a square of Infantry and in him we have experienced a severe Loss. One Lieut. was killed by his side, but in other respects our Loss is trifling considering we were solely engaged with Infantry and Artillery. The Brigade marched off nine Pieces of Artillery and about 500 Prisoners.

Another officer, Lieutenant Norcliffe Norcliffe of the 4th Dragoons, told a similar story of the same charge in a letter dated 10 August 1812:

We were pursuing the French Infantry, which were broken and running in all directions. I was cutting them down as well as I could, when in the hurry and confusion I lost my regiment and got with some soldiers of the 5th Dragoon Guards; on looking behind me, I could only see a few of the 4th, and we were in the centre of the enemy's infantry, amongst whom were a few Chasseurs and Dragoons. Nothing now remained but to go on, as we were in as much danger by going any other way.

I rode up to a French officer, who was, like the rest, taking to his heels, and cut him just behind his neck; I saw the blood flow, and he lost his balance, and fell from his horse. I perceived my sword was giving way in the handle, so I said to the officer who lay on the ground: "Donnez-moi votre epee" – I really believe he was more

> frightened than hurt; I sheathed my sword and went on with his. I had not gone 10 yards further before my horse was wounded in the ear by a gunshot; he turned sharp round, and the same instant I was shot in the head. I turned giddy and fell off. I can recollect a French Dragoon taking away my horse.

Eventually, Norcliffe was rescued by British soldiers who got him to a surgeon. By the time he wrote the letter he was recovering well, and had no regrets:

> It was a glorious day for our Brigade. They behaved nobly; four men killed of the troop I commanded, and several men and horses wounded. It was a fine sight to see the fellows running, and as we held our swords over their heads fall down on their knees, drop their muskets, and cry: "Prisonnier, monsieur."

Private William Brown was in the British 45th at Salamanca when his regiment was attacked by cavalry:

> As our brigade was marching up to attack a strongly posted column of infantry, a furious charge was made by a body of cavalry upon our Regiment, and, not having time to form square, we suffered severely. Several times the enemy rode through us, cutting down with their sabres all that opposed them. Our ranks were broken and thrown into the utmost confusion. Repeatedly our men attempted to reform, but all in vain they were as often cut down and trampled upon by their antagonists. At length, however, the enemy was driven off by some squadrons of our cavalry, who came up in time to save us from being totally destroyed. Numerous and severe were the wounds received on this occasion. Several had their arms dashed from their shoulders, and I saw more than one with their heads completely cloven. Among the rest I received a wound, but comparatively slight, although well aimed. Coming in contact with one of the enemy he brandished his sword over me, and standing in his stirrup-irons, prepared to strike; but, pricking his horse with my bayonet, it reared and pranced, when the sword fell, the point striking my forehead. He was, however, immediately brought down, falling with a groan to rise no more.

Late in the day, Ferey's division tried to cover the French retreat and was attacked by the British and Portuguese troops of Clinton's 6th Division. James FitzGibbon was a British officer in that division.

> It was half-past seven when the 6th Division, under General Clinton, was ordered to advance a second time and attack the enemy's line in front, supported by the 3rd and 5th Divisions. The ground over which we had to pass was a remarkably clear slope, like the glacis of a fortification – most favourable for the defensive fire of the enemy, and disadvantageous to the assailants, but the division advanced towards the position with perfect steadiness and confidence. A craggy ridge, on which the French infantry was drawn up, rose so abruptly that they could fire four or five deep; but we had approached within 200 yards of them before the fire of musketry began, which was by far the heaviest that I have ever witnessed, and was accompanied by constant discharges of grape. An uninterrupted blaze was then maintained, so that the crest of the hill seemed to be one long streak of flame. Our men came down to the charging position, and commenced firing from that level, at the same time keeping their touch to the right, so that the gaps opened by the enemy's fire were instantly filled up.

Although the French opened fire at relatively long range, "within 200 yards," the British were unable to press on with their attack, resulting in a prolonged firefight. A French officer continued the tale:

> The cruel fire cost us many lives, and at last, slowly, and after having given near an hour's respite to the remainder of the army, Ferey gave back, still protected by his flanking squares, to the very edge of the forest, where he halted our half-destroyed division. Formed in line it still presented a respectable front, and halted, despite the English batteries, which enfiladed us with a thundering fire.

Clinton attacked this second position with a strong Portuguese brigade, supported by troops from other divisions and some cavalry. The French were now shaken and the same French officer admitted that, "*We fired first, the moment they got within range.*"

The Battle of Vittoria 21 June 1813

In 1813 the French were suffering from the disaster in Russia. Prussia joined the alliance against Napoleon in March. Consequently Napoleon was unable to send any reinforcements to Spain. Many of the forces available to King Joseph and Marshal Jourdan were pinned down by guerillas. Wellington had an Allied army of 79,000 men. In May Wellington advanced. His Allied army was able to reach Burgos before the French could concentrate their forces against them. From Burgos the Allied army moved through the mountains to the north. Marshal Jourdan was in command of a French army of 66,000. He placed his army in a defensive position facing west, near the town of Vittoria.

At 8 a.m. on 21 June, Wellington's army made a co-ordinated attack. This began with a frontal attack from the west. This was the direction from which the French expected to be attacked. The attack, under the command of Sir Rowland Hill, was made by the British 2nd Division, Morillo's division of Spanish infantry and Cadogan's Brigade. These troops crossed the Zadorra at Puebla to attack the heights overlooking the French position. Although they took serious casualties, these attacks caused Marshal Jourdan to strengthen his left. The transfer of troops from the French right left the bridges over the Zadorra unguarded. Wellington's second attack came from the North; the attack was made by the 1st and 5th Divisions, Pack's and Bradford's Portugese Brigades and Longa's Spanish Brigade. Not only was this a flank attack but it could cut off the French army by reaching the road from Vittoria back to France.

At Vittoria, O'Callaghan's brigade of Hill's Division captured the village of Subijana with little opposition and was then instructed to hold off the French troops facing it. According to Edward Macarthur of the 39th:

> The companies of the brigade were ordered independently to the front, to skirmish with the Enemy. The ground on which they stood was open, and exposed to the Artillery of the Enemy who had lined the opposite coverts with a swarm of light troops. In the short space of ten minutes my company lost in killed and wounded two Officers, and 29 men. Every Company maintained its ground till its ammunition was exhausted, when it was succeeded by another.

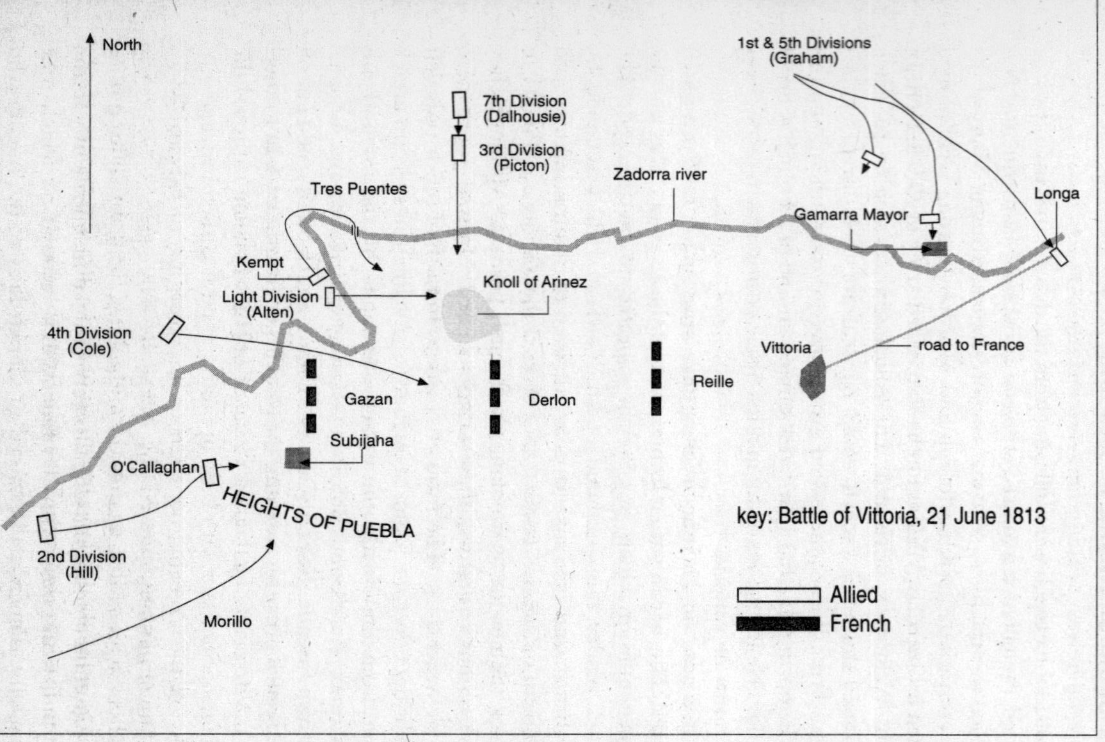

Map of the Battle of Vittoria

O'Callaghan's three battalions lost 48 men killed and no fewer than 443 officers and men wounded in the battle, many of them in this incident.

Wellington learned late in the morning that the French had left the bridge across the Zadorra at Tres Puentes unguarded. The Light Division was nearby, in the centre of the Allied army Kempt's Brigade was immediately dispatched from the Light Division to seize the bridge. Concealed by high ground on the hairpin bend of the Zadorra, the light infantry were able to take the bridge virtually unopposed. John Kincaid was in Kempt's Brigade:

> Our division got under arms this morning before daylight, and passed the base of the mountain by its left, through the Camp of the fourth division, who were still asleep in their tents, to the banks of the river Zadora, at the village of Tres Puentes. The Opposite side of the river was occupied by the enemy's advanced posts, and we saw their army on the hills beyond, while the spires of Vittoria were visible in the distance. We felt as if there was likely to be a battle; but as that was an event we were never sure of; until we found ourselves actually in it, we lay for some time just out of musket shot, uncertain what was likely to turn up, and waiting for orders. At length a sharp fire of musketry was heard to our right; and, on looking in that direction, we saw the head of Sir Rowland Hill's corps, together with some Spanish troops, attempting to force the mountain which marked the enemy's left. The three battalions of our regiment were, at the same moment, ordered forward to feel the enemy, who lined the opposite banks of the river, and with whom we were quickly engaged in a warm skirmish. The affair with Sir Rowland Hill became gradually warmer, but ours had apparently no other object than to amuse those who were opposite to us, for the moment; so that, for about two hours longer, it seemed as if there would be nothing but an affair of outposts. About twelve o'clock, however, we were moved rapidly to our left, followed by the rest of the division, till we came to an abrupt turn of the river, where we found a bridge, unoccupied by the enemy, which we immediately crossed, and took possession of what appeared to me to be an old field-work, on the other side. We had not been many seconds there before we observed the bayonets of the 3rd and 7th Divisions glittering above the standing corn, and advancing upon another bridge, which stood about a quarter of a mile further to our left, and

where, on their arrival, they were warmly opposed by the enemy's light troops, who lined the bank of the river (which we ourselves were now on) in great force, for the defence of the bridge. As soon as this was observed by our division, Colonel Barnard advanced with our battalion, and took them in flank with such a furious fire as quickly dislodged them, and thereby opened a passage for these two divisions free of expense, which must otherwise have cost them dearly. What with the rapidity of our movement, the colour of our dress, and our close contact with the enemy, before they would abandon their post, we had the misfortune to be identified with them for some time, by a battery of our own guns, who, not observing the movement, continued to serve it out indiscriminately, and all the while admiring their practice upon us; nor was it until the red coats of the 3rd Division joined us that they discovered their mistake.

The battle now commenced in earnest; and this was perhaps the most interesting moment of the whole day. Sir Thomas Graham's artillery, with the 1st and 5th Divisions, began to be heard far to our left, beyond Vittoria. The bridge which we had just cleared stood so near to a part of the enemy's position that the 7th Division was instantly engaged in close action with them at that point.

On the mountain to our extreme right the action continued to be general and obstinate, though we observed that the enemy were giving ground slowly to Sir Rowland Hill. The passage of the river by our division had turned the enemy's outpost at the bridge on our right, where we had been engaged in the morning, and they were now retreating, followed by the 4th Division. The plain between them and Sir Rowland Hill was occupied by the British cavalry, who were now seen filing out of a wood, squadron after squadron, galloping into form as they gradually cleared it. The hills behind were covered with spectators, and the 3rd and the Light Divisions, covered by our battalion, advanced rapidly upon a formidable hill in front of the enemy's centre, which they had neglected to occupy in sufficient force.

In the course of our progress, our men kept picking off the French videttes, who were imprudent enough to hover too near us; and many a horse, bounding along the plain, dragging his late rider by the stirrup-irons, contributed in making it a scene of extraordinary and exhilarating interest.

Old Picton rode at the head of the 3rd Division, dressed in a blue coat and round hat, and swore as roundly all the way as if he had been wearing two cocked ones. Our battalion soon cleared the hill in question, of the enemy's light troops; but we were pulled up on the opposite side of it by one of their lines, which occupied a wall at the entrance of a village immediately under us. During the few minutes that we stopped there, while a brigade of the 3rd Division was deploying into line, two of our companies lost two officers and 30 men, chiefly from the fire of the artillery bearing on the spot from the French position. One of their shells burst immediately under my nose, part of it struck my boot and stirrup iron, and the rest of it kicked up such a dust about me that my charger refused to obey orders; and, while I was spurring and he capering, I heard a voice behind me, which I knew to be Lord Wellington's, calling out in a tone of reproof, "Look to keeping your men together, sir!" and though, God knows, I had not the remotest idea that he was within a mile of me at the time, yet so sensible was I that circumstances warranted his supposing that I was a young officer, cutting a caper, by way of bravado, before him, that worlds would not have tempted me to look round at the moment. The French fled from the wall as soon as they received a volley from a part of the 3rd Division, and we instantly dashed down the hill, and charged them through the village, capturing three of their guns; the first, I believe, that were taken that day. They received a reinforcement, and drove us back before our supports could come to our assistance; but, in the scramble of the moment, our men were knowing enough to cut the traces, and carry off the horses, so that when we retook the village, immediately after, the guns still remained in our posession. The battle now became general along the whole line, and the cannonade was tremendous. At one period we held one side of a wall, near the village, while the French were on the other, so that any person who chose to put his head over from either side, was sure of getting a sword or a bayonet put up his nostrils. This situation was, of course, too good to be of long endurance. The victory, I believe, was never for a moment doubtful. The enemy were so completely out-generalled, and the superiority of our troops was such, that to carry their positions required little more than the time necessary to march to them. After forcing their centre, the 4th Division and our own got on the flank and rather in rear of the enemy's left wing, who were retreating before Sir Rowland Hill, and who, to effect their escape, were now obliged to fly in one confused mass.

Had a single regiment of our dragoons been at hand, or even a squadron to have forced them into shape for a few minutes, we must have taken from 10 to 20,000 prisoners. After marching along side of them for nearly two miles, and as disorderly body will always move faster than an orderly one, we had the mortification to see them gradually heading us, until they finally made their escape. I have no doubt but that our mounted gentlemen were doing their duty as they ought in another part of the field; yet, it was impossible to deny ourselves the satisfaction of cursing them all, because a portion had not been there at such a critical moment. Our elevated situation, at this time, afforded a good view of the field of battle to our left, and I could not help being struck with an unusual appearance of unsteadiness, and want of confidence among the French troops. I saw a dense mass of many thousands occupying a good defensible post, who gave way in the greatest confusion, before a single line of the 3rd Division, almost without feeling them. If there was nothing in any other part of the position to justify the movement, and I do not think there was, they ought to have been flogged, every man, from the general downwards.

The ground was particularly favourable to the retreating foe, as every half-mile afforded a fresh and formidable position, so that, from the commencement of the action to the city of Vittoria, a distance of six or eight miles, we were involved in one continued hard skirmish.

On passing Vittoria, however, the scene became quite new and infinitely more amusing, as the French had made no provision for a retreat; and, Sir Thomas Graham having seized upon the great road to France, the only one left open was that leading by Pampeluna and it was not open long, for their fugitive army, and their myriads of followers, with baggage, guns, carriages, &c. being all precipitated upon it at the same moment, it got choaked up about a mile beyond the town, in the most glorious state of confusion; and the drivers, finding that one pair of legs was worth two pair of wheels, abandoned it all to the victors.

Further allied attacks from the north followed. Picton's 3rd Division – supported by a flanking attack by Kempt's Brigade – stormed over the Zadorra to the east of Tres Puentes. In the centre, the Allied 4th Division and the rest of the Light Division crossed the Zadorra. This maintained the pressure from the west. Meanwhile, the British 2nd Division and its supporting troops continued to press from the south.

After the siege of Badajoz Harry Smith of the Light Division had married a young Spanish lady. His wife lived and travelled with the army. His brigade of the Light Division was commanded by General Vandeleur. It came into action later than Kempt's brigade:

> At the Battle of Vittoria [21 June] my Brigade, in the middle of the action, was sent to support the 7th Division, which was very hotly engaged. I was sent forward to report myself to Lord Dalhousie, who commanded. I found his lordship and his Q.M.G., Drake, an old Rifle comrade, in deep conversation. I reported pretty quick, and asked for orders (the head of my Brigade was just getting under fire). I repeated the question, "What orders, my Lord?" Drake became somewhat animated, and I heard His Lordship say, "Better to take the village," which the French held with twelve guns (I had counted by their fire), and seemed to be inclined to keep it. I roared out, "Certainly, my Lord," and off I galloped, both calling to me to come back, but, as none are so deaf as those who hear, I told General Vandeleur we were immediately to take the village. There was no time to lose, and the 52nd Regiment deployed into line as if at Shorncliffe, while our Riflemen were sent out in every direction, five or six deep, keeping up a fire nothing could resist. I galloped to the officer commanding a Battalion in the 7th Division (the 82nd, I think). "Lord Dalhousie desires you closely to follow this Brigade of the Light Division."
>
> "Who are you, sir?" "Never mind that; disobey my Lord's order at your peril." My Brigade, the 52nd in line and the swarms of Riflemen, rushed at the village, and although the ground was intersected in its front by gardens and ditches, nothing ever checked us until we reached the rear of the village, where we halted to reform – the twelve guns, tumbrils, horses, etc., standing in our possession. There never was a more impetuous onset – nothing could withstand such a burst of determination. Before we were ready to pursue the enemy – for we Light Division ever reformed and got into order before a second attack, thanks to poor General Bob Craufurd's most excellent tuition – up came Lord Dalhousie with his Q.M.G., Drake, to old Vandeleur, exclaiming, "Most brilliantly achieved indeed! Where is the officer you sent to me for orders?" "Here I am, my lord." Old Drake knew well enough. "Upon my word, sir, you receive and carry orders quicker than any officer I ever saw." "You said, 'Take the village.'

My lord, there it is," I said, "guns and all." He smiled, and old Drake burst into one of his grins. "Well done, Harry."

We were hotly engaged all the afternoon pursuing the French over very broad ditches. Until we neared Vittoria to our left, there was a plain free from ditches. The confusion of baggage, etc., was indescribable. Our Brigade was moving rapidly on, when such a swarm of French Cavalry rushed out from among the baggage into our skirmishers, opposite a company of the 2nd Battalion Rifle Brigade, commanded by Lieutenant Tom Cochrane, we thought they must have been swept off. Fortunately for Tom, a little rough ground and a bank enabled him to command his Company to lie down, and such a reception they gave the horsemen, while some of our Company were flying to their support, that the French fled with a severe loss. Our Riflemen were beautiful shots, and as undaunted as bulldogs. We knew so well, too, how to support each other, that scarcely had the French Dragoons shown themselves when Cochrane's rear was supported, and we had such mutual confidence in this support that we never calculated on disaster, but assumed the boldest front and bearing.

A rather curious circumstance occurred to me after the first heights and the key of the enemy's central position was carried. I was standing with Ross's Brigade of guns sharply engaged, when my horse fell as if stone dead. I jumped off, and began to look for the wound. I could see none, and gave the poor animal a kick on the nose. He immediately shook his head, and as instantly jumped on his legs, and I on his back. The artillerymen all said it was the current of air, or, as they call it, the wind, of one of the enemy's cannon-shot. On the attack on the village previously described, Lieutenant Northey (52nd Regiment) was not knocked off as I was, but he was knocked down by the wind of a shot, and his face as black as if he had been two hours in a pugilistic ring.

The fall of my horse had been observed by some of our soldiers as they were skirmishing forward, and a report soon prevailed that I was killed, which, in the course of the afternoon, was communicated to my poor wife, who followed close to the rear on the very field of battle, crossing the plain covered with treasure. Her old groom, West, proposed to carry off some on a led horse. She said, "Oh, West, never mind money. Let us look for your master." She had followed the 1st Brigade men, the 2nd having been detached, unobserved by her, to aid the 7th Division. After the battle, at dusk, my Brigade was ordered to join the 1st Brigade, with

General Alten's head-quarters. I had lost my voice from the exertion of cheering with our men (not cheering them on, for they required no such example), and as I approached the 1st Brigade, to take up the ground for mine, I heard my wife's lamentations. I immediately galloped up to her, and spoke to her as well as I could, considering the loss of my voice. "Oh, then, thank God, you are not killed, only badly wounded." "Thank God," I growled, "I am neither," but, in her ecstasy of joy, this was not believed for a long while.

The French were being attacked in front flank and rear. Their retreat became a rout in which they lost virtually all their artillery and transport.

Wellington's casualties from the battle were 5,100. The French not only lost 8,000 casualties but also virtually all their artillery and transport. They retreated into Pampeluna which was blockaded by the allies.

News of Wellington's victory reassured both Prussia and Austria after they had been defeated by Napoleon, in the north, at Lutzen and Bautzen. It also helped Austria to decide to rejoin the alliance against France in August.

By mid-July Wellington's army had reached the Pyrenees. Joseph and Jourdan had been replaced by Soult.

Wellington sent part of his army under Sir Thomas Graham to besiege San Sebastian. San Sebastian was a port on the north coast of Spain through which the army could be supplied by sea. Soult counter-attacked.

John Kincaid and the Light Division were involved in the action in the mountain passes:

> Marshal Soult having succeeded to the command of the French army, and finding, towards the end of July, that St Sebastian was about to be stormed, and that the garrison of Pampeluna were beginning to get on short allowance, he determined on making a bold push for the relief of both places; and assembling the whole of his army, he forced the pass of Maya, and advanced rapidly upon Pampeluna. Lord Wellington was never to be caught napping. His army occupied too extended a position to offer effectual resistance at any of their advanced posts; but, by the time that Marshal Soult had worked his way up to the last ridge of the Pyrenees, and within sight of "the haven of his wishes", he found

his lordship waiting for him, with four divisions of the army, who treated him to one of the most signal and sanguinary defeats that he ever experienced.

Our division, during the important movements on our right, was employed in keeping up the communication between the troops under the immediate command of Lord Wellington and those under Sir Thomas Graham, at St Sebastian. We retired, the first day, to the mountains behind Le Secca; and, just as we were about to lie down for the night we were again ordered under arms, and continued our retreat in utter darkness, through a mountain path, where, in many places, a false step might have rolled a fellow as far as the other world. The consequence was, that, although we were kept on our legs during the whole of the night, we found, when daylight broke, that the tail of the column had not got a quarter of a mile from their starting post.

On a good broad road it is all very well; but, on a narrow bad road, a night march is like a nightmare, harassing a man to no purpose.

On the 26th, we occupied a ridge of mountain near enough to hear the battle, though not in a situation to see it; and remained the whole of the day in the greatest torture, for want of news.

About midnight we heard the joyful tidings of the enemy's defeat, with the loss of 4,000 prisoners. Our division proceeded in pursuit, at daylight, on the following morning.

We moved rapidly by the same road on which we had retired; and, after a forced march, found ourselves, when near sun-set, on the flank of their retiring column, on the Bidassoa, near the bridge of Janca, and immediately proceeded to business.

The sight of a Frenchman always acted like a cordial on the spirits of a rifleman; and the fatigues of the day were forgotten, as our three battalions extended among the brushwood, and went down to "knock the dust out of their hairy knapsacks", as our men were in the habit of expressing themselves; but, in place of knocking the dust out of them, I believe that most of their knapsacks were knocked in the dust; for the greater part of those who were not floored along with their knapsacks shook them off by way of enabling the owner to make a smarter scramble across that portion of the road on which our leaden shower was pouring; and, foes as they were, it was impossible not to feel a degree of pity for their situation: pressed by an enemy in the rear, an inaccessible mountain on their right, and a river on their left, lined by an invisible foe, from whom there was no escape but the desperate one of running the gauntlet. However, "as every dog has his day", and this was ours, we must stand accused of making the most of it. Each company, as they passed, gave us a volley; but as they had nothing to guide their aim, except the smoke from our rifles, we had very few men hit.

Amongst other papers found on the road that night, one of our officers discovered the letter-book of the French military secretary, with his correspondence included to the day before. It was immediately sent to Lord Wellington.

We advanced, next morning, and occupied our former post, at Bera. The enemy still continued to hold the mountain of Echelar, which, as it rose out of the right end of our ridge, was, properly speaking, a part of our property; and we concluded, that a sense of justice would have induced them to leave it of their own accord in the course of the day; but when, towards the afternoon, they showed no symptoms of quitting, our division, leaving their kettles on the fire, proceeded to eject them. As we approached the mountain, the peak of it caught a passing cloud, which gradually descended in a thick fog, and excluded the enemy from our view. Our three battalions, however, having been let loose, under Colonel Barnard, we soon made ourselves "Children of the Mist", and, guided to their opponents by the whistling of their balls, made them descend from their "high estate"; and, handing them across the valley into their own position, we then retired to ours, where we found our tables already spread, and a comfortable dinner awaiting us.

This was one of the most gentleman-like day's fighting that I ever experienced, although we had to lament the vacant seats of one or two of our messmates.

On 7 October Wellington and the Allied army crossed the Bidassoa river into France. On 10 November they broke through the French defences along the Nivelle river. John Kincaid:

The fall of Pampeluna having, at length, left our further movements unshackled by an enemy in the rear, preparations were made for an attack on their position, which, though rather too extended, was formidable by nature, and rendered doubly so by art.

Petite La Rhune was allotted to our division, as their first point of attack; and, accordingly the 10th being the day fixed, we moved to our ground at midnight, on the 9th. The abrupt ridges in the neighbourhood enabled us to lodge ourselves, unperceived, within half-musket-shot of their piquets; and we had left every description of animal behind us in camp, in order that neither the barking of dogs nor the neighing of steeds should give indication of our intentions.

Our signal of attack was to be a gun from Sir John Hope, who had now succeeded Sir Thomas Graham in the command of the left wing of the army.

We stood to our arms at dawn of day, which was soon followed by the signal gun; and each commanding officer, according to previous instructions, led gallantly off to his point of attack. The French must have been, no doubt, astonished to see such an armed force spring out of the ground almost under their noses; but they were nevertheless prepared behind their entrenchments, and caused us some loss in passing the short space between us; but the whole place was carried within the time required to walk over it; and, in less than half-an-hour from the commencement of the attack, it was in our possession, with all their tents left standing.

Petite La Rhune was more of an outpost than a part of their position, the latter being a chain of stupendous mountains in its rear; so that while our battalion followed their skirmishers into the valley between, the remainder of our division were forming for the attack on the main position and waiting for the co-operation of the other divisions, the thunder of whose artillery, echoing along the valleys, proclaimed that they were engaged, far and wide, on both sides of us. About midday our division advanced to the grand attack, on the most formidable-looking part of the whole of the enemy's position, and, much to our surprise, we carried it with more ease and less loss than the outpost in the morning, a circumstance which we could only account for by supposing that it had been defended by the same troops, and that they did not choose to sustain two hard beatings on the same day. The attack succeeded at every point; and, in the evening we had the satisfaction of seeing the left wing of the army marching into St Jean de Luz.

The allied army pushed the French back towards Bayonne. Wellington had invaded France from the south-west. In the north the allies were closing in from the east after victories at Dennewitz in

September 1813 and Leipzig in October 1813. In December 1813, John Kincaid observed some of Napoleon's foreign contingents changing sides:

> In the course of the night a brigade of Belgians, who were with the French army, having heard that their country had declared for their legitimate king, passed over to our side, and surrendered.
>
> On the 12th there was heavy firing and hard fighting, all day, to our left, but we remained perfectly quiet. Towards the afternoon, Sir James Kempt formed our brigade, for the purpose of expelling the enemy from the hill next the chateau, to which he thought them rather too near; but, just as we reached our different points for commencing the attack, we were recalled, and nothing further occurred.
>
> I went, about one o'clock in the morning, to visit our different piquets; and seeing an unusual number of fires in the enemy's lines, I concluded that they had lit them to make some movement; and, taking a patrol with me, I stole cautiously forward, and found that they had left the ground altogether. I immediately returned, and reported the circumstance to General Alten, who sent off a despatch to apprize Lord Wellington.
>
> As soon as day began to dawn, on the morning of the 13th, a tremendous fire of artillery and musketry was heard to our right. Soult had withdrawn every thing from our front in the course of the night, and had now attacked Sir Rowland Hill with his whole force. Lord Wellington, in expectation of this attack, had, last night, reinforced Sir Rowland Hill with the 6th Division; which enabled him to occupy his contracted position so strongly, that Soult, unable to bring more than his own front to bear upon him, sustained a signal and sanguinary defeat.
>
> Lord Wellington galloped into the yard of our chateau, soon after the attack had commenced, and demanded, with his usual quickness, what was to be seen? Sir James Kempt, who was spying at the action from an upper window, told him; and, after desiring Sir James to order Sir Lowry Cole to follow him with the 4th Division, he galloped off to the scene of action. In the afternoon, when all was over, he called in again, on his return to head-quarters, and told us, "that it was the 'most glorious affair that he had ever seen; and that the enemy had absolutely left upwards of 5,000 men, killed and wounded, on the ground."
>
> This was the last action in which we were concerned, near

> Bayonne. The enemy seemed quite satisfied with what they had got; and offered us no further molestation, but withdrew within their works.

On 27 February 1814 Wellington attacked Soult at Orthez. Harry Smith:

> At dark we withdrew all our posts out of Orthez but a picquet near the bridge in the town, and at daylight [27 February] we crossed by a pontoon bridge below Orthez, and marched over difficult ground. We saw the enemy very strongly posted, both as regards the elevation and the nature of the ground, which was intersected by large banks and ditches, while the fences of the field were most admirably calculated for vigorous defence. As we were moving on the right of the 3rd Division, Sir Thomas Picton, who was ever ready to find fault with the Light, rode up to Colonel Barnard. "Who the devil are you?" knowing Barnard intimately. "We are the Light Division." "If you are Light, sir, I wish you would move a little quicker," said in his most bitter and sarcastic tone. Barnard says very cool, "Alten commands. But the march of infantry is quick time, and you cannot accelerate the pace of the head of the column without doing an injury to the whole. Wherever the 3rd Division are, Sir Thomas, we will be in our places, depend on it."
>
> We were soon engaged, but less for some time than the troops to our right and left. I never saw the French fight so hard as this day, and we were actually making no advance, when the Duke came up, and ordered the 52nd Regiment to form line and advance. The Battalion was upwards of 700 strong. It deployed into line like clockwork, and moved on, supported by clouds of sharpshooters. It was the most majestic advance I ever saw. The French, seeing this line advance so steadily, were appalled; their fire, which at first was terrific, gradually decreased as we neared. The Divisions on our right and left also moved on. The battle was won.

In the north Napoleon was vigorously defending Paris against overwhelming numbers of allied troops. The allies finally entered Paris on 31 March 1814. The last battle of Wellington's peninsular campaign was fought on 10 April. The allied army forced the French off the Calvinet ridge overlooking the city of Toulouse.

Harry Smith:

When the enemy were driven from the heights, they retired within the town, and the canal then became their line of defence, which they maintained the whole of the next day; but in the course of the following night they left the town altogether, and we took possession of it on the morning of the 12th.

The inhabitants of Toulouse hoisted the white flag, and declared for the Bourbons the moment the French army left it; and, in the course of the same day, Colonel Cooke arrived from Paris, with the extraordinary news of Napoleon's abdication. Soult has been accused of having been in possession of that fact prior to the battle of Toulouse; but, to disprove such an assertion, it can only be necessary to think, a moment, whether he would not have made it public the day after the battle, while he yet held possession of the town, as it would not only have enabled him to keep it, but, to those who knew no better, it might have given him a shadow of claim to the victory, if he chose to avail himself of it; and I have known a victory claimed by a French marshal on more slender grounds. In place of knowing it then, he did not even believe it now; and we were absolutely obliged to follow him a day's march beyond Toulouse before he agreed to an armistice.

The British forces were sent into quarters to await being sent back to Great Britain. The Spanish and Portuguese elements of the Allied army marched home. John Kincaid took some leave in Scotland. Harry Smith took his young Spanish wife home to England but he himself was immediately sent to the war in North America.

Napoleonic Wars – the Hundred Days

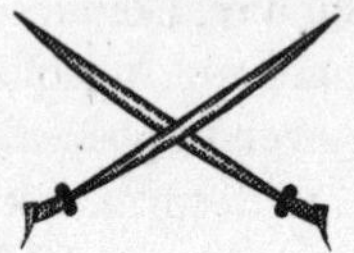

The Battle of Waterloo – Introduction

The nearest run thing you ever saw in your life.
The Duke of Wellington

The period between Napoleon's landing in France and his final defeat is known as "The Hundred Days".

Napoleon had landed near Cannes on 1 March 1815 with 1,000 men and four guns which he had been allowed as ruler of Elba. His path was blocked by one of his old regiments south of Grenoble. He won them over to his side by coolly walking up to them alone and addressing them. Every other French army unit sent to resist him joined him. On 20 March he entered Paris supported by the entire French army.

His former enemies, Great Britain, Prussia, Austria and Russia immediately formed an alliance, declared war, and mobilised their forces. France faced armies of up to 660,000 men. France had a standing army of just under 150,000 men. Many of Napoleon's former veterans volunteered and the 1813 class of conscripts was recalled. Napoleon decided to attack the Allied armies nearest to him. These were an Allied army under the Duke of Wellington and a Prussian army under Field Marshal Blücher.

The Duke of Wellington's army was made up of British, German, Dutch and Belgian troops. The Dutch and the Belgians were united under the King of the Netherlands. Some of the Belgian troops in the Allied army had been serving Napoleon the previous year. The Allied army was assembling around Brussels. Field Marshal Blücher's Prussian army of 117,000 men was nearby, around Liege. They were mostly inexperienced conscripts. On 3 May Wellington and Blücher had agreed that if Blücher was attacked Wellington would move to his support.

Napoleon succeeded in keeping his preparations secret. He had assembled an army of 122,721 men and 366 guns. They were mostly experienced soldiers. They crossed the frontier at Charleroi on 15 June. That evening Wellington realized that Napoleon was trying to separate him from Blücher. Both Allied armies were spread out. Despite this Wellington ordered his available troops forward to support Blücher. The allies needed to hold a crossroads at a place called Quatre Bras. If they lost it they would be cut off from each other and could be defeated in turn by the French. A Dutch-Belgian brigade got there just before the French but needed reinforcement if the allies were to keep it. Blücher's Prussian army fell back before the French advance. The French army advanced in three formations. The left wing was under the command of Marshal Ney. The right wing was under the command of Marshal Grouchy. The third formation was a central reserve under Napoleon himself.

Each wing was to advance from Charleroi towards one of the two Allied armies. The larger Allied force (the Prussian) was to be brought to battle and decisively defeated by one of the wings strengthened by the reserve. The other wing was to contain the smaller Allied force, and send assistance if necessary. As soon as the first Allied army had been beaten, the second Allied army would be attacked in force. The Prussian units spread out north of Charleroi retreated, fighting, while the rest of the Prussian army marched towards Ligny. On 16 June Napoleon began to show signs of lethargy. He did not realise the Prussians were waiting, on the defensive at Ligny until 11 a.m. He sent Ney with the left wing to take the crossroads at Quatre Bras and to prevent Wellington coming to help the Prussians. Wellington himself arrived at Quatre Bras about 10.30 a.m. Once he had given some necessary orders there he rode across to see Blücher. When defending, Wellington preferred to position his men on the reverse slope of any hill or ridge they were defending. Wellington noticed that the Prussians were positioned on a forward slope. He warned Blücher and his chief of staff and rode away saying:

I will come; provided I am not attacked myself.

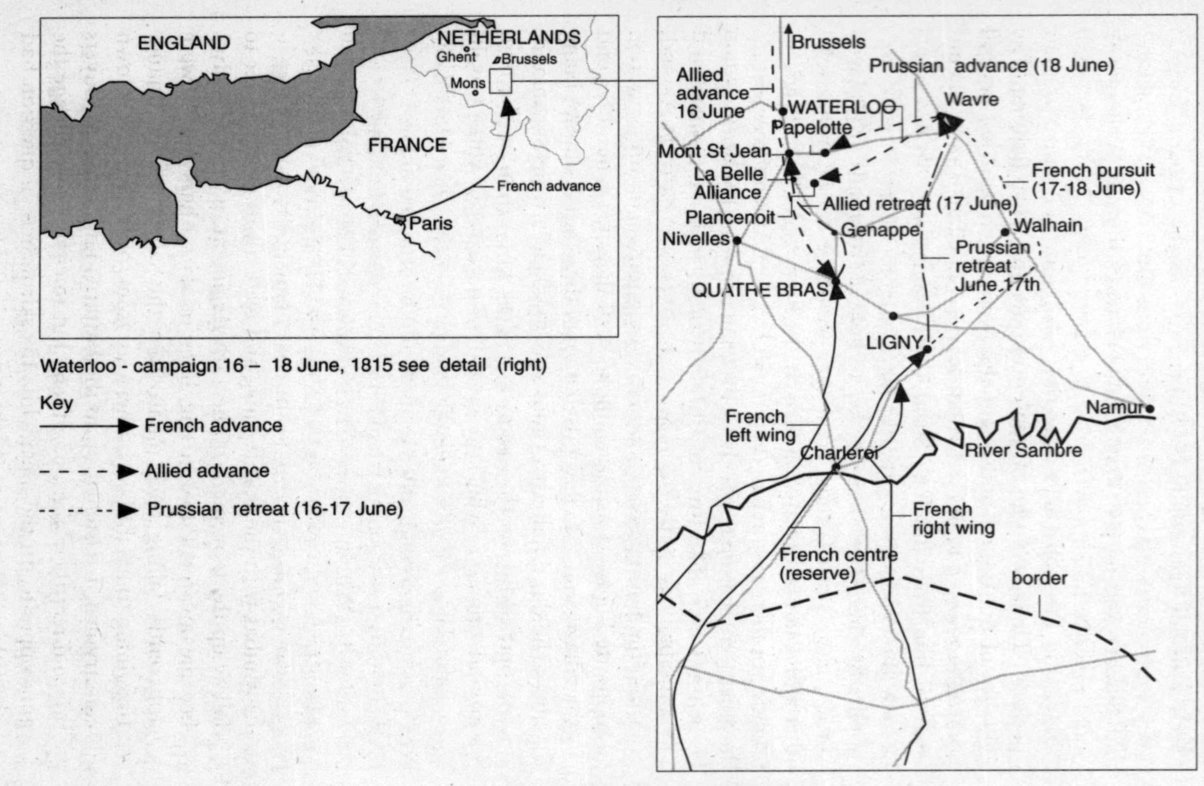

Maps of the Waterloo campaign

Battle of Ligny 16 June 1815

Napoleon's aim was to drive the Prussians to the north-east, away from Wellington. At 2.30 the troops of Vandamme's corps began to attack the Prussians defending the villages in the centre of their position. There was a lot of house-to-house and street fighting. The villages of St Amand and Wagnelée were taken and lost several times. Napoleon had begun the battle with 71,000 men and 242 guns against Blücher's 83,000 men and 224 guns. Neither side had all its available men on the battlefield.

Lieutenant Reuter was a Prussian junior artillery officer. At Ligny, Lieutenant Reuter's gunners were trying to support an infantry attack when they were fired at by skirmishers:

> I suppose it was between two and three o'clock in the afternoon when I received an order to take four guns of my battery and accompany the 14th Regiment in its advance towards St Amand, while the howitzers and two remaining guns took up a position opposite Ligny, so as to be able to shell the open ground beyond the village, and the village itself, too, in the event of our not being able to hold it. I halted my guns about 600 paces from St. Amand, and opened fire on the enemy's artillery in position on the high ground opposite, which at once began to reply with a well-sustained fire of shells, and inflicted heavy losses on us. Meanwhile the 14th Regiment, without ever thinking of leaving an escort behind for us, pressed gallantly forward to St Amand, and succeeded in gaining possession of a part of that village. I myself was under the impression that they had been able to occupy the whole of it. The battery had thus been engaged for some hours in its combat with the hostile guns, and were awaiting the order to follow up the movement of the 14th Regiment, when suddenly I became aware of two strong lines of skirmishers which were apparently falling back on us from the village of St Amand. Imagining that the skirmishers in front of us were our own countrymen, I hastened up to the battery and warned my layers not to direct their aim upon them, but to continue to engage the guns opposite. In the meanwhile the skirmishers in question had got within 300 paces of the battery.
>
> I had just returned to the right flank of my command when our surgeon, Zinkernagel, called my attention to the red tufts on the shakos of the sharpshooters. I at once bellowed out the order,

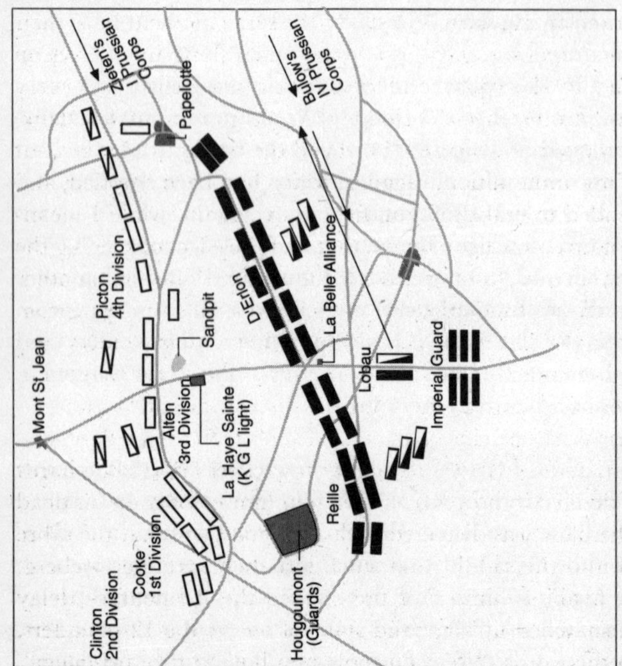

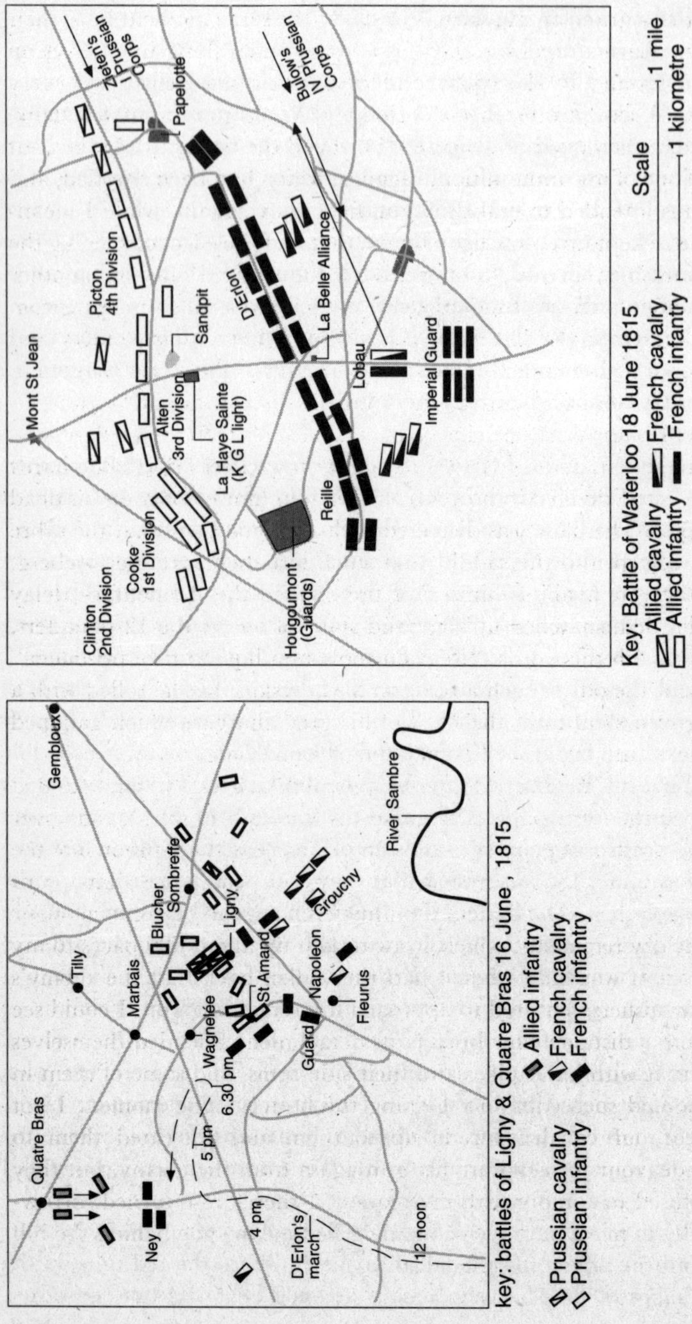

Maps of the Battle of Waterloo, Ligny, Quatre Bras

"With grape on the skirmishers!" At the same moment both their lines turned upon us, gave us a volley, then flung themselves on the ground. By this volley, and the bursting of a shell or two, every horse, except one wheeler belonging to the gun on my left flank, was either killed or wounded. I ordered the horses to be taken out of one of my ammunition waggons, which had been emptied, and thus intended to make my gun fit to move again, while I meanwhile kept up a slow fire of grape that had the effect of keeping the marksmen in my front glued to the ground. But in another moment, all of a sudden, I saw my left flank taken in rear, from the direction of the Ligny brook, by a French staff officer and about 50 horsemen. As these rushed upon us the officer shouted to me in German, "Surrender, gunners, for you are all prisoners!" With these words he charged down with his men on the flank gun on my left, and dealt a vicious cut at my wheel driver, Borchardt . . . who dodged it, however, by flinging himself over on his dead horse. The blow was delivered with such good will that the sabre cut deep into the saddle, and stuck fast there. Gunner Sieberg, however, availing himself of the chance the momentary delay afforded, snatched up the hand spike of one of the 12-pounders, and with the words, "I'll soon show him how to take prisoners!" dealt the officer such a blow on his bearskin that he rolled with a broken skull from the back of his grey charger, which galloped away into the line of skirmishers in our front.

The 50 horsemen, unable to control their horses which bounded after their companion, followed his lead in a moment, rode over the prostrate marksmen, and carried the utmost confusion into the enemy's ranks. I seized the opportunity to limber up all my guns except the unfortunate one on my left, and to retire on two of our cavalry regiments, which I saw drawn up about 600 paces to my rear. It was only when I had thus fallen back that the enemy's skirmishers ventured to approach my remaining gun. I could see from a distance how bravely its detachment defended themselves and it with handspikes and their side-arms, and some of them in the end succeeded in regaining the battery. The moment I got near our cavalry I rode up to them and entreated them to endeavour to recapture my gun again from the enemy, but they refused to comply with my request. I therefore returned sorrowfully to my battery, which had retired meanwhile behind the hill with the windmill on it near Ligny.

The French corps of D'Erlon had been ordered by Ney to come to Quatre Bras. Ney only had one corps (Reille's) at Quatre Bras. At 4 p.m. D'Erlon intercepted a message from Napoleon ordering him to go to Ligny. He sent a message to Ney informing him of this. D'Erlon had almost got there when a furious message from Ney reached him. Consequently his corps failed to participate in either battle.

At Ligny the Prussians were still resisting the French attacks at 7 p.m. Both sides were desperately weary. A Prussian officer described the appearance of his men:

> The light of the long June day was beginning to fail . . . The men looked terribly worn out after the fighting. In the great heat, gunpowder smoke, sweat and mud had mixed into a thick crust of dirt, so that their faces looked almost like those of mulattos, and one could hardly distinguish the green collars and facings on their tunics. Everybody had discarded his stock; grubby shirts or hairy brown chests stuck out from their open tunics; and many who had been unwilling to leave the ranks on account of a slight wound wore a bandage they had put on themselves. In a number of cases blood was soaking through.
>
> As a result of fighting in the villages for hours on end, and of frequently crawling through hedges, the men's tunics and trousers had got torn, so that they hung in rags and their bare skin showed through.

Napoleon finally used his reserve. This consisted of his veterans, the Imperial Guard and Milhaud's cuirassiers, heavy cavalry. The Prussians fell back under the weight of this attack. They retreated in good order. Lieutenant von Reuter helped to form a rearguard in the centre, where the French had broken the Prussian line:

> It was now about 8 p.m., and the growing darkness was increased by heavy storm clouds which began to settle down all around us. My battery, in order to avoid capture, had, of course, to conform to this general movement of retreat. I now noticed that there was an excellent artillery position about 1,500 paces behind the village of Brye, close to where the Roman road intersects the road to Quatre Bras . . . I made for this point with all haste, so that I might there place my guns and cover with their fire the retreat of my comrades of the other arms. A hollow road leading to Sombreffe delayed my progress some minutes. At length I got

over this obstacle and attained my goal; but just as I was going to give the word, "Action rear," Von Pirch's (II) infantry brigade began to debouch from Brye. The general saw in an instant what he took for a selfish and cowardly movement of retreat on my part, dashed his spurs into his horse, and galloped up to me nearly beside himself with passion, and shouting out, "My God! Everything is going to the devil! "Truly, sir," said I, "matters are not looking very rosy, but the 12-pounder battery, No. 6, has simply come here to get into a position from whence it thinks it may be able to check the enemy's advance." "That, then, is very brave conduct on your part," answered the general, at once mollified; "cling to the position at all hazards, it is of the greatest importance. I will collect a few troops to form an escort to your guns." While this short but animated discussion had been going on his brigade had come up close to where we were. He formed it up to cover us, and sent everyone who was mounted to collect all retreating troops in the neighbourhood for the same purpose, while, as they came up, he called out to them, "Soldiers, there stand your guns, are you not Prussians!"

During the time that a sort of rear-guard was thus formed, the battery had opened fire on the enemy's cavalry, which was coming up rather cautiously, and had forced them to fall back again. Later on, a 6-pounder field battery and half a horse artillery battery came up and joined us. The fight then became stationary, and as the darkness came on, fighting gradually ceased on both sides.

Christian Nagel, whose regiment had fared badly in the fighting, also insisted that morale remained good:

We were defeated, we knew that; but far from looking upon ourselves as beaten, all of us were filled with a steadfast spirit, full of unshaken confidence in ourselves and the coming day, and we spoke a good deal with each other.

The Prussian army did withdraw in good order, despite the severity of the fighting at Ligny, and the retreat was well managed. Perhaps 8,000 or 10,000 men fled eastwards, away from the main army. These were mostly recruits from Prussia's new provinces, so their loss probably did the army little real harm.

Although they had been beaten, the Prussians were able to retreat in the right direction, due north towards Wavre. This was the direction which would enable them to join forces with Wellington's army. Colonel von Rieche was chief of staff in Zieten's Prussian corps. He helped direct the Prussian retreat from Ligny. Gneisenau was the overall chief of staff of the Prussian army. Colonel von Rieche:

> Although it was almost dark I could still see my map clearly enough to realize that Tilly was not marked on it. Thinking it likely that a number of other officers would have the same map, and that uncertainty and confusion could easily result, I proposed that instead of Tilly another town lying further back but on the same line of march should be named as the assembly point – somewhere which we could assume would be shown on every other map. I remarked that even if two withdrawal points were detailed, they were both in the same direction, so there would be no fear of confusion. Gneisenau agreed. On his map I found that Wavre was just such a place.
>
> How far my suggestion contributed to the fact that the retreat extended as far as Wavre I must leave open.
>
> Next I stationed the staff officer I had with me, Lieutenant von Reisewitz, at the point on the Roman road where the track now to be taken branched off, and instructed him to direct any troops who arrived to follow it. The detachments which had already taken the Roman road or the Namur road could not, of course be recalled. In itself this was a bad thing, yet it had the advantage that the enemy would be deceived as to the line of our withdrawal.
>
> As the troops directed on to the road were all split up, General Gneisenau ordered me to collect them and form them up. Anyone who has ever been given such a task, in similar circumstances, will know the endless difficulties one has to contend with in order to carry it out. I tried to deal with the problem by first halting the head of the throng and letting the rest of the men fall in on this. When, after a great deal of trouble, I had managed to get one group halted and was trying to stop the men who were going past in the meantime, the group broke up again; and this went on for a while until I succeeded in attracting a few officers and non-commissioned officers to assist me. Particularly helpful in this business was my hat with its white plume, because in the dark people mistook me for a general, an error I was glad to put up with.

When I had disentangled the skein to the point where the men stood grouped under regiments and formed up in ranks and files, they marched off in good order. Feeling worn out, I lay down under a tree, holding onto the bridle of my poor horse, which had had nothing to eat or drink all day and all night. I could scarcely have credited such an animal with so much endurance, but it seems to have been one of those occasions, with him as with human beings, when one is so keyed up that one can stand unbelievable strains.

Although he had been injured, Blücher remained cheerful. He said:

We have taken a few knocks and shall have to hammer out the dents!'

His mood was widespread in his army. Christian Nagel wrote:

Shortly after midnight, we decamped; it appeared the enemy was approaching. At the village of Tilly we encountered troops around invigorating fires, near which we also encamped. That did us good; soon I lay fast asleep. Towards daybreak everything was again in movement and after covering several miles, all the troops bivouacked near the town of Wavre, where Blücher had his main headquarters.

The Prussians had lost 16,000 men and 21 guns. The French had lost 11,000 men. The most significant fact was that, from Wavre, the Prussians could move towards Wellington.

The Battle of Quatre Bras 16 June 1815

At Quatre Bras Wellington's troops managed to hold off Ney's attacks. By the evening enough of Wellington's troops had arrived for the Allies to outnumber the French. Each side had lost 4,000 casualties. John Kincaid was there with his battalion of the 95th Rifles:

Lord Wellington, I believe, after leaving us at Waterloo, galloped on to the Prussian position at Ligny, where he had an interview with Blücher, in which they concerted measures for their mutual co-operation. When we arrived at Quatre Bras, however, we found him in a field near the Belgian outpost; and the enemy's guns were just beginning to playing on the spot where he stood, surrounded by a numerous staff.

We halted for a moment on the brow of the hill; and as Sir Andrew Barnard galloped forward to the head-quarter group; I followed, to be in readiness to convey any orders to the battalion. The moment we approached, Lord Fitzroy Somerset, separating himself from the duke, said, "Barnard, you are wanted instantly; take your battalion and endeavour to get possession of that village," pointing to one on the face of the rising ground, down which the enemy were moving; "but if you cannot do that, secure that wood on the left, and keep the road open for communication with the Prussians." We instantly moved in the given direction; but, ere we had got half-way to the village, we had the mortification to see the enemy throw such a force into it, as rendered any attempt to retake, with our numbers, utterly hopeless; and as another strong body of them were hastening towards the wood, which was the second object pointed out to us, we immediately brought them to action, and secured it. In moving to that point, one of our men went raving mad, from excessive heat. The poor fellow cut a few extraordinary capers, and died in the course of a few minutes.

While our battalion-reserve occupied the front of the wood, our skirmishers lined the side of the road, which was the Prussian line of communication. The road itself, however, was crossed by such a shower of balls, that none but a desperate traveller would have undertaken a journey on it. We were presently reinforced by a small battalion of foreign light troops with whose assistance we were in hopes to have driven the enemy a little further from it; but they were a raw body of men, who had never before been under fire; and, as they could not be prevailed upon to join our skirmishers, we could make no use of them whatever. Their conduct, in fact, was an exact representation of Mathews's ludicrous one of the American militia, for Sir Andrew Barnard repeatedly pointed out to them which was the French, and which our side; and, after explaining that they were not to fire a shot until they joined our skirmishers, the word "March!" was given; but march, to them, was always the signal to fire, for they stood fast, and began blazing away, chiefly at our skirmishers too, the officers on each occasion sending back to say that we were shooting at them; until we were, at last, obliged to be satisfied with whatever advantages their appearance could give, as even that was of some consequence, where troops were so scarce.

Bonaparte's attack on the Prussians had already commenced, and the fire of artillery and musketry in that direction was tremendous; but the intervening higher ground prevented us from seeing any part of it.

The plain to our right, which we had just quitted, had likewise become the scene of a sanguinary and unequal contest. Our division, after we left it, deployed into line, and, in advancing, met and routed the French infantry; but, in following up their advantage, they encountered a furious charge of cavalry and were obliged to throw themselves into squares to receive it. With the exception of one regiment, however, which had two companies cut to pieces, they were not only successful in resisting the attack, but made awful havock in the enemy's ranks, who, nevertheless, continued their forward career, and went sweeping past them, like a whirlwind, up to the village of Quatre Bras, to the confusion and consternation of the numerous useless appendages of our army, who were there assembled, waiting the result of the battle.

The forward movement of the enemy's cavalry gave their infantry time to rally; and, strongly reinforced with fresh troops, they again advanced to the attack. This was a crisis in which, according to Bonaparte's theory, the victory was theirs, by all the rules of war, for they held superior numbers, both before and behind us; but the gallant old Picton, who had been trained in a different school, did not choose to confine himself to rules in those matters; despising the force in his rear, he advanced, charged, and routed those in his front, which created such a panic among the others, that they galloped back through the intervals in his division, with no other object in view but their own safety.

After this desperate conflict, the firing, on both sides, lulled almost to a calm for nearly an hour, while each was busy in renewing their order of battle. The Duke of Brunswick had been killed early in the action, endeavouring to rally his young troops, who were unable to withstand the impetuosity of the French and, as we had no other cavalry force in the field, the few British infantry regiments present, having to bear the full brunt of the enemy's superior force of both arms, were now considerably reduced in numbers.

The battle, on the side of the Prussians, still continued to rage in an unceasing roar of artillery. About four in the afternoon, a troop of their dragoons came as a patrol to inquire how it fared with us, and told us in passing that they still maintained their position. Their day, however, was still to be decided, and indeed, for that matter, so was our own; for, although the firing, for the moment, had nearly ceased, I had not yet clearly made up my mind which side had been the offensive, which the defensive, or which the winning. I had merely the satisfaction of knowing that we had not lost it; for we had met fairly in the middle of a field (or, rather unfairly, considering that they had two to one) and after the scramble was over, our division still held the ground they fought on. All doubts on the subject, however, began to be removed about five o'clock. The enemy's artillery once more opened; and, on running to the brow of the hill to ascertain the cause, we perceived our old light-division general, Count Alten, at the head of a fresh British division, moving gallantly down the road towards us. It was indeed a joyful sight; for, as already mentioned, our division had suffered so severely that we could not help looking forward to a renewal of the action, with such a disparity of force, with considerable anxiety; but this reinforcement gave us new life, and, as soon as they came near enough to afford support, we commenced the offensive, and, driving in the skirmishers opposed to us, succeeded in gaining a considerable portion of the position originally occupied by the enemy, when darkness obliged us to desist. In justice to the foreign battalion, which had been all day attached to us, I must say that, in this last movement, they joined us cordially, and behaved exceedingly well. They had a very gallant young fellow at their head; and their conduct in the earlier part of the day can, therefore, only be ascribed to its being their first appearance on such a stage.

Leaving Count Alten in possession of the ground which we had assisted in winning, we returned in search of our division, and reached them about eleven at night, lying asleep in their glory, on the field where they had fought, which contained many a bloody trace of the day's work.

The firing, on the side of the Prussians, had altogether ceased before dark, but recommenced, with redoubled fury, about an hour after; and it was then, as we afterwards learnt, that they lost the battle.

At 9 a.m. on 17 June Wellington received a message from Blücher and began to retreat. He sent the infantry first. The rearguard was formed by the cavalry and horse artillery. Helped by the rain which began during the afternoon, the allied army got back safely to the position Wellington intended to hold until the Prussians came to his support. This was just south of the village of Waterloo where Wellington himself made his headquarters. Napoleon did not know which way the Prussians had gone. He sent Marshal Grouchy with 33,000 men in the direction of Gembloux. Napoleon himself seems to have delayed Grouchy's departure. Grouchy obediently marched to Gembloux where he camped for the night without news of the Prussians or further communication with Napoleon.

John Kincaid observed the retreat from Quatre Bras and the rearguard action by the Household Cavalry:

> About nine o'clock, we received the news of Blücher's defeat and of his retreat to Wavre. Lord Wellington therefore immediately began to withdraw his army to the position of Waterloo. Sir Andrew Barnard was ordered to remain as long as possible with our battalion, to mask the retreat of the others; and was told, if we were attacked, that the whole of the British cavalry were in readiness to advance to our relief. I had an idea, however, that a single rifle battalion in the midst of 10,000 dragoons would come but indifferently off in the event of a general crash, and was by no means sorry when, between eleven and twelve o'clock, every regiment had got clear off, and we followed, before the enemy had put anything in motion against us.
>
> After leaving the village of Quatre Bras, and passing through our cavalry, who were formed on each side of the road, we drew up at the entrance of Genappe. The rain, at that moment, began to descend in torrents, and our men were allowed to shelter themselves in the nearest houses; but we were obliged to turn out again in the midst of it in less than five minutes, as we found the French cavalry and ours already exchanging shots, and the latter were falling back to the more favourable ground behind Genappe; we therefore retired with them en masse through the village, and formed again on the rising ground beyond.
>
> While we remained there, we had an opportunity of seeing the different affairs of cavalry; and it did one's heart good to see how cordially the life-guards went at their work: they had no idea of any thing but straightforward fighting, and sent their opponents flying in all directions. The only young thing they showed was in every one who got a roll in the mud (and, owing to the slipperiness

of the ground, there were many) going off to the rear, according to their Hyde-Park custom, as being no longer fit to appear on parade; I thought, at first, that they had been all wounded, but, on finding how the case stood, I could not help telling them that theirs was now the situation to verify the old proverb, "the uglier the better soldier!"

The roads, as well as the fields, had now become so heavy, that our progress to the rear was very slow; and it was six in the evening before we drew into the position of Waterloo. Our battalion took post in the second line that night, with its right resting on the Namur-road, behind La Haye Sainte, near a small mud-cottage, which Sir Andrew Barnard occupied as a quarter. The enemy arrived in front, in considerable force, about an hour after us, and a cannonade took place in different parts of the line, which ended at dark, and we lay down by our arms. It rained excessively hard the greater part of the night; nevertheless, having succeeded in getting a bundle of hay for my horse and one of straw for myself, I secured the horse to his bundle by tying him to one of the men's swords stuck in the ground and, placing mine under his nose, I laid myself down upon it, and never opened my eyes again until daylight.

The Battle of Waterloo 18 June 1815

On Sunday 18 June Wellington's Allied army took up its positions. These faced south on a ridge at right angles to the main road to Brussels. Some units were still arriving direct from overseas. Harry Smith had arrived in the Netherlands two days before. He came with General Lambert's brigade direct from North America. General Lambert was given command of the Allied 6th Division which formed part of Wellington's reserve. Harry Smith:

As we anticipated, our march from Ghent was very sudden. In an hour after the order arrived we moved en route for Brussels. We reached Asche on the afternoon of the 16th June. The rapid and continuous firing at Quatre Bras, as audible as if we were in the fight, put us in mind of old times, as well as on the *qui vive*. We expected an order every moment to move on. We believed the firing to be at Fleurus. As we approached Brussels the next day [17 June], we met an orderly with a letter from that gallant fellow De Lancey, Q.M.G., to direct us to move on Quatre Bras.

In the afternoon, after we passed Brussels, the scene of confusion, the flying of army, baggage, etc., was an awful novelty to us. We were directed by a subsequent order to halt at the village of Epinay, on the Brussels side of the forest of Soignies, a report having reached his Grace that the enemy's cavalry were threatening our communication with Brussels (as we understood, at least). The whole afternoon we were in a continued state of excitement. Once some rascals of the Cumberland Hussars, a new Corps of Hanoverians (not of the style of our noble and gallant old comrades, the 1st Hussars) came galloping in, declaring they were pursued by Frenchmen. Our bugles were blowing in all directions, and our troops running to their alarm-posts in front of the village. I went to report to Sir John Lambert, who was just sitting quietly down to dinner with my wife and his A.D.C. He says very coolly, "Let the troops—; this is all nonsense; there is not a French soldier in the rear of his Grace – depend on it, and sit down to dinner." I set off; though, and galloped to the front, where a long line of baggage was leisurely retiring. This was a sufficient indication that the alarm was false, and I dismissed the troops and started for the débris of a magnificent turbot which the General's butler had brought out of Brussels. This was in the afternoon.

Such a thunderstorm and deluge of rain now came on, it drenched all that was exposed to it, and in a few minutes rendered the country deep in mud and the roads very bad. All night our baggage kept retiring through the village.

In the course of the night, Lambert's Brigade were ordered to move up to the position the Duke had taken up in front of the forest of Soignies, and our march was very much impeded by waggons upset, baggage thrown down, etc. [18 June]. We met Sir George Scovell, an A.Q.M.G. at head-quarters, who said he was sent by the Duke to see the rear was clear, that it was choked between this and the Army, and the Duke expected to be attacked immediately; our Brigade must clear the road before we moved on. Our men were on fire at the idea of having to remain and clear a road when an attack was momentarily expected, and an hour would bring us to the position. The wand of a magician, with all his spells and incantations, could not have effected a clear course sooner than our 3,000 soldiers of the old school.

This effected, General Lambert sent me on to the Duke for orders. I was to find the Duke himself, and receive orders from no other person. About 11 o'clock I found his Grace and all his staff near Hougoumont. The day was beautiful after the storm, although the country was very heavy. When I rode up, he said, "Hallo, Smith, where are you from last?" "From General Lambert's Brigade, and they from America." "What have you got?" "The 4th, the 27th, and the 40th; the 81st remain in Brussels." "Ah, I know, I know; – but the others, are they in good order?" "Excellent, my lord, and very strong." "That's all right, for I shall soon want every man. One of his staff said, "I do not think they will attack today." "Nonsense," said the Duke. "The columns are already forming, and I think I have discerned where the weight of the attack will be made. I shall be attacked before an hour. Do you know anything of my position, Smith?" "Nothing, my lord, beyond what I see – the general line, and right and left." "Go back and halt Lambert's Brigade at the junction of the two great roads from Genappe and Nivelles. Did you observe their junction as you rode up?" "Particularly, my lord." "Having halted the head of the Brigade and told Lambert what I desire, ride to the left of the position. On the extreme left is the Nassau Brigade those fellows who came over to us at Arbonne, you recollect. Between them and Picton's Division (now the 5th) I shall most probably require Lambert. There is already there a Brigade of newly raised Hanoverians, which Lambert will give orders to, as they and your Brigade from the 6th Division. You are the only British Staff Officer with it. Find out, therefore, the best and shortest road from where Lambert is now halted to the left of Picton and the right of the Nassau troops. Do you understand?" "Perfectly, my lord." I had barely turned from his Grace when he called me back. "Now, clearly understand that when Lambert is ordered to move from the fork of the two roads where he is now halted, you are prepared to conduct him to Picton's left." It was delightful to see his Grace that morning on his noble horse Copenhagen – in high spirits and very animated, but so cool and so clear in the issue of his orders, it was impossible not fully to comprehend what he said; delightful also to observe what his wonderful eye anticipated, while some of his staff were of opinion the attack was not in progress.

John Kincaid's battalion was in Sir James Kempt's brigade of General Picton's 5th Division. Several rifle companies, including his, were placed in a sandpit in front of the Allied line on the ridge.

> Our battalion stood on what was considered the left centre of the position. We had our right resting on the Namur road, about a hundred yards in the rear of the farmhouse of La Haye Sainte, and our left extending behind a broken hedge, which ran along the ridge, to the left. Immediately in our front, and divided from La Haye Sainte only by the great road, stood a small knoll, with a sand-hole in its farthest side, which we occupied, as an advanced post, with three companies. The remainder of the division was formed in two lines; the first, consisting chiefly of light troops, behind the hedge, in continuation from the left of our battalion reserve; and the second, about a hundred yards in its rear. The guns were placed in the intervals between the brigades, two pieces were in the roadway on our right, and a rocket-brigade in the centre.

As Kincaid described, the Allied artillery was positioned in the gaps between the infantry formations and in front of them so they could fire down the slope. The cavalry was placed behind the infantry line.

> The left of the Allied position was at Papelotte where two light cavalry brigades awaited the arrival of the Prussians and some Dutch Belgian troops garrisoned the village. Towards the centre was Picton's 5th Division which had been weakened by its losses at Quatre Bras. To the right of Picton's 5th Division was Alten's 3rd Division. This Division included Major-General C. Halkett's brigade and Major-General Kielmansegge's brigade of the King's German Legion (KGL) The farmhouse of La Haye Sainte, in front of the Allied position was fortified by light infantry of the KGL. This enabled its defenders to fire into the flanks of any attacking force.

According to Kincaid, on the Allied right was the:

> 1st Division under General Cooke, this included two British Guards brigades. The guards were responsible for defending the chateau of Hougomont which was at the right hand end of the Allied line. Behind the 1st Division was the 2nd Division under Lt. General Clinton. The 2nd Division was both a reserve and a flank guard.

After all the rain, the ground was so soft and muddy that the French delayed their attack. At about 11.30 a.m. Napoleon ordered Reille's corps to attack Hougoumont which protected the Allied right. The Guards in and around Hougoumont held it firmly. Reille had to commit more and more of his corps. John Kincaid was able to see the beginning of the struggle for Hougoumont:

> Shortly after we had taken up our ground, some columns, from the enemy's left, were seen in motion towards Hugoumont, and were soon warmly engaged with the right of our army. A cannon-ball, too, came from the Lord knows where, for it was not fired at us, and took the head of our right hand man. That part of their position, in our own immediate front, next claimed our undivided attention. It had hitherto been looking suspiciously innocent, with scarcely a human being upon it; but innumerable black specks were now seen taking post at regular distances in its front, and recognising them as so many pieces of artillery, I knew, from experience, although nothing else was yet visible, that they were unerring symptoms of our not being destined to be idle spectators.

Soon after 1 p.m. the guns Kincaid had observed began their bombardment of the Allied position. Wellington kept his men back out of sight, and ordered them to lie down. By this time Napoleon knew that the Prussians were on their way. He ordered D'Erlon's corps to advance towards the Allied left centre. The four divisions of D'Erlon's corps were deployed in columns up to 200 men wide with limited cavalry support. The men of the KGL Light companies had to retire inside La Haye Sainte and the 95th Rifles, in the sandpit, had to fall back to their battalion on the ridge. Picton's division held the line in front of D'Erlon's attack. The British infantry fired at less than 50 yards. Picton himself was killed, shot in the head as he ordered his men to bayonet charge the 8,000 Frenchmen. John Kincaid was one of the riflemen who had to fall back:

> The scene at that moment was grand and imposing, and we had a few minutes to spare for observation. The column destined as our particular friends first attracted our notice, and seemed to consist of about 10,000 infantry. A smaller body of infantry and one of cavalry moved on their right; and, on their left, another huge column of infantry, and a formidable body of cuirassiers, while beyond them it seemed one moving mass.

We saw Bonaparte himself take post on the side of the road, immediately in our front, surrounded by a numerous staff; and each regiment, as they passed him, rent the air with shouts of "Vive Empereur!" nor did they cease after they had passed; but, backed by the thunder of their artillery, and carrying with them the rubidub of drums, and the tantarara of trumpets, in addition to their increasing shouts, it looked, at first, as if they had some hopes of scaring us off the ground; for it was a singular contrast to the stern silence reigning on our side, where nothing, as yet, but the voices of our great guns, told that we had mouths to open when we chose to use them. Our rifles were, however, in a very few seconds required to play their parts, and opened such a fire on the advancing skirmishers as quickly brought them to a stand-still; but their columns came steadily through them, although our incessant tiralade was telling in their centre with fearful exactness, and our post was quickly turned in both flanks, which compelled us to fall back and join our comrades, behind the hedge, though not before some of our officers and theirs had been engaged in personal combat.

When the heads of their columns showed over the knoll which we had just quitted, they received such a fire from our first line that they wavered, and hung behind it a little; but, cheered and encouraged by the gallantry of their officers, who were dancing and flourishing their swords in front, they at last boldly advanced to the opposite side of our hedge, and began to deploy. Our first line, in the meantime, was getting so thinned that Picton found it necessary to bring up his second, but fell in the act of doing it. The command of the division, at that critical moment, devolved upon Sir James Kempt, who was galloping along the line, animating the men to steadiness. He called to me by name, where I happened to be standing on the right of our battalion, and desired "that I would never quit that spot." I told him that he might depend upon it: and in another instant I found myself in a fair way of keeping my promise more religiously than I intended; for, glancing my eye to the right, I saw the next field covered with the cuirassiers, some of whom were making directly for the gap in the hedge where I was standing. I had not hitherto drawn my sword, as it was generally to be had at a moment's warning; but, from its having been exposed to the last night's rain, it had now got rusted in the scabbard, and refused to come forth! I was in a precious scrape! Mounted on my strong Flanders mare, and with my good old sword in my hand, I would have braved all the chances without a moment's hesitation; but, I confess that I felt considerable doubts as to the propriety of standing there to be sacrificed, without the means of making a scramble for it. My mind, however, was happily relieved from such an embarrassing consideration, before my decision was required; for the next moment the cuirassiers were charged by our household brigade; and the infantry in our front giving way at the same time under our terrific shower of musketry, the flying cuirassiers tumbled in among the routed infantry, followed by the life-guards, who were cutting away in all directions. Hundreds of the infantry threw themselves down and pretended to be dead, while the cavalry galloped over them, and then got up and ran away. I never saw such another scene in all my life.

Lord Wellington had given orders that the troops were, on no account, to leave the position to follow up any temporary advantage; so that we now resumed our post, as we stood at the commencement of the battle, and with three companies again advanced on the knoll.

Two thousand British heavy cavalry had charged and shattered the French infantry attack. Sergeant Charles Ewart was in 2nd Regiment of Dragoon Guards (also known as the Royal North British, the Scots Greys). His regiment was part of one of the cavalry brigades which broke D'Erlon's attack. Ewart captured a French Eagle, the regimental standard of the 45th Infantry Regiment. He was subsequently made an officer for his achievement.

It was in the charge I took the Eagle from the enemy: he and I had a hard contest for it; he made a thrust for my groin, I parried it and cut him down through the head. After this a lancer came at me; I threw off the lance by my right side and cut him through the chin and upwards through the teeth. Next a foot soldier fired at me, then charged me with his bayonet, which I also had the good luck to parry, and then I cut him down through the head; thus ended the contest.

By 3.30 p.m. D'Erlon had reformed his shattered troops. Napoleon ordered Ney to resume the assault. The French artillery fire was at its heaviest. A soldier named Thomas in the 71st Highland Light Infantry described being under this fire:

> The artillery had been tearing away since day-break, in different parts of the line. About 12 o'clock we received orders to fall in for attack. We then marched up to our position, where we lay on the face of a brae, covering a brigade of guns. We were so overcome by the fatigue of the two days' march, that, scarce had we lain down until many us fell asleep. I slept sound, for some time, while the cannon-balls plunging in amongst us, killed a great many. I was suddenly awakened. A ball struck the ground a little below me, turned me heels-over-head, broke my musket in pieces and killed a lad at my side. I was stunned and confused and knew not whether I was wounded or not. I felt a numbness in my arm for some time.
>
> We lay thus, about an hour and a half a under a dreadful fire, which cost us about 60 men, while we never fired a shot. The balls were falling thick amongst us. The young man I lately spoke of lost his legs by a shot at this time. They were cut very close: he soon bled to death. "Tom," said he, "remember your charge: my mother wept sore when my brother died in her arms. Do not tell her all how I died; if she saw me thus, it would break her heart: farewell, God bless my parents!" He said no more, his lips quivered, and he ceased to breathe.

Ney apparently thought that the Allied army was beginning to retreat. He ordered 5,000 French cavalry to attack Wellington's unbroken troops. Thomas:

> About two o'clock, a squadron of lancers came down, hurraying, to charge the brigade of guns: they knew not what was in the rear. General Barnes gave the word, "Form square." In a moment the whole brigade were on their feet, ready to receive the enemy. The General said, "Seventy-first, I have often heard of your bravery, I hope it will not be worse than it has been today." Down they came upon our square. We soon put them to the right about.

Captain Alexander Cavalie Mercer was in command of G Troop Royal Horse Artillery. This was a mobile unit of six 9-pounder horse-drawn guns which were capable of changing position during a battle. They had only arrived that morning. They had been ordered to change position several times when:

> How long we had been in this position, I know not, when at length we were relieved from it by our adjutant (Lieutenant Bell), who

brought orders for our removal to the right of the second line. Moving, therefore, to our right, along the hollow, we soon began a very gentle ascent, and at the same time became aware of several corps of infantry, which had not been very far from us, but remained invisible, as they were all lying down. Although in this move we may be said to have been always under a heavy fire, from the number of missiles flying over us, yet were we still so fortunate as to arrive in our new position without losing man or horse. In point of seeing, our situation was much improved; but for danger and inactivity, it was much worse, since we were now fired directly at, and positively ordered not to return the compliment – the object in bringing us here being to watch a most formidable looking line of lancers drawn up opposite to us, and threatening the right flank of our army.

The back of the principal ridge on which our army was posted descended by a pretty regular slope in the direction of Waterloo, and but just in rear of its right another shorter and lower ridge ran a little way almost parallel to it. The high road to Nivelle passed along the hollow between the two. Both ridges terminated in a ravine that enclosed our right flank, running down from the Chateau de Hougoumont . . .

Mercer's troop had been under fire from French artillery when they were ordered to change position again. Not all the Allied infantry was as steady as the 71st.

It might have been, as nearly as I can recollect – about 3 p.m., when Sir Augustus Frazer galloped up, crying out, "Left limber up, and as fast as you can." The words were scarcely uttered when my gallant troop stood as desired – in column of subdivisions, left in front, pointing towards the main ridge. "At a gallop, march!" and away we flew as steadily and compactly as if at a review. I rode with Frazer, whose face was as black as a chimney-sweep's from the smoke, and the jacket sleeve of his right arm torn open by a musket-ball or case-shot, which had merely grazed his flesh. As we went along, he told me that the enemy had assembled an enormous mass of heavy cavalry in front of the point to which he was leading us (about one-third of the distance between Hougoumont and the Charleroi road), and that in all probability we should immediately be charged on gaining our position. "The Duke's orders, however, are positive," he added, "that in the event of their persevering and charging home, you do not expose your men but retire with them into the adjacent squares of infantry." As he spoke, we were ascending the reverse slope of the main position. We breathed a new atmosphere – the air was suffocatingly hot, resembling that issuing from an oven. We were enveloped in thick smoke, and, malgré the incessant roar of cannon and musketry, could distinctly hear around us mysterious husting noise, like that which one hears of a summer's evening proceeding from myriads of black beetles; cannon-shot, too, ploughed the ground in all directions, and so thick was the hail of balls and bullets that it seemed dangerous to extend the arm lest it should be torn-off. In spite of the serious situation in which we were, I could not help being somewhat amused at the astonishment expressed by our kind-hearted surgeon (Hitchins), who heard for the first time this sort of music. He was close to me as we ascended the slope, and, hearing this infernal carillon about his ears, began staring round in the wildest and most comic manner imaginable, twisting himself from side to side, exclaiming, "My God, Mercer, what is that? What is all this noise? How curious! – how very curious!" And then when a cannon-shot rushed hissing past, "There! – there! What is it all?" It was with great difficulty that I persuaded him to retire: for a time he insisted on remaining near me, and it was only by pointing out how important it was to us, in case of being wounded, that he should keep himself safe to be able to assist us, that I prevailed on him to withdraw. Amidst this storm we gained the summit of the ridge, strange to say, without a casualty; and Sir Augustus, pointing out our position between two squares of Brunswick infantry, left us with injunctions to remember the Duke's order and to economize our ammunition. The Brunswickers were falling fast – the shot every moment making great gaps in their squares, which the officers, and sergeants were actively employed in filling up by pushing their men together, and sometimes thumping them ere they could make them move. These were the very boys whom I had but yesterday seen throwing away their arms, and fleeing, panic-stricken, from the very sound of our horses' feet. Today they fled not bodily, to be sure but spiritually, for their senses seemed to have left them. There they stood, with recovered arms, like so many logs, or rather like the very wooden figures which I had seen them practising at in their cantonments. Every moment I feared they would again throw down their arms and flee; but their officers and sergeants behaved nobly, not only keeping them together, but managing to keep their squares closed in spite of the carnage made amongst them. To have sought refuge amongst men in such a state were madness – the very moment our men ran from their guns I was convinced, would be the signal for their disbanding. We had better, then, fall at our posts than in such a situation. Our coming up seemed to reanimate them, and all their eyes were directed to us – indeed, it was providential, for had we not arrived as we did, I scarcely think there is a doubt of what would have been their fate. Our first gun had scarcely gained the interval between their squares, when I saw through the smoke the leading squadrons of the advancing column coming on at a brisk trot, and already not more than one hundred yards distant, if so much, for I don't think we could have seen so far. I immediately ordered the line to be formed for action – case-shot! and the leading gun was unlimbered and commenced firing almost as soon as the word was given: for activity and intelligence our men were unrivalled. The very first round, I saw, brought down several men and horses. They continued, however, to advance. I glanced at the Brunswickers, and that glance told me it would not do; they had opened a fire from their front faces, but both squares appeared too unsteady, and I resolved to say nothing about the Duke's order, and take our chance – a resolve that was strengthened by the effect of the remaining guns as they rapidly succeeded in coming to action, making terrible slaughter, and in an instant covering the ground with men and horses. Still they persevered in approaching us (the first round had brought them to a walk), though slowly, and it did seem they would ride over us. We were a little below the level of the ground on which they moved – having in front of us a bank of about a foot and a half or two feet high, along the top of which ran a narrow road – and this gave more effect to our case-shot, all of which almost must have taken effect, for the carnage was frightful. I suppose this state of things occupied but a few seconds, when I observed symptoms of hesitation, and in a twinkling, at the instant I thought it was all over with us, they turned to either flank and filed away rapidly to the rear. Retreat of the mass, however, was not so easy. Many facing about and trying to force their way through the body of the column, that part next to us became a complete mob, into which we kept a steady fire of case-shot from our six-pieces. The effect is hardly conceivable, and to paint this scene of slaughter and confusion impossible. Every discharge was followed by the fall of numbers, whilst the survivors struggled with each other, and I actually saw them using the pommels of their swords to fight their way out of the melée. Some, rendered desperate at finding themselves thus pent up at the muzzles of our guns, as it were, and others carried away by their horses, maddened with wounds, dashed through our intervals – few thinking of using their swords, but pushing furiously onward, intent only on saving themselves. At last the rear of the column, wheeling about, opened a passage, and the whole swept away at a much more rapid pace than they had advanced, nor stopped until the swell of the ground covered them from our fire. We then ceased firing; but as they were still not far off, for we saw the tops of their caps, having reloaded, we stood ready to receive them should they renew the attack.

One of, if not the first man who fell on our side was wounded by his own gun. Gunner Butterworth was one of the greatest pickles in the troop, but, at the same time, a most daring, active soldier; he was No. 7 (the man who sponged, etc.) at his gun. He had just finished ramming down the shot, and was stepping back outside the wheel, when his foot stuck in the miry soil, pulling him forward at the moment the gun was fired. As a man naturally does when falling, he threw out both his arms before him, and they were blown off at the elbows. He raised himself a little on his two stumps, and looked up most piteously in my face. To assist him was impossible – the safety of all, everything, depended upon not slackening our fire, and I was obliged to turn from him. The state of anxious activity in which we were kept all day, and the numbers who fell almost immediately afterwards, caused me to lose sight of poor Butterworth; and I afterwards learned that he had succeeded in rising and was gone to the rear; but on inquiring for him next day, some of my people who had been sent to Waterloo told me that they saw his body lying by the roadside near the farm of Mont St Jean – bled to death! The retreat of the cavalry was succeeded by a shower of shot and shells, which must have annihilated us had not the little bank covered and threw most of them over us. Still some reached us and knocked down men and horses.

At the first charge, the French column was composed of grenadiers a cheval and cuirassiers, the former in front. I forget whether they had or had not changed this disposition, but think, from the number of cuirasses we afterwards found, that the cuirassiers led the second attack. Be this as it may, their column reassembled. They prepared for a second attempt, sending up a cloud of skirmishers, who galled us terribly by a fire of carbines and pistols at scarcely 40 yards from our front. We were obliged to stand with port-fires lighted, so that it was not without a little difficulty that I succeeded in restraining the people from firing, for they grew impatient under such fatal results. Seeing some exertion beyond words necessary for this purpose, I leaped my horse up the little bank, and began a promenade (by no means agreeable) up and down our front, without even drawing my sword, though these fellows were within speaking distance of me. This quieted my men; but the tall blue gentlemen, seeing me thus dare them, immediately made a target of me, and commenced a very deliberate practice, to show us what very bad shots they were and verify the old artillery proverb, "The nearer the target, the safer you are." One fellow certainly made me flinch, but it was a miss; so I shook my finger at him, and called him coquin, etc. The rogue grinned as he reloaded, and again took aim. I certainly felt rather foolish at that moment, but was ashamed, after such bravado, to let him see it, and therefore continued my promenade. As if to prolong my torment, he was a terrible time about it. To me it seemed an age. Whenever I turned, the muzzle of his infernal carbine still followed me. At length bang it went, and whiz came the ball close to the back of my neck, and at the same instant down dropped the leading driver of one of my guns (Miller), into whose forehead the cursed missile had penetrated.

The column now once more – the plateau, and these popping gentry wheeled off right and left to clear the ground for their charge. The spectacle was imposing, and if ever the word sublime was appropriately applied, it might surely be to it. On they came in compact squadrons, one behind the other, so numerous that those of the rear were still below the brow when the head of the column was but at some 60 or 70 yards from our guns. Their pace was a slow but steady trot. None of your furious galloping charges was this, but a deliberate advance, at a deliberate pace, as of men resolved to carry their point. They moved in profound silence, and the only sound that could be heard from them amidst the incessant roar of battle was the low thunder-like reverberation of the ground beneath the simultaneous tread of so many horses. On our part was equal deliberation. Every man stood steadily at his post, the guns ready, loaded with a round-shot first and a case over it; the tubes were in the vents; the port-fires glared and sputtered behind the wheels; and my word alone was wanting to hurl destruction on that goodly show of gallant men and noble horses. I delayed this, for experience had given me confidence. The Brunswickers partook of this feeling, and with their squares – much reduced in point of size – well closed, stood firmly with arms at the recover, and eyes fixed on us, ready to commence their fire with our first discharge. It was indeed a grand and imposing spectacle! The column was led by an officer in a rich uniform, his breast covered with decorations whose earnest gesticulations were strangely contrasted with the solemn demeanour of those to whom they were addressed. I thus allowed them to advance the head of the column might have been 50 or 60 yards from us, and then gave the word, "Fire!" The effect was terrible. Nearly the whole leading rank fell at once; and the round-shot, penetrating the column confusion throughout its extent. The ground, already encumbered with victims of the first struggle, became now almost impassable. Still, however, these devoted warriors struggled on intent only on reaching us. The thing was impossible. Our guns were served with astonishing activity, whilst the running fire of the two squares was maintained with spirit. Those who pushed forward over the heaps of carcasses gained but a few paces in advance, there to fall in their turn and add to the difficulties of those succeeding them. The discharge of every gun was followed by a fall of men and horses like that of grass before the mower's scythe. When the horse alone was killed, we could see the cuirassiers divesting themselves of the encumbrance and making their escape on foot. Still, for a moment, the confused mass (for all order was at an end) stood before us, vainly trying to urge their horses over the obstacles presented by their fallen comrades, in obedience to the now loud and rapid vociferations of him who had led them on and remained unhurt. As before many cleared everything and rode through us; many came plunging forward only to fall, man and horse, close to our guns; but the majority again turned at the very moment when, from having less ground to go over, it was safer to advance than retire, and sought a passage to the rear. Of course the same confusion, struggle amongst themselves, and slaughter prevailed as before, until gradually they disappeared over the brow of the hill. We ceased firing, glad to take breath. Their retreat exposed us, as before, to a shower of shot and shells: these last, falling amongst us with very

> long fuses, kept burning and hissing a long time before they burst, and were a considerable annoyance to man and horse. The bank in front, however, again stood our friend, and sent many over us innocuous.

The Allied army made some tactical adjustments to their formations to repel the attacks. What remained of the Allied cavalry charged the French cavalry. Thomas:

> We soon received orders to move to the heights. Onwards we marched and stood, for a short time, in square, receiving cavalry every now and then. The noise and the smoke were dreadful.
>
> At this time I could see but a very little way from me; but all around, the wounded and slain lay very thick. We then moved on in column, for a considerable way, and formed line; gave three cheers, fired a few volleys, charged the enemy, and drove them back.
>
> At this moment a squadron of cavalry rode furiously down upon our line. Scarce had we time to form. The square was only complete in front when they were upon the points of our bayonets.
>
> Many of our men were out of place. There was a good deal of jostling, for a minute or two, and a good deal of laughing. Our quarter-master lost his bonnet, in riding into the square; got it up, put it on, back foremost, and wore it thus all day. Not a moment had we to regard our dress. A French General lay dead in the square; he had a number of ornaments upon his breast. Our men fell to plucking them off; pushing each other as they passed, and snatching at them.
>
> We stood in square for some time, whilst the 13th dragoons and a squadron of French dragoons were engaged. The 13th dragoons retiring to the rear of our column, we gave the French a volley, which put them to the right about; then the 13th at them again. They did this, for sometime; we cheering the 13th, and feeling every blow they received. When a Frenchman fell, we shouted; and when one of the 13th, we groaned. We wished to join them, but were forced to stand in square.

By 5 p.m. 9,000 French cavalry had been committed against the Allied line and there were no reserves left. Most of the Allied cavalry had either been lost or were committed. Shortly after 6 p.m. Ney organized his infantry, artillery and remaining cavalry in an attack on the Allied centre around La Haye Sainte. The light companies of the KGL holding it fought until they ran out of ammunition. They then escaped. Ney placed guns at La Haye Sainte, 300 yards from the Allied line. He pleaded for reinforcements which would bring victory. Napoleon replied:

> Des troupes! Ou voulez-vous que j'en prenne? Voulez-vous que j'en fasse? (Troops! Where do you want me to get them? Do you want me to make them?)

Napoleon had troops, 6,000 infantry of the Imperial Guard. But he was now concerned about his right, around Plancenoit. The Prussians had been attacking Plancenoit since 4 p.m. Bulow's IV corps were the first Prussians to arrive. Napoleon had failed to hold them with the rest of his reserve, Lobau's corps. So he refused to let Ney have the Guard to break through in the Allied centre when it was at its weakest. The Prussians had actually captured Plancenoit when Napoleon sent some of the Imperial Guard to push them back. By 7 p.m. they had done so. By this time Zieten's I Prussian corps was finally arriving on the Allied left at Papelotte. They drove the French out of Papelotte and advanced towards La Belle Alliance and Plancenoit. Their arrival was vital for Wellington who was able to strengthen his centre by bringing his own troops across from his left. John Kincaid described the Allied centre at about 7 p.m.:

> I shall never forget the scene which the field of battle presented about seven in the evening. I felt weary and worn out, less from fatigue than anxiety. Our division, which had stood upwards of 5,000 men at the commencement of the battle had gradually dwindled down into a solitary line of skirmishers. The 27th regiment were lying literally dead, in square, a few yards behind us.
>
> My horse had received another shot through the leg, and one through the flap of the saddle which lodged in his body, sending him a step beyond the pension-list. The smoke still hung so thick about us that we could see nothing. I walked a little way to each flank, to endeavour to get a glimpse of what was going on; but nothing met my eye except the mangled remains of men and horses, and I was obliged to return to my post as wise as I went.
>
> I had never yet heard of a battle in which everybody was killed; but this seemed likely to be an exception, as all were going by turns. We got excessively impatient under the tame similitude of the latter

part of the process, and burned with desire to have a last thrust at our respective vis-à-vis; for, however desperate our affairs were, we had still the satisfaction of seeing that theirs were worse. Sir John Lambert continued to stand as our support, at the head of three good old regiments, one dead (the 27th) and two living ones; and we took the liberty of soliciting him to aid our views; but the Duke's orders on that head were so very particular that the gallant general had no choice.

Napoleon finally allowed some of the Imperial Guard to be used to drive the Prussians back far enough for a last attack on the Allied army. Ney led the Imperial Guard towards the Allied right where Wellington himself was waiting. The Allied artillery gave the approaching columns devastating frontal fire. Maitland's First British Guards brigade was lying down, in silence, when the first column of the Imperial Guard was less than 50 yards from them. Wellington himself broke the silence: "Now, Maitland now's your time!" Then he gave the direct order, "*Stand up Guards*."

600 muskets fired at the unprepared Imperial Guardsmen. With the support of two British regiments to their left, they drove the Grenadiers and Chasseurs of the Imperial Guard down the slope. The Imperial Guard rallied. With the support of another Imperial Guard battalion and some heavy French cavalry, they managed to force the British to retreat back to their original position. The fresh battalions of the Imperial Guard continued to attack until a superb act of initiative by Colonel Colborne of the 52nd regiment proved decisive.

General Adam's brigade were to the right of Maitland's Guards brigade. The 52nd regiment were on the right of Adam's brigade. They were concealed by the ground from the advancing French. On his own initiative Colborne advanced his men, halted them and wheeled them so that they formed a line facing the flank of the French column. They opened fire. General Adam ordered the rest of the brigade, the 71st and the 95th Rifles to support the 52nd. They charged the French. It was too much, even for the Imperial Guard. The cry was heard, "La Garde recule." (The Guard falls back).

When he saw the Guard in retreat, Napoleon himself was reported to have exclaimed "*Mais ils sont en melée!" (But they are a mob!)*

Thomas, in the 71st, was not fully aware what was happening:

The whole army retired to the heights in the rear; the French closely pursuing to our formation, where we stood, four deep, for a considerable time. As we fell back, a shot cut the straps of the knapsack of one near me: it fell, and was rolling away. He snatched it up, saying, "I am not to lose you that way, you are all I have in the world;" tied it on the best manner he could, and marched on.

Lord Wellington came riding up. We formed square, with him in our centre, to receive cavalry. Shortly the whole army received orders to advance. We moved forwards in two columns, four deep, the French retiring at the same time.

John Kincaid, in the Allied centre, was aware of the action to his right:

Presently a cheer, which we knew to be British, commenced far to the right, and made every one prick up his ears; it was Lord Wellington's long wished-for orders to advance; it gradually approached, growing louder as it grew near; we took it up by instinct, charged through the hedge down upon the old knoll, sending our adversaries flying at the point of the bayonet. Lord Wellington galloped up to us at the instant, and our men began to cheer him; but he called out, "No cheering, my lads, but forward, and complete your victory!"

John Kincaid and Harry Smith agreed that they could see little because of the smoke which hung over the ridge. Harry Smith:

Late in the day, when the enemy had made his last great effort on our centre, the field was so enveloped in smoke that nothing was discernible. The firing ceased on both sides, and we on the left knew that one party or the other was beaten. This was the most anxious moment of my life. In a few seconds we saw the red-coats in the centre, as stiff as rocks, and the French columns retiring rapidly, and there was such a British shout as rent the air. We all felt then to whom the day belonged. It was time the "Crisis" should arrive, for we had been at work some hours, and the band of death had been most unsparing. One Regiment, the 27th, had only two officers left – Major Hume, who commanded from the beginning of the battle, and another – and they were both wounded, and only 120 soldiers were left with them.

Wellington gave the signal for the general advance. Harry Smith:

> At this moment I saw the Duke, with only one Staff officer remaining, galloping furiously to the left. I rode on to meet him. "Who commands here?" "Generals Kempt and Lambert, my lord." "Desire them to get into a column of companies of Battalions, and move on immediately." I said, "In which direction, my lord?" "Right ahead, to be sure." I never saw his Grace so animated. The Crisis was general, from one end of the line to the other.

John Kincaid:

> This movement had carried us clear of the smoke; and, to people who had been for so many hours enevloped in darkness, in the midst of destruction, and naturally anxious about the result of the day, the scene which now met the eye conveyed a feeling of more exquisite gratification than can be conceived. It was a fine summer's evening, just before sunset. The French were flying in one confused mass. British lines were seen in close pursuit, and in admirable order, as far as the eye could reach to the right, while the plain to the left was filled with Prussians. The enemy made one last attempt at a stand on the rising ground to our right of La Belle Alliance; but a charge from General Adam's brigade again threw them into a state of confusion, which was now inextricable, and their ruin was complete. Artillery, baggage, and every thing belonging to them, fell into our hands. After pursuing them until dark, we halted about two miles beyond the field of battle, leaving the Prussians to follow up the victory.

Some of the Allied army was incapable of pursuing the defeated French.

In the evening, Mercer's troop had been fired at by an advancing Prussian battery. They lost so many men and horses to this "friendly fire" that they were unable to join the general advance at the end of the battle:

> Our situation was indeed terrible: of 200 fine horses with which we had entered the battle, upwards of 140 lay dead, dying, or severely wounded. Of the men, scarcely two-thirds of those necessary for four guns remained, and these so completely exhausted as to be

totally incapable of farther exertion. Lieutenant Breton had three horses killed under him; Lieutenant Hincks was wounded in the breast by a spent ball; Lieutenant Leathes on the hip by a splinter; and, although untouched myself, my horse had no less than eight wounds, one of which – a graze on the fetlock joint – lamed him for ever. Our guns and carriages were, as before mentioned, altogether in a confused heap, intermingled with dead and wounded horses, which it had not been possible to disengage from them. My poor men, such at least as were untouched, fairly worn out, their clothes, faces, etc., blackened by the smoke and spattered over with mud and blood, had seated themselves on the trails of the carriages, or had thrown themselves on the wet and polluted soil, too fatigued to think of anything but gaining a little rest. Such was our situation when called upon to advance! It was impossible, and we remained where we were. For myself, I was also excessively tired – hoarse, making speech painful, and deaf – from the infernal uproar of the last eleven hours. Moreover, I was devoured by a burning thirst, not a drop of liquid having passed my lips since the evening of the 16th; but although, with the exception of the chicken's leg last night, I may be said to have eaten nothing for two whole days, yet did I not feel the least desire for food.

Thomas and the 71st were also incapable of pursuing the French far:

We moved on towards a village, and charged right through killing great numbers, the village was so crowded. We then formed on the other side of it and lay down under the canopy of heaven, hungry and wearied to death. We had been oppressed all day, by the weight of our blankets and greatcoats, which were drenched with rain, and lay on our shoulders like logs of wood.

Scarce was my body stretched out on the ground, when sleep closed my eyes.

John Kincaid concluded:

This was the last, the greatest, and the most uncomfortable heap of glory that I ever had a hand in, and may the deuce take me if I think that everybody waited there to see the end of it, otherwise it never could have been so troublesome to those who did. We were, take us all in all, a very bad army. Our foreign auxiliaries, who constituted more than half of our numerical strength, with some exceptions, were little better than a raw militia – a body without a soul, or like an inflated pillow, that gives to the touch, and resumes its shape again when the pressure ceases – not to mention the many who went clear out of the field, and were only seen while plundering our baggage in their retreat.

Our heavy cavalry made some brilliant charges in the early part of the day; but they never knew when to stop, their ardour in following their advantages carrying them headlong on, until many of them "burnt fingers," and got dispersed or destroyed.

Of that gallant corps, the royal artillery, it is enough to say, that they maintained their former reputation – the first in the world – and it was a serious loss to us, in the latter part of the day, to be deprived of their more powerful cooperation, from the causes already mentioned.

The British infantry and the King's German legion continued the inflexible supporters of their country's honour throughout, and their unshaken constancy under the most desperate circumstances showed that, though they might be destroyed, they were not to be beaten.

If Lord Wellington had been at the head of his old Peninsular army, I am confident that he would have swept his opponents off the face of the earth immediately after their first attack; but with such a heterogeneous mixture under his command, he was obliged to submit to a longer day.

Harry Smith:

That evening at dark we halted, literally on the ground we stood on; not a picquet was required, and our whole cavalry in pursuit. Then came the dreadful tale of killed and wounded; it was enormous, and every moment the loss of a dear friend was announced. To my wonder, my astonishment, and to my gratitude to Almighty God, I and my two brothers – Tom, the Adjutant of the 2nd Battalion Rifle Brigade, who had, during the day, attracted the Duke's attention by his gallantry, and Charles, in the 1st Battalion, who had been fighting for two days – were all safe and unhurt, except that Charles had a slight wound in the neck. In the thunderstorm the previous evening he had tied a large silk handkerchief over his stock; he forgot to take it off; and probably owed his life to so trifling a circumstance. There was not an instance throughout the Army of two brothers in the field escaping. We were three, and I could hardly credit my own eyes. We had nothing to eat or drink. I had some tea in my writing-case, but no sugar. It had been carried by an orderly, although in the ranks. He found me out after the battle, and I made some tea in a soldier's tin for Sir James Kempt, Sir John Lambert, and myself; and while we were thus regaling, up came my brother, of whose safety I was not aware.

Pursued by the Allied army and the Prussians, the French retreat became a rout. A Prussian who had been taken prisoner earlier in the battle was caught up in the rout:

The things I witnessed exceeded anything I had expected, and were beyond belief. Had I not actually seen it all, I should have considered it impossible for a disciplined army – an army such as the French was – to melt away to such an extent. Not only the main road, as far as one could see in either direction, but also every road and footpath was covered with soldiers of every rank, of every arm of the service, in the most complete and utter confusion. Generals, officers, wounded men – and these included some who had just had limbs amputated: everybody walked or rode in disorder. The entire army had disintegrated. There was no longer anyone to give orders, or anyone to obey. Each man appeared bent on nothing but saving his own skin. Like a turbulent forest stream this chaotic mass surged around the waggon in which I was sitting with several companions in misfortune . . .

Very occasionally someone would shout to us: "Sauvez-vous! We are lost! Thank God we shall have peace at long last! We shall be going home!" Several times the cry came up from the rear, "He's coming! The enemy's coming! Sauve qui peut!" and then everyone ran in desperate haste. Some threw down their weapons, others their knapsacks, and they took refuge in the corn or behind hedges, until the reassuring shout of: "No, no, it's all right! They're our own men!" calmed the panic.

A single cavalry regiment could have taken many thousands of prisoners here, because there was no question of offering resistance or of sticking together. Along this road I saw no guns at all, though near Beaumont a solitary cannon lay abandoned. Even in Beaumont there were no longer any regular authorities, as they had all fled.

The allies marched to Paris without further serious resistance. Thomas:

> In the morning we got half an allowance of liquor; and remained here until midday, under arms; then received orders to cook. When cooking was over we marched on towards France. Nothing particular happened before reaching Paris, where we lay in the lines until the French capitulated.

Napoleon abdicated for the second time and surrendered to the captain of a British battleship. He was exiled to St Helena in the South Atlantic. He died there in 1821.

Wars of 1812–15

The Battle of New Orleans 23 December 1814–8 January 1815

> Pay no attention to the rockets, boys. They're nothing but toys to amuse children.
>
> Major-General Andrew Jackson

On 18 June 1812 the United States declared war on Great Britain. The popular slogan was "Free Trade and sailor's rights!". Great Britain was fighting a world war against the French Empire of Napoleon Bonaparte. Anglo-American relations had steadily worsened since 1807.

Great Britain had the world's largest navy. Both Great Britain and the United States had small standing armies. The British army was committed to the war in Europe. Canada was then a British province. Only a few regiments were stationed there for garrison duties. The United States attempted to invade Canada without success in 1812 and 1813.

US overseas trade was stopped by a British naval blockade. American victories in single ship actions hurt the pride of Great Britain's Royal Navy but could not lift the blockade. When the conflict with Napoleon ended, British troops were reassigned to the war with the United States.

The capture of New Orleans was to be the decisive stroke of the war, cutting off the access of the mid-western and western states to the sea.

News of British plans was readily available and by September 1814 Major-General Andrew Jackson, commander of the military

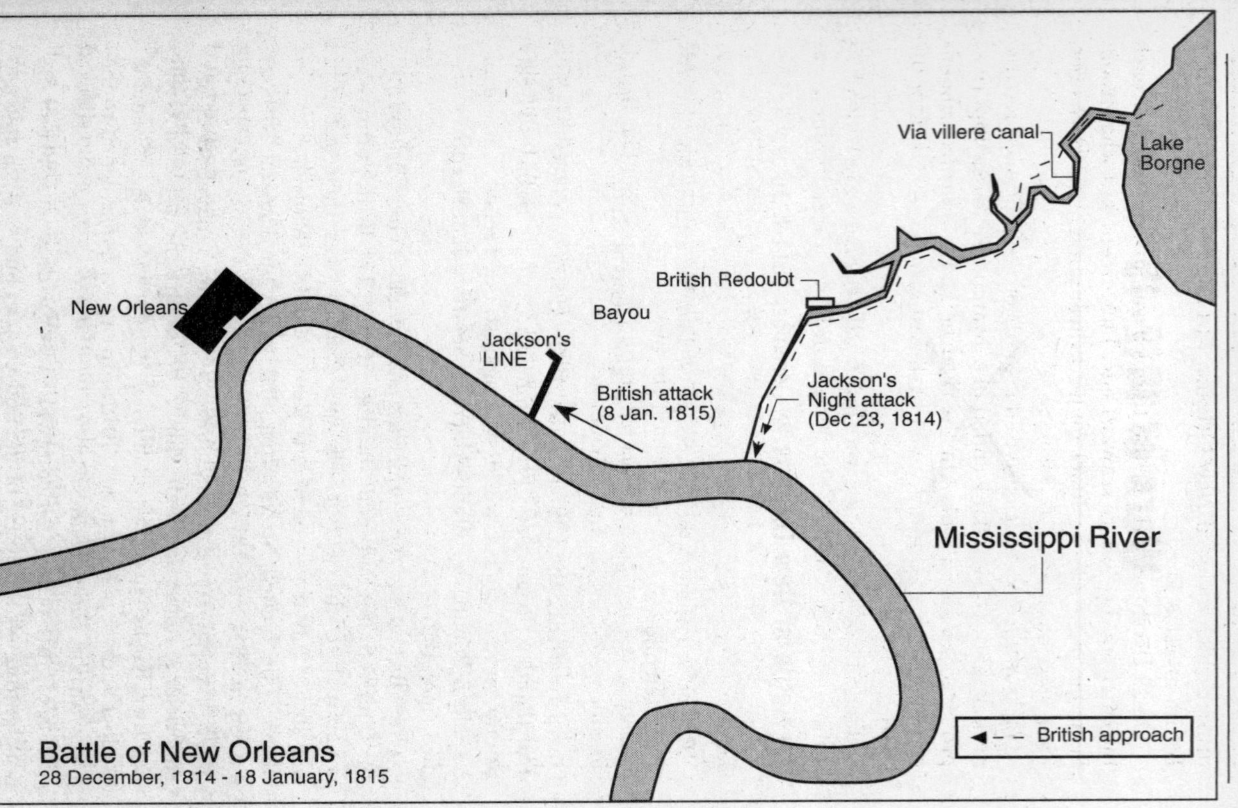

Map of the Battle of New Orleans

district which included New Orleans, was awaiting the arrival of a British invasion force.

On 23 December 1814 British troops began to land and approach the city from the Eastern seaward side. Jackson ordered what troops he had to make a night attack on the British camp on 23 December. Each side took about 30 prisoners.

Jackson formed a defensive line south of the city on a narrow neck of land. His left flank ended in a swamp; the Mississippi river protected his right flank. On the river he had two armed schooners. One of them was destroyed by British artillery fire before the battle.

The American defenders were protected by earthworks which had a ditch in front of them. The ground in front of their position was open.

The newly arrived British commander-in chief, Sir Edward Pakenham, planned an assault which was to begin with a barrage to silence the American artillery and reduce their earthworks. This was to be followed by a frontal assault in two columns.

The battle of New Orleans began on 28 December. The British assault went forward in two columns.

From the river, the American schooner, *Louisiana*, opened fire with her broadside guns at the British column nearest the river, one shot killing 15 men at once.

A British officer in that column recorded:

> Scarce a bullet passed over, or fell short of its mark, but all striking full into the midst of our ranks occasioned terrible havoc. The shrieks of the wounded, the crash of the firelocks, and the fall of such as were killed, caused at first some little confusion; and what added to the panic was, that from the houses beside which we stood, bright flames suddenly burst out. The Americans expecting this attack, had filled them with combustibles for the purpose; and directing one or two guns against them, loaded with red-hot shot, in an instant set them on fire.

Lieutenant George Gleig was also caught in the barrage and shocked by the knowledge that "the Americans are excellent shots, as well with artillery as rifles." He added:

> A tremendous cannonade mowed down our ranks, and deafened us with its roar; while the two large chateaux and their out-

> buildings almost scorched us with the flames, and blinded us with the smoke that they emitted.

The column broke ranks and took cover in the ditches or lay prone on the grass. The British returned fire with Congreve rockets. Jackson's comment summed up their effect.

Losses had been light on the American side with 16 killed and wounded. British casualties totalled 60. Pakenham decided to regard the engagement as a "reconnaissance in force".

The British had learnt that the American earthworks were stout, and it would take much heavier guns to break them down. The ditch in the foreground would have to be filled and spanned, an operation to be executed at the moment of attack.

Pakenham gave orders to bring up heavier guns to batter down the ramparts. It would take some days to bring the heavier artillery from the fleet, anchored outside Lake Borgne. Meanwhile his troops would remain where they were.

They were subjected to night-time raids and sniping at sentinels.

While the British were obviously getting ready for another major effort, the Americans used these last days of the year to strengthen their earthworks. More logs and earth were piled along the modest ridge. The half-mile stretch from swamp to river had stood up well, but needed patching. The batteries, which had been a target for the British guns, had suffered from lack of adequate protection. As more guns were brought up from the naval arsenal, some salvaged from one of the schooners, Jackson approved the use of cotton bales for platforms and embrasures.

> "Well, General," a major told him, "it's not in any military manual I know of." "We'll rewrite the book," said Jackson.

The nearest bales of cotton were confiscated, brought ashore and packed in embrasures around the batteries.

Vincent Nolte, the owner of the cotton bales, observed:

> I was somewhat vexed at the idea of their taking cotton of the best sort, and worth from ten to eleven cents, out of a ship already loaded and on the point of sailing, instead of procuring the cheaper kind, which was to be had in plenty throughout the suburbs of the city, at seven or eight cents, and said as much to Livingston. He, who was never at a loss for a reply, at once

> answered: "Well, Mr Nolte, if this is your cotton, you at least will not think it any hardship to defend it."

On 1 January 1815 the British began an artillery bombardment which was to be followed by an infantry assault. The American artillery replied. The prolonged bombardment became known as the battle of "the Bales and Hogsheads". It was inconclusive. The cotton bales were ineffective at strengthening the embrasures. The sugar barrels (hogsheads) used by the British as gun-platforms on the soft mud were equally ineffective.

Captain Hill of the British Artillery noted:

> Our men, both those working the guns and the infantry lying down in the rear, suffered heavily. By half-past eleven or after the enemy's fire had been maintained about 40 minutes, five of our guns were dismounted completely. They had to be left on the field. Eight more were so disabled in their carriages that they could not be pointed. This left us with only nine serviceable guns and of these but one was a 12-pounder.

The only infantry to move forward were a company of riflemen and an engineer, Lieutenant Wright. They attempted to outflank the American left.

Quartermaster Surtees of the 95th Regiment reported:

> Both himself and nearly all his party perished; for it seems they fell in with a body of American riflemen who, being much better acquainted with traveling in the woods than our people were, fell on them and . . . nearly cut off the whole party.

Around noon General Pakenham gave the order to withdraw and observed:

> seeing that our position was not tenable and that any attempt at further holding out would merely expose our men and guns to further destruction.

Captain Hill confirmed the wisdom of this bitter decision:

> We could not see that we had silenced so much as one of their guns; and their fire grew more and more accurate with every discharge.

Casualties among the British during the hour-and-a-half exchange had come to 26 killed and 41 wounded.

One American soldier wrote:

> Although New Orleans troops are constantly under arms, such is the spirit which prevails among them, that they submit to the fatigues of the camp with the greatest cheerfulness, and it appears more like a party of pleasure than the encampment of an army in hourly expectation of being led into battle . . . Indeed, an aide-de-camp of the general said he could not get a man of them to keep clear of the shot and rockets which were flying among them. They volunteer and go out in parties of 20 or 30 men, and pick off the British when they get a chance . . . The deserters say there would be many more coming over to our lines, if they were not afraid of "those fellows with the dirty shirts."

A British soldier wrote a letter:

> It was a sad day for men who, a year before, had marched through France from the Pyrenees to the sea. We retired not only baffled and disappointed, but in some degree disheartened and discontented . . . All our plans had proved abortive. Even this artillery attack, upon which so much reliance had been placed, was found to be of no avail . . . Provisions are scanty and coarse. Cannon and mortar from the enemy's position play unremittingly upon us day and night . . . With such experience the army almost as one man has settled down to the conclusion that nothing short of a grand assault at any cost of life can extricate us from our difficulties.

On 4 January 2,300 Kentuckians under General Carroll arrived to reinforce Jackson. By the end of the first week in January Jackson had 5,400 soldiers on both sides of the river. On 6 January, General Lambert arrived with 2,700 reinforcements for the British army.

The climax of the battle came on Sunday 8 January. The day began in thick fog. When the fog cleared, Harry Smith, on General Pakenham's staff, disliked the position so much that he tried, unsuccessfully, to persuade Pakenham to delay the attack:

> While we were talking, the streaks of daylight began to appear, although the morning was dull, close, and heavy, the clouds almost touching the ground. He said, "Smith, order the rocket

to be fired." I again ventured to plead the cause of delay. He said, and very justly, "It is now too late: the columns would be visible to the enemy before they could move out of fire, and would lose more men than it is to be hoped they will in the attack. Fire the rocket, I say, and go to Lambert." This was done. I had reached Lambert just as the stillness of death and anticipation (for I really believe the enemy was aware of our proximity to their position) [was broken by the firing of the rocket]. The rocket was hardly in the air before a rush of our troops was met by the most murderous and destructive fire of all arms ever poured upon column. Sir Edward Pakenham galloped past me with all his Staff, saying, "That's a terrific fire, Lambert." I knew nothing of my General then, except that he was a most gentlemanlike, amiable fellow, and I had seen him lead his Brigade at Toulouse in the order of a review of his Household Troops in Hyde Park. I said, "In 25 minutes, General, you will command the Army. Sir Edward Pakenham will be wounded and incapable, or killed. The troops do not get on a step. He will be at the head of the first Brigade he comes to, and what I say will occur."

His troops began to advance in formations 60 men wide and four men deep.

Quartermaster E. N. Burroughs saw a British officer shot from his horse and marveled at the marksmanship that brought him down:

At a distance of nearly 300 yards! As if to warn us of the fate in store! . . . The bullet cut about half its diameter in the upper rim of his left ear, passed through his head, out at the right temple and went on. Instantly the whole American line, from the swamp to a point past its center, was ablaze. In less time than one can write it, the 44th Foot was literally swept from the face of the earth. In the wreck and confusion that ensued within five minutes the regiment seemed to vanish from sight – except the half of it that lay stricken on the ground. Every mounted officer was down at the first fire. No such execution by small arms has ever been seen or heard of.

There were gallant attempts to scale the earthworks, an effort impossible without ladders. A British officer reported:

Some few, indeed, by mounting one upon another's shoulders, succeeded in entering the works, but these were instantly over-

> powered, most of them killed, and the rest taken; while as many as stood without were exposed to a sweeping fire which cut them down by whole companies . . . They fell by the hands of men whom they absolutely did not see; for the Americans, without so much as lifting their faces above the rampart, swung their firelocks by one arm over the wall, and discharged them directly on their heads.

Pakenham rode to the front and his troops resumed their advance. He was hit by a cannon ball in the shoulder, while another knocked his horse from under him.

Pakenham was carried off the field and laid down under a tree.

The 93rd Highlanders followed their Colonel in a last magnificent charge towards the ramparts. They were shot down by several thunderous volleys.

It only remained for General Lambert, the senior unwounded British officer, to order his remaining troops to cover the retreat of those on the field.

General Pakenham's dying words were:

> Lost for lack of courage.

Jackson was heard to observe of the red lines advancing to meet their fate:

> Magnificent. But is it war?

Captain John Cooke, as he crouched among the fallen, observed:

> Some of the wounded managed to crawl away; but every now and then, some unfortunate man was lifted off the ground by round shot, and lay killed or mangled . . . A wounded soldier, who was lying amongst the slain 200 yards behind us continued without any cessation, for two hours, to raise his arm up and down with a convulsive motion, which excited the most painful sensations amongst us; and as the enemy's balls every now and then killed some soldiers, we could not help casting our eyes toward that moving arm, which really was a dreadful magnet of attraction.

The siege continued until 18 January when the British began to withdraw. The British were regrouping for a second advance from the landward side via Mobile when the news that Great Britain and the United States were at peace finally arrived. The Peace treaty had been signed in Europe on 24 December 1814, the day after Jackson's night attack on the first wave of advancing British soldiers.

On 16 March General Jackson paraded his men on the battlefield, before leaving them. In a proclamation issued by his Adjutant-General Rob Butler, he included the citizens and troops of New Orleans:

> You have secured to America a proud name among the nations of the earth, a glory which will never perish. Go, then, my brave companions to your homes, to those tender connections and those blissful scenes which render life so dear – full of honor and crowned with laurels which will never fade. The expression of your General's thanks is feeble; but the gratitude of a country of freemen is yours; yours the applause of an admiring world!

Jackson later made his judgement of the significance of the battle:

> If General Pakenham and his 10,000 matchless veterans could have annihilated my little army, as he expected to do, he would have captured New Orleans and sentried all the contiguous territory, though technically the war was over. It was the purpose of Great Britain to have held that territory.
>
> She would immediately have abrogated the Treaty of Ghent and would have ignored Jefferson's transaction with Napoleon.

Andrew Jackson went on to become Military Commander of the southern United States. While holding this command he invaded Florida with the result that Spain ceded it to the United States. He became President in 1828. During his second term as President, Texas become independent from Spain.

Crimean War

The Battle of Balaclava 25 October 1854

In 1853 Turkey declared war on Russia to prevent Russian expansion into the Balkans. In support, Great Britain and France sent a combined army to the Crimea.

William Howard Russell accompanied the British Army. For two years, he sent back accounts for *The Times* newspaper.

On the 25 October, 1854 a Russian force crossed the Tchernaya river and threatened the Allied camp and their main supply port of Balaclava. The Turks held a line of redoubts on the Woronzov heights, between Balaclava and the Tchernaya river. They abandoned them and retreated. Sir Colin Campbell was in command of Balaclava. He positioned the 93rd Highlanders to cover the town and the camp. In front of them were British cavalry, under Lord Lucan; the Light Brigade, under Lord Cardigan; and the Heavy Brigade, under Lord Scarlett. Three famous incidents occurred during the battle of Balaclava. William Howard Russell described the first incident, the "thin red line".

> As the Russian cavalry on the left of their line crown the hill, across the valley they perceive the Highlanders drawn up at the distance of some half-mile, calmly awaiting their approach. They halt, and squadron after squadron flies up from the rear, till they have a body of some 1,500 men along the ridge – lancers and Dragoons and Hussars. Then they move *en echelon* in two bodies, with another in reserve. The cavalry who have been pursuing the Turks on the right are coming up the ridge beneath us, which conceals our cavalry from view. The Heavy Brigade in advance is

drawn up in two columns. The first column consists of the Scots Greys and of their old companions in glory, the Enniskillens; the second of the 4th Royal Irish, of the 5th Dragoon Guards, and of the 1st Royal Dragoons. The Light Cavalry Brigade is on their left in two lines also. The silence is oppressive; between the cannon bursts, one can hear the champing of bits and the clink of sabres in the valley below. The Russians on their left drew breath for a moment, and then in one grand line dashed at the Highlanders. The ground flies beneath their horses' feet – gathering speed at every stride they dash on towards that thin red streak topped with a line of steel. The Turks fire a volley at 800 yards, and run. As the Russians come within 600 yards, down goes that line of steel in front, and out rings a rolling volley of Minie musketry. The distance is too great. The Russians are not checked, but still sweep onwards with the whole force of horse and man, through the smoke, here and there knocked over by the shot of our batteries above. With breathless suspense everyone awaits the bursting of the wave upon the line of Gaelic rock; but ere they came within 150 yards, another deadly volley flashes from the levelled rifles, and carries death and terror into the Russians. They wheel about, open files right and left, and fly back faster than they came.

"Bravo Highlanders! Well done!" shout the excited spectators; but events thicken. The Highlanders and their splendid front are soon forgotten. Men scarcely have a moment to think of this fact that the 93rd never altered their formation to receive that tide of horsemen.

"No," said Sir Colin Campbell, "I did not think it worth while to form them even four deep!"

The second incident was the charge of the Heavy Brigade. William Howard Russell:

The ordinary British line, two deep, was quite sufficient to repel the attack of these Muscovite chevaliers. Our eyes were, however, turned in a moment on our own cavalry. We saw Brigadier General Scarlett ride along in front of his massive squadrons. The Russians – evidently corps d'elite – their light-blue jackets embroidered with silver lace were advancing on their left at an easy gallop, towards the brow of the hill. A forest of lances glistened in their rear, and several Squadrons of grey-coated

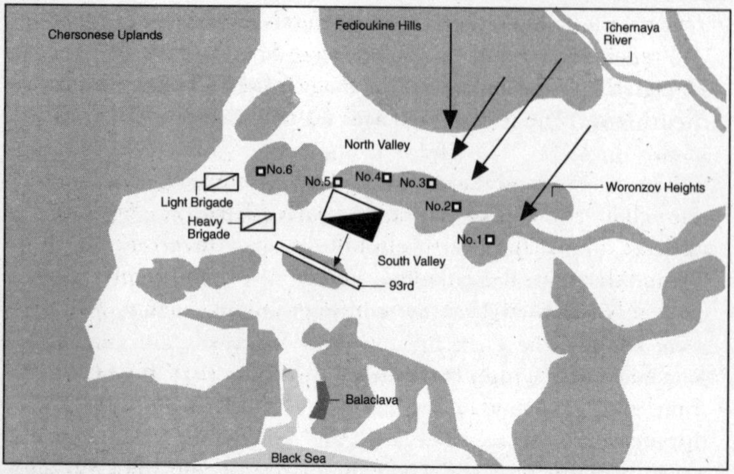

Battle of Balaclava 1 - the Russian advance & the 'Thin Red Line' - key ▫ Turkish redoubt
direction of the Russian advance British infantry British cavalry Russian cavalry
high ground

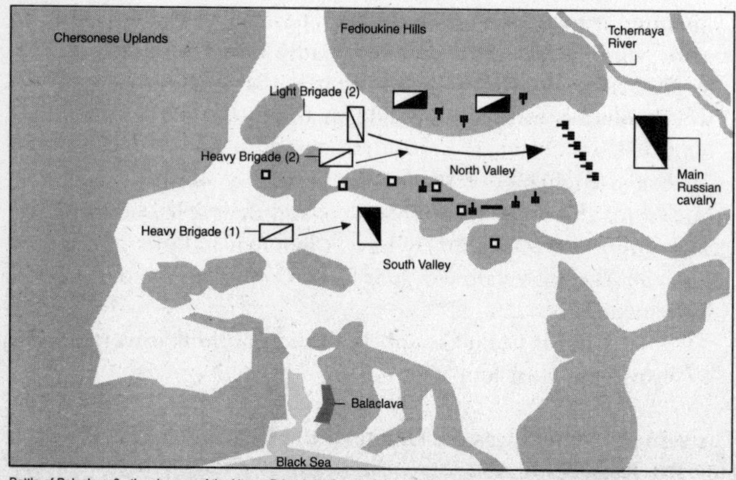

Battle of Balaclava 2 - the charges of the Heavy Brigade(1) & Light Brigade(2) ▫ captured Turkish redoubt Russian guns
direction of British charges Russian infantry British cavalry Russian cavalry
high ground

Map of the Battle of Balaclava

dragoons moved up quickly to support them as they reached the Summit. The instant they came in Sight the trumpets of our cavalry gave out the warning blast which told us all that in another moment we would see the shock of battle beneath our very eyes. Lord Raglan, all his staff and escort, and groups of officers, the Zouaves, the French generals and officers, and bodies of French infantry on the height, were Spectators of the scene as though they were looking on the Stage from the boxes of a theatre. Nearly everyone dismounted and sat down, and not a word was said.

The Russians advanced down the hill at a slow canter, which they changed to a trot and at last nearly halted. The first line was at least double the length of ours – it was three times as deep; behind them was a similar line, equally strong and compact. They evidently despised their insignificant-looking enemy, but their time was come.

The trumpets rang out through the valley, and the Greys and Enniskillens went right at the centre of the Russian cavalry. The space between them was only a few hundred yards; it was scarce enough to let the horses "gather way", nor had the men quite space sufficient for the full play of their sword arms. The Russian line brings forward each wing as our cavalry advance and threaten to annihilate them as they pass on. Turning a little to their left, so as to meet the Russians' right, the Greys rush on with a cheer that thrills to every heart – the wild shout of the Enniskillens rises through the air at the same moment. As lightning flashes through a cloud the Greys and Enniskillens pierced through the dark masses of the Russians. The shock was but for a moment. There was a dash of steel and a light play of sword blades in the air, and then the Greys and the redcoats disappear in the midst of the shaken and quivering columns. In another moment we see them merging and dashing on with diminished numbers, and in broken order, against the second line, which is advancing against them to retrieve the fortune of the charge.

It was a terrible moment. "God help them! They are lost!" was the exclamation of more than one man, and the thought of many. With unabated fire the noble hearts dashed at their enemy – it was a fight of heroes. The first line of Russians which had been smashed utterly by our charge, and had fled off at one flank and towards the centre, were coming back to swallow up our handful of men. By sheer steel and sheer courage Enniskillen and Scot were winning their desperate way right through the enemy's squadrons, and already grey horses and redcoats had appeared right at the rear of the second mass, when, with irresistible force, like one bolt from a bow, the 1st Royals, the 4th Dragoon Guards, and the 5th Dragoon Guards rushed at the remnants of the first line of the enemy, went through it as though it were made of pasteboard, and dashing on the second body of Russians, as they were still disordered by the terrible assault of the Greys and their companions, put them to utter rout. This Russian horse in less than five minutes after it met our dragoons was flying with all its speed before a force certainly not half its strength.

A cheer burst from every lip – in the enthusiasm officers and men took off their caps and shouted with delight – thus keeping up the scenic character of their position, they clapped their hands again and again . . .

Lord Raglan, the British commander, wished to prevent the removal of the guns from the captured Turkish redoubts. He sent a written message to Lord Lucan:

Cavalry to advance and take advantage of any opportunity to recover the heights. They will be supported by the infantry, which have been ordered to advance on two fronts.

Lord Raglan then sent a second written message to Lord Lucan:

Lord Raglan wishes the cavalry to advance rapidly to the front, and to try to prevent the enemy carrying away the guns. Troop of horse artillery may accompany. French cavalry is on your left.

William Howard Russell:

I should premise that, as the Russian cavalry retired, their infantry fell back towards the head of the valley, leaving men in three of the redoubts they had taken and abandoning the fourth. They had also placed some guns on the heights over their Position, on the left of the gorge. Their cavalry joined the reserves, and drew up in six solid divisions, in an oblique line, the entrance to the gorge. Six battalions of infantry were placed behind them, and about 30 guns were drawn up along their line, while masses of infantry were also collected on the hills behind the redoubts on our right. Our cavalry had moved up to the ridge across the valley, on our left, as the ground was broken in front, and had halted in the order I have already mentioned.

When Lord Lucan received the order from Captain Nolan and had read it, he asked, we are told, "Where are we to advance to?"

Captain Nolan pointed with his finger to the line of the Russians, and said, "There are the enemy, and there are the guns, sir, before them. It is your duty to take them," or words to that effect, according to the statements made since his death.

Lord Lucan with reluctance gave the order to Lord Cardigan to advance upon the guns, conceiving that his orders compelled him to do so. The noble Earl, though he did not shrink, also saw the fearful odds against him. Don Quixote in his tilt against the windmill was not near so rash and reckless as the gallant fellows who prepared without a thought to rush on almost certain death.

J. W. Weightman was a trooper in the 17th Lancers; this regiment was at the front of the Light Brigade:

As the line at the trumpet sound broke from the trot into the gallop, Lord Cardigan, almost directly behind whom I rode, turned his head leftward toward Captain Morris and shouted hoarsely, "Steady, steady, Captain Morris!" The injunction was no doubt pointed specially at the latter, because he, commanding the regiment one of the squadrons of which had been named to direct, was held in a manner responsible to the brigade commander for both the pace and direction of the whole line. Later, when we were in the midst of our torture, and, mad to be out of it and have our revenge, were forcing the pace, I heard again, high above the turmoil and din, Cardigan's sonorous command, "Steady, steady, the 17th Lancers!" and observed him check with voice and outstretched sword Captain White, my squadron leader, as he shot forward abreast of the stern, disciplined chief leading the brigade. But, resolute man though he was, the time had come when neither the commands nor the example of Cardigan availed to restrain the pace of his brigade; and when to maintain his position in advance, indeed, if he were to escape being ridden down, he had to let his charger out from the gallop to the charge. For hell had opened upon us from front and either flank, and it kept open upon us during the minutes – they seemed hours – which passed while we traversed the mile and a quarter at the end of which was the enemy. The broken and fast-thinning ranks raised rugged peals of wild fierce cheering that only swelled the louder as the shot and shell from the battery tore gaps through us, and the enfilading musketry fire from the Infantry in both flanks brought down horses and men. Yet in this stress it was fine to see how strong was the bond of discipline and obedience. "Close in! Close in!" was the constant command of the squadron and troop officers as the casualties made gaps in the ragged line, but the order was scarcely needed, for of their own instance and, as it seemed, mechanically, men and horses alike sought to regain the touch.

We had not broke into the charging pace when poor old John Lee, my right-hand man on the flank of the regiment, was all but smashed by a shell; he gave my arm a twitch, as with a strange smile on his worn old face he quietly said, "Domino! chum," and fell out of the saddle. His old grey mare kept alongside of me for some distance, treading on and tearing out her entrails as she galloped, till at length she dropped with a strange shriek. I have mentioned that my comrade, Peter Marsh, was my left-hand man; next beyond him was Private Dudley. The explosion of a shell had swept down four or five men on Dudley's left, and I heard him ask Marsh if he had noticed "what a hole that b – shell had made" on his left front. "Hold your foul-mouthed tongue," answered Peter, "swearing like a blackguard, when you may be knocked into eternity next minute!" Just then I got a musket-bullet through my right knee, and another in the shin, and my horse had three bullet wounds in the neck. Man and horse were bleeding so fast that Marsh begged me to fall out; but I would not, pointing out that in a few minutes we must be into them, and so I sent my spurs well home, and faced it out with my comrades. It was about this time that Sergeant Talbot had his head clean carried off by a round shot, yet for about 30 yards further the headless body kept the saddle, the lance at the charge firmly gripped under the right arm. My narrative may seem barren of incidents of the charge but amid the crash of shells and the whistle of bullets, the cheers and the dying cries of comrades, the sense of personal danger, the pain of wounds, and the consuming passion to reach an enemy, he must be an exceptional man who is cool enough and curious enough to be looking serenely about him for what painters call "local colour". I had a good deal of "local colour" myself, but it was running down the leg of my overalls from my wounded knee.

Well, we were nearly out of it at last, and close on those cursed guns. Cardigan was still straight in front of me, steady as a church, but now his sword was in the air; he turned in his saddle for an instant, and shouted his final command, "Steady! Steady! Close in!" Immediately afterwards there crashed into us a regular volley from the Russian cannon. I saw Captain White go down and Cardigan disappear into the smoke. A moment more and I was within it myself. A shell burst right over my head with a hellish crash that all but stunned me. Immediately after I felt my horse under me take a tremendous leap into the air. What he jumped I never saw or knew; the smoke was so thick I could not see my arm's length around me. Through the dense veil I heard noises of fighting and slaughter, but saw no obstacle, no adversary, no gun or gunner, and, in short, was through and beyond the Russian battery before I knew for certain that I had reached it.

I then found that none of my comrades were close to me. There was no longer any semblance of a line. No man of the Lancers was on my right, a group was a little way on my left. Lord Cardigan must have increased his distance during or after passing through the battery, for I now saw him some way ahead, alone in the midst of a knot of Cossacks. At this moment Lieutenant Maxse, his Lordship's aid-de-camp, came back out of the tussle, and crossed my front as I was riding forward. I saw that he was badly wounded; and he called to me, "For God's sake, Lancer, don't ride over me! See where Lord Cardigan is," pointing to him, "rally on him!" I was hurrying on to support the brigade commander, when a Cossack came at me and sent his lance into my right thigh. I went for him, but he bolted; I overtook him, drove my lance into his back and unhorsed him just in front of two Russian guns which were in possession of Sergeant-Majors Lincoln and Smith, of the 18th Light Dragoons, and other men of the Brigade. When pursuing the Cossack I noticed Colonel Mayow deal very cleverly with a big Russian cavalry officer. He tipped off his shako with the point of his sword, and then laid his head right open with the old cut seven. The chase of my Cossack had diverted me from rallying on Lord Cardigan; he was now nowhere to be seen, nor did I ever again set eyes on the chief who had led us down the valley so grandly. The handful with the guns, to which I momentarily attached myself, were presently outnumbered and overpowered, the two sergeant-majors being taken prisoners, having been dismounted. I then rode towards Private Samuel Parkes, of the 4th Light Dragoons, who, supporting with one arm the wounded trumpet-major (Crawford) of his regiment, was with the other cutting and slashing at the enemies surrounding them. I struck in to aid the gallant fellow, who was not overpowered until his sword was shot away, when he and the trumpet-major were taken prisoners, and it was with difficulty I was able to cut my way out. Presently there joined me two other men, Mustard, of my own corps, and Fletcher, of the 4th Light Dragoons. We were now through and on the further side of a considerable body of the Russian cavalry, and so near the bottom of the valley that we could well discern the Tchernaya river. But we were all three wearied and weakened by loss of blood; our horses wounded in many places; there were enemies all about us, and we thought it was about time to be getting back. I remember reading in the regimental library of an officer who said to his commander, "We have done enough for honour," that was our humble opinion too, and we turned our horses' heads. We forced our way through ring after ring of enemies, fell in with my comrade Peter Marsh, and rode rearward, breaking through party after party of Cossacks, until we heard the familiar voice of Corporal Morley, of our regiment, a great, rough, bellowing Nottingham man. He had lost his lance hat, and his long hair was flying out in the wind as he roared, "Coom ere! Coom ere! Fall in, lads, fall in!" Well, with shouts and oaths he had collected some 20 troopers of various regiments. We fell in with the handful this man of the hour had rallied to him, and there joined us also under his leader-ship Sergeant Major Ranson and Private John Penn, of the 17th. Penn, a tough old warrior who had served with the 3rd Light in the Sikh war, had killed a Russian officer, dismounted, and with great deliberation accoutred himself with the belt and sword of the defunct, in which he made a great show. A body of Russian Hussars blocked our way. Morley, roaring Nottingham oaths by way of encouragement, led us straight at them, and we went through and out at the other side as if they had been made of tinsel paper. As we rode up the valley, pursued by some Hussars and Cossacks, my horse was wounded by a bullet in the shoulder, and I had hard work to put the poor beast along. Presently we were abreast of the Infantry who had blazed into our right as we went down; and we had to take their fire again, this time on our left. Their firing was very impartial; their own Hussars and Cossacks following close on us suffered from it as well as we. Not many of Corporal Morley's party got back. My horse was shot dead, riddled with bullets. One bullet struck me on the forehead, another passed through the top of my shoulder; while struggling out from under my horse a Cossack standing over me stabbed me with his lance once in the neck near the jugular, again above the

> collar-bone, several times in the back and once under the short rib; and when, having regained my feet, I was trying to draw my sword, he sent his lance through the palm of my hand. I believe he would have succeeded in killing me, clumsy as he was, if I had not blinded him for the moment with a handful of sand. Fletcher at the same time lost his horse, and, it seems, was wounded. We were very roughly used. The Cossacks at first hauled us along by the tails of our coatees and our haversacks. When we got on foot they drove their lance-butts into our backs to stir us on. With my shattered knee and the other bullet wound on the shin of the same leg, I could barely limp, and good old Fletcher said, "Get on my back, chum!" I did so, and then found that he had been shot through the back of the head. When I told him of this, his only answer was, "Oh, never mind that, it's not much, I don't think." But it was that much that he died of the wound a few days later; and here he was a doomed man himself, making light of a mortal wound, and carrying a comrade of another regiment on his back. I can write this, but I could not tell of it in speech, because I know I should play the woman.

Weightman was captured but was released after the end of the war.

Joseph Grigg joined the 4th Light Dragoons, (later the 4th Hussars) aged 18 in 1843. He took part in the charge of the Light Brigade, in the second line. When the 4th Light Dragoons arrived in the Crimea, the regiment was under the command of Lieutenant-Colonel Lord George Paget. Joseph Grigg:

> One day I was mounted with my troop, waiting for orders from Lord Raglan, who was on a hill behind us, from whence he could see the greater part of the battlefield, and send an aide-de-camp with an order whenever necessary.
>
> From where we were formed up, we watched the enemy place nine field guns across the valley at about half a mile from us; and two field batteries of two guns each were put into position, one on a slope on the left of the guns, and one on the right. Two squares of infantry were also posted on the left of the guns, under cover of the guns on the hillside, while others were in possession of the redoubts which the Turks had deserted.
>
> I saw Captain Nolan, of the 15th Hussars, come galloping down from Lord Raglan to where Lord Lucan and Lord Cardigan were, and we knew then that there was something for us to do.

Our men of the Light Brigade were the 17th Lancers (Duke of Cambridge's Own), as fine a regiment as ever carried lances; the 8th Hussars, – nice lot of fellows, always ready for anything in the fighting way; the 11th Hussars, who all did their duty well; the 13th Light Dragoons, as good as any in the fight; and our 4th Queen's Own Light Dragoons, who were as ready for it as the others.

The Earl of Cardigan shouted out, "The Brigade will advance-march!" and Trumpet-Major Joy, who was orderly, sounded the "Trot" when we had got into walking order, and we then broke into a trot. Soon the trumpet sounded "Gallop," and afterwards "Charge," and away we went at a splendid pace. As we got nearer the guns our pace was terrific; the horses were as anxious to go as we were; mine snorted and vibrated with excitement, and I could hardly keep my seat, for we seemed to go like the wind.

We were in three lines: in the first, as nearly as I can remember, were the 13th Light Dragoons and 17th Lancers; second line, 4th Light Dragoons and 11th Hussars; third line, 8th Hussars. The lines were about 100 yards apart, so that when a man went down with his horse, the man behind him had time to turn his horse on one side or jump him over the obstacle. Every man thus had all his work to do to look before him, and there were not many chances to watch the dreadful work of the shots, shells, and bullets, which were showered at us from all directions.

The first man to fall was Captain Nolan, who went down directly we got within the range of their guns; but soon afterwards men and horses began to fall fast; the man on my right hand went down with a crash, and soon afterwards the man on my left went down also.

I remember, as we neared the guns, Captain Brown, who was in command of our squadron, called out to the men in the second line, who were getting too, near the front, "Steady, men, steady you shall have a go in directly."

Just before we got to the guns, we gave three loud cheers, and then, in a moment, we were among the enemy.

As I passed the wheel of the gun-carriage the gun was fired, and I suppose some of the 8th Hussars got that shot, or shell, or whatever it was. The wind was blowing from behind us, and the smoke from the guns prevented us from seeing very well what work there was for us to do.

The first man I noticed was a mounted driver. He cut me across the eyes with his whip, which almost blinded me, but as my horse flew past him, I made a cut at him and caught him in the mouth, so that his teeth all rattled together as he fell from his horse. I can fancy I hear the horrible sound now. As he fell I cut at him again; and then I made for another driver, and cut him across the back of his neck, and gave him a second cut as he fell.

A few gunners stood in a group with their rifles, and we cut at them, as we went rushing by. Beyond the guns the Russian cavalry, who should have come out to prevent our getting near the gunners, were coming down upon us howling wildly, and we went at them with a rush. I selected a mounted Cossack, who was making for me with his lance pointed at my breast. I knocked it upwards with my sword, pulled up quickly, and cut him down across the face. I tried to get hold of his lance, but he dropped it.

As he was falling, I noticed that he was strapped to the saddle, so that he did not come to the ground, and the horse rushed away with him. His lance, like all the others used by the Cossacks, had a black tuft of hair, about three inches from the blade, to hide a hook having a sharp edge, with which the reins of their enemies are cut when the lance is withdrawn after a thrust.

Some men of the 4th and I made for several other cossacks who were there in a body, cutting our way through them as through a small flock of sheep; and thus engaged, the batteries on the slopes fired upon us, and their own men also, which was strange warfare, to say the least of it!

Just then I heard Lord George Paget call out, "Rally on me!" I turned and saw him holding up his sword, and we all turned our horses towards where he had taken up a position in front of the guns. On arriving we noticed a regiment of Polish lancers, which had come out from an opening in the hills behind us and was preparing to charge our rear; we thereupon charged through the guns again, killing several Russian Hussars who were still there. It seemed to me then, in the terrible din, confusion, and excitement, that all the gunners and drivers were on the ground, either dead or wounded.

Before the Polish Lancers had time to form line and attack us, the Chasseurs d'Afrique (a French regiment), who were coming down the valley at a sweeping pace, drove them back with great loss.

After a short engagement with the Russian Hussars, we turned our horses in the direction of our starting place and rode back the best way we could, under fire of the infantry and the batteries on the hills.

I was in company with a comrade belonging to my own troop, and all of a sudden down went his horse, and he pitched over its head and lay helpless on the ground. I immediately dismounted and picked him up, when I found his shoulder was dislocated. Regimental Sergeant Major Johnson of the 13th Light Dragoons, who was coming up behind us, rode towards us, calling out, "What's the matter?" and between us we got him back in safety.

Captain Portal, who did not get a wound, rode an Irish horse called "Black Paddy". A large piece of a shell struck it in the shoulder, and directly we got back the poor animal fell dead. The captain had the hoofs cut off and preserved. I saw them some time afterwards beautifully polished, shoes and all.

Captain Hutton, I believe, was wounded in several places, and so was his horse, which also fell dead directly it returned from the charge.

Private Samuel Parks, Lord Paget's orderly, who dismounted to pick up Trumpet-Major Crawford, was taken prisoner with several others. After 13 months he was exchanged, and Lord George Paget asked all about his doings. He told us that General Menschikoff said to him, "Did they make all your men drunk before the charge?" "No, sir," he answered, "unless a pen'orth of rum in an evening would do it, for we only pay a penny a day for our allowance." "Well," said, the General, as he walked away, "I never saw a prettier charge in all my life."

Joseph Grigg left the army, as a sergeant, after 25 years' service, in 1869.

American Civil War

American Civil War – Introduction

> In your hands my dissatisfied fellow-countrymen and not in mine, is this momentous issue of civil war. The government will not assail you. You can have no conflict without yourselves being the aggressors. You have no oath registered in heaven to destroy the government, while I have the most solemn one to protect and defend it.

These were the words of President Lincoln, soon after his inauguration. Between his election in November 1860 and his inauguration, South Carolina seceded (left) the Union. This meant that South Carolina no longer considered itself to be part of the United States. Mississippi, Alabama, Florida, Georgia, Louisiana and Texas left shortly afterwards. In February 1861 the seceding states formed a Confederacy of sovereign states. Jefferson Davis, a former US Senator, was chosen as its President.

President Lincoln disclaimed all intention of invading the south. He announced that he would not interfere with slavery in the southern states. He attempted to revive the common memories of the North and the South which:

> Like mystic chords, stretch from every battlefield and patriot grave to every living heart over this broad land.

Individual soldiers, like Robert E. Lee, serving in the regular army of the United States had to choose between remaining loyal to the Union (United States), or resigning and offering their services to the

Confederacy. Entire garrisons also had to decide which side they supported. Many of the regular army garrisons in the southern states decided to change their allegiance from the Union to the Confederacy. One garrison which remained loyal to the Union was situated in Charleston, South Carolina. This garrison refused to surrender its arms to the Confederacy. Despite problems with its food supply the garrison eventually moved into the uncompleted Fort Sumter in Charleston harbour. President Lincoln diplomatically informed the Governor of South Carolina that he intended to resupply the garrison with food. President Davis ordered General Beauregard, in command of the local Confederate forces, to demand the surrender of the garrison. The regular army garrison commander, Major Anderson, refused. On 12 April 1861 Confederate batteries began a two-day bombardment of the fort. The garrison surrendered and was allowed to depart for the North. No blood had been shed but the bombardment was a clear act of rebellion. This action started the American Civil War.

The bombardment of Fort Sumter roused and united the North. President Lincoln issued a proclamation calling for:

> The militia of the union to the number of 75,000 (to suppress) combinations (in seven states) too powerful to be suppressed in the ordinary course of judicial proceedings.

In protest at Lincoln's call to arms, Virginia also seceded. Virginia seceded on the principle that the United States government had no right to prevent states from leaving the Union. Virginia placed her military forces at the disposal of the Confederacy. Arkansas, Tennessee and North Carolina followed Virginia's lead. West Virginia actually broke away from Virginia and gave its allegiance to the Union. It was admitted to the Union as the state of West Virginia. There were four other border states in which slavery was practised: Kentucky, Missouri, Maryland and Delaware. These were eventually secured for the Union.

The United States had been divided into those states which supported the Union; these were in the north. On the other side were those states which supported the Confederacy; these were in the south. On the Union side were 23 states with a population of 22 million. Against them, on the Confederate side, were 11 states with a population of 9 million, including 4 million slaves. The northern states had most of the industrial capacity and far greater resources

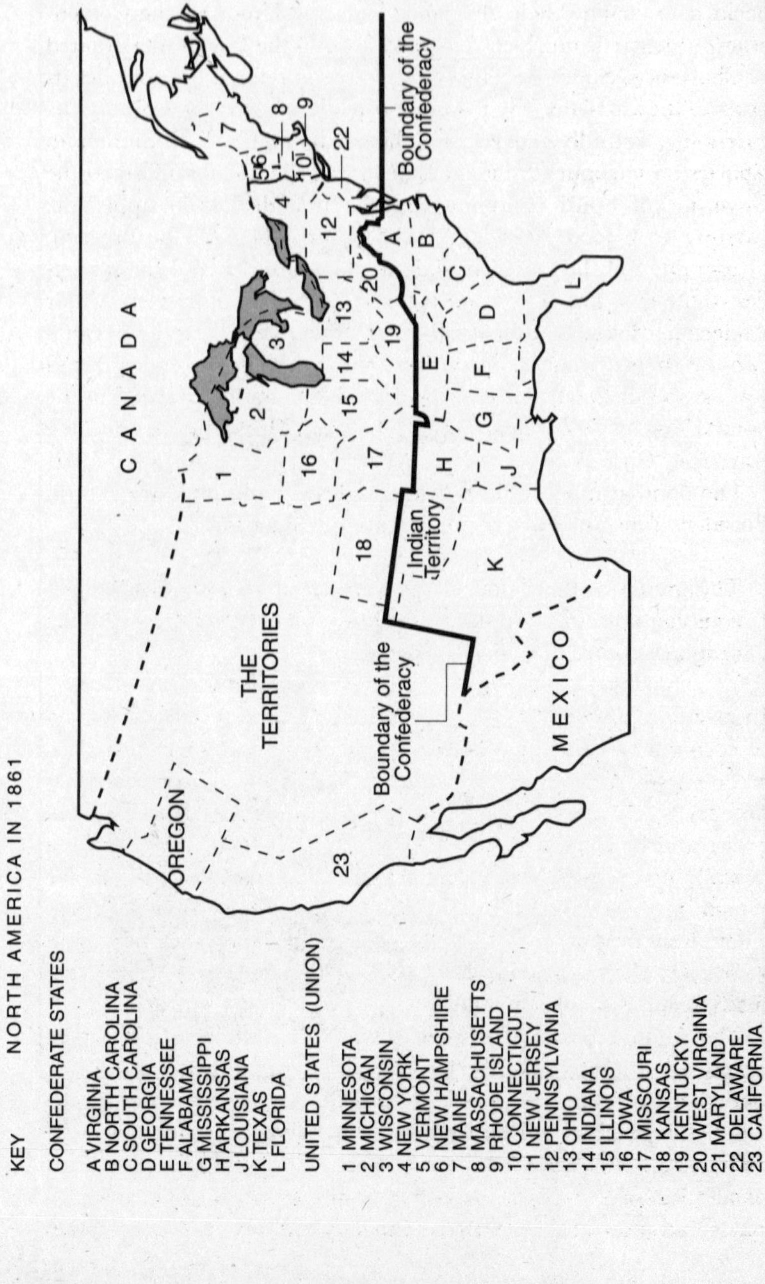

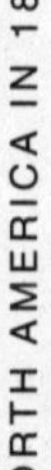

Map of North America in 1861

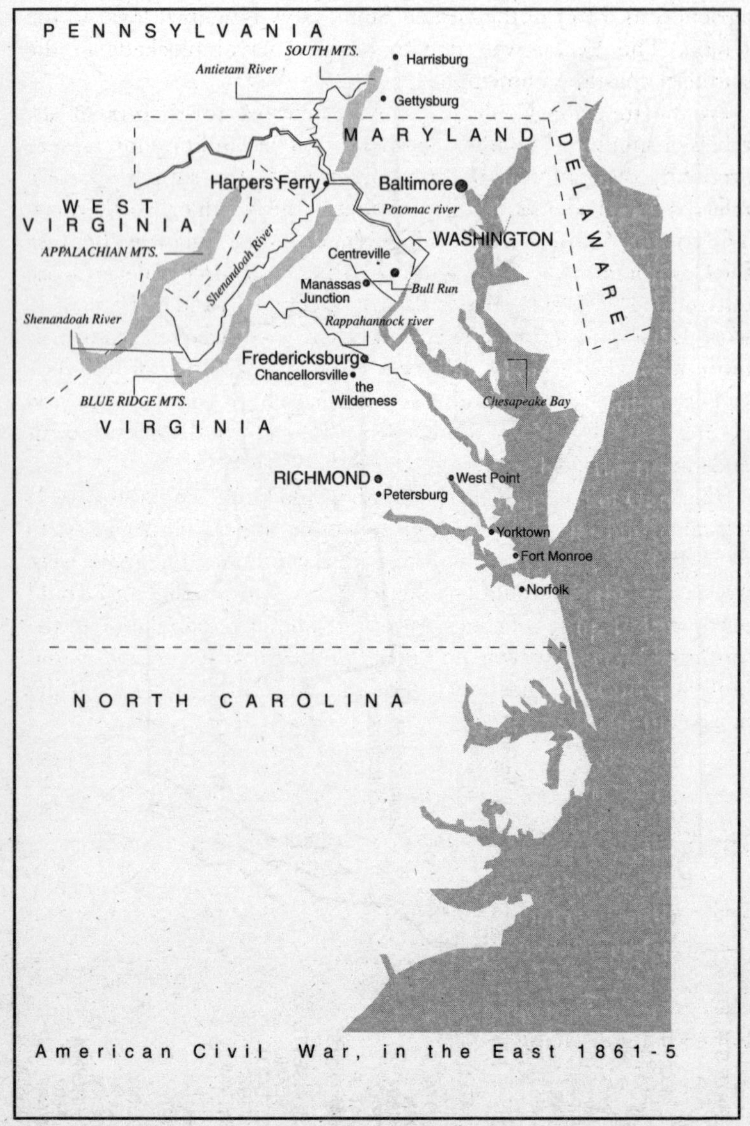

Map of the War in the East 1861–5

than the southern states. The economy of the southern states was agricultural. Most of the United States navy remained loyal to the Union. The Union was able to begin a naval blockade of the southern coastline immediately.

At the time the Confederates were referred to as secessionists, rebels or simply the South or southerners. Their military forces were originally distinguished by grey uniforms. Union supporters were referred to as Federals, Yankees or simply the North or Northerners. Their military forces were distinguished by blue uniforms. Because the Confederates had fewer resources, their uniforms frequently wore out and they either used captured Union uniforms and equipment or wore homespun garments. These were a brown colour known as butternut. They were occasionally referred to as "the butternuts".

The southern states merely claimed the right to go their own way. Naturally, their strategy was defensive. The North denied this right and therefore had to take the offensive.

The subjugation of the entire South would be a formidable task. It was an area 800 miles from top to bottom and 1,200 from east to west. The railways were few and in poor condition. The roads were worse. An invader would have to bring his own supplies and would need very long lines of communication. The slave population of the south was an asset which continued to raise the crops, maintain and build roads and fortifications, releasing a large number of their white masters for military service.

The Battle of Bull Run 1861

> To my utter astonishment, (I) saw our whole body retreating in utter confusion and disorder.
>
> Edwin S. Barrett

Public opinion, in 1861, asked:

> How long should the United States tolerate this insolent challenge?

At the outbreak of the American Civil War both sides set about raising armies. The two capitals, Washington and Richmond, were only 100 miles apart. The land between them was divided into two by the Blue Ridge Mountains. The broader route was over the Potomac river. The Shenandoah valley, west of the Blue Ridge Mountains, provided a second possible invasion route. It was necessary to guard both routes whether attacking or defending.

The Confederates sent their main forces to defend the line of the Potomac river which marked the northern frontier of Virginia. The railway station which served the Confederate position, Manassas Junction, was only 30 miles from Washington. General Beauregard was sent to this position with 22,000 men. General Joseph E. Johnston was given 11,000 defend the Shenandoah valley.

President Lincoln, unlike the Southern President, had no military experience and put pressure on his general-in chief, Winfield Scott, to advance on Richmond. Despite their numbers the Union armies were largely untrained. The main force was 35,000 men under Irvin McDowell, a competent soldier. The Union General in the Shenandoah valley, Patterson, was given 15,000 men to hold off Johnston and prevent him from joining Beauregard.

When the Union advance took place, both Confederate generals were expecting to be attacked and were asking for reinforcements. Patterson lost contact with Johnston's forces. This allowed Johnston to reinforce Beauregard by rail. He arrived with two brigades the day before the battle.

The night before the Battle of Bull Run the Union army was encamped at Centreville. The southern army was waiting for them at the Bull Run creek, positioned across the northern army's line of advance near the railway junction at Manassas. Part of the Confederate army had dug entrenchments; other units had taken up positions in the woods.

McDowell got his attack in first and his superior numbers threatened to overwhelm the numerically weaker Confederates before further reinforcements could arrive. It was in this crisis that Jackson's brigade made its stand "like a stonewall" on the Henry Hill. Then the arrival, by rail, of another of Johnston's brigades turned the tide of the battle. The Union troops were being fired at from their flank and taking casualties when they were ordered to retreat.

When the news of the defeat reached the camp meeting at Desplaines, Illinois, Rev. Henry Cox, who was preaching at the time the intelligence was received, remarked, on closing his sermon:

> Brethren, we had better adjourn this camp meeting, and go home and drill.

Edwin S. Barrett was a civilian attached to the 5th Massachusetts regiment. This regiment took part in the initial successful advance against the Confederates. As his account explains, the Confederates had prepared some defensive positions and also had the advantage of woods where their superior fieldcraft showed its value. At the critical point in the battle the 5th Massachusetts regiment entered a wood, engaged with the enemy in front of them. While they were in this wood, the Union army began to retreat. By the time they emerged the retreat had become a rout which affected troops miles back which were still marching towards the front:

> Until this time I supposed that everything had been swept before us, as the fire from the batteries had been nearly silenced on their right and only an occasional discharge was heard. On the enemy's left, the firing was not nearly as vigorous as half an hour previous. I came out of the woods, and to my utter astonishment, saw our whole body retreating in utter confusion and disorder – no lines, no companies, no regiments could be distinguished. I stood still a few moments, unable to comprehend the extraordinary spectacle, heard my name called, and turning around a Lieutenant of the Massachusetts 5th came towards me. "My God, Ed! What are you here for?" he exclaimed. Without replying, I asked if the 5th had suffered much. He said that the Colonel was dangerously wounded. I waited to find others of my friends, but the whole line was drifting back through the valley. I fell in with them and went slowly up the hill, occasionally halting and looking back. I stopped on the brow of a hill while the volume drifted by, and I can compare it to nothing more than a drove of cattle, so entirely broken and disorganized were our lines. The enemy had nearly ceased firing from the batteries on their right and centre, but still, on our extreme right, beyond a patch of woods, the fight was going on, and their cannonading was kept up with vigor.
>
> The line where the main battle was fought was a half to three quarters of a mile in length, the ground uneven and broken by knolls and patches of wood. At no time did we have a fair chance at the enemy in the open field. They kept behind their intrenchments, or under cover of the woods. Our comparatively slight loss can be attributed to the fact that the great body of our troops were posted in the valley in front of the enemy's batteries, but by keeping as close to the ground as possible, the enemy's shot passed

over their heads, while the cross fire of infantry from their flanks caused us the most damage.

I did not leave the hill until the enemy's infantry came out from their intrenchments, and slowly moved forward, their guns glistening in sun; but they showed no disposition to charge, and only advanced a short distance. Had they precipitated their columns upon our panic-stricken army, the slaughter would have been dreadful, for so thorough was the panic that no power on earth could have stopped the retreat, and made our men turn and fight. They were exhausted with 12 hours' marching and having had little to eat, their mouths parched with thirst, and no water in their canteens – what could be expected of them then? Our men did fight like heroes, and only retreated when they had no officers to control and command them.

I found my horse tied to the tree where I left him in the morning. Mounting him, I rode to the hospital headquarters, and stopped some time watching the ambulances bringing their loads of wounded, fearing I might discover a friend or acquaintance. As these loads of wounded men were brought up, blood flowed from the ambulances like water from an ice cart, and their multilated limbs protruding from the rear had no semblance of humanity. I left these scenes of blood and carnage, and fell into this retreating mass of disorderly and confused soldiery. Then commenced my retreat. None who dragged their weary limbs through the long hours of that night will ever forget it. Officers of regiments placed themselves in front of a body of their men, and besought them to halt and form, for if they did not make a stand, their retreat would be cut off. But they might as well have asked the wind to cease blowing. The men heeded them not, but pressed on in retreat. The regiments two or three miles to our rear, which had not been in action, exhorted our men to halt, as we drifted by, but all to no pupose. No power could stop them. The various regiments tried to collect as many as possible by calling out the number of their regiment and their State. In some instances, they collected together two or three hundred men.

Barrett joined the "dreadful night march" towards Centreville.

A Southern correspondent related:

General Jackson's brigade had been lying for hours sustaining with unflinching courage a most terrific fire. The general had his horse shot under him, and a finger of the left hand shot off; but, cool as a cucumber, he still urged his "boys" to be steady; and steady they were, when they charged and butchered the Fire Zouaves and other regiments right and left. The General has a way of holding his head up very straight; as his almost invariable response to any remark, "Very well," whilst his chin seems trying to get up towards the top of his head. The writer remembers, in the midst of the fight, to have seen the General rallying his men, while his chin seemed to stick out farther, and his "Very wells" seemed to sound more euphoniously than ever and when the writer wished to pour a little whiskey upon the shattered finger, he was told that it was "of no consequence", and away went the general, with a battery following him, to take position in some advantageous spot. If ever anyone was entitled to a sobriquet, the General certainly deserved that of cool.

The Battle of Antietam 17 September 1862

The first battle of Bull Run left the Confederacy secure in the East for a while. The day after the battle, Irvin McDowell was replaced as General in Chief of the Union army by George B. McClellan, a regular army officer who had served in the Mexican War of 1846–7.

In the West, the Mississippi river and its tributaries, the Cumberland and Tennessee rivers, allowed the Union an opportunity to take the war into the heart of the Confederacy. As well as the powerful Unites States Navy, the Union had flotillas of armoured river gunboats.

The Confederate forces in the Mississippi valley were commanded by Albert Sidney Johnston. Against him was the Union General Henry W. Halleck. Under Halleck was a retired regular army officer, Ulysses S. Grant. Grant took Fort Donelson on the Cumberland River in February 1862, capturing 14,000 prisoners and 60 guns.

The Union was able to begin to blockade the Confederate coast and its ports. The Union still held some posts on the Confederate coast. These included Fort Monroe on the Yorktown peninsula, close to the Confederate capital, Richmond. McClellan took his army by sea to the Yorktown peninsula, landing at Fort Monroe. He advanced to within 25 miles of the Confederate capital before being engaged in a series of battles known as the Seven Days' Battle. In 1862, the main Confederate army defending Richmond became known as the Army of Northern Virginia. It was commanded by General Robert E. Lee. Lee's most distinguished subordinate was Thomas "Stonewall" Jackson. The United States government recalled McClellan and his army to Washington.

As soon as Lee was sure McClellan had taken his army back to Washington, Lee moved north. He sent Jackson with part of the Army of Northern Virginia to advance on Washington. Jackson and his forces arrived at Manassas Junction by the direct route overland. He was attacked by the Union forces covering Washington under the command of General Pope. This was the battle of Manassas (also known as Second Bull Run). On the first day of this battle Jackson held off superior numbers of Union forces. The next day the rest of the Army of Northern Virginia began to arrive. General Pope ordered his forces to retreat to their entrenchments outside Washington.

Lee then led the Army of Northern Virginia into Maryland. This was an attempt to win the war by capturing Washington. By circling around the entrenchments south of Washington, the Army of Northern Virginia was able to approach the Union capital from its undefended Northern side.

By this time McClellan had arrived from the Yorktown peninsula. McClellan's army was combined with the Union forces defending Washington. The combined force was entitled the Army of the Potomac. McClellan and the Army of the Potomac set off in pursuit of Lee. McClellan forced back Lee's rearguard at the South Mountain passes. On 13th September, 1862, Lee turned to fight at the Antietam Creek. McClellan delayed his attack; meanwhile Jackson arrived with reinforcements for the Confederate army.

Sources disagree on how many men fought on each side at the Antietam Creek on 16 and 17 September 1862. In his official report, McClellan wrote that he had 87,164 at the battle of Antietam. Confederate numbers have been estimated at 35 to 40,000. Confederate sources referred to this battle as Sharpsburg, the nearest town.

George W. Smalley wrote this account of the Battle of Antietam on the battlefield itself, on the evening of Wednesday, 17 September 1862. It was intended for the *New York Daily Tribune*. He expected the fight would be resumed the next day. George W. Smalley was a journalist attached to the staff of the Army of the Potomac. His

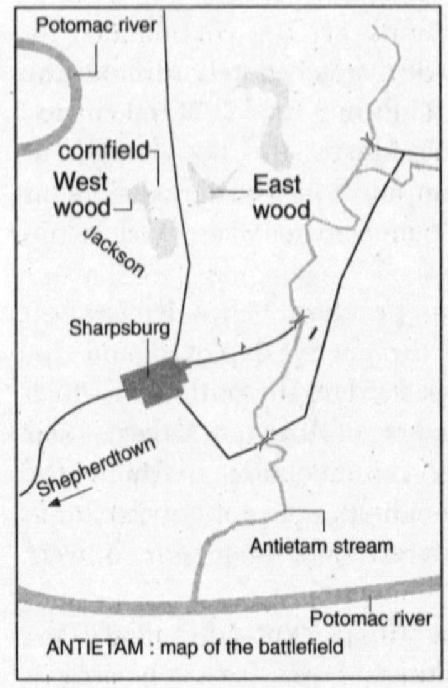

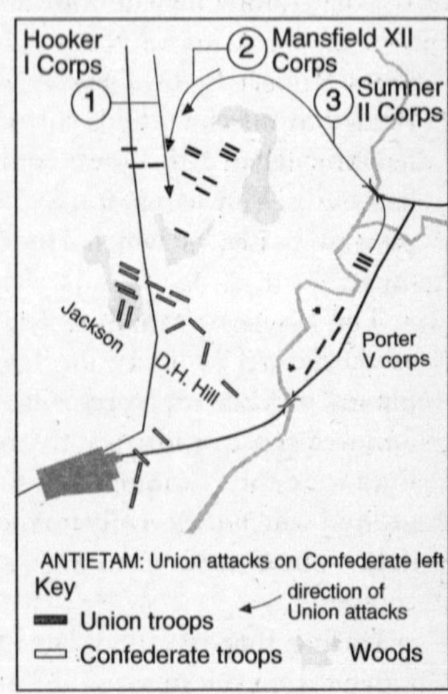

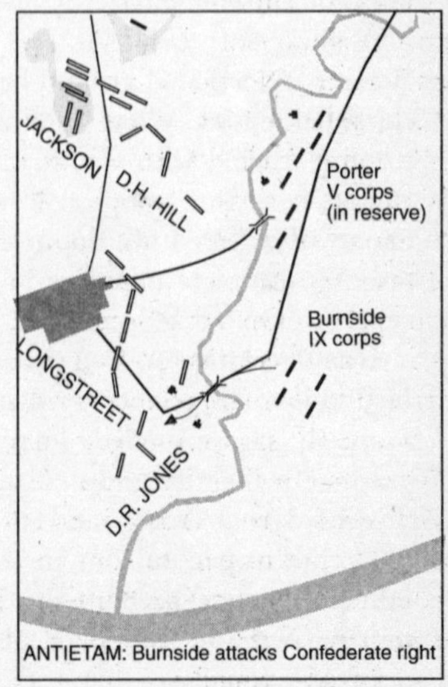

Map of the Battle of Antietam

courage under fire was remarkable and he was respected enough to be asked to assist the staff-officers by taking messages:

> On the evening of Tuesday, Hooker was ordered to cross the Antietam Creek with his corps, and, feeling the left of the enemy, to be ready to attack next morning. During the day of apparent inactivity, McClellan, it may be supposed, had been maturing his plan of battle, of which Hooker's movement was one development.
>
> The position on either side was peculiar. When Richardson advanced on Monday, he found the enemy deployed and displayed in force on a crescent-shaped ridge, the outline of which followed more or less exactly the course of Antietam Creek. Their lines were then forming, and the revelation of force in front of the ground which they really intended to hold, was probably meant to delay our attack until their arrangements to receive it were complete.
>
> During that day they kept their troops exposed, and did not move them even to avoid the artillery-fire, which must have been occasionally annoying. Next morning the lines and columns which had darkened cornfields and hill-crests had been withdrawn. Broken and wooded ground behind the sheltering hills concealed the rebel masses. What from our front looked like only a narrow summit fringed with woods was a broad tableland of forest and ravine; cover for troops everywhere, nowhere easy access for an enemy. The smoothly sloping surface in front and the sweeping crescent of slowly mingling lines was all a delusion. It was all a rebel stronghold beyond.
>
> Unaided attack in front was impossible. McClellan's forces lay behind low, disconnected ridges in front of the rebel summits, all, or nearly all, unwooded. They gave some cover for artillery, and guns were therefore massed on the centre. The enemy had the Shepherdstown road, and the Hagerstown and Williamsport road, both open to him in rear for retreat. Along one or the other, if beaten, he must fly. This, among other reasons, determined, perhaps, the plan of battle which McClellan finally resolved upon.
>
> The plan was generally as follows: Hooker was to cross on the right, establish himself on the enemy's left if possible, flanking his position, and to open the fight. Sumner, Franklin, and Mansfield were to send their forces also to the right, co-operating with and

sustaining Hooker's attack, while advancing also nearer the centre. The heavy work in the centre was left mostly to the batteries, Porter massing his infantry supports in the hollows. On the left, Burnside was to carry the bridge already referred to, advancing then by a road which enters the pike at Sharpsburg, turning at once the rebel flank, and destroying his line of retreat. Porter and Sykes were held in reserve. It is obvious that the complete success of a plan contemplating widely divergent movements of separate corps, must largely depend on accurate timing – that the attacks should be simultaneous, and not successive.

The battle began with the dawn. Morning found both armies just as they had slept, almost close enough to look into each other's eyes. The left of Meade's reserves and the right of Ricketts' line became engaged at nearly the same moment, one with artillery, the other with infantry. A battery was almost immediately pushed forward beyond the central woods, over a ploughed field, near the the top of the slope where the cornfield began. On this open field, in corn beyond, and in the woods, which stretched forward into the broad fields, like a promontory into the ocean were the hardest and deadliest struggles of the day.

For half an hour after the battle had grown to its full strength, the line of fire swayed neither way. Hooker's men were fully up to their work. They saw their General everywhere in front, never away from the fire; and all the troops believed in their commander, and fought with a will. Two thirds of them were the same men who, under McDowell, had broken at Manassas.

The half hour passed; the rebels began to give way a little – only a little; but at the first indication of a receding fire, "Forward" was the word and on went the line with a cheer and a rush. Back across the cornfield, leaving dead and wounded behind them, over the fence, and across the road, and then back again into the dark woods which closed around them, went the retreating rebels.

Meade and his Pennsylvanians followed hard and fast – followed till they came within range of the woods, among which they saw their beaten enemy disappearing – followed still, with another cheer, and flung themselves against the cover.

But out of those gloomy woods came suddenly and heavily terrible volleys – volleys which smote and bent, and broke in a moment that eager front – and hurled them swiftly back for half the distance they had won. Not swiftly, nor in panic, any farther. Closing up their shattered lines, they came slowly away; a regiment where a brigade had been; hardly a brigade where a whole division had been victorious. They had met at the woods the first volleys of musketry from fresh troops – had met them and returned them till their line had yielded and gone down before the weight of fire, and till their ammunition was exhausted.

In ten minutes the fortune of the day seemed to have changed; it was the rebels now who were advancing, pouring out of the woods in endless lines, sweeping through the cornfield from which their comrades had just fled. Hooker sent in his nearest brigade to meet them, but it could not do the work. He called for another. There was nothing close enough, unless he took it from his right. His right might be in danger if it was weakened; but his centre was already threatened with annihilation. Not hesitating one moment, he said to Doubleday, "Give me your best brigade instantly."

The best brigade came down the hill to the right on the run, went through the timber in front through a storm of shot and bursting shell, and crashing limbs, Over the open field beyond, straight into the cornfield, passing, as they went, the fragments of three brigades shattered by the rebel fire, and streaming to the rear. They passed by Hooker, whose eyes lighted as he saw these veteran troops, led by a soldier whom he knew he could trust. "I think they will hold it" he said.

General Hartsuff took his troops very steadily, but, now that they were under fire, not hurriedly, up the hill from which the cornfield begins to descend, and formed them on the crest. Not a man who was not in full view – not one who bent before the storm. Firing at first in volleys, they fired then at will with wonderful rapidity and effect. The whole line crowned the hill and stood out darkly against the sky, but lighted and shrouded ever in flame and smoke. They were the 12th and 13th Massachusetts, and another regiment which I cannot remember – old troops all of them.

There for half an hour they held the ridge, unyielding in purpose, exhaustless in courage. There were gaps in the line, but it nowhere bent. Their general was severely wounded early in the fight, but they fought on. Their supports did not come – but they determined to win without them. They began to go down the hill and into the corn; they did not stop to think that their ammunition was nearly gone; they were there to win that field and they won it. The rebel line for the second time fled through the corn and into the woods. I cannot tell how few of Hartsuff's brigade were left when the work was done; but it was done. There was no more gallant, determined, heroic fighting in all this desperate day. General Hartsuff is very severely wounded; but I do not believe he counts his success too dearly purchased.

The crisis of the fight at this point had arrived. Ricketts' division, vainly endeavoring to advance, and exhausted by the effort, had fallen back. Part of Mansfield's corps was ordered in to their relief; but Mansfield's troops came back again and their General was mortally wounded. The left nevertheless was too extended to be turned, and too strong to be broken. Ricketts sent word he could not advance, but could hold his ground.

Doubleday had kept his guns at work on the right, and had finally silenced a rebel battery that for half an hour had poured a galling enfilading fire along Hooker's central line. There were woods in front of Doubleday's hill which the rebels held, but so long as those guns pointed towards them they did not care to attack.

With his left, then, able to take care of itself, with his right impregnable, with two brigades of Mansfield still fresh and coming rapidly up, and with his centre a second time victorious, General Hooker determined to advance. Orders were sent to Crawford and Gordon – the two Mansfield brigades – to move forward at once, the batteries in the centre were ordered to advance; the whole line was called on, and the General himself went forward.

To the right of the cornfield and beyond it was a point of woods. Once carried and firmly held, it was the key of the position. Hooker determined to take it. He rode out in front of his farthest troops on a hill to examine the ground for a battery. At the top he dismounted and went forward on foot, completed his reconnaissance, returned, and remounted. The musketry fire from the point of woods was all the while extremely hot. As he put his foot in the stirrup a fresh volley of rifle bullets came whizzing by. The tall, soldierly figure of the general, the white horse which he rode, the elevated place where he was, all made him a most dangerously conspicuous mark. So he had been all day, riding often without a staff officer or an orderly near him – all sent off on urgent duty – visible everywhere on the field. The rebel bullets had followed him all day, but they had not hit him, and he would not regard them.

Remounting on this hill, he had not ridden five steps when he was struck in the foot by a ball. Three men were shot down at the same moment by his side. The air was alive with bullets. He kept on his horse a few minutes, though the wound was severe and excessively painful, and would not dismount till he had given his last order to advance. He was himself in the very front. Swaying unsteadily on his horse, he turned in his seat to look about him. "There is a regiment to the right. Order it forward! Crawford and Gordon are coming up. Tell them to carry those woods and hold them – and it is our fight!" It was found that the bullet had passed completely through his foot. The surgeon, who examined it on the spot, could give no opinion whether bones were broken; but it was afterwards ascertained that though grazed they were not fractured. Of course the severity of the wound made it impossible for him to keep the field, which he believed already won, so far as it belonged to him to win it. It was nine o'clock. The fight had been furious since five. A large part of his command was broken, but with his right still untouched, and with Crawford's and Gordon's brigades just up, above all, with the advance of the whole central line, which the men had heard ordered with cheers, and with a regiment already on the edge of the woods he wanted, he might well leave the field, thinking the battle was won – that his battle was won, for I am writing only about the attack on the rebel left.

I see no reason why I should disguise my admiration of General Hooker's bravery and soldierly ability. Remaining nearly all the morning on the right, I could not help seeing the sagacity and promptness of his movements, how completely his troops were kept in hand, how devotedly they trusted him, how keen was his insight into the battle, how every opportunity was seized and every reverse was checked and turned into another success. I say this the more unreservedly because I have no personal relation whatever with him, never saw him till the day before the fight and don't like his politics or opinions in general. But what are politics in such a battle?

Sumner arrived just as Hooker was leaving and assumed command. Crawford and Gordon had gone into the woods, and were holding them stoutly against heavy odds. As I rode over towards the left I met Sumner at the head of his column, advancing rapidly through the timber opposite where Crawford was fighting. The veteran General was riding alone in the forest, far ahead of his leading brigade, his hat off; his gray hair, and beard, and mustache strangely contrasting with the fire in his eyes and his martial air, as he hurried on to where the bullets were thickest.

Sedgwick's division was in advance, moving forward to support Crawford and Gordon. Rebel reinforcements were approaching also, and the struggle for the roads was again to be renewed. Sumner sent forward two divisions – Richardson and French – on the left. Sedgwick, moving in column of divisions through the woods in rear, deployed and advanced in line over the cornfield. There was a broad interval between him and the nearest division, and he saw that if the rebel line were complete, his own division was in immediate danger of being flanked. But his orders were to advance, and those are the orders which a soldier – and Sedgwick is every inch a soldier – love best to hear.

To extend his own front as far as possible, he ordered the Thirty-fourth New York to move by the left flank. The maneouvre was attempted under a fire of the greatest intensity, and the regiment broke. At the same moment, the enemy perceiving their advantage, came round on that flank. Crawford was obliged to give way on the right, and his troops, pouring in confusion through the ranks of Sedgwick's advance brigade, threw it into disorder, and back on the second and third lines. The enemy advanced, their fire increasing.

General Sedgwick was three times wounded; in the shoulder, leg, and wrist, but he persisted in remaining on the field so long as there was a chance of saving it. His Adjutant-General, Major Sedgwick, bravely rallying and trying to reform the troops, was shot through the body, the bullet lodging in the spine, and fell from his horse. Severe as the wound is, it is probably not mortal – Lieutenant Howe, of General Sedgwick's staff endeavored vainly to rally the Thirty-fourth New York. They were badly cut up, and would not stand. Half their officers were killed or wounded, their colors shot to pieces, the color-sergeant killed – every one of the color-guard wounded. Only 32 were afterwards got together.

The Fifteenth Massachusetts went into action with 17 officers and nearly 600 men. Nine officers were killed or wounded, and some of the latter are prisoners. Captain Simons, Captain Saunders of the sharpshooters, Lieutenant Derby, and Lieutenant Berry are killed. Captain Bartlett and Captain Jocelyn, Lieutenant Spurr, Lieutenant Gale, and Lientenant Bradley are wounded. 134 men were the only remains that could be collected of this splendid regiment.

General Dana was wounded. General Howard, who took command of the division after General Sedgwick was disabled, exerted himself to restore order; but it could not be done there. General

Sumner ordered the line to be reformed. The test was too severe for volunteer troops, under such a fire. Sumner himself attempted to arrest the disorder, hut to little purpose. Lieutenant-Colonel Revere and Captain Audenried, of his staff, were wounded severely, but not dangerously. It was impossible to hold the position. General Sumner withdrew the division to the rear, and once more the cornfield was abandoned to the enemy.

French sent word he could hold his ground. Richardson, while gallantly leading a regiment under a heavy fire, was severely wounded in the shoulder. General Meagher was wounded at the head of his brigade. The loss in general officers was becoming frightful.

At one o'clock affairs on the right had a gloomy look. Hooker's troops were greatly exhausted and their general away from the field. Mansfield's were no better. Sumner's command had lost heavily, but two of his divisions were comparatively fresh. Artillery was yet playing vigorously in front, though the ammunition of many of the batteries was entirely exhausted and they had been compelled to retire.

Doubleday held the right inflexibly. Sumner's headquarters were now in the narrow field where, the night before, Hooker had begun the fight. All that had been gained in front had been lost. The enemy's batteries, which, if advanced and served vigorously, might have made sad work with the closely massed troops, were fortunately either partially disabled or short of ammunition. Sumner was confident that he could hold his own, but another advance was out of the question. The enemy, on the other hand, seemed to be too much exhausted to attack.

At this crisis Franklin came up with fresh troops and formed on the left. Slocum, commanding one division of the corps, was sent forward along the slopes lying under the first ranges of the rebel hills while Smith, with the other division, was ordered to retake the cornfields and woods which all day had been so hotly contested. It was done in the handsomest style. His Maine and Vermont regiments, and the rest, went forward on the run, cheering as they went, swept like an avalanche through the cornfields, fell upon the woods, took them in ten minutes, and held them. They were not again retaken.

The field and its ghastly harvest which the reaper had gathered in those fatal hours remained finally with us. Four times it had been lost and won. The dead are strewn so thickly that as you ride over it you cannot guide your horse's steps too carefully. Pale and bloody faces are everywhere upturned. They are sad and terrible but there is nothing which makes one's heart beat so quickly as the imploring look of wounded men, who beckon wearily for help which you cannot stay to give.

General Smith's attack was so sudden that his success was accomplished with no great loss. He had gained a point, however, which compelled him to expect every moment an attack, and to which, if the enemy again brought up reserves, would task his best energies and best troops. But the long strife, the heavy losses, incessant fighting over the same ground repeatedly lost and won inch by inch, and more than all, perhaps the fear of Burnside on the left and Porter in front, held the enemy in check. For two or three hours there was a lull even in the Cannonade on the right, which hitherto had been incessant. McClellan had been over on the field after Sumner's repulse, but had speedily returned to headquarters. Sumner again sent word that he was able to hold his position, but could not advance with his own corps.

Meantime where was Burnside, and what was he doing? On the right, where I had spent the day until two o'clock, little was known of the general fortunes of the field. We had heard Porter's guns in the centre, but nothing from Burnside on the left. The distance was, perhaps, too great, to distinguish the sound of his artillery from Porter's. There was no immediate prospect of more fighting on the right, and I left the field which all day long had seen the most obstinate contest of the war, and rode over to McClellan's headquarters. The different battlefields were shut out from each other's view, but all partially visible from the central hill, which General McClellan had occupied during the day. But I was more than ever impressed, on returning, with the completely deceitful appearance of the ground the rebels had chosen, when viewed from the front.

Hooker's and Sumner's struggle had been carried on over an uneven and wooded surface, their own line of battle extending in a semicircle of less than a mile aud a half. Perhaps a better notion of their position can be got by considering their right, centre and left as forming sides of a square. So long, therefore, as either wing was driven back, the centre became exposed to a very dangerous enfilading fire, and the farther the centre was advanced the worse it was, unless the lines on its side and rear are firmly held. This formation resulted originally from the efforts of the enemy to turn both flanks. Hooker at the very outset threw his column so far into the heart of the rebel lines that they were compelled to threaten him on the flank to secure their own centre.

Nothing of all this was perceptible from the hills in front. Some directions of the rebel lines had been disclosed by the smoke of their guns, but the whole interior formation of the country beyond the hills was completely concealed. When McClellan arranged his order of battle, it must have been upon information, or have been left to his corps and division commanders to discover for themselves.

Up to three o'clock Burnside had made little progress. His attack on the bridge had been successful, but the delay had been so great that to the observer, it appeared as if McClellan's plans must have been seriously disarranged. It is impossible not to suppose that the attacks on right and left were meant in a measure to correspond, for otherwise the enemy had only to repel Hooker on the one hand, then transfer his troops, and push them against Burnside.

This is an anonymous account of the charge of the Second Maryland regiment which finally took the bridge:

There was no noise, no cheering in the ranks; but, on the other hand, there was no wavering or faltering as they moved sternly and silently forward into the conflict. The measured and heavy tread of the battalion, falling in dull cadence on the ear, was the only sound audible as it entered the head of the bridge. Suddenly the enemy's cannon opened at short range, pouring upon it a tempest of round shot and shell, sweeping away whole files, and ploughing bloody furrows through the ranks. But it faltered not. At the sharp, short order of the officers, "Close up, boys," the bloody gaps were filled and the heroic battalion pressed on. Standard-bearer after standard-bearer went down before iron hurricane; but scarcely was he down when the standard, wrenched from his dying grasp, was borne aloft by his nearest comrade in the strife.

The way over the bridge was filled with corpses. Most of the officers had fallen. Captain Wilson, of a family that had sent five brothers to the war, for the moment commanding the regiment, had gone down, pierced through the middle of his forehead by a minie ball. Captain Martin, succeeding him, fell mortally wounded; but there was no check, no faltering or sign of confusion or hesitation. With their heads bent, their shoulders a little forward, at the charge step, they moved steadily on, until the

> bridge was cleared, and the way opened to the regiments in the rear. It was only when the bridge was won, and room obtained to deploy the column, that the old, lusty Maryland cheer which more than 80 years before had been heard at Brandywine, at Guilford and Eutaw, rang out on the sulphureous air of that dread September day, attesting that those who sent it were the legitimate sons of sires who had fought for freedom, and won immortal fame under Howard and Williams. They are no more forever the despised "Plug Uglies" of Baltimore, but a "new Maryland line", indomitable as the "old", baptized anew in fire and blood, which has washed away all former transgressions.

Smalley's account continues, noting Burnside's caution:

> Here was the difference between Smith and Burnside. The former did his work at once, and lost all his men at once – that is, all whom he lost at all; Burnside seems to have attacked cautiously in order to save his men, and sending successively insufficient forces against a position of strength, distributed his loss over a greater period of time, but yet lost none the less in the end.
>
> Finally, at four o'clock, McClellan sent simultaneous orders to Burnside and Franklin – to the former to advance and carry the batteries in his front at all hazards and at any cost; to the latter to carry the woods next in front of him to the left, which the rebels still held. The order to Franklin, however, was practically countermanded, in consequence of a message from General Sumner that, if Franklin went on and was repulsed, his own corps was not yet sufficiently reorganized to be depended on as a reserve. Franklin, thereupon, was directed to run no risk of losing his present position, and, instead of sending his infantry into the woods, contented himself with advancing his batteries over the breadth of the fields in front, supporting them with heavy columns of infantry, and attacking with energy the rebel batteries immediately opposed to him. His movement was a success, so far as it went, the batteries maintaining their new ground, and sensibly affecting the steadiness of the rebel fire. That being once accomplished, and all hazard of the right being again forced back having been dispelled, the movement of Burnside became at once the turning point of success, and the fate of the day depended on him.
>
> How extraordinary the situation was may be judged from a moment's consideration of the facts. It is understood that from the

outset Burnside's attack was expected to be decisive, as it certainly must have been if things went well elsewhere, and if he succeeded in establishing himself on the Sharpsburg road in the rebel rear. Yet Hooker and Sumner and Franklin and Mansfield were all sent to the right three miles away, while Porter seems to have done double duty with his single corps in front, both supporting the batteries and holding himself in reserve. With all this immense force on the right, but 16,000 men were given to Burnside for the decisive movement of the day.

Still more unfortunate in its results was the total failure of these separate attacks on the right and left to sustain, or in any manner co-operate with, each other. Burnside hesitated for hours in front of the bridge, which should have been carried at once by a coup de main. Meantime Hooker had been fighting for four hours, with various fortune, but final success. Sumner had come up too late to join in the decisive attack which his earlier arrival would probably have converted into a complete success; and Franklin reached the scene only when Sumner had been repulsed. Probably before his arrival the rebels had transferred a considerable number of troops to their right to meet the attack of Burnside, the direction of which was then suspected or developed.

Attacking first with one regiment, then with two, and delaying both for artillery, Burnside was not over the bridge before two o'clock perhaps not till three. He advanced slowly up the slopes in his front, his batteries in rear covering, to some extent, the movements of the infantry. A desperate fight was going on in a deep ravine on his right; the rebel batteries were in full play, and apparently very annoying and destructive, while heavy columns of rebel troops were plainly visible, advancing, as if careless of concealment, along the road and over the hills in the direction of Burnside's forces. It was at this point of time that McClellan sent him the order above given.

Burnside obeyed it most gallantly. Getting his troops well in hand, and sending a portion of his artillery to the front, he advanced with rapidity and the most determined vigor straight up the hill in front, on top of which the rebels had maintained their most dangerous battery. The movement was in plain view of McClellan's position and as Franklin, on the other side, sent his batteries into the field about the same time, the battle seemed to open in all directions with greater activity than ever.

The fight in the ravine was in full progress, the batteries in the centre were firing with new vigor, Franklin was blazing away on the right, and every hilltop, ridge, and woods along the whole line was crested and veiled with white clouds of smoke. All day had been clear and bright since the early cloudy morning; and now this whole magnificent, unequalled scene shone with the splendor of an afternoon September sun. Four miles of battle, its glory all visible, its horrors all hidden, the fate of the republic hanging on the hour – could any one be insensible of its grandeur?

There are two hills on the left of the road, the farthest the lowest. The rebels have batteries on both. Burnside is ordered to carry the nearest to him, which is the farthest from the road. His guns, opening first from this new position in front, soon entirely controlled and silenced the enemy artillery. The infantry came on at once, advancing rapidly and steadily, their long, dark lines and broad masses plainly visible without a glass as they moved over the green hillside.

The next moment the road in which the rebel battery was planted was canopied with clouds of dust swiftly descending into the valley. Underneath was a tumult of wagons, guns, horses and men, flying at speed down the road. Blue flashes of smoke burst now and then among them; a horse or a man, or half a dozen, went down, then the whirlwind swept on.

The hill was carried; but could it be held? The rebel columns, before seen moving to the left, increase their pace. The guns on the hill above send an angry tempest of shell down among Burnside's guns and men. He has formed his columns apparently in the near angles of fields bordering the road – high ground above them everywhere except in rear.

In another moment a rebel battle-line appears on the brow of the ridge above them, moving swiftly down in the most perfect order, though met by incessant discharges of musketry, of which we plainly see the flashes, does not fire a gun. White spaces show where men are falling, but they close up instantly, and still the line advances. The brigades of Burnside are in heavy column; they will not give way before a bayonet charge in line, and the rebels think twice before they dash into those hostile masses.

There is a halt; the rebel left gives way and scatters over the field; the rest stand fast and fire. More infantry comes up; Burnside is outnumbered, flanked, compelled to yield the hill he took so bravely. His position is no longer one of attack; he defends himself with unfaltering firmness, but he sends to McClellan for help.

McClellan's glass for the last half hour has seldom been turned away from the left. He sees clearly enough that Burnside is pressed – needs no messenger to tell him that. His face grows darker with anxious thought. Looking down into the valley where 15,000 troops are lying, he turns a half-questioning look on FitzJohn Porter, who stands by his side, gravely scanning the field. They are Porter's troops below, are fresh, and only impatient to share in this fight. But Porter slowly shakes his head, and one may believe that the same thought is passing through the minds of both generals. "They are the only reserves of the army; they cannot be spared."

McClellan remounts his horse, and with Porter and a dozen officers of his staff rides away to the left in Burnside's direction. Sykes meets them on the road – a good soldier, whose opinion is worth taking. The three generals talk briefly together. It is easy to see that the moment has when everything may turn on one order given or withheld, when the history of the battle is only to be written in thoughts and purposes and words of the general.

Burnside's messenger rides up. His message: "I want troops and guns. If you do not send them, I cannot hold my position half an hour." McClellan's only answer for the moment is a glance at the western sky. Than he turn speaks very slowly: "Tell General Burnside this is the battle of the war. He must hold his ground till dark at any cost. I will send him Miller's battery. I can do nothing more. I have no infantry." Then, as the messenger was riding away, he called him back. "Tell him if he cannot hold his ground, then the bridge, to the last man! – always the bridge! If the bridge is lost, all is lost."

The sun is already down; not half an hour of daylight is left. Till Burnside's message came it seemed plain to every one that the battle could not be finished today. None suspected how near was the peril of defeat, of sudden attack on exhausted forces – how vital to the safety of the army and the nation were those 15,000 waiting troops of FitzJohn Porter in the hollow. But the rebels halted instead of pushing on; their vindictive cannonade died away as the light faded. Before it was quite dark the battle was over. Only a solitary gun of Burnside's thundered against the enemy, and presently this also ceased, and the field was still.

The peril came very near; but it has passed, and in spite of the peril, at the close the day partly a success; not a victory, but an advantage, had been gained. Hooker, Sumner, and Franklin held all the ground they had gained and Burnside still held the bridge

> and his position beyond. Everything was favorable for a renewal of the fight in the morning.

Smalley was wrong. Instead of resuming the battle, McClellan preferred to regroup and reorganize his own army. His subordinates, particularly Burnside, felt the same. They allowed Lee and his army to withdraw southward, back to Confederate territory.

This account of the experience of a wounded soldier may have occurred in the cornfield at Antietam:

> I remember no acute sensation of pain, not even any distinct shot, only an instantaneous consciousness of having been struck; then my breath came hard and labored, with a croup-like sound, and with a dull, aching feeling in my right shoulder; my arm fell powerless at my side, and the Enfield dropped from my grasp. I threw my left hand up to my throat, and withdrew it covered with the warm, bright-red blood. The end had come at last! But, thank God, it was death in battle. Only let me get back out of the deathly storm, and breathe away the few minutes that were left me of life in some place of comparative rest and security. It all rushed into my mind in an instant. I turned and staggered away to the rear. A comrade brushed by me, shot through the hand, who, a moment before, was firing away close at my side. I saw feeble reinforcements moving up, and I recollect a thrill of joy even then, as I thought that the tide of battle might yet be turned, and those rebel masses beaten back, broken, foiled, disheartened.
>
> But my work was done. I was growing faint and weak, although not yet half way out of range of fire. A narrow space between two massive bowlders, over which rested lengthwise the trunk of a fallen tree, offered refuge and hope of safety from further danger. I crawled into it, and lay down to die. I counted the minutes before I must bleed to death. I had no more hope of seeing the new year on the morrow than I now have of outliving the next century. Thank God, death did not seem so dreadful, now that it was come. And then the sacrifice was not all in vain, falling thus in God's own holy cause of freedom. But home and friends! O, the rush of thought then!
>
> Let the veil be drawn here. The temple of memory has its holy place, into which only one's own soul may, once in a great season, solemnly enter.
>
> And so I lay there, with my head pillowed on my blanket, while

the battle swelled again around and over me – bullets glancing from the sides of stone that sheltered me, or sinking into the log above me, and shot and shell crashing through the tree-tops, and falling all about me. Two shells, I remember, struck scarcely ten feet from me, and in their explosion covered me with dirt and splinters; but that was all. Still I lived on. I smile now as I think of it, how I kept raising my left hand to see if the fingernails were growing white and purple, as they do when one bleeds to death, and wondering to find them still warm and ruddy. Hemorrhage must have ceased almost, and the instincts of existence said, "Live!"

Then came the agony of waiting for removal from the field. How I longed and looked for some familiar face, as our men twice charged up into the wood, directly over me! But they belonged to another division, and had other work to do than bearing off the wounded.

In his diary, Lorenz A. Miears of the 3rd Arkansas Company E, wrote:

Next day, September 17, the battle of Sharpsburg was. I believe the yanks called it Antetum. Our regiment pased through a cornfield (with) fodder just right for pulling. The way bullets cut that corn down & as they would hit the blades (came) off like fodder. As we was going in we met a batry coming out. Just as it was passing us a shell hit one of the horses. As far as I could see him, (he) was going with his head up & his intrels dragging on the ground.

When we got over the hill, we formed (a) line of battle and was ordered (to lie) down. We as much exposed lying down as standing up. They was killing us faster than the litter bearers could carry them. Louis Pumphry, my good old neighbor-boy friend, was positioned in (the) rear of (the) lines to keep them closed up. When I did not hear him talking to the boys to keep close and be brave, I looked behind to see where he was. He was lying on his side looking up at me (with) the blood running out of his mouth and nose. I stooped down, took his hand & said, "Louie, are you shot bad?" But he could not speak. I and George Pender layed him at the foot of a mulberry tree 10 or 12 feet (away). He was dead. The ball had passed entirely threw his body. I never saw him again.

> Just then, Capt. Cook, commanding a battery in our left, came. Seeing the destruction, (he) ran down the line hollowing "Charge them!" Our regement, the 30th Virginia and 27th N. Carolina regements charged, thinking it was (a) general order for the hole line. We routed them back one-fourth mile, but finding we was all that had charged, we had to get back in line & they came near us taking us prisoners.

It was the bloodiest single day's conflict of the entire war. The result was a draw. Lee's hope of a decisive victory was thwarted. Lee and his army retreated south. He did so gradually, destroying railway lines as he went. As he marched south he was joined by further reinforcements. By 20 October his forces amounted to nearly 68,000. In November McClellan was replaced as commander of the Army of the Potomac by General Burnside.

The Battle of Fredericksburg 13 December 1862

> Six times, did the enemy, notwithstanding the havoc caused by our batteries, press on with great determination, to within one hundred yards of the foot of the hill, but here encountering the deadly fire of our infantry, his columns were broken, and fled in confusion to the town.
>
> Robert E. Lee

After the Battle of Antietam, the Confederate Army of Northern Virginia under Robert E. Lee retreated southwards. Ambrose Burnside had been appointed commander of the Union Army of the Potomac. Burnside followed Lee's retreating army. He hoped to seize Fredericksburg and use it as a base for an advance upon Richmond. Lee decided to make a stand at Fredericksburg and prepared defensive positions on the heights to the west of the town. These had been completed by 13 December 1862. The Union army crossed the Rappahannock river and moved through the town. The battle of Fredericksburg consisted of a series of Union frontal attacks on prepared defensive positions. The attacks were quite determined but were repulsed with very heavy casualties. Meade's division on the Union left actually penetrated the Confederate position before it was forced to withdraw.

General Humphreys commanded the Third Division of the Union Fifth Corps. His division attacked during the afternoon as it was becoming dusky. The Confederate defenders were protected by a stone wall. He directed his men to go in with the bayonet and to ignore the survivors of earlier attacks, who were sheltering behind a natural embankment 150 yards from the stone wall. He ordered the officers to the front, and led one of his two brigades himself. In Humphreys' own words:

> With a hurrah, the brigade, led by General Tyler and myself, advanced gallantly over the ground, under the heaviest fire yet opened, which poured upon it from the moment it rose from the ravine.
>
> As the brigade reached the masses of men referred to, every effort was made by the latter to prevent our advance. They called to our men not to go forward, and some attempted to prevent by force their doing so. The effect upon my command was what I apprehended – the line was somewhat disordered, and in part forced to form into a column, but still advanced rapidly. The fire of the enemy's musketry and artillery, furious as it was before, now became still hotter. The stone wall was a sheet of flame that enveloped the head and flanks of the column. Officers and men were falling rapidly, and the head of the column was at length brought to a stand when close up to the wall. Up to this time, not a shot had been fired by the column, but now some firing began. It lasted but a minute, when, in spite of all our efforts, the column turned and began to retire slowly. I attempted to rally the brigade behind the natural embankment so often mentioned, but the united efforts of General Tyler, myself, our staffs, and the other officers, could not arrest the retiring mass.

F. W. Palfrey of the Twentieth Massachusetts was there. Palfrey continued:

> General Humphreys had one horse disabled by wounds and another killed under him. He had but one staff officer remaining mounted, and his horse was wounded in three places. His force being now too small to try another charge, he was directed to bring in Allabach's men from the line of natural embankment. This was well done, two of his regiments in particular, the 123rd

> and 155th Pennsylvania, "retiring slowly and in good order, singing and hurrahing."

The retreat of Allabach's men may have been what the Confederate General Ransom referred to when he said,

> This last desperate and maddened attack met the same fate which had befallen those which preceded, and his hosts were sent, actually howling, back to their beaten comrades in the town.

Palfrey added some of his own memories:

> Those who have been in battle know how much and how little they saw and heard. They remember how the smoke and the woods and the inequalities of ground limited their vision when they had leisure to look about them, and how every faculty was absorbed in their work when they were actively engaged; how the deafening noise made it almost impossible to hear orders; what ghastly sights they saw as men and horses near them were torn with shell; how peacefully the men sank to rest whom the more merciful rifle-bullet reached in a vital spot; how some wounded men shrieked and others lay quiet; how awful was the sound of the projectiles when they were near hostile batteries, how incessant was the singing and whistling of the balls from rifles and muskets; how little they commonly knew of what was going on a hundred yards to their right or left. Orderly advances of bodies of men may be easily described and easily imagined, but pictures of real fighting are and must be imperfect. Participants in real fighting know how limited and fragmentary and confused are their recollections of work after it became hot. The larger the force engaged, the more impossible it is to give an accurate presentation of its experiences. We can follow the charge of the 600 at Balaclava, from which less than one in three came back unharmed, better than we can follow the advance of Hancock's 5,000 at Fredericksburg, from which not quite three in five came back unharmed. And Hancock's advance was only one of many.

The Union losses were 12,353 killed, wounded and missing.

The Battle of Chancellorsville 1863

> It is permissible for an officer to be defeated; but never to be surprised.
>
> A French military writer quoted by Abner Doubleday

The battle of Chancellorsville began as a Union attempt to destroy the main Confederate army, the Army of Northern Virginia. The Union commanders' tactical errors on the battlefield nearly resulted in their own army being destroyed. The result of the battle was a second opportunity for a Confederate invasion of Union territory. If the Confederates either destroyed the main Union army or captured one of its major cities, such as Baltimore, the Union might be compelled to make peace and the Confederacy would have won the war.

Abner Doubleday was a regular officer who, before the war, had been in the same regiment as "Stonewall" Jackson and A. P. Hill, Robert E. Lee's Corps commanders. Doubleday began 1863 in command of the Third Division of the Union First Corps.

1863 began with the opposing armies in approximately the positions they had held after the battle of Fredericksburg. Burnside was replaced by Hooker as commander of the Army of the Potomac. Hooker wanted to trap the main Confederate army in a pincer movement. This would involve attacks from both front and rear of the Confederate positions around Fredericksburg. The Union army had been reinforced. The main Confederate army had been weakened by President Davis' policy of detaching forces to any point which appeared to be under threat.

Hooker left one Union Corps in front of Fredericksburg. He sent the main body of the Union army around Lee's flank, to Chancellorsville where it could cut off his line of retreat, back to Virginia. Lee was not deceived and advanced towards Chancellorsville, leaving a rearguard of two divisions at Fredericksburg.

On 1 May Hooker moved out to attack Lee. The countryside made movement very difficult. It consisted of dense, impenetrable thickets. The two armies encountered each other about two and a half miles from Chancellorsville.

On 2 May Hooker expected to fight a defensive battle. Doubleday described the ground:

> . . . a plain, covered by dense thickets, with open spaces in the vicinity of the houses, varied by the high ground at Talley's on the

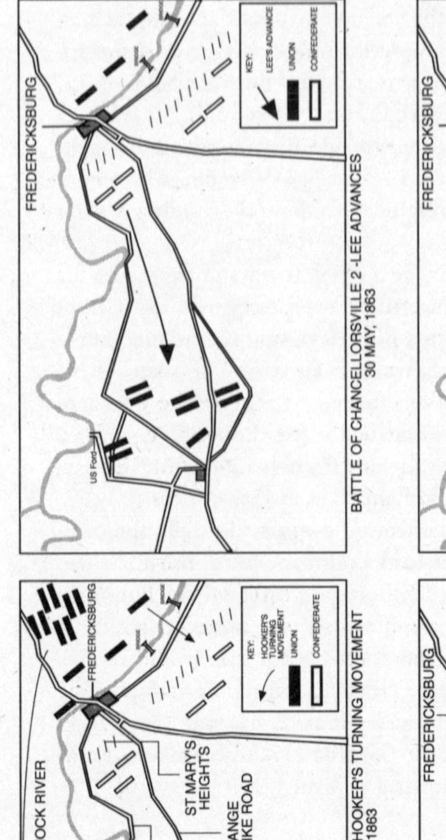

Map of the Battle of Chancellorsville

west and by the hills of Fairview and Hazel Grove on the south, and terminating in a deep ravine near the river. Our general line was separated from that of the enemy by small streams, which principally ran through ravines, forming obstacles useful for defensive purposes. This was the case on the east and south, but on the west, where Howard's line terminated, there was nothing but the usual thickets to impede the enemy's approach.

When night set in, the sound of the axe was heard in every direction, for both armies thought it prudent to strengthen their front as much as possible.

The prospect for Lee as darkness closed over the scene was far from encouraging. He had examined the position of the Union army carefully, and had satisfied himself that as regards its centre and left it was unassailable. Let any man with a musket on his shoulder, encumbered with a cartridge-box, haversack, canteen, etc., attempt to climb over a body of felled timber to get at an enemy who is coolly shooting at him from behind a log breast-work, and he will realize the difficulty of forcing a way through such obstacles. Our artillery, too, swept every avenue of approach, so that the line might be considered as almost impregnable. Before giving up the attack, however, Stuart was directed to cautiously reconnoitre on the right, where Howard was posted, and see if there was not a vulnerable point there.

J.E.B. Stuart, the Confederate cavalry commander, obeyed his orders. When night fell, his cavalrymen discovered the Union right flank was open. It would be possible to march around it and attack the troops on the Union right from behind.

Lee detached Jackson's Corps to do this. While the two halves of the Confederate army were separated there was a danger that either half could be overwhelmed. Doubleday:

Hooker was expecting to be attacked on his left and his centre.

As soon as Jackson was en route, Lee began to demonstrate against our centre and left, to make Hooker believe the main attack was to be there, and to prevent him from observing the turning column in its progress toward the right. A vigorous cannonade began against Meade, and a musketry fire was opened on Couch and Slocum; the heaviest attack being on Hancock's position, which was in advance of the main line.

Hooker could not make up his mind what he should do

> although his enemy's movements were visible. He neither attacked nor ensured that his weak flank was strengthened.

When Jackson's men reached a position where it overlapped the Union right and were in position to attack it from behind. The Union right consisted of the 11th Corps under General Howard. He actually ignored the reports he was given of the enemy's approach.

The 17th Connecticut Infantry had two companies on picket duty on the Union right. The Colonel of the regiment wrote:

> The disaster resulted from Howard's and Devens' utter disregard and inattention under warnings that came in from the front and flank all through the day. Horseman after horseman rode into my post and was sent to headquarters with the information that the enemy were heavily marching along our front and proceeding to our right; and last of all an officer reported the rebels massing for attack. Howard scouted the report and insulted the informants, charging them with telling a story that was the offspring of their imaginations or their fears.

A cavalry captain, George E. Farmer, reported to Howard that he had discovered Confederate artillery on the flank of the 11th Corps. In his own words his report was "courteously received," but disbelieved. Doubleday:

> It would seem from all accounts that nothing could vanquish Howard's incredulity. He appeared to take so little interest in Stonewall's approach that when Captain George E. Farmer, one of Pleasonton's staff (Pleasonton was the Union cavalry commander), reported to him that he had found a rebel battery posted directly on the flank of the 11th Corps, he was, to use his own language, "courteously received, but Howard did not seem to believe there was any force of the enemy in his immediate front." Sickles and Pleasonton were doing all they could to ascertain Jackson's position, for at this time a small detachment of the 3rd Corps were making a reconnaissance on the Orange Court House Plank Road, and Rodes states that our cavalry was met there and skirmished with Stuart's advance. Farmer said he saw no Union pickets, but noticed on his return that Howard's men were away from their arms, which were stacked, and that they were playing cards, etc., utterly unsuspicious of danger and unprepared for a

contest. Notwithstanding the reports of Jackson's movement from spies and scouts, Howard ordered no change in his lines.

The fierce rush of the rebels, who came in almost simultaneously with the pickets, first struck General Von Gilsa's two small regiments and the two guns in the road, the only force that actually fronted them in line.

Von Gilsa galloped at once to Howard's Headquarters at Dowdall's Tavern to ask for immediate reinforcements. He was told, "he must hold his post with the men he had, and trust to God", information which was received by the irate German with objurgations that were not at all of an orthodox character.

Devens' division, thus taken in flank, was driven back upon Schurz's division, and that being unable to form, was heaped after some resistance on Steinwehr's division, in the utmost confusion and disorder. Steinwehr had only Buschbeck's brigade with him; the other – that of Barlow – been sent out to reinforce Sickles; but he formed line promptly, behind a weak intrenchment, which had been thrown across the road, and with the aid of his artillery kept Jackson at bay for three-quarters of an hour. Howard exerted himself bravely then, and did all he could to rally the fugitives, but Rodes' division, which attacked him, was soon reinforced by that of Colston, and the two together folded around his flanks, took his line in reverse, and finally carried the position with a rush; and then Buschbeck's brigade retired in good order through the flying crowd, who were streaming in wild disorder to the rear past Hooker's headquarters.

And now, with the right of our line all gone, with a yawning gap where Sickles' corps and Williams' division had previously been posted, with Lee thundering against our centre and left, and Jackson taking all our defences in reverse, his first line being close on Chancellorsville itself, it seemed as if the total rout of the army was inevitable.

Just before this attack Hooker had decided to interpose more force between the wings of the rebel army, in order to permanently dissever Jackson from the main body. If Sickles had been allowed to attack the left flank of the enemy opposite the Furnace, as he requested permission to do earlier in the afternoon, this co-operative movement could hardly have failed to produce great results; afterward it was too late to attempt it. As already stated, Williams' division struck Anderson in front on Birney's left, and Geary attacked McLaws' across the Plank Road to the right of

Hancock. Geary found the enemy strongly posted, and as he made no progress, returned to his works. When the rout of the 11th Corps took place, Williams also hastened back, but was fired on by Jackson's troops, who now occupied the intrenchments he had left. Sickles thinks if this had not occurred several regiments of the enemy would have been cut off from the main body.

The constantly increasing uproar, and the wild rush of fugitives past the Chancellorsville House, told Hooker what had occurred, and roused him to convulsive life. His staff charged on the flying crowd, but failed to stop them, and it became necessary to form a line of fresh troops speedily, for Jackson in his onward march was sweeping everything before him. It was not easy to find an adequate force for this emergency, for the whole line was now actively engaged, Slocum being attacked on the south, and Couch and Meade on the east. Fortunately, Berry's division was held in reserve, and was available. They were true and tried men, and went forward at once to the rescue. Berry was directed to form across the Plank Road, drive the rebels back, and retake the lost intrenchments; an order easy to give, but very difficult to execute. In fact, the most he could do under the circumstances, was to form his line in the valley opposite Fairview, and hold his position there, the enemy already having possession of the higher ground beyond.

Before Berry went out Warren had already stopped several of the Eleventh Corps batteries, and had formed them across the Plank Road behind the position the infantry assumed. The fire of these guns was very destructive and was the principal agent in checking the enemy. As soon as they formed in line, Warren gave orders to Colonel Brest, Chief of Artillery to the Twelfth Corps, to post more batteries on the eminence called Fairview, to the rear and left of the others.

Few people appreciate the steadiness and courage required, when all around is flight and confusion, for a force to make its way through crowds of fugitives, advance steadily to the post of danger in front, and meet the exulting enemy, while others are seeking safety in the rear. Such men are heroes, and far more worthy of honor than those who fight in the full blaze of successful warfare.

The thickets being unfavorable to cavalry, Sickles had sent Pleasonton back to Hazel Grove with two mounted regiments, the 8th New York, the 17th Pennsylvania, and Martin's battery, while the 6th New York was scouting the woods dismounted. Upon reaching the open space which he had left when he went to the front, Pleasonton found the place full of the debris of the combat-men, horses, caissons, ambulances – all rushing furiously to the rear. To clear the way he charged on the flying mass, at Sickles' suggestion, who had ridden in advance of his troops which were still behind at the Furnace. Sickles directed Pleasonton to take command of the artillery and the latter hastily collected 22 guns, consisting of his own and the 3rd Corps batteries. Unfortunately there was no time to load or aim, for the rebels were close at hand, and their triumphant yells were heard as they took possession of the works Buschbeck had so gallantly defended. In another moment our troops would have been compelled to give up this advantageous position, which was on an eminence overlooking Chancellorsville and the Plank Road, and which was really the key of the battle field. There was but one way to delay Jackson, some force must be sacrificed, and Pleasonton ordered Major Peter Keenan, commanding the 8th Pennsylvania Cavalry, to charge the 10,000 men in front with his 400. Keenan knew if he threw his little force into that seething mass of infantry, horses and men would go down on all sides, and there would be few left to tell the tale. A sad smile lit up his noble countenance, as he said, "General, I will do it."

A large part of his command were lost, but the short interval thus gained was of priceless value. Pleasonton was enabled to clear a space in front of him and to bring 22 guns loaded with double canister to bear upon the enemy. They came bursting over the parapet they had just taken with loud and continuous yells, and formed line of battle within 300 yards of Pleasonton, displaying a United States flag to deceive him. He soon detected the imposture, and fired into their masses with all his guns at once. The discharge seemed fairly to blow them back over the works from which they had just emerged. Their artillery under Colonel Crutchfield which had been brought up to sweep the Plank Road was almost annihilated by the fire of the battery on the Plank Road. This gave time to reload the guns.

Unfortunately for the Confederates, Jackson himself was mortally wounded during the night. Jackson was looking for a position where his men could cut off a Union retreat:

Jackson therefore halted his men in the edge of the woods, about a mile and a half from Chancellorsville, posted two brigades on the two roads that came in from the south, and sent for Hill's division, which was in rear and which had not been engaged, to take the front, while the other two divisions fell back to the open space at Dowdall's Tavern to reform their lines. Pending this movement he rode out on the Plank Road with part of his staff and a few orderlies to reconnoitre, cautioning his pickets not to fire at him on his return.

When he came back new men had been posted and his approach was mistaken for the advance of Pleasonton's cavalry. His own troops fired into him with fatal effect. Nearly all his escort were killed or wounded and he received three balls, which shattered both arms. His horse ran toward the Union lines and, although he succeeded in turning him back, he was dashed against the trees and nearly unhorsed. He reached the Confederate lines about the time our artillery again opened up the Plank Road with a fire which swept every thing from its front. Several of his attendants were killed and others wounded. The rebels found the utmost difficulty in keeping their men in line under this tremendous fire. Sentries had to be posted, and great precautions taken to prevent the troops from giving way. General Pender recognized Jackson as he was carried past and complained of the demoralizing effect of this cannonade, but Jackson replied sharply and sternly, "You must hold your ground, General Pender." He was removed to the Wilderness Tavern and, as General Lee was in some fear that Averell's cavalry, then at Elley's Ford, might make a dash and capture him, he was sent on to Guiney's Station, on the Fredericksburg and Richmond Railroad, where he died on 10 May.

Doubleday's own Corps, the 1st, had been sent to a ford to cut off Lee's retreat. They were now summoned to stop the rout and hold off Jackson's attack. Doubleday himself was getting ready for bed:

At sunset the 1st Corps went into bivouac on the south side of United States Ford, about four miles and a half from Chancellorsville. The men were glad enough to rest after their tedious march on a hot day, loaded down with eight days' rations. General Reynolds left me temporarily in charge of the corps, while he rode on to confer with Hooker. We heard afar off the roar of the battle caused by Jackson's attack, and saw the evening sky reddened with the fires of combat, but knowing Hooker had a large force, we felt no anxiety as to the result, and took it for granted that we would not be wanted until the next day. I was preparing a piece of india-rubber cloth as a couch when I saw one of Reynolds' aids, Captain Wadsworth, coming down the road at all speed. He brought the startling news that the 11th Corps had fled, and if we did not go forward at once, the army would be hopelessly defeated. We were soon on the road, somewhat oppressed by the news, but not dismayed. We marched through the thickening twilight of the woods amid a silence at first only broken by the plaintive song of the whip-poor-will, until the full moon rose in all its splendor. As we proceeded we came upon crowds of the 11th Corps fugitives still hastening to the rear. They seemed wholly disheartened. We halted for a time, in order that our position in line of battle might be selected, and then moved on. As we approached the field a midnight battle commenced, and the shells seemed to burst in sparkles in the trees above our heads, but not near enough to reach us. It was Sickles fighting his way home again. When we came nearer and filed to the right to take position on the Elley's Ford road, the men struck up John Brown's song, and gave the chorus with a will. Their cheerful demeanor and proud bearing renewed the confidence of the army, who felt that the arrival of Reynolds' corps, with its historic record, was no ordinary reinforcement.

We were now on the extreme right of the other forces, on the Elley's Ford road, with the right flank thrown back behind Hunting Creek.

Hooker was very much discouraged by the rout of the 11th Corps. An occurrence of this kind always has a tendency to demoralize an army and render it less trustworthy; for the real strength of an armed force is much more in opinion than it is in numbers. A small body of men, if made to believe the enemy are giving way, will do and dare anything; but when they think the struggle is hopeless, they will not resist even a weak attack, for each thinks he is to be sacrificed to save the rest. Hence Hooker did not feel the same reliance on his men as be did before the disaster. He determined, nevertheless, to continue the battle, but contract his lines by bringing them nearer to Chancellorsville. The real key of the battle-field now was the eminence at Hazel Grove. So long as we held it the enemy could not advance without presenting his right flank to our batteries, and if they obtained possession of it they could plant guns which would enfilade Slocum's line and fire directly into our forces below. Birney's division at this time was posted in advance of Best's guns on the left, Berry was on the right, with Williams' division of the 12th Corps behind Birney, and Whipple's division in rear of Berry.

The position of Hazel Grove commanded Chancellorsville, where all the roads meet, and which it was vital to Hooker to hold. For if he lost that, he could not advance in any direction, and only his line of retreat to the Ford would remain open to him. Pleasonton spent the night in fortifying this hill, and placed 40 guns in position there; but it was of no avail, for it was outside of the new line Sickles' was directed to occupy at daylight, and Hooker was not aware of its importance. A request was sent to the latter to obtain his consent to hold it, but he was asleep, and the staff-officer in charge, who had had no experience whatever in military matters, positively refused to awaken him until daylight, and then it was too late, for that was the time set for the troops to fall back to the new line.

Hooker then ordered Sedgwick's corps, at Fredericksburg, to attack Lee's rearguard. Sedgwick had 26,000 men against 9,000 Confederates under General Jubal Early. The Confederates were in the positions they had held at the battle in December 1862.

On the next day, 3 May, the Confederates captured Hazel Grove in the centre of the Union position. Hooker's orders required the Union troops at Hazel Grove to change position. The Confederate attack arrived just as the Union troops were leaving.

Stuart, who was now in command of Jackson's corps, saw at a glance the immense importance of this capture, and did not delay a moment in crowning the hill with 30 pieces of artillery, which soon began to play with fatal effect upon our troops below; upon Chancellorsville; and upon the crest occupied by Slocum, which it enfiladed, and as McLaws' batteries also enfiladed Slocum's line from the opposite side; it seems almost miraculous that he was able to hold it at all.

Simultaneously with the attack against Hazel Grove came a fierce onslaught on that part of Sickles' line to the left of the road, accompanied by fierce yells and cries of "Remember Jackson!" a watchword which it was supposed would excite the rebels to strenuous efforts to avenge the fatal wound of their great leader.

It was handsomely met and driven back by Mott's brigade, which had come up from the Ford, and now held the front on that part of the line. A brilliant counter-charge by the 5th and 7th New Jersey captured many prisoners and colors.

Sickles' men fought with great determination but, being assailed by infantry in front and battered almost in flank by the artillery posted at Hazel Grove, the line was manifestly untenable. After an obstinate contest the men fell back to the second line, which was but partially fortified, and soon after to the third line, which was more strongly intrenched, and which they held to the close of the fight.

McGowan's, Lane's, and Heth's brigades of A. P. Hill's division charged resolutely over this line also; but they suffered heavily from Best's guns at Fairview, and were driven back by Colonel Franklin's and Colonel Bowman's brigades of Whipple's division, which made an effective counter-charge. Whipple's other brigade, that of Graham, had been sent to relieve one of Slocum's brigades on the left of the line, which was out of ammunition. It held its position there for two hours.

While this attack was taking place on the left of the road, Pender's and Thomas' brigades, also of Hill's division, charged over the works on the right, but when the others retreated they were left without support and were compelled to retire also. They reformed, however; tried it again, and once more succeeded in holding temporary possession of part of the line, but were soon driven out again.

The struggle increased in violence. The rebels were determined to break through the lines, and our men were equally determined not to give way. Well might De Trobriand style it "a mad and desperate battle". Mahone said afterward: "The Federals fought like devils at Chancellorsville." Again Rodes' and Hill's divisions renewed the attempt and were temporarily successful, and again was the bleeding remnant of their forces flung back in disorder. Doles' and Ramseur's brigades of Rodes' division, managed to pass up the ravine to the right of Slocum's works and gain his right and rear, but were unsupported there, and Doles was driven out by a concentrated artillery and musketry fire. Ramseur, who now found himself directly on Sickles' left flank, succeeded in holding on until the old Stonewall brigade under Paxton came to his aid, and then they carried Fairview again, only to be driven out as the others had been.

The battle had now lasted several hours, and the troops engaged, as well as the artillery, were almost out of ammunition. There should have been some staff officer specially charged with this subject, but there seemed to be no one who could give orders in relation to it.

The last line of our works was finally taken by the enemy, who having succeeded in driving off the 3rd Maryland of the 12th Corps, on Berry's left, entered near the road and enfiladed the line to the right and left. Sickles sent Ward's brigade to take the place of the 3rd Maryland, but it did not reach the position assigned it in time, the enemy being already in possession. In attempting to remedy this disaster, Berry was killed, and his successor, General Mott, was wounded. The command then devolved upon General Bevere, who, probably considering further contest hopeless, led his men out of the action without authority – an offence for which he was subsequently tried and dismissed the service.

Our front gradually melted away and passed to the new line in rear through Humphreys' division of the 5th Corps, which was posted about half a mile north of the Chancellorsville House in the edge of the thicket, to cover the retreat. At last only indomitable Hancock remained, fighting McLaws with his front line, and keeping back Stuart and Anderson with his rear line.

The enemy, Jackson's Corps, showed little disposition to follow up their success. The fact is, these veterans were about fought out, and became almost inert. They did not, at the last, even press Hancock, who was still strong in artillery, and he withdrew his main body in good order, losing however, the 27th Connecticut regiment, which was posted at the apex of his line on the south, and was not brought back in time, in consequence of the failure of a subordinate officer to carry out his orders.

Before Hancock left, his line was taken in reverse, and he was obliged to throw back part of his force to the left to resist Anderson, who was trying to force the passage of Mott Run. The line in that direction was firmly held by Colonel Miles of the 61st New York, who was shot through the body while encouraging his men to defend the position.

Hooker was injured at this point in the battle. Two Union corps were not currently involved in the battle. At Fredericksburg, Sedgwick was following Hooker's orders to attack the Confederate rearguard. Sedgwick took the heights but he followed up so cautiously that the

Confederates were able to regroup and counter attack. Doubleday:

> As Hooker seemed disposed to be inactive, Lee thought he might venture to still further augment the force in front of Sedgwick, with a view to either capture the 6th Corps or force it to recross the river. He therefore directed Anderson to reinforce McLaws with the remainder of his division, leaving only what was left of Jackson's old corps to confront Hooker. Anderson had gone over to the right, opposite the 11th and 12th Corps, and had opened with a battery upon the wagon trains which were parked in that vicinity, creating quite a stampede, until his guns were driven away by the 12th Corps. In this skirmish, General Whipple, commanding the 3rd division of Sickles' Corps, was killed. In the meantime, Early had retaken the heights of Fredericksburg, which were merely held by a guard of Gibbons' division, so that, when Anderson arrived and took post on the right of McLaws, parallel to Plank Road, Sedgwick found himself environed on three sides by the enemy; only the road to Banks' Ford remained open, and even that was endangered by bands of rebels, who roamed about in rear of our forces. At one time it is said they could have captured him and his headquarters. Fortunately the tents which constituted the latter were of so unpretending a character, that they gave no indication of being tenanted by the commanding general.

Lee showed the decision that the Union Generals so often lacked. He reinforced the rearguard at Fredericksburg so that Sedgwick's corps was not only outnumbered but in danger of being destroyed. It was now faced by 25,000 Confederates. Sedgwick's corps retreated and crossed the Rappahannock river as night fell. Nightfall brought the end of the battle. It was another Union defeat. They had lost 17,197 killed, wounded and missing. The Confederates had lost 13,619.

The Battle of Gettysburg 1–3 July 1863

> The situation was very peculiar.
>
> Abner Doubleday, division commander, Union First corps

After the Confederate victory at Chancellorsville, Lee invaded Pennsylvania. In the West, Vicksburg on the Mississippi was near to falling to Union troops unless Joseph E. Johnston could be reinforced. Lee's invasion plans were approved despite the need for some of his troops on the Mississippi. Lee's goal was to destroy the Army of the Potomac. Lee hoped to do this by getting his army between the Army of the Potomac and Washington and fighting a defensive battle on ground of his own choosing.

After the death of Jackson, Longstreet became Lee's senior corps commander. Lee's army consisted of three infantry corps, a cavalry corps and an artillery corps, 82,000 men with 190 guns.

The Army of Northern Virginia;

Longstreet's corps consisted of the divisions of McLaws, Hood and Pickett. Ewell's corps consisted of the divisions of Early, Rhodes and Johnson. A.P. Hill's corps consisted of the divisions of Anderson, Heth and Pender. Plus J. E. B. Stuart's cavalry corps.

The Army of the Potomac consisted of seven corps with a total of 135,000 men and 300 guns.

The 1st Corps was commanded by Reynolds, who was also commander of the left wing of the Army of the Potomac. This meant that he had immediate control of the 1st, 3rd and 11th Corps and was second in command of the Army of the Potomac. Abner Doubleday was the senior division commander of the 1st Corps. When Reynolds was killed on 1 July, Doubleday took over as commander of the 1st Corps. General Meade had been in overall command of the Army of the Potomac since 28 June, after Hooker's resignation. After Reynolds' death, Meade appointed Newton to the command of the 1st Corps so Doubleday reverted to command of the 3rd division of the 1st Corps.

The Army of the Potomac: 1st Corps commanded by Reynolds (on 1 July Reynolds was killed; Doubleday took over); Newton was in command on 2 July and 3 July. 1st Division commanded by Wadsworth; 2nd Division commanded by Robinson; 3rd Division commanded by Doubleday.

2nd Corps commanded by Hancock; 1st Division commanded by Caldwell; 2nd Division commanded by Gibbon (Harrow); 3rd Division commanded by Hays.

3rd Corps commanded by Sickles (when Sickles was wounded, Birney took command); 1st Division commanded by Birney; 2nd Division commanded by Humphreys.

5th Corps commanded by Sykes; 1st Division commanded by Barnes; 2nd Division commanded by Ayres; 3rd Division commanded by Crawford.

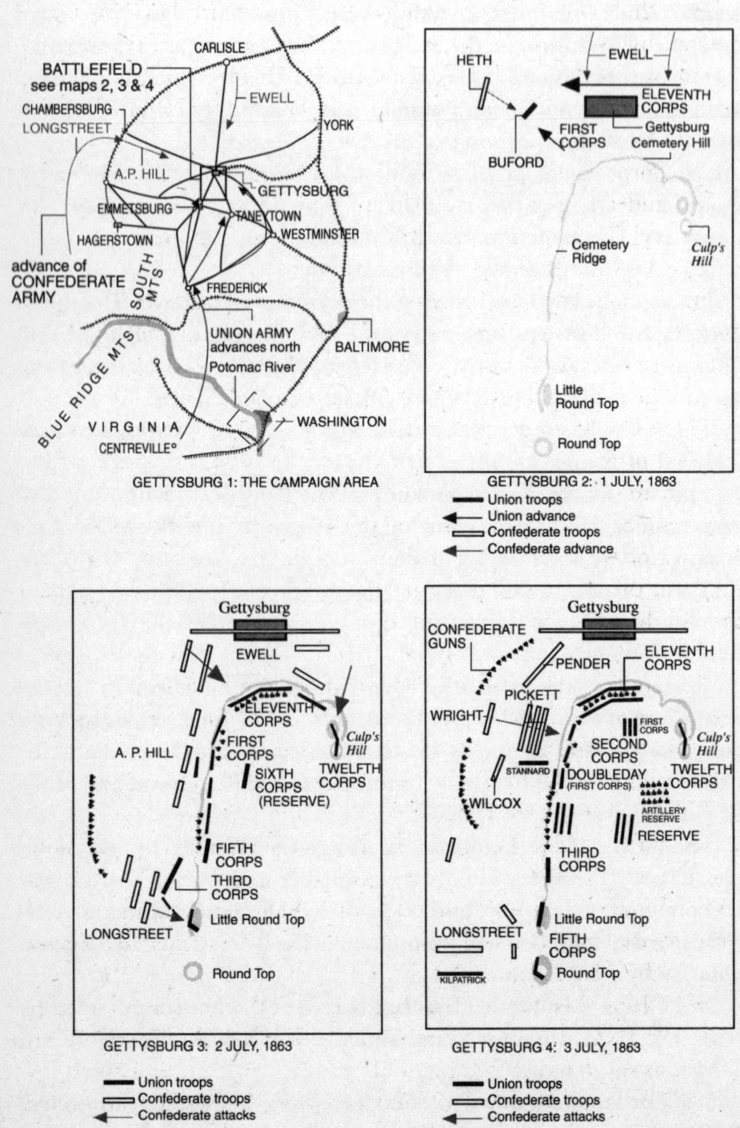

Map of the Battle of Gettysburg

6th Corps commanded by Sedgwick; 1st Division commanded by Wright; 2nd Division commanded by Howe; 3rd Division commanded by Wheaton.

11th Corps commanded by Howard; 1st Division commanded by Barlow; 2nd Division commanded by Steinwehr; 3rd Division commanded by Schurz.

12th Corps commanded by Williams; 1st Division commanded by Ruger; 2nd Division commanded by Geary.

Cavalry Corps commanded by Pleasonton; 1st Division commanded by Buford; 2nd Division commanded by Gregg.

The Confederate cavalry corps under Stuart had 11,000 cavalry and 16 guns. The cavalry was responsible for scouting ahead of the main force to find the enemy, identifying his strength and reporting back to the army. Stuart began to ride north on 25 June. He did not rejoin the Confederate army until 2 July. For a whole week Lee was deprived of the "eyes" of his army. Lee expected the Army of the Potomac to stay near Washington, south of the Potomac. Part of the purpose of Stuart's ride was to detain the Army of the Potomac near Washington. To get between the Army of the Potomac and Washington, the Army of Northern Virginia had to march north then turn southward when the Army of the Potomac advanced towards them.

The Union cavalry under Pleasonton gave better service in the Gettysburg campaign. They informed the Union army of enemy movements and fought vital delaying actions.

According to Doubleday Stuart crossed the Potomac and found the Union troops were now all north of the river; he resumed his march north, capturing some supply trains. He did not send any reports back to Lee.

Lee remained ignorant of the location of the Union army he had come to destroy. He was also unaware that Hooker had been replaced by Meade.

On 28 June, Lee learnt that that the Union army was already at Frederick. He realized that they could cut off his line of retreat. This was not as serious as the threat to his supplies, especially of ammunition. He ordered his army to concentrate on Gettysburg.

Meade was fully informed, by telegrams and Buford's scouts, that the enemy were concentrating on Gettysburg. The left wing of the Union army was under Reynolds. Reynolds himself was only about six miles from Hill's troops. Doubleday described Reynolds' reactions:

> Reynolds had the true spirit of a soldier. He was a Pennsylvanian and, inflamed at seeing the devastation of his native State, was most desirous of getting at the enemy as soon as possible. I speak from my own knowledge, for I was his second in command, and he told me at Poolesville soon after crossing the river that it was necessary to attack the enemy at once, to prevent his plundering the whole State. As he had great confidence in his men, it was not difficult to divine what his decision would be. He determined to advance and hold Gettysburg. He directed the 11th Corps to come up as a support to the 1st, and he recommended, but did not order, the 3rd Corps to do the same.

Buford had two cavalry brigades. He positioned one facing west and the other facing north. Doubleday:

> On the morning of July 1, General Buford . . . held the ridges to the west of Gettysburg, with his cavalry – composed of Gamble's and Devens's brigades. His vedettes were thrown far out toward the enemy to give timely notice of any movement, for he was determined to prevent the rebels from entering the town if possible, and knew the 1st Corps would soon be up to support him. The enemy were not aware that there was any considerable force in the vicinity, and in the morning sent forward Heth's division of Hill's corps to occupy the Place, anticipating no difficulty in doing so Buford in the meantime had dismounted a large part of his force, had strengthed his line of skirmishers, and planted his batteries at the most commanding points.
>
> General Reynolds, in consequence of the duties devolving upon him as commander of the Left Wing of the army, that is of the 1st, 3rd, and 11th Corps, had turned over the command of the 1st Corps to me. He now made immediate dispositions to go forward to assist Buford.
>
> Reynolds sent for me about six o'clock in the morning, read to me the various despatches he had received from Meade and Buford and told me he should go forward at once with the nearest division – that of Wadsworth – to aid the cavalry. He then instructed me to draw in my pickets, assemble the artillery and the remainder of the corps, and join him as soon as possible. Having given these orders he rode off at the head of the column, and I never saw him again.
>
> Heth's division, which started early in the morning to occupy

the town, soon found itself confronted by Buford's skirmishers, and formed line of battle with Archer's and Davis's brigades in front, followed by those of Pettigrew and Brockenborough. At 9 a.m. the first gun was heard. Buford had three cannon-shots fired as a signal for his skirmish line to open on the enemy, and the battle of Gettysburg began.

As the rebels had had several encounters with militia, who were easily dispersed, they did not expect to meet any serious resistance at this time, and advanced confidently and carelessly. Buford gave way slowly; taking advantage of every accident of ground to protract the struggle. After an hour's fighting he felt anxious, and went up into the steeple of the Theological Seminary from which a wide view could be obtained, to see if the 1st Corps was in sight. One division of it was close at hand, and soon Reynolds, who had preceded it, climbed up into the belfry to confer with him there, and examine the country around. Although there is no positive testimony to that effect, his attention was doubtless attracted to Cemetery Ridge in his rear, as it was one of the most prominent features of the landscape.

There are two roads coming into Gettysburg from the west, making a considerable angle with each other. Each is intersected by ridges running north and south; on that nearest to the town, and about three-fourths of a mile from the central square, there is a large brick building, which was used as a Lutheran Theological Seminary. A small stream of water called Willoughby's Run winds between the next two ridges. The battle on the first day was principally fought on the heights on each side of this stream.

Buford being aware that Ewell's corps would soon be on its way from Heidlersburg to the field of battle was obliged to form line facing north with Devens's brigade, and leave Gamble's brigade to keep back the overpowering weight of Hill's corps advancing from the west.

Doubleday himself:

caught up with Meredith's brigade of Wadsworth's division, commonly called "The Iron Brigade", just as it was going into action.

In the meantime the enemy approaching from the west were pressing with great force against Buford's slender skirmish line, and Reynolds went forward with Cutler's brigade to sustain it. He skilfully posted Hall's 2nd Maine battery in the road, and threw forward two regiments, the 14th Brooklyn and 95th New York, a short distance in advance on the left. At the same time he directed General Wadsworth to place the remaining three regiments of the brigade, the 147th New York, the 76th New York, and the 56th Pennsylvania on the right of the road. When this formation was completed the cavalry brigade under Gamble, which had been fighting there, withdrew and formed in column on the left of the infantry, but the other cavalry brigade under Devens, which was not facing in that direction, still held its position, awaiting the advance of Ewell's corps from the north.

As Davis' rebel brigade of Heth's division fronting Wadsworth were hidden behind an intervening ridge, Wadsworth did not see them at first, but formed his three regiments perpendicularly to the road, without a reconnaissance. The result was that Davis came over the hill almost directly on the right flank of this line, which being unable to defend itself, was forced back and directed by Wadsworth to take post in a piece of woods in rear on Seminary Ridge. The two regiments on the right accordingly withdrew, but the 147th New York, which was next to the road, did not receive the order, as their Colonel was shot down before he could deliver it. They were at once surrounded and very much cut up before they could be rescued from their perilous position.

The two regiments on the right, which were forced back, were veterans, conspicuous for gallantry in every battle in which the Army of the Potomac had been engaged since the Peninsula campaign. As Wadsworth withdrew them without notifying Hall's battery in the road, or the two regiments posted by Reynolds on the left, both became exposed to a disastrous flank attack on the right. Hall finding a cloud of skirmishers launched against his battery which was now without support, was compelled to retreat with the loss of one gun, the horses of which had all been killed. The non-military reader will see that while a battery can keep back masses of men it cannot contend with a line of skirmishers. To resist them would be very much like fighting mosquitoes with musket-balls. The two regiments posted by Reynolds, the 14th Brooklyn and 95th New York, finding their support gone on the right, while Archer's rebel brigade was advancing to envelop their left, fell back leisurely under Colonel Fowler of the 14th Brooklyn, who assumed command of both as the ranking officer present.

I reached the field just as the attack on Cutler's brigade was going on, and at once sent my adjutant-general, Major Halstead, and young Meredith L. Jones, who was acting as aide on my staff, to General Reynolds to ask instructions. Under the impression that the enemy's columns were approaching on both roads, Reynolds said, "Tell Doubleday I will hold on to this road," referring to the Chambersburg road, "and he must hold on to that one," meaning the road to Fairfield or Hagerstown. At the same time he sent Jones back at full speed to bring up a battery.

The rebels, however, did not advance on the Fairfield road until late in the afternoon. They must have been in force upon it some miles back, for the cavalry so reported, and this caused me during the entire day to give more attention than was necessary to my left, as I feared the enemy might separate my corps from the 3rd and 11th Corps at Emmetsburg. Such a movement would be equivalent to interposing between the 1st Corps and the main army. The cavalry probably referred to Pettigrew's brigade, which Buford met early in the morning.

There was a piece of woods between the two roads, with open ground on each side. It seemed to me this was the key of the position, for if this woods was strongly held, the enemy could not pass on either road without being taken in flank by the infantry, and in front by the cavalry. I therefore urged the men as they filed past me to hold it at all hazards. Full of enthusiasm and the memory of their past achievements they said to me proudly, "If we can't hold it, where will you find the men who can?"

As they went forward under command of Colonel Morrow of the 24th Michigan Volunteers, a brave and capable soldier, who, when a mere youth, was engaged in the Mexican War, I rode over to the left to see if the enemy's line extended beyond ours, and if there would be any attempt to flank our troops in that direction. I saw, however, only a few skirmishers, and returned to organize a reserve. I knew there was fighting going on between Cutler's brigade, and the rebels in his front, but as General Reynolds was there in person, I only attended to my own part of the line; and halted the 6th Wisconsin Regiment as it was going into action under Lieutenant-Colonel R. B. Dawes, and the Brigade Guard under Captain Glenn, 149th Pennsylvania, to post them in the open space between the Seminary and the woods, as a reserve.

It is proper to state that General Meredith, the permanent commander of the brigade, was wounded as he was coming up, some time after its arrival, by a shell which exploded in front of his horse. Colonel Morrow of the 24th Michigan therefore remained in command during the day.

Both parties were now trying to obtain possession of the woods. Archer's rebel brigade, preceded by a skirmish line, was crossing Willoughby's Run to enter them on one side as the Iron Brigade went in on the other. General Reynolds was on horseback in the edge of the woods, surrounded by his staff. He felt some anxiety as to the result, and turned his head frequently to see if our troops would be up in time. While looking back in this way, a rebel sharpshooter shot him through the back of the head, the bullet coming out near the eye. He fell dead in an instant without a word. I felt the great loss the country had sustained in his death, and lamented him as almost a life-long companion, for we were at West Point together, and had served in the same regiment – the old 3rd Artillery – upon first entering service, along with our present Commander-in-Chief, General Sherman, and General George H. Thomas. When quite young we had fought in the same battles in Mexico. I had little time, however, to indulge in these recollections. The situation was very peculiar. The rebel left under Davis had driven in Cutler's brigade and our left under Morrow had charged into the woods, preceded by the 2nd Wisconsin under Colonel Fairchild, swept suddenly and unexpectedly around the right flank of Archer's brigade, and captured a large part of it, including Archer himself. The fact is, the enemy were careless and underrated us, thinking, it is said, that they had only militia to contend with. The Iron Brigade had a different head-gear from the rest of the army and were recognized at once by their old antagonists. Some of the latter were heard to exclaim, "There are those d – d black-hatted fellows again! 'Taint no militia. It's the Army of the Potomac."

Having captured Archer and his men, many of the Iron Brigade kept on beyond Willoughby's Run, and formed on the heights on the opposite side.

The command now devolved upon me, with its great responsibilities. The disaster on the right required immediate attention, for the enemy, with loud yells, were pursuing Cutler's brigade toward the town. I at once ordered my reserve under Lieutenant-Colonel Dawes to advance against their flank. If they faced Dawes, I reasoned that they would present their other flank to Cutler's men so that I felt quite confident of the result. In war, however, unexpected changes are constantly occurring. Cutler's brigade had been withdrawn by order of General Wadsworth, without my knowledge, to the suburbs of Gettysburg. Fortunately, Fowler's two regiments came on to join Dawes, who went forward with great spirit, but who was altogether too weak to assail so large a force. As he approached, the rebels ceased to pursue Cutler, and rushed into the railroad cut to obtain the shelter of the grading. They made a fierce and obstinate resistance, but, while Fowler confronted them above, Dawes brought a gun to enfilade their position, and formed his men across the cut, by Fowler's order, to fire through it. The rebels could not resist this; the greater number gave themselves up as prisoners, and the others scattered over the country and escaped.

This success relieved the 147th New York, which, as I stated, was surrounded when Cutler fell back, and it also enabled us to regain the gun which Hall had been obliged to abandon.

The enemy having vanished from our immediate front, I withdrew the Iron Brigade from its advanced position beyond the creek, reformed the line on the ridge where General Reynolds had originally placed it, and awaited a fresh attack, or orders from General Meade. The two regiments of Cutler's brigade were brought back from the town, and, notwithstanding the check they had received, they fought with great gallantry throughout the three days' battle that ensued.

There was now a lull in the combat. I was waiting for the remainder of the First Corps to come up, and Heth was reorganizing his shattered front line, and preparing to bring his two other brigades forward.

During the lull, Doubleday perceived the importance of the position and resolved to hold it. The remainder of the 1st corps came up.

It was a hot place for troops; for the whole position was alive with bursting shells, but the men went forward in fine spirits and, under the impression that the place was to be held at all hazards, they cried out, "We have come to stay!" The battle afterward became so severe that the greater portion did stay, laying down their lives there for the cause they loved so well. Morrow's brigade remained in the woods where Reynolds was killed, and Biddle's brigade was posted on its left in the open ground along the crest of the same ridge, with Cooper's battery in the interval. Cutler's brigade took up its former position on the right of the road. Having disposed of Wadsworth's division and my own division, which was now under command of Brigadier-General Rowley, I directed General Robinson's division to remain in reserve at the Seminary, and to throw up a small semicircular rail intrenchment in the grove in front of the building. Toward the close of the action this defence, weak and imperfect as it was, proved to be of great service.

The death of Reynolds temporarily left Doubleday in command of the Union 1st Corps. Meade appointed Hancock to replace Reynolds as commander of the left wing and Newton as commander of the 1st Corps. The Union 11th Corps began to arrive before Ewell's Confederate corps could attack the right flank of the Union forces.

The first indication I had that Ewell had arrived, and was taking part in the battle, came from a battery posted on an eminence called Oak Hill, almost directly in the prolongation of my line, and about a mile north of Colonel Stone's position. This opened fire about 1.30 p.m., and rendered new dispositions necessary; for Howard had not guarded my right flank as proposed, and indeed soon had more than he could do to maintain his line. When the guns referred to opened fire, Wadsworth, without waiting for orders, threw Cutler's brigade back into the woods on Seminary Ridge, north of the railroad grading; a movement I sanctioned as necessary. Morrow's brigade was concealed from the view of the enemy, in the woods where Reynolds fell, and Biddle's brigade, by my order, changed front to the north. It could do so with impunity, as it was behind a ridge which concealed its left flank from Hill's corps, and was further protected in that direction by two companies of the 20th New York State Militia, who occupied a house and barn in advance, sent there by the colonel of that regiment, Theodore B. Gates, whose skill and energy were of great service to me during the battle.

It would of course have been impossible to hold the line if Hill attacked on the west and Ewell assailed me at the same time on the north; but I occupied the central position, and their converging columns did not strike together until the grand final advance at the close of the day, and therefore I was able to resist several of their isolated attacks before the last crash came.

About 3.30 p.m. Early's division of Ewell's corps attacked and forced the Union troops to retreat. The right flank of the Union 1st Corps was left exposed:

So far I had done all that was possible to defend my front, but circumstances were becoming desperate. My line was very thin and weak, and my last reserve had been thrown in.

Doubleday's 1st Corps was forced back to Seminary Ridge:

What was left of the 1st Corps after all this slaughter rallied on Seminary Ridge. Many of the men entered a semi-circular rail entrenchment which I had caused to be thrown up early in the day, and held that for a time by lying down and firing over the pile of rails. The enemy were now closing in on us from the south, west, and north, and still no orders came to retreat. Buford arrived about this time and, perceiving that Penin's brigade in swinging around to envelop our left exposed its right flank, I directed him to charge. He reconnoitered the position they held, but did not carry out the order; I do not know why. It was said afterward he found the fences to be an impediment; but he rendered essential service by dismounting his men and throwing them into a grove south of the Fairfield road, where they opened a severe fire, which checked the rebel advance and prevented them from cutting us off from our direct line of retreat to Cemetery Hill.

The first long line that came on from the west was swept away by our artillery, which fired with very destructive effect, taking the rebel line en echarpe.

Although the Confederates advanced in such force, our men still made strong resistance around the Seminary, and by the aid of our artillery, which was most effective, beat back and almost destroyed the first line of Scales' brigade, wounding both Scales and Pender. The former states that he arrived within 75 feet of the guns, and adds: "Here the fire was most severe. Every field officer but one was killed or wounded. The brigade halted in some confusion to return this fire." My Adjutant-Generals Baird and Halstead, and my aids Lee, Marten, Jones, and Lambdin had hot work carrying orders at this time, and it is a marvel that any of them survived the storm of bullets that swept the field.

Hancock arrived and took control of the Union army:

In sending Hancock forward with such ample powers, Meade virtually appointed him commander-in-chief for the time being, for he was authorized to say where we would fight, and when, and how. In the present instance, in accordance with his recommendation, orders were immediately sent out for the army to concentrate on Cemetery Ridge. Two-thirds of the 3rd Corps and all of the 12th came up, and by six o'clock the position became tolerably secure. Stannard's 2nd Vermont brigade also arrived, and as they formed part of my command, reported to me for duty; a very welcome reinforcement for my shattered division. Sickles had taken the responsibility of joining us without orders, knowing that we were hard pressed. His command prolonged the line of the 1st Corps to the left. Slocum's Corps – the 12th – was posted, as a reserve, also on the left.

Hancock now relinquished the command of the field to Slocum and rode back to Taneytown to confer with Meade and explain his reasons for choosing the battlefield.

Longstreet's corps soon arrived and joined Ewell and Hill; so that the whole rebel army was ready to act against us the next morning, with the exception of Pickett's division.

At the close of the day General John Newton rode up and took charge of the 1st Corps by order of General Meade, and I resumed the command of my division.

2 July, the second day of the battle:

The two armies were about a mile apart. The Confederates – Longstreet and Hill – occupied Seminary Ridge, which runs parallel to Cemetery Ridge, upon which our forces were posted. Ewell's corps, on the rebel left, held the town, Hill the centre, and Longstreet the right.

Lee could easily have manoeuvred Meade out of his strong position on the heights, and should have done so. When he determined to attack, he should have commenced at daybreak, for all his force was up except Pickett's division; while two corps of the Union army, the 5th and 6th, were still far away, and two brigades of the 3rd Corps were also absent.

The latter were marching on the Emmetsburg road, and as that was controlled by the enemy, Sickles felt anxious for the safety of his men and trains, and requested that the cavalry be sent to escort them in. This was not done, however. The trains were warned off the road, and the two brigades were, fortunately, not molested.

There has been a great deal of bitter discussion between Longstreet, Fitz Lee, Early, Wilcox, and others as to whether Lee did or did not order an attack to take place at 9 a.m., and as to whether Longstreet was dilatory, and to blame for not making it. When a battle is lost there is always an inquest, and a natural desire on the part of each general to lay the blame on somebody else's shoulders. Longstreet waited until noon for Law's brigade to come up, and afterward there was a good deal of marching and countermarching to avoid being seen by our troops. There was undoubtedly too much delay. The fact is, Longstreet saw we had a strong position and was not well pleased at the duty assigned him, for he thought it more than probable his attempt would fail. He had urged Lee to take up a position where Meade would be forced to attack him, and was not in very good humor to find his advice disregarded. The rebel commander, however, finding the Army of the Potomac in front of him, having unbounded confidence in his troops, and elated by the success of the first day's fight, believed he could gain a great victory then and there, and end the war, and determined to attempt it. He was sick of these endless delays and constant sacrifices, and hoped one strong, sword-thrust would slay his opponent, and enable the South to crown herself queen of the North American continent.

There had been a Council of War, or Conference of Corps Commanders, called at Meade's headquarters, and it was universally agreed to remain and hold the position. As the 3rd Corps, in answer to the guns of Clark's battery, was suddenly assailed by a terrible concentrated artillery fire, General Sickles rode back to his command and General Meade went with him. The latter objected to Sickles's line, but thought it was then too late to change it.

Lee intended to make simultaneous attacks on the Union right and left. The attack on the Union right would be made by Ewell's corps and on the Union left by Longstreet's corps. (Only McLaws and Hood's divisions of Longstreet's corps had arrived. Pickett's division which had been the last in the column was still marching to join the army).

The Union army was defending a position in the form of a right-angle. Its left and centre was the vertical arm along a ridge with two hills at the end. The centre and right formed the horizontal arm of the right-angle, south of the town.

Longstreet formed his two divisions into a line of battle which overlapped the Union line. Some Union troops had advanced down from the ridge, but were forced back. The Confederates advanced to seize Little Round Top, the hill at the end of the Union line. General Warren, the Chief Engineer of the Union army, saw the danger:

> Without losing a moment he rode down the Slope, over to Barnes, took the responsibility of detaching Vincent's brigade and hurried it back to take post on Little Round Top. He then sent a staff officer to inform General Meade of what he had done and to represent the immense importance of holding this commanding point.
>
> Vincent's brigade rapidly formed on the crest of a small spur which juts out from the hill and, not having time to load, advanced with the bayonet, in time to save the height. The contest soon became furious and the rocks were alive with musketry. General Vincent sent word to Barnes that the enemy were on him in overwhelming numbers, and Hazlett's regular battery, supported by the 140th New York under Colonel O'Rorke of Weed's brigade, was sent as a reinforcement. The battery was dragged with great labour to the crest of Little Round Top, and the 140th were posted on the slope on Vincent's right. They came upon the field just as the rebels, after failing to penetrate the centre, had driven back the right. In advancing to this exposed position, Colonel O'Rorke, a brilliant young officer who had just graduated at the head of his class at West Point, was killed and his men thrown into some confusion, but Vincent rallied the line and repulsed the assault. In doing so he exposed himself very much and was soon killed by a rebel sharpshooter. General Weed, who was on the crest with the battery, was mortally wounded in the same way and, as Hazlett leaned over to hear his last message, a fatal bullet struck him also and he dropped dead on the body of his chief. Colonel Rice of the 44th New York now took command in place of Vincent. The enemy, having been foiled at the centre and right, stole around through the woods and turned the left of the line, but Chamberlain's regiment, the 20th Maine, was folded back by him, around the rear of the mountain, to resist the attack. The rebels came on like wolves, with deafening yells, and forced Chamberlain's men over the crest, but they rallied and drove their assailants back in their turn. This was twice repeated and then a brigade of the Pennsylvania Reserves and one of the 5th Corps dashed over the hill. The 20th Maine made a grand final charge and drove the rebels from the valley between the Round Tops,

capturing a large number of prisoners. Not a moment too soon, for Chamberlain had lost a third of his command and was entirely out of ammunition. Vincent's men in this affair took two colonels, fifteen officers, and 500 men prisoners, and 1,000 stand of arms. Hill in his official report says "Hood's right was held as in a vise."

The regiment holding the end of the Union line was the 20th Maine. The 20th Maine was a volunteer regiment which had been 1,000 strong when it was raised. It had dwindled to 300 men. It was commanded by Colonel Joshua L. Chamberlain. Chamberlain had been a college professor until he volunteered. He was a thoughtful and perceptive officer. He realised that the regiment could be outflanked so he extended his line as far as he could and positioned his left wing at right angles to his main line. His regiment was attacked by an Alabama regiment from Hood's division of Longstreet's corps. The Alabamians charged repeatedly and twice closed to hand-to-hand combat.

Chamberlain himself recalled:

> The edge of conflict swayed to and fro, with wild whirlpools and eddies. At times I saw around me more of the enemy than of my own men; gaps opening, swallowing, closing up again with sharp convulsive energy; squads of stalwart men who had cut their way through us, disappearing as if translated. All around, strange, mingled roar . . .

And the Colonel saw something else he was always to remember:

> I saw through a sudden rift in the thick smoke our colors standing alone. I first thought some optical illusion imposed upon me. But as forms emerged through the drifting smoke, the truth came to view. The cross-fire had cut keenly; the center had been almost shot away; only two of the color guard had been left, and they fighting to fill the whole space; and in the center, wreathed in battle smoke, stood the color-sergeant, Andrew Tozier. His color staff planted in the ground at his side, the upper part clasped in his elbow, so holding the flag upright, with musket and cartridges seized from the fallen comrade at his side, he was defending his sacred trust in the manner of the songs of chivalry.

The 20th Maine had begun the fight with 60 rounds per man. In an hour and a half they had fired nearly every round.

Colonel Oates of the Alabama regiment (the 15th Alabama) attacking up hill saw his officers falling; first he saw a bullet strike Captain J. Henry Ellison in the head:

> He fell upon his left shoulder, turned upon his back, raised his arms, clenched his fists, gave one shudder, his arms fell, and he was dead.

Then he saw more of his officers falling:

> Captain Brainard, one of the bravest and best officers in the regiment, in leading his company forward, fell, exclaiming, "O, God! That I could see my mother," and instantly expired. Lieutenant John A. Oates, my dear brother, succeeded to the command of the company, but was pierced through by a number of bullets, and fell mortally wounded. Lieutenant Cody fell mortally wounded, Captain Bethune and several other officers were seriously wounded, while the carnage in the ranks was appalling.

And, later:

> My dead and wounded were then nearly as great in number as those still on duty. They literally covered the ground. The blood stood in puddles in some places on the rocks.

Oates believed that his men drove the Union troops from their position five times but each time they rallied and drove the Confederates back, twice closing to hand-to-hand combat.

The 20th Maine had lost one-third of their strength; they had only 200 men left. The regiment next to them agreed to extend so that the 20th Maine could move men from its right companies to its left. Chamberlain decided that when they finally ran out of ammunition, they would make a bayonet charge. The bent back left wing would begin the charge before the rest of the line.

Private Theodore Gerrish of the 20th Maine:

> Our line is pressed so far that our dead are within the lines of the enemy. The pressure made by the superior weight of the enemy's line is severely felt. Our ammunition is nearly all gone, and we are using the cartridges from the boxes of our wounded comrades. A critical moment has arrived, and we can remain as we are no

longer; we must advance or retreat. It must not be the latter, but how can it be the former? Colonel Chamberlain understands how it can be done. The order is given "Fix bayonets!" and the steel shanks of the bayonets rattle upon the rifle barrels. "Charge bayonets, charge!" Every man understood in a moment that the movement was our only salvation, but there is a limit to human endurance, and I do not dishonor those brave men when I write that for a brief moment the order was not obeyed, and the little line seemed to quail under the fearful fire that was being poured upon it. O, for some man reckless of life, and all else save his country's honor and safety, who would rush far out to the front, lead the way, and inspire the hearts of his exhausted comrades! In that moment of supreme need the want was supplied. Lieut. H. S. Melcher, an officer who had worked his way up from the ranks, and was then in command of Co. F., at that time the color company, saw the situation and did not hesitate, and for his gallant act deserved as much as any other man of the honor of the victory on Round Top.

With a cheer, and a flash of his sword that sent an inspiration along the line, full ten paces to the front he sprang – ten paces – more than half the distance between the hostile lines. "Come on! Come on! Come on, boys!" he shouts. The color sergeant and the brave color guard follow, and with one wild yell of anguish wrung from its tortured heart, the regiment charged.

The rebels were confounded at the movement. We struck them with a fearful shock. They recoil, stagger, break and run, and like avenging demons our men pursue. The rebels rush toward a stone wall, but, to our mutual surprise, two scores of rifle barrels gleam over the rocks, and a murderous volley was poured in upon them at close quarters. A band of men leap over the wall and capture at least a hundred prisoners. This unlooked-for reinforcement was Company B whom we supposed were all captured.

Our Colonel's commands were simply to hold the hill, and we did not follow the retreating rebels but a short distance. After dark an order came to advance and capture a hill in our front. Through the trees, among the rocks, up the steep hillside, we made our way, captured the position, and also a number of prisoners.

On the morning of 3 July we were relieved by the Pennsylvania reserves, and went back to the rear. Of our 350 men, 135 had been killed and wounded. We captured over 300 prisoners, and a detachment sent out to bury the dead found 50 dead rebels upon the ground where we had fought.

Colonel Oates of the Alabama regiment:

> I . . . had the officers and men advised the best I could that when the signal was given that we would not try to retreat in order, but every one should run in the direction from whence we came . . . When the signal was given we ran like a herd of wild cattle, right through the line of dismounted cavalrymen . . . As we ran, a man named Keils, of Company H, from Henry County, who was to my right and rear, had his throat cut by a bullet, and he ran past me breathing at his throat and the blood spattering.

The 20th Maine had received 130 casualties, killed or wounded 150 Confederates and took 400 prisoners. Corporal William T. Livermore wrote in his diary:

> The Regiment we fought and captured was the 15th Alabama. They fought like demons and said they never were whipped before and never wanted to meet the 20th Maine again. . . . Ours was an important position and, had we been driven from it, the tide of battle would have been turned against us and what the result would have been we cannot tell.

Fresh Union regiments came up to reinforce the position during the night.

The fighting continued around the broken ground in front of the Union left. Hill's corps was still attacking the Union centre. Some Confederate troops actually broke into the Union centre. Doubleday:

> . . . the great effort of Wilcox and Wright, which would have been ruinous to us if followed up, was fruitless of results. Both were repulsed for lack of support, but Wright actually reached the crest with his Georgians and turned a gun, whose cannoneers had been shot, upon Webb's brigade of the 2nd Corps. Webb gave them two staggering volleys from behind a fence, and went forward with two regiments. He charged, regained the lost piece, and turned it upon them.
>
> Wright, finding himself entirely isolated in this advanced position, went back again to the main line, and Wilcox did the same. On this occasion Wright did what Lee failed to accomplish the next day at such a heavy expense of life, for he pierced our centre,

and held it for a short time, and had the movement been properly supported and energetically followed up, it might have been fatal to our army, and would most certainly have resulted in a disastrous retreat.

Lee's divisions seemed never to strike at the hour appointed. Each came forward separately, and was beaten for lack of support.

Wright attained the crest and Wilcox was almost on a line with him. The latter was closely followed up and nearly surrounded, for troops rushed in on him from all sides. He lost very heavily in extricating himself from his advanced position. Wilcox claims to have captured temporarily twenty guns and Wright eight.

As they approached the ridge a Union battery limbered up and galloped off. The last gun was delayed and the cannoneer, with a long line of muskets pointing at him within a few feet, deliberately drove off the field. The Georgians manifested their admiration for his bravery by crying out "Don't shoot," and not a musket was fired at him. I regret that I have not been able to ascertain the man's name.

In the morning General Tidball, who was attached to the cavalry as Chief of Artillery, rode along the entire crest from Little Round Top to Culps Hill to make himself familiar with the lines. As he passed my headquarters he noticed some new troops, the 2nd Vermont brigade under General Stannard, which formed part of my command. They were a fine-looking body of men, and were drawn up in close column by division, ready to go to any part of the field at a moment's notice. After inquiring to what corps they belonged he passed over to the right. On his return late in the day he saw Sickles' whole line driven in and found Wright's rebel brigade established on the crest barring his way back. He rode rapidly over to Meade's headquarters and found the general walking up and down the room, apparently quite unconscious of the movements which might have been discerned by riding to the top of the hill, and which should have been reported to him by some one of his staff. Tidball said, "General, I am very sorry to see that the enemy have pierced our centre." Meade expressed surprise at the information and said, "Why, where is Sedgwick?" Tidball replied, "I do not know, but if you need troops, I saw a fine body of Vermonters a short distance from here, belonging to the 1st Corps, who are available." Meade then directed him to take an order to Newton and put the men in at once; the order was communicated to me and I went with my division at double quick

> to the point indicated. There we pursued Wright's force as it retired, and retook, at Hancock's instigation, four guns taken by Wright earlier in the action. When these were brought in I sent out two regiments, who followed the enemy up nearly to their lines and retook two more guns.

According to Lee's plan, Ewell's corps should have attacked the Union right at the same time as Longstreet's corps was attacking the Union left. Ewell did nothing until Longstreet's attack had been repulsed:

> To supplement this attack on the (Union) right, and prevent reinforcements from being sent there, Early's division was directed to carry Cemetery Hill by storm. Before it advanced, a vigorous artillery fire was opened from four rebel batteries on Benner's Hill, to prepare the way for the assault, but our batteries on Cemetery Hill, which were partially sheltered by earthworks, replied and soon silenced those of the enemy. Then Early's infantry moved forth, Hays's brigade on the right, Hoke's brigade on the left, under Colonel Avery, and Gordon's brigade in reserve. It was supposed Johnson's division would protect Early's left flank, while Rodes' and Pender's divisions would come forward in time to prevent any attack against his right. The enemy first struck Von Gilsa's brigade, which was posted behind a stone fence at the foot of the hill. Still farther to its left, at the base of the hill, was Ames's brigade, both enclosing Rickett's and Weidrick's batteries on higher ground above. Stuart's, Reynolds's and Stevens's batteries, which had been a good deal cut up on the first day, were now brought to bear on the approaching enemy. Colonel Wainwright, Chief of Artillery to the 1st Corps, gave them orders not to attempt to retreat if attacked, but to fight the guns to the last. The enemy advanced up the ravine which was specially commanded by Stevens's battery. Weidrick, Ricketts, and Stevens played upon the approaching line energetically. The rebel left and centre fell back, but the right managed to obtain shelter from houses and undulating ground, and came on impetuously, charging over Von Gilsa's brigade, and driving it up the hill, through the batteries. In doing so Hays says the darkness and smoke saved his men from a terrible slaughter. Weidrick's battery was captured, and two of Ricketts's guns were spiked. The enemy, in making this movement, exposed their left flank to Stevens's battery, which poured a

terrible fire of double canister into their ranks. The 33rd Massachusetts also opened a most effective oblique fire. The batteries were penetrated but would not surrender. Dearer than life itself to the cannoneer is the gun he serves, and these brave men fought hand to hand with handspikes, rammer, staves, and even stones. They shouted, "Death on the soil of our native state rather than lose our guns!" Hancock, all this time, should have been kept busy on his own front repelling an attack from Rodes and Pender, but as they did not come forward, and as he felt that there was great danger that Howard would lose Cemetery Hill and his own right be turned, he sent Carroll's brigade to the rescue. Carroll was joined by the 106th Pennsylvania and some reinforcements from Schurz's division. For a few minutes, Hays says, there was an ominous silence and then the tramp of our infantry was heard. They came over the hill and went in with a cheer. The enemy, finding they were about to be overwhelmed, retreated, as no one came to their assistance. When they fell back our guns opened a very destructive fire. It is said that out of 1,750 men of the organization known as "The Louisiana Tigers," only 150 returned. Hays attributes his defeat to the fact that Gordon was not up in time to support him.

The failure to carry the Hill isolated Johnson's division on our extreme right. As it could only be reached by a long circuit it was not easy for Lee to maintain it there, without unduly weakening other parts of his line. That Rodes's division did not reach Cemetery Hill in time to co-operate with Early's attack was not owing to any lack of zeal or activity on the part of that energetic officer. He was obliged to move out of Gettysburg by the flank, then change front and advance double the distance Early had to traverse, and by the time he had done so Early had made the attack and had been repulsed.

The day closed with the rebels defeated on our left, but victorious on our right. Fortunately for us, this incited Lee to continue his efforts. He could not bear to retreat after his heavy losses, and acknowledge that he was beaten. He resolved to reinforce Johnson's division, now in rear of our right, and fling Pickett's troops, the elite of his army, who had not been engaged, against our centre. He hoped a simultaneous attack made by Pickett in front and Johnson in rear, would yet win those heights and scatter the Union army to the winds. Kilpatrick, who had been resting the tired men and horses of his cavalry division at

Abbotsford after the conflict at Hanover, went on the afternoon of the 2nd to circle around and attack the left and rear of the enemy by way of Hunterstown. This plan was foiled, however, by the sudden arrival of Stuart's cavalry from its long march. They reached that part of the field about 4 p.m. After a fierce combat, in which Farnsworth's and Custer's brigades and Estes's squadron were principally engaged against Hampton's brigade supported by the main body, darkness put an end to the fight. Kilpatrick then turned back and bivouacked at Two Taverns for the night.

At night a council of war was held, in which it was unanimously voted to stay and fight it out. Meade was displeased with the result, and although he acquiesced in the decision, he said angrily, "Have it your own way, gentlemen, but Gettysburg is no place to fight a battle in."

3 July, third day of the battle.
Doubleday:

At dawn on the 3rd the enemy opened on us with artillery, but the firing had no definite purpose, and after some hours it gradually slackened. The principal interest early in the day necessarily centred on the right, where Johnson's position not only endangered the safety of the army, but compromised our retreat. It was therefore essential to drive him out as soon as possible. To this end batteries were established during the night on all the prominent points in that vicinity. Geary had returned with his division about midnight, and was not a little astonished to find the rebels established in the works he had left. He determined to contest possession with them at daylight. In the meantime he joined Greene and formed part of his line perpendicular to our main line of battle, and part fronting the enemy.

On the other hand, Ewell, having obtained a foothold, swore he would not be driven out, and hastened to reinforce Johnson with Daniels's and O'Neill's brigades from Rodes's division.

As soon as objects could be discerned in the early gray of the morning our artillery opened fire. As Johnson, on account of the steep declivities and other obstacles, had not been able to bring any artillery with him, he could not reply. It would not do to remain quiet under this fire, and he determined to charge, in hopes of winning a better position on higher ground. His men – the old Stonewall brigade leading – rushed bravely forward, but were as gallantly met by Kane's brigade of Geary's division and a close and severe struggle ensued for four hours among the trees and rocks. Ruger's division of the 12th Corps came up and formed on the rebel left, taking them in flank and threatening them in reverse. Indeed, as the rest of our line were not engaged, there was plenty of support for Geary. Shaler's and Wheaton's brigades and other troops were sent him as a reserve force.

At about 11 a.m., finding the contest hopeless, and his retreat threatened by a force sent down to Rock Creek, Johnson yielded slowly and reluctantly to a charge made by Geary's division, gave up the position and withdrew to Rock Creek, where he remained until night.

Having failed at each extremity, it only remained to Lee to retreat, or attack the centre. Such high expectations had been formed in the Southern States in regard to his conquest of the North that he determined to make another effort. He still had Pickett's division, the flower of Virginia, which had not been engaged, and which was full of enthusiasm. He resolved to launch them against our centre, supported on either flank by the advance of the main portion of the army. He had hoped that Johnson's division would have been able to maintain its position on the right, so that the Union centre could be assailed in front and rear at the same time, but Johnson having been driven out, it was necessary to trust to Pickett alone, or abandon the whole enterprise and return to Virginia.

Everything was quiet up to 1 p.m., as the enemy were massing their batteries and concentrating their forces preparatory to the grand charge – the supreme effort – which was to determine the fate of the campaign, and to settle the point whether freedom or slavery was to rule the Northern States.

It seems to me there was some lack of judgment in the preparations. Heth's division, now under Pettigrew, which had been so severely handled on the first day, and which was composed in a great measure of new troops, was designated to support Pickett's left and join in the attack at close quarters. Wilcox, too, who one would think had been pretty well fought out the day before, in his desperate enterprise of attempting to crown the crest, was directed to support the right flank of the attack. Wright's brigade was formed in rear, and Pender's on the left of Pettigrew, but there was a long distance between Wilcox and Longstreet's forces on the right.

At 1 p.m., a signal gun was fired and 115 guns opened against

Hancock's command, consisting of the 1st Corps under Newton, the 2nd Corps under Gibbon, the 3rd Corps under Birney, and against the 11th Corps under Howard. The object of this heavy artillery fire was to break up our lines and prepare the way for Pickett's charge. The exigencies of the battle had caused the 1st Corps to be divided, Wadsworth's division being on the right at Culps Hill, Robinson on Gibbon's right, and my own division intervening between Caldwell on the left and Gibbon on the right. The convex shape of our line did not give us as much space as that of the enemy, but General Hunt, Chief of Artillery, promptly posted 80 guns along the crest – as many as it would hold – to answer the fire, and the batteries on both sides suffered severely in the two hours' cannonade. Not less than eleven caissons were blown up and destroyed; one quite near me. When the smoke went up from these explosions rebel yells of exultation could be heard along a line of several miles. At 3 p.m. General Hunt ordered our artillery fire to cease, in order to cool the guns, and to preserve some rounds for the contest at close quarters, which he foresaw would soon take place.

My own men did not suffer a great deal from this cannonade, as I sheltered them as much as possible under the crest of the hill, and behind rocks, trees, and stone fences.

The cessation of our fire gave the enemy the idea they had silenced our batteries, and Pickett at once moved forward, to break the left centre of the Union line and occupy the crest of the ridge. The other forces on his right and left were expected to move up and enlarge the opening thus made, so that finally, the two wings of the Union Army would be permanently separated, and flung off by this entering wedge in eccentric directions.

This great column of attack, it was supposed, numbered about 17,000 men. The force that now advanced would have been larger still had it not been for a spirited attack by Kilpatrick against the left of Longstreet's corps, detaining some troops there which otherwise might have co-operated in the grand assault against our centre.

It necessarily took the rebels some time to form and cross the intervening space, and Hunt took advantage of the opportunity to withdraw the batteries had been most injured, sending others in their place from the reserve artillery, which had not been engaged. He also replenished the ammunition boxes, and stood ready to receive the foe as he came forward – first with solid shot, next with shell, and lastly, when he came to close quarters, with canister.

The distance to be traversed by Pickett's column was about a mile and a half from the woods where they started, to the crest of the ridge they desired to attain. They suffered severely from our artillery, which opened on them with solid shot as soon as they came in sight; when half way across the plain they were vigorously shelled; double canisters were reserved for their nearer approach.

At first the direction of their march appeared to be directly toward my division. When within 500 yards of us, however, Pickett halted and changed direction obliquely about 45 degrees, so that the attack passed me and struck Gibbon's division on my right. Just here one of those providential circumstances occurred which favored us so much, for Wilcox and Lang, who guarded Pickett's right flank, did not follow his oblique movement, but kept on straight to the front, so that soon there was a wide interval between their troops and the main body, leaving Pickett's right fully uncovered.

The rebels came on magnificently. As fast as the shot and shell tore through their lines they closed up the gaps and pressed forward. When they reached the Emmetsburg road the canister began to make fearful chasms in their ranks. They also suffered severely from a battery posted on Little Round Top, which enfiladed their line. One shell killed and wounded ten men. Gibbon had directed his command to reserve their fire until the enemy were near enough to make it very effective. Pickett's advance dashed up to the fence occupied by Hays' brigade of the 2nd Corps in front of our main line; then the musketry blazed forth with deadly effect, and Pettigrew's men began to waver on the left and fall behind; for the nature of the ground was such that they were more exposed than other portions of the line.

Before the first line of rebels reached the fence it was obliged to pass a demi-brigade under Colonel Theodore B. Gates of the 20th New York State Militia and a Vermont brigade under General Stannard, both belonging to my command, and holding my front line parallel to that of the enemy and some distance below the crest, in advance of the main line of battle.

When Pickett's right became exposed in consequence of the divergence of Wilcox's command, Stannard seized the opportunity to make a flank attack, and while his left regiment, the 14th, poured in a heavy oblique fire, he changed front with his two right regiments, the 13th and 16th, which brought them perpendicular to the rebel line of march. In cases of this kind when struck directly on the flank, troops are quite unable to defend themselves, and Kemper's brigade crowded in toward the centre to avoid Stannard's energetic and deadly attack. They were closely followed up by Gates's command, who continued to fire into them at close range. This caused many to surrender, others to retreat outright, and others simply to crowd together. Nevertheless, the next brigade – that of Armistead – united to Garnett's brigade, pressed on, overpowered Hays' brigade of the 2nd Corps, and drove it from its advanced position at the fence, back through the batteries on the crest, and in spite of death-dealing bolts on all sides, Pickett determined to break Gibbon's line and capture his guns.

Although Webb's front was the focus of the concentrated artillery fire, and he had already lost 50 men and some valuable officers, his line remained firm and unshaken. It devolved upon him now to meet the great charge which was to decide the fate of the day. It would have been difficult to find a man better fitted for such an emergency. He was nerved to great deeds by the memory of his ancestors, who in former days had rendered distinguished services to the Republic, and felt that the results of the whole war might depend upon his holding his position. His men were equally resolute. Cushing's battery, "B", 4th United States Artillery, which had been posted on his left, and Brown's Rhode Island Battery on his right, were both practically destroyed by the cannonade. The horses were prostrated, every officer but one was struck, and Cushing had but one serviceable gun left.

As Pickett's advance came very close to the first line, young Cushing, mortally wounded, holding on to his intestines with one hand, ran his only gun down to the fence with the other, and said: "Webb, I will give them one more shot!" At the moment of the last discharge he called out, "Good-bye!" and fell dead at the post of duty.

Webb sent for fresh batteries to replace the two that were disabled, and Wheeler's 1st New York Independent Battery came up just before the attack, and took the place of Cushing's battery on the left.

Armistead pressed forward, leaped the fence, waving his sword with his hat on it, followed by about a hundred of his men, several of whom carried battle-flags. He shouted, "Give them the cold steel, boys!" and laid his hands upon one of the guns. The battery for a few minutes was in his possession, and the rebel flag flew triumphantly over our line. But Webb was at the front, very near Armistead, animating and encouraging his men. He led the 72nd Pennsylvania regiment against the enemy, and posted a line of wounded men in rear to drive back or shoot every man that deserted his duty. A portion of the 71st Pennsylvania, behind a stone wall on the right, threw in a deadly flanking fire, while a great part of the 69th Pennsylvania and the remainder of the 71st made stern resistance from a copse of trees on the left, near where the enemy had broken the line, and where our men were shot with the rebel muskets touching their breasts.

Then came a splendid charge of two regiments, led by Colonel Hall, which passed completely through Webb's line, and engaged the enemy in a hand-to-hand conflict. Armistead was shot down by the side of the gun he had taken. It is said he had fought on our side in the first battle at Bull Run, but had been seduced by Southern affiliations to join in the rebellion; and now, dying in the effort to extend the area of slavery over the free States, he saw with a clearer vision that he had been engaged in an unholy cause, and said to one of our officers who leaned over him: "Tell Hancock I have wronged him and have wronged my country."

My command being a little to the left, I witnessed this scene, and, after it was over, sent out stretcher-bearers attached to the ambulance train, and had numbers of wounded Confederates brought in and cared for. I was told that there was one man among these whose conversation seemed to indicate that he was a general officer. I sent to ascertain his rank, but he replied: "Tell General Doubleday in a few minutes I shall be where there is no rank." He expired soon after, and I never learned his name.

The rebels did not seem to appreciate my humanity in sending out to bring in their wounded, for they opened a savage fire against the stretcher-bearers. One shell burst among us, a piece of it knocked me over on my horse's neck, and wounded Lieutenant Cowdry of my staff.

When Pickett – the great leader – looked around the top of the ridge he had temporarily gained, he saw it was impossible to hold the position. Troops were rushing in on him from all sides. The 2nd Corps were engaged in a furious assault on his front. His men were fighting with clubbed muskets, and even banner staves were intertwined in a fierce and hopeless struggle. My division of the 1st Corps were on his right flank, giving deadly blows there, and the 3rd Corps were closing up to attack. Pettigrew's forces on his left

> had given way, and a heavy skirmish line began to accumulate on that flank. He saw his men surrendering in masses and, with a heart full of anguish, ordered a retreat. Death had been busy on all sides, and few indeed now remained of that magnificent column which had advanced so proudly, led by the Ney of the rebel army, and these few fell back in disorder, and without organization, behind Wright's brigade, which had been sent forward to cover the retreat. At first, however, when struck by Stannard on the flank, and when Pickett's charge was spent, they rallied in a little slashing, where a grove had been cut down by our troops to leave an opening for our artillery. There two regiments of Rowley's brigade of my division, the 151st Pennsylvania and the 20th New York State Militia, under Colonel Theodore B. Gates, of the latter regiment, made a gallant charge, and drove them out. Pettigrew's division, it is said, lost 2,000 prisoners and 15 battle-flags on the left.
>
> While this severe contest was going on in front of Webb, Wilcox deployed his command and opened a feeble fire against Caldwell's division on my left. Stannard repeated the manoeuvre which had been so successful against Kemper's brigade by detaching the 14th and 16th Vermont to take Wilcox in flank. Wilcox thus attacked on his right, while a long row of batteries tore the front of his line to pieces with canister, could gain no foothold. He found himself exposed to a tremendous cross fire, and was obliged to retreat, but a great portion of his command were brought in as prisoners by Stannard and battle-flags were gathered in sheaves.

Despite the failure of "Pickett's charge", the battle continued on the flanks, Union troops pushed the Confederates back to their own own lines. Lee sent Stuart's cavalry around the Union flank to attack their rear. General G. A. Custer's cavalry brigade helped hold them off.

Meade sent forward a brigade preceded by skirmishers. Longstreet's remaining troops were well fortified and resisted so strongly that Meade gave up all idea of a counter-attack Doubleday:

> The fact is, Meade had no idea of leaving the ridge. I conversed the next morning with a corps commander who had just left him. He said: "Meade says he thinks he can hold out for part of another day here, if they attack him."

This language satisfied me that Meade would not go forward if he could avoid it, and would not impede in any way the rebel retreat across the Potomac. Lee began to make preparations at once and started his trains on the morning of the 4th. By night Rodes' division, which followed them, was in bivouac two miles west of Fairfield. It was a difficult task to retreat burdened with 4,000 prisoners, and a train 15 miles long, in the presence of a victorious enemy, but it was successfully accomplished as regard his main body.

CSS *Alabama* v USS *Kearsage* 1864

The United States (Union) Navy imposed an effective blockade of Confederate ports, strangling Confederate commercial shipping. In retaliation the Confederacy sent to sea individual armed ships to cruise against Union merchant ships. Few of these cruisers were properly adapted for ocean-going voyages. But the Confederate States Steamer *Alabama* did enough damage to persuade Union merchants to consign their cargoes to neutral British vessels.

In her two year cruise the C S S *Alabama* captured and burnt 57 merchant vessels. She sailed 75,000 miles. Her depredations drew off some of the most effective Union warships from their blockade. The CSS *Alabama* was a screw (propeller) steamer with full sail-power. She could hoist her propeller up into a well which allowed her to sail without drag. Her two engines were coal-powered and capable of 13 knots. Her armament consisted of one rifled 7-inch and one rifled 8-inch gun with six 32-pound smooth-bore guns in each broadside. In her trial voyage she sailed from the British shipyard where she was built to the Azores where Confederate officers took her over and most of the original crew signed on with the Confederate States Navy. She was commanded by by Captain Raphael Semmes.

Arthur Sinclair went to sea, aged 13, with the United States Navy. He joined the Confederate States Navy as a master's mate in 1861. He served as an aid to the captain of the *Merrimac* in her battle with the *Monitor*. He joined the *Alabama* at sea between Liverpool and the Azores. He was promoted to Lieutenant by Captain Semmes.

The C S S *Alabama* sailed from Liverpool on 24 August 1862. She began to cripple and demoralize Union commercial shipping.

On 10 June 1864 she ended her two-year cruise and entered harbor in Cherbourg, France. News of her reached a nearby Union warship, the USS *Kearsage*. The USS *Kearsage* arrived at Cherbourg three days later. Captain Semmes challenged the *Kearsage* to fight. 19 June was agreed as the date. The *Kearsage* had armour plating and heavier guns.

Captain Semmes intended to board the *Kearsage* but was unable to do so. *Kearsage*'s superior armament and *Alabama*'s defective ammunition brought about her end. The action lasted for one and a half hours. Arthur Sinclair described the fight:

> The *Kearsage* suddenly turns her head inshore and steams towards us, both ships being at this time about seven or eight miles from the shore. When at about one mile distant from us, she seems from her sheer-off with helm to have chosen this distance for her attack. We had not yet perceived that the *Kearsage* had the speed of us. We open the engagement with our entire starboard battery, the writer's 32-pounder of the port side having been shifted to the spare port, giving us six guns in broadside; and the shift caused the ship to list to starboard about two feet, by the way, quite an advantage, exposing so much less surface to the enemy, but somewhat retarding our speed. The *Kearsage* had pivoted to starboard also; and both ships with helms a-port fought out the engagement, circling around a common centre, and gradually approaching each other.
>
> The enemy replied soon after our opening; but at the distance her pivot shell-guns were at a disadvantage, not having the long range of our pivot-guns, and hence requiring judgment in guessing the distance and determining the proper elevation. Our pivots could easily reach by ricochet, indeed by point-blank firing, so at this stage of the action, and with a smooth sea, we had the advantage.
>
> The battle is now on in earnest; and after about fifteen minutes' fighting, we lodge a 100-pound percussion shell in her quarter near her screw; but it fails to explode, though causing some temporary excitement and anxiety on board the enemy, most likely by the concussion of the blow. We find her soon after seeking closer quarters (which she is fully able to do, having discovered her superiority in speed), finding it judicious to close so that her 11-inch pivots could do full duty at point-blank range. We now ourselves noted the advantage in speed possessed by our enemy;

and Semmes felt her pulse, as to whether very close quarters would be agreeable, by steering towards her to close the distance; but she had evidently reached the point wished for to fight out the remainder of the action, and demonstrated it by sheering off and resuming a parallel to us. Semmes would have chosen to bring about yard-arm quarters, fouling, and boarding, relying upon the superior physique of his crew to overbalance the superiority of numbers; but this was frustrated, though several times attempted, the desire on our part being quite apparent. We had therefore to accept the situation, and make the best of it we could, to this end directing our fire to the midship section of the enemy, and alternating our battery with solid shot and shell, the former to pierce, if possible, the cable chain-armor, the latter for general execution.

Up to the time of shortening the first distance assumed, our ship received no damage of any account, and the enemy none that we could discover, the shot in the quarter working no serious harm to the *Kearsage*.

At the distance we were now fighting (point-blank range), the effects of the eleven-inch guns were severely felt, and the little hurt done the enemy clearly proved the unserviceableness of our powder, observed at the commencement of the action.

The boarding tactics of Semmes having been frustrated, and we unable to pierce the enemy's hull with our fire, nothing can place victory with us but some unforeseen and lucky turn. At this period of the action our spanker-gaff is shot away, bringing our colors to the deck; but apparently this is not observed by the *Kearsage*, as her fire does not halt at all. We can see the splinters flying off from the armor covering of the enemy; but no penetration occurs, the shot or shell rebounding from her side. Our colors are immediately hoisted to the mizzenmast-head.

The enemy having now the range, and being able with her superior speed to hold it at ease, has us well in hand, and the fire from her is deliberate and hot. Our bulwarks are soon shot away in sections; and the after pivot-gun is disabled on its port side, losing, in killed and wounded, all but the compresser-man. The quarter-deck 32-pounder of this division is now secured, and the crew sent to man the pivot-gun. The spar-deck is by this time being rapidly torn up by shells bursting on the between-decks, interfering with working our battery; and the compartments below have all been knocked into one. The *Alabama* is making water fast, showing severe punishment; but still the report comes from the engine-room that the ship is being kept free to the safety-point.

She also has now become dull in response to her helm, and the sail-trimmers are ordered out to loose the head-sails to pay her head off. We are making a desperate but forlorn resistance, which is soon culminated by the death-blow. An eleven-inch shell enters us at the waterline, in the wake of the writer's gun, and passing on, explodes in the engine-room, in its passage throwing a volume of water on board, hiding for a moment the guns of this division. Our ship trembles from stem to stern from the blow. Semmes at once sends for the engineer on watch, who reports the fires out, and water beyond the control of the pumps. We had previously been aware our ship was whipped, and fore-and-aft sail was set in endeavor to reach the French coast; the enemy then moved in shore of us, but did not attempt to close any nearer, simply steaming to secure the shore-side and await events.

It being now apparent that the *Alabama* could not float longer, the colors are hauled down, and the pipe given, "All hands save yourselves."

The *Alabama*'s boats had been destroyed in the action. Most of her crew was picked up by an English yacht, *Deerhound*, which was allowed to rescue her sailors.

The Battle of the Wilderness 1864

I need this man. He fights.
Abraham Lincoln

After the battle of Gettysburg, the Confederate army of Northern Virginia retreated into Virginia and took up positions south of the Rappahannock river. Meade, in command of the Union Army of the Potomac, followed them.

On 9 March 1864 President Lincoln appointed Ulysses S. Grant commander of all the Union armies. In response to criticism of Grant, Lincoln replied, "I need this man. He fights." Grant had won victories in the West at Fort Donelson, Fort Henry and Vicksburg. He perceived that the way to win the war was to destroy the enemy's armies; in his own words:

> Conquering the organised armies of the enemy is vastly more important than the mere acquisition of their territories.

Grant was persevering, calm and flexible. He firmly believed in discipline, the sound preparation of supplies, ordnance and planning.

Morris Schaff had been with the Army of the Potomac since 1862. He was a regular officer of the corps of Ordnance. He had graduated from West Point in 1862.

In 1864 it was by no means certain that the war would result in victory for the Union. It was still possible for the Confederates to strike a decisive blow which would end the war in their favour. Schaff described this possibility:

> This being the state of affairs, let us suppose that Lee, at the outset of the campaign of 1864, had defeated the Army of the Potomac decisively, and had driven Grant back across the Rappahannock, as he had driven Burnside, Pope, and Hooker – how loud and almost irresistible would have been the cry for an armistice, supported (as it would have been) by Wall Street and all Europe! Where, then, would have been the victory of Gettysburg? In view of the disparity of numbers and the depleted resources of the Confederacy, was it possible for Lee to have given such a blow? Yes, and had not Fate registered her decree that at the critical moment Longstreet was to fall in the Wilderness as Jackson had fallen at Chancellorsville, he would have come near doing so.
>
> And so, great as was the victory at Gettysburg, I am not at all convinced that it was decisive, remembering, as I do, how the balance trembled more than once in the campaign from the Rapidan.
>
> After several abortively offensive movements by each of the armies during the autumn of 1863, they went into winter quarters: Lee, with his army well in hand, on the south bank of the Rapidan; Meade, between the Rapidan and the Rappahannock. The former's headquarters were among some pines and cedars at the foot of Clarke's Mountain, near Orange Court House; the latter's were on a knoll covered with tall young pines about a mile and a half northwest from Brandy Station. The bulk of the army of the Potomac was around Culpeper and Stevensburg; one corps, the 5th, under Warren, stretched northward along the Orange and Alexandria Railroad at present the Southern as far as Calverton; the 6th was

between the railroad and Hazel River, a little tributary of the Rappahannock, the 2nd around Stevensburg, the 1st and 3rd, consolidated before we moved with the other three, were about Culpeper. Lee's principal depot for supplies was at Orange Court House, ours at Brandy, where I passed the greater part of the winter in charge of the ordnance depot.

Slavery was finally abolished in May 1864. President Lincoln needed to be renominated as Republican candidate and, then, re-elected in November. His opponent was McClellan, the original commander of the Army of the Potomac. McClellan was standing as the Democratic candidate with the declared intention of an end to the war and a negotiated settlement with the Confederacy.

Grant's plan was to impose the Union's advantages in men and materials on the Confederates by attacking on all fronts. Grant ordered Sherman, in the West, to defeat the Confederates under Johnston and to move into the interior of the "enemy's country" to damage their war resources. He gave Phil Sheridan two infantry Corps and three cavalry divisions to suppress Confederate activity in the Shenandoah valley. Grant, himself, joined Meade and the Army of the Potomac whom he had ordered to go wherever Lee went.

A sergeant of the 5th Massachusetts battery wrote on April 30, 1864:

> The next battle will be a rouser! The rebels of Lee's army are all ready for us, and are said to be 90,000. They will give us a tough pull if my opinion amounts to anything.
>
> Today I was up to Brandy Station. You can form no idea of the bustle and confusion at this depot when the army is getting ready to move. It looked to me as if 1,000 or more wagons were waiting to load, and there were immense piles of ammunition and all kinds of Ordnance Stores, etc., etc., and piles of boxes of hard bread as high as two and three-story houses. It reminded me some of a wharf in New York with 12 or 15 ships loading and unloading.

Morris Schaff's estimates of the strength of the Army of the Potomac, in men and material, demonstrates Grant's emphasis on sound logistical preparations:

> While I do not wish to encumber the narrative with a burden of figures, yet it may interest the reader to know that we had in the

> Army of the Potomac, the morning we set off on the great campaign, 4,300 wagons and 835 ambulances. There were 34,981 artillery, cavalry, and ambulance horses, and mules, making an aggregate of 57,509 animals. The strength of the Army of the Potomac was between 99 and 100,000 men. Burnside, who caught up with us the second day of the Wilderness, brought with him about 20,000 more.

At the beginning of May 1864 the Army of the Potomac crossed the Rapidan river and entered an area of dense forest. Lee intended to use this country where the Union advantages in numbers and artillery would be less effective. The Confederates had to the advantage of local knowledge. Morris Schaff:

> What is known as the Wilderness begins near Orange Court House on the west and extends almost to Fredericksburg, 25 or 30 miles to the east. Its northern bounds are the Rapidan and the Rappahannock and, owing to their winding channels, its width is somewhat irregular. At Spotsylvania, its extreme southern limit, it is some 10 miles wide. There, as along most of its southern border, it gives way to a comparatively open country.
>
> This theatre of bloody conflicts is a vast sea, so to speak, of dense forest – a second growth more than a century old. It is made up chiefly of scrubby, stubborn oaks, and low limbed, disordered, haggard pines – for the soil is cold and thin – with here and there scattering clumps of alien cedars. Some of the oaks are large enough to cut two railroad ties, and every once in a while you come across an acre or two of pines some 10 to 12 inches in diameter, tall and tapering, true to the soaring propensities of their kind. But generally, the trees are noticeably stunted, and so close together, and their lower limbs so intermingled with a thick underbrush, that it is very difficult indeed to make one's way through them.

On 2 May Grant ordered Meade to advance. On 4 May Lee became aware of this. Lee had 65,000 men against Grant's 120,000. Grant expected Lee to retreat rather than attack.

On 5 May 1864 Union troops to came into contact with the Confederates. Schaff:

> It was extraordinarily difficult to form troops into battle order in the dense forest and undergrowth. Once a division left the roads or

fields it disappeared utterly, and its commander could not tell whether it was in line with the others or not. As it turned out, they were almost as disconnected when they struck the enemy as if they had been marching in the dark. Yet it took nearly four hours to get ready to form, and when the orders came to go ahead, divisions were still looking for each others' flanks.

The leading Union corps was Hancock's 2nd Corps. They were trying to advance in two lines of battle when they came under a determined attack. Wadsworth's division was brought up in support. It was trying to advance in line of battle to join Bartlett's left. Cutler is on the right with the Iron Brigade, the 24th Michigan on its left. Stone is in the centre of the division, Rice on the left. Daniel W. Taft, a brave, one-armed Vermont veteran, who was with Rice in the 95th New York, tells me that, as they advanced, a wild turkey, the first and only one he ever saw, broke from a thicket ahead of them.

The Maryland brigade of Robinson's division is in reserve behind Stone, Robinson's other division ready to support Griffin.

Getty at the head of his division has reached the junction of the Brock and Plank roads. He was there just in time, for with his staff and escort, although under fire of the tall North Carolinians who had driven Hammond back, he held them off till Wheaton coming up at run formed across the Plank Road, saving the key of the battle-field. There were bodies of Confederate dead within less than 200 feet of this vital point. Hancock, urged by orders from Meade, is riding rapidly ahead of his corps up the Brock Road to join Getty. His troops are coming on, too, as fast as they can, sometimes at double-quick, but all are greatly delayed by artillery, trains, and horsemen, the road being very narrow and bordered by such thick woods that they cannot draw off into them to clear the way for the infantry.

For three or four miles this side of Todd's Tavern the road is packed with his sweltering troops, for it is very hot in the still woods. The main heavy supply trains that had followed Hancock's troops to Todd's Tavern have faced about and are making all speed for Chancellorsville, where the artillery reserve is going into park.

Wadsworth's division had the same difficulties experienced by everyone in the battle of the Wilderness.

Well, as already stated, when they began to move, it was almost noon. The troops tried at first to advance in line of battle from the temporary works which had been thrown up while the reconnaissances and preparations had been going on; but, owing to the character of the woods, they soon found that was out of the question, and had to break by battalions and wings into columns of fours. So by the time they neared the enemy, all semblance of line of battle was gone and there were gaps everywhere between regiments and brigades. Regiments that had started in the second line facing west found themselves facing north, deploying ahead of the first line. As an example of the confusion, the 6th Wisconsin had been formed behind the 7th Indiana, with orders to follow it at a distance of 100 yards. By running ahead of his regiment, the colonel of the 6th managed to keep the 7th in sight till they were close to the front; but when the firing began, the 7th set out at double-quick for the enemy and disappeared in a moment; and the next thing was an outburst of musketry and the enemy were coming in front and marching by both flanks.

But there was almost the same state of affairs on the other side, except that the Confederates, being more used to the woods, observed the general direction better and handled themselves with much more confidence and initiative than ours, when detached from their fellows. For instance, the 45th North Carolina, of Daniels' brigade, having lost all connection with the rest of its brigade, stumbled right on to Stone or Rice, and before they knew it were within a few rods, only a thickety depression between them. Ours were the first to fire, but the aim was too high and scarcely any one hurt; the return volley, however, so says the regiment's historian who was present, was very fatal, and our men broke, leaving a row of dead. Cases of this kind could be repeated and re-repeated of what took place in the Wilderness . . . As a proof of the savage and unexpected encounterings, a line of skeletons was found just after the war, half-covered in the drifting leaves, where some command, Northem or Southern, met with a volley like that of the 45th North Carolina, from an unseen foe.

Lieutenant Holman S. Melcher, of the 20th Maine, described the heavy fire:

The bugles sounded the "Charge" and, advancing to the edge of the field, we saw the first line of battle about halfway across it, receiving a terribly fatal fire from an enemy in the woods on the farther side, This field was less than a quarter of a mile across, had been planted with corn the year before, and was now dry and dusty. We could see the spurts of dust started up all over the field by the bullets of the enemy, as they spattered on it like the big drops of a coming shower you have so often seen along a dusty road.

By evening reports were coming back to Grant who ordered renewed attacks:

The countryside of woods and the occasional small fields meant that units lost touch with each other and could find the enemy on their flank or rear. Units were forced to retreat to avoid being captured.

At ten minutes of six the sun dropping toward the tree-tops, and twilight, owing to the density of the woods, gathering fast. Lyman, who had stayed at Hancock's side to give Meade timely information as to the progress of events, reported: "We barely hold our own; on the right the pressure is heavy. General Hancock thinks he can hold the Plank and Brock roads, but he can't advance."

The battle raged on. Wheaton's men on the north, and the Vermonters on the other or south side of the road, with Ward's brigade, were still standing up to it, although suffering terribly. The Confederates in front of them had the advantage of a slight swell in the ground, and every attempt to dislodge them had met with slaughter. Birney sent a couple of regiments to their support. About sundown the commanding officer of the 5th Vermont was asked if he thought, with the help of Birney's men, he could break the enemy's line. "I think we can," replied the stout-hearted man. And when Birney's men were asked if they would give their support, they answered, "We will," with a cheer. And again they went at the enemy's line, which partially gave way it was probably Scales; but so dense were the woods that a break at one point had mighty little moral effect to the right or left, with troops as steady as theirs and ours.

The sun having gone down, darkness soon settled around them all, but the struggle did not end. Never was better grit shown by any troops. They could not see each other and their positions were disclosed only by the red, angry flashes of their guns. Their line stretched from about two-thirds of a mile north of the Plank Road to a distance of a mile and a half south of it. And so, shrouded in the smoke, and standing or kneeling among their dead, both sides kept on. All other sounds having died away, the forest now at every discharge roared deeply.

The history of the Confederate 46th North Carolina recorded:

All during that terrible afternoon, the regiment held its own, now gaining, now losing, resting at night on the ground over which it had fought, surrounded by the dead and wounded of both sides.

The history of the Confederate 55th North Carolina stated:

84 lay dead on the line where we fought, and 107 were wounded. They were on one side of a morass and we on the other.

A butchery pure and simple, it was unrelieved by any of the arts of war in which the exercise of military skill and tact robs war of some of its horrors.

The history of the 11th North Carolina reported:

At one time during the fighting of the 5th, the brigade lay down behind a line of dead Federals so thick as to form partial breastworks, showing how stubbornly they had fought and how severely they had suffered.

Schaff:

Bear in mind that they did all their fighting amid the umbrage and terror of the woods, and not under the eye of a single general officer; not one in 20 could see his colors or his colonel. There was none of the inspiration of an open field with stirring scenes. No, they fought the battle alone, their only companion the sense of Duty who was saying to them, to those obscure boys from the Green Mountains of Vermont, from Connecticut, Pennsylvania, New York, and Ohio: "Stand fast for your country, stand fast for the glory of the old home, for the honor of the gray-haired father and mother." Let garlands be given, too, to Heth's and Wilcox's men, and if I were the son of one who stood there that day under the banner of the Confederacy, I'd feel proud of my blood.

At last, about eight o'clock, the volleys that had been so thundering and dreadful stopped almost suddenly. No one who was with the Army of the Potomac that night will ever forget the immediate silence.

Grant was not troubled by the success of Lee's attack and ordered the Army of the Potomac to attack all along the line the next day. Neither Burnside's Union corps nor Longstreet's Confederate corps had arrived to reinforce their comrades. Schaff himself saw Grant:

> . . . yet seemingly Grant at the close of the day – and I saw him once or twice – was not troubled, and he issued orders with the same even, softly warm voice, to attack Lee impetuously early the next morning all along his line.

Schaff recorded an act of compassion during the night:

> The incident is found in the diary of Captain Robert E. Park, Company F, 12th Alabama, Battle's brigade, Rodes' division.
>
> "Crawled over the works with two canteens of water to relieve some of the wounded, groaning and calling aloud in front of the line. Night dark, no moon and few stars, and as I crawled to the first man and offered him a drink of water, he declined; and, in reply to my inquiries, told me that he was shot through the leg and body and was sure he was bleeding internally. I told him that I feared he would not live till morning, and asked him whether he was making any preparation for leaving this world. His reply was that he had not given it a thought, as his life had not been one of sin, and that he was content. He was about 20 years of age, and from a northwestern state."

The next morning, 6 May, Schaff himself was given a despatch to take to General Warren:

> Shortly after arriving there, Meade's instruction through Warren for Wadsworth to report for orders – Hancock while detached from the Fifth Corps, was given me to deliver, and with an orderly I started up the Parker's Store Road, encumbered with Burnside's troops moving sluggishly into position, the ground being very difficult to form on speedily. By this time it was about 8 o'clock. The general had passed through them to the front, where Potter was deploying but he had no sooner arrived there than his big staff caught the eye of a Confederate battery somewhere on the right of Ewell's line, and it opened on them, making it so uncomfortable that they had to edge away. I left the road about where the uppermost eastern branch comes in, and struck off through the

woods in the direction Wadsworth had taken the night before. I had not gone a great way when my orderly, a German, riding behind me, said, "Lieutenant, you are bearing too much to the right, you will run into the rebel lines." I sheered to the left; here and there were stragglers and wounded, and at a point alongside the run, propped against a beech tree, his head resting on his right shoulder, his cap on the ground beside him, was a dead fair-faced boy, 18 or 19 years old, holding in his bloodless hand a few violets which he had picked. A shot had struck him in the arm, or the leg, I have forgotten which, and he had slowly bled to death. I fancy that, as he held the little familiar wild-flowers in his hand, his unsullied eyes glazed as he looked down into them, and his mind was way off at home.

After passing him, the orderly again cautioned me, but this time I paid no attention to him and went on, guided by the firing.

The woods were very thick, and unknowingly we were approaching quite a little rise, when suddenly came the command, "Get off that horse and come in." I lowered my head to the left, and there stood a heavy skirmish line with uplifted guns. It did not take me one second to decide. I suspect that as usual I did not think at all, but gave my horse a sudden jerk to the right, then the spur, and as he bounded they let drive at us. A shot, I suppose it was one from their 58-calibre Enfields, grazing my sabre-belt, struck the brass "D" buckle on my left side and tore the belt apart. My Colt's pistol in its holster began to fall and I grabbed it with my left hand. Just then a limb knocked off my hat and with my right hand I caught it as it was passing my right boot top. Meanwhile the horse was tearing his way along the course we had come.

The orderly disappeared instantly, and that was the last I saw of him till the next morning, just after I had returned Grant's despatches that will be mentioned later. When I met him, with unfeigned surprise he exclaimed, "Why, my God! lieutenant, I thought sure you were killed up there yesterday."

I hardly know why he should have thought so unless he concluded I was falling when I was reaching for my hat. His judgment was better than mine, however, and had I followed it neither of us would have had such a close call.

Well, as soon as I could get control of my horse and both of us could breathe a bit easier, for the dear old fellow was no more anxious to go to Richmond that way than I, apparently, I struck

> off more to the left, and in a little while ran into swarms of stragglers, and pretty soon met a group falling back under some discipline. Upon inquiring, I found that they belonged to Cutler's brigade of Wadsworth's division, and they told me that the division had been driven with heavy losses. I gave to the officer who said he was going back to the open ground, that is, to the Parker's Store Road or the Lacy fields, the despatch, which will be found in the War Records, dated May 5 by mistake; the hour given is 8.30. In this despatch to Warren I reported the enemy's skirmish-line as being about a mile from the field, that they had tried Wadsworth's left, and that I would go on till I found him. The person to whom this despatch was handed either delivered it in person or sent it by some one to Warren's headquarters, and it was forwarded from there to Humphreys in a despatch dated 9.05. Soon I fell in with Cutler himself, leading back fragments of his broken command. There may have been 700 or 800 of them, and possibly twice that number, for they were scattered all through the woods. He was rather an oldish, thin, earnest looking Roundhead sort of a man, his light stubby beard and hair turning gray. He was bleeding from a wound across his upper lip, and looked ghastly, and I have no doubt felt worse; for he was a gallant man, and to lead his men back, hearing every little while the volleys of their comrades still facing the enemy, must have been hard. On my asking him where Wadsworth was, he said, "I think he is dead,"; and one or two of his officers said, "Yes, we saw him fall."
>
> Relying on what they told me, I started back for Meade's headquarters. When I reached there and reported the serious break in Wadsworth's lines, no one could believe it; but just then Cutler's men began to pour out of the woods in full view on the ridge east of the Lacy house, and the seriousness of the situation at once appeared to all. As to Wadsworth's death, Cutler and his officers were mistaken; he was not mortally wounded until about two hours later, but just before they broke the general's horse was killed and that led them to believe, I think, that he was killed also.

Despite appearances the Confederates did not seriously break the Union line, neither did they follow the retreating Union infantry.

The Army of the Potomac was actually attacking all along the line and pushing the Confederates back when Longstreet's Confederate corps arrived. A Confederate source, soon after the war, wrote that:

Just as they start, Lee catches sight of them and gallops up and asks sharply, "What brigade is this?"

"The Texas brigade," is the resolute response. General Lee raised himself in his stirrups, uncovered his gray hairs, and with an earnest yet anxious voice exclaimed above the din, "My Texas boys, you must charge." A yell rent the air, and the men dashed forward through the wreckage of Hill's corps and under a stinging fire from our sharpshooters. On they go, and now they have passed through Williams's guns, their muzzles still smoking, when suddenly they hear, "Charge, charge, men!" from a new, full voice, and there behind them is Lee himself, his warm brown eyes aflame. "Come back, come back, General Lee!" cry out the cannoneers earnestly; he does not heed and rides on; but a sergeant now takes hold of Traveller's rein. It is a great pity that we have not a picture of that sergeant's face as he turns the big gray horse around and exchanges a firm, kindly glance with his rider. Lee yields to his better judgment and joins Longstreet who, on the knoll near by, is throwing his brigades in as he did at Gettysburg, with the calmness of a man who is wielding a sledge.

Schaff:

The intrepid Wadsworth, returning to the front, and seeing the 20th Massachusetts athwart the road where Webb had left it, his vehement spirit set on fire by Hancock's ardent and communicative aggressiveness, asked in pungent, challenging tones, "Cannot you do something here?" Abbott hesitating, mindful of Webb's order to hold that point at all hazards, the high-spirited Wadsworth, who by nature was more an individual combatant than the cool and trained commander, leaped the little barrier of rotten planks torn from the decaying road-bed, and of course Abbott and the 20th followed him. Wadsworth's second horse was killed, and the regiment was met immediately with a withering volley. After striving in vain to drive the enemy, Abbott had to desist from further efforts. He then ordered the men to lie down so as to escape a wicked, sputtering fire; but he himself, young and handsome, coolly and without bravado walked back and forth before his line, his eyes and face lit by the finest candle that glows in the hand of Duty. "My God, Schaff," said to me the brave Captain Magnitsky of the 20th, with moistened eyes, "I was proud of him as back and forth he slowly walked before us." A shot soon struck him and he fell. They tenderly picked up the mortally wounded, gallant gentleman and carried him to the rear. Bartlett reached Webb about the time he had changed front forward onto the sorely stricken 20th and formed in rear of his left centre. It was now about 9.30. Wadsworth, catching sight of Bartlett's colors flying defiantly in the face of Field's oncoming veterans, called on him in person to charge over some troops weakened by repulses, who were hesitating – and he and his men responded well. I can hear Bartlett's voice ringing, "Forward," and see his spare, well-bred face lit up dauntlessly by those intense blue eyes; eyes I have seen glint more than once with pleasant humor, for he had, besides courage, the spirit of comradeship, that pleasant, cloud-reflecting stream, rippling and green banked, that flows through our natures. But in a little while a shot struck him in the temple, and he followed his college friend, Abbott, to the field hospital; he had already lost his left leg at Yorktown, and been seriously wounded in two places leading an assault at Port Hudson. The regiment lost 252 killed and wounded.

Wadsworth, after the charge, exclaimed, "Glorious!" but, like all the gains, theirs was temporary.

As soon as Carroll, Lewis A. Grant, Birney, Webb, and Wadsworth heard Sorrel's quick volleys, they were all on their feet at once, for the character of the firing and the cheers told them that Peril had snapped its chain and was loose. In a few minutes fleeing individuals, then squads, and then broken regiments, began to pour through the woods from the left.

Kershaw and Field, being notified by Longstreet to resume the offensive as soon as they should hear Sorrel, now pressed forward, seriously and exultingly active. Wadsworth, to stay the threatening disaster (for that lunatic, Panic, travels fast, and every officer of experience dreads its first breath), flew to the 37th Massachusetts at the head of Eustis's brigade, which was just getting back from the junction, and ordered Edwards, a resolute man, to throw his regiment across the front of Field, who, with several pieces of artillery raking the road, was advancing. The 37th moved quickly by flank into the woods, and then, undismayed, heard the command, "Forward." And with it went my friends, Lieutenants Casey and Chalmers, and that pleasant and true one of many a day, Captain "Tom" Colt of Pittsfield, whose mother was a saint. "You have made a splendid charge!" exclaimed Wadsworth, and so they had – the ground behind them showed it; they thrust Field back, gaining a little respite for all hands before disaster; and very valuable it proved to be, for some of the broken commands thereby escaped utter destruction.

While Field and Kershaw assailed Carroll, Birney, and Wadsworth fiercely, fire was racing through the woods, adding its horrors to Sorrel's advance; and with the wind driving the smoke before him, he came on, sweeping everything. Seeing his lines falter, Sorrel dashed up to the color-bearer of the 12th Virginia, "Ben" May, and asked for the colors to lead the charge. "We will follow you," said the smiling youth spiritedly, refusing to give them up; and so they did. In the midst of the raging havoc, Webb, under instructions from Wadsworth, now in an almost frantic state of mind, tried to align some troops beyond the road so as to meet Sorrel, whose fire was scourging the flanks of Carroll and the Green Mountain men, through whom and around whom crowds of fugitives, deaf to all appeals to rally, were forcing their way to the rear. But the organizations, so severely battered in the morning, were crumbling so fast, and the tumult was so high, that Webb saw it was idle to expect they could hold together in any attempted change of position; he therefore returned to his command, and quickly brought the 56th Massachusetts, Griswold's regiment, alongside the road. Fortunately his 19th Maine, withdrawn during the lull to replenish its ammunition, had been wheeled up by the gallant Connor at the first ominous volley from the South. They had barely braced themselves on the road before Carroll, and then the old Vermont brigade, had to go; and now Connor and Griswold open on Sorrel, checking him up roundly.

Wadsworth undertook to wheel the remnants of Rice's regiments who had stood by him, so as to fire into the enemy on the other side of the road. In trying to make this movement he ran squarely onto Perrin's Alabama brigade, of Anderson's division, which had relieved a part of Field's, who rose and fired a volley with fatal effect; breaking Wadsworth's formation, the men fleeing in wild confusion. In this Alabama brigade was the 8th Regiment, commanded that morning by Hilary A. Herbert who lost his arm. This gallant man, soldier, member of Congress, and distinguished lawyer was Mr Cleveland's Secretary of the Navy.

The heroic Wadsworth did not or could not check his horse till within 20-odd feet of the Confederate line. Then, turning, a shot struck him in the back of the head, his brain spattering the coat of Earl M. Rogers, his aide at his side. The U-rein of Wadsworth's

> horse, after the general fell, caught in a snag, and, Rogers's horse having been killed by the volley, he vaulted into the saddle, and escaped through the flying balls. Wadsworth lies unconscious within the enemy's lines; his heart, that has always beaten so warmly for his country, is still beating, but hears no response now from the generous, manly, truth-viewing brain. I believe that morning, noon, and night the bounteous valley of the Genesee; with its rolling fields and tented shocks of bearded grain, holds Wadsworth in dear remembrance.

At this critical point in the battle Longstreet and his divisional commanders were shot by a volley fired by their own men:

> A few words will explain it all. The 61st Virginia of Mahone's brigade – Mahone, a small, sallow, keen-eyed, and fleshless man had approached within 40 or 50 yards of the road, and, through the smoke and intervening underbrush, seeing objects emerging on it from the bushes on the opposite side, mistook them for enemies and let drive a scattering volley. What they saw was a part of their fellow regiment, the 12th Virginia, who with the colors had crossed the road in pursuit of Wadsworth's men and were returning. The volley intended for them cut right through Longstreet, Kershaw, Jenkins, Sorrel, and quite a number of staff and orderlies, who just then came riding by, killing instantly General Jenkins, Captain Foley, several orderlies, and two of the 12th's color-guard. But of all the bullets in this Wilderness doomsday volley the most fated was that which struck Longstreet, passing through his right shoulder and throat, and almost lifting him from his saddle. As the unfortunate man was reeling, about to fall, his friends took him down from his horse and propped him against a pine tree. Field, who was close by, came to his side, and Longstreet, although faint, bleeding profusely and blowing bloody foam from his mouth, told him to go straight on; and then despatched Sorrel with this message to Lee: "Urge him to continue the movement he (Longstreet) was engaged on; the troops being all ready, success would surely follow, and Grant, he firmly believed, be driven back across the Rapidan."

The Confederate attack was delayed by three or four hours. During the delay, Hancock was able to organize and strengthen a defensive line. Artillery fire had been little used previously in the battle because of the limited vision and difficulty in handling guns in the woods. A combination of artillery fire and counter-attacks held the Union defensive line. Schaff's summary of 5 and 6 May:

> Two days of deadly encounter; every man who could bear a musket had been put in; Hancock and Warren repulsed, Sedgwick routed, and now on the defensive behind breastworks; the cavalry drawn back; the trains seeking safety beyond the Rapidan; thousands and thousands of killed and wounded – he can almost hear the latter's cries, so hushed is the night – and the air pervaded with a lurking feeling of being face to face with disaster. What, what is the matter with the Army of the Potomac? Was an evil, dooming spirit cradled with it, which no righteous zeal or courage can appease? And he shifts his position.

The Union had 18,000 casualties. The Confederates had about 11,000 casualties. Previously after a stalemate and heavy losses both sides had withdrawn. Grant ordered an advance. This was a turning point. The Union army would continue to drain Lee's strength. The Union army was elated by the order to advance. The Confederates retreated in front of them.

An officer of the 83rd Pennsylvania remembered that:

> they yelled as they went, and as their voices kept going further and further away, this was the first evidence we had that they were also on the move. They even got started in advance of us.

The Confederates were retreating, the Union were advancing. Grant had not won but he was acting as if he had. Both armies raced towards a crossroads at Spotsylvania Court House. It was to be the last open battle of the Civil War. In all subsequent engagements the Confederates fought from entrenchments. At the time these were called rifle pits.

The advance towards Richmond continued with Grant making flanking movements, usually countered by Lee. At Cold Harbor on 3 June the Union army lost 6,000 casualties in one hour.

Lee's veterans were confused by being forced to retreat, as this contemporary anecdote illustrates:

> A war-beaten veteran of Longstreet's corps made a funny remark to a prominent politician who conversed with him while coming in

> from the front. Said he, "I do not understand this; Lee has won a big victory over Grant on the Rapidan, and told us so, and that night we retreated. Then he won another in the Wilderness, and told us so, and we retreated to Spottsylvania. Then he won another tre-men-jus victory, and I got tuk prisoner; but I reckon he has retreated ag'in. Now when he used to lick them, the Yanks fell back and claimed a victory, and we understood it. Now Lee claims victories, and keeps falling back, and I can't understand it."

Grant tried to capture Petersburg, south of Richmond, to cut it off from the rest of Confederate territory and its supplies. When the attack on Petersburg failed the Union army also resorted to trench warfare. In April 1865 the Confederate lines were finally turned. Sheridan got behind Lee and captured his remaining supply trains. Unable to feed his men, Lee sent a message to President Davis to evacuate Richmond. At Appomattox Court House Lee asked on what terms he might surrender. Grant's terms were:

> The officers and men of the Army of Northern Virginia should surrender their arms and return on parole to their homes. They would not to be molested while they observed the laws of the United States. Lee's officers were to keep their swords. Food would be provided from the Union wagons.

Grant added:

> Your men must keep their horses and mules. They will need them for the spring ploughing.

The Army of Northern Virginia, which so long had "carried the Confederacy on its bayonets", surrendered, 27,000 strong; and a fortnight later, despite the protests of President Davis, Sherman, in the West, accepted Johnston's surrender on terms similar to those granted to Lee.

The officer Grant chose to command the parade at which the Army of Northern Virginia would lay down its arms was Joshua Chamberlain, ex-Colonel of the 20th Maine, now a Brigadier General.

Chamberlain was convinced that the men of the Army of Northern Virginia deserved a salute of arms. He was well aware that criticism might follow. He resolved to order the Union troops on parade to salute them, because, as he explained it:

> My main reason . . . was one for which I sought no authority nor asked forgiveness. Before us in proud humiliation stood the embodiment of manhood; men whom neither toils and sufferings, nor the fact of death, nor disaster, nor hopelessness could bend from their resolve; standing before us now, thin, worn, and famished, but erect, and with eyes looking level into ours, waking memories that bound us together as no other bond; was not such manhood to be welcomed back into a Union so tested and assured?

All the Union regimental commanders present had been instructed. The Confederate cavalry and artillery had already handed over their weapons. Shortly after sunrise on 12 April 1865, as the grey column of the Confederate infantry came opposite the right of the Chamberlain's Brigade, a signal was given; there was the soft, ordered slapping of hands on wood and metal, and along the whole line, regiment by regiment in succession, muskets rose with a simultaneous gleaming to the position of the old "carry" – the marching salute.

The general John B. Gordon was riding disconsolately with bowed head at the head of the Confederate column. As he caught the sound of shifting arms, he realized what it meant and the spirit of the occasion changed. Gordon wheeled toward Chamberlain's Brigade. The Confederate general dropped his sword point to the toe of his boot to return Chamberlain's compliment.

Then, facing his own command, Gordon ordered his troops to pass with the same position of the manual, the two armies honoring one another in a final salute.

In Chamberlain's own words:

> On our part not a sound of trumpet more, nor roll of drum; not a cheer, nor word nor whisper of vain-glorying, nor motion of man standing again at the order, but an awed stillness rather, and – breath-holding, as if it were the passing of the dead!

President Davis was captured by a cavalry squadron. The armed resistance of the Confederate States ended.

Lincoln had entered Richmond with Grant, and on his return to Washington learned of Lee's surrender. To those who spoke of hanging Jefferson Davis, Lincoln replied, "*Judge not that ye be not judged.*"

Lincoln urged reconciliation with the defeated. At Cabinet, on 14 April he spoke of Lee and other Confederate leaders with kindness, and pointed to the paths of forgiveness and goodwill.

That evening as he sat in his box at Ford's Theatre he was shot through the head from behind by an actor. The actor escaped from the theatre, exclaiming, "Sic semper tyrannis." He escaped to Virginia, where he was hunted down and shot to death in a barn. Another member of the government, Seward, the Secretary of State, was also stabbed at his home, though not fatally, as part of the same plot.

Lincoln died next day, without regaining consciousness.

In 1868 Grant was elected President. He served two terms. He died in 1885.

Machine Gun
Modern Period

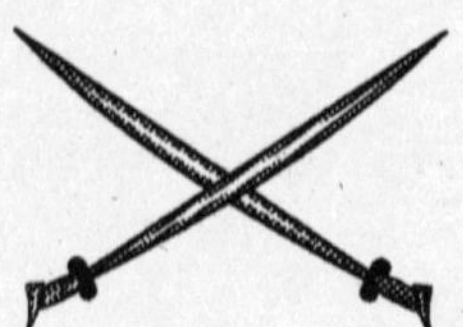

Spanish–American War 1898

Popular revolts against Spanish colonial rule had taken place in Cuba and the Philippines in 1895. Protests against Spanish repression were strongly expressed in American newspapers but the United States did not intervene until an American battleship, USS *Maine*, was blown up in Havana harbour in 1898. President McKinley declared war on Spain. The United States had a tiny standing army. This was expanded by the raising of volunteer regiments.

On 20 April 1898 armed intervention in Cuba was sanctioned. Theodore Roosevelt was Assistant Secretary to the Navy. He quickly became involved in raising a volunteer force composed of cowboys and mountaineers. This force was designated the First United States Volunteer Cavalry Regiment. Informally they were known as the Rough Riders. They were mounted infantry who fought on foot with pistols and rifles.

On 20–25 June the US expeditionary force to Cuba landed on the beach at Daiquiri, near Guantanamo, without opposition. They made camp for a few days and then advanced towards Santiago de Cuba.

The US expeditionary force was commanded by General Wheeler. The Rough Riders advanced as part of the right wing which was commanded by General Young. Theodore Roosevelt was second in command of the Rough Riders.

They advanced along trails through an area of jungle. At a place called Las Guasimas they encountered the Spaniards. Two squadrons of regular cavalry led the advance. As they climbed the ridges the Spaniards broke and fled. The fight cleared the way toward Santiago, and they experienced no further resistance on the way to Santiago.

The Battle of Las Guasimas

That afternoon we made camp and dined, subsisting chiefly on a load of beans which we found on one of the Spanish mules which had been shot. We also looked after the wounded. Dr Church had himself gone out to the firing-line during the fight, and carried to the rear some of the worst wounded on his back or in his arms. Those who could walk had walked in to where the little field-hospital of the regiment was established on the trail. We found all our dead and all the badly wounded. Around one of the latter the big, hideous land-crabs had gathered in a grewsome ring, waiting for life to be extinct. One of our own men and most of the Spanish dead had been found by the vultures before we got to them; and their bodies were mangled, the eyes and wounds being torn. The Rough Rider who had been thus treated was in Bucky O'Neill's troop; and as we looked at the body, O'Neill turned to me and asked, "Colonel, isn't it Whitman who says of the vultures that 'they pluck the eyes of princes and tear the flesh of kings'?" I answered that I could not place the quotation. Just a week afterward we were shielding his own body from the birds of prey. One of the men who fired first, and who displayed conspicuous gallantry, was a Cherokee half-breed, who was hit seven times, and of course had to go back to the States. Before he rejoined us at Montauk Point he had gone through a little private war of his own; for on his return he found that a cowboy had gone off with his sweetheart, and in the fight that ensued he shot his rival. Another man of L Troop who also showed marked gallantry was Elliot Cowdin. The men of the plains and mountains were trained by life-long habit to look on life and death with iron philosophy. As I passed by a couple of tall, lank, Oklahoma cow-punchers, I heard one say, "Well, some of the boys got it in the neck!" to which the other answered with the grim plains proverb of the South: "Many a good horse dies."

We improvized litters, and carried the more sorely wounded back to Siboney that afternoon and the next morning; the others walked. One of the men who had been most severely wounded was Edward Marshall, the correspondent, and he showed as much heroism as any soldier in the whole army. He was shot through the spine, a terrible and very painful wound, which we supposed meant that he would surely die; but he made no complaint of any kind, and while he retained consciousness persisted in dictating the story of the fight.

Next morning they buried seven Rough Riders. General Young was "struck down with the fever". Wood, the commander of the Rough Riders, took charge of the brigade and Roosevelt took command of the Rough Riders:

> There was nothing like enough transportation with the army, whether in the way of wagons or mule-trains; exactly as there had been no sufficient number of landing-boats with the transports. The officers' baggage had come up, but none of us had much, and the shelter-tents proved only a partial protection against the terrific downpours of rain. These occurred almost every afternoon, and turned the camp into a tarn, and the trails into torrents and quagmires. We were not given quite the proper amount of food, and what we did get, like most of the clothing issued us, was fitter for the Klondyke than for Cuba. We got enough salt port and hardtack for the men, but not the full ration of coffee and sugar, and nothing else. I organized a couple of expeditions back to the seacoast, taking the strongest and best walkers and also some of the officers' horses and a stray mule or two, and brought back beans and canned tomatoes. These I got partly by great exertions on my part, and partly by the aid of Colonel Weston of the Commissary Department, a particularly energetic man whose services were of great value. A silly regulation forbade my purchasing canned vegetables, etc., except for the officers; and I had no little difficulty in getting round this regulation, and purchasing (with my own money, of course) what I needed for the men.
>
> The army was camped along the valley, ahead of and behind us, our outposts being established on either side. From the generals to the privates all were eager to march against Santiago. At daybreak, when the tall palms began to show dimly through the rising mist, the scream of the cavalry trumpets tore the tropic dawn; and, in the evening, as the bands of regiment after regiment played the "Star-Spangled Banner", all, officers and men alike, stood with heads uncovered, wherever they were, until the last strains of the anthem died away in the hot sunset air.
>
> On 30 June we received orders to hold ourselves in readiness to march against Santiago, and all the men were greatly over joyed, for the inaction was trying. The one narrow road, a mere muddy track along which the army was encamped, was choked with the marching columns. As always happened when we had to change

camp, everything that the men could not carry, including, of course, the officers' baggage, was left behind.

Our brigade was drawn up on the hither side of a kind of half basin, a big band of Cubans being off to the left. As yet we had received no orders, except that we were told that the main fighting was to be done by Lawton's infantry division, which was to take El Caney, several miles to our right, while we were simply to make a diversion. This diversion was to be made mainly with the artillery, and the battery which had taken position immediately in front of us was to begin when Lawton began.

It was about six o'clock that the first report of the cannon from El Caney came booming to us across the miles of still jungle. It was a very lovely morning, the sky of cloudless blue, while the level, shimmering rays from the just-risen sun brought into fine relief the splendid palms which here and there towered above the lower growth. The lofty and beautiful mountains hemmed in the Santiago plain, making it an amphitheatre for the battle.

Immediately our guns opened, and at the report great clouds of white smoke hung on the ridge crest. For a minute or two there was no response. Wood and I were sitting together, and Wood remarked to me that he wished our brigade could be moved somewhere else, for we were directly in line of any return fire aimed by the Spaniards at the battery. Hardly had he spoken when there was a peculiar whistling, singing sound in the air, and immediately afterward the noise of something exploding over our heads. It was shrapnel from the Spanish batteries. We sprung to our feet and leaped on our horses. Immediately afterward a second shot came which burst directly above us; and then a third. From the second shell one of the shrapnel bullets dropped on my wrist, hardly breaking the skin, but raising a bump about as big as a hickory-nut. The same shell wounded four of my regiment, one of them being Mason Mitchell, and two or three of the regulars were also hit, one losing his leg by a great fragment of shell. Another shell exploded right in the middle of the Cubans, killing and wounding a good many, while the remainder scattered like guinea-hens. Wood's led horse was also shot through the lungs; I at once hustled my regiment over the crest of the hill into the thick underbrush, where I had no little difficulty in getting them together again into column.

Meanwhile the firing continued for 15 or 20 minutes, until it gradually died away. As the Spaniards used smokeless powder, their artillery had an enormous advantage over ours, and, moreover, we did not have the best type of modern guns, our fire being slow.

As soon as the firing ceased, Wood formed his brigade, with my regiment in front, and gave me orders to follow behind the 1st Brigade, which was just moving off the ground. In column of fours we marched down the trail toward the ford of the San Juan River. We passed two or three regiments of infantry, and were several times halted before we came to the ford. The 1st Brigade, which was under Colonel Carroll – Lieutenant-Colonel Hamilton commanding the 9th Regiment, Major Wessels the 3rd, and Captain Kerr the 6th – had already crossed and was marching to the right, parallel to, but a little distance from, the river. The Spaniards in the trenches and block-houses on top of the hills in front were already firing at the brigade in desultory fashion. The extreme advance of the 9th Cavalry was under Lieutenants McNamee and Hartwick. They were joined by General Hawkins, with his staff, who was looking over the ground and deciding on the route he should take his infantry brigade.

Our orders had been of the vaguest kind, being simply to march to the right and connect with Lawton – with whom, of course, there was no chance of our connecting. No reconnaissance had been made, and the exact position and strength of the Spaniards was not known. A captive balloon was up in the air at this moment, but it was worse than useless. A previous proper reconnaissance and proper look-out from the hills would have given us exact information. As it was, Generals Kent, Sumner, and Hawkins had to be their own reconnaissance, and they fought their troops so well that we won anyhow.

I was now ordered to cross the ford, march half a mile or so to the right, and then halt and await further orders; and I promptly hurried my men across, for the fire was getting hot, and the captive balloon, to the horror of everybody, was coming down to the ford. Of course, it was a special target for the enemy's fire. I got my men across before it reached the ford. There it partly collapsed and remained, causing severe loss of life, as it indicated the exact position where the 10th and the 1st Cavalry, and the infantry, were crossing.

As I led my column slowly along, under the intense heat, through the high grass of the open jungle, the 1st Brigade was to our left, and the firing between it and the Spaniards on the hills grew steadily hotter and hotter. After awhile I came to a sunken lane, and as by this time the 1st Brigade had stopped and was engaged in a stand-up fight, I halted my men and sent back word for orders. As we faced toward the Spanish hills my regiment was on the right with next to it and a little in advance the 1st Cavalry, and behind them the 10th. In our front the 9th held the right, the 6th the centre, and the 3rd the left; but in the jungle the lines were already overlapping in places. Kent's infantry were coming up, farther to the left.

Captain Mills was with me. The sunken lane, which had a wire fence on either side, led straight up toward, and between, the two hills in our front, the hill on the left, which contained heavy blockhouses, being farther away from us than the hill on our right, which we afterward grew to call Kettle Hill, and which was surmounted merely by some large ranch buildings or haciendas, with sunken brick-lined walls and cellars. I got the men as well-sheltered as I could. Many of them lay close under the bank of the lane, others slipped into the San Juan River and crouched under its hither bank, while the rest lay down behind the patches of bushy jungle in the tall grass. The heat was intense, and many of the men were already showing signs of exhaustion. The sides of the hills in front were bare; but the country up to them was, for the most part, covered with such dense jungle that in charging through it no accuracy of formation could possibly be preserved.

The fight was now on in good earnest, and the Spaniards on the hills were engaged in heavy volley firing. The Mauser bullets drove in sheets through the trees and the tall jungle grass, making a peculiar whirring or rustling sound; some of the bullets seemed to pop in the air, so that we thought they were explosive; and, indeed, many of those which were coated with brass did explode, in the sense that the brass coat was ripped off, making a thin plate of hard metal with a jagged edge, which inflicted a ghastly wound. These bullets were shot from a .45-calibre rifle carrying smokeless powder, which was much used by the guerillas and irregular Spanish troops. The Mauser bullets themselves made a small clean hole, with the result that the wound healed in a most astonishing manner. One or two of our men who were shot in the head had the skull blown open, but elsewhere the wounds from the minute steel-coated bullet, with its very high velocity, were certainly nothing like as serious as those made by the old large-calibre, low-power rifle. If a man was shot through the heart, spine, or brain he was, of course, killed instantly; but very few of the wounded died – even under the appalling conditions which prevailed, owing to the lack of attendance and supplies in the field-hospitals with the army.

While we were lying in reserve we were suffering nearly as much as afterward when we charged. I think that the bulk of the Spanish fire was practically unaimed, or at least not aimed at any particular man, and only occasionally at a particular body of men; but they swept the whole field of battle up to the edge of the river, and man after man in our ranks fell dead or wounded, although I had the troopers scattered out far apart, taking advantage of every scrap of cover.

My orderly was a brave young Harvard boy, Sanders, from the quaint old Massachusetts town of Salem. The work of an orderly on foot, under the blazing sun, through the hot and matted jungle, was very severe, and finally the heat overcame him. He dropped; nor did he ever recover fully, and later he died from fever. In his place I summoned a trooper whose name I did not know. Shortly afterward, while sitting beside the bank, I directed him to go back and ask whatever general he came across if I could not advance, as my men were being much cut up. He stood up to salute and then pitched forward across my knees, a bullet having gone through his throat, cutting the carotid. When O'Neill was shot, his troop, who were devoted to him, were for the moment at a loss whom to follow. One of their number, Henry Bardshar, a huge Arizona miner, immediately attached himself to me as my orderly, and from that moment he was closer to me, not only in the fight, but throughout the rest of the campaign, than any other man, not even excepting the color-sergeant, Wright.

The Battle of San Juan Hill

Roosevelt finally received the command "to move forward and support the regulars in the assault on the hills in front."

The instant I received the order I sprang on my horse and then my "crowded hour" began. The guerillas had been shooting at us from the edges of the jungle and from their perches in the leafy trees, and as they used smokeless powder, it was almost impossible to see them, though a few of my men had from time to time responded. We had also suffered from the hill on our right front, which was held chiefly by guerillas, although there were also some Spanish regulars with them, for we found their dead. I formed my men in column of troops, each troop extended in open skirmishing order, the right resting on the wire fences which bordered the sunken lane. Captain Jenkins led the first squadron, his eyes literally dancing with joyous excitement. I started in the rear of the regiment, the position in which the colonel should theoretically stay. Captain Mills and Captain McCormick were both with me as aides; but I speedily had to send them off on special duty in getting the different bodies of men forward. I had intended to go into action on foot as at Las Guasimas, but the heat was so oppressive that I found I should be quite unable to run up and down the line and superintend matters unless I was mounted; and, moreover, when on horseback, I could see the men better and they could see me better.

I soon found that I could get that line, behind which I personally was, faster forward than the one immediately in front of it, with the result that the two rearmost lines of the regiment began to crowd together; so I rode through them both, the better to move on the one in front. This happened with every line in succession, until I found myself at the head of the regiment.

Both lieutenants of B Troop from Arizona had been exerting themselves greatly, and both were overcome by the heat; but Sergeants Campbell and Davidson took it forward in splendid shape. Some of the men from this troop and from the other Arizona troop (Bucky O'Neill's) joined me as a kind of fighting tail. The 9th Regiment was immediately in front of me, and the 1st on my left, and these went up Kettle Hill with my regiment. The 3rd, 6th, and 10th went partly up Kettle Hill (following the Rough Riders and the 9th and 1st), and partly between that and the block-house hill, which the infantry were assailing. General Sumner in person gave the 10th the order to charge the hills; and it went forward at a rapid gait. The three regiments went forward more or less intermingled, advancing steadily and keeping up a heavy fire. Up Kettle Hill Sergeant George Berry, of the 10th, bore not only his own regimental colors but those of the 3rd, the color-sergeant of the 3rd having been shot down; he kept shouting, "Dress on the colors, boys, dress on the colors!" as he followed

Captain Ayres, who was running in advance of his men, shouting and waving his hat. The 10th Cavalry lost a greater proportion of its officers than any other regiment in the battle – 11 out of 22.

By the time I had come to the head of the regiment we ran into the left wing of the 9th Regulars, and some of the 1st Regulars, who were lying down; that is, the troopers were lying down, while the officers were walking to and fro. The officers of the white and colored regiments alike took the greatest pride in seeing that the men more than did their duty; and the mortality among them was great.

I spoke to the captain in command of the rear platoons, saying that I had been ordered to support the regulars in the attack upon the hills, and that in my judgment we could not take these hills by firing at them, and that we must rush them. He answered that his orders were to keep his men lying where they were, and that he could not charge without orders. I asked where the Colonel was, and as he was not in sight, said, "Then I am the ranking officer here and I give the order to charge" – for I did not want to keep the men longer in the open suffering under a fire which they could not effectively return. Naturally the Captain hesitated to obey this order when no word had been received from his own Colonel. So I said, "Then let my men through, sir," and rode on through the lines, followed by the grinning Rough Riders, whose attention had been completely taken off the Spanish bullets, partly by my dialogue with the regulars, and partly by the language I had been using to themselves as I got the lines forward, for I had been joking with some and swearing at others, as the exigencies of the case seemed to demand. When we started to go through, however, it proved too much for the regulars, and they jumped up and came along, their officers and troops mingling with mine, all being delighted at the chance. When I got to where the head of the left wing of the 9th was lying, through the courtesy of Lieutenant Hartwick, two of whose colored troopers threw down the fence, I was enabled to get back into the lane, at the same time waving my hat, and giving the order to charge the hill on our right front. Out of my sight, over on the right, Captains McBlain and Taylor, of the 9th, made up their minds independently to charge at just about this time; and at almost the same moment Colonels Carroll and Hamilton, who were off, I believe, to my left, where we could see neither them nor their men, gave the order to advance. But of all this I knew nothing at the time. The whole line, tired of waiting, and eager to close with the enemy, was straining to go forward; and it seems that different parts slipped the leash at almost the same moment. The 1st Cavalry came up the hill just behind, and partly mixed with my regiment and the 9th. As already said, portions of the 3rd, 6th, and 10th followed, while the rest of the members of these three regiments kept more in touch with the infantry on our left.

By this time we were all in the spirit of the thing and greatly excited by the charge, the men cheering and running forward between shots, while the delighted faces of the foremost officers, like Captain C. J. Stevens, of the 9th, as they ran at the head of their troops, will always stay in my mind. As soon as I was in the line I galloped forward a few yards until I saw that the men were well started, and then galloped back to help Goodrich, who was in command of his troop, get his men across the road so as to attack the hill from that side. Captain Mills had already thrown three of the other troops of the regiment across this road for the same purpose. Wheeling around, I then again galloped toward the hill, passing the shouting, cheering, firing men, and went up the lane, splashing through a small stream; when I got abreast of the ranch buildings on the top of Kettle Hill, I turned and went up the slope. Being on horseback I was, of course, able to get ahead of the men on foot, excepting my orderly, Henry Bardshar, who had run ahead very fast in order to get better shots at the Spaniards, who were now running out of the ranch buildings. Sergeant Campbell and a number of the Arizona men, and Dudley Dean, among others, were very close behind. Stevens, with his platoon of the 9th, was abreast of us; so were McNamee and Hartwick. Some 40 yards from the top I ran into a wire fence and jumped off Little Texas, turning him loose. He had been scraped by a couple of bullets, one of which nicked my elbow, and I never expected to see him again. As I ran up to the hill, Bardshar stopped to shoot, and two Spaniards fell as he emptied his magazine. These were the only Spaniards I actually saw fall to aimed shots by any one of my men, with the exception of two guerillas in trees. Almost immediately afterward the hill was covered by the troops, both Rough Riders and the colored troopers of the 9th, and some men of the 1st.

No sooner were we on the crest than the Spaniards from the line of hills in our front, where they were strongly intrenched, opened a very heavy fire upon us with their rifles. They also opened upon us with one or two pieces of artillery, using time fuses which burned very accurately, the shells exploding right over our heads. On the top of the hill was a huge iron kettle, or something of the kind, probably used for sugar refining. Several of our men took shelter behind this. We had a splendid view of the charge on the San Juan block-house to our left, where the infantry of Kent, led by Hawkins, were climbing the hill. Obviously the proper thing to do was to help them, and I got the men together and started them volley-firing against the Spaniards in the San Juan block-house and in the trenches around it. We could only see their heads; of course this was all we ever could see when we were firing at them in their trenches. Stevens was directing not only his own colored troopers, but a number of Rough Riders; for in a melée good soldiers are always prompt to recognize a good officer, and are eager to follow him. We kept up a brisk fire for some five or ten minutes; meanwhile we were much cut up ourselves. Gallant Colonel Hamilton, than whom there was never a braver man, was killed, and equally gallant Colonel Carroll wounded. When near the summit Captain Mills had been shot through the head, the bullet destroying the sight of one eye permanently and of the other temporarily. He would not go back or let any man assist him, sitting down where he was and waiting until one of the men brought him word that the hill was stormed. Colonel Veile planted the standard of the 1st Cavalry on the hill, and General Sumner rode up. He was fighting his division in great form, and was always himself in the thick of the fire. As the men were much excited by the firing, they seemed to pay very little heed to their own losses.

Suddenly, above the cracking of the carbines, rose a peculiar drumming sound, and some of the men cried, "The Spanish machine-guns!" Listening, I made out that it came from the flat ground to the left, and jumped to my feet, smiting my hand on my thigh, and shouting aloud with exultation, "It's the Gatlings, men, our Gatlings!" Lieutenant Parker was bringing his four Gatlings into action, and shoving them nearer and nearer the front. Now and then the drumming ceased for a moment; then it would resound again, always closer to San Juan hill, which Parker, like ourselves, was hammering to assist the infantry attack. Our men cheered lustily. We saw much of Parker after that, and there was never a more welcome sound than his Gatlings as they opened. It was the only sound which I ever heard my men cheer in battle.

The infantry got nearer and nearer the crest of the hill. At last we could see the Spaniards running from the rifle-pits as the Americans came on in their final rush. Then I stopped my men for fear they should injure their comrades, and called to them to charge the next line of trenches.

To Roosevelt's dismay, his men were distracted and did not follow him immediately:

Long before we got near them the Spaniards ran, save a few here and there, who either surrendered or were shot down. When we reached the trenches we found them filled with dead bodies in the light blue and white uniform of the Spanish regular army. There were very few wounded. Most of the fallen had little holes in their heads from which their brains were oozing; for they were covered from the neck down by the trenches.

While I was reforming the troops on the chain of hills, one of General Sumner's aides, Captain Robert Howze, as dashing and gallant an officer as there was in the whole gallant cavalry division, by the way came up with orders to me to halt where I was, not advancing farther, but to hold the hill at all hazards. Howze had his horse, and I had some difficulty in making him take proper shelter; he stayed with us for quite a time, unable to make up his mind to leave the extreme front, and meanwhile jumping at the chance to render any service, of risk or otherwise, which the moment developed.

The Spaniards who had been holding the trenches and the line of hills, had fallen back upon their supports and we were under a very heavy fire both from rifles and great guns. At the point where we were, the grass-covered hillcrest was gently rounded, giving poor cover, and I made my men lie down on the hither slope.

At this particular time it was trying for the men, as they were lying flat on their faces, very rarely responding to the bullets, shells, and shrapnel which swept over the hill-top, and which occasionally killed or wounded one of their number.

The firing stopped by night fall. Roosevelt's men dug trenches and went to sleep. They remained in this position until Santiago surrendered:

In the attack on the San Juan hills our forces numbered about 6,600. There were about 4,500 Spaniards against us. Our total loss in killed and wounded was 1,071. Of the cavalry division there were, all told, some 2,300 officers and men, of whom 375 were killed and wounded. In the division over a fourth of the officers were killed or wounded, their loss being relatively half as great again as that of the enlisted men – which was as it should be.

I think we suffered more heavily than the Spaniards did in killed and wounded (though we also captured some scores of prisoners). It would have been very extraordinary if the reverse was the case, for we did the charging; and to carry earthworks on foot with dismounted cavalry, when these earthworks are held by unbroken infantry armed with the best modern rifles, is a serious task.

First World War

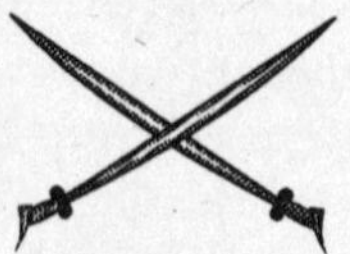

On 3 August 1914 Germany declared war on France and invaded Belgium. On 4 August, Great Britain declared war on Germany for violating Belgian neutrality. By 18 August a British army of 80,000 men had been landed in France.

First World War – chronology

1914

28 June 1914 Archduke Franz Ferdinand assasinated in Sarajevo
28 July Austria-Hungary declares war on Serbia
1 August Germany declares war on Russia
3 August Germany declares war on France, Germany invades Belgium
4 August Great Britain declares war on Germany
6 August Austria-Hungary declares war on Russia
13 August Austria-Hungary invades Serbia
14 August Battle of the Frontiers French versus German forces
23 August Battle of Mons
26 August Battle of Le Cateau
6 September Battle of the Marne
13 September Battle of the Aisne
19 October First Battle of Ypres
5 November Great Britain and France declare war on Turkey

1915

10 March Battle of Neuve Chapelle
18 March Allied naval attempt to force the Dardanelles

23 April Second Battle of Ypres (First use of Poison Gas by the Germans)

23 April British & ANZAC landings at Gallipoli

23 May Italy declares war on Austria-Hungary

6 August British landings at Suvla Bay, Gallipoli

23 September Allied offensive in Artois and Champagne

19 October Sir Douglas Haig replaces Sir John French as Commander in Chief British Army in France

1916

9 January evacuation of British & ANZAC forces at Gallipoli completed

25 January First Military Service Bill (Conscription of unmarried men aged 18–41)

21 February Battle of Verdun begins

24 April Easter Rising begins in Dublin

16 May Second Military Service Bill (Conscription of married men aged 18–41)

1 July Battle of Somme begins

15 September First use of tanks at Efflers Courlette on the Somme

7 December Lloyd George succeeds Asquith as British Prime Minister

1917

1 February Germany begins unrestricted submarine warfare

14 March Provisional Government takes power in Russia

15 March Tsar Nicholas II abdicates

6 April United States of America declares war on Germany

9 April Battle of Arras begins (Canadian attack on Vimy Ridge)

16 April French offensive on the Aisne begins

15 May Petain succeeds Nivelle as French Commander in Chief

20 November Battle of Cambrai begins

2 December Hostilities between Russia & Germany suspended

1918

3 March Peace of Brest-Litovsk between Russia and Germany

21 March German offensive in Picardy begins

1 April Royal Air Force formed from Royal Flying Corps and

Royal Naval Air Service

9 April German offensive in Flanders begins

14 April Foch appointed Commander-in-Chief of Allied Armies in France

9 June German offensive versus French on the Matz

15 June German offensive on Champagne – Marne

18 July Allied counter-offensive on Champagne – Marne

8 August Battle of Amiens

26 September Franco-American offensive in Meuse-Argonne sector

30 September Bulgaria accepts an Armistice

30 October Turkey accepts an Armistice

3 November Austria-Hungary accepts an Armistice

9 November Kaiser Wilhelm II abdicates

11 November Armistice – ceasefire on all fronts

1919

20 June Versailles Treaty concluded and signed

The Western Front 1914

The British Expeditionary Force (BEF) which landed in France was composed of regular army soldiers. The German Emperor, Kaiser Wilhelm II, described them as "a contemptibly small army". They brought with them a small number of aircraft and airmen, the Royal Flying Corps. On 20 August, the Royal Flying Corps discovered the Germans. The BEF moved into Mons on the left of the French Fifth Army. The French retreated, leaving the BEF outnumbered 2:1.

The British army had learnt from its experiences in South Africa during the Boer war (1899–1902). Its professional soldiers had a high degree of skill at arms. At Mons, the weakest point in the British line was held by two battalions from the Royal Fusiliers and Middlesex regiments.

The British took position on the bank of the Mons-Condé canal. A bend in the canal was held by two British battalions: the 4th Middlesex and the 4th battalion, Royal Fusiliers. They were firing at a steady 15 rounds a minute – rapid fire

Corporal W. Holbrook was in the 4th battalion, Royal Fusiliers:

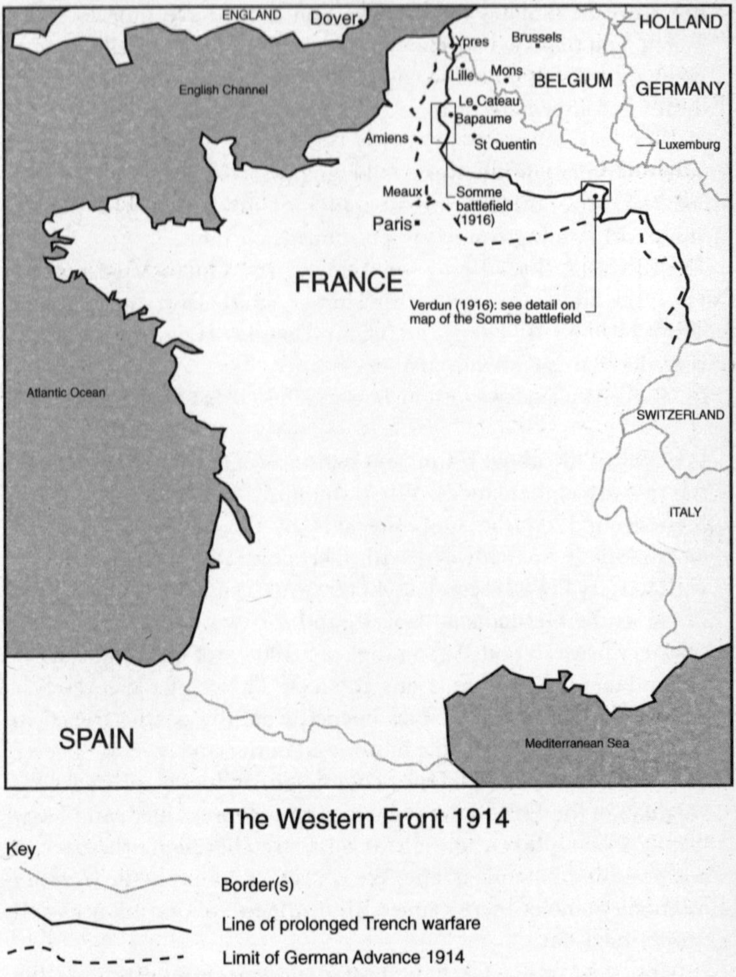

ENGLAND
Dover
HOLLAND
Ypres
Brussels
Lille
Mons
BELGIUM
GERMANY
English Channel
Le Cateau
Bapaume
Amiens
St Quentin
Luxemburg
Meaux
Somme battlefield (1916)
Paris
FRANCE
Verdun (1916): see detail on map of the Somme battlefield
Atlantic Ocean
SWITZERLAND
ITALY
SPAIN
Mediterranean Sea
The Western Front 1914
Key
Border(s)
Line of prolonged Trench warfare
Limit of German Advance 1914

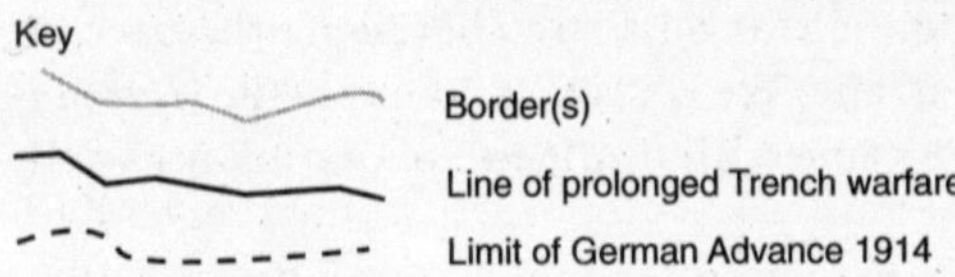

Map of The Western Front in 1914

Bloody Hell! You couldn't see the earth for them there were that many. Time after time they gave the order "Rapid Fire". Well, you didn't wait for the order, really! You'd see a lot of them coming in a mass on the other side of the canal and you just let them have it. They kept retreating, and then coming forward, and then retreating again. Of course, we were losing men and a lot of the officers, especially when the Germans started this shrapnel shelling and, of course, they had machine-guns – masses of them!

But we kept flinging them back. You don't have time to think much. You don't even feel nervous – you've got other fellows with you, you see. I don't know how many times we saw them off. They didn't get anywhere near us with this rapid fire.

Another German army was advancing west of Mons to cut the British off. The British retreated in carefully calculated moves, turning and fighting from new positions each time.

The BEF was divided into two Army Corps. On 26 August, at Le Cateau, the 2nd Corps, under Sir Horace Smith-Dorrien stood and fought while the 1st Corps, under Sir Douglas Haig, continued to retreat. Le Cateau was an artillery battle.

Lt. R.A. Macleod was in 80 Battery, XV Brigade, RFA:

We opened fire about 6 a.m. and registered a few targets including the railway embankment. When the mist lifted, we saw that the high ground on the Opposite side of the valley beyond the embankment was crowded with Germans. We opened on them with battery fire 20 seconds at 4,000 yards, gradually reducing the range as the Germans advanced, and for two hours we kept up "battery fire 5 seconds" at a range of 2,400 yards on the line of the embankment they were trying to cross. They suffered severely.

The German artillery soon opened frontally on the trench in front of us. The fire became hotter and hotter and several "overs" fell among our batteries. One of our first casualties was Lieutenant Coghlan of the 11th Battery on our right. He was killed, and I saw his body being taken to the rear on a stretcher along the back of our position to a sunken lane. We continued to fire at the German infantry. Some of them came within rifle fire of our infantry and were wiped out.

More and more German batteries came into action, a big concentration of them was Rambourlieux Farm which was now visible on our left flank (it had been concealed by the early-morning mist) and from there they could enfilade our position. A German aeroplane came overhead about 9 a.m. and started dropping stuff like streamers of silver paper over our trenches. Whenever he did this the German guns opened up on the spot he was flying over. He came over our brigade and did the same. A ranging round fell near the 11th Battery from a German battery enfilading from the left. Salvoes then began to fall on the 11th Battery, and their casualties started mounting up, we could hear them calling for stretchers, and many shells also fell on the 37th Battery on our left, knocking out some guns and detachments. We, behind our low ridge, were more fortunate and only had comparatively few shells on the position. Wounded infantry and gunners began to trickle past us on their way back to the dressing station in Reumont.

Our infantry were splendid. They had only scratchings in the ground made with their entrenching tools, which didn't give much cover, but they stuck it out and returned a good rate of fire. The German infantry fired from the hip as they advanced, but the fire was very inaccurate.

The 2nd Corps held the Germans for six hours, They were able to withdraw from their positions in daylight. They had lost 7,812 men and 38 guns.

The Germans assumed that the British would retreat south-west, towards the Channel coast. Instead the British retreated due south, alongside the French. A British officer asked one of his men, "How are your boots?" He replied, "Very full of feet, sir."

The French covered the retreat, losing 300,000 men in the "battle of the Frontiers". They had another army forming east of Paris.

By 5 September, the Germans under Von Kluck had reached the Marne. The French under Joffre counter-attacked. The BEF joined in. Corporal W. Holbrook:

We gradually advanced a bit. Of course the Germans were trying to attack there too. One day I was sent with another fellow to a bit of high ground looking over the field where our Brigade was, because they expected the Germans to come along this road, or to send a patrol along it anyhow. And I and this other fellow were undercover on this road. We had to warn the troops further down if any advance was made and they'd got their eye on us looking for a signal. While we were there I saw a sight I'd never seen before and I don't imagine anyone ever saw it again. A German Uhlan regiment – the whole regiment – attacked the Lincolns (they were in our Brigade, they were on our left) and I saw these Germans from where I was. I looked down this little bit of a valley and I saw all these German cavalry attack the Lincolns. And the Lincolns held their fire until they were just 200 or 300 yards away and then they let go. The Germans got nowhere near them, they got absolutely slaughtered. They slaughtered hundreds. I saw every bit of it as if I was watching a film. It lasted about half an hour.

I says to the other fellow, "Just look at that!" And there were cavalry falling everywhere and wounded staggering about. An hour or two later I think every man in the Lincolns had a German helmet he'd picked up.

The Germans retreated.

Sgt F.M. Packham was in the 2nd Battalion of the Royal Sussex:

On the morning of 10 September we found ourselves right in the forefront of the army and my platoon was leading the advance. We stopped on the road in front of a village called Priez. We had an idea that something was afoot. The Colonel and the adjutant rode up and conversed with our company officer. Then our platoon was ordered to "advance at the double". With our platoon officer in the lead, we started to advance and we had to cross a small brook. Some of us were able to jump across but others jumped in and waded across. We kept on going, across a field and up a slight rise. When we reached the top we could see some Germans taking cover among some wheat stooks. We were ordered to lay down and open fire on them. We had a great time firing at them as they dodged from stook to stook, but very soon afterwards the German artillery opened fire on us.

They found our position with the first salvo. I saw the blinding flash as the shells burst in the air just in front of us and I could hear the shrapnel whistling past me. There were shouts and screams and I knew that some had been hit. I looked behind me and saw one of our corporals with his face covered with blood. We started again, firing at the enemy, then someone called behind us for us to get back. As I went to get up I was knocked down. I thought at first that someone had pushed me down, so I got to my feet again and started moving back. My shoulder strap was loose. I put my hand to the back of my shoulder to find out what was wrong with it and felt that it was wet. I was amazed to find that it was blood on my hand and that I'd been hit. I asked the man next to me to have a look at it and he said that I had quite a gash in my shoulder. So I went back to look for the First Aid squad, but it was a long time before I could locate one. I found one at last in the village, Priez. There were a lot of casualties waiting to be seen.

> The medical officer looked at my wound and the orderly put a dressing on it. That night some of us were taken by lorry to a rear field hospital. It was a very rough journey. One of the men had a stomach wound and had to lay on the hard floor of the lorry. He died just as we arrived at the hospital.

The French and British advanced to the River Aisne. The Germans dug in on a ridge, north of the River Aisne, called the "Chemin de Dames". It was the beginning of trench warfare. They counter-attacked the BEF who were still in the open. The BEF hung on, waiting for reinforcements and supplies.

The BEF moved from its position between two French armies to a position on the left of the line, in Flanders. After the loss of Antwerp, the Belgian army stopped its retreat on the river Yser. The BEF was reinforced by the last regular division of the British army. On 14 October this division entered Ypres. The line now extended from Belfort in Alsace, on the Swiss border, to the coast, in Flanders.

The Battle of the Somme 1 July–18 November 1916

In January 1916, the commanders of the French and British armies, Joffre and Haig, agreed to mount a joint attack on the Western Front in the coming summer. They decided to attack along a wide front at the point where the French and British met, close to the Somme river. The ground there was chalk-based. This allowed the Germans to construct deep underground shelters, largely untouchable by artillery. North of the Somme river, the German lines ran along the higher ground, protected by dense concentrations of barbed wire and linked by heavily fortified villages and redoubts.

In February, the Germans attacked at Verdun. By June, the French had already lost 200,000 casualties. This forced a change in the plans for the attack. The bulk of the attack was now to be made by the British army on a 15-mile front extending south from Serre to Fricourt, then east to Maricourt on the north bank of the Somme river. The preliminary bombardment began on 24 June. By 1 July 1.5 million shells had been fired. It failed to destroy the German machine guns.

Freiwilliger Eversman was in a German infantry regiment sheltering in a deep dugout during the bombardment:

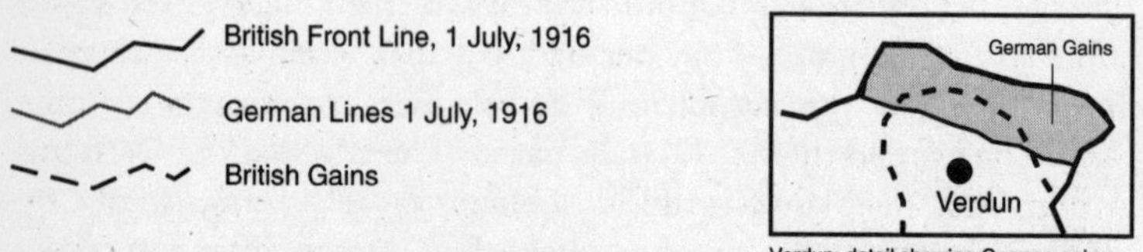

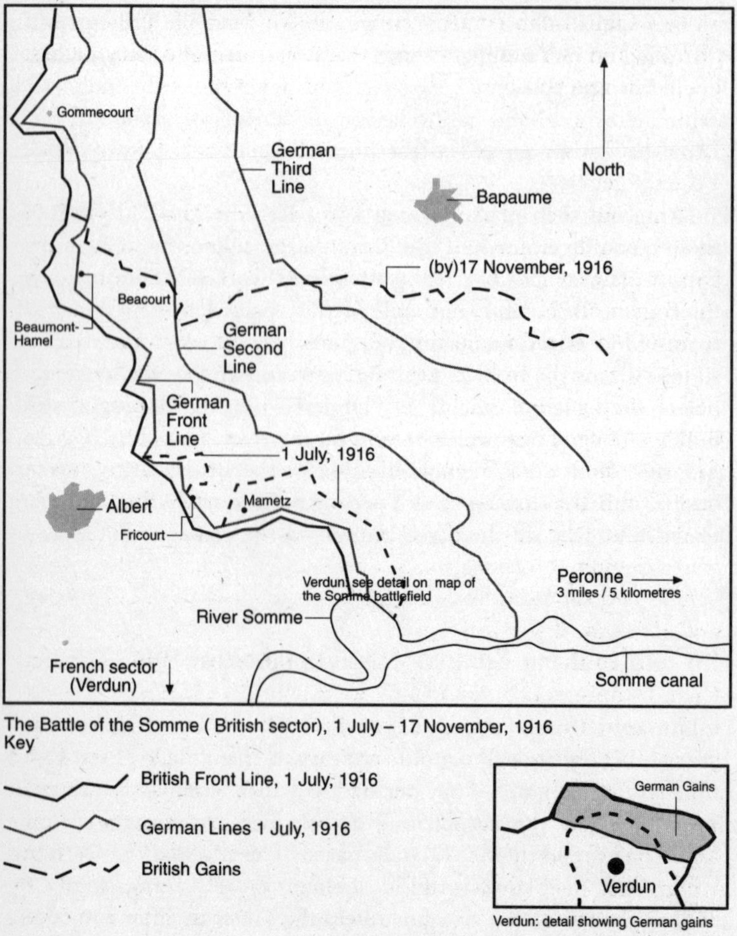

Gommecourt
German
Third
Line
North
Bapaume
(by)17 November, 1916
Beacourt
Beaumont-
Hamel
German
Second
Line
German
Front
Line
1 July, 1916
Albert
Mametz
Fricourt
Verdun: see detail on map of
the Somme battlefield
Peronne
3 miles / 5 kilometres
River Somme
French sector
(Verdun)
Somme canal
The Battle of the Somme (British sector), 1 July – 17 November, 1916
Key
British Front Line, 1 July, 1916
German Lines 1 July, 1916
British Gains
German Gains
Verdun
Verdun: detail showing German gains

Map of the Battle of the Somme

It is night. Shall I live till morning? Haven't we had enough of this frightful horror? Five days and five nights now this hell concert has lasted. One's head is like a madman's; the tongue sticks to the roof of the mouth. Almost nothing to eat and nothing to drink. No sleep. All contact with the outer world cut off. No sign of life from home nor can we send any news to our loved ones. What anxiety they must feel about us. How long is this going to last?

Eversman's diary was later found and handed to a British officer.

Ernest Deighton was a sniper in the 8th battalion of the Royal

Yorkshire Light Infantry. He was lying in No-Man's Land, between the British and German front line trenches, waiting to join the first line when it reached him:

> I thought I was a goner. I didn't think I'd get back. I didn't think I'd ever get back.
>
> Lying out there that morning I were within 25 or 30 yards of the German front line, looking through this telescopic sight at the gap in their trench. I could have touched it. I had my finger on the trigger all the time, not moving, and I saw a few of them laid to rest. But it didn't do our lads much good. As soon as they started across the machine-guns opened up. It seemed like hours before they got up near to me, but they kept on coming. I still dursn't move. These bullets are flying all over the place. It were Maxims they were firing and they were shooting across each other, with this hissing noise as they went past. I dursn't turn round, but I heard the noise behind me and I knew our fellows were coming. Some of them were getting hit and they were yelling and shouting, but they came on, and when the first wave got up to me I jumped up.
>
> I were in the first row and the first one I saw were my chum, Clem Cunnington. I don't think we'd gone 20 yards when he got hit straight through the breast. Machine-gun bullets. He went down. I went down. We got it in the same burst. I got it through the shoulder. I hardly noticed it, at the time, I were so wild when I saw that Clem were finished. We'd got orders: "Every man for himself and no prisoners!" It suited me that, after I saw Clem lying there.
>
> I got up and picked up my rifle and got through the wire into their trench and straight in front there was this dugout – full of Jerries, and one big fellow was on the steps facing me. I had this Mills bomb. Couldn't use my arm. I pulled the pin with my teeth and flung it down and I were shouting at them, I were that wild.
>
> "There you are! Bugger yourselves! Share that between you!" Then I were off! It was hand-to-hand! I went round one traverse and there was one – face to face. I couldn't fire one-handed, but I could use the bayonet. It was him or me and I went first! Jab! Just like that. It were my job. And from there I went on. Oh, I were wild! Seeing Clem like that!
>
> We were climbing out of the trench, making for the second line, and that's where they got me again just as I were climbing out,

through the fingers this time, on the same arm. I still managed to get on. I kept up with the lads nearly to the second line. Then I got another one. It went through my tin hat and down and straight through my foot. Well, that finished it!

After a bit, lying there, I saw two fellows drop into some shell-hole. I crawled after them and, of course, you couldn't see much for the smoke but, next thing we did know, the Germans had taken back all their front line again. There were no more of our fellows about. So there we had to stop. When night came I were in a deuce of a state. I must have been fainting off and on, what with the loss of blood. You'd no idea of the passage of time. I didn't know where I were. I only knew there were Germans in front and Germans behind and I had no idea which way were the British lines.

What with having nothing to eat and nothing to drink all day, my tongue was getting as big as two. I could hardly close my mouth. My water-bottle was gone. I couldn't realize where I was. Lights going up all the time. All this noise. Them shelling from their side and us shelling from ours, and machine-gun in between. What worried me was getting caught in our own shellfire. I bothered more about that. Well, they dropped in front of me and they dropped behind me but they never put one into the shell-hole.

Local attacks continued. The Germans counter-attacked to regain lost ground. They were able to hold many of the strong points in their lines.

The attacks continued, trying to capture German strong points. Corporal Joe Hoyles went "over the top" on 10 July as part of an attempt to capture the village of Contalmaison. He was in the 13th battalion of the Rifle Brigade:

It was a very bright hot day and we'd seen Contalmaison go up in the air. We'd seen the church go up in the air. Marvellous gunnery it was, our gunnery. We had to take to the left of Contalmaison. I was a section leader and Colonel Pinney came by the Platoon and he said, "We're going over at 8.45. Set your watches." Those of us in charge of sections had to take our sections over. Where I got my courage from I don't know. I suppose, being young, one had an "Up Guards and at 'em" sort of feeling. Some men funked it of course. They went over all right, they had to or they'd have got my bayonet up their arse. But you could tell from their faces that a lot of people dreaded it. We went over with fixed bayonets and we all had a Mills bomb in our hands. It was a quarter or a third of a mile to the first German trench.

I always remember saying to my section, "Come on, Rifle Brigade! The first time Over the Top. Here we go!" And off we went. We were in the first wave, and our platoon officer, Fitzgibbon, was out in front of us. They just mowed us down! People were falling on your right and your left and of course you had to keep going forward.

The British lost 175,000 casualties in July, 1916. The next big "push" was on 18 August. Edward Gale was an acting Lance-Corporal in the 7th battalion of the Rifle Brigade:

It was the waiting to go over that was the worst, because we didn't go over until almost three o'clock in the afternoon. There was a whole brigade waiting to go over on a battalion front, so we were crowded up like anything. During the morning, the sergeant came round with the old rum jar and gave us a dessertspoonful of rum, just to put Dutch courage in us. It was strong, that Army rum, and I think he had two or three spoonfuls to our one – or more!

We really needed that rum, waiting to go over the top! Our own guns had put down this terrific barrage but, because we were a bit higher up than the Germans, in order to hit them they'd had to sight the guns so that they would just skim the top of our trenches and there we were, crouching in this terrible noise, and these terrible shells going over us just inches above. You can't describe the feeling! You can't describe the noise! A couple of our own chaps were killed. One fellow had the top of his head took off with one of our own shells. His brains were all over the place. But the artillery couldn't help it. They had a terrible job to get the elevation right and just had to try and skim the top of our trenches and this poor chap Dixon got it. He was only five or six yards away from me. It didn't do much for us to see that sort of thing before we went over!

Five minutes after we went over the top we were finished! The German machine-guns went through our lines just like a mow goes through a field of corn. I don't think we got 200 yards before we were so mucked up that we just had to lay out in No-Man's Land. I was in a shell-hole with the sergeant – the one who'd been sampling the rum. We were absolutely pinned down but he kept jumping up and shouting, "Why don't we advance? Why don't we advance?" He was absolutely hollering. How could you advance when there was three of you there and you couldn't see anybody else? I shouted back at him, "Why don't you keep down? You'll be drawing the guns on us!"

D Company had gone across first and C Company were supposed to be following behind us. From this shell-hole we looked back and we could see C Company there lying on the ground spread out in extended order, just as they'd gone across. We couldn't understand why they weren't coming up to support us. There was just the three of us in the shell-hole – the platoon sergeant and Jack Hall, who was the Lance-Corporal, and myself. And the sergeant said, "Why the hell don't they come on and give us a hand? We can't go in there on our own!"

This old sergeant wasn't half going on, nothing would keep him quiet. He was an enlisted man – he wasn't a Regular. There was only two of us Regulars in the 7th Battalion, but the sergeant had been in the Marines before the war, so he should have known better. Of course he had all this rum in him. Then the third time he jumped up they got him! A bullet went straight in his ear and blew half his face away. Me and Jack had to lay there with him. We lay there for hours and hours and hours with all this clatter going on around us and when it got dusk we started to crawl back.

The Germans had to transfer five divisions to their Eastern front. The French were attacking at Verdun. The British had made some small gains. Despite their losses, the British continued the battle into September. On 15 September they introduced a new weapon designed to suppress barbed-wire and machine guns: the tank. Lance-Corporal Len Lovell was following one of the tanks:

It was marvellous. That tank went on, rolling and bobbing and swaying in and out of shell-holes, climbing over trees as easy as kiss your hand! We were awed! We were delighted that it was ours. Up to now Jerry had supplied all the surprises. Now it was his turn to be surprised!

The tank waddled on with its guns blazing and we could see Jerry popping up and down, not knowing what to do, whether to stay or to run. We Bombers were sheltering behind the tank, peering round

> and anxious to let Jerry have our bombs. But we had no need of them. The Jerries waited until our tank was only a few yards away and then fled – or hoped to! The tank just shot them down and the machine-gun post, the gun itself, the dead and wounded who hadn't been able to run, just disappeared. The tank went right over them. We would have danced for joy if it had been possible out there. It seemed so easy! Hop Trench was "kaput" and in a very few minutes Ale Alley got the same treatment. We were elated!

There were less than 50 tanks. Some broke down, others lost their sense of direction. The gains they made were lost to counter-attacks. Communication was so slow and difficult that it was impossible to bring up supporting troops to hold the ground gained.

Each series of attacks was made by a different formation of the British Army until its manpower was too weak to continue. On 12 November Gough's 5th Army, the reserve, attacked with partial success. They captured Beaucourt but the Germans still held the high ground between Beaumont Hamel and Beaucourt. This limited success was enough to persuade the English and French governments to continue the war into 1917.

The British had lost 420,000 casualties in the battle of the Somme. They had gained 10 kilometres of ground.

Aerial Warfare

The use of aircraft in the First World War was, initially, for reconnaissance. Aircraft also proved themselves useful for artillery observation. Three weeks after the war began, Sir John French, commander of the BEF, wrote:

> I wish particularly to bring to your notice the admirable work done by the Royal Flying Corps. Their skill, energy and perseverance have been beyond all praise. They have furnished me with the most complete and accurate information which has been of incalculable value in the conduct of operations.

Early types of aircraft were unarmed and were unable to deny enemy aircraft the use of the skies for the same purpose.

In 1915 this changed. A French aviator, Roland Garros, had his Morane single-seater aircraft fitted with a machine gun which was able to fire through the propeller. He shot down six German aircraft. After several weeks it became clear to the Germans that there was only one Allied machine equipped to do this. Garros' aircraft developed engine trouble behind the German lines and he was forced to land. He was captured before he could destroy his aircraft. The Germans recognized the aircraft as the one that had been doing the damage. Examination revealed how it had been done. It was a crude and dangerous device. Each blade of the propeller was fitted with a triangular steel wedge which would deflect any bullets which hit the blade. The aircraft was flown to Germany where it was handed to the young Dutch designer, Anthony Fokker. Within 48 hours he had solved the problem of how to synchronize the firing of the gun so that the bullets would pass between the blades of the propeller. He had the device installed in one of his Fokker E1 monoplanes. He was ordered to prove it worked by shooting down an Allied aircraft.

Fokker protested that he was a neutral.

But before long he was in the air. At about 6,000 feet he saw an Allied Farman two-seater observation aircraft. He dived towards it. Fokker wrote afterwards:

> This aircraft had no reason to fear me. I was going straight for it, my nose aimed at it, and they couldn't possibly have any reason to fear bullets fired through my propeller.
>
> While approaching, I thought of what a deadly accurate stream of lead I could send into the aircraft. It would be just like shooting a sitting rabbit because the pilot couldn't shoot back through his propeller at me.
>
> As the distance between us narrowed the aeroplane grew larger in my sights. My imagination could visualize my shots puncturing the petrol tanks in front of the engine. The tank would catch fire. Even if my bullets failed to kill the pilot and observer, the machine would fall down in flames. I had my finger on the trigger . . . I had no personal animosity towards the French. I was flying merely to prove that a certain mechanism I had invented would work. By this time I was near enough to open fire, and the French pilots were watching me curiously . . . In another instant, it would be all over for them.
>
> Suddenly, I decided that the whole job could go to hell. It was

too much like "cold meat" to suit me. I had no stomach for the whole business, nor any wish to kill Frenchmen for Germans. Let them do their own killing!

Returning quickly to the Douai flying field, I informed the commander of the field that I would do no more flying over the Front. After a brief argument, it was agreed that a regular German pilot would take up the machine. Lieutenant Oswald Boelcke, later to be the first German ace, was assigned to the job. The next morning I showed him how to manipulate the machine-gun while flying the aircraft, watched him take off for the Front, and left for Berlin.

By the time Fokker arrived in Berlin, Boelcke had shot down an Allied aircraft using the synchronized gun. The next day another German pilot, Max Immelman, shot down a second Allied aircraft. Other German pilots demanded the guns. Fokker went back to his factory to make them.

For a while the skies were almost clear of Allied aircraft. But four months later a German pilot, lost in a fog, landed behind the French lines. He was captured and his aircraft with its synchronized gun was examined. The Allies were able to copy it. They combined its techniques with a device which used hydraulic pressure to improve the gun. The war in the air was, once again, an even struggle.

Oswald Boelcke and Max Immelman became Germany's first air aces. Air aces became newsworthy items. Soon the French were celebrating the feats of Georges Guynemer. Immelman crashed and died on 18 June 1916. On 28 October 1916 Boelcke died, leading his squadron in an attack on two British aircraft. One of his young pilots, Manfred von Richthofen, wrote in his diary:

Had they been 20, Boelcke would have given us same signal. I attacked one aircraft and he the other. I had to let go because one of the German machines got in my way. I looked around and noticed Boelcke settling his victim about 200 yards away from me.

It was the usual thing. Boelcke would shoot down his opponent and I had to look on. Close to Boelcke flew a good friend of his. It was an interesting struggle. Both men were shooting. It was probable that the Englishman would fall at any moment. Suddenly I noticed an unnatural movement of the two German flying machines. Immediately I thought: collision. I had not yet seen a collision in the air. I had imagined that it would look quite different. In reality, what happened was not a collision. The two machines merely touched one another. However, if two machines go the tremendous pace of flying machines, the slightest contact has the effect of a violent concussion.

Boelcke drew away from his victim and descended in large curves. He did not seem to be falling, but when I saw him descending below me I noticed that part of his aeroplane had broken off. Now his machine was no longer steerable. It fell accompanied all the time by Boelcke's faithful friend.

When we reached home we found the report, "Boelcke is dead!", had already arrived. We could scarcely realize it. The greatest pain was, of course, felt by the man who had the misfortune to be involved in the accident.

Manfred von Richthofen became Germany's most famous pilot. He was shot down by Flight Lieutenant Arthur Roy Brown on 21 April 1918. Brown was trying to protect another pilot, "Wop" May. May:

I kept dodging and spinning, I imagine from about 12,000 feet until I ran out of sky and had to hedgehop over the ground. Richthofen was firing at me continually. The only thing that saved my life was my poor flying. I didn't know what I was doing myself and I do not suppose that Richthofen could figure out what I was going to do. We came over the German lines, troops firing at us as we went over. This was also the case coming over the British lines.

I got on the Somme River and started up the valley at a very low altitude, Richthofen very close on my tail. I went around a curve in the river just near Corbie. Richthofen beat me to it and came over the hill. At that moment I was a sitting duck. I was too low down between the banks to make a turn away from him, I felt that he had me cold, and I was in such a state of mind at this time that I had to restrain myself from pushing my stick forward into the river, as I knew that I had had it.

Then, Brown got behind von Richthofen and fired at 40 yards' range. Von Richthofen's plane crashed on the Allied side of the lines. His body was recovered and buried with military honours.

The Western Front 1918

In 1917 the Germans retreated to newly constructed positions – the Hindenburg Line. The British attacked at Ypres (the Third Battle of Ypres, which they called Passchendaele). They lost 250,000 casualties. In November they attacked the Hindenburg Line using tanks. They broke through but lacked the reserves to exploit their gains. The Germans counter-attacked with fresh troops and retook the lost ground.

In December 1917 the Russians made peace. German troops from the Eastern Front were now available for the Western Front. Until the Americans arrived, the Germans had an advantage in manpower. They had an opportunity to strike decisively before they lost their advantage. On 21 March 1918 they attacked the British where they were weakest, between Arras and St Quentin, with the aim of advancing north-east to the channel coast.

The Germans used new tactics; their initial bombardment was aimed at command posts and supporting artillery. They mixed high explosive with gas shells. This cut telephone lines and weakened the defenders. When their infantry attacked, they infiltrated between strongpoints which they could then attack from the flank or behind. Their intention was to reinforce where they had broken through. To add to the confusion, the area was covered by thick mist.

Leutenant Herman Wedekind was a German company commander:

> Five or ten Englishmen without weapons and with strange expressions came towards us. They had not quite reached us when their own artillery dropped some shells between them and us. Several of them fell down, and the rest ran past us. We ran over to the first, shot-up English trench. As far as we could see, the enemy was not putting up any resistance at all and had evacuated his positions. We quickly pushed on. There were no Englishmen in the second trench either. We were in an empty field.

Alwein Hitzeroth was a Musketier in a Minenwerfer (mortar) company:

> We joined up with the infantry again and continued forward over a flat field, then down into a slightly sloping valley. Here we came

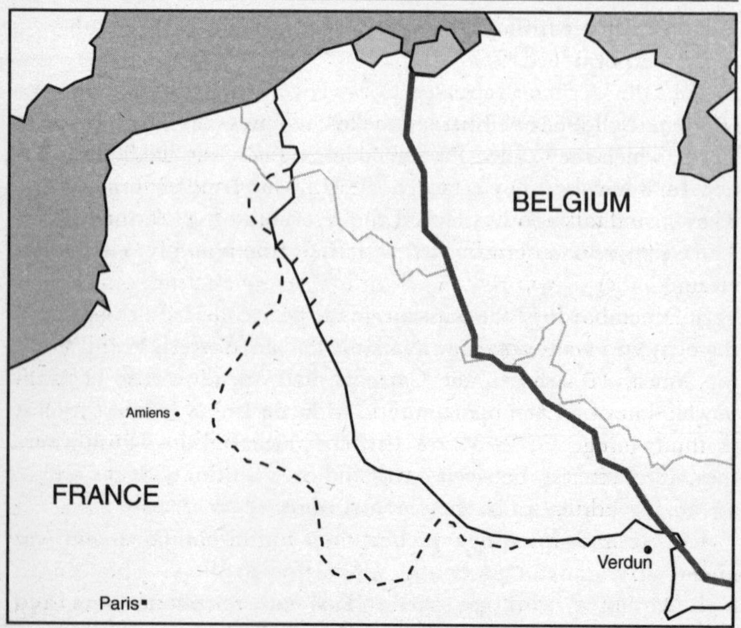

The Western Front 1918

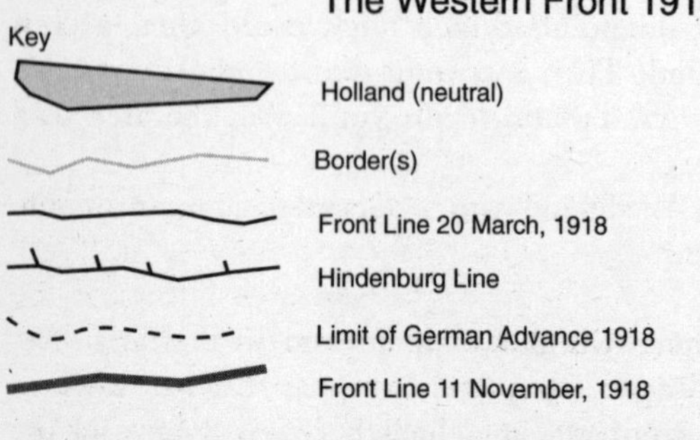

Map of the Western Front in 1918

under enemy artillery fire and scrambled for cover. Although the shelling soon stopped, we lost one man dead and three wounded. As soon as it did, the Regiment's 1st and 3rd Battalions attacked and, after fierce hand-to-hand fighting, broke through the English position. It seemed that the enemy's resistance was broken here, and again we pushed forward, capturing all sorts of guns and ammunition and supplies. The supplies were especially welcomed by us lowly privates – milk, cigarettes, white bread and real coffee! Our bread-bags soon were stuffed full.

Some British troops, in forward positions, were captured without a fight. Corporal Ted Gale:

> We were holding this part of the line. There was three companies up there, and A Company was back behind alongside Essigny-Le-Grand. I was in D Company. They'd been bombarding all night long, and talk about a London fog! We couldn't see the next sentry next door to us standing in the trench. We honestly couldn't see each other, it was that thick with the German guns and the fog. The bombardment was moving on and it was full daylight, but there was no Germans coming over or anything.
>
> Well, we stand to for hours in our battle positions! Then the Captain of the company comes along the line. He said, "Funny thing going on. It's very unusual. There's no sign of an attack. You'd better all go down in the dugouts and have something to eat, something to drink. Leave a couple of sentries up here." So we left a couple of sentries on top and went down into the dugouts.
>
> We got a brew going but, damn it, we hadn't been in the dugout for more than about 10 minutes when the Captain popped his head in the dugout door. He said, "You can all come up. You won't want your rifles." He said it quite calm, like. Anyway, we came walking up the dugout steps, and there was all these Jerries round us!
>
> Of course, we realized what had happened. Jerry had broken through on the right and left of us. This was a mopping-up party coming. They'd never attempted a frontal attack. That was the strategy, you see: they went through on the right and left.
>
> Our whole battalion was caught. A Company was back in Essigny-Le-Grand. They were just cooking their breakfast for the Company, because they hadn't had a chance to have any, and Jerry walked in just as they were starting to dish up breakfast for the troops. Fried bacon and bread.

After midday, the mist cleared. British gunners in the third line had to shoot directly at the Germans advancing towards their positions. Gunner Walter Lugg:

> We had this chap Charlie Drake, and he was a good friend of mine. (Both my mates were called Charlie – the other was Charlie Stone.) Charlie Drake had very good eyesight, marvellous eye-

sight, and he was looking over, and all of a sudden he shouted to our captain, who by this time was standing on top of the gun-pit, because we'd pulled our guns into the open, and he shouted to him, "Here they are! Hordes of them!" So I looked through my telescope sight and all of a sudden I saw the blooming Germans 300 yards away from us. Well, we didn't have to be told! We started letting fly at them, firing at short range. We had a .2 fuse on her, and they had a muzzle velocity of 1,610 feet a second, so you can work out as soon as we fired they were exploding. Point blank over open sights.

The gunners had to abandon their guns. They disabled them before retreating to another position. Walter Lugg:

The chaps who weren't handling the guns lay out with rifles to hold the Jerries off when we stopped firing. I was handling one of the guns, so I had to help to get the breech-block out, take the No. 7 sights away. Most of us managed to get back all right, creeping away in ones and twos. Captain Heybittel didn't go until nearly the end, because he wanted to see everyone away. We all got away except for Lieutenant Patterson and three other chaps. They were on the other gun, and possibly they'd had more of a struggle with their breech-block, but they were a bit behind and to our right as we were moving back. Next thing, I heard Captain Heybittel give a shout and he was standing pointing his revolver. When I looked over my shoulder, it must have been 50 or more yards away, Lieutenant Patterson was being marched away with two or three other chaps – marched away by a bunch of Germans who must have worked round the side of us. The skipper just pointed his revolver and fired. They say he hit one of them.

The rest of us got back to the next position all right, where there were another two guns, so we helped them and kept firing, and the lads who had rifles kept firing. They were glad to have us, I can tell you. When we got back there we buried the breech-blocks we'd carried back.

The Captain gave the order and we all knew that we didn't have much time, so we started to disable the gun. It was absolutely burning hot – and what a job we had to get that breech-block out! Of course, more haste less speed! But we managed it and dumped it in a sandbag, which I was given the job of carrying – not for the first time that day! We decided we would give the Germans one more surprise, so we took out the pins that held the wheels on, so that when the Germans drove them away the blooming wheels would fall off. Ha ha! We did that with malice aforethought, and we did it off our own bat.

While we were there, someone spotted a movement just on our right and shouted out, "Who's there?" No answer. So we realized that they were Germans. Charlie Stone was lying there covering us, and he got up and went out – he'd got his rifle – and he walked right out towards the place. He said in a kindly voice, "Come on, Fritz. Come on, Fritz." Next thing, they fired a shot and Charlie Stone fired back, and then somebody else fired. The Jerries started running away, but Charlie ran after them, right out into No-Man's Land. I was right by him, but I couldn't go with him because I had the breech-block in a sandbag on my back, so obviously I couldn't go. But he went. "Come on, Fritz," he said – just like that! These Germans were actually in the rear of us, and Charlie went right after them – chasing after them. He chased one for about 100 yards before he caught him. Of course some other fellows had followed by then. They captured two prisoners, and Charlie even brought in their old machine-gun on the way back. He got the Victoria Cross for that, and if ever a man earned it it was Charlie Stone. He was a coal miner in civil life, and a great friend of mine.

We started making our way back, prisoners and all. It took us a long time in the dark, and then when we got back to our wagon lines they were completely deserted. All our horses had gone, the wagons had gone, and of course we'd lost all our guns. They'd all been captured – but we'd made sure that they wouldn't be much use to the Jerries.

On 22 March Ludendorff, the German Commander-in-Chief, had to decide where to reinforce his attacks. He sent reinforcements south of St Quentin. The British Army was retreating, fighting. Second Lieutenant E. Hakewill-Smith was in command of a platoon of the Royal Scots Fusiliers:

I collected some odd men coming back, and this brought the strength of the platoon up to about 60. I was lucky enough to get hold of a stray Vickers machine-gun and its team, and I also got another Lewis-gun off one of our aeroplanes, which was forced to land near my trench. This meant that I now had three machine-guns and about 60 rifles and, but for the fact that my trench was unwired, I should have felt very confident.

Shortly after four o'clock in the afternoon the enemy began to push on again. There were simply swarms of them – line after line, coming about five paces apart. I counted 30 lines and then got tired of counting, there were so many of them. Just at this time we got a very nasty enfilade machine-gun fire from our left, which I didn't like a bit, but luckily we spotted the gun, fired at it like billy-o, and managed to make it shift. The Boche came slowly plodding along, simply thousands of them! I waited until they were 600 yards away and then opened up with machine-guns and rapid rifle fire. There were so many of them that we couldn't miss! We simply mowed them down, and they weren't making much ground. But suddenly we saw more Boche behind us, coming through Etreillers and working round our rear. I turned a Lewis-gun on them and this held them up, but only for about two minutes, and then I saw the Boche on our right flank pushing on . . .

The next day, 23 March, they retreated. The German effort weakened. Allied reserves were brought up to deal with the crisis. Lieutenant Robert Watson Kerr was in the Tank Corps. 25 tanks were available. His section commander:

. . . shouted, "Look slippy! You're going into action at once!" That made us jump, and in a moment or two we had got our tunics and Sam Browne belts on, pocketed our loaded Colts, and crossed the road to our tanks. "Here!" I shouted to the reconnaissance officer when I had got my tank under way, "where's the front line?" "There isn't one," he replied. "Well, where's the Boche, then?" He pointed over the sunny fields ahead. "Just walk right on and you'll find them soon enough!"

We set off walking beside our tanks, with our crews inside them, but after we had covered some distance across country there was a slight tension in the air. Guns were firing somewhere near. Then suddenly, to our right, about 100 yards or so away, we caught sight of a battery of British field guns firing in the open.

We stopped. So did the battery. Then to our amazement we heard the artillerymen shout, "The tanks! The tanks!" and they followed this up with enthusiastic cheers, led by the officer waving his cap above his head. We waved back – a little embarrassed –

thinking that the gunners must have been feeling pretty desperate to cheer us like that.

Pipsqueaks were now dropping unpleasantly around and beyond us, and so we separated to our own tanks. It was safer there, and any minute now we might come on the infantry who were supposed to support us. But that was where we made a mistake! There were no infantry ahead of us. We were on our own, and the battery of artillery had apparently been the front line. No wonder they had cheered!

Only nine tanks returned. The gunners and the tank crews had gained some time in which a stronger defensive line could be formed. Dick Gammell was a Second Lieutenant in the Black Watch. His responsibilities were usually communications, telephones lines:

There were stragglers all over the place and we collected them all together, and when we assembled things really were chaotic. There was quite high ground in front of us, and the Jocks were simply streaming back. Wilson and I decided to become infantry officers, as it were, and try to steady things. So far as I was concerned, signals didn't matter any more! So we went forward and collected some Jocks and formed a sort of line. They were all from different units, so we were in complete disorder.

It was the bush telegraph that saved the whole thing, and it was quite extraordinary. They'd managed to get the field kitchens up just behind us, and the rumour went round, and before we knew where we were the men began to congregate. They say that if a man's hungry he'll find out where the food is, and that's quite true, because that is really how the Division assembled – what was left of it!

The British retreated over the Somme battlefield. Alex Jamieson was a private in the Royal Scots:

Even when we managed to get away the day before our troubles weren't over, because we were shelled all the way back. In fact it seemed that we'd become a target for the German artillery! We moved up quite a stiff incline to some old British trenches of 1916, and my exhaustion had got to such a stage that I didn't even attempt to drop to the ground, even when the shells were bursting quite close. But someone nearby did, and then he started kicking and yelling, so in spite of the state I was in myself I managed to drag him into a trench. He was only shell-shocked, but it was having such a bad effect on everyone that a sergeant ordered me to take him to a field dressing station we could see across the valley. By the time we got there it had moved on, so there was nothing for it but to follow. I was supporting this chap, and carrying his rifle as well as my own, because he was so shocked and his legs were just like jelly, but gradually I was getting to the stage of being as bad as he was, or even weaker. We found a medical aid post on the Combles road, and they wouldn't take him in, but I asked the doctor to give me a note that I had reported, so that I wouldn't be charged as a deserter.

Eventually we reached a casualty clearing station at Maricourt (this was the place where we had detrained a month or so earlier), and they took my casualty over and directed me to a compound for regimental stragglers. When I got there I was given some hot food, but as soon as I got the plate in my hand and sat down to eat it I promptly fell asleep. I was as hungry as could be, but I don't remember if I ever ate that food at all. A few hours later I went off again – with another chit from the stragglers post, of course – and I joined up with what was left of the battalion at Bray.

On 26 March the New Zealand division was rushed south to help. They prevented the Germans advancing through a gap in the British line north of Albert. George Mackay was in a machine gun section of the New Zealand Rifle Brigade:

Well, we had hardly got settled when over they came. Band out in front and all, just marching. They had taken France, in other words, and they were home and dry. So I gave them the first blast at 1,000 yards. And, of course, as soon as they come under fire they scattered, broke up their formation, and took to the long grass. Well, then all I had to do was just pick out bunches of them, and that's what I was doing. I looked on that as one of the best day's sport I've ever had! Loads of ammunition and plenty of Huns. And you can see that parties of Huns at 1,000 yards coming towards us was quite good shooting.

We got them slowed up a bit in the long grass, and they started using smoke bombs. A rifle grenade would fire forward, and it would burst and the smoke would just gradually pass through, and when it cleared these buggers would be a bit closer. Well,

Lieutenant Nees paid us a visit at one point, and he's looking at the smoke. "Ah," he says, "I can see through that with these glasses. You can see the figures coming forward. Here, take my glasses and put an observer on and fire in their direction." So we did that from then on. We slowed them down a bit more. When there would be a curl of smoke, this fellow would say, "Under the third curl to the right there's a bunch coming forward." And I would shoot at them. I was shooting on the blind, of course, but we slowed them down.

Well, that went on a bit, and eventually they got right down to this road and there was a trench along there, and they were all waiting to jump across and get into dead ground. Had they got across that road they could have come around the back and shot us in the rear, and that was my danger. I didn't think there was anybody in there to stop them. If they had got through, they would have come round and sniped us. They would have been shooting down on us. That's when my experience stood me in good stead. I'd been fired on when a road was frozen and I knew what a ricochet could do, so I let them have a ricochet deliberate. The party was going to cross there, bunched up, and I would hit the road about 30 yards on the nearside and let them have the broken-up bullets. Of course the bullets howl and shriek – a ricochet bullet can make all sorts of noises – but it slowed them down. But soon I saw the whole lot of them come up and start firing across the road, so I fired up and down and among them. Then I could see what they were firing at: the one and only bayonet charge that I've ever seen. A party of anything between 30 and 50 of our fellows with their bare bayonets, rifle and bayonet, charged down across the road and into them. Of course as soon as they got to the road I stopped firing on the Germans, so the New Zealanders crossed the road and into them. That put us safe! They stopped it!

On 28 March Ludendorff attacked further north near Arras, without success. The same day, the American General Pershing offered his troops wherever they were needed. The American troops began to use British and French equipment which enabled them to arrive sooner. In March, 84,000 arrived in France. In May, 264,000 and, in June, over 306,000 arrived.

The Germans made a last attempt to capture Amiens on 4–5 April. They had lost 250,000 casualties. On 8 April they attacked on a part of the front held by a Portuguese division. By 18 April the attack had been held. They had advanced 28 miles and taken 70,000 prisoners since 21 March. They were holding a longer defensive line with fewer men.

From 27 May the Allies began a series of limited attacks along their line. On 8 August, the British attacked on the Somme with 450,000 men supported by over 400 tanks, 2,000 guns and aircraft. The Germans collapsed so badly that Ludendorff called it "the blackest day of the German army in the history of this war". The tanks were mechanically unreliable, slow and vulnerable to artillery fire so that on 9 August only 145 were active. By 13 August none were available. The British were unable to keep attacking. The Germans were able to patch up a new front. The Allies kept up attacks along the line. By 5 October the British had broken through some sections of the Hindenburg Line. On 4 October the German Chancellor had requested an armistice on the basis of the peace proposals suggested by President Wilson in January 1918. On 8 November the delegations met to agree terms. The German delegation accepted the terms they were offered. The Kaiser's rule was to be replaced by a democratic republic. The next day the Kaiser abdicated and fled to Holland. At 5 a.m. on 11 November the German delegation signed. At 11 a.m. the fighting stopped.

Second World War

Introduction

In 1938 Nazi Germany invaded Czechoslovakia. Great Britain and France then guaranteed to support Poland if Poland was attacked by Germany. The Germans invaded Poland in August 1939. The British Government demanded that they withdraw. The German leader, Adolf Hitler would not promise to withdraw. Great Britain and France declared war on Germany.

The Fall of France 1940

After the Germans completed their conquest of Poland; apart from at sea, a period of inactivity followed. The British called it the "phoney war". In April and May 1940, the Germans overran Norway, Denmark and the Netherlands. Belgium remained neutral. The British had sent an army to France. This army, the British Expeditionary Force (BEF), was positioned on the French frontier near the Belgian border. French armies were positioned on either side of the BEF. Britain and France expected a German thrust through Belgium. The Belgians would not allow them to enter their territory. When the expected German thrust through Belgium came in May 1940, the BEF advanced to meet it. Another German thrust punched right through to the French coast between the BEF and the French forces to the South. The British and French forces to the North retreated to the only port on the French coast still open to them – Dunkirk. They had to abandon their vehicles and heavy equipment to get their men back to England.

The French surrendered on 21 June.

The Battle of Britain 1940

> What General Weygand called the Battle of France is over. I expect that the Battle of Britain is about to begin. The whole fury and might of the enemy must very soon be turned on us. Hitler knows that he will have to break us in this island or lose the war. If we can stand up to him, all Europe may be free and the life of the world may move forward to broad sunlit lands.
>
> But if we fail, then the whole world, including the United States, including all we have known and cared for, will sink into the abyss of a new Dark Age made more sinister and perhaps more protracted, by the lights of perverted science.
>
> Let us therefore brace ourselves to our duties and so bear ourselves that, if the British Empire and its Commonwealth last for a thousand years, men will still say, "This was their finest hour."
>
> Winston Spencer Churchill, 18 June 1940

After the fall of France in June 1940, Great Britain faced Germany alone. On 16 July 1940 Hitler issued Fuhrer Directive No. 16: on preparations for a landing operation against England. The tasks of the German air force, the Luftwaffe, were to "prevent air attacks, engage approaching naval vessels, destroy coastal defences . . . break the initial resistance of the enemy's land forces and annihilate reserves behind the front." The Luftwaffe was able to use bases on the French coast to try to gain control of the air over Britain. This would have allowed the Germans to invade Britain. The Germans gave their invasion plans the code-name Operation Seelöwe (Sealion).

The Luftwaffe began by attacking British shipping and convoys along the south and east coasts of England combined with large fighter sweeps across the south-east. These attacks weakened the British defences and drew Royal Air Force (RAF) fighters into combat. On 1 August Hitler issued Fuhrer Directive No. 17. This ordered the Luftwaffe to overpower the Royal Air Force with all the forces in its command in the shortest possible time.

During the second week in August, the Luftwaffe changed tactics. They began heavy bombing raids on airfields and radar stations throughout southern England. Their aim was to destroy RAF fighter defences.

The Luftwaffe bombing raids were extended throughout Great Britain. The raids were both by day and night. On the night of

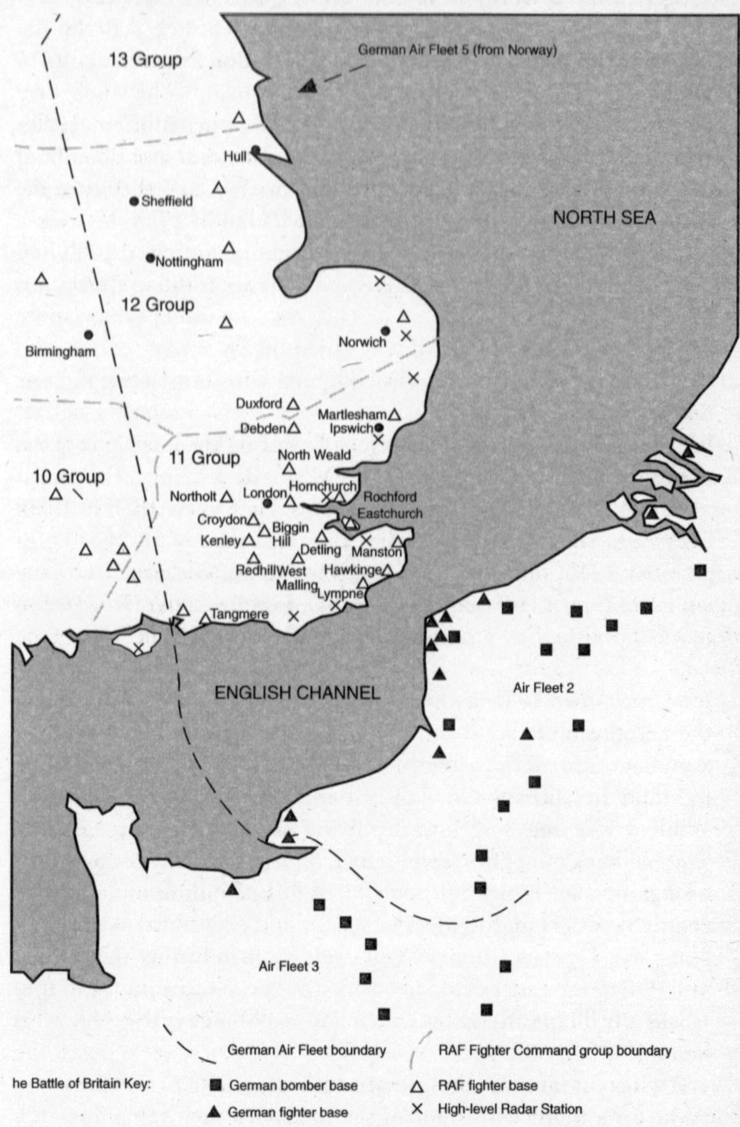

Map of the Battle of Britain

24 August 1940 a German bomber crew, off-course, dropped their bombs on London. In retaliation RAF bombers attacked Berlin the following night. Outraged, Hitler ordered London and other cities to be bombed.

By early September 1940 the Luftwaffe had switched their attacks from airfields and radar stations to London. Day and night bombing had started on the capital, concentrating mainly on the docklands.

After John Maurice Bentley Beard left school in 1936, he took a job in a bank. While working there he became interested in flying. He joined the RAF Volunteer Reserve for flying training during his weekends.

When the war began, Beard was called up for active service with an RAF fighter squadron. It was equipped with Hurricane fighters and based near London.

Beard was in action almost continually during the later part of the Battle of Britain. He won a medal (DFM) for destroying a confirmed total of eight enemy aircraft, over London. He had married in 1939.

Beard described his part during the final part of the battle, in September 1940, on a day in which the Germans claimed to have flown more than 1,000 planes against the London area. His description was published in a national newspaper in 1940:

> I was supposed to be away on a day's leave but dropped back to the aerodrome to see if there was a letter from my wife. When I found out that all the squadrons had gone off into action I decided to stand by, because obviously something big was happening. While I was climbing into my flying kit, our Hurricanes came slipping back out of the sky to refuel, reload ammunition, and take off again. The returning pilots were full of talk about flocks of enemy bombers and fighters which were trying to break through along the Thames Estuary. You couldn't miss hitting them, they said. Off to the east I could hear the steady roll of anti-aircraft fire. It was a brilliant afternoon with a flawless blue sky. I was crazy to be off.
>
> An instant later an aircraftman rushed up with orders for me to make up a flight with some of the machines then reloading. My own Hurricane was a nice old kite, though it had a habit of flying left wing low at the slightest provocation. But since it had already accounted for 14 German aircraft before I inherited it, I thought it had some luck, and I was glad when I squeezed myself into the same old seat again and grabbed the "stick".

We took off in two flights (six fighters), and as we started to gain height over the station we were told over the R.T. (radio-telephone) to keep circling for a while until we were made up to a stronger force. That didn't take long, and soon there was a complete squadron (12 machines) including a couple of Spitfires which had wandered in from somewhere.

Then came the big thrilling moment: ACTION ORDERS. Distantly I heard the hum of the generator in my R.T. earphones and then the voice of the ground controller crackling through with the call signs: "[Censored]." Then the order: "50 plus bombers, 100 plus fighters over Canterbury at 15,000 heading north-east. Your vector [steering course to intercept] nine zero degrees. Over!"

We were flying in four V formations of three. I was flying No. 3 in Red flight, which was the squadron-leader's and thus the leading flight. On we went, wing-tips to left and right slowly rising and falling, the roar of our 12 Merlins drowning all other sound. We crossed over London which, at 20,000 feet, seemed just a haze of smoke from its countless chimneys, with nothing visible except the faint glint of the barrage balloons and the wriggly silver line of the Thames.

I had too much to do watching the instruments and keeping formation to do much thinking. But once I caught a reflected glimpse of myself in the windscreen – a goggled, bloated, fat thing with the tube of my oxygen supply protruding gruesomely sideways from the mask which hid my mouth. Suddenly I was back at school again, on a hot afternoon when the Headmaster was taking the Sixth and droning on and on about the later Roman Emperors. The boy on my right was showing me surreptitiously some illustrations which he had pinched out of his father's medical books during the last holidays. I looked like one of those pictures.

It was an amazingly vivid memory as if school was only yesterday. And half my mind was thinking what wouldn't I then have given to be sitting in a Hurricane belting along at 350 miles an hour and out for a kill. Me defending London! I grinned at my old self at the thought.

Minutes went by. Green fields and roads were now beneath us. I scanned the sky and the horizon for the first glimpse of the Germans. A new vector came through on the R.T. and we swung round with the sun behind us. Swift on the heels of this I heard Yellow flight leader call through the earphones: "[Censored].” I looked quickly towards Yellow’s position and there they were!

It was really a terrific sight and quite beautiful. First they seemed just a cloud of light as the sun caught the many glistening chromium parts of their engines, their windshields and the spin of their airscrew discs. Then as our squadron hurtled nearer, the details stood out. I could see the bright-yellow noses of Messerschmitt fighters sandwiching the bombers, and could even pick out some of the types. The sky seemed full of them, packed in layers thousands of feet deep. They came on steadily, wavering up and down along the horizon. “Oh, golly,” I thought, “golly, golly.”

And then any tension I had felt on the way suddenly left me. I was elated but very calm. I leaned over and switched on my reflector sight, flicked the catch on the guns button from “Safe” to “Fire”, and lowered my seat till the circle and dot on the reflector sight shone darkly red in front of my eyes.

The squadron-leader’s voice came through the earphones giving tactical orders. We swung round in a great circle to attack on their beam – into the thick of them. Then, on the order, down we went. I took my hand from the throttle lever so as to get both hands on the stick and my thumb played neatly across the gun button. You have to steady a fighter just as you have to steady a rifle before you fire it.

My Merlin screamed as I went down in a steeply-banked dive on to the tail of a forward line of Heinkels. I knew the air was full of aircraft flinging themselves about in all directions but, hunched and snuggled down behind my sight, I was conscious only of the Heinkel I had picked out. As the angle of my dive increased, the enemy machine loomed larger in the sight field, heaved towards the red dot, and then he was there!

I had an instant’s flash of amazement at the Heinkel proceeding so regularly on its way with a fighter on its tail. “Why doesn’t the fool move!” I thought, and actually caught myself flexing my muscles into the action I would have taken had I been he.

When he was square across the sight I pressed the button. There was a smooth trembling of my Hurricane as the eight-gun squirt shot out. I gave him a two-second burst and then another. Cordite fumes blew back into the cockpit, making an acrid mixture with the smell of hot oil and the air compressors.

I saw my first burst go in and just as I was on top of him and turning away I noticed a red glow inside the bomber. I turned tightly into position again and now saw several short tongues of flame lick out along the fuselage. Then he went down in a spin, blanketed with smoke and with pieces flying off.

I left him plummeting down and, hauling back on my stick, climbed up again for more. The sky was clearing but ahead towards London I saw a small tight formation of bombers completely encircled by a ring of Messerschmitts. They were still heading north. As I raced forward three flights of Spitfires came zooming up from beneath them in a sort of Prince of Wales feathers manoeuvre. They burst through upwards and outwards, their guns going all the time. They must have each got one for an instant later I saw the most extraordinary sight of eight German bombers and fighters diving earthward together in flames.

I turned away again and streaked after some distant specks ahead. Diving down, I noticed that the running progress of the battle had brought me over London again. I could see the network of streets with the green space of Kensington Gardens, and I had an instant's glimpse of the Round Pond where I sailed boats when I was a child. In that moment and as I was rapidly over-hauling the Germans ahead, a Dornier 17 sped right across my line of flight closely pursued by a Hurricane. And behind the Hurricane came two Messerschmitts. He was too intent to have seen them and they had not seen me! They were coming slightly towards me. It was perfect. A kick at the rudder and I swung in towards them, thumbed the gun button and let them have it. The first burst was placed just the right distance ahead of the leading Messerchmitt. He ran slap into it and he simply came to pieces in the air. His companion, with one of the speediest and most brilliant "get-outs"! have ever seen, went right away in a half lmmelmann turn. I missed him completely. He must almost have been hit by the pieces of the leader but he got away. I hand it to him.

At that moment some instinct made me glance up at my rear-view mirror and spot two Messerschmitts closing in on my tail. Instantly I hauled back on the stick and streaked upwards. And just in time. For as I flicked into the climb I saw the tracer streaks pass beneath me. As I turned I had a quick look round the "office" [cockpit]. My fuel reserve was running out and I had only about a second's supply of ammunition left. I was certainly in no condition to take on two Messerschmitts. But they seemed no more eager than I was. Perhaps they were in the same position, for they turned away for home. I put my nose down and did likewise.

Only on the way back did I realize how hot I was. I had forgotten to adjust the ventilator apparatus in all the stress of the fighting, and hadn't noticed the thermometer. With the sun on the windows all the time, the inside of the "office" was like an oven. Inside my flying suit I was in a bath of perspiration, and sweat was cascading down my face. I was dead tired and my neck ached from constantly turning my head on the look-out when going in and out of dog-fights. Over east the sky was flecked with A.A. puffs, but I did not bother to investigate. Down I went, home.

At the station there was only time for a few minutes' stretch, a hurried report to the Intelligence Officer and a brief comparing of notes with the other pilots. So far my squadron seemed to be intact in spite of a terrific two hours in which we had accounted for at least 30 enemy aircraft.

But there was more to come. It was now about 4 p.m., and I gulped down some tea while the ground crews checked my Hurricane. Then with about three flights collected we took off again. We seemed to be rather longer this time circling and gaining height above the station before the orders came through on the R. T. It was to patrol an area along the Thames Estuary at 20,000 feet. But we never got there.

We had no sooner got above the docks when we ran into the first lot of enemy bombers. They were coming up in line about 5,000 feet below us. The line stretched on and on across the horizon. Above, on our level, were assorted groups of enemy fighters. Some were already in action with our fellows spinning and twirling among them. Again I got that tightening feeling at the throat, for it really was a sight to make you gasp.

But we all knew what to do. We went for the bombers. Kicking her over I went down after the first of them, a Heinkel 111. He turned away as I approached chiefly because some of our fellows had already broken into the line and had scattered it. Before I got up he had been joined by two more. They were forming a V and heading south across the river.

I went after them. Closing in on the tail of the left one I ran into a stream of cross-fire from all three. How it missed me I don't know. For a second the whole air in front was thick with tracer trails. It seemed to be coming straight at me only to curl away by the windows and go lazily past. I felt one slight bang however and, glancing quickly, saw a small hole at the end of my starboard wing. Then, as the Heinkel drifted across my sights, I pressed the button once . . . twice . . . Nothing happened.

I panicked for a moment till I looked down and saw that I had forgotten to turn the safety catch knob to the "Fire" position. I flicked it over at once and in that instant saw that three bombers, to hasten their getaway, had jettisoned all their bombs. They seemed to peel off in a steady stream. We were over the southern outskirts of London now and I remember hoping that most of them would miss the little houses and plunge into fields.

But dropping the bombs did not help my Heinkel. I let him have a long burst at close range which got him right in the "office". I saw him turn slowly over and go down, and followed to give him another squirt. Just then there was a terrific crash in front of me. Something flew past my window, and the whole aircraft shook as the engine raced itself to pieces. I had been hit by A.A. fire aimed at the bombers, my airscrew had been blown off and I was going down in a spin.

The next few seconds were a bit wild and confused. I remember switching off and flinging back the sliding roof almost in one gesture. Then I tried to vault out through the roof. But I had forgotten to release my safety belt. As I fumbled at the pin the falling aircraft gave a twist which shot me through the open cover. Before I was free the airstream hit me like a solid blow and knocked me sideways. I felt my arm hit something, and then I was falling over and over with fields and streets and sky gyrating madly past my eyes.

I grabbed at the rip-cord on my 'chute. Missed it. Grabbed again. Missed it. That was no fun. Then I remember saying to myself, "This won't do. Take it easy, take it slowly." I tried again and found the rip-cord grip and pulled. There was a terrific wrench at my thighs and then I was floating still and peacefully with my "brolly" canopy billowing above my head.

The rest was lovely. I sat at my ease just floating gradually down, breathing deep, and looking around. I was drifting across London again at about 2,000 feet. Just below me I spotted another parachute, a German, from the bomber I had shot down. I shouted to him but he did not appear to hear me; he was about 500 feet lower and falling faster than me.

I drifted toward the river. Lower now and over the crowded Dockland area I could plainly see the wreck of houses which the bombers had left in their wake, and the smoke of fires. At one point I could actually see fire-engines hurtling along a street. There was no other traffic visible. The northward fringe of London's houses came nearer. I could see that I had plenty of room to miss the crowded roofs and land in open fields.

I actually landed in an allotment garden, my trailing body and the parachute harness simply massacring whole rows of runner-beans. I brought up finally in a compost heap festooned with tendrils and the peas and beans I dragged with me.

I lay there for a minute or two, just glad to be alive. In that short while a whole posse of Home Guards and air raid wardens burst into the allotment and surrounded me. I think I was a little bit screwy because I just lay there and smiled at them, although they were looking so wary and ferocious. Nice ordinary little blokes. I could have kissed them.

Then I said, "Help me out of this harness, will you?" I found I could not move my right arm which hurt a lot from that bump I felt as I had bailed out. They obliged cheerfully, handling me as carefully as if I was made of glass. I started to say how sorry I was that I had made such a mess of the runner-beans when someone stuck a cigarette in my mouth.

They helped me to get my tunic off while I had a look at my arm. It wasn't bad. My shoulder was out a bit and that was all except for a few bruises on my leg. We walked in a procession to the allotment entrance where the chief warden said his car was waiting. By coincidence I had landed only three or four miles from my own station, and the warden offered to drive me there. But just as we got to the road an ambulance drove up. "That's service for you," said one of the wardens. So I had to climb in and be driven back to the station Medical Officer. I was minus my Hurricane, I had a slightly damaged shoulder, but I was plus two German bombers and a fighter. It was the end of a perfect day.

The RAF had prevented the Luftwaffe from gaining control of the air over Britain. On 17 September Hitler announced the postponement of Operation Seelöwe.

Eventually, the British and their allies were able to take the offensive against Germany. Night bombing of English cities continued. Later this became known as "The Blitz". Daylight attacks were confined to fighter and fighter-bomber sweeps across southern England.

On 20 August 1940 Winston Churchill, the British Prime Minister, said in Parliament:

> The gratitude of every home in our island, in our Empire, and indeed throughout the world, except in the abodes of the guilty, goes out to the British airmen, who, undaunted by odds, unwearied in their constant challenge and mortal danger, are turning the tide of the world war by their prowess and devotion.
>
> Never in the field of human conflict was so much owed by so many to so few.

Pearl Harbor 7 December 1941

The Japanese had been aggressively expanding in China and south-east Asia since 1931. As in Europe, the US administration gave covert aid to the Chinese war effort, including American pilots. The United States increased diplomatic pressure on the Japanese to withdraw from China. The United States' commercial treaty with Japan was suspended during 1939. After this, economic restrictions were imposed. These restrictions included oil supplies. The Japanese had few raw materials and no oil supplies of their own. In July 1941 Japanese assets in the United States were frozen; this meant a virtual embargo on all trade, including oil. To fulfill their strategic goals the Japanese would have to seize oilfields by force. Obviously the United States would oppose this. The United States was effectively blocking Japanese ambitions in Asia and the Pacific.

On 7 December 1941 the Japanese damaged the United States Pacific fleet in a surprise attack at Pearl Harbor in Hawaii. The aircraft carriers of the United States Navy were not in port. The United States declared war on Japan. Hitler declared war on the United States.

Lieutenant Clarence Dickinson was a regular naval officer. Two years before the attack on Pearl Harbor he had transferred from destroyers to flying duties. He joined Scouting Squadron Six in April 1941 after completing his training as an aviator, a naval-pilot. Scouting Squadron Six formed part of the carrier air group of the USS *Enterprise*. The USS *Enterprise* was returning to Pearl Harbor after completing a mission to fly fighters to the US Marine base on

Wake Island. Their return to port was delayed by bad weather. This had held up the *Enterprise*'s carrier group due to their inability to refuel their escorting destroyers. But for this delay they would have arrived in Pearl before the Japanese attack.

In the United States Navy, it was standard practice to fly the planes ashore and land them at the airfield nearest their home port. On 7 December Dickinson was flying an SBD Douglas Dauntless back to the airfield on Ford Island. The SBD Douglas Dauntless was a two-seat dive bomber. It was the type then used by the United States Navy for carrier based reconnaissance (scouting) and dive-bombing. Hence the initials SBD. Clarence Dickinson:

> Planes returning from our carriers have an invisible portal to Pearl Harbor. When we took off the task force was still 210 miles from the south-west tip of the Island of Oahu. This is called Barber's Point and it is about 10 miles west of Pearl Harbor. When I finally altered course to head for Pearl Harbor I cut no corners because I had to identify myself as a friendly plane by my manner of flying. Flying wing on me and slightly astern was the other plane of my section, piloted by young Ensign McCarthy. We came to 1,500 feet while we were well out at sea and then started towards land on a northerly course. This was the aerial equivalent of a password. Just to be sure we were on the prescribed course I had Miller take a bearing with his direction finder on a Honolulu radio station. This he did several times and the last time was around five minutes past eight when we were 20 or 25 miles off Barbers Point. It seems amazing now but they were still broadcasting Hawaiian music from Honolulu as I noticed a big smoke cloud near my goal.
>
> There were, as a matter of fact, two distinct columns of smoke swelling into cloud shapes. The smaller column was somewhat closer to the northerly course I was following into Barber's Point. Remember, we were flying towards the Island fast, probably three miles a minute and in the space of seconds insignificant things would expand and our viewpoint would change.
>
> Smoke clouds are familiar things above the Hawaiian landscape. It is customary to set fire to vast fields of sugar cane in the harvest seasons. Above the cane is a solid mass of straw-dry leaves. The leaves burn, leaving bare, rodlike stalks ready for the knives of the harvesters. So I paid small heed to the smoke. I observed four ships off the entrance to Pearl Harbor: one cruiser and three destroyers. Even from 20 miles away I could tell they were our

ships by their silhouettes and I no longer gave them any thought. Then ahead, well off to my right, I did see something unusual, a rain of big shell splashes in the water off the entrance to Pearl Harbor, and recklessly close to shore. It couldn't be target practice; it was Sunday. Those batteries would shoot fast enough at any unidentified submarine but the ragged pattern of the silvery splashes disposed of that half-formed notion. For about as long as it took me to express an opinion to my rear seat man I supposed some Coast Artillery batteries had gone stark mad and were shooting wildly. I remarked to Miller, through my microphone, "Just wait! Tomorrow the Army will certainly catch hell for that." Then, when we were scarcely three minutes from land, I noticed something that gave a significant and terrible pattern to everything I had been seeing. Abruptly it was revealed that the base of the biggest smoke cloud was in Pearl Harbor itself. I lifted my gaze to the mile-high top and up there I distinguished black balls of smoke, thousands of them, changing into ragged fleecy shapes. This was the explanation of the splashing in the water. Those thousands of smoke balls were anti-aircraft bursts. Pearl Harbor was under air attack.

Dickinson and McCarthy sighted a Japanese four-engine patrol bomber and chased it. Dickinson thought it was taking photographs. The Japanese bomber evaded them by flying into the smoke clouds above Pearl Harbor. Dickinson and McCarthy were attacked by Japanese fighters:

In a few minutes we were over Barber's Point at 4,000 feet flying wing to wing. A glance to the right at Ensign McCarthy's plane was almost like seeing Miller and myself in a mirror; in yellow rubber life-jackets, parachute harness, and almost faceless behind black goggles and radio gear fixed on white helmets. Mac's rear seat man, like mine, was on his seat in his cockpit, alert to swing his twin machine guns on the ring of steel track that encircled him. Thereafter everything happened in split-second sequences. Two fighters popped out of the smoke cloud in a dive and made a run on us.

Mac dipped his plane under me to get on my left side so as to give his gunner an easy shot at the oncoming enemy fighters. But the bullets they were shooting at me were passing beneath my plane and poor Mac went right into them. It was when I put my plane into a left-hand turn to give my gunner a better shot that I saw Mac's plane below, smoking; it was losing speed and altitude. In that brief glance I saw it burst into yellow flame. Then the enemy fighter who had done this zipped past me to the left and I rolled my plane to get a shot at him with my fixed guns. As he pulled up in front of me and to the left I saw painted on his fuselage a telltale insignia, the red disc on the white wing reminding me of a big fried egg with a red yolk. That was when, for the first time, I confirmed what my common sense had told me; these were Jap fighters, Zeros. I missed him, I'm afraid.

Those Zeros had so much more speed than I did that they could afford to go rapidly out of range before turning to swoop back after McCarthy. In that same second four or five more Zeros dove out of the smoke cloud and sat on my tail. Miller was firing away and was giving me constant reports on what was happening behind me. It was possibly half a minute after I had seen the Jap insigne for the first time that Miller in a calm voice said: "Mr Dickinson, I have been hit once, but I think I have got one of these sons of bitches."

I looked back and saw with immense satisfaction what Miller had shot. One of the Jap fighters was going down in flames. This was corroborated later by a Marine captain near Ewa Field. It was in that interval, watching the Jap go down, that below me I saw McCarthy's flaming plane again, making a slow turn to the right. Then I saw a parachute open just above the ground and I knew that either Mac or his rear-seat man had gotten out. The chances were it would be the pilot because it is pretty hard for the rear seat man to get himself and his parachute clear of the machine gun track that encircles him, unless he starts climbing out while he has plenty of altitude. It is definitely easier to get out from the front seat. Of course there was no time for a lingering look then but I found out later it was Mac's parachute that opened, that as he jumped he had been thrown against the tail surfaces of his plane, breaking his leg. He was in the hospital for months afterward.

I am trying to relate this part of my experience as it might be recorded in slow motion by a movie camera. Nevertheless it happened almost as swift as thought. In one glance I saw our Jap go down in flames, saw Ensign McCarthy's parachute open, and then again my eyes were wide for those Jap fighters behind us. There were four or five, the nearest less than 100 feet away. A Jap fighter has two machine guns, .26 calibre, right above the motor and at the front edge of each wing a twenty-millimetre automatic cannon. You get a queer feeling looking at those guns when they are shooting. They seem to be winking at you with jewelled eyes, and it's pretty to watch but you know each wink is an effort which may kill you very, very dead.

They were putting bullets into the tail of my plane, right and left, but even so I was causing them to miss a lot. The best defense in such a situation is to make a hard turn. For a few seconds a lot of their tracers were swishing harmlessly past my tail, so I know my turns were hard. They were having a field day, no formation whatever, all of them in a scramble to get me, each one wildly eager for the credit. Then one or more of them got on the target with cannon. They were using explosive and incendiary bullets that clattered on my metal wing like hail on a tin roof. I was fascinated by a line of big holes creeping across my wing closer and closer to us. I could hear those bullets explode and I saw the first tongue of yellow as that bullet fire went into the gasoline tank in my left wing. I know there was only a lapse of seconds after Miller told me he had been hit when he reported again and I think it was just as the wing caught fire.

"Are you all right, Miller?"

"Mr Dickinson, I've expended all six cans of ammunition." Then he screamed. It was as if he opened his lungs and just let go. I have never heard any comparable human sound. It was a yell of agony. I believe that Miller died right then. When I called again there was no reply. It seemed to me that we were in one hell of a fix. I had to go from a left-hand into a right-hand turn because the fast Japanese fighters had pulled up ahead of me on the left. I was still surprised because these amazing Zeros could turn inside a dive-bomber. I kicked my right rudder and tried to put my right wing down but the plane did not respond to the stick. The controls had been shot away. With the left wing down and the right rudder on and only 800 or 900 feet from the ground, I went into a spin.

I yelled at Miller but got no reply. Then I started to get out, and although it was the first time I had ever jumped I found myself behaving as if I were using a check-off list. I was responding to indoctrination and training. I remember that I started to unbutton my radio cord with my right hand and unbuckle my belt with my left. But I couldn't unfasten my radio cord with one hand, so, using both hands, I broke it. Then I unbuckled my belt, pulled my feet underneath me, put my hands on the sides of the cockpit, leaned out on the right-hand side and as I shoved clear the rush of wind was peeling my goggles off.

I had shoved out on the right side because that was the inside of the spin. I was facing the revolving ground because the plane was close to being vertical, spinning around its nose. It is funny, but it is easiest to get out of a plane's cockpit when it is in a spin, provided you go on the inside; then the tail is blown away from you. Right in that vortex I was thinking, "I hope I don't have to pay for those goggles; they weren't any good in the first place." They were an experimental kind we had been testing. I was in the air tumbling over and over grabbing and feeling for the ripcord's metal handle. Pulling it, I flung my arm wide.

There was a savage jerk. From where I dangled my eyes followed the shroud lines up to what I felt was the most beautiful sight I had ever seen, the stiff-bellied shape of my white silk parachute. I heard a tremendous thud; my plane had struck the ground nose first, and exploded. Then I struck the ground feet first, seat next and head last. My feet were in the air and the wind had been jarred out of me. Fortunately I had jumped so low that neither the Japs overhead nor the Marines defending Ewa Field had time to get a shot at me.

I had come to earth on the freshly graded dirt of a new road, a narrow aisle through the brush to the west of Ewa Field. I didn't realize it then but I had had the luck to hit the only road bisecting that brush area for five miles. In the backward somersault I made in landing, my head had struck a bush and afterward the doctor pulled out a thorn that he found imbedded in a sore spot on my head. That had been my only injury except for the slightest of nicks on the ankle bone right where machine gun bullets had made horizontal cuts in my sock.

Dickinson was given a lift by a civilian couple out for a picnic. They were strafed by a Japanese plane:

We saw other automobiles that had been strafed by Japs; bullet-torn cars that had either rolled or been pushed into ditches and fields along the way we came. Then the road brought us out on a low bluff at the back of Pearl Harbor and from the car we could see all of it, an expanse of land-locked salt water broken into bays channels by peninsulas, islands and marshes. From where we were it was about six miles in a beeline to the harbor, and probably an area six miles wide would fix the dimensions of the stage on which we were seeing most of the show. Terrible though it was, it was like a show; a Hollywood super-colossal spectacle directed by Cecil B. DeMille. Indeed, if they had let him in there with unlimited money he could have invented nothing so much like a nightmare in Technicolor.

We were just in time to see the big dive bombing attack that was going on about nine o'clock in the morning. It had been 55 minutes since Miller, at my back, using his direction-finder had taken that final bearing by tuning in on the Honolulu radio station. The leaning column of smoke I had seen then was now close enough for us to really see its source. I could see that the fire was erupting from battleship row and from its position I was pretty sure it was the *Arizona*, right there in the middle of Pearl Harbor.

There was so much smoke the sun was obscured. Consequently the lemon-yellow flashes of the guns seemed all the more vivid against the sombre background. Except for the fiercely burning *Arizona* there was gunfire from all the ships; from the battleships, cruisers, destroyers, submarines and little boats; and the whole system of shore defenses was wonderfully in action. From Fort Weaver, clear around the landscape, where this couple with me had planned to spend a lazy day, the army had angry guns shooting at the darkened sky. In a lot of places I could see army guns going. But where were all our planes, navy and army?

When I had been brought to the south-east segment of the harbor plain, to the entrance of Hickam Field, I left the blue sedan and that admirable couple. I hope I thanked them adequately in my hurry. All over Hickam Field there were fires, answers to the questions in my mind as to why there appeared to be only Jap planes overhead. Rows of planes were blazing on the field; also hangars, barracks and other buildings. Guns were rattling and pounding around the field. Men were fighting fires. But these were things I saw on the run.

I ran a quarter of a mile to the entrance gate of the navy reservation, a shore entrance to everything we mean when we speak of Pearl Harbor: a great stronghold of the fleet, unlike anything else in the world. It is a specialized domain, a place where the fleet sorts itself out, where battleships keep to themselves in an exclusive two-mile, double row in an estuary well removed from where the more ordinary cruisers ride at their moorings. Destroyers in finger piers here keep a little off from submarines. Each species of fighting ship has its own haven and its own beauty parlor somewhere in the harbor reaches. There are wonderful facilities for repairs to all manner of ships and gear. There are stupendous docks to accommodate ships greater than any yet built, docks streaked by shadows of gigantic cranes.

When Dickinson reached Ford Island, the sight he saw "got him by the throat":

Towering before our eyes, about 30 yards or so out in the channel was the slowly moving vast gray bulk of a battleship. Beyond her, farther up the channel, I could see the *Arizona*. She lay at the far end of battleship row, her broken twisted wreckage amidships belching the blackest smoke, which kept expanding into bigger shape. One fighting top and tripod mast canted out of this incredible disorder. But on all the ships in that double two-mile lane, right to the old battleship before our eyes, guns were blasting at the planes above the harbor. Yet, all the terrific power of the biggest guns on those battleships, of turreted main and secondary batteries, of 16-inch and lesser guns was futile now. They were made to fight things like themselves, not gadflies in the sky. However, there on Hospital Landing the ship in front of us filled our eyes. Anywhere you looked her guns were going; eight five-inch anti-aircraft guns; lesser stuff and machine guns. Along the deck I saw wounded and men with stretchers were rushing to carry them away.

The battleship was trying to get out to sea and a lot of Jap dive-bombers had been detailed to get her where she was, in the channel, where her 29,000 tons of steel hull, machinery and guns – if sunk – would choke Pearl Harbor; with the fleet inside. Where we stood, the old ship's great side seemed to loom higher than a ball park fence and her length was such (580 feet overall) you simply could not see what was happening from stem to stern with just one look. But everywhere I looked I saw organization, men under control.

There was a tremendous ear-splitting explosion. A bomb had struck on her deck close to one of her anti-aircraft guns. 1,300 men, I guess, were aboard the ship. Some were killed, more were hurt; but only one anti-aircraft gun had stopped firing. All the

> others were spewing lemon-colored fire in high angles. Machine guns were rattling on the decks and on high platforms. For the first time in my life I was seeing a naval vessel in action and I was just watching in that futility in which you find yourself caught in dreams. But this was real and what was striking at the old ship was a newer weapon, my kind of weapon – dive bombers.

Dickinson noted the Japanese dive-bombers' angle of dive was shallower than that of his fellow United States Navy pilots. While on the Hospital Landing, he found the answer to his own question. Can a man dodge a bomb dropped from an airplane? He found that he could. He managed to get a boat across to Ford Island:

> Ford Island is that part of Pearl Harbor devoted to navy flying. Familiar things there were so altered I was stricken with amazement. I couldn't believe what I was seeing. The hangars were afire and their glass wall fronts were black with holes. A bomb had hit one hangar. In front of the nearest was appalling wreckage of the patrol planes, of those big PBY's. Up on one corner of the hangar in front of which I stepped ashore there is a steel water tank painted orange and white in enormous checkerboard squares, so no flyer can fail to see it. On the roof of that tank is the control tower for the airfield. By radio from there you get your signals taking off or landing, and any careless pilot is sure to hear a scolding voice because the air station is organized like a ship and everything about it is kept shipshape. But now there was nothing shipshape anywhere in sight.
>
> As we stood there on the ramp where the Catalinas in their cradles go in and out of the water there was a great flaring across the channel, and while I stared, with a tremendous blast the destroyer *Shaw* blew up. Fire had reached her magazine and what I saw rise out of her was a big ball of red fire – just clear fire – fringed with black. With rocket speed it rose about 400 or 500 feet straight up and, spell-bound, I saw it burst open from the middle. I was thinking: "It is like a gigantic rotten orange exploding" when I was knocked flat by the explosion. Somewhat dazed, I was in the act of picking myself up and observing others who had been knocked down when someone yelled, "Here comes a Jap plane."
>
> We swarmed into the undamaged hangar, and as not one, but a number of planes roared across Ford Island with their guns going, I was behind a steel column in that hangar. In a few minutes I was

on my way again to the other side of the airfield where the carrier planes are based. The island is a little more than a mile long and in places about three quarters of a mile wide. Right down its middle is a runway. Sprinting on that stretch of concrete I saw that it was strewn with pieces of shrapnel, misshapen bullets from Jap machine guns and empty cartridges that had fallen from their planes. I could guess from the quantity of this stuff that they had done a lot of systematic strafing here to keep our flyers on the ground. However, they love to strafe. It seems to be characteristic of them, a thing that has been noticed in many of the battle areas. Repeatedly that morning I saw their dive-bombers pull out of dives with strafing an obvious part of their design. A rear-seat gunner could not strafe much after a dive unless the pilot deliberately prepared a chance for him. A Jap pilot would strafe with his fixed guns, then pull out extremely low after a dive and "kick" his tail around, banking to give the gunner easy shooting. With wings almost at right angles to the ground or a ship's deck the rear gunner would have his fun, spraying bullets down into helpless people.

Dickinson found some other pilots from his own squadron who had landed safely. The Japanese mounted their attack in two waves. In the lull between the first and second Japanese waves, defences were improvized:

All over the Island right after the first attack guns had been taken out of damaged planes and set up on tripods hastily improvised out of pipe. Sandbags had been piled around some of these. As a consequence a lot of Jap planes were shot down when they came back at nine o'clock. It must have been about half past nine when, with a whoop of delight and relief, I saw Earl Gallaher walk into the Command Center; he was reporting for instructions. Lieutenant Gallaher was the executive officer of Scouting Squadron Six. As flight officer I was third in the squadron; that is, next to Gallaher who was second in command. Although we had been together in our ready room (in the "island". just off the flight deck of the carrier) only a little more than three hours before, we shook hands in an effusive greeting and then just stood there, grinning at each other. There was no time to say much about what had happened; our immediate concern was getting ready for what would happen. We were

> expecting to be sent after those Jap carriers as soon as they were located. So we went back to see what planes we could find, and managed to get together nine planes that we could man. We had bombs put on them and kept the rear guns manned. There were still a lot of Jap planes overhead.

Dickinson and the other pilots from his squadron took off to see if they could find the Japanese aircraft carriers.

On their return they had to share their quarters with other survivors. The next day they flew back to their own aircraft carrier. Back aboard the aircraft carrier, his fellow sailors were seething with indignation and eager for a crack at the enemy "no matter what it cost".

The USS *Lexington* was the first US aircraft carrier to fight the Japanese aircraft carriers at the Battle of the Coral Sea.

The Battle of the Coral Sea 7–8 May 1942

> Scratch one flat-top!
> Commander Bob Dixon USN

The battle of the Coral Sea was the first naval battle fought between aircraft carriers. In fact it began a new era of naval fighting – one in which the opposing fleets were never in sight of each other. Stanley Johnston, sailed aboard the USS *Lexington* as a war correspondent. Johnston's articles appeared in the *Chicago Tribune*.

After Pearl Harbor, the Japanese captured Malaya, Singapore, Sumatra, Java and the Phillipines. By the early summer of 1942 they had reached the limit of their territorial conquests. They made a forward thrust towards Port Moresby, a strategic base in Papua, New Guinea. They intended to build up their air-power there until they had control of the air over Australia. The United States Navy was operating two aircraft carrier groups, nearby in the seas around the Solomon Islands, north-east of New Guinea and Australia. Each aircraft carrier group had a single large aircraft carrier. The two aircraft carrier groups combined at the end of February and made successful air strikes on Japanese forces at Lae and Salamua in Papua, New Guinea and, on 4 May, 1942, Tulagi, near Guadalcanal in the Solomons. The combined carrier group was under the

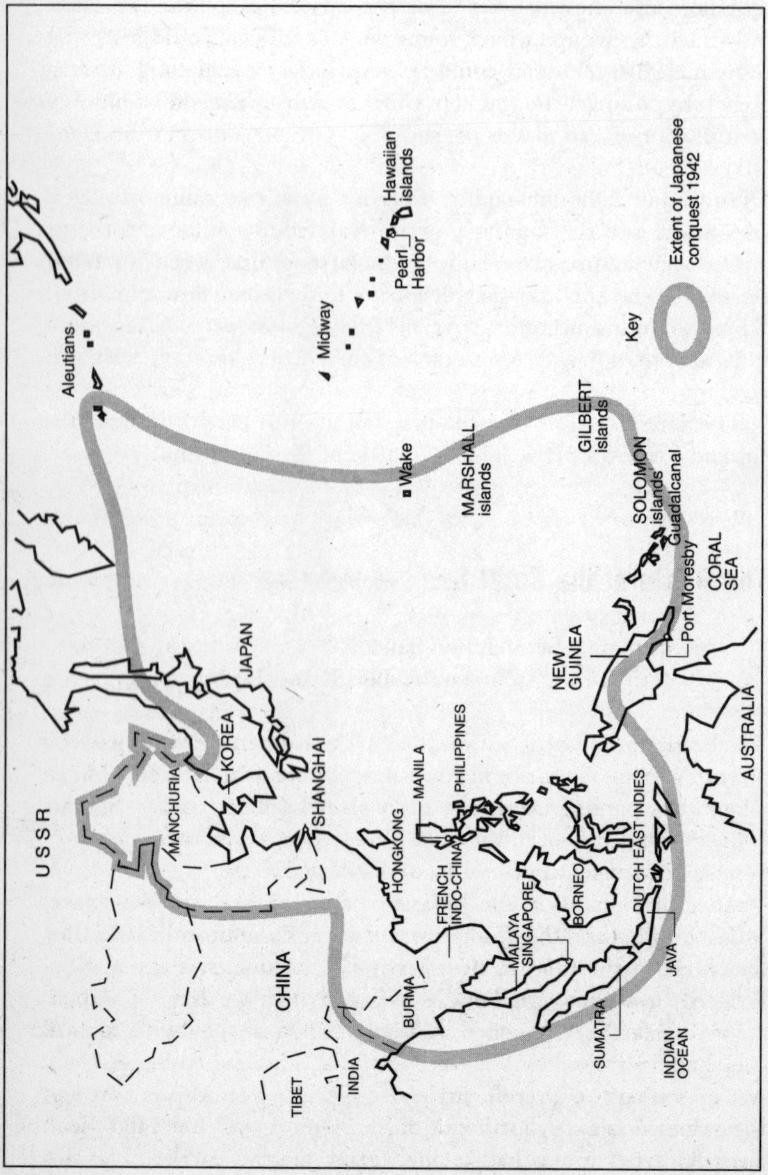

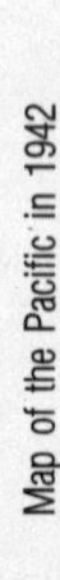

Map of the Pacific in 1942

command of Admiral Frank Fletcher. His flagship was the other carrier in the group, which Johnston, in his account, refers to as Carrier II. The *Lexington* could be named because she had already been sunk. Carrier II was the USS *Yorktown*. The other big US carriers, *Hornet* and *Enterprise*, had not yet returned from the Doolittle raid on Tokyo.

On 6 May 1942 the combined carrier group was sailing north in response to reports of a Japanese carrier group similar in force to their own. So strong were the opposing Japanese forces that the Americans regarded themselves as sailing in Japanese waters.

Stanley Johnston:

> The entire ship's company was awake on the morning of 7 May for a good hour before dawn. We had been steaming northward at a steady clip all night long, and every man knew that we were within range of an enemy force as powerful as our own. We had no way of knowing whether they had been aware of our presence the afternoon before – we rather suspected they had. And they, too, might well be planning to make the same sort of dawn assault we would attempt.
>
> All the plans, however, for getting the dive-bomber and torpedo bomber squadrons off early fell through. Our scouts, off and ranging the surrounding sea in the half-light before sun-up could find no trace of the Japs. Their precision quartering of the sea still was bringing no results at 7 a.m.; and they were beginning to get out toward the limit of their ranges – which also was toward the maximum limit of our squadrons' fighting distances.
>
> "The Japs couldn't have seen us and run away," one officer told me. "We're in their waters, and they'll want to press the attack first if they can. They probably missed us entirely and during the night turned aside to go in some direction that has taken them outside our zone of search."
>
> His estimate, I thought, was probably correct – but it turned out that we were both wrong.

A Japanese long-range reconnaissance aircraft was shot down near the fleet:

> About 8 o'clock a long-range scout from Carrier II called his vessel:
>
> "Jap fleet-one carrier, three heavy cruisers, six destroyers – 180

miles, course 120, speed 20 knots. West-north-west." Quick glances at our charts showed us the enemy was about 50 miles north of Misima. We were standing a little south of the island of Rossel. The scout's cryptic language indicated that the Japs were 180 miles from us, and that they then were steering a course of 120 degrees at a 20-knot speed. From the scout's report it was evident that the Jap fleet had split up. On the previous evening the *Lexington's* scouts had seen a flotilla of two carriers, five cruisers and a dozen destroyers. Possibly this force split during the night into two formations with one carrier to each group.

. . . our pilots were all set for take-off at the time the Jap fleet's location was pin-pricked on our charts. A few minutes were required for our navigators to plot the courses our squadrons should fly to intercept the Japanese, and to chalk this and some last-minute weather information on the ready-room blackboard.

Getting all this information to the pilots and stowing them into their aircraft required only 20 minutes. And not more than 30 had elapsed by the time the last of the air-striking group was speeding on its way. In all, 76 aeroplanes were sent off. They consisted of 24 torpedo planes and 36 scouts and dive-bombers, most of which were carrying a 1,000-pound bomb load. A few of the scouts carried one 500-pounder and two 100-pounders. Finally, there was a unit of 16 fighter planes to escort the others and to deal with the Japanese fighter-plane defences.

Hardly had our attack squadrons cleared the deck when the scouts reappeared with landing gear and hook down. This was the unspoken signal that they wanted to come aboard. The first crew in reported that they had been in combat over the Japanese formation. Biplane float fighters had intercepted them and they were forced to shoot their way out. None of the scouts was lost, and they managed to shoot down two of these interfering Japs. There was no sign, they said, of any of the Zero monoplane fighters from the Japanese carriers.

The bombing, torpedo-plane and fighter formations meanwhile were climbing up to cruising altitude. Flying through the overcast they level off in clear air. In a few minutes they passed the edge of the cloud layer, as Lieutenant Raring had predicted they would, and from there on the trip was made in cloudless skies with a visibility as wide as 60 miles.

Lieut.-Commander Weldon Hamilton, the dive-bomber skipper, was at the front of his formation which had climbed up to

15,000 feet and was slightly ahead and above Dixon's scout-bombers, who were at 12,000. Underneath these two groups were Brett's torpedo planes. The fighters had split up, four pairs in the high-level group flying slightly above and behind Hamilton, and the other four idling along with the torpedo squadron.

"Our course led us along the island of Tagula for 60 miles," Hamilton later told me. "From our height in the clear air this island with its coral reefs, its tiny aits (islets), with the breakers combing over them like whipped cream, was a sight to behold. The blue of the sea, the green of the island, and the cream and silver of the surf and sand were truly magnificent.

"After we had passed Tagala we went northward to bring up past the eastern tip of Misima. The flight up to that point had been uneventful, but now we were within 30 miles of where the enemy should be. A few minutes later we were over the area where we expected to find them, so I began to search the horizon with my powerful binoculars.

"Visibility was remarkable, the sky cloudless, and eventually I found, almost 40 miles to the eastward, at right-angles to our course, a number of thin white hairs on the blue sea. A careful look at these showed them to be the wakes of the Japanese fleet we were seeking.

"I radioed to the other squadron commanders, and we all altered course to fly toward them."

"Little was said over the air," Hamilton told me. "When I first sighted the enemy I radioed: "Bob from Ham, Bob from Ham (he was calling Commander Bob Dixon, who was leading the scout-bombers), enemy ships sighted 20 miles north of our present position."

"I underestimated the actual distance. At that time I could only see those white wakes in the light blue distance. Bob sent a message to Brett (Lieut-Commander Jimmy Brett, torpedo-squadron skipper): "Did you get that, Jimmy?" When Jimmy said yes, but he couldn't see "em, Bob said: "I'll coach you in, boy." He did that as soon as he was able to sight the enemy. Remember, Bob was somewhat lower than I was and had no binoculars.

"I came out of the sun and almost exactly downwind, and could only see those white wakes in the light blue distance. When I was finally able to distinguish the ships I recognized the carrier from the reflection of the sun on its light-coloured flight-deck. I then radioed: "I see one flat-top rotter." Then Bob saw it. Little else was said that I remember until after the attack. There was some fighter talking about Japanese seaplane fighters, which I did not pay much attention to.

"I came out of the sun and almost exactly downwind, and cornmenced my attack immediately after Bob Dixon's squadron was finished. The Japanese had made a turn to the left as Dixon's crew attacked. They made a second turn while I was waiting for our torpedo planes to take station for their co-ordinated attack with us. I went down at the start of the third turn the carrier made. The torpedo squadron attacked at the same time.

"We began from 16,500 feet and pushed over in our dive at 12,000. The Jap was exactly downwind as I nosed down, simplifying my problem tremendously. My bomb, which was the first 1,000-pounder to hit, struck in the middle of the flight-deck's width, just abaft amidships. As I looked back the entire after-portion of the flight-deck was ablaze and pouring forth heavy black smoke. Pulling up, I heard Bob's voice (Dixon's on the radio): "Mighty fine, mighty fine."

"Watching the rest of my squadron come down, I observed some of the boys missing the carrier with their bombs. I called them on the radio, saying: 'Use the wind, boys, use the wind' because their bombs were hitting downwind of the ship.

"My rear gunner told me later that a Jap fighter followed me in my dive and made three attacks on my plane after the pull-out. But evidently his guns had jammed, as my gunner never saw him fire. At that time I was a sitter, as I did not know he was there, and was busy watching the Japanese carrier exploding. My radioman believes he disabled the Jap, but did not actually see him crash.

"During their dives, rear gunners in my squadron definitely got two Jap fighters which attacked them.

"The assault on this Jap carrier should go down in naval history as a most successful co-ordinated dive-bombing – torpedo attack. The two co-ordinating squadrons, VB-2 and VT-2, did not lose a single plane."

The arrival of the squadrons over the Japs was also recounted by Lieut.-Commander Bob Dixon, who that day was leading his scouts as dive-bombers. (These were the planes with single 500- and two 100-pound bombs.)

"We came over at 12,000 feet. Enemy fighter patrols were in the air, but they barely reached us, as we eased off into our almost vertical dives.

"To be really effective against dive-bombers fighter planes have to reach them before they get to the turn-over point. Ordinarily fighters can't stay with us in the dive because with our airbrakes we keep our speed at about 250 miles an hour. The streamlined fighters with noses down go right on past us and pick up speed toward 400 miles an hour.

"But these Japs wouldn't give up. They were Zeros, and that means they were very clean jobs. But the pilots put their flaps down, dropped their landing gear, and did everything they could to keep their speed low. Nevertheless, they would go on past us. But that didn't keep them out, either. They would pull up, do a zooming chandelle, and come right back in to fire at the next planes diving past. The commander added that the result was a terrific free-for-all. The Zeros stayed with us right down to the water.

"Naturally, we went for the carrier first. It was obvious we had caught them by surprise. In the dive I could see a number of planes on deck, and one was coming up from the interior hangar deck in the elevator.

"When we first saw the Japs," Dixon continued, "the carrier was downwind. It immediately made a sharp turn to the port trying to get back into the wind to launch its planes. I could see it all clearly as I peered through my telescopic sight, lining myself up for the bomb release."

A dozen or more pilots told of that "fighting dive" the scouts made that day. Imagine a huge cascade 15,000 feet in height, with every few seconds a mighty salmon flashing down its course! Our dive-bombing pilots were following just such a track, almost like salmon flashing over an immense waterfall. They were changing formation at the top to echelon – which means they were stringing out one behind the other. They would then push off, each man following his leader or taking his own special target during the approximate 40-second interval between the commencement of the descent and the recovery after dropping their bombs 1,000 feet above the water.

The Japanese fighters, to give them their due, were tenaciously battling, even during the 40-second dives, to distract the pilots throughout this aiming period. Often there would be a chain of diving planes with a scout bomber at the bottom, a Zero just above him, a second scout bomber on the Zero's tail, with a second Zero above the second scout. Above that there would be other similarly mingled chains of Jap fighters and our scouts.

The Japanese ships around the carrier had thrown up a heavy curtain of bursting shells from their anti-aircraft guns. All the planes, scouts, Zeros, and our heavy dive-bombers, which by now were coming down from about 16,000 feet, went right through the shell curtain, in most cases without ever knowing it. Our pilots' eyes were glued to their sights, and our rear gunners in both the scouts and heavy dive-bombers were firing at the Zeros. The Japs probably were equally intent, for they were using their 20-mm cannon and machine-guns every time they were lined up, even momentarily, on one of our planes.

Some of our fighters, sitting up at 16,000 feet, where they were protecting the last of the dive-bombers at their most vulnerable point (a few seconds before they turn over in their dive), reported that Commander Dixon's dive was perfectly made. They saw his 500-pound bomb – the first one dropped – hit the Jap carrier amidships, wrecking the flight-deck and preventing the launching of any of the planes still aboard.

Right behind Dixon followed Ensign P. F. Neely, whose 500-pounder hit near the carrier's port side. It was a near miss, but the blast from this bomb tossed two burning planes from the carrier's decks into the sea.

The third bomber, flown by Ensign Smith, scored a direct bit on the carrier's starboard anti-aircraft battery. The explosion of this bomb silenced this group of guns and blew three more planes over board. The fourth bomber, flown by Ensign J. A. Leppla, was one of those attacked by the Zeros almost as soon as his dive steepened to the near vertical. His rear gunner, John Liska, facing backwards and firing his twin .30-calibre machine-guns, fought off this particularly persistent attack. In a duel with two of the Zeros that quickly overhauled the scout and closed to point-blank range, firing their cannon, Liska got hits that caused flames to burst from their fuel tanks. Both these Zeros crashed into the sea.

Ensign Leppla was busy during his dive, too. He saw a Zero go on past him and begin shooting at Smith's plane. Easing out of his dive slightly, Leppla got the Zero into his sights and shot that one down also.

The carrier was well into its turn by that time and, besides, Leppla had been distracted. The best he could do with his 500-pounder was to lay it close beside the carrier in a near miss. This, however, didn't satisfy him. He zoomed away, climbed back to

4,090 feet, and dive bombed one of the Japanese cruiser escorts with both his 100-pounders. One of these hit the cruiser on the stern, which invariably is the target at which dive-bombers aim their bombs.

But let us return to this dive which was completed by the entire scout squadron in less time than it takes you to read these few paragraphs.

Ensign O. J. Schultz, fifth in line in that attack, secured a hit on the carrier with his bomb, but was attacked by four Zero fighters as he recovered from his dive. His rear gunner, whose name I never learned, but who was, you may be sure, as much a hero as any of the pilots, broke up the attack by shooting one down and making it so hot for the others that they turned away. When that plane got back to the carrier 29 bullet-holes were counted in it, but neither pilot nor gunner were wounded.

The scouts' dives had taken away the enemy's fighter protection aloft, and the heavier dive-bombers with 1,000-pounders in their belly rack had little opposition as they delivered their attacks. But the two or three minutes during which the scouts were attacking had enabled the Jap fleet to spread out so that each vessel would have plenty of water in which to manoeuvre and to get their heaviest anti-aircraft guns into action.

Co-ordinated with the commencement of the heavy dive-bomber assault was Lieut-Commander Jimmy Brett's torpedo-squadron attack. The Zeros that had survived the battle with the scouts during the dive now stayed down on the sea and flew out to intercept the torpedo planes, now making their final approaches.

"Hey, fighters, come and get these Zeros off me," Brett radioed to our Grumman pilots, as the first of the Japs began playing leapfrog across the torpedo planes, now fanned out almost in a squadron-front formation.

Lieutenant Baker and his wingman, whose contribution to the battle up to that point had been the downing of a Jap seaplane fighter, answered Brett's call. In two runs they shot down two Zeros and held off the rest to free the torpedo formation.

The first of the heavy dive-bombers, which we left a moment ago just starting their dives, was piloted by Lieut-Commander Hamilton. "Ham" had been over-carried by the wind in his dive at a Jap cruiser at Salamaua, and had vowed before he started his fight that morning of the 7th that he would get a bull's-eye.

"My ambition in life is to put my big bomb clean through the deck and into the vitals of the biggest Japanese carrier I can find," Ham had been telling us all in the wardroom mess.

"Hamilton did just what he wanted," Paul Ramsey later said. "I watched his dive, and saw that he plonked his bomb into the exact centre of the flight-deck, just slightly abaft of midships. There was a tremendous explosion; flames seemed to leap 400 feet into the air."

Another fighter pilot, Lieut-Commander Flatley, skipper of Carrier II's fighters, told me later:

"I was sitting upstairs at 5,000 feet watching them come down. The heavy bombs began exploding at three- and four-second intervals. Flames, and sea-water were being thrown hundreds of feet high from each explosion. The 1,000-pound bombs seemed to be pattering down like rain, and those big babies do four times as much damage as the 500-pounders.

"The sight of those heavy bombs smashing that carrier was so awful it gave me a sick feeling. Every second bomb was landing and exploding aboard the ship. Those powerful blasts were literally tearing the big ship apart. She burst into flames from bow to stem. I don't see how anybody aboard that ship could have survived."

While this split-second action was going on, Commander Brett – now free of the fighters – was dropping his own "fish". He is a wily one. He used the smoke pouring out of the wounded Jap to screen his squadron's approach. They sneaked in from downwind under the smoke. When so close they couldn't miss they made an "S" turn so that their torpedoes finally dropped full into the starboard side of their victim. The Navy's remarkable photographs of this action show exactly how this was done, and in many of these pictures Brett's planes can be seen following his trail.

One after another these deadly fish zipped in and blasted against the carrier's hull. 12 actual torpedo hits were scored, literally tearing the whole side out of the vessel. Almost at the same time 16 bombs of the 1,000-pound size, plus three 500-pounders, were slamming into her from above. The result was that this vessel disappeared in a huge cloud of smoke and steam almost as if a giant heel had crunched her beneath the surface.

Back on the *Lexington* all of us were anxious to know the results of the attack. We were confident the squadrons would do a good job, but this was, after all, the first such attack ever made on a carrier by American crews. In the radio-room we could hear some of the pilots talking, but static was bad and much of it was inaudible. By watching the clock we knew they must have gone into action, and our natural anxiety was heightened by this knowledge.

All the tension on the carrier exploded the moment we heard Commander Dixon's voice come in strong and clear:

"Scratch one flat-top! Dixon to carrier. Scratch one flat-top!"

It meant that the Navy could scratch one more Japanese flat-top (carrier) off the lists of the enemy's fleet. In other words, the boys had done the job and the carrier was sunk – news which brought forth resounding cheers and applause throughout the ship from stem to stern and keel to truck.

The Japanese aircraft carrier was the light carrier *Shoho*. It was destroyed as a result of the attack. Stanley Johnston:

Commander Hamilton got back to the carrier with his engine vibrating severely and with bullet holes in his propeller-drilled by bullets from his own guns. He told the story this way:

"As I came through the anti-aircraft pattern and released my bomb, inadvertently I squeezed the 'Mickey Mouse' (the gun- and bomb-release trigger) a little too hard, and my guns fired. Of course, at the time I didn't know this, but the plane began to vibrate violently, and I assumed I had been hit by Jap fire. I throttled back as I pulled out, and found I could amble along home at reduced speed. I took a look to see where I'd been hit as soon as I landed. Only then did I find that the synchronization gear on one gun had slipped and the prop was perforated by my own slugs."

As the planes started to return we could see by the way some of them were flying that they had been damaged. And as they came into the landing circle I saw tears in their metal skins that later proved to be cannon-shot holes in wings and tail fins on several of the ships. One came in asking to land out of his turn, and the ship's physician, always on duty on the flight deck, was waved up to the plane. And as this plane was taxied into parking position the doctor was standing on the wing cutting away the shirt of the rear gunner, who had been drilled through his upper left lung. They put him into the special Navy wire stretcher and carried him below – the Lex's first man wounded in action.

Practically everyone else in the squadrons had routine flights back to the carrier except Ensign Leppla and his gunner, D. K. Liska.

These two, who already had accounted for three Zeros in this battle – and remember, they were flying in a comparatively slow scout bomber, which should have been cold meat to any fighter – had flown about half the 180 miles of the homeward trek when they spotted a Jap seaplane fighter. It was then several miles off their course, and interfering with no one.

But to these two boys a Jap is a Jap wherever he is. Leppla turned after the seaplane and rapidly overhauled it. The Jap was waiting for them, and he, too, was a two-seater. The result was a short but violent air duel that ended when the Japanese plane crashed into the sea. It gave Leppla and Liska a day's total of four.

When their plane finally alighted on the Lex all of us went out and walked around it, examining it closely. Parts of it looked like my wife's colander. There were bullet holes in the wings, fuselage, the tail, the ailerons. It must have whistled a cheerful tune as the wind whipped through these holes while flying. The other pilots wondered how and why it answered to the controls. Its return at all is a testimonial to the builders of the ship and engine.

When I looked into the cockpit I found that other shots had gone through the plexiglass cockpit covers, missed the pilot and gunner by inches, and then completely smashed some of the instrument board. One bullet tore the heel off the pilot's right shoe, and another, after coming through the plane and "buzzing round the cockpit like a bee", to quote Leppla, went through the leg of his flying suit and was found stuck in the knee of his trousers.

Our pilots were home in time for lunch, which turned into a celebration. There was a good deal of satisfaction over many things, first the destruction of the enemy carrier and all the aircraft aboard her at the time; the sinking of a heavy cruiser and the shooting out of the air of 17 aircraft. All of this had been accomplished for the loss of three SBDs – the Douglas scout-bombers; the crew of one – Quigley and his gunner – being saved.

Another important point for all the airmen was the fact that they had encountered the vaunted Zero and found that even scout-bombers could handle it. The fighters got little chance at the Zeros, which went down with the dive-bombers and stayed down to hit at the torpedo planes. Only two Zeros, as a matter of fact, were credited to the fighters, the rest going to dive-bombers, torpedo planes and scouts.

The weather deteriorated rapidly as we turned southward that afternoon. We got into rain squalls, low scud, and some fog. Visibility was at times zero, and at others lifted to only several miles – tricky flying weather in which carrier pilots work hard and run the risk of losing their carrier.

All of us felt that with daylight would come the world's first battle between two strong aircraft carrier forces, each being aware of the other's presence, so the surprise element was out. And all of us felt that history was in the making as our vessels groped through the inky night.

We were anticipating an air assault on the Lex and Carrier II almost as soon as it was light, so there was real point to the preparations we then made.

I wandered around the *Lexington*'s quarters for a time, being too uncomfortably hot to sleep. I finally fell asleep at 4 a.m. So exhausted was I that when the pre-dawn battle stations call came at 5.30 I just rolled over and dug into the pillow again. But the "clang, clang, clang" of the scouts going off finally roused me. And suddenly I was wide awake. I had just remembered there was a very good reason for getting up this morning – there were Japs round and about us and a battle in the offing.

It turned out that the *Lexington* remained in clear weather throughout the hours of daylight. It was the Japanese who had the position of advantage, for their fleet was in ideal carrier weather – it was running from one patch of low scud and rain to another all day long. It had these natural curtains to hide in and its ships split up most skilfully to take all the benefits the weather afforded.

There had been every likelihood that the two fleets would be close together at dawn. It could have been possible that they might be almost within sight of us, and we of them. We of the Lex stood to general quarters in all departments, ready to bounce into action the minute our scouts took the air just before daylight. Maybe they would find the enemy in their first 15 minutes of flying. If that was the case the battle would go to the force that struck the earliest blow. We intended to be that force.

15 minutes, 30 minutes, then an hour went by and none of the scouts reported a thing. They had flown out from the ship in all directions like spokes of a wheel radiating from the hub. After that first hour we relaxed somewhat on the ship and got a good breakfast under our collective belts.

It was not until 8.10 that Ensign Smith, one of the scouts who had gone out due north-east, radioed a contact report. He had completed the full limit of 225 mile outbound course, had flown his 900 cross leg and 25 miles of his return course, when he sighted the enemy.

"Two carriers, four heavy cruisers, many destroyers, steering 120 degrees, 20 knots. Their position 75 miles, roughly north-east," he reported.

The US Carrier group finally sent off their attacking force about 9.30 a.m. In total there were 73 aircraft – 21 torpedo planes, 37 dive-bombers and 15 fighters. Commander Dixon himself stayed over the Japanese fleet to guide the attacking force. The US fleet was in condition Zed, in anticipation of being itself attacked. Johnston:

After we fired our air "shot" at the Japs at 9.30 that morning I wandered up on the signal bridge and stood around. Our flotilla was in tight formation, charging north-east at 20 knots on the trail of our planes. There were several reasons for this, the principal one being that of reducing the length of their flight back to the carrier. In going out more than 200 miles to hit the Japanese, they were operating at the extreme limit of their range and needed any help we could give to shorten that return trip.

Captain Sherman, who was living on the bridge in his emergency cabin these days, told me we had steam raised so that our speed could be stepped up to 30 knots at short order, should this be deemed necessary. We sat in his quarters speculating on what the morning might hold for us.

"There's a possibility," he said, "that the striking forces from both sides (ours and the Japanese) are right now in the air flying to the attack, and that both will get through.

"I feel that at the present time an air attack group cannot be stopped. It's likely that the position will be similar to that of two boxers, both swinging a knock-out punch at the same time and both connecting."

Later in the day I was to think of these words and the accuracy with which they summed up the situation. The captain knew his stuff, and very evidently had weighed all the chances. He was fully aware of the facets in this sea-air war that is so new to the rest of the world, but not to these two opponents.

The bridge of an aircraft carrier is the place from which to see the action, because everything of importance occurs either in the air around the ship or on the long, narrow flight deck that stretches away toward the bow and the stern. The signal bridge on the Lex was a six-foot-wide "open verandah" around the island on the starboard side. It was 25 feet above the flight deck, which itself rose 50 feet above the sea. Ten or 12 feet above the signal bridge was a smaller open verandah affording the admiral and his staff a post of observation. Finally, above that was a tiny little "crow's nest" known as the "sky forward" lookout.

The Island was a light, unarmoured structure. From the deck, about 30 feet behind the Island, arose the vast smoke funnel, which consolidated within its steel structure the tubes carrying smoke and fumes from the ship's 16 huge boilers, from her ventilating system and from her galleys. The funnel was carried to 60 feet above the flight deck and around its upper rim was an iron catwalk with a platform at either end. The after platform was a lookout position known as "sky aft". Round the catwalk were searchlights, signal lights, camera mounts for the ship's photographers, and other posts.

The signal bridge is the captain's country. Connected to it from every compartment in the ship are telephone lines and voice tubes. It is the heart and brain of the ship. Everything that happens on the vessel is reported directly to the captain. From inside the ship the reports come by telephone. From outside, where lookouts and signalmen always are on duty, they come in the form of notes written on signal pads. The bridge itself extends clear around the island.

The enclosed portion to the bow is the wheelhouse, where the helms men and officer of the watch are for ever on duty. With them are messengers.

The captain's emergency cabin is just behind the wheelhouse. And behind that again is the chartroom – the office of the ship's navigating officer.

This morning the bridge was "stripped" for action. It meant that the heavy plate-glass windows around the wheelhouse had been unlatched and slid down into the sills, leaving it open all round.

Today the ship's navigating officer, Commander James R. Dudley, was on duty in the wheelhouse, where he was noting every change of course. With him were Commander Seligman, the ship's executive officer, and the communications officer, Commander Winthrop Terry. Outside on the bridge was the ship's air officer, Commander Herbert ("Ducky") Duckworth and Lieut-Commander Edward H. Eldredge, ship's air staff. Marines, orderlies and signalmen made the bridge a crowded place.

In the chartroom an Ensign and the Chief Quartermaster logged in the permanent "big book" the speed and direction of the ship with every change, plus the time these changes were made.

A stranger looking on could not have identified the officers from the enlisted men. Everyone habitually there was deeply tanned. And everyone, from the admiral down to the newest orderly, that morning wore working clothes. For Admiral Fitch and Captain Sherman this consisted of khaki, Navy issue canvas windbreakers with a zipper front over a khaki shirt, cotton drill trousers of khaki, and battle bonnets, the new round-head type steel helmets.

So was everyone else on the bridge wearing helmets and either blue denim coveralls or khaki shirt and pants. The helmets are particularly good in the tropics because they have a papier-maché liner which can be worn as a sun helmet when there is no danger of flying fragments. But today, by order, everyone on the flight deck or above wore a helmet. And everyone had to keep nearby his post the Navy issue life-jacket. Most of these are kapok vests. The flyers, and anyone with wings – which included the captain, Seligman and, of course, everyone connected with flying operations – had the new rubberized "Mae Wests" which can be inflated either with little compressed gas bottles – the kind used in a soda siphon – or blown up by lung power. These are worn deflated until needed.

In addition to zigzagging the *Lexington* was frequently moving out of the centre of the fleet formation when she turned into the wind – which happened to be about north-north-west – to launch or take aboard aircraft of her defence screen. This meant a left turn for the big ship every time, and frequently carried her outside of the cruiser and destroyer screen on our port side. These ships were holding their fleet position and disregarding the *Lexington*'s manoeuvres.

Captain Sherman had at his command, for the defence of his vessel, eight fighters and eight scouts. A similar force had been retained by Carrier II, and, in addition to the primary job of guarding the carriers (inevitably the most important targets), these planes also were guarding to some extent the escort vessels in the flotilla.

This day Captain Sherman cut his fighter and scout groups in half. Four fighters and four scouts were constantly aloft while their counterparts were refuelling on deck, rotating at brief intervals so all could fight at any time with maximum loads of fuel and ammunition. The fighters with their supercharged engines were given the high-level watches whence enemy dive-bombers probably would appear, and the scouts were ordered to watch for low-level torpedo planes.

The first alarm on the Lex came at 10 o'clock, when twelve "ghosts" – unidentified planes – were reported approaching from ahead. These never did come into sight, and we never knew who or what they might have been. During the next half hour, after we were certain they were not coming our way, I dropped below for a cup of coffee. I found the ship absolutely emptied of her crew. Battle stations take every man, right down to the mess boys, who pass ammunition, to some fighting post. And I had a quiet few minutes in the senior wardroom.

I returned to the bridge in time to hear the second alarm, which came in at 10.50 a.m. One of the scouts called: "Katie to carrier. Big force of enemy aircraft coming in from right ahead. They are 60 miles away."

The message went out over the ship's loud-speaker system and every man aboard instantly realized we were in for a knock-down, drag-out battle with the Japanese air squadrons. I remembered that Captain Sherman, while we were talking in his cabin, had told me he believed the Japs would arrive, if at all, about 11 o'clock. Just one more point on which the skipper was dead right.

The Lex, following the Captain's orders, began a port turn into wind so that all the aeroplanes then in reserve on the decks could get off. While we were launching the last of our scouts and fighters I looked over at Carrier II, two miles away on our starboard beam, where the same scene was being enacted. Both ships were getting every plane and gun into the air, for both captains realized that the only real defence against an aeroplane is another aeroplane.

I could feel the change in vibration as the Lex's big propeller speeded up to give us the last knot. This greater speed is needed for swift manoeuvring, which is really a ship's best defence. And as I looked down from the bridge into the nests of light automatic cannon on the flight deck, I saw the gun teams standing by their pieces holding extra shell clips and eagerly looking ahead and upward in the direction from which the enemy was expected.

About this time a great deal began to happen. Thinking back later I realize a thousand and one impressions were registering that I wasn't even conscious of at the time. Chiefly I was busy for the next few minutes getting my microphone and telephone circuits straightened out. With lightning suddenness the fleet was in the direst danger. One minute we had been shouldering our way through the Coral Sea billows in what might have been a pleasure cruise, the next we were prepared to fight for our lives. Such is the speed of sea-air war in this year of our Lord. Perhaps the only way to give an approximately true picture of the speed of events in the next crowded minutes is to take the time-table of the action as I jotted it into my little pocket book as the battle thundered all around. From these jottings, some hours later I reconstructed everything I had seen and heard, and it is some of this expanded material that the reader will get here.

While we were commencing our starboard turn back into the fleet formation, after having launched our last aeroplane, we heard the voice of Paul Ramsey coming in over the loud-speakers:

"Agnes to carrier. Enemy planes, 17,000 feet, four groups of nine each. Two groups dive-bombers, each with mixed group of Messerschmitt 109s and Zero fighters in escort.

"I'm at 14,000, twelve miles north-east of you, climbing hard. They are going awfully fast. Doubt if I can intercept."

Almost simultaneously we had a call from a scout, off in the same direction.

"Nora to carrier. Enemy torpedo planes, Nakajima 975, spilling out of a cloud eight miles out. They are at 6,000 feet in a steep glide. We're intercepting now."

Red Gill, in the fighter control room, was calling all our dispersed defence planes, and directed them to concentrate against these oncoming enemies. The loud-speaker was full of orders, calls and notations as the Japs were sighted by our planes and coming closer by the minute.

I can fix the action of the next few minutes accurately from my own and the *Lexington*'s official notes:

11.06 a.m. – A huge column of smoke is seen falling into the sea far out on our port beam. Almost instantly we are told a scout has shot down another of those ubiquitous Kawanishi four-motor snoopers. The crew of this big plane evidently has been directing the Jap dive- and torpedo-bombers toward us. This is the third Kawanishi we downed in four days, every one of them within sight of the fleet. Each one made a beautiful bonfire in the sky and left a heavy smoke trail.

11.15 a.m. – the Lex, still increasing her speed gradually, is not quite back within the fleet formation. There is only one cruiser on our port side, slightly off our quarter. The destroyers and other cruisers that should be covering that side are astern, ahead, or to starboard of us. Might be better if they were keeping station on us rather than on each other.

11.16 a.m. – I am watching that cruiser and suddenly see flaming and belching smoke as they fire at something I can't see.

Not until seconds later does the thunder-clap of the first shots, and then the steady roll of firing, as the cruiser's smaller weapons join in and keep pumping shells, reach me. I see winks of flame all over that cruiser from those guns.

11.16 and a half a.m. – "Here they come," sing the look-outs. "Enemy torpedo planes off the port beam." The skipper with a calm glance in that direction speaks quietly to the helmsman: "Hard a starboard." The manoeuvre is intended to swing the Lex so that she will present only her comparatively narrow stern and beam to the torpedo craft. But in comparison to the speed of those diving silver midges I can now discern low behind the cruiser, the gallant old Lex seems to be standing still. Even as the captain speaks they are getting larger, and fanning out to cover a wide front as they approach. They are coming in at a scorching pace – I judge that with their dive and wide-open throttles they probably are doing almost 300 miles an hour.

As yet the *Lexington*'s guns are silent. Now the gunners are beginning to distinguish the nine planes of this first wave. Two of them are following a course that will bring them right across that blessed cruiser out there, 2,000 yards off our port quarter. These two planes are so low that they have to zoom slightly to pass over her. As they do one disintegrates in the air, simply disappears as if snatched away by some giant magician. Evidently it has been struck by one of the cruiser's heavier shells, which also exploded the torpedo. The flash of this Jap blowing up is a beautiful sight: "Pretty shooting, boys. That's one that won't make it."

About this time the *Lexington*'s own batteries of more than 100 guns break into flame. There is the sharp, "Wham, wham, wham, wham, wham" of the 5-inchers, the staccato bark of the 1.1-inchers

(37-mm), and the rushing yammer of the 20-mm batteries. A hellish chorus, uneven, jerky, but so forceful that it leaves us, there on the bridge; gasping in the partial vacuums created by the blasts. Out on the open bridge we are above the gun muzzles, and with the first firing our nostrils are stung by the reeking cordite of the driving charges. Up from the port side of the ship goes a curtain of tracer, winking red and white in the brilliant sunlight. Our light-automatics are firing.

11.17 a.m. – The *Lexington* is still swinging. As her slender stern comes round more and more toward them, the Japs change slightly, parallel us, and when abreast turn once more toward our port beam. They are riding right in on a hail of the smaller weapons' tracer, but they don't seem to falter once. Not even the destruction of their leading plane by our cruiser appears to faze them.

By now they are in close to us. The first couple is not more 800 yards off and the last within about a 1,000 yards. We can see the black blobs of the torpedoes fall away from the and their splash as they hit the water, and their trailing foam as their own internal machinery begins to drive their twin propellers and sends them shooting on toward us at 50 knots, just under the surface of the sea.

There are still eight of them coming on, in spite of our fire. Each one drops its torpedo. But instead of turning away they continue straight on in toward us, with the leading pair right down on the water, so low they have to pull up slightly to get over us, following a track that will pass over the fore-part of our flight deck.

Right here I see the results of all our battery training. The forward battery has the range on that first Jap. I see their shells, bright crimson tracers, tearing through the wings and fuselage. This plane wavers, begins a slow roll to its left, and veers off just enough to pass in an inverted position just under our bow. As it glides by I see flames coming from the tail, and the machine smashes itself into the water 50 feet off our starboard bow.

The port forward 5-inch battery, manned by Marines, concentrates its fire on the second Jap. As this plane zooms to cross almost directly over these guns they hit it squarely with a shell. The explosion blows it to bits, its engine plunging into the water almost at the foot of the battery. Shreds of its wings and tail surfaces slither along the carrier's deck like sheets of paper swept in front of a gale. I can't see what happens to the crew – and I'm not interested.

The remaining six silver planes are trying to pass astern.

Similar fusillades of fire from our after-guns are concentrating on them, but they seem to be weathering it, and in a second they have zipped past and rapidly are diminishing, snaking in sharp banks to throw off the gunners' aim, and staying low as they scuttle away.

This first wave has hardly passed when a second appears. They, too, come from our port quarter. But instead of being low they are at 1,000 feet or better. I can just make them out, coming down in a 45-degree-angle glide.

11.18+ a.m. – The *Lexington* shudders under our feet, and a heavy blast spouts mingled flame and water on our port side forward. A torpedo explosion, and we can see the wakes of others streaking toward us. These missiles dropped by those first eight Japs are only just now reaching us. I notice that some of them are porpoising (nosing up out of the water and then diving deeply as if their levelling control mechanism had been damaged). Their wicked noses look to me like death incarnate. I have the illusion they are alive, and breaking water to peek at us, only to dive again after having made sure of their courses.

11.20 a.m. – "Wham" – again the whole ship is shaken. Another torpedo. And at the same place, on our port bow. Another spout of flame enclosed in sea-water. While we are still staggering under the lurch as the great old ship heaves and shakes itself, a lookout in "sky-forward" (just above the bridge) calls out, "Dive-bombers."

Looking upward into the sun I see the first dive-bomber flattening out, having just released its bomb. The plane is very low, no more than about 800 feet, and I look up in time to see the long black bomb separate from the plane. There is a terrific "boom" and a blinding flash on the port forward gun gallery. A 1,000-pound bomb had hit among the three 5-inch guns there-wrecking them all, starting a fire, and killing most of the Marines in the gun teams.

The second wave of torpedo planes, still untouched by all the fire directed at them, are now dropping their fish. They have come on down to about 200 feet off the water, and are still 1,000 yards away. I notice that they are not straightening out, nor flying parallel to the water surface when dropping their missiles. Instead, they are still in their dive, and going very fast.

This group also comes straight on in toward us, and opens up with their machine-guns. Their fire, incidentally, is pretty accurate: it killed and wounded some of the men on our after-port gun platforms. Can't see whether any of these planes are finally knocked down by us, I don't know, for the action by now is at white heat, and all around us are geysers of water several hundred feet high from the dive-bombers' near misses. The planes themselves are coming over us at not much more than funnel height, all of them bouncing their machine-gun bullets off the decks, the sides of the ships, and the lookout positions. At times the whole deck is sprayed with their bright tracers, but most of this fire seems a little too high to hit the exposed gun crews.

11.21 a.m. – "Baloom!!" – another torpedo hit. Also on the port side, almost amidships. More torpedoes are coursing toward us, their white wakes ghastly warnings of the disaster in the water. The seas seem full of them on our port side.

This new batch of torpedoes is porpoising even more than the first lot. Two of them appear to be certain to hit us right amidships.

The trail behind them shows they have been aimed as bull's-eyes. I glimpse their nasty black noses about a hundred yards out. They looked like sure hits. I brace myself for the explosion – but they do not come.

I look out to starboard and see two torpedoes break the surface running away from us, still porpoising. They must have passed right under the ship which means they dived more than forty feet, because the old Lex, loaded down as she is for war, is drawing at least this much.

About this time a light bomb hits the Lex's funnel. It explodes and kills or wounds several men on the catwalk. A moment later some of the dive-bombers' machine-gun fire wounds some more men stationed there. All in all this turns out to be a pretty dangerous post in the battle.

. . . a quite illogical thought passes through my mind: "There's so damned much noise here I can't hear any single explosion – it's almost like a complete silence."

Hardly has this thought intruded when there is a new sound – the moaning, eerie wail of the *Lexington*'s steam siren. It seems a heavy bomb has passed through the 30-foot gap between the island and the funnel, missed the ship, and fallen into the sea on the starboard side. In its passage it struck and kinked the metal tube in which the lanyard, operating the whistle from the bridge, is housed. This glancing blow bent the tube and pulled the lanyard tight, causing the whistle to continue to hoot and moan – the cry of something stricken – which continues until the last of the Japs have passed over us – only then someone turned off the steam.

11.22 a.m. – "Whooom!" once more the *Lexington* lurches – the fourth torpedo hit.

11.22 and a half a.m. – "Baloom!!!" – the fifth torpedo, all on the port side – amidships and forward.

Captain Sherman is watching the torpedoes and dive-bombers and swinging the ship now to starboard, now to port in a snake-dance in an effort to evade the missiles. His orders to the navigating officer and helmsman continue to be in a tone of voice that might have been used in any drawing-room.

About this time I am passing in front of the wheelhouse. The skipper is standing in front of the wheel looking out and listening intently to the reports being made to him from all round. As I pass I catch his eye and brashly enough put my hand out. The Captain takes it and as we shake hands I remark: "I think it's going to be all right, Captain." He smiles back and squeezes my hand: "I hope so, I hope so," he says in his quick, quiet way.

Looking out to starboard to see how the rest of the ships are faring, I count five planes burning on the water. Japanese planes escaping after having dropped their torpedoes or bombs are being followed by our starboard guns pouring tracers into and after them. A huge waterspout leaps up near Carrier II; my immediate reaction is, "She's hit." (Later I discover it was a near miss by a huge bomb.)

Suddenly I see a Grumman following a Jap as he dives down toward Carrier II. They disappear into the smoke of the umbrella of bursting, heavy anti-aircraft shells and emerge into a literal hail of the machine-gun fire thrown up from her decks. The Jap releases his bomb and begins to flatten out – he bursts into flame as the bullets from our fighter rip into his petrol tanks. The Jap flames into the sea and the Grumman zooms back into the fight.

Dive-bombers are still coming down, only a second or so apart. Most of the missiles are falling towards the after-end of the ship, close, but not quite hitting. Above we see the Jap machines diving in a chain. Watching closely I see the bombs leave each plane. The aircraft follow, gradually flattening out. Their machine-guns and wing cannon wink momentarily. Each plane sweeps over the deck and then becomes a tiny shape, swiftly diminishing in size as it speeds away.

11.25 a.m. – "Seven more torpedo planes from the port side," the lookouts call. Our anti-aircraft fire is so hot now that the pilots in these planes are anxious to drop their fish and get away. They fail to press home their attack like the first groups. All of them are dropping their torpedoes while still in a 45-degree glide, and more than 200 feet above the water. They then turn away instead of boring in. They never come closer than within 1,500 yards of the Lex.

Again we swing to avoid the torpedoes. This time it is back to starboard. All the torpedoes seem to be porpoising badly.

"Hold her steady, Captain, hold her steady," Commander Duckworth suddenly shouts. He is out on the navigation bridge dancing up and down in his excitement, his arms spread out to each beam as if pressing the torpedoes away with his hands. "We've got three alongside two to port and one to starboard – they are exactly paralleling us.

"If we veer," Ducky yells, "we'll collect one sure." The skipper "holds her" straight, and the torpedoes churn slowly on past us. We are doing 25 knots and they are doing 50, so they seem slow anyway.

11.26 a.m. – A signalman reports to Captain Sherman that one of our airmen (having been forced to bale out during the fighting) is floating on his little yellow inflated raft through the centre of the speeding fleet. He is just off our starboard bow and only 100 yards from our track. As we sweep past him I can see him on his knees wildly cheering and waving us on. He is paying absolutely no attention to the Jap aircraft all around us and to the flying anti-aircraft stuff zipping past him from our own guns and other guns in the fleet.

Captain Sherman glances his way, instantly understanding, and over his shoulder directs a signalman to have our plane-guard destroyer – the last one in the fleet – "pick that boy up." This is done. The destroyer draws alongside him, spins quickly, and as it slides past, engines in reverse, makes a sharp turn, drops him a line, and jerks him aboard.

11.27 a.m. – Five more Jap torpedo planes suddenly appear. In the confusion we have not seen them until they are right in the midst of the fleet. But now our anti-aircraft have opened up on them, too. These new enemies are almost at water level. They single us out, spread fanwise, and bore into our starboard side the first attack of the day on our right.

With the entire fleet firing on them they drop their fish a long way out. The old *Lexington*, still charging ahead despite her wounds, turns once again and all these torpedoes miss her, their feathery wakes lacing the water wide off our bow.

Two more Jap planes slide in through the fleet's fire, but these turn aside from the Lex, pass astern of us under the barrage of our A.A. guns, and drop their fish at the cruiser on our port quarter. Accepting the challenge, this smartly handled ship swings quickly, avoiding both torpedoes. The cruiser's gun crew, meanwhile, is pouring stuff at both the planes and someone gets a direct hit on one of them. The plane disappears in a clap of thunder and fire. Commander Seligman is intently watching the diving Jap planes when a Marine approaches, gives a smart salute, and hands him a paper. The Commander reluctantly takes his eyes off the attackers and hastily reads the message. Crumpling the paper in his hand he disgustedly exclaims. "This is a swell time to worry me with this – as if I didn't have enough disturbance already."

I ask, "What's the bother now?"

Without taking his eyes from the bombers, he replies, "Someone wants me to worry because we have a case of measles aboard."

11.32 a.m. – The last of the dive-bombers roars by, raking us with his machine-guns as he passes. His bomb falls close, but definitely not aboard. The guns trail him out of sight. Suddenly there is silence. The attack is over, and despite the hits suffered the *Lexington* is afloat, steering normally, and her engines are giving Captain Sherman the speed he asks for.

By now we have a six-degree list to port, and the lookouts report we are spilling oil in our wake astern. Smoke rising from the gun ports indicates fire inside the hull.

The whole assault has lasted only 16 minutes. More than 103 Japanese aircraft have passed over us. Our gunners have made an all-time record by shooting down 19 of the Jap planes – 19 that we could see from the *Lexington*'s decks. How many more were so badly damaged that they crashed after passing over the horizon, we will never know. Ten minutes after the attack ended, and while our gunners still had itchy trigger fingers, one of our scouts came back. He was flying somewhat erratically and went immediately into the landing circle with wheels and hook down – the landing signal. As the plane flew the downward leg of the landing circle some of our after-port machine-gunners fired a few shots in its direction They were stopped by others who recognized the type and the insignia.

The plane came up astern, too high and too fast, and though waved off by the landing officer the flyer cut out his motor, dropped down on the wet, sloping deck, bounced once, touched the left wing tip and then flipped over the port side. This plane was flown by Ensign R. F. McDonald with C. H. O. Hamilton as rear gunner. The two had formed part of our anti-torpedo-plane screen and had been in some hot air fighting over the horizon. While duelling McDonald had been badly wounded in the shoulder and was now trying to land before he lost consciousness.

The wound was in his right shoulder (his stick shoulder), and in the ensuing crash he broke his right arm as well. Both men were picked out of the sea by our plane-guard destroyer coming along behind us. McDonald was sent to a naval hospital to recover from his hurts and Hamilton was not injured.

Now the fighters and scouts began coming back. They were being rearmed and refuelled and sent off once more – because we had no assurance there would not be another Jap wave.

Shortly after noon Commander Brett's torpedo squadron returned. As they flew forward on our starboard to get into the landing circle, one of our destroyers let fly a few rounds at them. Fortunately, all these shots missed, and the over-anxious gunner was quietened. Brett's 11 plane squadron had only 10 planes when it landed. All his boys had come through the attack safely except the missing plane which was forced down into the sea with dry fuel tanks 30 miles out. A destroyer was sent to get the crew, and all three were picked up.

The stories of the air fighting which took place in defence of the Lex began to filter in as reports from our patrols were brought to the bridge. They indicated that our air screens were probably more important to the defence of the ship than the anti-aircraft fire.

Ramsey and his fighters had told us earlier that they tried, unsuccessfully, to intercept the first two units of Jap dive-bombers.

They never caught these planes because the Japs were above and ahead of Ramsey before they were seen. The fighter escort of the following wave of Jap dive-bombers mixed it with Ramsey's units.

One of our fighter pilots told how Ramsey had found himself momentarily in an advantageous firing position near one of the Japanese Messerschmitts in the ensuing melée. He dived on it and fired almost all his ammunition before it started to fall in a spin. In Ramsey's own words:

"That fellow was all painted up with yellow and red stripes. He looked like a Christmas tree, almost too pretty to shoot at, but I thought I'd better try him. He never did burn, and he took an awful lot of shooting. If they're all going to be like that: it's going to be tough to collect these things."

While the flight deck crews were busy servicing the *Lexington*'s air-defence planes, Captain Sherman on the bridge began getting the first reports from below decks by approximately 11.45. They came from men who had spent the battle period in engine-rooms, battery-rooms, the hospital, the various hull compartments, and all the departments necessary for the efficient functioning of a ship.

These men, officers and crew, had been busy long before the battle was ended, trying to offset the damage the Japanese inflicted on the *Lexington*. Their work began with the fall of the first close bombs and the first torpedo hits. It involved, foremost, a check-up on all compartments, to isolate those flooded from the rest. It meant they had to struggle, often far below the waterline, cutting and jamming timbers to strengthen bulkheads against the rush and pressure of the invading sea.

In the case of the *Lexington*, five torpedoes struck her within a four-minute period, all of them on the port side forward of amidships. In one section two of these hits were so close together that the second torpedo seriously damaged the main hull. The net total of loss of buoyancy, plus the weight of water that entered many of the damaged port-side compartments caused the list (about 6 degrees) mentioned earlier.

The structural damage had not slowed the *Lexington* down or prevented her from launching or landing aircraft. The worst damage was a fire in the hold near her fuel tanks. The crew were unable to put the fire out. Then there was a series of huge internal explosions. The explosions were caused by the ignition of petrol vapour escaping from ruptured fuel tanks:

During the next five hours we suffered more casualties than we had in all the fighting against the Japanese. The bravery and gallantry of the crew was above and beyond the sort of valour that actuates men in the heat of killing.

Lieutenant H. E. Williamson, who was standing just outside the doorway to Central Control when the main blast shook us:

"There was a terrific explosion that seemed to be either in the Internal Communications (telephone switchboard) or Central Station," he reported. "The concussion hurled me against the guard rail – which broke – and against the switchboard. Immediately following the explosion a gale of wind, with the force of a hurricane, blew through the door from Central and pinned me to the board. The wind seemed to be made up of streams of flame and myriads of sparks, very similar to the flames of an explosion in a petrol engine cylinder.

"The flames were between a cherry red and white, and the sparks were crimson. The gale lasted for only a few seconds, and left nothing but heavy choking fumes I was already partially blinded by the flash, and could not breathe because of the fumes. There were cries from the surrounding rooms, so I shouted at the top of my voice: 'Take it easy and hold your breath, and we'll all get out.'"

His conclusion that the blasts were gas fumes was borne out by the later analysis of our engineers. Their investigation showed the first explosion had been caused by the ignition of the highly volatile vapours escaping from our damaged 100-octane spirit tanks, which seeped through fractured bulkheads.

This first heavy blast tore strong steel watertight doors from their hinges and twisted massive steel hatches from bolts, thus opening up the decks below the water-line. Particularly it smashed down every steel door in the compartments extending forward from Central Control right through the Junior Officers' Mess, the Chief Petty Officers' Mess, and to the main hospital 300 feet away right in the bow.

The crew fought the fires for five hours. After the ship had lost all electrical power, the Captain gave his final orders.

At 4.30 p.m. Captain Sherman sent a message to Seligman to get the men up from below. Then commenced a hunt through smoke-filled smouldering passages to make sure that every man on duty in the various compartments received the order. The loud-speaker system which made it so easy to transmit orders while the ship was functioning normally had gone when the electricity failed, so the job was done methodically by men who groped from door to door and deck by deck.

Some of these messengers went down to down to decks around and below the fires to pass on the word for there were men in those lower regions on pumping stations and watching the waterlevels in the bilges.

A destroyer now came alongside to take off our wounded and give assistance to our fire-fighters. When it was found after the hoses had been rigged up that the flow of water was inadequate, the order came to have all men brought up to the flight deck.

About 5 o'clock I was standing on the bridge when I saw Admiral Fitch lean over his upper balcony and call down to Captain Sherman: "Well, Ted, let's get the men off."

Meanwhile, Admiral Fletcher on Carrier II, his flagship, had been notified of the decision to abandon the Lex. He answered by asking what assistance Captain Sherman would require, and after the captain signalled his reply, three cruisers and four destroyers were directed to stand in close and prepare to aid in taking the *Lexington*'s crew off.

The rest of the fleet continued on out towards the horizon; Carrier II had to keep moving to keep her patrols in the air; these were now doubly important, because they formed the only air screen for the rest of us. Some of our own pilots were flying these patrols, for with his usual foresight Captain Sherman, hours earlier, had ordered that as many of his aircraft as could be accommodated aboard Carrier II be flown to its deck. In this way about 25 per cent of all the *Lexington*'s squadrons were saved for later battle. Only aircraft that had escaped battle damage were chosen. They represented a material reinforcement to Carrier II – and more than replaced her losses.

Almost as soon as the ropes had been rigged over the 50-foot-high sides, men began dropping into the sea, where they climbed on to the rafts. It was about 5.15 o'clock. One of the destroyers came alongside to starboard, and took between 400 and 500 men aboard, who climbed down the ropes to her deck.

As this destroyer, loaded with the *Lexington*'s wounded and hundreds of her men, pulled away from us, there came spontaneously from her a roar which developed into three lusty cheers for Captain Sherman. It was an amazing and uplifting thing there in those grim moments. The men who cheered were the men the skipper had led into battle. They knew he was the stuff, and they cheered him to the end.

Most of the men lowered themselves to water level on the port side aft. The ship drifted away from them as she floated downwind, and left a stream of swimmers and loaded rafts strung out for nearly 1,000 yards. All the vessels, except one cruiser and the destroyer standing to our starboard, formed up along this line of men and pulled them aboard as quickly as possible.

It took two hours to get the crew off. Then Admiral Fletcher gave orders to sink the *Lexington*. A US destroyer put four torpedoes into her. As she sank one of her officers commented:

"There she goes. She didn't turn over. She is going down with her head up. Dear old Lex. A lady to the last!"

US and Japanese forces both withdrew. The United States had lost more tonnage, including the *Lexington*. The Japanese lost the carrier *Shoho*, the carrier *Shokaku* was heavily damaged, and the carrier *Zuikaku*, although unscathed, lost most of her planes and air crews. Neither would be able to take part in the next battle, the Battle of Midway.

It was the first major setback in the war for the Japanese. They would sail to Midway with their air striking power reduced by one-third. There would be no more expansion, no more bases, or victories for Japan. They would never again threaten Australia and New Zealand.

The Battle of the Coral Sea was a significant triumph for United States communications intelligence (Comint). It had proved it could provide accurate, timely intelligence.

The Battle of Midway 3–4 June 1942

Had we lacked early information of the Japanese movement, and had we been caught with Carrier Task Forces dispersed, possibly as far away as the Coral Sea, the Battle of Midway would have ended far differently.

Admiral Chester W. Nimitz

Admiral Isoruku Yamamoto, Commander-in-Chief of the Combined Japanese fleet, wanted to lure the United States fleet into a battle in which its aircraft carriers could be destroyed. He considered it likely that the Americans would come out to fight for Midway Island. Midway is a western part of the Hawaiian islands chain. If the Japanese took Midway, the United States fleet in the Pacific would be threatened. Surely, if Midway was attacked, the American fleet would have to come out, in force, to defend it. The Japanese (Army) General Staff were not convinced by Yamamoto's arguments.

General James Doolittle led a daring raid on Tokyo, using modified B-25 bombers, launched from the carrier *Hornet*. They succeeded in bombing Tokyo. Because of the raid, the Japanese General Staff approved the Midway operation. Yamamoto released two carriers, the *Shokaku* and the *Zuikaku*, for the army's attack on Port Moresby. Neither made it to Midway.

The Midway operation was intended to be an ambush. The Japanese would send some 200 ships and 700 planes, including 11 battleships, 8 carriers, 23 cruisers, 65 destroyers and 20 submarines. The First Carrier Striking Force was to soften up Midway, which would then be taken by the Occupation Force. The Main Body, commanded by Admiral Yamamoto, would stand well to the rear. When the American fleet rushed to the defense of Midway, the Main Body, alerted by submarines, would move into position and the desired battle would be joined. Elements of the Northern Force would then close on the flanks, and, due to overwhelming superiority of numbers, the Japanese would destroy the United States fleet.

The United States Navy was on the defensive; their only real chance for success was to concentrate their forces at the right place at the right time.

On 13 March 1942 American cryptanalysts had broken the Japanese Navy's Code (JN 25). So the United States Navy could read Japanese signals. By a piece of deception they tricked the Japanese into revealing their target – Midway Island.

The Commander-in-Chief of the United States Pacific Fleet, Admiral Chester W. Nimitz, was responsible for anticipating where the next Japanese strike would come. On the basis of Communications Intelligence (Comint) he became convinced that the next Japanese strike would come at Midway. Late in May 1942 he told Admiral King, Commander-in-Chief of the entire United States fleet, that he expected a major attack against Midway.

Admiral Nimitz had only three carriers; *Yorktown*, *Hornet* and *Enterprise*.

On 17 May, Admiral Nimitz ordered his forces in the South Pacific back to Pearl Harbor. The *Yorktown* had been badly damaged in the Battle of the Coral Sea. It seemed unlikely that she would be available. *Enterprise* and *Hornet* were ordered to return to Pearl Harbor.

Enterprise and *Hornet* left Pearl Harbor on 28 May to take up a position north-east of Midway. *Yorktown* was quickly repaired and sailed from Pearl two days later. The two task forces joined about 350 miles north-east of Midway on 2 June. Rear Admiral Frank Jack Fletcher became officer in tactical command.

Aboard the *Enterprise* was Lieutenant Clarence Dickinson:

> When we were 500 or 600 miles north of Midway our force began cruising back and forth. Three or four days passed and nothing happened and in our squadron's ready room we were becoming a little dubious as to whether anything was going to happen. However, on the morning of 3 June we received a report that electrified everybody on our carrier.
>
> We learned that navy seaplanes, those big Catalina flying boats, the PBY's, while scouting some 700 or 800 miles west of Midway, had sighted a great fleet consisting of numerous battleships, cruisers and destroyers, escorting at least six large troop transports. We did not have any ships where these had been sighted. Therefore the report could mean only one thing. The Japanese were coming.

Only when he was confident that he had found the enemy did Admiral Fletcher order his planes to attack. His pilots were impatient to take off. Dickinson:

> We tried to settle down. Finally they gave us a new position for the enemy carriers and in about five minutes the talker for the second time yelled to us the order to man the planes. On the flight deck every man stood in his plane adjusting his gear, knowing this was the big day. We took off about nine o'clock and began flying around the ship, rendezvousing. Finally at 9.30 we were in good formation; the two squadrons of dive-bombers, Scouting Six and Bombing Six, and with us ten planes from Fighting Six. The new group commander was Lieutenant Commander McCluskey, al-

ways called "Mac" aboard the carrier. His was the 47th plane.

In the meantime one of the other two carriers in our force had launched her planes and these joined up with us. In some manner those planes soon became separated from ours and I saw no more of them. We climbed rapidly; at 10,000 feet we started using oxygen. When we reached 20,000 feet, we levelled off and from there on we were flying at practically our top speed on what we supposed was a course that would soon bring the Japs in sight. We were unaware that the Jap carriers, after launching their initial attack, had turned north-west. They were to the north of us and going north-west as we flew on towards Midway.

After the US carrier planes had been searching for over two hours, they were on a north-easterly course. It was shortly after midday.

About a quarter past twelve Lieutenant Commander McClus-key at the front and top of the formation picked up the enemy some 40 or 45 miles ahead and to the left. We headed for them as fast as we could go. What Mr McCluskey had distinguished first, almost halfway to the far horizon, on that dense ocean blue were thin, white lines; mere threads, chalk-white. He knew those must be the wakes of the Japanese ships. You can always distinguish the wake before you pick up a ship. Because I was less high, it was not until about five minutes after Mr McCluskey saw them that I could see them, too.

This was the Japanese striking force. I could see a huge fleet, so many ships that I knew it was their main body. I wanted to keep looking at it but I was obliged to make sure we kept close formation on the skipper's division ahead of me, watch out for my own pilots and also keep an eye out for enemy planes. The enemy combat patrol should have been up at the altitude where we were flying, around 20,000 feet. I expected them and kept looking around. We were rapidly trading altitude for speed. The closer you come to a fighter's speed the less differential he has to make runs on you. So we were making for the enemy fleet "downhill", the pull of gravity adding to the power of our engines. We made a slight change to the left to get on a course that would bring us ahead of the enemy. Consequently, within a few minutes, off to my right I had an intoxicating view of the whole Japanese fleet. This was the culmination of our hopes and dreams. Among those ships, I could see two long, narrow, yellow rectangles, the flight decks of carriers. Apparently they leave the decks either the natural wood color or possibly they paint them a light yellow. But that yellow stood out on the dark blue sea like nothing you have ever seen. Then farther off I saw a third carrier. I had expected to see only two and when I saw the third my heart went lower. The south-west corner of the fleet's position was obscured by a storm area. Suddenly another long yellow rectangle came sliding out of that obscurity. A fourth carrier!

I could not understand why we had come this far without having fighters swarming over and around us like hornets. But we hadn't seen a single fighter in the air and not a shot had been fired at us.

Every ship in that fleet bore a distinguishing mark, resembling that tell-tale symbol of the heathen that I had first seen on a fighter plane at Pearl Harbor, each battleship, cruiser and destroyer advertised itself as Japanese with this marking painted on the forward turret. The turret top appeared as a square of white with a round, blood-red center. But on the deck of each carrier, bow or stern, the marking was exactly like that which appears on their planes, and which invariably suggests to me a fried egg with a red yolk. On the nearest carrier I could see that this symbol probably would measure 60 feet across; a 5-foot band of white, enclosing a 50-foot disk of red. An enticing target!

There were planes massed on the deck of each carrier and I could clearly see that the flight decks were undamaged, in perfect condition to launch.

"DeLuca, stand by for anything. There ought to be fighters coming." "I've got everything under control back here, Mr Dickinson." The calmness with which he spoke pleased me.

"Okay, DeLuca. We'll be going down in a few seconds."

The fleet was passing under us now; we were almost at the middle of its position. Some of the craft below us were recognizable because on our own ships we had collections of scale models of many Japanese ships; our own kind of voodoo. I had studied them thoroughly. Sometimes, to get a dive-bomber's view, I had placed a model on the deck and then, standing on a chair, looked down on it. So I was confident I could recognize at least some Japanese ships of war that I never before had seen. Certain characteristics of her silhouette made me feel sure that the most distant, that fourth carrier I had first seen coming out of the storm area, was the *Hiryu* and I guessed one of the nearer ones to be her sister ship, the *Soryu*. Now we were at an altitude between 15,000 and 16,000 feet. The next thing I heard through my headphones was the voice of Mr McCluskey.

"Earl Gallaher, you take the carrier on the left and Best, you take the carrier on the right. Earl, you follow me down."

Lieutenant Best, assigned to the other target, was the skipper of Bombing Six. I had been unaware of it but Bombing Three, from a third carrier in our force, had been launched after we left. They had arrived at the same time and fortunately their commander had picked the one uncovered carrier in the group of three below us. I continued to be amazed by our luck. We had dreamed of catching Jap carriers but none of us had ever imagined a situation like this where we could prepare for our dive without a trace of fighter opposition; we had supposed the Jap fighters would be coming at us from all angles. I did not understand why they were not, because those bright yellow decks below were absolutely unblemished. Then I saw some of their fighters milling about, close to the water. They were finishing a job. It seems that our torpedo squadrons, one from each of the American carriers, had made an attack at noon. In considerably less than the 25 minutes that elapsed before we made our attack they had been destroyed, except for a few who got back to the fleet. Undoubtedly the Jap fighters I saw flying close to the water had just finished the destruction of those squadrons, and probably the fighters we saw on the carriers' decks had returned aboard for refueling. This must be the reason our bombing squadrons were able to come in unopposed.

I saw Mr McCluskey's plane and those of his two wing men nose up and we passed under.

Right after the skipper and his division had started I kicked my rudders back and forth to cause a ducklike twitching of my tail. This was the signal for my division to attack. In my turn I pulled up my nose and in a stalled position opened my flaps. We always do this, throw the plane up and to the side on which we are going to dive, put out the flaps as brakes and then peel-off. I was the ninth man of our squadron to dive.

By the grace of God, as I put my nose down I picked up our carrier target below in front of me. I was making the best dive I had ever made. The people who came back said it was the best dive they had ever made. We were coming from all directions on the port side of the carrier, beautifully spaced.

Going down, I was watching over the nose of my plane to see

the first bombs land on that yellow deck. At last her fighters were taking off and that was when I felt sure I recognized her as the *Kaga*; and she was enormous. The *Kaga* and the *Akagi* were sister ships and had been converted from battleships as our *Lexington* and *Saratoga* had been converted from battle cruisers. To us *Kaga* and *Akagi* were the big names in the Japanese fleet. Very likely one, or more, of their newer carriers was better, but to us those two symbolized that which we had trained ourselves to destroy.

The carrier was racing along at 30 knots, right into the wind. She made no attempt to change course. I was coming at her a little bit astern, on the left-hand side. By the time I was at 12,000 feet I could see all the planes ahead of me in the dive. We were close together but no one plane was coming down in back of another as may easily happen.

The target was utterly satisfying. The squadron's dive was perfect. This was the absolute. After this, I felt, anything would be just anti-climax.

I saw the bombs from the group commander's section drop. They struck the water on either side of the carrier. The explosions probably grabbed at her like an ice man's tongs. Earl Gallaher was the next man to drop. I learned later that his big bomb struck the after part of the flight deck, among the parked planes, and made a tremendous explosion which fed on gasoline. I had picked as my point of aim the big red disk with its band of white up on the bow. Near the dropping point I began to watch through my sight.

The only bombsight we use in a dive bomber is an optical tube about two feet long, mounted so that the axis of the tube coincides more or less with the axis of the plane. Coming in, we get what we call a position angle. The whole of the dive is really an aiming period but you do not put your eye to the sight until near the end of the dive; that is when you make minute corrections in the course of your plane, striving to keep the pipper at the middle of the optical sight just short of the target until the instant when you are going to drop. Then, allowing for the wind, you get the pipper right on the target. You are pointing the plane. As I was almost at the dropping point I saw a bomb hit just behind where I was aiming, that white circle with its blood red center; I found out later the bomb was one dropped by Ensign Stone. I saw the deck rippling, and curling back in all directions exposing a great section of the hangar below. That bomb had a fuse set to make it explode about four feet below the deck. I knew the last plane had taken off or landed on that carrier for a long time to come. I was coming a little abaft the beam on the port side on a course that would take me diagonally across her deck to a point ahead of her island.

I dropped a few seconds after the previous bomb explosion. After the drop you must wait a fraction of a second before pulling out of the dive to make sure you do not "throw" the bomb, spoil your aim as certainly as when you jerk, instead of squeeze, the trigger of a rifle.

I had determined during that dive that since I was dropping on a Japanese carrier I was going to see my bombs hit. After dropping I kicked my rudder to get my tail out of the way and put my plane in a stall. So I was simply standing there to watch it. I saw the 500-pound bomb hit right abreast of the island. The two 100-pound bombs struck in the forward area of the parked planes on that yellow flight deck. Then I began thinking it was time to get myself away from there and try to get back alive.

I realized that I had seen three Zero fighters taking off the *Kaga* during my dive. As I pulled out over the carrier I saw them again some 300 or 400 feet below me and to the right. You do not see Zeros unmoved. Frantically I pulled levers to close my diving flaps which give the wings a Y shape; the stem of the Y is the wing. The flaps are perforated with many dollar-size holes. They are twelve inches wide along the backs of the wings. So, in diving you are feathered like an arrow by these brakes, the purpose of which is to give you better control and keep you from going down too fast. There is a lever that works your landing flaps, the bottom half of your diving flaps. There is a lever which controls the raising and lowering of your wheels.

So far DeLuca had seen nothing coming from behind or above but any one of those three below was in a position in which, simply by pulling up his nose he could kill me very easily. However, two had passed underneath me, going to the left. When the third passed underneath and went to the left I took a deep breath. The other two had gone after a group of our planes already retiring from the action. The group might well deal with them but I felt quite naked. This third Zero climbed. And how they climb! He went rapidly astern and started a run on us from the rear and above. He started firing when he was 800 yards away, which is much too far. When he was closer, 600 or 700 hundred yards away, DeLuca threw a burst at him. The Jap quit at once and went off to play with something else.

Over on my right a destroyer was shooting at me. He had my range all right but his bursts were popping about 1,000 yards ahead of me. He could correct that easily. So each time he would shoot I would pull up, then duck right down to the water.

For some reason I was outguessing him even more easily than I had believed possible at the speed of my plane. Then I looked at the instrument panel. Instead of making between 220 and 250 knots I was crawling. I was only doing about 95! I looked around and discovered with a shock that my landing flaps were down.

Undoubtedly I had grabbed the wrong handle after my dive but at this time I really did some grabbing. Some of our people who were still around told me later on that to them it seemed as if I were demonstrating my Douglas dive-bomber. Landing flaps were opening; diving flaps were opening; my wheels were up and down and my activity was like a three-ring circus. Finally everything was closed and, happily for me, somebody put a couple of small bombs on the destroyer that was shooting at me. But I did not know that right then.

Another fighter had passed to the right of me and had slowly drawn ahead. He was stalking a group of our planes that were crossing my course, and his. When this fighter was only a short distance ahead of my fixed guns, I must admit I caught myself thinking, "If I miss him he'll be alive and awfully mad at me." But he was too good an opportunity to let go. I took a good bead on him and began shooting. I fired 10 or 20 rounds from each of the two guns, two armor piercing bullets for each visible tracer. The Jap pilot must have been hit because suddenly his plane fell off on the left wing and went down, spun into the water, and disappeared.

DeLuca had seen that plane go by us and had heard my guns firing. He yelled over the radio: "Do you think you got him, Mr Dickinson? Did you get him?"

"Yes, DeLuca. I think I did."

"That's good, Mr Dickinson."

"Can you see any more back there? I'll take care of the front. You take care of the rear. For Christ's sake keep a good lookout."

"Sure, Mr Dickinson. I'm looking out mighty good."

Dickinson remembered his impression of the Japanese fleet after their attack:

As we went away from the *Kaga* I could see five big fires in the middle of the Japanese fleet. One was either a battleship or a big cruiser. The destroyer that had been shooting at me was lying still and smoking heavily amidships where her boilers are. But the three biggest fires were the carriers. They were burning fiercely and exploding. I looked back when I was a couple of miles away. In spite of the succession of incidents this was no more than a few minutes after my bombs had landed on the *Kaga*. She was on fire from end to end and I saw her blow up at the middle. From right abreast the island a ball of solid fire shot straight up. It passed through the fleecy lower clouds which we estimated to be 1,200 feet above the water. Some of our flyers who were up higher saw this solid mass of fire as it burst up through the clouds, and they said the fire rose 300 or 400 feet still higher. Probably that was gasoline but many of the explosions I was seeing in those three carriers were, I think, from their own bombs parked below on the hangar decks in readiness for planes to be rearmed.

I could not afford to wait another second. My gasoline gauges had suddenly assumed an importance greater than the blazing, ruined carriers. I was dubious about our chances from here on. There was no plane for me to join on the flight back towards our carrier. Those who had been behind me in the dive had passed me during that interval when my flaps were down. I could see some of our planes ahead of me streaking for the carrier but I couldn't afford the gasoline to go wide open trying to catch up with them. When I left the enemy my inboard tanks registered, each one, 30 gallons. If we had to go more than 150 or 175 miles on the return flight 60 gallons ought to be enough, if I was careful. It might not get me aboard but it would get me back.

Except for my concern about the gasoline my feeling was one of intense satisfaction. I had great admiration for the Marines and I was sure they were taking care of Midway Island. I knew the army had done some damage. But it is only natural that the source of my satisfaction was the performance of our carrier group, and of that of the other carrier's squadron which I had just seen in action. As matters stood, I was convinced that what we had done to those three carriers had spoiled the invasion plans. There was scarcely room on Midway Island for six transport loads of soldiers. So it appeared obvious that the heathen had been bent on an invasion of the Hawaiian Islands. My guess was that we had stopped them cold. As DeLuca and I got farther and farther away from the enemy and could still see those five great fires astern, I reasoned that, as far as the Jap striking force was concerned, it was pretty well shot.

There had been an interval when I did not care greatly if we did have to go down and take our chances in the little rubber boat. But as I flew on, more and more I wanted to get back to the carrier and live through this day's work again. I was greedy for details of what others had seen. With each mile my eagerness to get back increased.

Trying to bring myself home, I kept watching my gas gauges. But the right-hand tank, which I was using, suddenly quit. Yet the gauge registered 17 gallons. Seventeen from 30 – there must have been only 13 gallons in that tank as we started away from the enemy. I felt as if the devil had just stolen 17 gallons from me. I switched to the left-hand inboard tank then, and immediately began to worry over how much there really was in that one.

I spoke to DeLuca. I told him I did not think we could get back and to make preparations for a landing any time. I made sure he had put his guns in their housing and removed and stowed that cabinet shape of armor plates designed to screen the gunner's vitals. In a crash landing these objects may rob the gunner of his chance if he strikes his head against them. Several officers had been lost trying to get an unconscious man out of the rear cockpit. There are only seconds rather than minutes after you crash before a plane goes down. Of course, these land planes have no flotation gear whatever in war time.

DeLuca accepted the situation very quietly. Rather quickly he informed me he was ready at the rear. All the way I had been using just the thinnest mixture of gas possible. Then DeLuca reported that there was a plane behind us, coming after us rapidly. I spent about five minutes worrying about that and then DeLuca recognized it as one of our own. It proved to be one of the squadron. In a little while Lieutenant Norman West was flying beside me and I was awfully glad to see him.

Presently we sighted our own fleet, 50 miles away, dead ahead. They were crossing my bow from left to right. We changed course to try to get ahead of them and then, in 12 or 13 minutes when there was only about 20 miles of blue water to cross, my engine began to sputter and miss. I grabbed my radio microphone and told them I was going down in the water about 20 miles ahead of them.

"Will you please pick me up as you come by?"

There was no acknowledgment. I called again and repeated the message. This time it was acknowledged and Norman West flew closer, to stand by and see how I made out. The engine was going on I don't know what. The arrow on the gauge was bouncing on zero. As I got 10 miles off the carrier to my surprise and horror I saw the fleet turn and head away from me. Instead of being on a course that would intercept them I was following them. I did not see how I could possibly catch them. Any second I expected the engine to quit. Instead of bouncing, the gauge mark was frozen on zero. It looked as if it could not be moved with a hammer.

There was one destroyer slightly astern of the fleet. I headed towards it, scarcely daring to be thankful yet. That was when the tank gave out. As the engine gasped a warning I switched back to the tank that had previously failed me.

There was a little there, a little that I needed urgently. You can make a much slower landing with your engine going. You must be sure your wheels are retracted because if they are down you will be flipped over on your back. You must put down your landing flaps, then just above the water lift your nose high and have a lot of throttle on.

I had unbuckled my parachute and thrown the harness off and detached my radio cord from my helmet as I headed into the wind; going lower and lower until I was right over the water. Because the torque of the engine is to the left, in a stall the tendency of the plane is to fall over on the left wing. I was giving it quite a bit of right rudder. Just after I cut the throttle I put my hand against the dashboard. At 80 miles an hour water is about as yielding as a brick wall. Then we hit and my cheek banged against the end of the bombsight. In about three seconds after we became quiet, I, was out on the right wing, inflating my life jacket. DeLuca was getting out on the left wing, hauling out the rubber boat. But I wasn't disposed to bother with the boat. I could see the destroyer not far off.

"Come on, DeLuca. Jump. Let's get clear before she sinks and the tail surface gets you."

The water was around his ankles and this good gunner was peering into it. I jumped in and found the temperature pleasing. DeLuca took another look, possibly to see that no shark was waiting for him. Then he jumped in and came paddling over to join me. We watched the plane sinking. The engine disappeared first, the tail rising a little. Then this brand-new plane, delivered by Douglas only a month before, went under. As a kind of farewell it sent up a tub-sized bubble.

DeLuca looked at me. We said nothing yet I know we both felt a pang. This had been one that we had boasted was a queen of the sky.

"Nice swimming, DeLuca."

"Feels fine. I'm glad we're back, Mr Dickinson. Just enough gasoline."

"Gasoline! DeLuca, I prayed that plane back the last 20 miles."

The truth is, I had not expected to get back.

This heavy destroyer was coming up. I felt sure I knew her even before I read the number on her bow.

Dickinson and his gunner DeLuca were picked up by the destroyer. By a coincidence it was the ship he had served aboard before he went to Pensacola to learn to fly.

Dickinson himself took no further active part in the battle. The next day he witnessed the Japanese air attack in which the *Yorktown* was hit:

Through the loud-speaker on the bridge we heard an American voice yelling in an almost joyful tone, "Tally-ho!" He had sighted enemy planes. From then on we caught occasional bits of their conversation. "Jim, take the one on the left." "I've got the one on the right, George." Suddenly the officer beside me at the bridge rail began to point as he exclaimed, "Look at that plane!" It must have been 12 miles away as we saw a streak of flame in the sky seem to burst wide into a ball of red fire. As this fell, stretching behind it was a plume of red smoke. I knew that was the gasoline of the falling Jap dive-bomber. What had been his plane and now was like a ball of fire vanished as it plunged into the sea, but even after the plane was gone there was hanging in the air a vertical streamer of red, which changed to black smoke.

We saw plane after plane go tumbling into the sea. Out of 18 Jap planes making that attack, 11 were shot down by our fighters before their bombs were dropped. Seven of the attacking planes got through the fighters. A fighter plane shot down one of these. Anti-aircraft fire destroyed another. A third presumably while under fire dropped its bombs into the sea and fell after them. But four aimed and dropped their bombs and then got away. We could see two or three of these bombers as they started their dives; saw them pull out and knew they had dropped. A great column of smoke rose from the carriers and mushroomed. Then there were two hits. It seemed to us the third one had struck amidships and there was another big flash out of which a column of smoke arose. The *Yorktown* appeared to slow down and come to a stop. But those two big columns of smoke made it difficult for us to see what was going on there. We were greatly worried.

At that time two cruisers and two destroyers were dispatched from our task force to go and help the *Yorktown* with their anti-aircraft. We were expecting to sight more enemy planes any minute and believed that our other ships would be attacked. There was no wind over the water so the columns of smoke from the fires aboard the *Yorktown* were rising straight up, 2000 or 3,000 feet. Happily, in about half an hour, we saw one of those columns of smoke seem to detach itself from the *Yorktown*, except for a tattered end, and leave her. In a little while there was no smoke whatever, and we knew the fires must be out.

The Jap planes, I felt sure, must have been launched from the yellow deck of that fourth carrier, the *Hiryu*. They certainly had not come from the three we had bombed. The rapidity with which they had followed us back makes me sure that all four Jap carriers were ready to launch their attack groups against us when we hit them. How it had all hung in the balance!

The *Yorktown* was under way again when the second alarm was given. In the previous attack the gunners on the destroyer had been disappointed because no Jap plane came within their range. But again they were looking hopefully at the sky to the left of the destroyer. Almost at once we saw the Jap planes coming toward the *Yorktown*. Again the sky over there was spotted with black bursts, almost twice as many as before. There was an incessant thundering and rumbling from the guns throwing up those bursts. At intervals fighters freshly armed and fueled could be seen taking off from the decks of our other two carriers to replace those giving out of gas or ammunition. Then, once more, we saw Jap planes tumbling out of the skies.

Once I saw three falling at the same time. Each as it fell was trailing behind it a long plume of red smoke. As each falling plane splashed into the sea its red plume changed to black smoke as if by some kind of wizardry. The black smoke quickly thinned and disappeared. Seemingly the Japs had put neither self-sealing tanks nor armor in these planes.

What we had seen was a torpedo attack. It was estimated there had been 12 to 15 planes escorted by fighters. Although some of the fighters may have gotten away, all the torpedo planes were shot down. Our fighters accounted for most of them but anti-aircraft was credited with three or more. Five of the planes got close enough to launch torpedoes. They were shot down but the *Yorktown* was hit. Of course, all we were sure of at the time was that as the attack petered out the *Yorktown* had stopped. Gradually we drew away and she was lost to view below the horizon, all of her, that is, except a column of smoke. Afterward we learned that she had a list which made her flight deck useless. In consequence her aircraft made landings on the other carriers in our fleet.

Meanwhile one of the *Yorktown*'s planes had found the fourth Japanese carrier:

One of the *Yorktown's* planes had found the Japanese carrier, *Hiryu*, together with battleships, cruisers and destroyers. Undoubtedly it was the *Hiryu's* planes that had crippled the *Yorktown*. So planes began taking off from my carrier and the other one. It was about a quarter past five and aboard the destroyer we estimated there would be daylight for more than four hours longer.

Finally the planes joined up and roared off to the north-west. Then a tedious wait began because absolute radio silence is maintained before an attack. Men were clustered wherever there was a radio. These had been connected and we were tuned in on the attack frequency.

Commodore Early, slight and scholarly but always smiling, at intervals would come in the crowded chart house and look at the radio, then look at the clock.

"Have you heard anything?"

"No, sir."

"Dickinson, what time do you think they should get there?"

"They had 175 miles to go. They should have been there five minutes ago."

"Well, let me know right away, if you hear anything."

"Yes, Commodore. We will."

Of course, I was the one aboard best able to interpret what we were waiting to hear. Finally the radio silence was broken. With great excitement I recognized the voice of my squadron commander, Earl Gallaher. So I knew he had gotten back from our first attack. But now he was leading this one.

Someone hastened to tell Commodore Early, and when he appeared the enlisted men on watch moved to let him approach the radio. Those grayish canvas life jackets the men of the navy wear in battle are thick from their kapok stuffing and each figure in the charthouse was bulky, except for me. From the Commodore down they coveted my aviation life jacket of yellow rubber, which would be cumbersome only when inflated.

Gallaher's voice could be heard reporting to the carrier that the enemy force now in sight of the attack group consisted of one carrier, the *Hiryu*, supported by battleships, cruisers and destroyers. He was meticulous in his report and then we heard him giving orders to the attack group. Of course, the primary objective was that carrier. The rest of the heathen ships could wait. Their previous successes had been won with carriers. We had to send their carriers to the bottom.

As I heard each order I was interpreting it in terms of that man's responsibility in the group. The dive seemed to take an interminable time. But then through their voices the excitement of the individuals in the attack group began to infect us there in the chart house, to infect all of the destroyer crew. It was apparent that the men in the attack group were trying to help us see they were doing.

"Right in the middle! The dirty –."

"Watch out, Joe! A bunch of fighters coming."

"Oh, boy! Look what my bomb did."

At times the attack group seemed to be howling in concert. We knew they had encountered some fighter opposition. So the wait for the dive-bombers to come back was another anxious time. I had counted the number that took off. By counting them as they landed on the flight deck ahead of us I would be able to tell what kind of a price we had paid for the *Hiryu*. Finally, after being in the air about three hours, the group reappeared.

I counted them before they started landing. There was one fewer than there should have been. We kept watching the horizon. That plane never returned. Afterward I learned that as our group approached the *Hiryu*, Jap fighters had shot it down. It was a plane from our carrier, out of Bombing Six.

The missing pilot and his gunner were picked up the next day.

A United States Navy submarine had finished off the last Japanese carrier still afloat during the night. By the morning the other three had sunk. The US fleet pursued the Japanese fleet as it retired and managed to sink two heavy cruisers, the *Mogami* and the *Mikuma*. Dickinson was transferred to an oil-tanker.

> On the tanker I began to get distressing news. Some officers and men came aboard who had seen the *Yorktown* during the morning hours of this day roll over on her side and then go down.

The four Japanese carriers, *Kaga*, *Akagi*, *Hiryu* and *Soryu*, which were sunk at the battle of Midway were the ones which had carried out the attack on Pearl Harbor. The Americans only lost one carrier, the *Yorktown*. The Japanese also lost over one hundred trained pilots, whom they were unable to replace. After the battle the Japanese would be on the defensive. The US and their allies would take the offensive in the Pacific.

Advance into Northern Europe 1944

On 6 June 1944 the Allies landed in Normandy, on the coast of France. By 7 June the Allies had consolidated their position. Without an existing port, their supplies were brought ashore over the beaches and by means of an artificial harbour, codenamed Mulberry.

On 17 August 1944 the Allies began to advance from the invasion area. Rex Wingfield came ashore about then. He was one of nine replacements who had come straight from training to join the infantry of the British 7th Armoured Division. Rex was 19 years old and had been a university student before entering his military service. He noticed the signs of the battle:

> German pill-boxes of heavy concrete lay smashed open as easily as their namesakes: on mounds already settling to the surrounding earth were sticks or rifles without bolts with helmets, both German and British, hanging from them. This had been the German frontline defences. Now the trenches were crumbling. An 88-mm gun stood forlornly in its emplacement, the muzzle shattered like a Hollywood explosive cigar. Beside it were the mounds of its gunners.

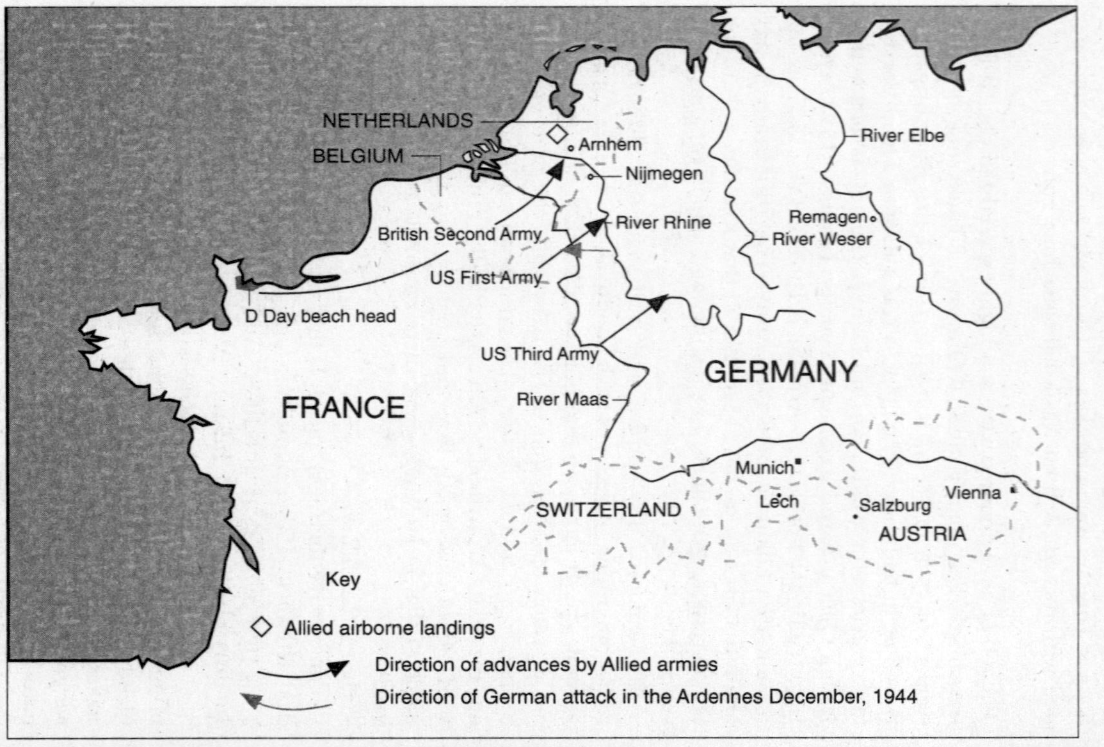

Map of Europe in 1944–5

When he and his fellow replacements reached their base camp a sergeant gave them an idea of what their life as infantry in an Armoured Division would be like. A "Tiffie" was a Typhoon fighter, armed with rockets. A Bren was a light machine gun:

> The job of an Armoured Div. is a highly specialized one. It is a spearhead. The point is three Regiments of Tanks and, in close support of each of them, is a Company of the Rifle Brigade, travelling in halftracks. The blade is you, riding in Troop-Carrying Vehicles – three battalions of Infantry. You now belong to the 1st/6th Queens Royal Regiment. You also belong to 131 Lorried Infantry Brigade of the 7th Armoured Division. You are now in the finest Battalion in the British Army. The 7th already has a reputation. It's up to you not to tarnish that reputation. Pardon the digression, gentlemen, but it's the most important thing for you to know.
>
> An Armoured Div. probes and pushes its way through or round opposition, it does not bash blindly ahead. It does not stop to 'mop up'. It moves on and hopes to God that its supplies last out or catch up. The limit of the advance is the limit of those supplies – not an inch further. The spearhead can't move without the shaft. An Armoured Div. is, basically, restricted to main roads. It can use good, firm tank-country, but there won't be much of that in Holland where there's a horrid canal every few yards.
>
> Here's the theory.
>
> Tanks make their way ahead. If they meet machine-guns, they deal with them. If they bump anti-tank guns or anti-tank ditches" – it's your job to deal with those. Anti-tank guns are cleared by Infantry flank attacks. Infantry also clear and hold anti-tank ditches; then Armoured Vehicles Royal Engineers bring up tank bridges or Fascine tanks fill up the ditch. Fascine tanks? They're bloody great Churchill tanks with a huge roll of brushwood and stakes on them. These bundles are dropped into the ditch and off we go! At night the tanks laager on some prominent feature or natural obstacle such a hill or a river. Round them, in all-round defence, are the Infantry. During the night supply columns battle their way to you-we hope! By next day your TCVs have brought up an ordinary Infantry Div. to relieve you, and on you go again. From dawn to dusk you have rocket-firing 'Tiffies' constantly circling round. They can be after anything you want cleaning up

inside three minutes. In addition to all this you have all the Div.'s Artillery to play with. Bleedin' tourists, that's what you are!

That, I repeat, is the theory.

You will have to learn a lot, and you will have to get rid of lot of the Blighty training ideas. For example: in Blighty they tell you that Bren magazines are distributed throughout a section. Each man who is killed means one or more mags short if the Bren needs them. Here they are all carried in a box by Number Two on the Bren. If he cops it, someone else takes the box, but that box always stays near the gun. Here's another thing of the same sort. You spent quite a long time learning how to give Fire Orders such as "Church Tower. Five o'clock. House. Bottom right-hand window. Range 00. Rapid fire!" By the time the dimmer members of the section have got on to the target, either they've been wiped out or the target's gone. We do it quicker. Whoever spots it shoves a round of tracer up the spout and says, as he fires, "Watch this bastard!" You learnt to search ground carefully, didn't you? Foreground, middle distance and background. Here you haven't got the time. When a shot is fired it cracks over your head. That isn't all. A second or two after the crack a thump sounds from the origin of that shot. Listen for that. That tells you where to look.

We don't have to worry much about wood or street clearing. That's not our job. That's for ordinary Infantry Divs. As you know, that sort of thing is very costly in men. In a Brigade we can't spare man-wastage like that. If our tanks go and play with someone else, we're taken out of the line because we're not strong enough to hold anything. All this does not mean we have an easier time than an ordinary Div.

We asked why no one in the Division seemed to wear steel helmets. The sergeant told us to drive along the road in a 15-hundredweight truck. The driver would show us. The truck pulled up on an embanked road. We jumped down. By the side of the road was a grave with a steel helmet on the neat white cross. The grave was that of a man from the 1st/7th Queens.

"Look at the back of that steel helmet."

We looked. There was no back. A piece of shrapnel had removed it.

"Now you know. A beret keeps the rain out just as well."

We drove back soberly.

"Now," said the sergeant, "you will realize that in this Div. you do things not from blind obedience, but because you know why."

They were driven north and crossed the frontier into Belgium. When they finally joined a rifle platoon, each replacement was paired with an experienced infantyman:

Next morning my education began.

Joe came over to me after breakfast as I sat cleaning my rifle.

"Right-ho! We'll start now, Rex. Where's your kit?"

I pointed. "Over there!"

He brought my webbing equipment over and emptied my pouches. A Bren magazine, grenades and cartridge clips poured out.

"That's the drill-book way. Now look at mine."

The pouches were further from the buckle than mine. I asked why.

"When you crawl, you may as well crawl comfortably without them sticking in your guts. Not too far round, mind, or they'll interfere with your arm movements. Now empty the pouches!"

I did so. In the left pouch were two bars of chocolate, boiled sweets and a tin of cigarettes In the right was a 77 smoke grenade and clips of ammunition were packed tightly on top. I looked at him questioningly.

"I'm right-handed, so, if I want anything, the right hand is the one I use. That's why ammo is in the right pouch. Fags are essential, but not a matter of life and death, so they go in the left-hand pouch. First things first, mate. No Bren mag? We always carry them in a box with the gun, so that we don't get them scattered in a hot spot. 36 grenades? Watch!"

He took two grenades and clipped them by the safety lever to his belt near his right buttock. The safety-pins were firmly splayed out.

"If I'm lying down or standing up I can get at them easily.

"Now, where do you keep your money?"

"Right-hand trouser pocket!" I said.

"OK. Feel mine! Much more important than money!"

I felt his pocket on his thigh. It wasn't there.

"Round the back, mate!"

The corner of his pocket was stitched to the back of the leg, drawing the whole leg round to the rear. The pocket contained more clips. The map pocket on his left thigh was full of letters. The field dressing pocket was empty. The dressing was tucked in his blouse.

In the blouse pockets were his "eating irons", cigarette-case and more ammo clips.

"May stop a bullet and easy to get at. OK? Let's do yours now."

When that job was done, he showed me his rifle. It was cocked and the safety-catch was on.

"Open the bolt!"

The bolt sprang back and a cartridge spun glittering out to the right.

"Count the rounds, including that one." Eleven.

"You load two full clips of five, the usual complement of the magazine. Press down the top round, put one more up the spout, and, keeping the cartridges in the magazine pressed down, close the bolt and apply the safety-catch. You've now got one more in there than a sniper may think you have, and one bullet equals one life. When recharging you're the perfect target, but, with that one extra, he may do something silly and you've got him. Don't look so cynical! It has been known for a sniper to wait patiently until the victim has emptied his magazine and then – you know what!

"Don't look so worried, as if you know nothing! I had to be taught all those dodges too. All this has been the theory. The main part of your education must wait till we get into action, but there are one or two more wrinkles I can give you.

"Come on!"

He took me outside to a TCV and showed me how to use the side and top bars to swing out over the side and back. We practised from all the seats in the truck. Next followed a short lecture on tank riding. When I climbed aboard a Cromwell I was to sit between the turret and the exhaust, in the middle. If I was too close to the turret, wireless static, words of command and loading would deaden or blot out the noise of an approaching shell or mortar-bomb. The same applied to the engine; only if mortars or shells burst in front of the tank was I to go near the turret, because that was the obvious target. Otherwise I was to lie flat in the middle. Shells burst up and out, so my best chance was to be low down in the middle.

My brain reeled with all this vital information. We went to dinner.

After the failure to capture a bridge over the river Rhine at Arnhem, he was involved in his first attack:

The Cromwells quested slowly down the road. We were pushing the Germans, expanding the Eindhoven–Grave–Nijmegen bulge towards the Maas. It looked like another easy Tank–Infantry co-operation job. We had had little trouble before. This was to be different.

The track debouched on to a road. Above the roar of the engine I heard the first shell I ever knew was coming for me. I have no recollection of getting down from the tank but came to find myself flat in a ditch 10 yards away. The shell exploded and I began to get up slowly, surprised that there was nothing much in a shell bursting a few feet away. I should have remembered the Escaut canal. As I got to my feet, I felt a heavy blow on my back. A furious voice hissed in my ear:

"Lie still, you bloody fool, and listen!" Shrapnel hummed and sighed through the sultry air. Pieces pattered down all round. My neighbour pointed to a bright, jagged, wicked sliver sticking in the bank.

"Touch it!" I did. It was white-hot. "See what I mean?"

My education was continuing. I had learnt one more important lesson. "Think what you're doing. Never forget a lesson once learnt!" I had forgotten the 25-pounder barrage at the Escaut canal. I was dozing. An Infantryman is allowed no chance to make a second mistake. The first mistake is usually enough.

Our advance continued.

He took part in a "fighting patrol". He was number two on the Bren.

"Right, lads! Last smoke!" There was no emphasis on that word "last". I looked back. Peter waved a jaunty farewell from his leafy eyrie. He represented safety, home. The bumping of the Bren box on my calf brought me to reality. The sergeant raised a hand and we melted into the ditch. He crawled cautiously to the next corner, looked carefully round, half-rolled over and waved us on. So we progressed, slowly, warily, guns ready, eyes shifting left, right, up, down. I looked back. At the end of the column was Bert, his Sten at the hip, moving backwards like an American gangster leaving a bank. The short snout of the weapon swung menacingly to left and right.

The track opened into a sandy clearing. In the middle was the derelict cottage. There was no smoke. Carefully we edged round it until the whole clearing was covered, half the patrol facing inwards, the other half peering intently outwards at the pine groves. The Sergeant crawled up. "Right-ho, Radcliffe! Cover me in. Anything moves, let 'em have it!"

We slid the Bren, bipod folded up, to the crest of the sand-dune. I took a spare magazine from the box. Radcliffe squirmed up to the butt. The fingers gripping it turned white. His eye peered through the sights. A round hole of sunshine glistened on the blue eyeball. The pale barrel pointed at the door. Something moved to our right. It was the sergeant crawling carefully to the top of the sand – a rush, a brown streak, and he was in! The Bren thundered in my ears and, as the smoke blew back, a running grey-green figure folded at neck, knee and ankle and hit the ground, still moved on by its momentum, and came to a sprawling stop.

"Blighter jumped out of the window!"

The sergeant removed the paybook and documents from the corpse for identification, rolled it on its back and folded the arms across the breast.

"That was an Observation Post – empty except for him. I've cut the telephone wire. Let's get out before they start mortaring."

The patrol shook down into its formation and moved away rapidly. Within three minutes the clearing shook to the roar of mortar-bombs. We watched the sandy dust-cloud billow above the trees. Five hundred yards away we sweated.

Now we decided to keep away from the track which was probably "zeroed" for mortars and move through a young pine grove with trees about seven feet high, their branches swinging and smacking into our faces. The advance slowed to a stop.

"Beggar this for a lark!" said the sergeant. "Back to the track!" We turned right and crunched our way through to the track, snapping pine-cones and branches with noisy abandon.

The trees were so closely packed that their branches would stop us from diving to the ground if we were mortared. I felt something tighten round my ankle.

"Trip-wire!" I yelled and dived flat, or as near flat as the branches would let me. I cringed, waiting for the mine to blow us to pieces. Nothing happened. A very cold, calm voice said above me: "Trip-wire, eh? Look at your ankle!"

I turned my head and looked. Wrapped round my ankle was a thin piece of copper wire – a rabbit snare.

The patrol continued, going forward, but always circling to the right. The sergeant now informed us that we were six miles out from the battalion. The thought didn't cheer us.

The sergeant stiffened. He motioned us to cover. From an isolated cottage 200 yards away came voices. We crawled along a ditch until we were all facing the cottage.

Sergeant Harris wriggled up to Jack and me, tapped us on the shoulder, and pointed to the building. Here we go!

Jack and I waved "good-bye" and squirmed over the lip of the ditch. On we crawled, well apart. Each inch was a mile, each second an age as we crawled slowly nearer. I wanted to tunnel under the earth to get away from the bullets I knew must be aimed at us now. I squinted from under my beret at the house, at Jack, and back at the steady weapons pointing right at the house. Jack looked and winked the confidence neither of us felt. He crept on all fours to the side of the house, beneath the window. He beckoned me on. We listened, each with a grenade in his hand. Nothing.

I pushed the door gently. It swung back. No creak. Nothing. The hall was dark. I crawled to the stairs. Still nothing. Up the stairs I remembered to keep my feet on the outside of each step to avoid creaking. The two bedrooms were empty. The ceilings were gashed with bullet-holes. By the side of a shattered cot lay a tiny teddy-bear. I went downstairs. Jack touched my shoulder. He pointed to the kitchen table. On it were a German rifle and cleaning kit. On it was a cigarette – still smoking. We heard a babble of voices from a clump of scrub 100 yards from the back door. We looked at each other. We heard something else – the metallic click of a Spandau being cocked. We ran madly back to cover, bullets picking puffs of dust from between our feet.

The patrol left, scampering down the ditch. Before we had gone a quarter of a mile we heard them. Someone wound a rusty gramophone handle – he wound six times and there came the nasty sound of a six-barrelled mortar, a "Moaning Minnie". We fell flat. The earth vibrated – but not badly. Jerry was bashing the ditch opposite the house. Before he switched targets we were away. The wireless man spoke into his mike. Within a minute we heard our own shells wobbling and scraping through the air. They hit with a hell of a crash. "Moaning Minnie" fell silent.

We felt carefree. We felt safe. The sergeant gathered us in a circle, facing outwards.

"Look, lads, we've been lucky up to now, but – and it's a big BUT – we're not home yet. We've got six more miles to go, and we shall be arriving in the dark at a strange Battalion. They've removed all booby-traps, but sentries are trigger-happy. We're not home yet. For God's sake, don't get careless now!"

We moved on, once more alert. Every bush might hold a sniper, every step might be mined. The wood stretched empty on every side. The "tide" we were following seemed endless. For hour after hour we went on, slowly, patiently, carefully. Now we were out of danger, as we thought, we realized how hungry we were, but to look in our pouches meant taking our eyes from our points of observation. That wasn't safe.

The sun sank down the sky. Shadows became longer, the trees more vague and indistinct, more menacing. This was the time patrols of both sides began to probe and push, looking for weak spots. Jerry patrols we expected, but – God, what if one of ours, briefed that day, should be coming in the opposite direction? The wireless squeaked. They'd thought of that. Each time we spotted the tracer and flares rising in the darkening sky, we tried to plot the position for Intelligence.

"Blacken up!" came the word. How the devil were we to darken our faces and hands? We could use earth, but we had no water. The sergeant gave us a withering look, picked up a handful of earth and turned modestly away. In a few seconds he turned round, his face and hands dark. We rumbled the idea very quickly, but – God, the smell!

We kept on our way, slowly moving right and wheeling back to the British lines. We felt more confident on our homeward journey. The night was our ally. To our right we saw the pale glow of "artificial moonlight" bouncing off the clouds. Some other sector must have patrols out. In front and to our left the dark forest stretched silent to the Maas. Behind was the enemy – we hoped.

The sergeant halted. The patrol slid to the ground, automatically observing their sectors. The night was still. A cool breeze had sprung from nowhere, bringing to us the pine-scent and the smell of the grass as it grew cool. I could hear the breathing of the man in front, magnified like all sounds at night. The toe-and heel-caps of his boots glinted palely. I looked to my right and peered into the dark wood. Across the track the trees stood mute. I looked away, for if you stared at anything long enough it moved. The patrol lay still. A strangely familiar smell came drifting down the "ride" – cigarette-smoke, and British at that. We were nearly home. Our stomachs became cold with hunger. God, how hungry we were! Our bodies felt cold with fatigue and motionless lying on the damp earth. The cigarette-smoke smelt stronger, sponged up by the earth and the pine grove. We peered ahead but, as we knew from our own experience, there was no glow. A cigarette held between the crook of the thumb and forefinger in the tightly-cupped palms did not show any glow, but the fragrant smoke was a dead "give-away". Authority frowned upon this navigational aid provided for enemy patrols, but it was evened up by the fact that Jerry did the same. Depending on the wind strength, the strange, pungent smell of "Wehrmacht" cigars or cigarettes gave us warning up to half a mile from enemy positions. Instinctively one knew the difference in the smell.

Each figure in the patrol turned its head and the message came whispered down:

"Dead on time. Sergeant's crawling out front to give our people two red Verys. The answer is one green. Faces down, hands concealed! Pass it on!" I turned and hissed at the face behind. The words moved on.

In front all was still – then – "Pouff!" bright gold, and a red Very sailed up – then another. We pressed our faces to the earth, still squinting at our sectors, for in that glare we should be sitting targets to an enemy. The red glow faded, went out. We sneaked a quick look to our front, then back to our sector. Nothing.

Silence. Yes! There it was, soaring pale at the end of the "ride". We got to our feet and moved, still well spaced, towards our lines. A whispered challenge, a reply, and we crept into safety. Only one thing remained. The sergeant counted us through. It had been known for Jerry to slip a sniper on the end of a careless incoming patrol, a sniper who created chaos behind the lines.

A guide took us through the rear areas. We swung along confidently, cigarettes glowing – Oh! the taste of that cigarette! So the happy, tired column clumped down the road, a firefly with boots.

The advance towards from the Maas to the Rhine continued. Wingfield was now a Lance-Corporal, in command of a section:

Now we advanced cautiously through the town of Udem. The streets were choked with rubble and splintered timber. Our tanks slowly ground their way up and over the debris of homes, spraying before them with Besa. Snipers in the rubble bounced bullets off the tanks and some ricocheted near us. We left the cover of the tanks and took our chance in the open, dodging from covet to covet in the rubble. The tanks thrashed up clouds of dust and their steel bodies ploughed through a smoky, choking fog. Sniper fire turned from the fruitless task of trying to pierce the tanks half-hidden in the dust, and sought out the units following us. The old, chilling cry of "Stretcher-Bearer!" echoed along what had been streets.

One sniper was spotted in the circular window of a church. A tank spat Besa fire at the wall. Puffs of dust spouted, moving steadily, inexorably up the building, inch by inch, flaming, leaping, leaden death. The sniper crouching in the circle was blasted to his feet, danced a jig on the bullets and slowly tilted and fell headlong, sprawling across the rubble.

He was soon avenged. A "Panzerfaust", the German Infantry anti-tank weapon like a flying gas-lamp, wobbled through the air and smashed into the back of the turret. Brown smoke gushed up from the turret and down the gun barrel, which drooped down lifeless. From the smoke the tank-commander spilled out of the turret. He was alone. We climbed up and dragged him from the smouldering steel. He wasn't injured, just dazed. We climbed up once more to rescue the others, but were stopped by a feeble cry from the commander.

"The rest have had it."

Tongues of flame came from the hatch. We backed away quickly and hit the ground as the tank "brewed up" with a muffled roar. Soon it was a mass of flame, rocked by the ammunition exploding inside the white-hot hull. A bursting shell blew the front away and we could see, silhouetted in the spitting flame, the driver sitting at his post, the hair on the back of the hands slowly burning.

"Let's get out!"

We did.

That night we dug in round the tanks against a glowing backcloth of burning tanks and homes. We patrolled to flush any snipers. None of our troops was in the town, so we shot at anything that moved. Panic-stricken animals from the farms, attracted by the glow, charged round the doomed town to make our task more difficult. So we carried on our deadly hide and seek in the rubble, figures flitting along the dying streets. If the snipers did but know that we were more scared than them, what a different picture it would have been. Finally we were driven out by the fumes and fire and withdrew to our positions on the outskirts. A wave of bombers droned over on their way home. Did they, I wonder, think of those tired men with the smoke-blackened faces lying in the glow of Udem, the men who had pushed their safety-zone from the coast of the Continent to the Rhine? Those men thought of you on your way home to civilization.

The night wore on. The fires in the town died down. We ate what we could when we could. We helped the tanks stock up with ammo. The shells seemed almost friendly in repose. Now the tanks came to life, twisting their turrets and testing the crackling wireless sets. Platoon commanders came round to put us in the picture. Things became clearer as we saw the little lines and bulges which were our advance. We had moved and fought for 16 hours. On the map it was an advance of three and a half miles.

The day's work was to advance still further to the Hochwald Forest. From Maas to Rhine the Germans had dug a huge anti-tank ditch. We had to capture and breach it. There were several snags. The country was open and it was daylight. Jerry was in strong defensive positions. We smoked incessantly, lighting one cigarette from the half-smoked remains of the previous one, anxious to finish that one and start another. Our tongues were sore from the smoke. Our stomachs began to rumble. We felt ill. We had had some rough stuff before and we knew that the "cold-stomach" feeling would vanish as soon as we moved off.

We waited. The tanks stood silent. Dawn came. The sun climbed. The morning was warm with a slight breeze – a nice day to die.

Our tanks started up and we climbed aboard. This put us six feet off the ground, but we had to give the Jerry snipers a sporting chance after their splendid but vain efforts to penetrate the tanks. We stood there, shuffling and stamping our feet impatiently. No one spoke.

Reluctantly the tanks moaned forward, chewed on the choke and settled to "line ahead". Even the great steel monsters seemed uneasy. There were innumerable starting troubles that morning. The engines were not cold – the burning town of Udem made sure of that.

Finally we moved off to the open fields, swerved off the road into the country and on again. Immediately a Spandau burst bounced off the tanks. So did we. I heard the crack overhead and listened for the thump which always echoed from the gun itself. Got it! That clump of bushes! I told one of my riflemen to put five rounds of tracer into it. The other two section-commanders did the same. The criss-cross rounds signalled the target to our three tanks. They heeled as they turned and hosed the scrub with their three Besas. The bushes jerked and shook beneath the leaden flail. The machine-gun stopped.

We crept on, keeping to the hedges. To our right a farmhouse went on fire. From the blazing building spilled German infantry, hands clasped behind their necks. One man came out by himself, a S.S. man, a leaping, hammering Schmeisser at his hip. He ran for a hayrick. Besa tracer stitched the air behind him. The earth at his heels boiled with dust. Now the Besa hit him and threw him into the haystack, which immediately "brewed up". The Besa cut off. Two German and two British Infantrymen rushed to save him. The heat was too great.

A hundred yards to the front a two-inch mortar bomb trailed smoke across a potato clamp. Probing tracer still came from it. The next mortar bomb was H.E. The tracer slowly tilted until it was vertical and stopped. Almost immediately it opened up again. An infantryman knelt on one knee and the black blob of a Mills bomb curved into the smoke – a pause and the explosion stamped out the tracer. The base plug of the "36" screamed off overhead.

Now the thrower stood up, waved on his section and vanished into the smoke.

I got to my feet and my section followed me. We skirted the potato clamp cautiously. By now the smoke had drifted away. The fins of the smoke bomb stuck up from the ground. Standing on its head against the clamp was a German corpse. There was no trace of anyone else, just half a steel helmet lying by the two scorched divots of the bomb and grenade. We passed hurriedly. Ahead, up a slight gradient 400 yards in front of us, was the anti-tank ditch.

They charged the anti-tank ditch, thinking it was held by the enemy. Just in time they found out that it was occupied by their own "B" company and some German prisoners:

In the middle of the curses and attempts to regroup Jerry defensive fire came down. We hit the ground, "B", "D" and the German prisoners in a hopeless jumble. The gunnery was, fortunately, of a low standard as no shells came in among us. One straggler on the edge of the ditch was hit in the shoulder as he dived into the trench, rolling to the bottom in a shower of earth and stones. We bandaged him as neatly as we could. He didn't seem too bad, so we said how much we envied him, wrapped him in his gas-cape to prevent shock and gave him a cigarette. From the smile on his face we gathered that "Jack" was certainly all right.

The barrage stopped.

Wingfield made a mistake; he used an enemy slit trench, near a prominent feature. This was doubly likely to be "zeroed in" by enemy mortars and artillery. They were shelled for nine hours. Wingfield smoked 180 cigarettes. The next morning, a runner came with an order for section commanders to report for orders. One of the other battalions in the brigade, the Monmouths, had "bumped it", encountered enemy anti-tank guns:

Throughout the day we waited. A runner came.

"Section-commanders to '0' Group!"

"The Monmouths have bumped it again. They always do. The survivors are hanging on by their eyebrows. Some companies are down to a dozen. They are approximately two miles to the west of us. We are passing through them at dusk. The plan is this. First, four flail tanks of 79th Armoured will clear the mines. We shall travel on tanks behind them, 'D' Company leading the battalion, 18 Platoon leading the company. 200 yards from the ditch, the flails will turn left and right and demine the approaches. The infantry will get off the tanks and fan out into the fields. They will then advance to the ditch, which they will hold till the engineers' Fascine tanks fill it in – then, back onto the tanks and keep going! The Yanks aren't very far away and Jerry is being heavily squeezed. Defensive fire is expected to be heavy. (Much later we discovered that Jerry had 1,054 guns in the area.) Everyone to be as quiet as possible. Check ammo and food. Pull out of your present positions one hour before dusk and report here to Company H.Q. You will be taken by guides to the 15th/19th Hussars, who, as usual, will be our playmates. Off you go!"

The light faded. Our feet moved automatically, left, right, left, right, winding through the wood. Our enemy was the weight of the pack, the stifling closeness of the pine forest, the unknown danger we had coming to us.

We came into a clearing. Stopped and silent lay the Cromwells, the crews sitting by the turrets, their boots tapping uneasily on the tracks. We moved past the sinister booms of the flails, their chains dangling lifeless, down the boom arm to the squat, steel boxes and on to the first Cromwell.

"OK, Rex! Your section on that one!" God! We're the first in! We gingerly climbed aboard and settled with our backs to the warm exhaust-chute. The clatter of boots climbing onto the tracks and so to the armoured hulls faded down the line as the rest of the battalion embarked.

A faint squealing came from the interior of the tank. The Wireless Op. slowly got to his feet and climbed reluctantly into the turret.

"Move in five minutes!" The voice came hollow from the turret.

The rest of the crew came to life and climbed inside.

"Start up!"

A whine, a thunderous cough, and the tank trembled as the Merlin engine fought its way to full power.

From up front there came a deep roar and a clashing of whipping chains as the flails ground forward. We jerked back. We were off.

The night roared and snarled with the engines. Dust came back in choking clouds. We swayed and rolled on the pulverized track. My section moved up to the turret and held on to its solid, comforting coldness. . . . The tank-commander put his head out.

"Happy?" A chorus of groans greeted him.

"Rather you than me, mates!"

Yet we felt much safer than the tank crew behind their armour. An infantryman may be more vulnerable, but he's a darned sight more mobile.

The tank column slowed and stopped.

"How's it going, mates?" asked a voice from below. We peered over the side of the hull. Two pale faces seemed to be resting on the ground. We shouted down from our height.

"You the Monmouths?"

"Yes."

"Had a good time?"

"Bloody awful, mates. We've been stonked and machine-gunned to hell. I think we're the only two left from our platoon. Didn't think we'd last out till you got here. I've never been so glad to see the dark. It's been very quiet for the last hour. You know what sort of quietness I mean. Best of luck, mates. You'll need it!"

We lurched on and stopped again.

The night was blasted by a sudden purple flash. The flails vanished in a roaring cataract of flame. I don't know to this day why they blew up. We had heard no shells.

I found myself with my section in a field 20 yards away. I don't remember getting off the tank. Our tank, stung to fury, blazed away with Besa tracer. The glowing beads sprayed at the trees, struck and whirled off, moved slowly left and right, up and down, blasting the whole of the front of the wood. We lay there with our weapons ready and pointing at the trees which leaped and dropped in the glare of the blazing flails. From our right a lazy burst of tracer sailed, 100 feet up, over our heads. My Bren-gunner rose to his knees and hammered back.

Simultaneous with the last round of the Bren burst, I felt a searing pain start at my left hip, flash across and numb my right thigh. There was a shout to my left and the dull burst of a "36" grenade.

Then I knew.

"Christ! I've been hit!" I panicked. I'd been hit internally, so I should be bleeding from the mouth. I coughed into my hand. It was dry. Thank God! I felt better.

It was puzzling. I'd been hit, all right, but apart from the first burning slash it wasn't too bad. I felt perfectly OK. I was disappointed. No mortal agony, no frenzied writhing and no shattering pain churning my body.

A thump by my side and Smoky was there.

"Where've you been hit, Corp?"

"In the guts."

"Can you move?"

"I don't know. I'll try."

I tried to move my legs but my thighs and legs wouldn't respond. Oh, God! I'm paralysed! Smoky sat up, and once more I heard that chilling sound echoing, picked up and relayed into the distance:

"Stretcher-bearers!" Only this time it was for me.

I hoped that I would soon be out of it, and appealed to passing shadows to send the Medics when they could. All the figures were moving forward. All of them showed a morbid interest in where I'd been hit. To my shame, I found myself answering very proudly. I was the great hero. I'd been hit. They all told me how lucky I was. I suddenly realized that there would be no more battle for me. I felt fine.

Now I tried to move, with Smoky helping me. Each time I levered myself up, a pain shot through my guts. I still had no right thigh. I tried to remain calm and take stock of my position. I couldn't move. I was prone on the ground, so I should be safe from any more damage. Then I suddenly realized that I'd been hit when lying on the ground. Next time anyone said, "When in doubt, fall flat," I'd have something to say to them!

The greatest danger from wounds was shock. "Keep the patient warm", the book said. I rolled on to my back and unclasped my belt. A surge of warmth flooded through my abdomen and thighs. My right leg came back to me. I thought that it was only a temporary cramp which had attacked me and I tried to stand. The pain started at my abdomen and welled up over my body to my head and armpits. I felt sick. I lay down again, took my gas-cape off my belt, put it on and rebuckled the belt. The pain abated. So, in some way, my belt was acting as a partial tourniquet. I still didn't know what had hit me or where it came from. I had seen nothing.

A curious silence had fallen since I had been hit. It was broken by a sound from my left – a bubbly, heavy breathing which got hoarsely stronger and stronger – and stopped. Someone else had gone. A figure crawled across.

"Fred's had it! Hit through the lungs. What hit you, Corp?"

"I don't know."

"Maybe it was the machine-gun over by us. Just before Fred stopped his he'd slung in a grenade. It cut short a burst – but that burst got him."

A curious mutter arose from the ground and swelled to a shout – a pleading, cursing hubbub.

"They're leaving us! Come back, you cowardly bastards!"

The tanks were withdrawing. With them went our hopes, our prayers. The tanks moved slowly back, hosing the woods. Tracer faded and cut out. The last spinning burst ebbed and died and the tanks were gone. Their motors turned to a distant hum.

All around voices came from the darkness, discussing, despairing. Slowly, painfully, I crawled over to a dark mound on my right to draw comfort from a fellow sufferer. Smoky came with me.

"Pretty bloody, isn't it, mate?" No answer.

"I said, 'Pretty bloody, isn't it, mate?' " No answer.

Smoky touched the figure and recoiled. I didn't see his face. I wish I had. The man was staring straight ahead, his rifle gripped in his hands. He still said nothing. I moved round to his front and peered at his face. The pale forehead was stitched with four neat black holes.

"Get me out, Smoky, for God's sake!" I moved, half-crawling, half-carried by Smoky. I shivered and was sick.

More figures moved through us, another company going forward. Suddenly tracer began to spray the area, probing towards the shadowy men. Some of them dived flat. One was late. The tracer vanished into the cardboard carton of P.I.A.T. bombs on his back. A split second of silence followed, then the most appalling crash and blossom of flame. I tucked my head to the ground, and round the edges of the steel helmet I felt the hot blast of the explosion hit my shoulders. Each of these six bombs could blow a hole in a tank. A body hit the ground heavily.

"Christ!" it said.

A miracle had happened. The man was only bruised by his long fall. There wasn't even a scorch on his battle-dress! Another man with him swore that he'd seen a blob sailing up in the air, turning over and over.

The man stumbled on.

A scuffing of boots sounded in the grass and a figure knelt by me – one of the Medics from Battalion H.Q. We recognized each other.

"I told you you were a bloody fool to come back to this. Now, where have you got it?"

I tried to tell him with as much accuracy as possible. By the light of a blue shaded lamp he wrote my name, number, company and where I thought I'd been hit.

"Do you want any morphia?"

"No, thanks. It doesn't hurt."

"Right! I'll take this back to the M.O. so that he knows what wounds to prepare for. We'll be back for you in half an hour."

"What's the time?"

"About nine o'clock." I'd been there for two hours already.

I turned to Smoky.

"Looks as though you can get moving. I'll be OK now! Thanks, mate, for staying with me."

"That's OK, mate. You'd have done the same for me." I

would. "I'll try to see you again before they move you any further back." He moved away and his shadowy figure advanced to be lost in the wood.

I felt thirsty and tried to get at my water-bottle, but it was just too far away. The stretcher-bearer came back, looked at me and without saying a word, took my Sten, dismantled it and threw the pieces away.

God! He thought I might commit suicide. Still, I suppose some people in their despair might do it. I had too much to live for. I also hadn't the guts.

"Don't drink," he said and walked away.

I didn't try to drink. I wondered whether it would be safe to suck a boiled sweet. Better not. It would be suicide to light a cigarette. Throughout the time since I had been wounded I had been mentally alert and I decided to try an experiment.

Many times I had heard that, in moments of danger, psychic messages could be sent to near ones. I concentrated very hard and tried to tell my mother that I had been hit. She heard me. There is no explanation.

In front I heard a sharp whistle, rapidly approaching, and over it went! The shell burst half a mile behind. I had been afraid of that. Defensive fire, cunningly directed, was plunging into our supply route and rear areas. The stretcher-bearers wouldn't get through that lot. A universal groan from the other wounded told me that others had thought of that too. Patience! Patience!

The barrage moved slowly from the rear area. It was moving backwards and we were in the way. Now the shells burst among us, threaded their way back again and settled to a steady beat one hundred yards behind me. Our escape route to the rear was gone. We could only go forward.

The shelling stopped and figures appeared on the edge of the wood, coming towards us.

Counter-attack!

We could only play dead and pray. The men moved carefully between us.

"Tod!" said a voice.

Several things happened at once. At that moment a Vickers cut loose from behind. The tracers flared three feet overhead, stopped and went on again – but the beat of the gun hadn't stopped. One of the men's boots was right by my head when the burst started. A horrid sound, midway between a cough and a belch, and a body fell heavily across my legs, quivered, thrashed and lay still. His Schmeisser toppled across my shoulders, clouting me over the ear.

The Vickers stopped. There was a sound of running, weaving, dodging feet as the counter-attack melted back to the wood. A green Very light spun up the sky, poised, and fell. The shell storm burst with renewed fury. The counter-attack had failed. Jerry was pulling out. It was a question of waiting.

I wriggled clear of my burden. The night wore on.

Another danger came. Our own counter-barrage sparkled and crashed amid the woods. In its bright glow we saw branches chopped down and whirled away.

Then it happened. Our barrage corrected itself at the anti-tank ditch and slowly walked back – and back – and back! 30 yards ahead a wounded man cried out. There was a cut-off scream as the body changed to a smoking crater. A steel helmet bowled off into the darkness.

God! Please, God! No More! No more! Save my miserable skin! I tried to deceive God that I was pleading for my family's sake. He knew better. So did I. The next shell bloomed ten yards ahead of me. Its scorching heat hit my shoulders and slammed me two yards backwards. A tiny piece of shrapnel spanged off my helmet. So these helmets were some use!

The shells plunged right amongst us. Their concussion threw me this way and that, forward and backward. The earth heaved. It shook. I seemed to bounce like a ball. I turned a complete somersault and landed on my knees with a crash. I buried my face in the ground. I closed my eyes. I daren't look any more. My helmet grated in the soil, dug itself a channel and was still. With my hands I gripped the turf, determined to stay down, to pull myself into the sheltering earth. Shells screamed and whooped, blew aloft. Earth pattered down. The groans stopped.

The warmth of the shells passed in front of me, moving further and further away. I looked up. 20 . . . 25 . . . 30 yards away, on to the ditch and into the wood.

Tearfully I poured out my thanks to God in an agony of relief. I stretched my fingers. I flexed my limbs. They worked. I shook the earth from my gas-cape. The dry crackle of its water-proofing was the first new sound I was aware of. Our barrage was now 50 yards in front and the German shells were 50 yards to the rear. We were stuck in the middle. I wriggled to look round at the German corpse. He wasn't there. In the next shell-flash I saw him, draped like a rag doll, hanging on a hedge 50 yards away.

The barrage seemed less violent. The noise changed to a steady rumble. Tracer jetted into the wood. Thank God! The tanks were back! Ragged cheers broke out all over the area. There they were, the great steel bastards, moving relentlessly on, an endless train snarling into the heart of the forest.

The barrage stopped.

I heard the sound of boots scuffling on the grass.

"Here we are, mate! The sheriff's bleedin'' posse always get through!'

The stretcher-bearers had arrived.

Rex Wingfield was taken to a Medical Officer. He had been shot by at least two tracer bullets. These had gone in at his left hip and out at the right thigh, leaving a clean hole. The tracer powder had cauterized the wound. He was discharged as an invalid and subsequently recovered.

Jet Fighters versus Allied Bombers 1945

The Germans were the first to develop a jet fighter, the Me 262. When it became operational, in 1945, the Allies had held overwhelming air superiority in Europe for years. By the time Adolf Galland flew fighter missions in an Me 262 it was too late to turn the tide. Galland belonged to a fighter unit designated J.V. 44:

During these last weeks of the war we were able to fit out some aircraft with additional weapons which gave a greater firing power to the Me 262: R4M rockets of 5-cm calibre and 500g explosives. A single hit from these was enough to bring down a multi-engined bomber. They were fixed beneath the wings in two racks that carried 24 rockets. In a feverish hurry, our mechanics and servicing crew loaded up a few jet fighters, I took off in one of them.

Somewhere near Landsberg on the Lech I met a formation about 16 Marauders. I opened fire from a distance of about 600 yards in half a second with a salvo of 24 rockets into the close-flying formation. There were two certain hits: one bomber immediately caught fire and exploded, while a second lost large parts of its right tail unit and wing and began to spiral earthwards. In the meantime, the three other planes which took off with me had also attacked successfully. My accompanying pilot, Edward Schallmoser, who once over Riem had rammed a Lightning because in his excitement he could not fire, waded into the Marauders with all his rockets. That evening he reported back to his base with his parachute under his arm and a twisted leg.

Our impression of the efficiency of this new weapon was indescribable. The rockets could be fired outside the effective range of the defensive fire of the bombers, and a well-aimed salvo would probably hit several of them simultaneously. That was the way to break up formations. But this was the end of April 1945! In the middle of our decline, at the beginning of our collapse! It does not bear thinking about that we could have had these jet-fighters, these 3-cm quick-firing cannons, and these 5-cm rockets years ago, before our war potential had been smashed and indescribable misery had come over Germany through the raids! We dared not think about it!

Now we could do nothing but fly and fight, and do our duty as fighter pilots to the last.

Service in action still demanded heavy and grievous losses. On 18 April, Steinhoff crashed on a take-off, but managed to free himself from the burning wreckage of his jet-plane with very severe burns. A few days later Günther Lützow did not return from a mission. Long after the end of the war we were still hoping that this splendid officer might not have left us for ever. In the same spirit and with the same devotion, many more young pilots of our unit fell.

In those days the fate of Germany was sealed. On 25 April American and Soviet soldiers shook hands at Torgau on the Elbe. The last defensive ring of Berlin was soon penetrated.

The red flag was flying over the Ballausplatz in Vienna. The last bomb of the 2,755,000 tons which the Western Allies had dropped on Europe during five years of war.

At that moment I called my pilots together and said to them: "Militarily speaking, the war is lost. Even our action here cannot change anything. . . . I shall continue to fight, because operating with the Me 262 has got hold of me, and I am proud to belong to the last fighter pilots of the German Luftwaffe . . . Only those who feel the same are to go on flying with me . . ."

In the meantime, the harsh reality of the war finally decided the question "Bomber or fighter action by the Me 262?" in our favour. The leaders were completely occupied with themselves in Berlin and at other places. Numerous departments which up to now had interfered with allocation and the operation of jet-fighters ceased to function or did not come through any more. Commanders of the units of bombers, reconnaissance planes, Army support fighters, night fighters and sundry testing units which had been fitted out with the coveted Me 262 passed their aircraft on to us. From all sides we were presented with jet-fighters, until finally we had 70 aircraft.

On 26 April I set out on my last mission of the war when I led six jet-fighters of the J.V.44 against a formation of Marauders. Our own little directing post brought us well in contact with the enemy; the weather report was: varying cloud at different altitudes, with gaps, ground only visible in about three-tenths of the operational area.

Sighting the enemy formation in the district of Neuburg on the Danube, I once again noticed how difficult it was with such a great difference of speed and with cloud over the landmarks to find the relative flying direction between one's own aircraft and the enemy's, and how difficult it was to judge the approach. This had already driven Lützow to despair. He had discussed it repeatedly with me, and every time he missed his run-in this most successful fighter commodore blamed his own inefficiency as a fighter pilot. Had there been any need for more confirmation as to the hopelessness of operations with the Me 262 by bomber pilots, our experiences would have sufficed.

But now there was no time for such considerations. We were flying in almost the opposite direction to the Marauder formation. Each second meant that we were 300 yards nearer. I will not say that I fought this action ideally, but I led my formation to a fairly favourable firing position. Safety-catch off the gun and rocket-switch! At a great distance we already met with considerable defensive fire. As usual in a dog-fight. I was tense and excited, and so forgot to release the second safety-catch for the rockets, which did not go off. I was in the best firing position, had aimed accurately, and pressed my thumb on the release button with no result – maddening for any fighter pilot. Anyhow, my four 3-cm cannons were working. They had much more firing power than we had been used to so far. At that moment, close below me,

Schallmoser, the "jet rammer", whizzed past. In ramming he made no difference between friend or foe.

This engagement had lasted only a fraction of a second – a very important second, to be sure. One Marauder of the last string was on fire and exploded. Now I attacked another bomber in the van of the formation, and saw it was heavily hit as I passed very close above it. During this breakthrough I got a few minor hits from the defensive fire, but I wanted to know definitely what was happening to the second bomber I had hit. I was not quite clear if it had crashed. So far I had not noticed any fighter escort.

Above the formation I had attacked last I banked steeply to the left, and at this moment it happened: a hail of fire enveloped me. A Mustang had caught me napping. A sharp rap hit my right knee, the instrument panel with its indispensable instruments was shattered, the right engine was also hit – its metal covering worked loose in the wind and was partly carried away – and now the left engine was hit too. I could hardly hold her in the air.

In this embarrassing situation I had only one wish: to get out of this "crate", which now apparently was only good for dying in. But then I was paralysed by the terror of being shot while parachuting down. Experience had taught us that we jet-fighter pilots had to reckon on this. I soon discovered that after some adjustments my battered Me 262 could be steered again, and after a dive through the layer of cloud, I saw the Autobahn below me; ahead lay Munich, and to the left Riem.

In a few seconds I was over the airfield. Having regained my confidence, I gave the customary wing-wobble and started to come in. It was remarkably quiet and dead below. One engine did not react at all to the throttle, and as I could not reduce it I had to cut out both engines just before the edge of the airfield. A long trail of smoke drifted behind me. It was only then I noticed that Thunderbolts in a low-level attack were giving our airfield the works. Now I had no choice. I did not hear the warnings of our ground post because my wireless had faded out when I was hit. There remained only one thing to do: straight down into the fireworks! Touching down, I realized that the tyre of my nose-wheel was flat. It rattled horribly as the earth received me again at a speed of 150 m.p.h. on the small landing strip.

Brake! Brake! The kite would not stop, but at last I was out of it and into the nearest bomb-crater. There were plenty of them on our runways. Bombs and rockets exploded all around, bursts of shells from the Thunderbolts whistled and banged. A new low-level attack. Out of the fastest fighter in the world into a bomb-crater – an unutterably wretched feeling! Through the fireworks an armoured tractor came rushing across to me and pulled up sharply close by. It was one of our mechanics. Quickly I sat behind him. He turned and raced off on the shortest route away from the airfield. In silence I slapped him on the shoulder. He understood better what I wanted to say about the unity between flying and ground personnel than any words could have expressed.

The other pilots taking part in this operation were directed to neighbouring airfields or came into Riem after the attack. We reported five certain kills without loss to ourselves. I had to go to a hospital in Munich for treatment to my scratched knee. The X-ray showed two splinters in the kneecap, which was put in plaster. A fine business!

The enemy, advancing from the north, had already crossed Danube at several places. The J.V.44 prepared for its last transfer. Bar, who had come to us with the remnants of his Volks Fighter test commando, took over the command in my place. About 60 jet-fighters flew to Salzburg. Orders came from the Reichs Chancellery and from the Luftwaffe Staff in Berchtesgaden for an immediate transfer to Prague in order to pursue from there the completely hopeless fight for Berlin. The execution of this order was delayed until it became purposeless.

On 3 May the aircraft of the J.V.44 were standing on the aerodrome of Salzburg without any camouflage. American fighters circled overhead. The pilots did not shoot or drop any bombs, for they obviously hoped soon to be flying the German jet-fighters which had given them so much trouble. Salzburg prepared for the capitulation. The advanced units of Devers' army approached the town. As the rattle of the first tank was heard on the airfield our jet-fighters went up in flames.

Vietnam War

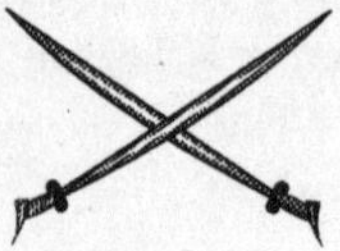

Introduction

Before the Second World War part of south-east Asia, known as Indochina, was under French control. In 1930 Ho Chi Minh and his followers began the Indochinese Communist Party. This was opposed to French colonial rule. From 1940 onwards, much of the area was controlled by the Japanese. After the Japanese surrender in 1945, Ho Chi Minh began to gather guerilla forces, the Viet Minh. They rebelled against French colonial rule. On 2 September 1945 Ho Chi Minh read Vietnam's Declaration of Independence and established the Democratic Republic of Vietnam in Hanoi. From December 1946 there was open war between the French and the Viet Minh. From 1950 the United States subsidized the French and the Chinese subsidised the Viet Minh. On 7 May 1954 the French were defeated at Dien Bien Phu.

In June 1954 the CIA established a military mission in Saigon.

In 1954 the Geneva Conference on Indochina ended French control of the area. It recognized the Democratic Republic of Vietnam in the North and the Republic of Vietnam in the South. It also declared a demilitarized zone at the 17th parallel.

On 24 October 1954 President Eisenhower pledged support to the Republic of Vietnam's government and military forces. In 1960 the National Liberation Front (NLF), the Viet Cong, was founded in South Vietnam. In 1961 the US began to build up its military forces in Vietnam. First it sent "combat advisors". On 8–9 March 1965 the first combat troops arrived. In April 1965 President Johnson authorized offensive operations by U.S. troops. The first battle between US troops and North Vietnamese forces took place 14–16 November 1965.

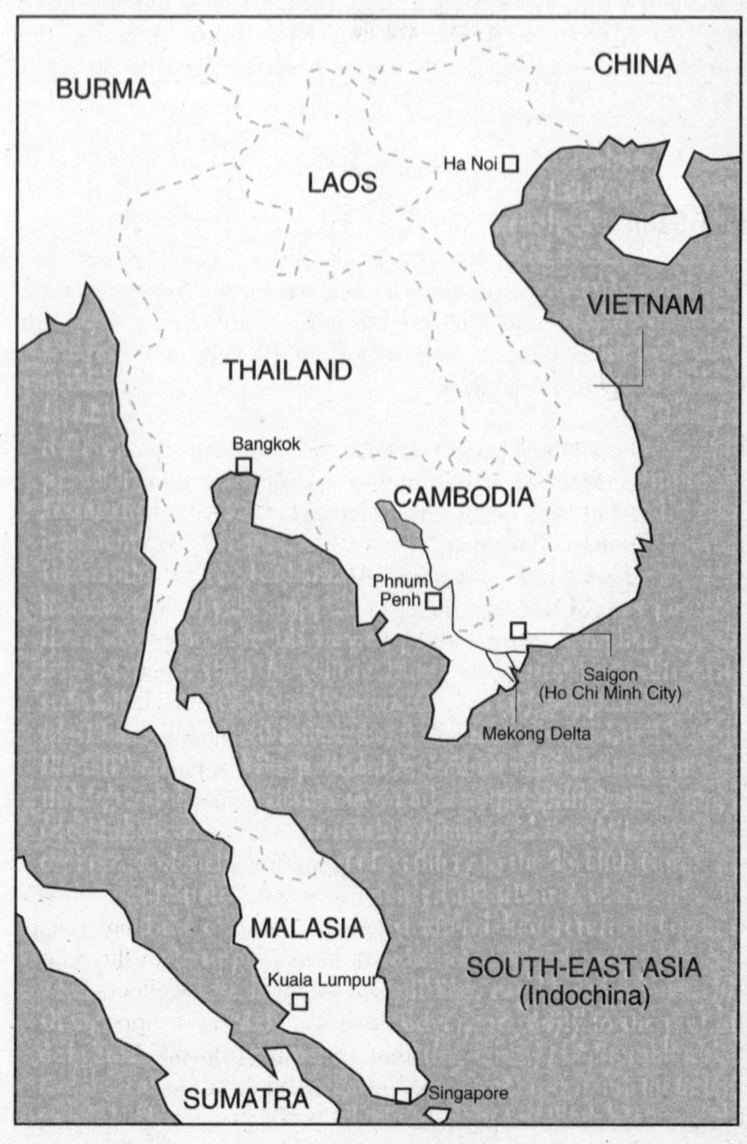

Map of South-East Asia (Indochina)

On 10 May 1968 peace talks began in Paris. On 8 June 1969 US troop withdrawals began. The last US troops did not leave until 29 March 1973. Despite the Paris Peace Accords, the war did not end until South Vietnam surrendered on 30 April 1975.

Khe Sanh

John T. Wheeler reported the Vietnam war for the Associated Press agency from 1965 until 1969. He was in Khe Sanh during the North Vietnamese Tet offensive. His report of 12 February 1968, was entitled "Life in the V Ring":

> The first shell burst caught the Marines outside the bunkers filling sandbags. More exploding rockets sent showers of hot fragments zinging. The Americans dove for cover.
>
> "Corpsman! Corpsman!"
>
> The shout came from off to the right.
>
> "We've got wounded here!"
>
> "Corpsman! Corpsman!" The shouts now came from the distance. You could see the men dragging a bleeding buddy toward cover.
>
> Inside the bunkers the Marines hugged their legs and their heads, unconsciously trying to make themselves as small as possible. The tempo of the shelling increased and the small opening to the bunker seemed in their minds to grow to the size of a barn door. The 5,000 sandbags around and over the bunker seemed wafer thin.
>
> Although it could increase their chances of survival only minutely, men shifted their positions to get closer to the ground.
>
> Some measured the angle to the doorway and tried to wriggle a bit more behind those next to them.
>
> There were no prayers uttered aloud. Two men growled a stream of profanity at the North Vietnamese gunners who might snuff out their lives at any moment.
>
> Near misses rocked the bunker and sent dirt cascading down everyone's neck.
>
> Outside the random explosions sent thousands of pounds of shrapnel tearing into sandbags and battering already damaged

mess halls and tent areas long ago destroyed and abandoned for life of fear and filth underground.

This is the life in the V Ring, a sharpshooter's term for the inner part of the bull's eye. At Khe Sanh the V Ring for the North Vietnamese gunners neatly covers the bunkers of Bravo Company, 3rd Reconnaissance Battalion. In three weeks, more than half the company had been killed or wounded. It was recon's bad luck to live in an area bordered by an ammunition dump, a flightline loading area, and the 26th Marine Regiment's command post.

Shrapnel and shell holes cover the area. The incoming rounds could hardly be noticed once the barrage stopped, such is the desolation.

And then the shells did stop. Silent men turned their faces from one to the other. Several men scrambled out of the bunker to see if more dead or wounded men from their unit were outside. Medics scurried through the area, crouching low.

Inside one bunker a Marine returned to his paperback book, a tale of a Wild West adventure. Another man whose hand had stopped in the midst of strumming a guitar resumed playing. Two men in a card game began flipping the soggy pasteboards again.

The shelling wasn't worth discussing. It was too commonplace and none from Bravo Company had been hit this time. Like jungle rot, snipers and rats, artillery fire was something to be hated and accepted at the same time.

But the sheilfire had taken its toll. Minutes before the barrage opened, Army Spec. 4 William Hankinson had drifted off from the other members of his communications team assigned to this Marine base.

When the first shell hit, he dived into a Marine bunker. After the explosions stopped, he talked with the Marines awhile before starting back to his bunker.

A white-faced Leatherneck joined the group.

"You look kind of sick," a Marine buddy said. "What happened?"

"The whole Army bunker got wiped out," he replied. "Jesus, what a mess."

Hankinson started to run toward the smashed bunker where his friends' shattered bodies lay. Marines caught and blocked him. Then, with a tenderness not at all out of place for hardened fighting men, they began to console the Army specialist, a man most had never spoken to before that day.

One dud mortar round was half-buried in the runway of the airstrip. Planes carrying priority supplies had to be waved off until the round could be removed.

Two demolition experts raced from shelter with fire axes and chopped it out of the aluminum sheet runway. Neither would give his name. Both had told their families they were safely out of the war zone.

"An awful lot of Marines are big liars on that point," one said. The men of No. 2 gun, Charlie Battery, didn't think of cover when the shelling began. After what they had been through when the main ammunition dump 200 yards away exploded during an earlier barrage, "This is coasting," one gunner said.

And alone of the Marines at Khe Sanh, the artillery could fire back at the enemy. No. 2 gun, commanded by Cpl Anthony Albo, kept pouring out 105-mm rounds even though a shell splinter had started a fire in the gun's ready ammo bunker.

At Charlie Med, the main casualty clearing station, wounded were coming in. Some were on stretchers, some hobbled by themselves, some were hauled in across the shoulder of a comrade.

One prayed, a few cried; some were unconscious. Many showed shock on their faces.

In between shellings, Lance Cpl Richard Noyes, 19, of Cincinnati, Ohio, rough-housed on the dirt floor of his bunker with a friend. Noyes lives with five buddies in the center of the V Ring. The war was pushed far into the background moment as ripples of laughter broke from the tangled, wrestling forms.

Then the first shell of a new barrage hit.

Both men recoiled as if a scorpion had been dropped between them. Even though they were underground in a bunker, everyone put on helmets. Across the front of his "brain pot", Noyes long ago had written in ink, "God walks with me."

A blank stare in the eyes of some is not uncommon at Khe Sanh where the Communists have fired up to 1,500 rounds of rockets, artillery and mortar shells in a single day.

It is called the 1,000-yard stare. It can be the sign of the beginning of combat fatigue.

For Noyes and thousands of others at this surrounded combat base, the anguish is bottled up within tolerable limits.

Noyes had had luck, lots of it. A rocket once drove through the bunker's sandbags and exploded, killing four and wounding 14 of the 20 men inside. Noyes was slightly wounded.

It was Noyes' second Purple Heart. One more and he automatically would be sent out of Vietnam under Marine regulations. Noyes doesn't want the third medal.

Despite heavy casualties, the survivors of the recon company are frightened but uncowed. When the call for stretcher bearers comes, the young Marines unhesitatingly begin wriggling through the opening in their bunker to help.

At night the men in Noyes' bunker sit and talk, sing, play cards, almost anything to keep from being alone with their thoughts. During a night when more than 1,000 rounds hit Khe Sanh, Noyes turned to a buddy and said:

"Man, it'll be really decent to go home and never hear words like incoming shells, mortars, rifles, and all that stuff. And the first guy who asks me how it feels to kill, I'll . . ." A pause. Then "You know, my brother wants me to go duck hunting when I get home. Man, I don't want to even see a slingshot when I get out of here."

Lt C.J. Slack of Carlsbad, Calif., said: "When I get back to California, I'm going to open a bar especially for the survivors of Khe Sanh. And any time it gets two deep at that bar, I'll know someone is lying."

Noyes smokes heavily and his hands never seem to be entirely still. Looking at the side of a cigarette pack. Noyes said with a wry smile, "Caution, Khe Sanh may be hazardous to your health. Oh, man, yeah."

Still later, he called out, "OK, we're going to sing now. Anyone who can't sing has to hum. Because I said so. OK, let's hear it."

Lance Cpl Richard Morris, 24, of North Hollywood, Calif., began playing a guitar. Two favorites that night were "Five Hundred Miles" and "Where Have All the Flowers Gone?"

A hard emphasis accompanied the verse that went: "Where have all the soldiers gone? To the graveyard every one. When will they ever learn? When will they ever learn?"

Finally the two small naked light bulbs were turned out and the Marines struggled toward sleep.

Falklands War

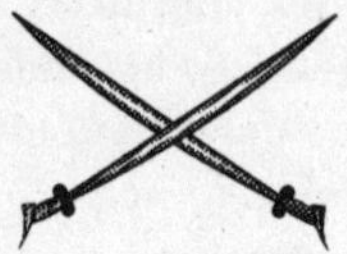

The Battle of Goose Green 27–28 May 1982

Talks between Great Britain and Argentina had failed to resolve the dispute over possession of the Falkland Islands. On 2 April 1982 Argentinian forces landed near Stanley, the capital. Their strength and numbers forced the British garrison of 40 Royal Marines to surrender.

The British Government decided to retake the islands, by force if necessary. A British Task Force was sent to the South Atlantic. The Task Force consisted of nearly 30,000 men, warships, merchant ships, aircraft, helicopter squadrons, and supporting arms.

The British landed on beaches east of Port San Carlos on 21 May. The Argentinian commander, General Benjamino Menendez, had been told that a landing at San Carlos was unlikely. He had done little to defend it. Major Carlos Esteban was in command of an Argentinian outpost at San Carlos:

> It was about ten to eight in the morning when one of my advance observers came running down and told me that there was a frigate coming in through the channel. I took the binoculars, ran forward with him, took up his position and observed that a considerable number of ships were entering. There was a large white ship in the middle of the bay of San Carlos; many frigates were protecting it and helicopters were flying around.

Barry Norman was a company sergeant major in the 2nd battalion of the parachute regiment (2 Para). They had to scramble down nets into the landing craft:

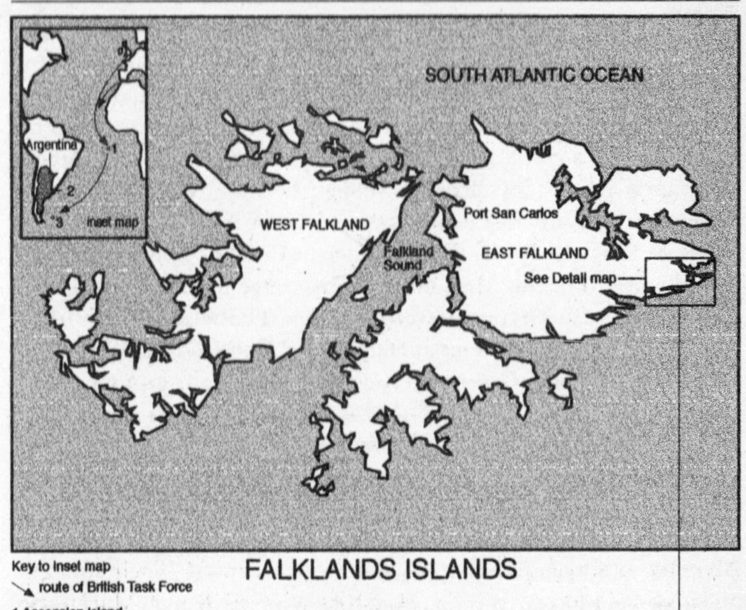

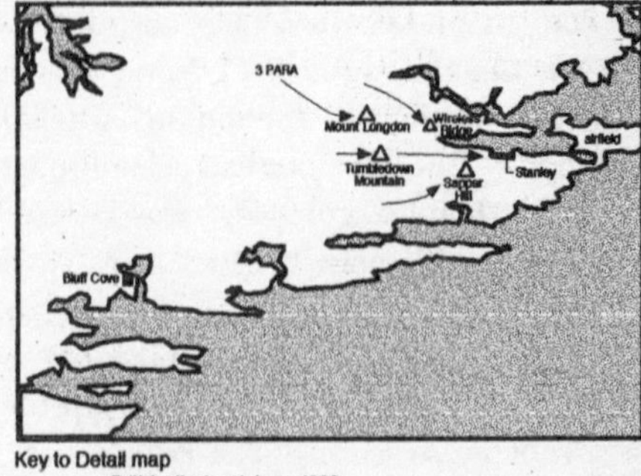

Map of the Falklands

> And seeing we had bergens (backpacks) of about 100 pounds plus on our backs at that particular time, it was lucky we only lost one bloke, who fell off and fell between the Norland and the landing craft, and he got quite substantial injuries. And that was his war finished, before it even started.

The ultimate objective of the British Task Force was to recapture the capital, Stanley. San Carlos was 86 miles from Stanley. The advance to Stanley was to be quick, using helicopters.

On 21 May, despite Argentinian air attacks, the British landed 3,000 men with their artillery and thousands of tons of supplies were safe ashore. The Argentinian air attacks continued. On 25 May they hit and destroyed the merchant ship Atlantic Conveyor. Atlantic Conveyor was a container vessel which was carrying the helicopters to be used in the advance on Stanley. Because of the loss of the helicopters, the advance would have to be on foot.

On 26 May the British Commander-in-Chief in London ordered the advance to begin. Most of the British force marched out of San Carlos on a northern route towards Stanley. 2 Para marched south to attack Argentinian positions at Darwin and Goose Green. There was an airstrip at Goose Green where some Pucara light ground attack aircraft were based. After a 15-mile night march 2 Para rested at an unoccupied farm at Camilla Creek.

Colonel H. Jones was in command of 2 Para. 2 Para consisted of four companies each of 110 men and a tactical Headquarters unit of 12 men, a total of 450 men. The British thought they were attacking a similar number of Argentinians.

There was high ground on either side of the route to Goose Green. The Argentinians held Darwin Hill to the east, above the small settlement at Darwin. They also held a ridge to the west at Boca House. On the night of 27 May, A company of 2 Para was sent to attack Darwin Hill. B company was sent to attack Boca House. D company and the tactical Headquarters unit were to advance between them. C company was in reserve.

The attack began before dawn. At first it went well but slowed down under heavy fire. At 8 a.m. an Argentinian captain, Jose Centurion, was ordered to take his men forward to help in the defence of Darwin Hill. They set up their machine gun positions in slit trenches in front of the hill:

> As the British tried to advance we opened fire. We fought a fairly intense battle, with some advantage because we managed to check the British detachment straight away and hold them back.

A company was pinned down in a gully. Colonel Jones took charge of the attack himself. Barry Norman:

> Colonel Jones said: "Right, the only way we're going to do it is over the top." So we lined up in extended line, and we went over the top with mortar smoke coming down onto the position to

> provide a screen. But that particular day, even for Falkland standards, the wind was exceptionally strong.

The wind blew the smoke screen away. Three paratroopers were killed. Colonel Jones shouted to Norman that he intended to make a flank attack on the Argentinian machine gun position ahead:

> He said, "Follow me", which I did. We then turned right and the Argentinians were firing at us from the high ground to the left. We ran across the top feature, as fast as we could, and then down, into dead ground from the Argentinian position. And I thought he was going to stop, but he didn't. He just continued running.

Norman followed Colonel Jones. He heard a warning about another machine gun position. He dived for cover and started firing at it. Colonel Jones did not take cover but kept going. Norman tried to warn Colonel Jones:

> To my utter amazement I looked again and he was just checking his sub-machine gun, to make sure he had a full magazine on, and he went charging up the hill, to the trench which I was firing at . . .
>
> I shouted to him, "Watch your fucking back!" And he totally ignored me. Whether or not he heard me, I don't know. I think he ignored me, personally. And the higher he went up, the nearer he was to this fall of shot. All of a sudden his body and the fall of shot coincided and he was hit in the back. The momentum of the shot actually forced him forward and he fell just within inches of the Argentinian trench he was actually going for.

Captain Centurion was amazed by Colonel Jones' participation in the attack:

> He (Colonel Jones) found my detachment by chance; I arrived not ten minutes before him, and took up the advantageous position, really by a stroke of luck. I think of Colonel Jones as someone who proved himself to be an excellent commander. Although he possessed innumerable resources: 66-mm rocket launchers, his unit had Milan anti-tank weapons, mortars, and some artillery support, he personally took part in a machine gun battle fighting with hand grenades.

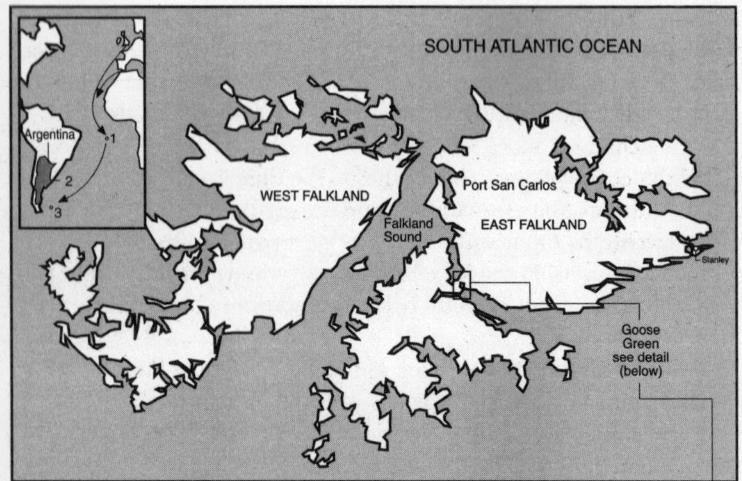

FALKLANDS ISLANDS Battle of Goose Green, 28-29 May 1982

Key to inset map (above)

route of British Task Force
1 Ascension Island
2 Buenos Aires
3 Falkland islands

Key to Goose Green detail (right)

1 Camilla Creek Farm

2 B company heading for Boca House

3 A company heading for Darwin Hill

4 D company & Tactical HQ

5 Colonel H Jones killed

6 D company attacks Boca House

7 & 8 attacks on airstrip & Goose Green

9 attack on School House by C company

10 airstrip

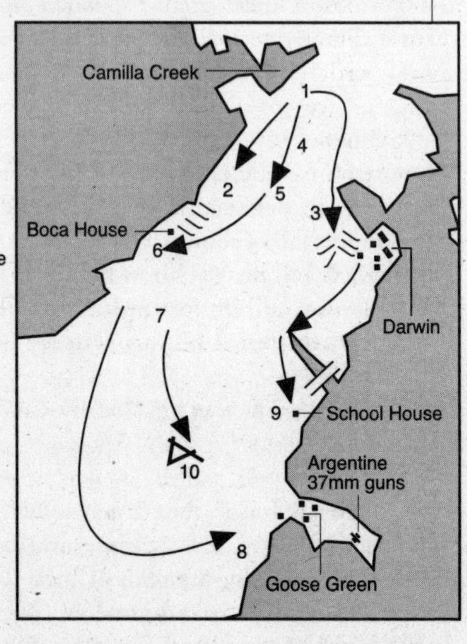

Map of the Battle of Goose Green

The second in command of 2 Para, Major Chris Keeble, was 1,500 yards behind with the tactical Headquarters unit. He heard a radio message "Sunray is down". He knew that meant something had happened to Colonel Jones and that he was in command of the battalion.

He decided that the Boca House ridge was the key to the battle.

Keeble changed tactics. He sent D company to help B company. Using the cover of the terrain, they were able to crawl along the beach to attack the Argentinian position at Boca House from the flank. Keeble brought up his supporting artillery (three 105-mm guns). By 11 a.m. both Argentinian positions were taken but the Argentinians at Goose Green had not yet surrendered. They had some 37-mm anti-aircraft guns on a strip of land beyond the settlement which had been used to fire directly on 2 Para. During the afternoon, an air strike by Harriers knocked out the 37-mm guns. Keeble decided to attack two positions: the School House, a strongly held position between Darwin and Goose Green, and the airstrip. He ordered B company to march south around the airstrip and approach Goose Green from the south. He ordered D company to advance directly towards Goose Green taking the airstrip on their way. He ordered C company to attack the School House. C and D companies were attacked by Pucaras. They shot one of them down with a "blowpipe", hand-held anti-aircraft missile. Three paratroopers were killed while taking the surrender of some Argentinians who had raised a white flag. Eventually the School House exploded, killing its remaining defenders.

Keeble was prepared to besiege the settlement firing at it with his artillery until it surrendered. A patrol reported that 112 civilians were being held in the community centre in Goose Green. Keeble took some time alone to decide what to do:

> I thrust my hands into my pockets, because they were so cold, and my fingers caught a piece of plastic that I had in my pocket, a laminated prayer, from a French soldier. I had a kind of bargain with God, you know, I'll carry this prayer, if you look after me. I knew this prayer well. And I suddenly thought, I need to say this, and in that darkness knelt down, in this gorse, and I said this prayer, which was essentially abandoning myself to God and seeking his will and whatever the outcome was, I'd live with that. And a most amazing kind of transformation occurred. From feeling cold and fearful, and uncertain and frightened, I suddenly

> felt joyful, hopeful, warm and very clear about what we should do. And I turned round and went back to the boys. I said, "I'll tell you what we're going to do. I'm going to seek a surrender, tomorrow morning." And they were astounded, inevitably, and I said, "Trust me", in the way in which I felt I needed to trust my God, in this case.

He sent some prisoners to open negotiations. The Argentinians offered to surrender if they could have a formal ceremony. The British were amazed when 1,500 Argentinians marched out. The British had lost 17 killed, including 13 officers and non-commissioned officers. They had learnt some lessons from the battle. All subsequent attacks were made at night.

On 14 June, the British reached Stanley; the Argentinian commander, General Menendez, surrendered.

The Gulf War

A tank battle at night is a curious affair.
Brigadier Chris Hammerbeck

On 2 August 1990 Iraqi troops invaded Kuwait. On 6 August the United Nations Security Council adopted Resolution 661 which called for the restoration of the legitimate government of Kuwait. The United States and Great Britain immediately sent aircraft to Saudi Arabia to deter any further Iraqi aggression.

On 29 November 1990 the United Nations passed Resolution 678. This Resolution ordered all Iraqi troops to withdraw from Kuwait by 15 January 1991. An international Coalition was formed. The Coalition's forces would defend any other states attacked by Iraq. The UN Resolution authorized the Coalition's forces to use "all necessary means" to expel the Iraqis from Kuwait if they would not withdraw peacefully.

The first phase of operations to expel the Iraqis from Kuwait consisted of air attacks. The aim of these air attacks was to reduce Iraqi fighting ability. The air attacks began on 17 January 1991. Among the 3,000 Coalition aircraft was 15 Squadron RAF, flying Tornado jet fighter-bombers. Their mission was to bomb the runways of the Iraqi airfields. The RAF used tactics which had been developed for a possible European war. They had been trained fly low to avoid detection by enemy radar. Low-level flying made the attacking aircraft vulnerable to anti-aircraft gun fire and hand-held missiles. The RAF lost five aircraft during the first week of the air war.

Flight Lieutenants John Nichol and John Peters were the navigator and pilot of a Tornado sent to attack Ar Rumaylah airfield in southern Iraq, in daylight on 17 January. They flew from an airbase

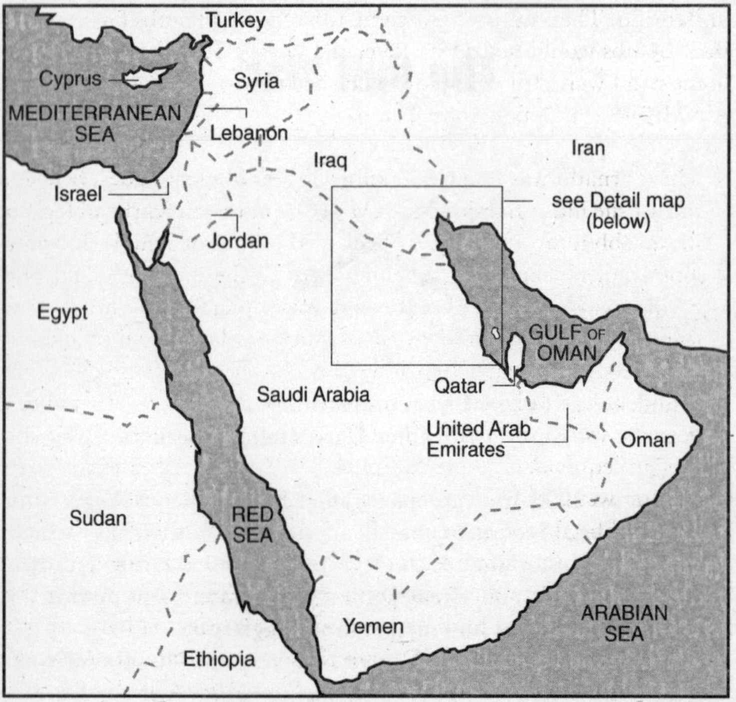

Turkey
Cyprus
Syria
MEDITERRANEAN SEA
Lebanon
Iran
Iraq
Israel
see Detail map (below)
Jordan
Egypt
GULF OF OMAN
Qatar
Saudi Arabia
United Arab Emirates
Oman
Sudan
RED SEA
ARABIAN SEA
Yemen
Ethiopia

The Gulf War area (above)

Iraq
Iran
Kuwait
Kuwait City
GULF OF OMAN
Coalition outflanking attack 24-28 February 1991
Bahrain
Saudi Arabia

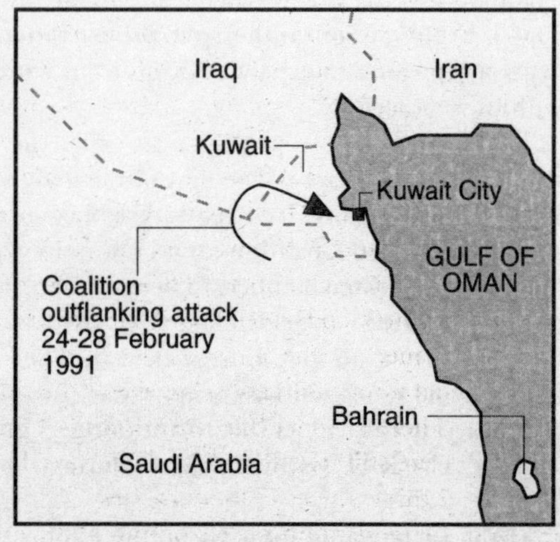

Map of the Gulf War

in Bahrain. Their attack with eight 1,000-pound bombs failed when their bombs would not release over the target. They jettisoned their bombs and were still flying low when they were hit by a Surface-to-Air Missile. The pilot, John Peters:

> The Tornado was doing 540 knots 50 feet above the desert when the missile hit. A hand-held SAM-16, its infra-red warhead locked inexorably onto the furnace heat of the aircraft's engines. Some lone Iraqi's lucky day. Travelling at twice the speed of sound, the SAM streaked into the bomber's tailpipe, piercing the heart of its right turbine. Five kilograms of titanium-laced high-explosive vaporized on impact, smashing the 30-ton aircraft sideways. It shuddered, a bright flame spurting from its skin; £15 million pounds, worth of high technology crippled in a moment by the modern equivalent of the catapult. The computerized fly-by-wire system went down, transforming the aircraft instantly from thoroughbred to cart-horse.
>
> We had just completed our attack run on the huge Ar Rumaylah airfield complex, in south-western Iraq; I was pulling the Tornado through a hard 4g turn, with 60 degrees of bank, to get onto the escape heading. The aircraft was standing on one wing, at the limits of controllable flight. The fly-by-wire loss sent it tumbling, the stick falling dead in my hands – a terrifying feeling for a pilot. I was pushing the controls frantically, the Tornado falling out of the sky, the ground ballooning up sickeningly in my windshield. The huge juddering force of the blast had knocked the wind out of me. Gasping, hanging off the seat straps, I yelled: "What the hell was that?"
>
> "We've been hit! We've been hit!" John Nichol, my navigator, shouted from the back seat. Urgently, he transmitted to the formation leader: "We've been hit! We're on fire! Stand by."
>
> "Prepare to eject, prepare to eject!" I yelled. "I can't hold it!" "Don't you bloody well eject! Get hold of it!" he shouted. It steadied me.
>
> Fast jet aircrew do not survive collision with the ground at 540 knots. There is a 100 per cent certainty of death. The Tornado's wings were still swept back at 45 degrees for the high-speed dash home. I threw the lever forward, desperate to prevent the looming crash. Incredibly, it worked: despite the fire and the enormous loss of power, the aircraft responded, lurching back under something like control as the wing surface, swept forward now at 25 degrees,

bit harder at the airflow. Still wallowing horribly, the aircraft began to climb, but with agonizing slowness. I nursed the stick back to gain precious altitude. Having avoided immediate collision with the ground, I had an awful awareness that the best thing would be to climb to a safe height. But we were still in a high threat area, not far from the target. We had to remain low until we were clear of the road, crawling with Iraqi troops, that we had crossed on the way in, before zooming to height for the return home.

It was then that our problems really started.

The deafening warble of the right engine fire warning blasted out, a Christmas tree panel of red failure lights flashing on.

At that moment a quadruple-barrelled 23-mm gun opened up from one of the dozens of anti-aircraft artillery (Triple-A) sites surrounding the target airfield that had been tracking and firing at us. Four of its shells peppered the AIM-9L Sidewinder missile nestling on our right inboard wing pylon, igniting the Sidewinder's rocket propellant. White-hot, the fuel began burning up through the top of the slender white missile, the airflow fanning it back in a die-straight, incandescent line. The Sidewinder had become a giant oxy-acetylene torch, slowly but surely severing the Tornado's wing.

During the few seconds since being hit, I had been utterly absorbed in the struggle to remain aloft. Now, as a crew, we had to get through the emergency action drills the pilot and navigator must carry out if they are to have any chance of survival.

"We have a right-hand engine fire. Give me the bold face checks!" I shouted.

John began reading off his check list. "Left throttle . . . HP [High Pressure fuel] shut!" he commanded.

"It's the right engine!" I screamed, closing the right throttle. This should starve the burning engine of fuel.

"Left LP cock, shut!" he persisted. Left LP cock? He was trying to get me to shut down the left engine, our only and dwindling chance of getting home in one piece.

"It's the fucking right engine!" I screamed at him. I glanced at the warning panel. The fire had not only not gone out, it was worsening.

"Sorry! Right LP cock, shut!"

"Right Low Pressure fuel cock is shut!"

"Right fire extinguisher, press!"

"Right fire extinguisher pressed."

Then I heard John shout, "We're on fire! We're on fire!"

"I know we're on fire," I said.

"No! We've got to get out of here! Look out the side of the aircraft!"

I glanced up. A bright orange glow in the rearview mirrors made me twist backwards sharply in the narrow seat. It wasn't just the wing: the back of the aircraft had disappeared. There was no sign of the Tornado's massive tailplane. In its place a huge fireball was devouring the fuselage whole. Already it was halfway along the aircraft's spine, just behind the UHF aerials – about three feet from where John sits. But it was the wing he was worried about. I could see him staring horrified at it. I, too, stared, transfixed for a second by the swiftness of the fire's progress. Its back end ablaze, the aircraft was like some comet, trailing orange fire and long grey plumes of leaking jet fuel.

John called up the formation leader again. "Ejecting, ejecting," he transmitted.

No one ever received the message.

John Nichol and John Peters ejected and were captured by the Iraqis. They were questioned, beaten up, kept in isolation and displayed on Iraqi television.

By 23 January low-level attacks were abandoned. By 27 January the Coalition had air supremacy.

The ground attack, Operation "Desert Storm", began on 24 February. The Iraqis had 100,000 troops in Kuwait. Their defences consisted of fixed positions behind minefields along the southern border of Kuwait, facing south. As well as attacking these directly and airborne assaults, Coalition armoured forces crossed the border into Iraq, west of Kuwait, to take the Iraqi positions in Kuwait from behind. Among the Coalition armoured forces was the British 4th Armoured Brigade. The Coalition armoured forces continued their attack by day and night from 24 February to 28 February. They had two pieces of equipment which enabled them to fight effectively at night. These were the Global Positioning System (GPS) and the Thermal and Optical gunsight (TOGS). Tank commanders knew their position to within 15 metres and could "see" enemy vehicles 2,500 metres away. Brigadier Chris Hammerbeck was the commander of the British 4th Armoured Brigade. He commanded his brigade from a Challenger tank. On the night of 25–26 February 4th

Armoured Brigade attacked an Iraqi position defended by about 20 tanks. For 18 hours Hammerbeck scarcely looked up from his TOGS sight.

Chris Hammerbeck:

> A tank battle at night is a curious affair, since the action is fought entirely on thermal sights and therefore in green, white and black, which removes much of the drama. You cannot see the enemy firing at your own tank, but you are aware that it is happening as a supersonic bang is heard as each round passes close by. A hit on the enemy is simply a black or white spot on the target, followed by a wisp of thermal smoke. In reality, this hides the catastrophic explosion of a tank, with the consequent loss of its crew.
>
> For my crew, the battle was a confused jumble of target acquisition followed by engagement sequences: "Fin [ammunition] . . . Tank . . . On . . . Fire!" Small groups of enemy who had baled out were sheltering in the blackness, which must have been broken by the flash of our gun . . . Inside the tank, pandemonium reigned as targets were spotted and engaged. The mix of smells ranged from the smoke of the main armament to that curiously acrid smell that humans give off when they are charged with adrenalin and, to be frank, scared.

By 28 February Coalition forces had reached Kuwait City and the Iraqis were in full retreat back to Iraq. Fighting ended on 28 February. Peace talks had begun by 4 March. These talks covered the exchange of prisoners. John Nichol and John Peters were handed over to the International Red Cross on 4 March.

Acknowledgments and Sources

The editor has made every effort to locate all persons having any rights in the selections appearing in this anthology and to secure permission from the holders of such rights. The editor apologises in advance for any errors or omissions inadvertently made. Queries regarding the use of material should be addressed to the editor c/o the publishers.

Ancient

The Gallic War, Julius Caesar, trans. H. J. Edwards (William Heineman Ltd 1970)

Civil Wars, Julius Caesar, trans. A. G. Peskett (William Heineman Ltd 1966)

Medieval

The Art of War, Sir Charles Oman (Methuen 1905)

Horse and Musket

Cromwell's Army, C. H. Firth (Methuen 1902)

The English Civil War, R. Holmes & P. Young (Wordsworth 2000)

Fire of Liberty, Esmond Wright ed. (Folio Society 1983)

The life of Admiral of the Fleet Sir W. Parker Augustus Philimore, William Parker (1876).

Nelsonian Reminiscences, G. S. Parsons, ed. W. H. Long (1905)

Letters & Despatches of Horatio Viscount Nelson. Selected & arranged by J. K. Laughton (1886)

The Narrative of Captain Coignet: Soldier of the Empire, Jean-Roch Coignet, trans. M. Carey (Chatto & Windus 1897)

From Valmy to Waterloo, C. Francois, trans R. B. Doulgas (London 1906)

The Death of Lord Nelson, W. Beatty (1807)

Recollections of Rifleman Harris, ed. H. Curling (London 1848)

Memoirs of a Sergeant, lately in the 43rd Regiment (London 1839)

Adventures in the Rifle Brigade, J. Kincaid (London 1838)

Autobiography of Harry Smith, ed. G. C. Moore Smith (1909)

Journal of the Waterloo Campaign, ed. C. A. Mercer (London 1870)

Journal of a soldier of the 71st Regiment, the Highland Light Infantry, from 1806 to 1815 (Edinburgh 1822)
Blaze of glory: the fight for New Orleans, 1814–15, S. T. Carter (Macmillan 1972)
Rank & File, T. H. McGuffie (Hutchinson 1964)
Told from the ranks, collecged by E. Milton Small (London 1898)
Anecdotes, poetry and incidents of the war 1860–65, ed. F. Moore (New York 1882)
Antietam and Fredericksburg, F. W. Palfrey (New York 1882)
Chancellorsville and Gettysburg, A. Doubleday (New York 1882)
Two years on the Alabama, A. Sinclair (London 1986)
The Battle of The Wilderness, M. Schaff (Boston 1910)

Machine gun

The Rough Riders, T. Roosevelt (1899)
1914, Lyn Macdonald (Michael Joseph 1987)
The Somme, Lyn Macdonald (Michael Joseph 1991)
They Fought for the Sky, Q. Reynold (Cassell 1958)
To the last man: Spring 1918, Lyn Macdonald (Michael Joseph 1998)
Their Finest Hour, J. M. Beard (Harcourt Brace 1941)
The Flying Guns, C. Dickinson (Simon & Schuster 1943)
Queen of the Flat Tops, S. Johnston (Jarrolds 1943)
The Only Way Out, R. Wingfield (Hutchinson 1955)
The First and the Last, A. Galland by permission of Cerberus Publishing
Life in the V Ring, J. T. Wheeler by permission of Associated Press
The Falklands War, D. Blakeway (Sidgwick & Jackson 1992) by permission of Pan Macmillan
Tornado Down, J. Peters & J. Nichol (Michael Joseph)
Storm Command, Sir Peter de la Billiere (Harper Collins 1992)

Other sources

Hoplites: The classical Greek battle experience, ed. V. D. Hanson (Routledge 1991)
The Crusades, A. Bridge (Granada 1985)
The Three Edwards, M. Prestwich (Routledge 1994)
History of the Royal Navy, W. Clowes (London 1897–1900)
Battles of the British Navy, J Allen (London 1852)
The American Civil War, W. S. Churchill (Cassell 1961)
The Twentieth Maine, J. J. Pullen (Yale University Press 1948)
Decisive factors in twenty great battles of the world, W. Seymour
Tactics & Experience in the age of Napoleon, R. Muir
The Face of Battle, J. Keegan (Cape 1977)
The Second World War, J. Keegan
The Falklands War, Sunday Times Insight Team (Sphere 1982)
Gardiner's Atlas of English History (Longmans 1910)
Muir's Atlas of Ancient and Classical History (George Phillip & Son 1971)
Muris' Historical Atlas Medieval & Modern (George Phillip & Son 1969)
The Illustrated Companion to Nelson's Navy, N. Blake and R. R. Lawrence (Chatham Publishing 2000)

Other titles available from Robinson Publishing

The Mammoth Book of The Titanic Ed. by Geoff Tibbals **£7.99 [ ]**

The Sinking of the Great ocean line, *Titanic*, has been recreated countless times, but none can give so graphic and revealing a picture as the accounts of those who were actually there. This new anthology strips away the Hollywood glss and tells the real story of the 'unsinkable' vessel. There are eyewitness accounts full of details that range from poignant to heartbreaking, stage by stage from the great ship's glorious launch in Belfast to the sombre sea burial services of those who perished on her first and only voyage.

The Mammoth Book of Science Fiction Ed. by Mike Ashley **£6.99 [ ]**

The best science fiction challenges our imagination, pushing it to extreme limits. In this terrific new anthology you will find some of the best and most challenging science fiction writing from the last fifty years – in these stories twenty leading authors of the genre ask the question 'What if . . .'? and then give their own very personal views of the changes and surprises that may befall humanity in the centuries to come.

The Mammoth Book of Travel in Dangerous Places
Ed. by John Keay **£7.99 [ ]**

Explorers were once the premier celebrities of their day – they captured the world's headlines and the public's imagination to a degree which would be unthinkable now. John Keay's classic collection includes the original first-hand accounts of many of these heroes including Ernest Shackleton, Sir Edmund Hillary and Roald Amundsen.

Robinson books are available from all good bookshops or can be ordered direct from the Publisher. Just tick the title you want and fill in the form below.

TBS Direct
Colchester Road, Frating Green, Colchester, Essex CO7 7DW
Tel: +44 (0) 1206 255777
Fax: +44 (0) 1206 255914
Email: sales@tbs-ltd.co.uk

UK/BFPO customers please allow £1.00 for p&p for the first book, plus 50p for the second, plus 30p for each additional book up to a maximum charge of £3.00.

Overseas customers (inc. Ireland), please allow £2.00 for the first book, plus £1.00 for the second, plus 50p for each additional book.

Please send me the titles ticked above.

NAME (Block letters). . . . .

ADDRESS . . . .

. . . .

POSTCODE . . . .

I enclose a cheque/PO (payable to TBS Direct) for . . . .

I wish to pay by Switch/Credit card

Number . . . .

Card Expiry Date . . . .

Switch Issue Number . . . .